Richard Pratt's exemplary commentary on 1 and 2 Chronicles is systematic, scholarly, sober and simple.

In his introduction Professor Pratt systematically sets forth the Chronicler's theology to address three primary concerns of the original Israelite readers. These are the people of God, the king and temple, and divine blessing and judgment. Our expositor's goal to write a theological commentary, not a scribal one, informs his whole work. References to these major themes and their sub-themes appear throughout the commentary. For example, instead of labeling the first nine chapters 'Genealogies', Pratt packages them 'The Identity, Privileges and Responsibilities of God's People.'

Our author's aim to write a theological commentary is based on the most recent scholarly literature. With reference to the Chronicler's differences from Samuel, he carefully distinguishes between intentional differences that reflect the inspired author's distinctive theology from that book and unintentional differences due to the Chronicler's using 'a version of Samuel that was not identical with the traditional Hebrew text on which our modern translations of Samuel are based'. Professor Pratt's theological presentation is always based on sound exegesis, interpreting the Chronicler's words in the light of his historical horizon. Moreover, few are as competent as to interpret narrative with a sensitivity to structure, characterisation, and plot development.

Professor Pratt's commentary is solid because he 'presupposes the infallibility of the Hebrew text which the Chronicler originally penned under the inspiration of the Holy Spirit'. He also presupposes that although the Chronicler addressed an original Israelite audience sometime between c. 515 and 390 BC, his theology has abiding value for contemporary Christian readers. Unfailingly, our author extends the Chronicler's theology into its development in the New Testament. The people of God become a reality in Christ. The hope for David's throne to be restored was fulfilled in Christ. The purposes of the temple are also fulfilled in him. Likewise, divine blessing and judgment is realised in Christ. Jesus bore the judgment of God on sin and set his people free to follow the path of blessed obedience.

Professor Pratt's style is simple and clear. In less than a page, and with a simple graphic, he sketches the complicated lineage of the high priesthood from Aaron to Joshua, the partner of Zerubbabel. The complicated genealogies are sketched so clearly that any reader can discern at a glance the lay of the land. Our commentator's artistic eye enables him to present graphically both the Chronicler's structure and his differences from his sources, Samuel and Kings. As a result, the reader always has the whole in view before taking on the word by word exposition.

In sum, Richard Pratt's commentary on Chronicles is written according to the ideals of the Reformed tradition.

Bruce Waltke
Reformed Theological Seminary
Orlando

Acknowledgements

This commentary has resulted from the efforts of a team with many members. My secretary, Diana Soule, has once again labored faithfully and expertly. Chuck Jacob, Rick Harper, and Adam Roberts deserve much thanks for their highly skilled research and assistance. Moreover, several classes of students have proofread this material and have offered many helpful suggestions.

I thank God for each of you. Your partnership on this project has been indispensable.

Richard L. Pratt, Jr.

30 June 97

Dedicated to my parents with much gratitude.

1 and 2 Chronicles

Richard L. Pratt, Jr.

Mentor

ISBN 1 85792 151 8

Published in the Mentor imprint in 1998 by Christian Focus Publications,
Geanies House, Fearn, Ross-shire, IV20 1TW, Great Britain.

Contents

Introduction

Part One: The Identity, Privileges and Responsibilities of God's People (1 Chr 1:1-9:34)

Part Two: The Ideal United Kingdom
(1 Chr 9:35–2 Chr 9:31)

Part Three: Judah During the Divided Kingdom
(2 Chr. 10:1–28:27)

Part Four: The Reunited Kingdom
(2 Chr. 29:1–36:23)

Dedicated to my parents with much gratitude.

Acknowledgements

This commentary has resulted from the efforts of a team with many members. My secretary, Diana Soule, has once again labored faithfully and expertly. Chuck Jacob, Rick Harper, and Adam Roberts deserve much thanks for their highly skilled research and assistance. Moreover, several classes of students have proofread this material and have offered many helpful suggestions.

I thank God for each of you. Your partnership on this project has been indispensable.

Richard L. Pratt, Jr.

30 June 97

Introduction

The book of Chronicles (1 and 2 Chronicles) is one of the most neglected portions of Scripture. Many students of the Bible find its complex history unfamiliar and assume that it is irrelevant for contemporary life. Despite these widespread assessments, Chronicles offers much to the Church today by providing perspectives on our Faith that we seldom consider.

To grasp the significance of Chronicles for our times, we must first understand its original meaning, the meaning intended for its first Israelite readers. Legitimate Christian applications must accord with the purposes for which the Holy Spirit first inspired this book. In this introduction, we sketch the contours of the original meaning of Chronicles by focusing on five issues: *1) Authorship and Date, 2) Historical and Theological Purposes, 3) Outline, 4) Major Themes,* and *5) Translation and Transmission.* Two appendices follow these topics.

Authorship and Date

The Holy Spirit inspired the book of Chronicles, but he spoke through the personality and purposes of a human writer. Chronicles does not explicitly identify this human instrument, but clues appear that help us limit possibilities.

Early Jewish traditions designated the scribe Ezra as the primary author of Chronicles (as well as the books of Ezra and Nehemiah). At least two considerations support this view: 1) The book was composed after Israel's return from exile to Babylon, near the time of Ezra's ministry. 2) Many passages in Chronicles have theological affinities with the focus of Ezra's ministry (see *Major Themes* below).

Other considerations, however, cast doubt on this traditional viewpoint: 1) The date of Chronicles' composition cannot be limited to Ezra's lifetime (see below). 2) Chronicles ties kingship and temple worship together in ways that do not appear in the teachings of Ezra. 3) Chronicles largely avoids a central issue in Ezra's ministry, intermarriage between Israelites and foreign women (Ezra 9:10-12; see Deut. 7:2-4; Neh. 10:30; 13:23-31).

For these reasons, most contemporary scholars remain unconvinced of the traditional outlook on the identity of Chronicles' human author. Ezra's ministry was certainly in harmony with this book. Moreover, he may have contributed to its composition or transmission in some unknown manner. Nevertheless, neither historical nor Scriptural evidences demonstrate that Ezra wrote Chronicles. As a result, we will follow the custom of most contemporary interpreters and simply refer to the inspired human author as 'the Chronicler'.

When did the Chronicler write? It is not possible to establish a precise date, but upon reflection a limited range of possibilities emerges.

The final verses of Chronicles provide us with the *earliest possible date* for final composition (2 Chr. 36:21-23; see Ezra 1:1-4). These verses record the edict of the Persian emperor, Cyrus, in which he ordered the return of Israelite exiles from Babylon. These events occurred in c. 539/8 BC.

The *latest possible date* for Chronicles is less certain. One important clue is that the style of Hebrew in the book gives no indication of influence from the Greek language. This evidence suggests that the book was written before Alexander the Great took control of Palestine in c. 330 BC.

The specific circumstances of Chronicles' composition become clearer in the light of the major events which took place in Palestine between these earliest and latest possible dates of composition (c. 538–c. 330 BC). We will summarize several crucial events which took place in this period (see Figure 1).

Composition of Chronicles

539/8	536	520	515	458-430	330
Return from Exile	Altar and Foundation of Temple	Haggai and Zechariah	Completion of Temple	Ezra and Nehemiah	Alexander the Great

Major Post-Exilic Events (Figure 1)

A number of Israelites returned from exile to Jerusalem following the Cyrus Edict (Ezra 2:1-64). A descendent of King David named Zerubbabel led the people in erecting an altar and a foundation for the new temple (Ezra 2:2; 3:2-3, 8-10). Nevertheless, disappointment, economic hardships, and trouble from foreigners quickly halted the reconstruction effort (Ezra 4:1-24).

The prophets Haggai and Zechariah preached in Jerusalem during this time (Ezra 5:1-2). They exhorted Zerubbabel and the people to continue the work on the temple. The returnees eventually complied with the prophetic word and completed the temple with great celebration in 515 BC (Ezra 6:14-15).

A generation later, however, the number of returnees remained few. Moreover, many men had intermarried with foreign women who served other gods (Ezra 9:1-2; Neh. 13:23-31; Mal. 2:11). These intermarriages led to widespread religious apostasy (Deut. 7:3; 1 Kgs. 11:1-13). Ezra (c. 458 BC) and Nehemiah (c. 445 BC) came to Jerusalem to call the people to repent of their failures and to conform to the Law of God.

Sadly, the reforms under Ezra and Nehemiah had only temporary effects. The sins of the people grew so great that Israel fell into centuries of spiritual darkness. This period of extended trouble we now call the Intertestamental Period (c. 425–c. 4 BC). Most of God's people remained scattered among the nations. The Israelites in Palestine first suffered under the rule of the Persians and Medes, then beneath Greek dominion, and finally under the iron fist of Rome. Intertestamental darkness continued until the inauguration of the Kingdom of God through the work of Christ and his apostles.

Where did the Chronicler and his book fit within this series of events? Two answers have come to the foreground in recent research. First, some interpreters have proposed that the Chronicler wrote as early as the ministries of Haggai and Zechariah (c. 520-515). At least three evidences support this view:

1) The book consistently presents the temple and its personnel in close partnership with the royal line of David (see *Major Themes* below). This dual emphasis on king and temple suggests that final composition took place near the days of Zerubbabel when expectations of Davidic and priestly partnership were still high (see Zech. 3:1-4:14; Hag. 1:14-2:9, 20-23). By the next generation, there is little evidence for hope of an imminent rise of the Davidic line to the throne of Jerusalem.

2) The Chronicler gave much attention to the details of priestly and Levitical duties (see *Major Themes* below). This concern also suggests a date of composition during the time when Zerubbabel and his priestly partner Joshua (Jeshua) were establishing the new temple order (see Zech. 3:1-4:14).

3) The striking omission of Solomon's downfall due to intermarriage (see 1 Kgs. 11:1-40 and commentary on 2 Chr. 1:1-9:31; 9:29-31) stands in sharp contrast with Nehemiah's appeal to the terrible results of Solomon's foreign marriages (see Neh. 13:26). This omission suggests that the Chronicler may have written in the generation before intermarriage had become a major problem in the post-exilic community.

Second, the majority of recent interpreters have argued that final composition took place during or just after the ministries of Ezra and Nehemiah (c. 450-390). The main evidence in favor of this view appears in the genealogy of 1 Chr. 3:17-24. This list extends to a number of generations after Zerubbabel. Some difficulties with interpretation make this evidence less than conclusive, but it would appear certain that the genealogy extends to at least two generations after Zerubbabel (see commentary on 1 Chr. 3:1-24).

In light of the ambiguity of the evidence, a specific date cannot be fixed for the final composition of Chronicles. It seems best to remain satisfied with a range of possibilities from sometime near the days of Zerubbabel to sometime soon after the ministries of Ezra and Nehemiah (c. 515-390). As our commentary will show, the emphases of the book fit well within these limits.

Historical and Theological Purposes

The Chronicler wrote to give his readers a true historical record of Israel's past. The historical nature of his book has been noted in the titles which have been attached to it. The traditional Hebrew title may be translated 'The Events of the Times', pointing to its historical quality. Some manuscripts of the Septuagint (ancient Greek versions of the Old Testament) entitled the book 'The Things Omitted', to suggest that it supplements the history of Samuel and Kings. Our English title, 'Chronicles' derives from Jerome and Luther who called the book 'The Chronicle of the Entire Sacred History'. These various titles indicate that even a cursory reading of Chronicles reveals its historical focus.

The Chronicler's careful handling of numerous written sources also points to his concern for historical veracity.

1) As he wrote of Israel's history, he relied primarily on the canonical books of Samuel and Kings for his information. The vast majority of materials in Chronicles comes from these authoritative Scriptures.

2) The Chronicler also referred to the Scriptures of the Pentateuch (e.g. 1 Chr. 1:1-2; [see Gen. 5:1-20]; 1 Chr. 4:24; [see Exod. 6:15; Num. 26:12-14]; 1 Chr. 5:1,2; [see Gen. 35:22; 49:3-4]; 1 Chr. 24:2 [see Lev. 10:1-2]), and the books of Joshua (e.g. 1 Chr. 2:7; [see Josh. 7:1]), Judges (1 Chr. 11:4; [see Judg. 1:21]), Ruth (1 Chr. 2:10-17; [see Ruth 4:18-22]), Psalms (1 Chr. 16:8-22; [see Ps. 105:1-15]), Isaiah (2 Chr. 32; [see Isa. 36:1-39:8]), and Jeremiah (2 Chr. 36:11-21; [see Jer. 52:1-30]).

3) Beyond this, he cited several unknown royal annals: 'the book of the annals of King David' (1 Chr. 27:24), 'the book of the kings' (2 Chr. 24:27), 'the book of the kings of Israel' (1 Chr. 9:1; 2 Chr. 20:34), and 'the book of the kings of Judah and Israel' (2 Chr. 16:11; 25:26; 28:26; 32:32), 'the book of the kings of Israel and Judah' (2 Chr. 27:7; 35:27; 36:8).

4) In addition, the Chronicler referred to prophetic writings which have since disappeared: the writings of Samuel (1 Chr. 29:29), Nathan (1 Chr. 29:29; 2 Chr. 9:29), Gad (1 Chr. 29:29), Ahijah (2 Chr. 9:29), Iddo (2 Chr. 9:29; 12:15; 13:22), Shemaiah (2 Chr. 12:15), and anonymous 'seers' (2 Chr. 33:19).

5) The content and style of many passages also suggest that the Chronicler used other unidentifiable sources (see 2 Chr. 9:29-31; 12:15-16; 16:11-17:1; 21:18-20; 24:23-27; 26:22-23; 28:26-27; 32:32-33; 35:20-27; 36:8). The Chronicler's use of these many sources indicates his strong desire to convey a true account of Israel's past.

As a book of history, Chronicles covers a wide range of events. It begins with Adam (1 Chr. 1:1) and traces the history of Israel to the period after return from exile in Babylon (1 Chr. 3:1-24). This historical record is fascinating in itself for it reveals much about the God of Israel whom we serve today.

In addition to informing his readers of the past, the Chronicler also wrote to convey theological perspectives. These purposes become especially evident when Chronicles is compared with the earlier records of Samuel and Kings. As our commentary will show, the Chronicler handled Samuel and Kings in different ways to focus his readers' attention on particular issues. He sometimes quoted long passages with little or no change, but at other times he made modifications, additions and omissions. These variations indicate that the Chronicler composed his history to convey theological lessons as well as historical information.

This commentary will concern itself primarily with the theological purposes of Chronicles. We will occasionally comment on historical issues, but our chief interest will be to discern the guidance Chronicles gave to its first readers. Only when we understand this theological focus will we correctly discern how the book also speaks to us today.

How may we summarize the Chronicler's theological concerns? What were the chief elements of his message? It helps to think of Chronicles' theology in terms of its message for the *Original Israelite Readers* as well as its application for *Contemporary Christian Readers*.

***Original Israelite Readers*:**
In general terms, the Chronicler originally wrote his history *to direct the restoration of the Kingdom during the early post-exilic period.* The people who had returned from exile faced many challenges. Although the prophets had predicted that return to the land would be a time of grand blessings (e.g. Amos 9:11-15; Joel 3:18-21; Ezek 34:26), the restoration had not brought about the blessings for which Israel hoped. Instead, the returnees endured discouraging economic hardship, foreign opposition, and domestic conflicts. The Chronicler wrote his history to offer guidance to this struggling community. He provided them with practical directions for attaining a greater realization of the blessings of the Kingdom of God in their time.

Contemporary Christian Readers:
The Chronicler's desire to direct the restoration of the Kingdom of God in his day connects the theology of his book to the concerns of the Christian Church today. Although post-exilic Israel's continuing sins brought failure in their day, the Kingdom of God did not fail utterly. As the New Testament teaches, the Chronicler's hopes were realized in Christ. Christ brings to fulfillment and exceeds all of the Chronicler's desires for God's people.

The New Testament also teaches, however, that Jesus did not accomplish this goal all at once. Instead, the restoration of the Kingdom of God comes in three stages. First, the *inauguration* of the Kingdom came through Christ's earthly ministry and the work of his apostles (see Mark 1:14-15; Luke 4:43; 10:11; Acts 1:3). Second, after the ministry of the apostles the *continuation* of the Kingdom of God extends to all the world through the ministry of the Church (see Acts 28:23; Rev. 1:6; 5:10). Third, in the future Jesus will bring the Kingdom to its *consummation* in the New Heavens and New Earth (see Rev. 21:1-22:21).

Christians may rightly apply the Chronicler's perspectives by asking how his message applies to these three phases of Christ's Kingdom. Chronicles presents theological themes which anticipate Christ's first coming, the continuing ministry of the church, and the return of Christ. In the next section we will illustrate how particular themes in Chronicles apply to both post-exilic Israel and to the three phases of Christ's Kingdom.

Outline

The book of Chronicles displays a well-conceived structure. The following outline provides an overview of the large patterns of the book (see figure 2). More detailed patterns are noted at the beginning of each section of the commentary.

Part One: The Identity, Privileges and Responsibilities of God's People (1 Chr. 1:1-9:34)

Part Two: The Ideal United Kingdom (1 Chr. 9:35-2 Chr. 9:31)
- David's Reign (1 Chr. 9:35-29:30)
- Solomon's Reign (2 Chr. 1:1-9:31)

Part Three: Judah During the Divided Kingdom (2 Chr. 10:1-28:27)
- Judgments and Increasing Blessings in Judah (10:1-21:3)
  - Rehoboam (10:1-12:16)
  - Abijah (13:1-14:1)
  - Asa (14:2-16:14)
  - Jehoshaphat (17:1-21:3)
- Northern Corruption in Judah (21:4-24:27)
  - Jehoram (21:4-21:20)
  - Ahaziah (22:1-9)
  - Athaliah (22:10-23:21)
  - Joash (24:1-27)
- Half-Hearted Obedience in Judah (25:1-28:27)
  - Amaziah (25:1-28)
  - Uzziah (26:1-23)
  - Jotham (27:1-9)
  - Ahaz (28:1-27)

Part Four: The Reunited Kingdom (2 Chr. 29:1-36:23)
- Hezekiah (29:1-32:33)
- Manasseh (33:1-20)
- Amon (33:21-25)
- Josiah (34:1-35:27)
- Final Events (36:2-23)

Outline of Chronicles (figure 2)

Major Themes

The post-exilic community faced a variety of challenges as they sought to re-establish the Kingdom of God in their day. These difficulties must have raised many important questions. 'Are we still heirs to the promises which God gave our forebears? What political and religious institutions should we embrace? How may we find the blessings of security and prosperity?' The Chronicler addressed these kinds of questions throughout his book.

The Chronicler wove together many theological motifs in order to respond to these questions. We will summarize his central theological concerns under the following headings.

1-3) People of God
- *1) All Israel*
- *2) Northern Israel*
- *3) International Relations*

4-9) King and Temple
- *4) Royal and Levitical Families*
- *5) Religious Assemblies*
- *6) Royal Observance of Worship*
- *7) Divine Kingship*
- *8) Music*
- *9) Temple Contributions*

10-28) Divine Blessing and Judgment
- *10-12) God and History*
  - *10) Divine Activity*
  - *11) Name of God*
  - *12) Divine Presence and Help*
- *13-22) Israel's Responsibilities*
  - *13) Covenant*
  - *14) Standards*
  - *15) Prophets*
  - *16) Motivations*
  - *17) Prayer*
  - *18) Humility*
  - *19) Seeking*
  - *20) Abandoning/Forsaking*
  - *21) Unfaithfulness*
  - *22) Repentance*
- *23-28) Divine Responses*
  - *23) Victory and Defeat*
  - *24) Building and Destruction*
  - *25) Increase and Decline of Progeny*
  - *26) Prosperity and Poverty*
  - *27) Disappointment and Celebration*
  - *28) Healing and Long Life / Sickness and Death*

References to these *Major Themes* appear throughout the commentary.

1-3) People of God

Throughout his history, the Chronicler explained who belonged among the people of God. The identity of God's people posed many difficulties for the post-exilic community. Whom should they count as heirs of God's promises? What geographical hopes were appropriate for the tribes of Israel? How inclusive or exclusive should they be? We will explore the Chronicler's answers to these questions under three rubrics: *1) All Israel,* 2) *Northern Israel,* and *3) International Relations.*

1) All Israel

Original Israelite Readers

The Chronicler's concern with clarifying the identity of God's people becomes evident in his frequent use of the terminology 'all Israel' and other closely related expressions (see commentary on 1 Chr. 11:1; 2 Chr. 10:1; 29:24). Six times the Chronicler simply copied this terminology from parallel passages in Samuel and

Kings (1 Chr. 18:14; 19:17; 2 Chr. 7:8,9; 10:16; 18:16). Four times he modified the text of Samuel and Kings to read 'all Israel' (1 Chr. 11:1; 14:8; 15:28; 2 Chr. 10:3). Beyond this, however, the expression occurs nineteen times in passages which are unique to Chronicles (1 Chr. 11:10; 12:38; 15:3; 21:5; 28:4; 28:8; 29:21; 29:23,25,26; 2 Chr. 1:2; 12:1; 13:4; 13:15; 24:5; 28:23; 29:24; 30:1; 35:3).

The Chronicler's emphasis on 'all Israel' reflected his deep commitment to including all the tribes of Israel among God's people. To be sure, the representatives of Judah, Benjamin, Ephraim, Manasseh, and Levi who had returned to the land were the chosen people (see commentary on 1 Chr. 9:3-9). As such, they played a seminal role in the restoration of the Kingdom.

At the same time, however, the Chronicler believed that God's people included more than the small population of the post-exilic community. He also identified the tribes of Israel who still remained outside the land as the people of God. In his view, the returnees in Judah needed to remember that the restoration was incomplete so long as some of the tribes remained exiled from the land. To express this broad vision of God's people, the Chronicler included both northern and southern tribes in his genealogies (1 Chr. 2:3; 4:24; 5:1,11,23; 6:1; 7:1,6,13,14,20,30; 8:1). He presented the ideal of all twelve tribes under David and Solomon. He spoke of both the North and South as the people of God (2 Chr. 10:3; 12:1; 13:4,15; 24:5). He also celebrated the reunification of the northern and southern kingdoms in the days of Hezekiah (see commentary on 2 Chr. 30:1-31:1). Finally, the Chronicler was so strongly committed to the return of all tribes to the land that he often pointed to geographical locations that belong to various tribes (see 1 Chr. 4:10,11-23; 5:23; 6:54-81; 7:28-29; 8:1-7; 8:8-13; 9:1-2; 2 Chr. 31:1b).

After the exile it was easy to settle for small results. Few exiles had returned; few districts of the land had returned to the appropriate tribes. The Chronicler insisted, however, that the blessings of God awaited his readers as they devoted themselves to the goal of re-establishing all the tribes of Israel to their rightful place in the land of promise.

Contemporary Christian Readers

The ideal of 'all Israel' anticipates a number of motifs that run throughout the New Testament. The inauguration of Christ's Kingdom was characterized by an inclusive focus. Jesus was emphatic in ministering to the rich (Matt. 27:57) and poor (Matt. 11:5), the religious and profane (Luke 7:36-38), the noble (John 4:46) and the despised (Luke 5:27; 17:12). From the announcement of the Kingdom to poor shepherds (Luke 2:8,9) to Christ's ministry to women and children (Luke 8:1-3; 23:55-56), the Kingdom of God included all of God's covenant people.

Jesus also expected the continuation of his Kingdom in the Church to emphasize the inclusiveness of the New Covenant. As Paul insisted, 'There is neither Jew nor Greek, slave nor free, male nor female, for you are all one in Christ Jesus' (Gal. 3:28). In a similar vein, James forbade any favoritism leading to discrimination in the Church (James 2:1-7).

The totality of God's people comes into focus throughout John's Revelation (see Rev. 19:6,7; 21:3,24). The Chronicler's desire that 'all Israel' constitute the restored Kingdom in his day will be fully realized when Christ returns.

2) Northern Israel

Original Israelite Readers

Chronicles gives special attention to the place of northern Israelites in the post-exilic community. The situation of the northern tribes was complex in the Chronicler's day. Most people from these tribes remained outside the land where the Assyrians had exiled them. Some Northerners had stayed in their traditional territories, but were mixed with exiles from other nations (see 2 Kgs. 17). Moreover, on several occasions in Judah's history, groups of Northerners joined themselves to Judah. Some descendants of these defectors had returned from the Babylonian exile with the first returnees (1 Chr. 9:3-9).

The book of Chronicles offers a balanced assessment on this complex situation. On the one hand, it strongly favors the political and religious structures of the South over those of the North. This loyalty to Judah becomes apparent by comparing the record of Kings and Chronicles. The Chronicler omitted large portions of Kings that dealt exclusively with events in the North. With one exception (2 Chr. 13:1 // 1 Kgs. 15:1-2), he omitted all North-South synchronizations from the book of Kings (see Asa, 2 Chr. 14:2 // 1 Kgs. 15:9; Jehoshaphat, 2 Chr. 17:1 // 1 Kgs. 22:41; Jehoram, 2 Chr. 21:4-5 // 2 Kgs. 8:16; Ahaziah, 2 Chr. 22:1 // 2 Kgs. 8:25; Joash, 2 Chr. 24:1 // 2 Kgs. 12:1; Amaziah, 2 Chr. 25:1 // 2 Kgs. 14:1; Jotham, 2 Chr. 27:1 // 2 Kgs. 15:32; Ahaz, 2 Chr. 28:1 // 2 Kgs. 16:1; Hezekiah, 2 Chr. 29:1 // 2 Kgs. 18:1). This nearly exclusive focus on events in Judah reveals that the institutions and peoples of the South were the heart of the Kingdom of God.

Along these same lines, the Chronicler asserted a strongly negative assessment of certain aspects of life in the North. This outlook appears in a number of ways.

1) Although the Chronicler acknowledged the legitimacy of Israel's initial political separation from Judah (2 Chr. 10:1-11:4), he strongly condemned northern worship practices and other forms of wickedness (2 Chr. 13:4-12;19:2; 21:6,12-15; 22:3; 22:10-23:21; 24:7; 25:7; 30:6-9).

2) The book makes it very plain that Judah was not to make political alliances with the wicked from northern Israel. To form such agreements was to reject reliance on God (2 Chr. 19:1-2; 20:35-37; 21:5,6, 12-15; 22:3-6; 25:7-10).

3) On several occasions, the Chronicler lamented that Judahite kings behaved like Israelite kings (2 Chr. 21:6,13; 22:4; 28:2-4). These comparisons also indicate a largely negative assessment of the North.

4) 2 Chr. 21:4-24:27 focuses on the corrupting influence of the North on Judah. This period was characterized by waywardness and the source of this trouble was too much involvement with northern Israel.

On the other hand, however, the Chronicler also sought to broaden the vision of his post-exilic readers to include the tribes of the North among the people of God. This emphasis becomes apparent in a number of ways.

1) Northern tribes appear in the opening genealogies and lists (1 Chr. 4:24-5:26; 7:1-40; 9:3).

2) At least twenty-three times the Chronicler's inclusive terminology 'all Israel' refers to the northern tribes.

3) The Chronicler noted that the division of Israel was by divine design (2 Chr. 11:1-4).

4) He reported approvingly several times that the faithful in the North defected to the southern kingdom (2 Chr. 11:17; 15:4,8; 30:11,18,21).

5) He once contrasted the North and South by pointing out that the Northerners obeyed God's prophet when Judah was in rebellion against God (2 Chr. 28:6-15).

6) Similarly, the Chronicler equated the moral conditions of Judah and Israel in the days of Hezekiah (2 Chr. 29:8-9). By this means, he indicated that Judah was not inherently superior to the North.

7) The exemplary religious reforms of three Judahite kings extended into the northern territories (2 Chr. 19:4; 31:1; 34:6-7) and the Chronicler condemned Asa's failure to reform the North (2 Chr. 15:17). These events pointed out that post-exilic Judahites should be concerned with religious reforms in the North.

8) The Chronicler also highlighted Hezekiah's symbolic reunion of the North and South at his Passover celebration (2 Chr. 30:1-31:1). His extraordinary patience toward the Israelites modeled the kind of actions the Chronicler's post-exilic readers were to exhibit toward their northern neighbors.

Contemporary Christian Readers

The outlook of Chronicles toward Northern Israel is confirmed for the Christian community in the teachings of the New Testament. Jesus inaugurated his Kingdom by ministering not only to Jerusalem (Luke 19:28), but to the Northern Israelites in Nazareth (Luke 4:16), Galilee (Luke 4:14), and Samaria (John 4:1-42). His commission to his apostles specifically mentioned Samaria (Acts 1:8). Moreover, descendants of northern Israel were among the 'Jews from every nation under heaven' (Acts 2:5) who were present at Pentecost.

In many respects, the Chronicler's emphasis on Northern Israel parallels Paul's insistence that every part of the body of Christ is essential to the edification of the Church (1 Cor. 12:12-26). Just as the post-exilic community needed true believers from the North, the Christian Church needs every part of the covenant community to be active and contributing to the work of the Kingdom today.

The inclusion of the northern tribes also appears in the consummation. At the end of this world, the Kingdom of Christ will include '144,000 from all the tribes of Israel' (Rev. 7:4). The Chronicler's desire for the return of the northern tribes will be fulfilled when the names of all twelve tribes are placed on the gates of New Jerusalem (Rev. 21:12). Every tribe will be represented in the consummation.

3) International Relations

Original Israelite Readers

In an attempt to define the people of God even further, the Chronicler also focused on relations between Israel and other nations. During the early post-exilic period, practical political realities forced the struggling community in Judah to deal with other nations (see for instance Ezra 3:7; Neh. 2:1-10). Questions as to the extent and nature of this involvement were of great importance. Chronicles touches on these matters in two important ways.

First, the book exhibits an openness toward foreigners to demonstrate that the post-exilic community should not entirely isolate itself from other nations.

1) The opening genealogies and lists include non-Israelites among the people of God. Kenites held a rightful place within the tribe of Judah (1 Chr. 2:55). Similarly, there may be Ishmaelite names in the records of Simeon (1 Chr. 4:25). Foreigners assisting the Levites were known as 'temple servants' (see Num. 31:30; Ezra 8:20); they were among those who first returned from exile (1 Chr. 9:1-34).

2) In much the same way, the Chronicler indicated that his ideal kings, David and Solomon, had economic ties with foreigners. David employed Hiram and foreign masons (1 Chr. 22:2). Solomon had many economic interactions with foreign nations (2 Chr. 8:17-9:26).

3) Beyond this, the Chronicler noted that foreigners were not to be excluded from Israel's religious life. For instance, he repeated material from Kings in which Solomon prayed that foreigners who come to the temple may know the God of Israel (2 Chr. 6:32-33). The amazement of the Queen of Sheba accordingly appears in his history as well (2 Chr. 9:1-12). In these ways, Chronicles displays a very positive outlook on foreign nations; total isolation was not an option for the restored community.

Second, a strong warning balanced these positive outlooks. On several occasions, the Chronicler insisted that Israel should never join in alliances with other nations. To do so was to turn from dependence on God. Dire consequences always followed for those who relied on foreign powers (2 Chr. 16:1-9; 28:16-21). The Chronicler believed that fidelity to God implied an exclusive reliance on him instead of other nations. In line with this belief, Chronicles adds that David did not help the Philistines when he was in their company (1 Chr. 12:19). Moreover, he demonstrated that only trusting in God caused the foreign nations to fear and to cease aggression against God's people (1 Chr. 14:17; 2 Chr. 9:1-12; 17:10; 20:29; 26:8). These passages reminded the post-exilic community to avoid relying on foreign human powers to sustain their newly restored nation; only divine power could secure the Kingdom.

Contemporary Christian Readers

The New Testament portrait of the Kingdom of God shares dual emphasis of openness and caution toward those outside of the covenant community. The faith of the Roman centurion (Matt. 8:5-13) and the fidelity of the Syro-Phoenician woman (Mark 7:24-30) exemplify this outward focus. Jesus even rebuked apostate Jews by warning them that people of Nineveh and the Queen of Sheba will judge them (Matt. 12:39-45). At the same time, however, Jesus warned against the evil influences of Gentile religions (Matt. 6:7).

Paul described the continuation of the Kingdom in terms of reaching foreign nations with the gospel (Acts 14:1,8; 17:12,34; 28:31). Paul was quick, however, to condemn any relationship with unbelievers that leads believers into apostasy (2 Cor. 6:14).

The themes of inclusion and separation find their greatest expression in the consummation of Christ's Kingdom. The final stage of the Kingdom will be a gathering of believers from all the nations of the earth. At that time, however, the wicked of all nations will be separated from the righteous and will suffer the eternal judgment of God (Rev. 21:24,26).

4-9) The King and Temple

The institutions of David's throne and the temple in Jerusalem form the Chronicler's second major theological concern. In the Chronicler's view these political and religious structures formed a two sided institutional center for the restored community. We will summarize his outlook by drawing attention to six motifs: *4) Royal and Levitical Families, 5) Religious Assembles, 6) Royal Observance of Worship, 7) Divine Kingship, 8) Music,* and *9) Temple Contributions.*

4) Royal and Levitical Families

Original Israelite Readers

The Chronicler's dual concern with Judah's throne and temple becomes evident in the detailed attention he gave to identifying the members of royal and Levitical families. His history reveals that God established specific families to fill these services.

1) The genealogies give more attention to David's lineage (1 Chr. 2:10-17; 3:1-24) and the families of the priests and Levites (1 Chr. 6:1-81) than to any other matters.

2) David's permanent dynasty over the nation (1 Chr. 17; 2 Chr. 13:5; 21:7; 23:3b) is described as a benefit, not a burden for Israel (1 Chr. 11:4-8, 10-11a, 18-19; 14:2; 18:14; 22:18; 2 Chr. 2:11; 7:10; 9:8).

3) The specific duties of particular priestly and Levitical families appear in a number of passages (1 Chr. 15:2; 23:28; 26:20; 2 Chr. 19:8, 23:7; 30:27; 31:2; 34:13). At times the instructions are very detailed, even specifying the ages of Levites who served (1 Chr. 23:3-5). These Levitical arrangements were to be observed in the post-exilic community (see 1 Chr. 6:48-53; 9:10-13; 16:39-42; 23:13; 29:22; 2 Chr. 29:34; 34:10).

These motifs spoke directly to concerns that troubled the post-exilic community. Judah's royal family bore a heavy responsibility for the destruction of Judah and the exile of her citizens (e.g. 2 Kgs. 21:10-15; 23:31-25:26). For this reason, at least some returnees must have wondered what role the family of David should play in their day. The Chronicler's focus on David's lineage asserted that David's sons belonged on Jerusalem's throne.

Moreover, disarray among the priests and Levites raised another important issue for the post-exilic community. When the Zadokite priest Joshua returned from Babylon to bring reforms to Levitical arrangements, other Levitical families did not immediately accept his leadership. The Chronicler, however, confirmed the teachings of other prophets by insisting on Zadokite leadership (see Ezek. 40:46; 44:10-16; 48:11; Zech 1-4). In this way, the Chronicler's focus on the priests and Levites had many practical implications for his readers.

Contemporary Christian Readers

The New Testament shares this concern with royal and priestly offices. In the first place, it plainly teaches that both of these offices are fulfilled in Christ.

Countless passages indicate that Jesus was the King of Israel (Matt. 2:2; 27:11; Luke 23:38; John 1:49; 12:13; 18:37; Rev. 17:14). He was acknowledged at his birth as the rightful heir of David's throne (e.g. Matt. 2:2). Beyond this, Christ continues to reign as King while he subdues his enemies and rules his people through his Word and Spirit (1 Cor. 15:25; Heb. 10:12-13). Moreover, at the consummation of the Kingdom every knee will bow to Christ's royal dominion and all people will submit to him (Rom. 14:11; Phil. 2:10-11). The enemies of the divine King will be punished forever and the followers of the King raised to glory (Rev. 7:14-17; 20:7-15).

Christ's ministry as priest also began at the inauguration of the Kingdom. Belonging to 'the order of Melchizedek' (Heb. 5:6), Christ endured the sufferings of this world without sin and graciously sacrificed himself on behalf of his people (Heb. 4:15). Moreover, Christ's priestly role continues throughout our time. He intercedes before the Father on behalf of the redeemed, looking after their interests and pleading their case (Heb. 4:14). Christ remains our advocate and representative before the Father (1 John 2:1). Moreover, priestly images of Christ also appear in association with the consummation. Christ is portrayed as the sacrificial lamb who stands at the center of the celestial throne room (Rev. 7:17). Christ will be exalted as our high priest throughout eternity (Heb. 7:3).

In a secondary way, the New Testament also applies the royal and priestly offices to all believers. As those who are in Christ we have been joined to his resurrection (Rom. 6:1-14). For this reason, we will reign with Christ when he returns (2 Tim. 2:12; Rev. 22:5). Moreover, we serve as priests today as well (Rev. 1:6). The body of Christ fulfills the sufferings of Christ (2 Cor. 1:5; Col. 1:24). We also form a spiritual temple for sacrifice (1 Pet. 2:1-5). The Church has become 'a royal priesthood' (1 Pet. 2:9). In these ways, the Chronicler's focus on kingship and priesthood not only applies to Christ himself, but to all believers as they are joined to Christ by faith.

5) Religious Assemblies

Original Israelite Readers

The Chronicler's focus on kingship and temple also comes to the foreground in his attention to religious gatherings called by Israel's monarchs. Usually he identified these events by the terminology of 'assemble' or 'assembly' (1 Chr. 13:2,4-5; 15:3; 28:1,8; 29:1,10,20; 2 Chr. 1:3,5; 6:3,12-13; 7:8-9; 20:5,14,26; 23:3; 24:6; 28:14; 29:23,28,31-32; 30:2,4,13,23-25; 31:18). The NIV occasionally translates related Hebrew expressions as 'summoned' (2 Chr. 5:2), 'came together' (2 Chr. 5:3), 'mustered' (2 Chr. 11:1) and 'community' (2 Chr. 31:18).

The Chronicler stressed religious assemblies as examples of mutual support between the king and temple. A number of assemblies served this function in the United Kingdom.

1) David's assembly to bring the ark into Jerusalem was a model for post-exilic worship reforms (1 Chr. 13:2,4-5; 15:3).

2) David called assemblies to encourage devotion to the temple (1 Chr. 28:1,8; 29:1,10,20). The Chronicler's readers were to do the same.

3) Solomon received wisdom as Israel's temple builder at an assembly; this event exalted Solomon's construction efforts as an ideal to be imitated (2 Chr. 1:3,5).

4) The assembly at Solomon's temple dedication spoke explicitly of the importance of the temple in Israel's future (2 Chr. 5:2-3; 6:3,12-13; 7:8-9).

During the Divided Kingdom a number of religious assemblies took place.

1) Rehoboam halted his unjustified attack on Israel in an assembly (2 Chr. 11:1-4).

2) Jehoshaphat responded to a serious military threat by calling for an assembly (2 Chr. 20:5,14,26). This exemplary gathering in worship led to great victory.

3) In addition, the importance of assemblies at the temple is evident in the reign of Joash. His national covenant renewal took place in an assembly (2 Chr. 23:3). Similarly, the exemplary account of Joash's reforms involved an assembly as well (2 Chr. 24:6).

The Reunited Kingdom also demonstrated the Chronicler's concern with religious assemblies by stressing worship events during Hezekiah's reign. The theme of assembly appears no less than eleven times in his largely positive record of Hezekiah (2 Chr. 29:23, 28, 31-32; 30:2, 4, 13, 23-25; 31:18). These accounts were designed to inspire the Chronicler's post-exilic readers to emulate Hezekiah's assemblies.

Contemporary Christian Readers

The Chronicler's concern with religious assemblies finds fulfillment in Christ and his Kingdom. Jesus came to earth to build his Church, a sanctified assembly belonging to God (Matt. 16:18). The apostles and prophets of the New Testament age form the foundation of the church for all time (Eph. 2:20).

The New Testament also calls for God's people to assemble with their King throughout the continuation of the Kingdom. Jesus said that he would be present whenever two or three are gathered in his Name (Matt. 18:20). God's people are called to fellowship by gathering as the church (Acts 14:27; 1 John 1:3). Assemblies of Christians are to devote themselves to worship and prayer, singing and giving thanks to the Lord (Eph. 5:19-20). Such assemblies are not to be forsaken (Heb. 10:25).

Religious assemblies in our times are but foretastes of our eternal gathering to God. The consummation of the Kingdom is described in terms of all believers joining countless angels in joyful heavenly assembly (Heb. 12:22). The return of Christ will mark the final call to worship as people from all ages are assembled in praise and adoration for their King (Rev. 21:1-4).

6) Royal Observance of Worship

Original Israelite Readers

The Chronicler also pointed to the centrality of David's throne and the temple by frequently noting how honorable kings of Judah devoted themselves to proper observance of temple worship. These notices appear in at least five different ways.

First, the strikingly positive record of David and Solomon draws attention to their exemplary devotion to the temple and its worship. Out of twenty-one chapters devoted to David, seventeen concentrate on his preparations for Solomon's temple (1 Chr. 13-29). In fact, the largest uninterrupted addition the Chronicler made to David's reign is exclusively concerned with his efforts on behalf of temple worship (1 Chr. 22-29). Similarly, Solomon's principal activity in Chronicles was the construction of the temple (2 Chr. 2-8).

Second, in the Divided and Reunited Kingdom the Chronicler focused on the extensive renovations and reforms of worship. Jehoshaphat (2 Chr. 17:3-6; 19:11), Asa (2 Chr. 15:8-15), Joash (2 Chr. 24:4-11), Hezekiah (2 Chr. 29:1-31:1), Manasseh (2 Chr. 33:16-17) and Josiah (2 Chr. 34:3b-35:19) are honored for their extensive worship reforms.

Third, to stress the importance of devotion to proper temple worship the Chronicler highlighted the numbers of sacrifices and offerings which honorable kings made (see 2 Chr. 1:6; 5:6; 7:4-5; 24:14; 29:32-35; 35:8-9). In each case, his intention was to convey that righteous kings enthusiastically supported the temple and its services.

Fourth, the Chronicler drew attention to the ways in which such kings often acknowledged the sanctity of the temple. This motif appears powerfully on many occasions in which kings insisted that temple personnel and the people consecrate themselves before approaching the temple (see 1 Chr. 15:4, 12, 14; 23:13; 29:5; 2 Chr. 5:11; 7:7, 16, 20; 23:6; 26:18; 29:5, 18, 19, 33, 34; 30:2, 3, 14, 17, 24; 35:3,6).

Fifth, Chronicles also notes the failure of some kings to give proper attention to temple worship. Two kings were not consistent in maintaining their reforms (2 Chr. 15:17; 20:33). Three kings actually built high places to other gods (2 Chr. 21:11; 28:4; 33:3). Beyond this, some kings defiled the temple (e.g. 2 Chr. 16:2) and its services (2 Chr. 26:16-21). The Chronicler condemned these actions in the strongest terms.

These aspects of Chronicles spoke directly to the needs of post-exilic Judah. In the early years of return from Babylon much work had to be done to rebuild the temple. After that task was completed, the worship practices of the post-exilic temple were still in need of reform. The reforms of Judah's kings in the past indicated not only the importance of the temple, but also stressed that proper temple worship was one of the chief responsibilities of the house of David in every age.

Contemporary Christian Readers

The perfect example of the royal observance of worship comes from the great King Jesus. Christ ushered in the Kingdom of God with a passion for holy worship. Even as a child, he was devoted to the temple practices (Luke 2:46). In his confrontation with Satan, Christ stated triumphantly that the only proper object of worship is God (Matt. 4:10). He drove out thieves from the temple courts (Matt. 21:12-13; John 2:14-15). Jesus' passion for worship becomes clear in his conversation with the Samaritan woman. There he explained that genuine worship is not confined to a geographic location, but must be done in Spirit and in truth (John 4:20-24).

The importance of worship extends throughout the continuation of the Kingdom as the church seeks to follow the teaching of Christ. Paul urged all believers to present themselves as 'living sacrifices' as a 'spiritual act of worship' (Rom. 12:1). It is the atoning work of Christ that enables believers to draw near and worship (Heb. 10:10). Paul also identified the New Testament church as those 'who worship by the Spirit of God' (Phil. 3:3).

The royal observance of worship becomes the great motif of the consummation of the Kingdom. John's revelation repeatedly portrays the worship of Christ the King (Rev. 5:14; 21:22). Obedience to the command to 'worship him who made the heavens, the earth, the sea, and the springs of water' will be the unbroken exercise of the children of God (Rev. 14:7). The angelic hosts are portrayed as serving him 'day and night in his temple' (Rev. 7:15).

7) Divine Kingship

Original Israelite Readers

The Chronicler emphasized the necessity of re-establishing the throne of David by developing a strong connection between David's dynasty and the reign of God. It was common in the ancient Near East to see a close relationship between the status of earthly human thrones and heavenly divine thrones. The peoples surrounding Israel believed that as their gods reigned, they established their chosen kings as powerful vice-regents. Unless a god was punishing his king, a weak or empty throne on earth called into question the power and authority of that king's god. Similar concepts are found throughout the Old Testament, but the Chronicler brought these beliefs to the foreground. Once God had ended the punishment of exile, the re-establishment of David's throne was a necessary demonstration that Israel's God reigned in heaven.

This theological conviction appears in a number of passages.

1) When speaking of the throne of Judah, the Chronicler shifted the wording from 'your (David's) house and kingdom' (2 Sam. 7:16) to 'my (God's) house and kingdom' (1 Chr. 17:14). This change exhibited the Chronicler's belief in a close connection between the divine and Davidic throne.

2) Similarly, the Chronicler changed the language of 1 Kings 10:9 ('on the throne of Israel') to 'on his [God's] throne as king to rule for the LORD your God' (2 Chr. 9:8). This variation also displayed the Chronicler's belief that a strong link existed between the throne of God and throne of David.

3) In material which the Chronicler added, King Abijah proclaimed that northern Israel was about to make war on 'the kingdom of the LORD ... in the hands of David's descendants' (2 Chr. 13:8). Abijah's words reflect the Chronicler's belief that the throne of David was the earthly representation of divine Kingship.

4) In two places (1 Chr. 29:1,19) the Chronicler designated the temple as God's 'palatial structure'. This royal terminology also revealed his view that God was Israel's King whose palace stood in Jerusalem alongside the human palace.

Chronicles stresses the relationship between the Davidic and divine thrones to meet a vital need in post-exilic times. Soon after the early returnees arrived in Jerusalem high hopes for the restoration of the Davidic line were put in Zerubbabel (see Hag. 2:20-23; Zech. 4). Despite these hopes, however, Zerubbabel never became king and disappeared from public life. Moreover, the lack of attention to royal matters in the ministries of Ezra and Nehemiah indicates that hopes for an immanent restoration of the line of David had faded. Messianic hopes were cast into the indefinite future along with other aspects of Israel's full restoration.

The Chronicler's outlook implied serious responsibilities in these situations. From his point of view, the restoration of Israel was not complete so long as the throne of David remained unoccupied. To lose hope for the restoration of David's throne was to deny the sovereignty of God himself.

Contemporary Christian Readers

The Chronicler's viewpoint on David's throne provides an essential background for understanding the New Testament teaching on the Kingdom of God (Heaven) (Matt. 12:22-28; Acts 2:22-36; 7:45-50). The darkness and discouragement of the post-exilic setting was dramatically reversed by the arrival of the great King. The divine and human Christ represents the conjoining of the divine and human thrones.

The apostles announced that Christ was 'exalted to the right hand of God' (Acts 2:22-36). There he sits on 'the throne of his father David' (Luke 1:32-33).

Christ is portrayed as the 'Most High' (Acts 7:45-50) who will reign until all his enemies are subdued (1 Cor. 15:25). The kingship of Christ is 'eternal' (1 Tim. 1:17). Upon his return, Christ will be acknowledged by all as the 'King of kings' (1

Tim. 6:15; Rev. 17:14; 19:16). The consummation will display his perfect human and divine kingship.

8) Music

Original Israelite Readers

The Chronicler's intense interest in the re-establishment of the temple and its services also appears in his extraordinary focus on music. Chronicles concentrates on the music of worship more than any other narrative portion of Scripture. For this reason, some interpreters have even suggested that the Chronicler himself was a Levitical musician. We will summarize his outlooks under two headings: the responsibility of music and the blessing of music.

First, the Chronicler took many opportunities to focus on the responsibility to perform music properly in the worship of God.

1) He made it clear which families of priests and Levites were to play instruments and sing (1 Chr. 6:33; 15:16,19,22,27; 16:4,7,42; 25:1-31; 2 Chr. 5:12; 7:6; 23:18; 29:25, 26, 27, 30; 30:21, 25; 31:2; 34:12; 35:15).

2) He noted that divine will was discerned in these matters by casting lots (1 Chr. 25:8).

3) Beyond this, he gave attention to such practical matters as the skills and training of Levitical musicians (1 Chr. 15:22; 25:7; 2 Chr. 34:12), as well as their rotation of responsibilities (1 Chr. 25:9-31).

4) The Chronicler also noted the wide range of instruments to be used in worship (e.g. 1 Chr. 13:8; 15:16).

5) He described some details of how and when music was performed in worship (2 Chr. 5:11-14; 7:6; 23:18; 29:27,28; 30:21).

6) Finally, the Chronicler noted that Levites and priests performed music to lead Israel into battle (1 Chr. 25:1; 2 Chr. 13:12,14; 20:21-22) and to celebrate victory (2 Chr. 20:28).

These descriptions of music indicated the importance of re-instituting proper musical practices in the post-exilic period. The Chronicler's emphasis suggests that his readers needed guidance in several matters. Who was to take responsibility for leading music? When and how was music to be used? He answered that direction in the matters could be found in Israel's past arrangements.

Second, Chronicles also drew attention to the wonder and joy associated with music. On many occasions, the Chronicler stressed that Israel rejoiced enthusiastically over the blessings of God. These celebrations nearly always involved music. At times the magnificence of the scenes overwhelm even modern readers (1 Chr. 15:16; 2 Chr. 5:12; 29:25-30; 30:21; 35:15).

The Chronicler repeatedly described scenes of musical celebration to offer positive incentive to his readers. For the most part, the post-exilic period was not characterized by rejoicing, singing, and dancing. Yet, Chronicles shows that when Israel served God faithfully in the past, God blessed them with the wonder of music. These scenarios encouraged the Chronicler's readers to move forward in the restoration of the Kingdom. The splendor of music awaited those who did not take their eyes off this goal.

Contemporary Christian Readers
As music and song were to be joyful expressions of devotion and celebration within Israel, so music plays an important role in the New Testament. Mary sang with joy when she realized her son was the Messiah (Luke 1:46-55). Angels announced the birth of the King in song (Luke 2:13-14). In many respects, the first coming of Christ's Kingdom was a musical event.

Musical responses from God's people also characterize Kingdom life for the New Testament Church. Believers are to make music in their hearts to the Lord with psalms and spiritual songs (Eph. 5:19; Col. 3:16). All of God's people are to celebrate the greatness of God in song (Rom. 15:11).

Music will also play a central role in the consummation of the Kingdom. When Christ returns, God's holy creatures will sing a new song unto the Lord (Rev. 5:9). Christians too will share in Christ's victory and sing the song of Moses and of the Lamb (Rev. 15:2-4).

9) Temple Contributions

Original Israelite Readers
One of the practical matters facing the post-exilic period was the need to fund the temple and its services. Although Cyrus had supplied the early returnees (Ezra 1:7-11), the prophecies of Haggai indicate that the people failed to contribute to the temple (Hag. 1). Malachi later rebuked the people for not fulfilling their tithes (Mal. 3:8-12). As a result of this kind of neglect, the Chronicler taught his readers the importance of supporting the temple by negative and positive examples from Israel's history.

First, Chronicles emphasizes a number of occasions when the treasuries of the temple were robbed. 1) Judah's king withdrew from the temple treasuries (e.g. 2 Chr. 16:2). 2) Moreover, the enemies of Judah took from the temple treasuries (e.g. 2 Chr. 12:9). The impoverishment of the temple represented judgment against God's people which the post-exilic community should avoid.

Second, the Chronicler also directed attention to occasions when the people of God devoted great quantities of money and materials to the temple.

1) He noted David's large contributions (1 Chr. 29:2-5) and the gifts of Israel (1 Chr. 29:6-9).

2) Solomon devoted resources to the temple construction (2 Chr. 2:1-5:1).

3) Joash collected and used much money for temple renovations (2 Chr. 24:5).

4) Hezekiah also gathered funds for temple services (2 Chr. 31:3-21).

5) Josiah raised temple finances as well (2 Chr. 34:9). In each case, such devotion to the temple led to times of great blessing and joy for the people of God. The same blessings would result for the post-exilic community, if it would devote financial resources to the temple.

Contemporary Christian Readers

The New Testament elaborates on the motif of temple contributions in a number of ways. Jesus was showered with gifts by the Magi as he was recognized as the great King of Israel (Matt. 2:11; John 12:3). This event exemplified enthusiastic and sacrificial giving to Christ as the final temple (John 2:18-22).

The necessity of gifts and offerings to the temple of God continues in the Kingdom after Christ's ascension. Now, however, contributions are made to the Church as the temple of the Holy Spirit. Early Christians zealously gave money to their brothers and sisters in Christ as well as to the poor (Acts 4:34-35: 11:29-30). The apostle Paul echoed the Chronicler's program by instructing Christians to set aside a sum of money 'in keeping with his income' that the Kingdom might be adequately financed (1 Cor. 16:1-4). Along these lines, he commended the Philippian Christians for their gifts and used temple language as he designated these gifts as 'an acceptable sacrifice, pleasing to God' (Phil. 4:18).

The consummation of the Kingdom will also be a time when great gifts are given to Christ. The 'honor and glory of the nations' will come to Christ and the Father who are the temple of the New Jerusalem (Rev. 21:26).

10-28) Divine Blessing and Judgment

A third major pillar in the book of Chronicles is the dynamic of divine blessing and judgment. The Chronicler's perspective on this matter was remarkably different from the writer of Kings. The book of Kings dealt with the judgment of God primarily to explain that the exile to Babylon was God's just judgment against his people. As a result, the author of Kings frequently pointed to the accumulation of divine wrath against Israel as the cause of the captivity (e.g. 2 Kgs. 17:1-41; 21:10-15). The recipients of Chronicles, however, had already returned to the land and needed to know how to avoid divine wrath and receive God's blessing in their time. The Chronicler met this need by repeatedly demonstrating that each generation of Israel faced choices which led to blessing or judgment.

The Chronicler's outlooks on divine judgment and blessing entailed many interrelated motifs. We will summarize his views in three major categories each of which will consist of smaller themes: *10-12) God and History, 13-22) Israel's Responsibilities,* and *23-28) Divine Responses.*

10-12) God and History

The Chronicler's outlooks on divine blessing and judgment rested on his convictions that God was intimately involved with his people. Israel and Judah had been the special object of redemption and judgment in the past. The post-exilic community to which he wrote was also the object of special divine attention. This perspective on Israel's relationship with God comes to expression in at least three important ways: *10) Divine Activity, 11) Name of God,* and *12) Divine Presence and Help.*

10) Divine Activity

Original Israelite Readers

God is very active in the book of Chronicles, but this divine activity takes a variety of forms. On one end of the spectrum, the Chronicler depicted God as dramatically intruding into history (1 Chr. 21:14-15; 2 Chr. 12:12; 18:31; 21:16; 28:5; 36:16-17). On the other end of the spectrum God often remained entirely in the background of events. His participation was merely implied by the remarkable nature of some incidents (2 Chr. 18:33; 20:23; 35:23).

Between these extremes, the Chronicler also described historical events in naturalistic terms and then added that God was actually behind them. He clarified that some incidents took place because God caused them (1 Chr. 10:13-14; 11:4; 2 Chr. 14:6; 22:7; 24:24; 25:20; 32:31). Similarly, he noted David's assurance of God's activity in his life (1 Chr. 11:9-10; 29:10-13). Chronicles also points out that many incidents occurred because they were fulfillment of the Word of God (1 Chr. 11:1-3; 11:10; 12:23; 2 Chr. 10:15; 36:22).

The Chronicler's purpose for drawing attention to this variety of divine activities was at least twofold. On the one hand, mentioning God's involvement in particular events indicated how his readers should evaluate those ancient events. When God caused something to happen the occurrence was to be approved or accepted by the readers. For instance, the Chronicler pointed out that Davidic claims to the throne were legitimate because God himself had caused Saul's death and transferred royal authority to David (1 Chr. 10:13-14). Similarly, the duties of priests and Levites were divinely ordained (1 Chr. 24:1-5). Likewise, God ordered Solomon to take the responsibility of temple building (2 Chr. 7:12).

On the other hand, the Chronicler wrote about the various ways God directed Israel's past to teach his post-exilic readers that God directed their history with similar variety. The activity of God in the book of Chronicles helped the readers see the many ways in which God was at work in their day. God acted in ordinary human efforts as well as extraordinary interventions. The post-exilic community needed to remember the full range of God's actions as they sought to rebuild the Kingdom.

Contemporary Christian Readers

The New Testament describes divine activity in ways that parallel the Chronicler's concerns. The inauguration of the Kingdom of Christ took place in the context of spectacular miraculous events. The virgin birth of Christ, his grand miracles, his death and resurrection, and the work of the apostles stand out among these mighty acts of God.

The New Testament also emphasizes the activity of God for the continuation of the Kingdom. Through the ministry of the Holy Spirit, the Church experiences the presence of God with power (John 14:15-21). Even so, day by day the Church must build the Kingdom even in ordinary times. God's actions often take place through normal means. In this sense, the providential activity of God continues for the Church's benefit in all ages (Rom. 8:28).

Finally, the consummation of Christ's Kingdom is the ultimate intrusion of God into human history. At the return of Christ, the entire cosmos will be destroyed and renewed (Rev. 21:1). This act of God will bring all the enemies of God to their knees and will grant great blessings to the people of God (Rev. 20:11-15).

11) Name of God

Original Israelite Readers

The activity of God also comes to expression in the Chronicler's doctrine of the Name of God. On two occasions, he mentioned God's Name simply to refer to his reputation or glory (1 Chr. 17:21,24). This use, however, was not his main interest. Instead, the Chronicler built upon a special theology of the divine Name that stemmed from earlier biblical traditions.

Simply put, Chronicles stresses that God's Name was the way of access to divine power. This concept appears no less than forty-three times (1 Chr. 13:6; 16:2, 8, 10, 29, 35; 21:19; 22:7-8, 10, 19; 23:13; 28:3; 29:13, 16; 2 Chr. 2:1, 4; 6:5-10, 20, 24, 26, 32-38; 7:14, 16, 20; 12:13; 14:11; 18:15; 20:8-9; 33:4, 7, 18; 36:13). The Chronicler believed that God himself is transcendent and unapproachable in his heavenly dwelling (2 Chr. 6:18). As a result, God had to condescend to Israel by putting his Name in the temple (2 Chr. 6:20). The presence of God's Name meant that God's 'eyes' and 'heart' were in the temple (2 Chr. 7:16).

Consequently, the Name of God was the source of power upon which God's people called when they were in trouble (1 Chr. 16:35; 2 Chr. 6:24, 26; 14:11). His Name was the object of their praise for displays of his power (1 Chr. 16:8, 10, 29; 29:13). The Name was also the authorizing power behind speeches on God's behalf (1 Chr. 16:2; 21:19; 23:13; 2 Chr. 33:18). Solemn oaths were to be taken in the Name of God for the same reason (2 Chr. 18:15; 36:13).

The Chronicler asserted this doctrine of God's Name not only to describe the past but to draw attention to the way of accessing divine power in the post-exilic period. Access to God and the hope of his blessing was available only for those who called on God's Name. This belief necessitated the reconstruction and full service of the temple which was the place of God's Name.

Contemporary Christian Readers

As the Chronicler claimed that Israel could only be strong by drawing upon the power of God's Name, so Christ taught that his Kingdom would succeed only by access to the Lord's power through his Name. Jesus established that his Name was central to life in the Kingdom. Salvation is only acquired by believing in the Name of the Lord (Acts 2:21; 4:12). Christians are 'justified in the name of the Lord Jesus Christ' (1 Cor. 6:11). Kingdom tasks are to be exercised in the Name of God: preaching (Luke 24:47), baptizing (Matt. 28:19), praying (John 14:13), fellowship (Matt. 18:20), driving out demons (Matt. 7:22) and worshipping in song (Rom. 15:9). The power behind these great works is located in the Name of Christ.

The consummation of the Kingdom will bring the great day of judgment upon humanity. Only those who have the Name of Christ written on their foreheads will be secured in the New Heavens and the New Earth (Rev. 22:4).

12) Presence and Help

Original Israelite Readers

The Chronicler often spoke of divine activity by means of the older biblical vocabulary of divine presence and help. These concepts touched vital aspects of the post-exilic experience.

First, Chronicles speaks of God being 'with' people. This language stems from Moses (e.g. Gen. 21:20, 22; 28:20; 31:5; Exod. 3:12; 34:9) and also appears in prophetic literature (e.g. Isa. 7:14; 8:10; Zeph. 3:17; Zech. 8:23). In 2 Chr. 13:12 Abijah indicated that for God to be 'with' someone meant he would fight for them. In line with this perspective, the Chronicler stressed that success is guaranteed when God is 'with' his people (1 Chr. 4:10; 9:20; 11:9; 17:2, 8; 22:11, 16, 18; 28:20; 2 Chr. 1:1; 13:12; 15:2, 9; 17:3; 19:6; 20:17; 25:7; 32:7, 8; 35:21; 36:23).

Second, the Chronicler expressed a similar concept by referring to 'help' from God. He derived this vocabulary from a number of earlier biblical traditions (Gen. 4:1; 49:25; Exod. 4:12; Deut. 33:29; Ps. 12:1; 18:6; 22:19; 30:10; 46:1; 54:4; 79:9; 86:17; 115:9-11; 118:7; 121:2; 124:8; 146:5). In one passage the help of God is explicitly tied to the concept of God being 'with' his people (2 Chr. 32:8). Put simply, the Chronicler believed that God helped Israel by intervening on her behalf in times of opposition and trouble. With only two exceptions (1 Chr. 5:26; 2 Chr. 16:12), the Chronicler associated divine help with military crises. On many occasions the people of God called out in prayer and God responded with help (1 Chr. 5:20; 2 Chr. 14:11; 18:31; 20:4; 26:7). For this reason, Amaziah assured David of God's help (1 Chr. 12:18) and Hezekiah assured Jerusalem of the same (2 Chr. 32:8). All human efforts were in vain without the help of God (2 Chr. 25:8).

The Chronicler employed these beliefs to inspire faithful dependence on God. He pointed to times when God was with his people and helped them in remarkable ways. He also noted that God sometimes withdrew from his rebellious people and gave them no help. These variations called the post-exilic community to seek God's presence and help in their day as they faced countless obstacles and threats.

Contemporary Christian Readers

The motif of God's presence and help in Chronicles speaks to Christian experience in a number of ways. The greatest expression of God's help came in the sending of Jesus Christ. Jesus came to save his people from sin and intervene on behalf of the redeemed through his incarnation. He became 'God with us' (Matt. 1:23). Luke records that the people were filled with awe at the works of Jesus and proclaimed, 'God has come to help his people' (Luke 7:16). The presence of God in Christ marked the onset of the Kingdom of God.

Throughout the continuation of the Kingdom, Christians must pray for the help of God (1 Tim. 5:5). As the risen Lord Jesus reigns over his Kingdom, he gives the Spirit of God to believers as a constant source of help (Acts 1:8; Phil. 1:19). The Christian experience is marked by the indwelling Spirit's protection, provision, power, and comfort.

The hope of every Christian lies in the consummation when God will be with his people forever (John 14:3). When God's presence with his people reaches its fullness, they will experience no more trouble (Rev. 21:2-4).

13-22) Israel's Responsibilities

The Chronicler's belief that God was involved in history led him to stress Israel's responsibility before God. True to earlier biblical traditions, his history points out that God's actions could often be explained as responses to Israel's actions. As a result, the Chronicler pointed to the kinds of human activities which resulted in God's judgment and blessing. We will describe his outlooks in ten motifs: *13) Covenant, 14) Standards, 15) Prophets, 16) Motivations, 17) Prayer, 18) Humility, 19) Seeking, 20) Abandoning/Forsaking, 21) Unfaithfulness, 22) Repentance.*

13) Covenant

Original Israelite Readers

Chronicles stresses that Israel was bound to God by covenant. On several occasions, the Chronicler used the term 'covenant' to describe an agreement among humans (1 Chr. 11:3; 2 Chr. 23:1,3,11), but his history concentrates on Israel's covenant with God.

First, the term 'covenant' appears most frequently with reference to Moses, especially as the Chronicler designated the ark of the temple as 'the ark of the covenant' (1 Chr. 15:25, 26, 28, 29;16:6, 37; 17:1; 22:19; 28:2, 18; 2 Chr. 5:2, 7, 10; 6:11). This traditional language from the Pentateuch described the ark as containing Moses' Law (2 Chr. 5:10; 6:11). The Mosaic Law was an indisputable covenant bond between Israel and God (see *Introduction: 14) Standards*).

Second, the Chronicler mentioned other divine covenants from the past to affirm their continuing significance for his readers. The Chronicler understood that each of God's covenants with Israel established permanent responsibilities before God. The Mosaic covenant remained authoritative beyond the days of Moses' covenant (see above). The covenant made with the patriarchs was fulfilled in blessings that came to David (1 Chr. 16:15-17). Similarly, David commanded Solomon to keep covenant with God (1 Chr. 28:9). Abijah appealed to David's dynastic covenant ('covenant of salt') to establish the legitimacy of his own throne

(2 Chr. 13:5). In much the same way, the Chronicler himself explained that the continuation of David's line in the days of Jehoram resulted from divine faithfulness to the covenant made with David (2 Chr. 21:7). These passages demonstrate that the Chronicler viewed the patriarchal, Mosaic, and Davidic covenants as valid for the people of God even after the exile.

Third, in several passages the Chronicler stressed the importance of covenant renewal. As Solomon noted, God's blessing came only to those who proved faithful to covenant responsibilities (2 Chr. 6:14). For this reason, after times of apostasy the people of God had to renew their allegiance to their covenant with God. Such reaffirmations took place in the days of Asa (2 Chr. 15:12), Joash and Jehoiada (2 Chr. 23:16), Hezekiah (2 Chr. 29:10) and Josiah (2 Chr. 34:32). Just as Jeremiah and Ezekiel spoke of the post-exilic times as one of covenant renewal (Jer. 31:31-33; Ezek. 34:25; 37:26), the Chronicler stressed exemplary covenant renewals from the past to guide covenant renewal in his day.

Contemporary Christian Readers

The coming of Jesus marked the institution of the New Covenant which built upon the patriarchal, Mosaic, and Davidic covenants. It also fulfilled the prophetic hopes of covenant renewal after return from exile.

Christ claimed that his own blood would seal and ratify this greater covenant (Luke 22:20; 1 Cor. 11:25; Heb. 7:22). This New Covenant would be accomplished by his mediating work on the cross and by his continuing intercession (Heb. 8:6; 9:15). As a result, those who trust in Christ are participants and beneficiaries of covenant blessings: eternal life (John 3:16; 10:28), assurance (1 Tim. 3:13), protection (John 17:11), and abundant life (Rom. 5:17). Christians are given the responsibility of being 'ministers of a new covenant' (2 Cor. 3:6) and are obligated to covenant fidelity and renewal (Rom. 3:31).

14) Standards

Original Israelite Readers

As a covenanted nation, Israel lived under divine standards. These standards governed the Chronicler's assessments of many situations in Israel's history and guided the evaluations he held before his post-exilic readers. At least three major standards appear in Chronicles.

First, the Chronicler relied heavily on the standard of Mosaic Law. In many cases, the actions of characters are approved or disapproved by appeals to the Law of Moses. Most often, these appeals focused on the regulations of worship (1 Chr. 6:49; 15:15; 16:40; 21:29; 22:13; 2 Chr. 8:13; 23:18; 24:6, 9; 30:16; 31:4, 21; 34:14, 19; 35:6, 12). Occasionally, the contexts have other matters in view (1 Chr. 22:12, 13; 2 Chr. 6:16; 12:1; 17:9; 19:8, 10; 25:4; 33:8; 35:26). While the Chronicler held forth the authority of Mosaic Law over the post-exilic community, he was not a pedantic legalist. On several occasions he wrote approvingly of times when extreme circumstances required actions which did not strictly conform to the Law of Moses (see 1 Chr. 21:28-22:1; 2 Chr. 5:11-12; 30:2).

Second, the Chronicler relied on many of David and Solomon's arrangements as standards to be observed by his readers. He often spoke of conformity to Moses and David together (1 Chr. 15:15; 22:13; 2 Chr. 8:13-14; 23:18; 33:7-8; 35:4,6). On a number of occasions the Chronicler upheld specific practices established by David and Solomon. For the most part, these references concerned practices of worship (1 Chr. 28:19; 2 Chr. 8:14; 23:18; 29:25, 27; 34:2; 35:4,15). At times, however, more general patterns are in view, especially when various kings are compared to David (2 Chr. 17:3; 28:1; 29:2; 34:2).

Third, the Chronicler set forth prophetic revelation as a standard which God's people must follow. As our discussion below indicates, the prophetic word was also an essential guide for life in the post-exilic period.

The Chronicler relied heavily on these standards as he sought to instruct his readers. He explained that compliance with the guidelines of Moses, David, Solomon, and the prophets had led Israel to blessing, but violations of these standards brought judgment. The Chronicler pointed to this dynamic to motivate his post-exilic readers to be faithful to these standards in their day.

Contemporary Christian Readers

These three standards of judgment are also reflected in the New Testament. First, the Mosaic Law is rigorously upheld as the moral standard for the Kingdom of Christ (Rom. 3:31; 1 Tim. 3:8). Jesus denied coming to abrogate the Law. Instead, he came to fulfill and obey it (Matt. 5:17; Rom. 10:4). When properly applied to the New Testament situation, the principles of the Law of Moses guide the people of God even today.

Second, certain figures are exalted as standards for others to follow. Hebrews 11:2-40 portrays a variety of Old Testament heroes of the faith that provide for us a standard of faith. As with the Chronicler, David (Matt. 12:3) and Moses (Heb. 11:24) are offered as ideals by which one's life should be patterned. As the final Moses and the last Son of David, Jesus provided the greatest standard of all.

Third, the authority of prophetic revelation in Chronicles is mirrored in the New Testament by the infallible revelation of the apostles and prophets of the church (Eph. 2:20). Their gospels and epistles are marked by revelatory character (John 21:24; 1 Cor. 14:37; 1 Thess. 2:13) and represent divine standards for Christians.

15) Prophets

Original Israelite Readers

The Chronicler placed particular emphasis on prophets. As emissaries of God's covenants, prophets applied divine standards to God's people by drawing attention to God's threats of judgment and offers of blessing. The Chronicler mentioned prophets or seers in his history no less than thirty-nine times. We will touch on three dimensions of his perspective.

First, the Chronicler revealed how much he valued prophets by referring his readers to a number of written prophetic records. The writings of Samuel, Nathan, and Gad recorded the events of David's life (1 Chr. 29:29). Nathan, Ahijah the Shilonite, and Iddo offered more information on Solomon's reign (2 Chr. 9:29). Shemaiah and Iddo had more to say about Rehoboam (2 Chr. 12:15). Iddo also described aspects of Abijah's reign (2 Chr. 13:22). Jehu the prophet kept records of Jehoshaphat's activities (2 Chr. 20:34). Isaiah reported on Uzziah (2 Chr. 26:22) and Hezekiah (2 Chr. 32:32). The Chronicler also introduced a letter from Elijah to Jehoram (2 Chr. 21:12). These repeated references to written prophetic sources indicate that prophetic perspectives from the past deeply influenced the Chronicler.

Second, the Chronicler highlighted the importance of prophecy by assigning a prophetic role to many Levites. On a number of occasions he designated Levites as 'prophets' and 'seers' (1 Chr. 25:1-5; 2 Chr. 20:14; 24:20; 29:30; 35:15). This identification appears in Chronicles more clearly than any other portion of the Old Testament. It probably reflects the conviction that the Levites, especially the musical Levites, had a prophetic role in the post-exilic community.

Third, Chronicles reports how the fate of Israel and Judah was often determined by their reactions to the prophetic word. God often sent prophets to warn of impending judgment (2 Chr. 12:5; 16:7-9; 18:8; 19:2; 21:12; 25:15; 28:9; 36:12), but reactions varied. David submitted to Nathan the prophet (1 Chr. 17:1-15) and Gad (1 Chr. 21:9-19) and received God's blessing. Rehoboam was blessed because he obeyed the prophet's prohibition against attacking Jeroboam (2 Chr. 11:1-23). Rehoboam also avoided complete defeat by responding with humility to Shemaiah (2 Chr. 12:1-12). Asa honored the prophet Azariah during his years of obedience and blessing (2 Chr. 15:8), but he rejected the prophet of God during his years of infidelity and judgment (2 Chr. 16:7-10). God spared Jehoshaphat from death because he searched for a true prophet of the Lord (2 Chr. 18:6f.). Ahab, however, died after mistreating Micaiah the prophet (2 Chr. 18:1-34). Jehoshaphat later submitted to prophetic rebuke and received blessings (2 Chr. 19:1-11; 20:1-29). Jehoram received a sharp rebuke from Elijah (2 Chr. 21:12-15). Amaziah listened to an unnamed prophet and won his battle (2 Chr. 25:5-13), but he suffered later for not listening to a prophetic rebuke (2 Chr. 25:14-28). In an unusual scenario, Northern Israelites shamed Judahites by giving heed to the prophetic word in the days of Ahaz (2 Chr. 28:9-21). Hezekiah sought Isaiah and received God's help (2 Chr. 32:20). Repentant Josiah inquired of the prophetess Huldah to his great benefit (2 Chr. 34:21f.). Finally, the Chronicler noted that one reason Zedekiah was the last king of Judah was because he refused to humble himself before Jeremiah the prophet (2 Chr. 36:12). Throughout the Chronicler's history each time the people of God disobeyed the prophetic word, judgment came against them. When they submitted to the Word of God through his prophets, they received blessings.

The implication of these scenarios would have been evident to the Chronicler's original readers. As they heard prophetic instructions in the post-exilic period (including the Chronicler's own words), they had to pay heed in order to receive the blessings of God.

Contemporary Christian Readers

The Christian faith holds similar outlooks on the prophetic word. New Testament writers repeatedly quoted or alluded to Old Testament prophets: Isaiah (Matt. 13:14; Mark 1:2; 7:6), Jeremiah (Matt. 2:17; 27:9), Jonah (Matt. 12:39), Daniel (Matt. 24:15), Joel (Acts 2:16), Samuel (Acts 13:20). Prophets are called 'servants' (Rev. 10:7) and 'brothers' (Rev. 22:9) and are understood in the New Testament as God's spokespersons (Matt. 1:22).

As the Chronicler assigned the prophetic office to priests, the New Testament grants the title of 'prophet' to the great high priest, Jesus Christ (Luke 1:76; Heb. 1:1-3). The apostle Paul performed the prophetic role as he was called to be a minister of the gospel (Rom. 1:1; 15:15-16). Timothy is called to be a prophetic voice in the Kingdom of God as he was ordained by Paul and the elders (1 Tim. 4:14). Acts 6 records the commissioning of New Testament Christians to be the heralds of God who are devoted to the ministry of the Word (Acts 6:1-7). New Testament believers are called to be prophets as they are to preach the good news to all creation throughout the continuation of the Kingdom (Mark 16:15).

As the Chronicler attached judgment and salvation to the response of Israel toward the prophetic word, so the New Testament depicts the destiny of individuals as contingent upon obedience to the Word of God. Paul warns against treating prophecy with 'contempt' (1 Thess. 5:20). Eternal life is contingent upon one's response to the Word of God (John 5:24). Those who hear and receive the Word of God are included 'in Christ' (Eph. 1:13). As with Israel, the Church is promised blessings if it heeds the prophetic word, but curses come to anyone who disregards or changes the Word of God (Rev. 22:18,19).

16) Motivations

Original Israelite readers

The Chronicler was a theologian of the heart. One of his chief concerns was to explain that service to God must not be reduced to mere external conformity. On the contrary, the blessings of God come to those who bring sincere and enthusiastic motivations to God.

In Chronicles as elsewhere in the Scriptures, the terms 'heart', 'soul', and 'mind' refer to the thoughts and motivations of people. These terms do not designate particular psychological faculties. All of the deeper dynamics of the inner person may be summed up as the heart, soul, or mind. For this reason, these terms are largely interchangeable.

Above all, the Chronicler held before his post-exilic readers the Mosaic ideal of obedience to God with a whole heart. Wholeheartedness appears in several contexts that shed light on what the Chronicler meant by the terminology. For instance, it is closely associated with being 'willing' to serve God (1 Chr. 28:9), giving money 'freely' (1 Chr. 29:9), doing 'everything' required for completing the temple (1 Chr. 29:19), seeking God 'eagerly' (2 Chr. 15:15), judging 'faithfully' in the fear of God (2 Chr. 19:9), and performing well 'in everything' (2 Chr. 31:21). In a word, to devote oneself wholeheartedly to God meant to render service with sincerity, enthusiasm and determination.

For this reason, the Chronicler often pointed out that certain kings did or did not serve God with their hearts. Zedekiah hardened his heart (2 Chr. 36:13). Pride is acknowledged as a condition of the heart (literally, 'proud of heart' [2 Chr. 25:19; 26:16; 32:25,26]). Repentance is said to involve the heart (2 Chr. 6:37). Seeking God should also stem from the heart (1 Chr. 22:19; 2 Chr. 11:16; 15:12; 19:3; 22:9).

It is important to note that the Chronicler explicitly distinguished between external behavior and the condition of the heart. Asa failed to destroy all 'the high places from Israel', but 'Asa's heart was fully committed ... all his life' (2 Chr. 15:17). In the Chronicler's thinking, wholehearted devotion to God was not synonymous with perfect practice. Conversely, Amaziah 'did right in the eyes of the LORD, but not wholeheartedly' (2 Chr. 25:2). In this case, the Chronicler distinguished between doing what was right and doing it sincerely and enthusiastically.

The Chronicler emphasized the importance of motivations because he believed that God examined the heart as well as behavior. David warned Solomon to evaluate his motives because God 'searches every heart and understands every motive behind the thoughts' (1 Chr. 28:9). David also confessed, 'You test the heart and are pleased with integrity' (1 Chr. 29:17). As Solomon said, God keeps covenant 'with those who continue wholeheartedly in your way' (2 Chr. 6:14). These passages warned the Chronicler's readers to examine their own motivations instead of simply conforming to a set of behaviors.

In the Chronicler's history, sincerity of heart often mollified the consequences of behavioral failures. The condition of the heart can be the basis of divine patience and forgiveness. Solomon asked God to 'forgive and deal with each man according to all he does, since you know his heart (for you alone know the hearts of men)' (2 Chr. 6:30). Similarly, Hezekiah prayed for God to forgive everyone 'who sets his heart on seeking God' (2 Chr. 30:19).

The Chronicler emphasized the heart to challenge his post-exilic readers. They were the restored community of whom it had been said, 'I will put my law on their hearts' (Jer. 31:33). His history called his readers to bring their hearts into conformity with the Law of God. Only then could they be assured of God's blessings.

Contemporary Christian Readers

The New Testament places a similar emphasis on the importance of the heart and motivations. Jesus taught that the greatest commandment was to love God 'with all of your heart' (Matt. 22:37-40). Moreover, salvation itself is described as the Spirit of Christ dwelling in the heart (Gal. 4:6). During the continuation of the Kingdom, God searches believers' hearts and minds as well as deeds (Rev. 2:23). In the consummation, judgment will not only focus on external behaviors, but God will also 'expose the motives' of the heart (1 Cor. 4:5).

17) Prayer

Original Israelite readers

The Chronicler exhibited a deep concern for prayer. The fullest expression of this concern appears in Solomon's temple prayer (2 Chr. 6:3-42 // 1 Kgs. 8:22-53) and God's response (2 Chr. 7:13-15 // 1 Kgs. 9:3-9). In his great temple prayer, Solomon asked God to hear prayers as the nation faced a variety of circumstances. In response, God agreed to hear such sincere prayers. These two passages established prayer as a principal means by which Israel could receive God's blessings.

This basic theology of prayer comes to expression throughout Chronicles as God answers prayers time and again. Although this pattern appears in Kings, it is much more extensive in Chronicles. In the opening genealogies and lists, the Chronicler mentioned the prayer of Jabez (1 Chr. 4:10) and of the Transjordanian tribes (1 Chr. 5:20). In both of these cases, the people of God cried out to him for help in times of conflict and he gave them victories. In the United Kingdom, both David (1 Chr. 16:7-36; 17:16-27; 29:10-20) and Solomon (2 Chr. 6:3-42) prayed. Their prayers modeled devotion and humility before God. In the Divided Kingdom, the record of the first four kings of Judah includes their prayers. Rehoboam and his nobles (2 Chr. 12:6), Asa (2 Chr. 14:11), Abijah (2 Chr. 13:14), and Jehoshaphat (2 Chr. 18:31; 20:6-12) asked for help in times of military crisis. Once again, God answered these prayers. In the Reunited Monarchy Hezekiah prayed for healing during Passover observance (2 Chr. 30:18), relief from Sennacherib's threat (2 Chr. 32:20-21), and deliverance from his sickness (2 Chr. 32:24). Moreover, Manasseh prayed for forgiveness while in exile and God returned him to the land (2 Chr. 33:12-13,18). All of these examples of prayer illustrated that God kept his promises to hear the prayers of his people.

These examples of prayer in Chronicles demonstrate the importance of prayer for the Chronicler's post-exilic readers. God's consistently gracious response to sincere prayers offered the returnees hope that God would answer their cries as well.

Contemporary Christian Readers

The centrality of prayer in the Chronicler's history foreshadows the importance of prayer in the teachings of the New Testament. Jesus prayed throughout his earthly ministry (Mark 6:46; Luke 6:12). Jesus also taught his followers how they should pray (Matt. 6:9-13). He encouraged them to pray that they 'may not fall' (Mark 14:38; Luke 22:40). He even commanded that his disciples pray for those who persecuted them (Matt. 5:44; Luke 6:28).

The apostles gave similar admonitions. We are to 'pray in the Spirit on all occasions' (Eph. 6:18) and to be devoted to prayer (1 Cor. 7:5). We are to pray continually (1 Thess. 5:17) as we surround 'everything by prayer' (Phil. 4:6). James emphasized the efficacy of the prayer of a righteous man (Jas. 5:16). Like post-exilic Israel, believers should pray to God when in trouble (Jas. 5:13), trusting that 'his ears are attentive to their prayer' (1 Pet. 3:12).

Jesus also instructed the church to pray earnestly for the consummation of the Kingdom when he prayed 'your Kingdom come' (Matt. 6:10). Following the example of John the apostle, we are to cry, 'Amen. Come, Lord Jesus' (Rev. 22:20). Our prayers will prove instrumental in the return of Christ.

18) Humility

Original Israelite Readers

Humility before God is another important responsibility which the Chronicler associated with divine blessing and judgment. The Chronicler used the verb 'to humble' eighteen times. The NIV translates this term 'subdued' (1 Chr. 17:10; 18:1; 2 Chr. 13:18), 'subjugated' (1 Chr. 20:4), 'humble' (2 Chr. 7:14; 12:6,7 [twice], 12; 28:19; 30:11; 33:12,19,23; 34:27 [twice]; 36:12). Once the NIV renders the same Hebrew word as 'repented' (2 Chr. 32:26). On three occasions in the United Kingdom (1 Chr. 17:10; 18:1; 20:4) and twice in the Divided Kingdom (2 Chr. 13:18; 28:19) the term is employed in the more ordinary sense of humbling through military defeat. Conquered nations were humbled in the sense that they lost the ability to resist and utterly surrendered to their conquerors.

The Chronicler employed this concept as a theological metaphor. He described a number of situations in which people humbled (or did not humble) themselves before God. On a number of occasions, the Chronicler placed humility in a four-step scenario.

- Israel was in rebellion against God.
- They were confronted with the need for change.
- They responded to the confrontation by surrendering themselves to God and submitting to his supremacy over them.
- This humility led to blessing from God.

First, several forms of rebellion gave rise to humility.

1) Rehoboam had abandoned the Law of God (2 Chr. 12:1,6,7).

2) Manasseh and Zebulun had not celebrated the Passover in Jerusalem according to the Law of God (2 Chr. 30:11).

3) Hezekiah 'humbled himself in his pride' ('repented of his pride' [NIV], 2 Chr. 32:26) because he had proudly failed to appreciate the kindness of God toward him (2 Chr. 32:25).

4) Manasseh humbled himself (2 Chr. 33:12,19) because he had worshipped other gods and resisted the prophets (2 Chr. 33:18).

5) Ammon is said not to have humbled himself as Manasseh did (2 Chr. 33:23); he continued his syncretistic practices throughout his life.

6) Josiah also humbled himself because he realized that Judah had forsaken God for idols (2 Chr. 34:27).

Second, humility resulted from several types of confrontation.

1) Three times the Chronicler pointed to prophetic confrontation. Rehoboam was humble when the prophet Shemaiah warned of defeat (2 Chr. 12:6,7). Josiah responded with humility at the word of Huldah (2 Chr. 34:27). Similarly, Zedekiah refused to humble himself in reaction to the word of God through Jeremiah (2 Chr. 36:12).

2) The northern Israelites in Hezekiah's day responded with humility to the king's couriers (2 Chr. 30:11).

3) In two situations, divine judgment brought about humility. Manasseh humbled himself only after defeat and exile (2 Chr. 33:10-13,23). Hezekiah also humbled himself after the Lord's wrath was on him (2 Chr. 32:25).

Third, humility resulted in surrender to God.

1) Humility gave rise to reforms during the reigns of Rehoboam (2 Chr. 12:6), Hezekiah (2 Chr. 30:12), Manasseh (2 Chr. 33:12), and Josiah (2 Chr. 34:27).

2) In the reigns of Rehoboam and Manasseh humility led to prayer for forgiveness and help (2 Chr. 12:6,7; 33:12,19).

3) In every case when people humbled themselves before God they ceased to rebel against him. Instead, they surrendered themselves to the will of God as their rightful Sovereign.

Fourth, humility before God brought dramatic blessings on no less than four occasions.

1) Rehoboam was spared utter defeat at the hand of Shishak and enjoyed many good things in his kingdom (2 Chr. 12:6,7,12).

2) Northern Israelites came to celebrate Hezekiah's Passover which resulted in the reunification of the nation (2 Chr. 30:11).

3) The destruction of Jerusalem was postponed because of Hezekiah's humility (2 Chr. 32:26).

4) Manasseh returned from exile in Babylon and experienced new prosperity when he humbled himself (2 Chr. 33:12,19).

The Chronicler's repeated emphasis on this theme inspired his post-exilic readers to humility. They too had a propensity to fall into rebellion against God. They had opportunities to receive God's warning against their rebellion. They were responsible to surrender themselves to God. Moreover, only humility could restore them to God's favor and bring a greater experience of his blessing.

Contemporary Christian Readers

The New Testament applies the theme of humility to Christians. Salvation is defined as humbling oneself before the Lord (Jas. 4:10; 1 Pet. 5:5). Entrance into the Kingdom of God is contingent upon the humbling of oneself with a child-like dependence upon God (Matt. 18:4).

Day by day Christians are to clothe themselves with humility (Eph. 4:2; Phil. 2:3; 1 Pet. 5:5). As with Israel, God blesses his people by giving grace to those who have sincere humility (Jas. 4:6).

The New Testament also projects humility into the consummation of the Kingdom. Upon the return of Christ those who attempted to exalt themselves will be humbled by the judgment of God (Matt. 23:12; Luke 14:11; 18:14). Even so, those who voluntarily humble themselves will ultimately be exalted (Luke 14:11; 14:14).

19) Seeking

Original Israelite Readers

Seeking God is another crucial responsibility of God's people in Chronicles. Two Hebrew verbs express this idea: *darash* (43 times) and *biqesh* (13 times). On one occasion the Chronicler indicated that these terms were closely related by using them together (1 Chr. 16:11). The NIV usually translates both terms 'seek', but 'inquire' also appears. Occasionally, 'search', 'consult', 'require', 'follow', 'want', and 'call into account' emerge in particular contexts.

'Seeking' appears in non-theological contexts (*darash* – 1 Chr. 26:31; 28:9; 2 Chr. 24:6,22; 31:9; 32:31; *biqesh* – 1 Chr. 4:39; 14:8; 21:3; 2 Chr. 9:23; 22:9). These uses are only tangentially related to the Chronicler's theological concept of seeking God.

The Chronicler wrote of 'seeking' in a theological sense with several specific objects.

1) On two occasions seeking focused on 'all the commands' (1 Chr. 28:8) and 'the counsel of the LORD' (2 Chr. 18:4).

2) In one passage seeking God was equivalent to inquiring for direction from a prophet (2 Chr. 18:6,7). By contrast, the opposite of seeking God was to consult a medium (1 Chr. 10:13).

3) Most frequently, however, the explicit object of seeking was God himself (e.g. *darash* – 1 Chr. 10:14; 13:3; 15:13; 16:11; 21:30; 22:19; 28:9; 2 Chr. 1:5; 12:14; 14:4; 14:7 [twice]; 15:2,12,13; 16:12; 17:3,4; 18:7; 19:3; 20:3; 22:9; 26:5 [twice]; 30:19; 31:21; 34:3, 21, 26; *biqesh* – 1 Chr. 16:10, 11; 2 Chr. 11:16; 15:4; 15:15; 20:4 [twice]). In these passages seeking was an expression of loyalty and devotion to God himself. For this reason, twice (1 Chr. 16:11; 2 Chr. 7:14) the object of seeking was the 'face' of God (i.e. his favor [see Num. 6:26]). Similarly, seeking God was the opposite of forsaking him or abandoning the covenant relationship between Israel and God (2 Chr. 15:2).

The concept of 'seeking' carried implicit connotations of intensity and commitment. The Chronicler highlighted this aspect of his concept by explicitly mentioning that seeking was to stem from the heart and soul (1 Chr. 22:19; 2 Chr. 11:16; 12:14; 19:3; 30:19). Mere outward conformity to the Law of God did not constitute seeking God. Seeking him required sincere inward devotion expressed in behavioral compliance to the Law.

The importance of seeking God with a sincere heart comes to light in the Chronicler's addition to God's response to Solomon's temple prayer (2 Chr. 7:14). God affirmed that when the people of God suffered the consequences of their sins, they could receive divine blessings if they sought the face of God (2 Chr. 7:14). This promise guided the Chronicler's repeated use of the concept of seeking God. Throughout his history he noted the dramatic results that occurred when people sought or did not seek God. Some people did not seek God or sought others instead of God (e.g. 1 Chr. 10:14; 13:3; 15:13; 2 Chr. 25:15,20). Without exception these people suffered divine judgment. Nevertheless, the Chronicler also indicated that other historical figures did seek God (e.g. 2 Chr. 14:4; 15:12). In each of these cases, the results were God's blessings.

The repetition of this motif throughout Chronicles called the post-exilic community to seek God in their own day. As troubles and disappointments mounted against those who had returned to the land, the way of divine blessing was made clear. Those who seek God could expect his blessing. To fail to seek him was to insure the failure of the post-exilic restoration.

Contemporary Christian Readers

The New Testament further reveals what it means to seek God. Jesus commanded that his followers seek the Kingdom of God (Matt. 6:33; Luke 12:31). Paul explained that seeking God is unnatural for sinful man and impossible for him to accomplish (Rom. 3:11). Even so, the regenerating work of the Holy Spirit enables man to 'seek to be justified in Christ' (Gal. 2:17) with the full assurance that 'he who seeks finds' (Matt. 7:8; Luke 11:10). The promise that God 'rewards those who earnestly seek him' extends to the consummation of the Kingdom (Heb. 11:6).

20) Abandoning / Forsaking

Original Israelite Readers

Chronicles also stresses that the people of God must not 'abandon' nor 'forsake' God. The NIV translates the same Hebrew term as 'abandon', 'forsake', 'reject', 'leave', and 'give up'. The basic significance of this terminology becomes apparent in non-theological contexts. On seven occasions, the Chronicler applied the concept of abandoning or forsaking to describe ordinary human affairs. When the people saw that Saul and his army had been defeated, they 'abandoned' their towns (1 Chr. 10:7). The Philistines 'abandoned' their gods by leaving them behind (1 Chr. 14:12). David 'left' Asaph to serve before the ark (1 Chr. 16:37). Rehoboam 'rejected' the advice of his elders (2 Chr. 10:8,13). In Ahaz's day, the soldiers of Israel 'gave up' their prisoners and plunder (2 Chr. 28:14). The Arameans 'left' Joash without helping him recover from his wounds (2 Chr. 24:25). These passages indicate that 'abandoning' implies concepts such as disowning, deserting and leaving something behind.

Throughout his history, the Chronicler used the concept of abandonment to describe Israel's disowning, deserting and leaving God behind. No less than nine times Israel's abandonment is stated in personal terms; Israel abandoned God himself (2 Chr. 7:22; 12:5; 13:10; 21:10; 24:20; 24:24; 28:6; 29:6; 34:25). In 2 Chr.

34:25 the personal character of Israel's abandonment of God becomes evident in that they left him 'for other gods'. For this reason, on two occasions abandoning God is set in opposition to seeking him (1 Chr. 28:9; 2 Chr. 15:2).

Despite this personal dimension, Chronicles is clear that forsaking God was to violate the Law of God. Israel abandoned God in two main ways. They flagrantly violated the Law of Moses in general terms (2 Chr. 7:19; 12:1; 24:20). Moreover, the nation also neglected divine regulations specifically governing worship (2 Chr. 13:10-11; 15:2-3; 21:10-11; 34:25).

To indicate the importance of not abandoning God, the Chronicler frequently pointed to dire consequences that came to those who did. In a word, when Israel abandoned God, he abandoned her (1 Chr. 28:9,20; 2 Chr. 15:5; 24:20). Divine abandonment took different forms. Maritime troubles (2 Chr. 20:37) and disease appear (2 Chr. 26:18-20). Yet, abandonment usually resulted in some kind of military trouble or defeat (2 Chr. 12:5; 21:10; 24:24; 32:21; 34:25). Exile was the most severe form of God's desertion (2 Chr. 7:19, 20).

The Chronicler emphasized the theme of abandoning God for at least two reasons. First, he explained to his post-exilic readers why they had not seen great blessings in the restoration. The early returnees had abandoned God in a number of ways and their actions brought them under a shadow of judgment. Second, he also pointed out the consequences of further violations of God's Law. The Chronicler's readers stood at a crossroads. If they continued to abandon God, they could expect only further abandonment from God.

Contemporary Christian Readers

The theme of abandonment continues to unfold in the New Testament. The Kingdom of Christ began with abandonment when Jesus cried, 'My God, my God, why have you forsaken me?' (Matt. 27:46; Mark 15:34). Absorbing the full judgment for the sins of his people, Christ was abandoned by God and painfully lamented. Nevertheless, God did not abandon Christ to the grave, but raised him up in victory through the resurrection (Acts 2:27-31).

Due to the redemption accomplished by Christ, those who are genuinely in Christ need not fear the abandonment of God. Christians may stumble and experience intense suffering, but Christ has promised 'Surely I will be with you always' (Matt. 28:20). True believers may be 'persecuted, but never abandoned' (2 Cor. 4:9). Neither the threats of death nor the attacks of the evil one can separate God's children from his love (Rom. 8:37-39).

Nevertheless, as in the Chronicler's day, not all who appear to be in Christ are genuinely in him. For this reason, the New Testament warns that some will abandon the Faith (1 Tim. 4:1). People within the Church must be careful not to abandon their 'first love' (Rev. 2:4).

The consummation of the Kingdom will infallibly demonstrate God's faithfulness to his people. He promised, 'Never will I forsake you' (Heb. 13:5). In the end, God's people will never forsake him and he will never forsake them.

21) Unfaithfulness

Original Israelite Readers

On fourteen occasions the Chronicler noted that the people of God had been 'unfaithful'. This description of rebellion against God brings to light another dimension of Israel's responsibility before God.

First, on many occasions the object of Israel's unfaithfulness is explicitly noted as God himself (1 Chr. 10:13; 2 Chr. 12:2; 28:19,22; 30:7). From the Chronicler's point of view, Israel was in a special relationship with God and rebellion was a direct and personal affront against him.

Second, unfaithfulness was also specified as acts of turning away from the Law of Moses, especially the Laws regarding worship (1 Chr. 2:7; 10:13; 2 Chr. 12:1; 26:16, 18; 28:22-23; 29:6,19; 33:19; 36:14). By this means the Chronicler drew attention to his keen interest in the Law and his high regard for proper worship.

Third, in every case of unfaithfulness, the Chronicler pointed to severe consequences of divine judgment. Achan (Achar) died (1 Chr. 2:7). The half-tribe of Manasseh went into exile (1 Chr. 5:25). Saul died (1 Chr. 10:13). Rehoboam suffered Shishak's attack (2 Chr. 12:2). Uzziah contracted a skin disease (2 Chr. 26:16-19). Ahaz was subjected to Assyrian domination (2 Chr. 28:19,22). Manasseh was exiled (2 Chr. 33:19). In fact, the Chronicler twice explained that Judah underwent the Babylonian exile because of unfaithfulness (1 Chr. 9:1; 2 Chr. 36:14).

This correlation between infidelity and severe consequences spoke to the post-exilic community in at least two ways. It reminded them that the troubles they had experienced were the result of their failure to remain faithful to God. Moreover, it warned that further infidelity would bring about severe consequences.

Contemporary Christian Readers

The New Testament often warned against infidelity. Jesus rebuked Israel for being 'unbelieving' (Matt. 17:17). The apostle Paul became 'astonished' at those who turn to a different gospel after confessing their faith in Christ (Gal. 1:6; 4:9). He further warned that many will turn from the truth and follow the way of Satan during the continuation of the Kingdom (1 Tim. 5:15; 2 Tim. 4:14). At the consummation, those who have been unfaithful will receive God's judgment (Heb. 10:26-31).

22) Repentance

Original Israelite Readers

On nine occasions Chronicles explicitly mentions the theme of repentance. The NIV translates the Hebrew term reflecting this concept as 'turn back' (2 Chr. 6:24), 'turn' (2 Chr. 6:26; 7:14; 15:4; 36:13), 'return' (2 Chr. 30:6, 9), 'bring back' (2 Chr. 24:19) and 'repent' (2 Chr. 6:37). The theme of repentance is not unique to Chronicles, but six of these nine occurrences appear in the Chronicler's additions to the book of Kings (2 Chr. 7:14; 15:4; 24:19; 30:6,9; 36:13). The motif was an important dimension of his concept of Israel's responsibility before God.

The Chronicler's concept of repentance was twofold. On the one hand, repentance was to turn away from evil. Solomon described it as turning 'from their sin' (2 Chr. 6:26). Similarly, God spoke of Israel turning 'from their wicked ways' (2 Chr. 7:14). On the other hand, repentance was an act of turning toward someone. Azariah the prophet referred to a time when Israel 'turned to the LORD' (2 Chr. 15:4). Prophets spoke to 'bring them back to him (the Lord)' (2 Chr. 24:19). Hezekiah called northern Israel to 'return to the LORD' (2 Chr. 30:6) and offered compassion from God if they would 'return to him' (2 Chr. 30:9). Finally, Zedekiah is condemned for not turning 'to the LORD' (2 Chr. 36:13). These expressions indicate the personal dimension of repentance. It did not amount simply to changing behaviors to match a set of regulations more thoroughly. Repentance was to approach God himself.

The results of repentance are also explicitly noted in Chronicles. On the one hand, those who refused to turn back to God would suffer his judgment. For instance, Zedekiah was sent to exile because he did not repent (2 Chr. 36:13). On the other hand, a number of blessings come to those who repent. The Chronicler stressed that God will have compassion, forgive sins, and answer the prayers of those who turn to him (2 Chr. 6:24, 26; 7:14; 30:9).

The purpose of this theme is evident. The failures of the post-exilic community had brought them to the point that the Chronicler called them to repentance. If his readers heeded this call, they would receive the mercy of God. If they refused, they could only expect further judgment from God.

Contemporary Christian Readers

The theme of repentance is also emphasized in the New Testament. Jesus declared that entrance into his Kingdom was contingent upon genuine repentance (Matt. 3:2). Christ explicitly warned that anyone who did not repent would certainly perish (Luke 13:3). Yet, the one who does repent inherits the Kingdom of God and causes much celebration in heaven (Luke 15:7).

The New Testament describes repentance much like the Chronicler. Paul preached that God requires repentance of everyone (Acts 17:30). Repentance includes the turning away from wickedness (Acts 3:19,26) and turning toward God (Acts 3:19; 26:20). True repentance is evident in the deeds of the repentant believer (Acts 26:20) and will be met with divine blessings (Acts 3:26). God himself is the one who grants the gift of repentance (2 Tim. 2:25).

At the consummation of the Kingdom, the presence or lack of repentance will determine eternal destiny. John anticipates the rebellion of those who refuse to repent, even in the face of judgment (Rev. 16:9,11). The Kingdom will belong to all who receive the word of God in repentance (Rev. 3:3).

23-28) Divine Responses

The Chronicler completed his doctrine of divine blessing and judgment by addressing the manner in which God would respond to his people. His history demonstrates that God's blessings and judgments take many different and unpredictable forms. By repeating some scenarios, however, the Chronicler pointed to patterns which God followed in the past to create a set of expectations for his post-exilic readers. We will touch on five of these patterns: *23) Victory and Defeat, 24) Building and Destruction, 25) Increase and Decline of Progeny, 25) Prosperity and Poverty, 27) Disappointment and Celebration,* and *28) Health, Long Life, Sickness and Death.*

23) Victory and Defeat

Original Israelite Readers

Victory and defeat appear as patterns of blessing and judgment on many occasions. The Chronicler focused on these themes because his readers faced many military threats. They had returned to Jerusalem, but then political security was tenuous at best. Just as the prophets had announced that return to the land would lead to war (see Isa. 11:11-16; 49:14-26; 54:1-3; Jer. 30:10-11; Ezek. 38-39; Amos 9:11-12), the Chronicler realized that the potential of warfare was great. For this reason, he set much of his discussion of divine judgment and blessing in the arena of warfare. He taught his post-exilic readers how to avoid defeat and to secure the blessing of victory in battle.

The following list indicates where the Chronicler dealt with victories and defeats.

Victories	*Defeats and Setbacks*
Transjordanian Tribes (1 Chr. 5:10,20-22)	Transjordanian Tribes (1 Chr. 5:24-26)
David (1 Chr. 11:4-9, 12-14; 14:8-17; 18:1-13;19:1-20:3; 20:4-8)	Saul (1 Chr. 10:1-14)
Abijah (2 Chr. 13:2b-21)	Rehoboam (2 Chr. 12:1-12)
Asa (2 Chr. 14:8-14)	Asa (2 Chr. 16:1-6)
Jehoshaphat (2 Chr. 20:1-30)	Jehoshaphat (2 Chr. 18:28-34)
Amaziah (2 Chr. 25:11-12)	Jehoram (2 Chr. 21:12-17)
Uzziah (2 Chr. 26:6-8)	Joash (2 Chr. 24:23-24)
Hezekiah (2 Chr. 32:9-21)	Amaziah (2 Chr. 25:20-24)
	Ahaz (2 Chr. 28:6-8)

On the one hand, military defeat was judgment for sin. The exile of the Transjordanian tribes was due to infidelity (1 Chr. 5:24-26). The Philistines defeated Saul because of his great sins (1 Chr. 10:1-14). Solomon acknowledged that sin often leads to military ruin (2 Chr. 6:24). Rehoboam forsook God and his Law only to find himself threatened by Shishak (2 Chr. 12:5-8). Infidelity and murder led to Jehoram's defeat (2 Chr. 21:12-17). Disobedience led to Joash's overthrow (2 Chr. 24:20-24). Amaziah refused to listen to God and suffered defeat (2 Chr. 25:20). Idolatry brought defeat to Ahaz (2 Chr. 28:1-8). Although the vast majority of examples indicate that defeat was God's response to the sins of his people, 2 Chr. 6:24 suggests that the Chronicler understood that not all defeats were because of sin.

The Chronicler's emphasis on military defeat as divine judgment followed the outlook of Moses and the prophets. Mosaic literature presents defeat as a covenant curse for rebellion against God (see Deut. 28:36-37,64; Lev. 26:17). The prophets affirmed the same perspective (e.g. Isa. 8:5-8; Jer. 5:10-17; Hab. 1:2-11). The Chronicler applied these theological perspectives to his analysis of Israel's history. The nation often suffered defeats because of rebellion against God.

On the other hand, the Chronicler also pointed to Israel's tremendous victories as a result of fidelity to God. He often stressed the wonder of these events by indicating the enormous sizes of the enemies whom Judah defeated. The Transjordanians took 100,000 captive (1 Chr. 5:10,20-22). David faced 32,000 chariots and charioteers along with others (1 Chr. 19:6-7). Rehoboam was attacked by 1,200 chariots, 60,000 horsemen and innumerable troops (2 Chr. 12:3). Jeroboam had 800,000 troops against Abijah's 400,000 (2 Chr. 13:3). Zerah lost to Asa even though he had a vast army with 300 chariots (2 Chr. 14:9). Jehoshaphat also faced a vast enemy whom God defeated (2 Chr. 20:2).

For the most part, the Chronicler noted the tremendous advantage of Israel's enemies to demonstrate that victory came not by human power but by divine intervention. From the Chronicler's perspective, victory in battle demonstrated that 'the battle is God's' (1 Chr. 5:22; 2 Chr. 20:15). By contrast, the Chronicler once mentioned that infidelity led to Israel's defeat despite her superior numbers (2 Chr. 24:24).

On many occasions, the Chronicler linked victory in battle with other major themes in his book. First, victory is often associated with prayer. In his dedicatory prayer, Solomon asked God to respond to prayers offered in times of battle (2 Chr. 6:24-25,28-31,34-35). Solomon's desire is fulfilled a number of times in Chronicles. The Transjordanian tribes receive victory because of their prayers (1 Chr. 5:20). Prayer delivered Rehoboam from total defeat (2 Chr. 12:1-12). Abijah and his men were delivered in battle because of prayer (2 Chr. 13:14). Asa was victorious because he cried out to God (2 Chr. 14:11). Jehoshaphat prayed in two different battles with positive results (2 Chr. 18:31;20:6-12). Hezekiah and Isaiah found deliverance for Jerusalem through prayer (2 Chr. 32:20). The Chronicler's purpose for repeating the connection between prayer and military victory is not difficult to discern. By drawing attention to the ways prayer delivered God's people in the past, the Chronicler instructed the post-exilic community on the necessity of prayer in their own day. When warfare threatened, the people of God were to pray.

Moreover, the Chronicler described the cessation of war as the gift of 'peace' (1 Chr. 4:40; 22:9, 18; 23:25; 2 Chr. 14:6,7; 15:15; 20:30), 'rest' (1 Chr. 19:19; 22:9; 2 Chr. 14:1,5,6; 20:30; 34:28), and 'quiet' (1 Chr. 22:9; 2 Chr. 23:21). The repetition of these positive motifs enabled the Chronicler to set positive goals before his post-exilic readers. They lived in a time of great insecurity. Nevertheless, through examples of God granting peace, rest and quiet to his people from time to time, the Chronicler depicted what his readers could expect to receive in their day as they were faithful to God and experienced victory from him.

Contemporary Christian Readers

The New Testament extends the Chronicler's concept of victory and defeat into the inauguration, continuation, and consummation of Christ's Kingdom. The inauguration marked the beginning of great victory. Through the death and resurrection of Jesus, death was 'swallowed up in victory' (1 Cor. 15:54). Satan fell from his position of authority (Luke 10:18), and was bound that the Kingdom might progress victoriously (Mark 3:27; Rev. 20:2). In his earthly ministry, Christ disarmed and made a mockery of the powers opposing God (Col 2:15).

Following the leadership of the Divine Warrior, Christians are to engage in battles that the Kingdom may advance. The war is not against 'flesh and blood' but 'against the powers of this dark world' and 'the spiritual forces of evil in the heavenly realms' (Eph. 6:12). Believers are to fight the good fight (1 Tim. 1:18; 6:12) by putting on the full armor of God and the armor of light (Rom. 13:12; Eph. 6:11). The weapons of the Christian soldier are not the weak weapons of this world. Rather the weapons of the Christian are filled with 'divine power' (2 Cor. 10:4). The principal empowerment of the believer is prayer (Eph. 6:18). Far from being a privilege of communication with God whereby we merely petition God for blessings, prayer is our access to the Divine Warrior himself. The prayers of believers are the powerful tools that God has issued to dismantle the forces of evil. As a result, Christians attain the victory through Christ (1 Cor. 15:57) and become 'more than conquerors' (Rom. 8:37). For everyone 'born of God overcomes the world' (1 John 5:4).

'Fighting' and 'victory' are central metaphors in John's description of the consummation. Occasionally, spiritual warfare appears bleak and uncertain for the Christian, but John's apocalyptic vision reassures every Christian that God will win the battle. Christ will return to earth to bring final defeat to all of his enemies (Rev. 19:11-21; 20:7-10).

24) Building and Destruction

Original Israelite Readers

The Chronicler also juxtaposed successful building projects and destruction as demonstrations of divine blessing and judgment. In the ancient Near East it was common for royal inscriptions to indicate divine blessings toward kings by recounting the king's successful construction efforts. City walls, roadways, fortifications, palaces, and temples were considered proof that a king was in the favor of his god. In much the same way, the Chronicler indicated his evaluation of kings at particular moments by noting their building projects.

Building projects do not play a major role in the opening genealogies. The Chronicler only pointed to successful efforts of Ephraimites (1 Chr. 7:24) and Benjamites (1 Chr. 8:12). These references note the blessings of God on particular families, but they do not function very importantly in these chapters.

By contrast, the record of David and Solomon's ideal reigns focuses on temple construction and the construction of their palaces. David was forbidden to build a temple, but the Chronicler maintained his honor by noting that he built a palace for himself (1 Chr. 14:1). Similarly, he also pointed out that Solomon had a splendid palace (2 Chr. 2:1,3; 7:11; 8:1). In line with the expectations of people in his day, the Chronicler indicated that David and Solomon were kings whose blessing from God was evident in their successful palace construction efforts.

In addition to their palaces, the Chronicler also noted that David and Solomon fortified their nation against enemies. David rebuilt and strengthened Jerusalem (1 Chr. 11:8). Solomon built a number of villages and established an elaborate system of defensive cities (2 Chr. 8:2-6).

Throughout the Divided and Reunited Kingdom, construction projects served as part of the Chronicler's portrayal of divine blessing and judgment. Put simply, successful construction projects indicated God's approval of a king. Rehoboam (2 Chr. 11:5-11), Asa (2 Chr. 14:6,7; 16:6), Jehoshaphat (2 Chr. 17:12), Uzziah (2 Chr. 26:2, 6, 9, 10), Jotham (2 Chr. 27:3-4) and Manasseh (2 Chr. 33:14) built up defensive fortifications of various sorts. In their contexts, these records clearly indicate that the completion of these projects was the result of divine blessing. They demonstrated that God had blessed his people at that particular time.

One example of fortification is problematic. During the Sennacherib invasion, Hezekiah prepared for the approaching Assyrian army by building defenses for Jerusalem (2 Chr. 32:5,29). Although the Chronicler did not explicitly condemn the king's actions, Isaiah the prophet spoke of Hezekiah's actions as a lack of trust in God (see commentary on 2 Chr. 32). The chief difference between Hezekiah's actions and other fortification projects was that Hezekiah turned to human ingenuity in response to a threat. Other fortifications in Chronicles took place after battles had been won (2 Chr. 16:6; 26:6) or as a result of faithfulness to God in some other matter (2 Chr. 11:5-11; 14:6, 7; 16:6; 17:12; 26:2, 6, 9, 10; 27:3-4; 33:14).

The Chronicler's outlook on building and fortification projects fit well with the needs of his post-exilic readers. Those who returned to the ruins of Jerusalem concentrated on building the temple. Ezra and Nehemiah were involved in the refortification of Jerusalem. The Chronicler instructed his readers on the proper outlook on these matters. Rebuilding Jerusalem and other sites was important, but these projects must not be motivated by reliance on human strength. Instead, success in fortifications and other building projects will come only as God's blesses his people for fidelity and trust. If the post-exilic community focused on faithfulness to God, then he would give them success in their construction efforts.

Contemporary Christian Readers

The post-exilic building and fortification projects anticipate the spiritual building of the Kingdom of God. Architectural imagery is pervasive throughout the New Testament as Christ the king announces the ultimate building program when he claims, 'I will build my church' (Matt. 16:18). The inauguration of the Kingdom also coincided with the destruction of the temple in Jerusalem (70 AD).

The continuation of the Kingdom is characterized by the building up of the people of God into his Kingdom (Jude 20). Paul exhorts the people of God to 'excel in the gifts that build up the church' (1 Cor. 14:12). Christian fellowship finds its purpose in the building up of one another (1 Thess. 5:11). The expansion of the Kingdom is accomplished through missionary efforts to lay a 'foundation' as 'expert' builders (1 Cor. 3:10).

As 'God is the builder of everything' (Heb. 3:4), the glory of the Kingdom's consummation will result from the efforts of the Divine builder (Heb. 3:4). While the enemies of God will ultimately suffer destruction (2 Thess. 1:9; 2 Pet. 2:1), the people of God will enter the great City 'whose architect and builder is God' (Heb. 11:10).

25) Increase and Decline of Progeny

Original Israelite Readers

Another way in which the Chronicler illustrated God's response to Israel was through the increase and decline of progeny. The Chronicler's focus on this theme stemmed from older Biblical traditions. Moses had made it clear that many children were the blessing of God for fidelity to the covenant (see Exod. 32:13; Deut. 30:2-6,9-10). Similar beliefs were expressed elsewhere in the Old Testament (e.g. Job 5:25; Ps. 127:3; Isa. 48:19).

In line with these traditions, the Chronicler noted that a number of tribes experienced significant increases of progeny. The tribe of Simeon is exalted by its large numbers (1 Chr. 4:38). Similarly, Issachar received the blessing of many children (1 Chr. 7:4). The Benjamites also found this blessing (1 Chr. 8:40; 9:7-9) as did David (1 Chr. 14:3-7). Rehoboam was blessed in this way after responding appropriately to the prophetic word (2 Chr. 11:18-23). Abijah had many children during his years of fidelity (2 Chr. 13:20-21). Jehoiada's progeny received attention in the Chronicler's record (2 Chr. 24:3).

By contrast, God judged Saul by killing both him and 'his house' (1 Chr.

10:14). The Chronicler pointed to divine judgment against Jehoram by noting that his children died (2 Chr. 21:14,16-17).

These passages demonstrate that the Chronicler sought to motivate his post-exilic readers by pointing to the blessing of a large progeny and the judgment of a decrease in progeny. As the prophet Zechariah indicated, the hope of restoration after exile included large numbers of children in Jerusalem (Zech. 8:5). The Chronicler held forth this ideal as well. Despite these hopes, the population of the post-exilic community remained relatively small. The Chronicler explained that the failure of this hope was due to infidelity and that its fulfillment depended on the faithful response of the post-exilic community.

Contemporary Christian Readers

The Old Testament's concern with physical progeny is developed in a number of directions in the New Testament. On the one hand, concern for children as the expected heirs of the covenant promises is evident in a number of New Testament passages (see Acts 2:39; 16:31; 1 Cor. 7:14). Beyond this, however, the Chronicler's emphasis on large numbers within Israel develops into the New Testament theme of multiplication through the proclamation of the gospel. In his first coming, Christ brought many to salvation (Matt. 4:23-25). The Church continues today to add to the numbers of the Church. At Christ's return the Chronicler's emphasis on the blessing of large numbers will find its final fulfillment. In the end, myriads of men and women will stand before God in the salvation of Christ (Rev. 7:9).

26) Prosperity and Poverty

Original Israelite Readers

The Chronicler also illustrated the dynamics of divine judgment and blessing in Israel's experience of poverty and prosperity. The returnees had suffered economic hardships when they returned (e.g. Hag. 1:6). These difficult conditions hardly compared with the portraits of Israel's glorious restoration found in the prophets (e.g. Isa. 60:1-22; 65:17-25). In response to these conditions, the Chronicler pointed to the steps necessary for avoiding economic deprivation and receiving the divine gifts of prosperity, wealth, and riches.

On the one hand, the Chronicler was convinced that post-exilic Israel's poverty resulted from serious violations of her covenant with God. This belief stemmed from Mosaic covenantal structures (Deut. 11:13-15). On a number of occasions, the Chronicler presented this negative assessment. For example, Zechariah made it plain to Joash that he 'will not prosper' (2 Chr. 24:20) because of disobedience. Similarly, Rehoboam suffered economic losses from his royal treasuries (2 Chr. 12:9). Along these same lines, the last kings suffered economically because of repeated rebellion against God (2 Chr. 36:3,7,10). These incidents explained the difficult economic conditions of post-exilic Israel as the result of infidelity. They also warned against continuing in disobedience.

On the other hand, prosperity was a gift from God for fidelity. Consequently, the Chronicler focused especially on the wealth and riches of the ideal United Kingdom. David gained great riches through his warfare (1 Chr. 18:7-8; 29:3-5). He also died with wealth and honor (1 Chr. 29:28). Solomon, however, exceeded the wealth of his father. From the beginning of his reign Solomon prospered (1 Chr. 29:23). God promised him even greater wealth in response to his request for wisdom to rule Israel (2 Chr. 1:11,12). In fact, the Chronicler described Solomon's riches as greater than any other king who ever lived (2 Chr. 9:22). The reigns of David and Solomon served as models for the post-exilic community. As a result, their reigns appear as times of great prosperity.

Similarly, the Chronicler highlighted the wealth and riches of certain kings during the Divided and Reunited Kingdom to teach his readers the way to prosperity. He noted the wealth gained in times of fidelity during the reigns of Asa (2 Chr. 14:7), Jehoshaphat (2 Chr. 17:5; 18:1) and Hezekiah (2 Chr. 31:21; 32:29). By this means, the Chronicler encouraged his readers to pursue righteousness in order to receive the gift of prosperity in their day.

Contemporary Christian Readers

The Kingdom of God marked the onset of a new era of spiritual riches (Eph. 1:3). Christ inaugurated his kingdom by offering the gift of eternal life and the full measure of joy (John 17:13; Rom. 10:13). To all who entered the kingdom of God, Christ promised an increasing abundance of blessing (Matt. 13:12).

The enduring blessing that Christ inaugurated for the believer is the gift of the Holy Spirit (John 16:13). The Spirit is given as a 'deposit' of our future inheritance in glory (Eph. 1:13-14). Although Christians may experience an enormous lack of material prosperity and blessing, the great blessing of the Holy Spirit enables them to further the work of the Kingdom (1 Cor. 7:7; 12:1-11; Eph. 4:7-13). Like Paul, Christians should not be surprised to find themselves deprived and persecuted (1 Thess. 2:9; 1 Pet. 4:12).

Even so, the riches which are not guaranteed during the continuation of the Kingdom will be given in full at its consummation. When Christ returns believers will inherit the earth (Matt. 5:5) and enjoy the riches of the New Heavens and New Earth (1 Tim. 6:19; Eph. 1:18).

27) Disappointment and Celebration

Original Israelite Readers

The Chronicler drew attention to God's responses to Israel by highlighting the themes of disappointment and celebration. According to prophetic hopes, the restoration of the kingdom was to be a joyous event (Isa. 60:1-22; 65:17-25). In reality, however, there were moments of celebration (Ezra 3:10-13; 6:16), but more often the restored community suffered (e.g. Ezra 3:12; 4:1-24; Neh. 1:4; 8:10-11). The Chronicler addressed this situation by identifying the causes of these disappointments and by pointing to the way of joy.

Incidents of disappointment appear in two ways in Chronicles. First, the

Chronicler pointed to scenes of disappointment simply by noting incidents that would ordinarily lead to sorrow and grief (e.g. 2 Chr. 20:35-37; 36:15-19). The emotional weight of these events was so obvious that no comment on emotions was necessary. Second, the Chronicler pointed explicitly to the sadness and disappointment of some events (e.g. 1 Chr. 10:10-14; 2 Chr. 33:12-14; 35:25). In each of the cases, the cause of disappointment is made plain. God's people had rebelled against him.

As important as these disappointing events may have been, it is evident that the Chronicler focused more on celebrative events. Joyous celebration played an especially prominent role in the idealized reigns of David and Solomon. Each of the major portions of David's reigns ended with celebration including festive eating (1 Chr. 12:40; 16:3; 29:22). Celebrations extend for lengthy portions of David's reign (1 Chr. 12:38-40; 15:25-16:43; 29:6-25). In much the same way, the central event of Solomon's life, the construction and dedication of the temple, ended in celebration in which the whole nation rejoiced in unison (2 Chr. 5:2-7:10).

The record of the Divided and Reunited Kingdom does not give as much attention to joyous celebration. Nevertheless, portions of five reigns stand out because they illustrate how certain actions brought celebration to the people of God. During Asa's reforms, the people rejoiced as they renewed the covenant with God (2 Chr. 15:10-15). The restoration of Joash to his rightful place as king and the covenant renewal that followed led to great celebration (2 Chr. 23:21). Hezekiah restored the temple with the result of joy (2 Chr. 29:36). The celebration of his Passover was so great that the festival had to be extended for a week (2 Chr. 30:23-31:1). Joy also resulted from the enormous contributions the people made to the temple services in Hezekiah's day (2 Chr. 31:8). Finally, Josiah's Passover observance also brought rejoicing to the nation (2 Chr. 35:1-19).

Once again, the Chronicler's motivations for highlighting these events is not difficult to discern. Covenant renewal, the re-establishment of the Davidic throne, and the restoration of national unity around the temple were among his highest ideals. He hoped to motivate his post-exilic readers to pursue these goals by displaying joys that resulted when they were attained in the past.

Contemporary Christian Readers

The New Testament also sets joyous celebration before Christians to motivate them to faithful living. The angels answered that the inauguration of the Kingdom brought 'great joy' (Luke 2:10). Celebration belongs to everyone who welcomes Jesus and his Kingdom.

At least two major threats come against Christian joy as the Kingdom continues. First, rebellion against God's Law and failure to trust Christ may cause severe disappointment. Jesus explained that the completion of joy is contingent upon obedience and remaining faithful (John 15:9-11). Furthermore, Paul warned that turning from the gospel, even in the midst of trial, would inevitably bring disappointment (Gal. 4:15). Second, the trials of this age also threaten to bring

disappointment instead of celebration. Jesus foretold that Christians will endure many trials, but he also promised that grief will eventually transform into joy (John 16:20).

Ultimately, the hope of every Christian is grounded in the consummation of the Kingdom. It will be marked by immeasurable celebration and festivity. Never again will the Christian's joy be lost (John 16:22; Heb. 12:22; Rev. 7:17).

28) Healing and Long Life / Sickness and Death

Original Israelite Readers

Chronicles also draws attention to the experience of sickness, death, healing, and long life as God responded to his people. Building on long-standing biblical traditions, the Chronicler noted that sickness and untimely deaths often result from the judgment of God (2 Chr. 15:13; 23:7). By contrast, healing from disease and long life stand as signs of God's blessing (1 Chr. 29:28; 2 Chr. 32:24-26).

The Chronicler also made it clear that death was often the consequence of disobedience. In the midst of Asa's reform, the punishment of death was extended to anyone who did not seek the Lord (2 Chr. 15:13). Death also ensued when an act of desecration toward the temple was committed (2 Chr. 23:7). Hezekiah experienced the threat of death but the Lord responded graciously to his repentance and faithfulness (2 Chr. 32:24-26).

It goes without saying that death was not always God's curse on his people. For this reason, the Chronicler often noted the honor or dishonor afforded kings in their burials. His reports vary in a number of ways. Some kings were highly honored in their burial notices by their close association with David: Solomon (2 Chr. 9:31), Rehoboam (2 Chr. 12:16), Abijah (2 Chr. 14:1), Asa (2 Chr. 16:14), Jehoshaphat (2 Chr. 21:1), Hezekiah (2 Chr. 32:33). The burials of other kings were qualified to indicate their dishonor: Jehoram (2 Chr. 21:20), Ahaziah (2 Chr. 22:9), Joash (2 Chr. 24:25), Uzziah (2 Chr. 26:23). Still other burial notices are relatively neutral: Amaziah (2 Chr. 25:28), Manasseh (2 Chr. 33:20), Josiah (2 Chr. 35:24).

These final burial notices shed light on the manner in which the Chronicler hoped his readers would respond to the actions of each king. They were not intended as categorical approvals or disapprovals; most kings in each grouping exhibited positive and negative actions. Yet, their burial notices indicated the Chronicler's last word on each king. A dishonorable burial notice drew attention to the king's actions which led to judgment. An honorable burial notice focused on the fidelity that led to that blessing.

Contemporary Christian Readers

The Kingdom of Christ began with dramatic displays of healing and other physical miracles. The ministries of Christ and his apostles demonstrated that the great Son of David brought with him the blessing for which the Chronicler hoped. Jesus came that we might have life more abundantly (John 10:10). At the same time, the

New Testament also testifies that the judgment of God during the inauguration and continuation of the Kingdom sometimes takes the form of physical death (e.g. Acts 5:1-11; 1 Cor. 11:30; 1 John 5:16). Finally, at the consummation of all things believers will enter eternal life and health (Rev. 22:1-5). The wicked, however, will undergo eternal death (Rev. 21:6-8).

Translation and Transmission

Reliable translations of Chronicles are readily available to English readers. Nevertheless, significant difficulties in translation appear from time to time. For the most part, this commentary follows the New International Version (NIV). When the commentary differs with the NIV, other major English translations (New King James [NKJ], New American Standard [NAS], and New Revised Standard [NRS]) are usually cited to illustrate and support an alternative rendering.

Beyond this, occasionally it is necessary to mention problems that arose in the transmission of ancient versions of Chronicles, Samuel, and Kings. The main witnesses to these books are the traditional Hebrew (Masoretic) text, versions of the Greek Old Testament (Septuagint), Syriac (Peshitta), and Latin (Vulgate) texts. Although this commentary presupposes the infallibility of the Hebrew text which the Chronicler originally penned under the inspiration of the Holy Spirit, none of the ancient versions of the book now available perfectly match the original. As a result, the commentary must deal with ancient witnesses in at least two different ways.

First, attention is given to possible corruptions of the ancient texts lying behind our modern translations. On a number of occasions it seems likely that one or more witnesses have suffered from intentional or unintentional changes. These corruptions are mentioned when they have a bearing on interpretation.

Second, recent discoveries at Qumran (the Dead Sea Scrolls) have provided much insight into the original text of Chronicles. Cave IV at Qumran (4Q) contained a number of fragments of the book of Samuel. Analyses of these fragments strongly suggest that the Chronicler used a version of Samuel that was not identical with the traditional Hebrew text on which our modern translations of Samuel are based. As a result, differences between our English translations of Samuel and Chronicles do not always represent intentional changes by the Chronicler. As we will see, some apparent differences between Samuel and Chronicles in our versions were not present in the Chronicler's original Hebrew texts of Samuel and Chronicles.

Appendix A – The Families of Levi

The genealogies and lists covering the tribe of Levi answered specific questions that had been raised in the Chronicler's day. The duties among the various families of Levi had shifted throughout the history of Israel, leaving much confusion in the minds of post-exilic Israelites. A brief sketch of these developments will make the Chronicler's purpose more evident. The following discussion is not comprehensive, but it points to the major contours of the tribe's history in six periods: Patriarchal, Mosaic, Davidic, Solomonic, Exilic, and Post-Exilic (see figure 3).

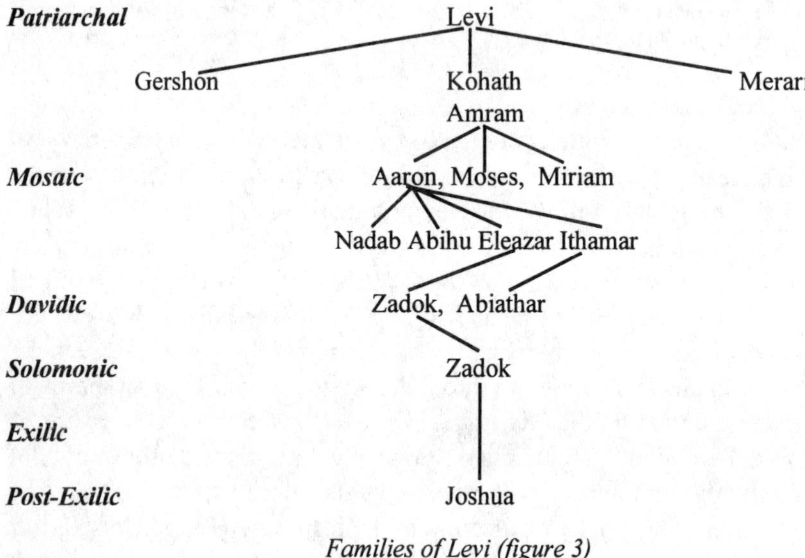

Families of Levi (figure 3)

Patriarchal Period

Levi was one of the twelve patriarchs and had three sons: Gershon, Kohath and Merari (1 Chr. 6:1; see Gen. 46:11). The Chronicler's genealogies deal with the Gershonites (6:17,20,62,71), Kohathites (1 Chr. 6:2,22,60-61,66), and Merarites (1 Chr. 6:19,29,63,77).

Mosaic Period

Kohath and his son Amram stood at the head of Levi's most prominent descendants. Moses, Aaron and Miriam descended from Amram (1 Chr. 6:3), and Moses consecrated Aaron and his sons as priests in distinction from all other Levites (see Exod. 28,29). The sons of Aaron had a variety of special duties in worship not shared by other Levites.

Not all the descendants of Aaron held this honored priestly role throughout history. Aaron had four sons: Nadab, Abihu, Eleazar, and Ithamar (6:3; see Exod. 6:23; Num. 3:2). The first two sons died without offspring in the wilderness because of sacrilege (see 24:2; Lev. 10:1-2). The sons of Eleazar and Ithamar alone continued the priestly line. All the descendants of Eleazar and Ithamar were to serve as priests, but Phinehas, a son of Eleazar, and his descendants were chosen as high priests because of Phinehas' zeal for God's honor (see Num. 25:10-13).

Davidic Period

David established two high priests to represent these two priestly families of Eleazar and Ithamar in his new capital of Jerusalem: Abiathar, a descendant of Ithamar

(15:11; 24:6), and Zadok, a descendant of Eleazar (6:4,12). These priests shared the high priestly office in David's day (18:16; see 2 Sam. 20:25).

Solomonic Period

During the struggle for the throne after David's death, Abiathar sided with Adonijah against Solomon (see 1 Kgs. 1:7). Therefore Solomon removed him from the priesthood, fulfilling the prophecy spoken by the Lord at Shiloh concerning the house of Eli (see 1 Sam. 2:27-36; 1 Kgs. 2:26-27,35). By contrast, Zadok supported Solomon and his descendants and held exclusive right to the high priestly service until the exile (29:22; see 1 Kgs. 2:35; 4:1-4).

Exilic Period

At the time of Judah's exile, many Zadokite priestly leaders were taken away to Babylon. As a result, other descendants of Levi who remained in the land served in their place among the ruins of the temple. The Zadokite priest Ezekiel prophesied that when the exiles returned, the Zadokite family would be restored to its previous status of leadership in the new temple. Other families of Levi were to hold subordinate positions, even as they had before the exile (see Ezek. 40:46; 43:19; 44:10-15).

Post-exilic Period

Naturally, Ezekiel's position caused trouble after the exile. Joshua (spelled 'Jeshua' in 1 Chr. 24:11; 2 Chr. 31:15), the Zadokite high priest, returned with David's descendant Zerubbabel to take charge of worship in Jerusalem. The prophet Zechariah supported Zadokite leadership. In his view, Joshua was Zerubbabel's indisputable partner (see Zech. 3-4). From the amount of attention given to these matters by Ezekiel and Zechariah it appears that not all the descendants of Levi were happy that the Zadokites were returning to their previous roles.

This background explains why the Chronicler took so much care to outline the duties given to each family of Levi. His genealogies and lists reach back to the Mosaic and Davidic periods to provide clear directions in the confusion of the post-exilic period. What families were supposed to be priests? What were the other Levitical families to do? The Chronicler addressed these kinds of issues in no uncertain terms. He supported the prominence of the Zadokite line, but also established duties of honor for the other families of Levi.

Appendix B – The Structures, Furnishings and Decorations of Solomon's Temple

The complexities of the Chronicler's records of Solomon's temple make it helpful to provide a brief overview of the matter.

Structures

First, of all the structures comprising the Temple complex, the Chronicler's primary concern was with the **temple of the LORD** (see 2 Chr. 3:1,3; 4:11,16,19; 5:1), the main building which was about 90 feet (27 meters) long and 30 feet (9 meters) wide. This central structure was divided into three parts.

1) The stairs leading to the front of the building rose to a large **portico** (see 2 Chr. 3:4,15-17; 8:12; 1 Kgs. 6:3; 7:6), a covered area (about 30 feet [9 meters] wide and high) adorned with two large pillars on either side.

2) Through the doors at the rear of the portico was the **main hall** (see 2 Chr. 3:5-7; 4:7-8,22; 1 Kgs. 6:5,17) which was about 60 feet [18 meters] long and 30 feet [9 meters] wide (see 1 Kgs. 6:17). This room corresponds to 'the Holy Place' of Moses' tabernacle (see Exod. 26:31-37).

3) Beyond the doors and curtain at the rear of the main hall was **the Most Holy Place** (see 2 Chr. 3:8,10-12; 4:22; 1 Kgs. 6:16, 23-28, 30-32), the innermost room which housed the ark of the covenant. This cubical room (about 30 feet [9 meters] in all dimensions) corresponds to the inner room by the same name in Moses' tabernacle (see Exod. 26:31-35).

Beyond these structures, the Chronicler also briefly mentioned **the courtyard of the priests** and **the large court** (2 Chr. 4:9). These areas were walled in courts surrounding the temple which were for priests and lay people respectively.

Furnishings

Second, in addition to the structures themselves, the Chronicler also remarked on many furnishings. A number of items in the courtyard of the priests appear.

1) The **bronze altar** (see 1 Kgs. 8:22,31,54,64; 9:25; 2 Kgs. 11:11; 12:9; 16:14-15; 23:9; 2 Chr. 4:1; 5:12; 6:12; 6:22; 7:7,9; 8:12; 15:8; 23:10; 29:18-27; 33:16; 35:16) stood directly in front of the stairs leading to the portico. It was used for burnt offerings and meal offerings (see Exod. 40:29).

2) The **Sea of cast metal** was an enormous basin placed just to the left of the stairs of the portico (2 Chr. 4:2). Its primary function was for priestly washings before ceremonies (2 Chr. 4:6b).

3) **Ten basins** (2 Chr. 4:6,14) flanked the temple, five on the southern side and five more on the northern side. They were used for washing the instruments **used for burnt offerings** (2 Chr. 4:6).

4) The Chronicler briefly mentioned **pots**, **shovels**, and **sprinkling bowls** (2 Chr. 4:11) which were presumably used by the priests in their courtyard.

Three furnishings were located in the main hall. 1) **Ten gold lampstands** (2 Chr. 4:20) stood alongside 2) **ten tables** (2 Chr. 4:8,19) placed on the northern and southern sides of the main hall. Only one lamp and table stood in Moses' tabernacle (see Exod. 25:23,31). 3) Along with these furnishings were **100 gold sprinkling bowls** (4:8) which were used for a variety of functions in the main hall.

Decorations

Third, the Chronicler recorded a number of decorations in the temple. To mention a few, the portico was **overlaid ... with pure gold** (2 Chr. 3:4b). The pillars on either side of the portico were elaborately decorated with **pomegranates attached** to **chains ... on top of the pillars** (2 Chr. 3:16; see also 4:12-13). The main hall was

paneled ... with pine and covered with fine gold (2 Chr. 3:5). Various artistic designs are also mentioned (2 Chr. 3:5), along with **precious stones** (2 Chr. 3:6). The Most Holy Place contained **gold nails** (or 'hooks'), each of which was **overlaid** in **its upward parts with gold** (2 Chr. 3:9). Two enormous golden **sculptured cherubim** stood behind the ark of the covenant **facing the main hall** (2 Chr. 3:10-13). The curtain separating the main hall and the Most Holy Place was **blue, purple, and crimson** with **cherubim** embroidered within it (2 Chr. 3:14). In the courtyard of the priests, the Sea stood on **twelve bulls** (2 Chr. 4:15) cast in bronze and facing in all directions; its rim was shaped **like a lily blossom** (2 Chr. 4:4-5).

Part One

The Identity, Privileges and Responsibilities of God's People (1 Chr 1:1-9:34)

Overview

The first chapters of Chronicles challenge the endurance of most modern readers. At first glance, we are tempted to pass over these ancient lists and genealogies as irrelevant, but such a stance toward these chapters does not match the Chronicler's outlook. He began his history with these materials to answer critical questions raised by the experience of post-exilic Israel. Who are the people of God? What privileges and responsibilities do they have? The Chronicler's answers to these questions revealed many important themes which characterize his entire history.

Israel's royal history, exile, and continuing troubles after the exile created a crisis of identity for many Israelites. In 922 BC the northern tribes broke away from Judah to establish their own monarchy and worship centers (see 2 Chr. 10:16-19; 1 Kgs. 12:16-33). Their sins were so great that the Lord sent the Assyrians to destroy the northern kingdom and to carry many of its citizens into exile in *c.* 722 BC (see 1 Chr. 5:25,26; 2 Kgs. 17:6-23). The Chronicler's original readers wondered about these events. Were these scattered tribes still to be counted among the people of God? What place did they hold in God's plan?

In the decades that followed the fall of northern Israel, the people of Judah also fell into flagrant disbelief. Consequently, the Lord sent the Babylonians to destroy Jerusalem in 586 BC and countless Judahites also went away into exile (see 1 Chr. 9:1b; 2 Chr. 36:17-21; 2 Kgs. 25:1-12). The Chronicler's readers faced a serious crisis. Had God forsaken Judah as well?

Even during the exile controversy grew between different groups of Israelites (see Ezek. 11:14-25). Those left in the land believed they were the rightful heirs of God's blessings. Those taken to Babylon argued they were the true people of God. This controversy became very practical for the Chronicler's post-exilic readers. In 538 BC the Persian emperor, Cyrus, permitted the exiles to return to Jerusalem (see 2 Chr. 36:22-23; Ezra 1:1-4), but critical questions still had to be settled. Who had a legitimate claim to God's blessings? What responsibilities did the various groups have?

In his genealogies and lists the Chronicler answered these and similar questions. In response to controversy and confusion in the post-exilic community, he gave an account of the identity, privileges, and responsibilities of God's people.

The book of Chronicles begins with nine chapters of genealogies. When we think of modern genealogies, we often picture a family tree containing the names of every family member. Genealogies in biblical times, however, were different from our modern genealogies. They followed a variety of forms and served many different functions. These variations also appear in the Chronicler's extensive use of genealogies.

The Chronicler's genealogies take on several forms. Some passages are linear and trace a single family line through many generations (e.g., 1 Chr. 2:34-41); other genealogies are segmented and sketch several family lines together (e.g., 1 Chr. 6:1-3). The Chronicler also omitted generations without notice, mentioning persons and events that were important to his concerns. In these cases, the expression 'son of' actually meant 'descendant of' and 'father of' meant 'ancestor of' (e.g., 1 Chr. 6:4-14). Beyond this, just as ancient genealogies often included brief narratives highlighting significant events, the Chronicler paused on occasion to tell a story (e.g. 1 Chr. 4:9-10; 5:18-22).

The functions of ancient genealogies also varied. They not only sketched familial relations, but political, geographical, and other social connections. In many cases, the expressions 'son of' and 'father of' had a broader meaning than immediate biological descent. In line with these ancient functions of genealogies, the Chronicler gave an assortment of lists, including families (e.g., 1 Chr. 3:17-24), political relations (e.g., 1 Chr. 2:24,42,45,49-52), and trade guilds (e.g., 1 Chr. 4:14,21-23).

Structure

The Chronicler's record divides into three main sections.

The Roots of Israel (1:1-2:2)
The Breadth and Order of Israel (2:1-9:1a)
The Continuation of Israel (9:1b-34)

Outline of 1 Chr. 1:1-9:34 (figure 4)

The symmetry of this presentation is evident. In the large center of these chapters the Chronicler focused on the breadth and order of the tribes of Israel (2:1-9:1a). As a prelude to this crucial material he quickly summarized the historical roots of Israel by noting the special ancestors of the twelve tribes (1:1-2:2). He then closed this portion of his book with a brief account of the descendants of the twelve tribes who stood at the center of the early post-exilic community (9:1b-34).

The Roots of Israel (1:1-2:2)

The first task before the Chronicler was to establish that his readers were descendants of a divinely selected people. To accomplish this end he drew from several chapters in Genesis to demonstrate that God had chosen the twelve tribes of Israel for special privileges and responsibilities which now belonged to his readers.

Structure

The Chronicler's account of Israel's roots divides into three main sections (see figure 5 on next page).

The people of Israel were not like other nations; they were beneficiaries of a divine program of narrowing selection. From all of Adam's descendants, Noah was selected as God's favored man. From all of Noah's descendants, Shem stood in special relationship with God. From all of Shem's descendants, God selected Abraham. From all the descendants of Abraham, Isaac was chosen. From the descendants of Isaac, God chose Israel and his children.

The history of humanity from Adam to Jacob proved that God had selected Israel to be his special people. The post-exilic readers of Chronicles had faced discouragements that caused many of them to wonder if God had utterly rejected

The Roots of Israel (1:1-2:2)
- Descendants of Adam (1:1-3)
- Descendants of Noah (1:4-27)
  - Introduction (1:4)
  - Descendants of Japheth (1:5-7)
  - Descendants of Ham (1:8-16)
  - Descendants of Shem (1:17-27)
- Descendants of Abraham (1:28-34a)
  - Introduction (1:28)
  - Descendants of Ishmael (1:29-31)
  - Descendants of Keturah (1:32-34a)
  - Descendants of Isaac (1:34b-2:2)
    - Introduction (1:34b)
    - Descendants of Esau (1:35-54)
    - Descendants of Israel (2:1-2)

Outline of 1 Chr. 1:1-2:2 (figure 5)

them. By tracing the special roots of Israel, the Chronicler demonstrated that Israel held a privileged relationship with the Creator.

Descendants of Adam (1:1-3)

By beginning his record with **Adam** to **Noah** (1:1-3), the Chronicler tied the people of God in his day to biblical primeval history (see Gen. 1:1-11:9). As children of Adam Israel had common origins with the entire human race. They were recipients of Adam's blessing and curse like all other peoples (see Gen. 1:26-29; 3:15-24; Rom. 5:12-21).

The names that follow Adam, however, indicate that a narrowing process of divine election was already at work in the earliest stages of human history. God chose to show special favor only to the line of **Seth** and **Noah** (1:1-3). While other primeval people rebelled against their Creator, the book of Genesis characterized these men as the first who 'called on the name of the LORD' (Gen. 4:26). They received the blessing of long life (see Gen. 5:5,8,11) and only Noah with his family was chosen to survive the flood (see Gen. 6:8-9,17-18).

The Chronicler's readers knew the biblical records of these primeval figures. Their mere mention as ancestors of the tribes of Israel made it evident that Israel was not an ordinary nation; her roots stretched from the most honored figures of primeval history.

Descendants of Noah (1:4-27)

The **sons of Noah** first appear here in the order of **Shem, Ham, and Japheth** (1:4), as they occur in Gen. 5:32. After introducing their names, however, the Chronicler reversed the order of Noah's sons to end with Shem (**Japheth** [1:5-7], **Ham** [1:8-16], **Shem** [1:17-27]), the ancestor of Israel. As on several other occasions, the Chronicler reversed the traditional order of the names to end with the man whom

God specially blessed (see 1:34a; 2:1-2). God favored the Shemites, or Semitic peoples, more than all other nations on earth. As Genesis 9:25-27 indicates, God promised that the Shemites would conquer the Canaanite descendants of Ham and provide blessings for the descendants of Japheth.

Nevertheless, God's favor did not extend equally to all Shemites. It was directed toward one special descendent of Shem, **Abram** (1:27). Abram was the father of the tribes of Israel; he became the heir of the privileges granted to Shem and the conduit of these blessings to the nation which he fathered (see Gen. 12:1-3).

Descendants of Abraham (1:28-34a)

The Chronicler turned next to **the sons of Abraham** to distinguish the chosen seed from Abraham's other descendants (1:28-34a). First, he mentioned **Isaac** and then **Ishmael** (1:28), but he reversed the order again by first listing the descendants of Ishmael (1:29-31), the father of the Arab nations, and the sons of **Keturah**, Abraham's second wife (1:32-33). This change of order indicated that only the descendants of **Isaac** (1:34) could rightfully claim Abraham's blessing (see 1:17-27; 2:1-2).

Isaac was the only child of Abraham born by divine promise instead of human design (see Gen. 17:15-21; 18:9-15; 21:1-8; Gal. 3:15-18,26-29). Isaac's supernatural birth reminded the Chronicler's readers that they were not like the other descendants of Abraham. Their heritage rested on Abraham's faith in God's promises, not in ordinary familial lineage (see Rom. 4:16-21).

Descendants of Isaac (1:34b-2:2)

The final step in the Chronicler's narrowing definition of God's people focuses on **the sons of Isaac** (1:34b-2:2). In usual fashion, the chosen line appears last (see 1:17-27, 34a). The text deals first with **Esau** (1:35-54) who sold his birthright to Jacob (see Gen. 25:27-34). Then it speaks of **the sons of Israel** (2:1-2) who inherited God's promises to Abraham.

The final verses in the record of Isaac's descendants (2:1-2) serve a literary function often called the 'Janus effect'. They function as the end of this material (1:34b-2:2), but they also introduce the passages that follow (2:1-9:1a).

In this context, the twelve tribes are explicitly identified as descendants of Isaac's son, **Israel** (2:1). The blessings of God came through the man Israel, but Genesis does not hide his imperfections (see Gen. 25:27-34; 27:1-36; 30:41-43; 31:20-21). Early in his life Jacob lived up to the meaning of his name, 'the supplanter' (see Gen. 25:26; 27:36). As God changed his character, however, he received the honorable name Israel, 'because you have striven with God and men and have overcome' (Gen. 32:28). Jacob cherished the birthright of Abraham and did all he could to acquire it.

By mentioning all twelve tribes of the nation Israel, the Chronicler reached the high point of this portion of his genealogies. His main purpose for the preceding material was to provide a reminder of the origins of the tribes. From his perspective, the post-exilic readers enjoyed a remarkable heritage of blessings and privileges.

The Breadth and Order of Israel (2:1-9:1a)

Having reminded the readers of their connection to the early people of God, the text turns next to lengthy records of the tribes of Israel. Comparisons with other biblical accounts reveal great selectivity in this material. These selections emphasize two important theological concerns. First, the breadth of God's people demonstrates that the privileges of divine election belonged not to a few but to all the tribes of the nation. Second, some tribes receive more honor than others. These accounts highlight certain groups who played important roles in national life before and after the exile.

Structure

The Chronicler's record of the tribes of Israel divides into five main parts which are enclosed by an introduction and summation (see figure 6 on pages 68 and 69).

Two general comments should be made about the arrangement of these genealogies. First, although they point to the breadth of God's people, these lists do not mention the tribes of Dan and Zebulun. The brevity and awkward Hebrew grammar of Naphtali's record (see 7:13) may indicate that the Chronicler's original text included a longer account of Naphtali as well as Dan and Zebulun. These materials may have been lost through transmission errors, but this explanation is uncertain (see *Introduction: Translation and Transmission*). The Chronicler himself may have omitted these tribes for other unknown reasons.

Even so, the complete list of Jacob's sons in 2:1-2 shows that these chapters express the Chronicler's insistence that all the tribes be counted among the people of God (see *Introduction: 1) All Israel*). Earlier prophets had already indicated that the restoration after exile would involve all twelve tribes (see Isa. 9:1-7; 11:12; 27:6,12-13; 43:1-7; 44:1-5,21-28; 49:5-7,14-21; 59:20; 65:9; 66:20; Ezek. 34:23-24; 37; 40-48; Hos. 1:11; 3:4-5; Amos 9:11-15; Mic 2:12-13; 4:6-8; 5:1-5a). The Chronicler also looked for a reunification of all Israel. From his point of view, the post-exilic restoration would remain incomplete until representatives of all the tribes were gathered in the promised land (see *Introduction: 1) All Israel*).

Second, the relative distribution of verses covering the tribes provides another important insight to the Chronicler's purposes. He alternated between long and short accounts (see figure 7). After an introduction (2:1-2), he began with a long text on **Judah** (2:3-4:23). This Judahite record precedes the relatively short records of **Simeon** (4:24-43) and the tribes who lived east of the Jordan River (5:1-26). Then another lengthy passage focuses on the sons of **Levi** (6:1-81), just before six short genealogies (**Issachar** ... **Asher** [7:1-40]). Finally, a relatively long account of **Benjamin** (8:1-40) closes the material.

These uneven distributions suggest that the Chronicler honored Judah, Levi, and Benjamin more than the other tribes. What did these three tribes have in common that warranted this honored status? Throughout history a great number of Judahites, Benjamites, and Levites remained committed to the Davidic king and the Jerusalem temple. Kingship and temple were the two essential institutions in

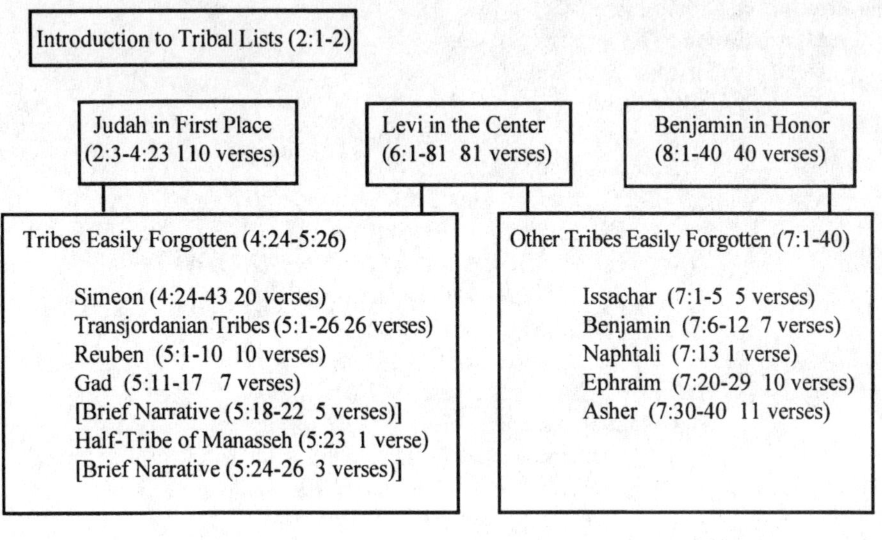

Distribution of Materials in 1 Chr. 2:1-9:1a (figure 7)

the Chronicler's ideal for restored Israel (see *Introduction: 4-9) King and Temple*). Judah, Levi, and Benjamin probably held extraordinary positions in the Chronicler's view because of their past loyalties to these institutions. As such, these tribes also played vital roles in the restoration efforts of post-exilic Israel. The last portion of the Chronicler's genealogies (9:1b-34) confirms this understanding of his purpose. In this description of the early returnees he once again emphasized the tribes of Judah, Benjamin, and Levi by drawing attention to their large numbers (see figure 6).

Introduction to Tribal Lists (2:1-2)
As mentioned above, these verses serve a double function. They close out the previous section of God's narrowing election (see 1:1-2:2), but they also introduce the following chapters which focus on the breadth and order of God's people (2:1-8:40).

The heads of Israel's twelve tribes appear in the order of Gen. 35:23-26 with the exception of Dan's placement. The Chronicler began with this list to acknowledge that all the tribes without exception were to be accepted as the heirs of Israel's blessing. This opening list balances with the closure of 9:1a (see figure 6).

Judah in First Place (2:3-4:23)
Judah appears first among the tribes. By order of birth, Reuben should have held this position, but the Chronicler later explained why he varied the order (see 5:1-2). He noted that Reuben lost his firstborn status because of incest (see Gen. 35:22; 49:3-4).

- The Breadth and Order of Israel (2:1-9:1a)
  - ■Introduction to Tribal Lists (2:1-2)
  - ■Judah in First Place (2:3-4:23)
    - ♦Judahite Families (2:3-9)
      - Descendants of Canaanite Woman (2:3)
      - Descendants of Tamar (2:4-9)
      - ♦Descendants of Ram (2:10-17)
        - Descendants of Caleb (2:18-24)
          - Descendants of Jerahmeel (2:25-33)
          - More Descendants of Jerahmeel (2:34-41)
        - More on Caleb (2:42-55)
          - Descendants of Caleb (2:42-50a)
          - Descendants of Hur (2:50b-55)
      - ♦More on Ram (3:1-24)
        - Descendants of David born in Hebron and Jerusalem (3:1-9)
        - Descendants of Solomon (3:10-16)
        - Descendants of Jeconiah (3:17-24)
    - ♦More on Judahite Families (4:1-23)
      - Perez (4:1-20)
        - Genealogy (4:1-8)
        - Territorial Expansion Narrative (4:9-10)
          - Introduction (4:9)
          - Jabez's Prayer (4:10a)
          - Jabez's Blessing (4:10b)
        - Genealogy (4:11-20)
      - Shelah (4:21-23)
  - ■Tribes Easily Forgotten (4:24-5:26)
    - ♦Tribe of Simeon (4:24-43)
      - Simeonite Genealogy (4:24-27)
      - Simeonite Geographical Notices (4:28-33)
      - Simeonite Territorial Expansions (4:34-43)
    - ♦Transjordanian Tribes (5:1-26)
      - Tribe of Reuben (5:1-10)
        - Reubenite Genealogy (5:1-8a)
        - Reubenite Geographical Notices (5:8b-9)
        - Reubenite Territorial Expansion (5:10)
      - Tribe of Gad (5:11-17)
        - Gadite Geographical Notices (5:11-12)
        - Gadite Genealogy (5:13-15)
        - Gadite Geographical Notice (5:16)
          - Notation of Source (5:17)
      - Transjordanian Victory Narrative (5:18-22)
        - Preparations for Battle (5:18)
          - Battle Waged (5:19)
            - Prayer and Divine Intervention (5:20)
          - Battle Won (5:21-22a)
        - Settlement After Battle (5:22b)

Half-tribe of Manasseh (5:23-26)
Manassehite Numbers and Territories (5:23)
Manassehite Deportation Narrative (5:24-26)
Manassehite Warriors in the Land (5:24)
Manassehite Apostasy (5:25)
Manassehite Deportation from the Land (5:26)

■Levi in the Center (6:1-81)
♦High Priestly Family (6:1-15)
High Priestly Line Distinguished (6:1-4a)
High Priestly Line Continued (6:4b-15)
♦Duties of Levites (6:16-47)
Ordinary Levites (6:16-30)
Musical Levites (6:31-47)
♦Duties of Priests (6:48-53)
Priestly Responsibilities (6:48-49)
Priestly Leadership (6:50-53)
♦Lands for Levi's Descendants (6:54-81)
Aaronic Lands (6:54-60)
Kohathite, Gershonite, Merarite Lands (6:61-65)
More Kohathite, Gershonite, Merarite Lands (6:66-81)

■Other Tribes Easily Forgotten (7:1-40)
♦The Tribe of Issachar (7:1-5)
♦The Tribe of Benjamin (7:6-12)
♦The Tribe of Naphtali (7:13)
♦The Tribe of Manasseh (7:14-19)
♦The Tribe of Ephraim (7:20-29)
Joshua's Genealogy (7:20-21a)
Ephraimite Defeat Narrative (7:21-24)
Ephraim's Sons Die in Battle (7:21)
Ephraim Mourns (7:22)
Ephraim's Progeny Settles (7:23-24)
More on Joshua's Genealogy (7:25-27)
Ephraimite Settlements (7:28-29)
♦The Tribe of Asher (7:30-40)
Sons of Asher (7:30)
Descendants of Beriah (7:31-39)
Asherite Military Strength (7:40)

■Benjamin in Honor (8:1-40)
Benjamites in Geba (8:1-7),
Benjamites in Moab, Ono and Lod, Aijalon and Gath (8:8-12)
Benjamites in Jerusalem (8:13-28)
More Benjamites Associated with Jerusalem (8:29-40)

■Summation of Tribal Lists (9:1a)

Outline of 1 Chr. 2:1-9:1a (figure 6)

The Chronicler also explained in a positive manner why Judah replaced Reuben as chief among the tribes. It was because **a ruler came from him** (5:2). The ruler in mind was none other than King David and his family (see 3:1). On several occasions it becomes evident that the Chronicler intentionally highlighted the family of David in these genealogies. He held before his readers the hope of re-establishing the Davidic throne in their day. The tribe of Judah held first place in these chapters to honor the family of David.

Structure

The Judahite material appears in a symmetrical pattern (see figure 6). It begins and ends with general descriptions of Judahite families (2:3-9; 4:1-23). Moreover, each portion of the first half is mirrored by additional information in the second half: Ram (2:10-17; 3:1-24), Caleb (2:18-24; 2:42-55), Jerahmeel (2:25-33; 2:34-41).

Judahite Families (2:3-9)

The Judahite genealogies begin with a broad introduction to the **sons of Judah** (2:3-9). The five sons are grouped according to their mothers: **a Canaanite woman, the daughter of Shua** (2:3; see Gen. 38:2), and **Tamar**, Judah's daughter-in-law (2:4-9; see Gen. 38:11-30).

The **five sons** of Judah (2:4) met with different fates.

1) **Er was wicked in the LORD's sight; so the LORD put him to death** (2:3). The record of this event appears in Gen. 38:7, but the nature of his sin is unknown.

2) The death of **Onan** (2:3) is not mentioned explicitly in Chronicles, but the death of his brother Er was closely connected to Onan's death (see Gen. 38:8-10).

3) Joshua 7:1 identifies **the son of Carmi, Achar** with the line of **Zerah** (2:4). The Chronicler shifted his name from 'Achan' (Josh. 7:1) to **Achar** for a word play. The name **Achar** sounds like the Hebrew word meaning **trouble** (2:7). Achar broke **the ban** and died under divine judgment (2:7; see Josh. 7:24-26). In fact, the Chronicler highlighted Achar's actions by using one of his typical terms for describing serious rebellion against God: Achar was **unfaithful** (2:7; see *Introduction: 21) Unfaithfulness*). The descendants of Zerah named **Ethan** and **Heman** (2:6) are among the wise men with whom Solomon was compared in 1 Kgs. 4:31. They are not to be confused with David's musicians of the same names.

4) **Shelah** (2:3) is only mentioned in this genealogy (2:3), but his descendants appear in 4:21.

5) By contrast with other descendants of Judah, the family of **Perez** (2:5,9) steadily increases numerically. As in a number of other passages, the Chronicler noted the increase of progeny to indicate that God had blessed the line of Perez above other families of Judah (see *Introduction: 25) Increase and Decline of Progeny*). No judgment on his house appears in this text. The Chronicler highlighted this branch of the tribe of Judah because it led to David, the great king of Israel.

The severe consequences of sin come to the foreground to introduce a guiding principle of his history. Time and again this history will point out that flagrant sins brought swift judgment from God. This motif warned the post-exilic readers against infidelity in their day. In much the same way, the emphasis on the relative purity of the family of Perez revealed the Chronicler's belief that fidelity to God brought about divine blessing (see *Introduction: 10-27) Divine Blessing and Judgment*).

Descendants of Ram (2:10-17)

In line with his special interest in David's royal family, the Chronicler broke with birth order and gave first place to the line of **Ram** (2:10-17). **Jesse** (2:12), the father of **David** (2:15), came from this branch of the tribe of Judah. This text depends on Ruth 4:18-22. It balances with information on Ram's descendants in 3:1-24 (see figure 6).

According to 1 Samuel 17:12-14 David was Jesse's eighth son, but here he is described as his **seventh** son (2:15). For some unknown reason, the Chronicler omitted David's brother Elihu, even though he mentioned him in 27:18. In line with the flexible standards for genealogies in the Chronicler's day, Elihu may have been dropped from this list because he died without progeny and was therefore unimportant for the post-exilic situation.

Descendants of Caleb (2:18-24)

The Chronicler proceeded next to the descendants of **Caleb** (2:18 [spelled 'Kelubai' in 2:9]) which balances with the later notices on this clan in 2:42-55 (see figure 6). This Caleb is not to be confused with the well-known 'Caleb son of Jephunneh' (Num. 13:6), whom the Chronicler clearly identified in 4:15.

As the preceding record of Ram gave the background of David the monarch (2:10-17), the lineage of Caleb provided the ancestry of another important character in the Chronicler's perspective. Caleb was the ancestor of **Bezalel** (2:20). Bezalel supervised tabernacle construction in the days of Moses (see Exod. 31:1-5; 35:30-36:7). The Chronicler focused on the family of this tabernacle artisan to express his belief in the close interconnection between the throne of David and temple worship as central institutions in Israel (see *Introduction: 4-9) King and Temple*).

Descendants of Jerahmeel (2:25-41)

The **sons of Jerahmeel** (2:25-41) stand at the center of the Judahite genealogies. The clan lived in southern Judah (see 1 Sam. 27:10; 30:27-29), but this material is the only genealogical information on the family.

The Jerahmeelites appear in two separate lists (2:25-33 and 2:34-41; see figure 6), which are distinguished by the summary statement: **These were the descendants from Jerahmeel** (2:33). The first list (2:25-33) provides a general orientation to the family. Many of these names are common in Scripture, but it is not possible to establish precise identifications. The second list (2:34-41) deals particularly with the family of **Sheshan** (2:34) and ends with his descendant **Elishama** (2:41).

This final name may provide a clue to the Chronicler's main concern with the Jerahmeelites. If there are no gaps in this genealogy, then **Elishama** appears near the generation of David. This temporal orientation suggests that he may have been David's contemporary. If this is true, the Chronicler may have wished to honor a family closely associated with David. Then again, because generations are skipped in biblical genealogies without notice, Elishama may have been a scribe of King Jehoiakim (see Jer. 36:12,20), or even a contemporary of the Chronicler himself. Whatever the case, the Chronicler felt it necessary to establish Elishama's pedigree as an important Judahite. Perhaps some of his readers questioned the status of this man or his descendants because **an Egyptian** (2:34) was among his ancestors. As such, the Chronicler demonstrated his inclusive outlook toward foreigners (see: *Introduction: 3) International Relations*).

More on Caleb (2:42-55)

The Chronicler moved next to a second record of **the sons of Caleb** (2:42) which balances with 2:18-24 (see figure 6). This material divides into two sections: **Caleb** (2:42-50a) and **Hur** (2:50b-55). These additional lists emphasize two issues.

First, the Chronicler mentioned **Ziph**, **Mareshah**, and **Hebron** (2:42), geographical sites beyond the borders of the province of Judah after the exile. In these geographical passages, 'father of' meant 'founder of' or 'leader of'.

By mentioning these places, the Chronicler touched on a theme which occurs on a number of occasions. He encouraged his post-exilic readers to expand their geographical hopes to include all the territories once occupied by these Judahites. The prophets had already announced that Israel would repossess the promised land after exile (see Isa. 34:17; 57:13; 60:21; Obad. 1:17-20). This passage is one among many which reaffirmed these hopes for the Chronicler's readers (see comments on 4:10,11-23,28-43; 5:23; 6:54-81; 7:28-29; 8:1-6,7-13; 9:1b-2; 10:7; 2 Chr. 20:7,11; 31:15).

Second, this section contains the names of Judahites whose legitimacy could easily have been called into question. They include the children of Caleb's concubines (2:46,48). Moreover, the text also mentions **Kenites** (2:55), foreigners who were adopted into Judah (see Judg. 1:16; 4:11). The Chronicler's vision of the people of God after the exile included non-Israelite converts as well (see 4:25; 9:2; see also *Introduction: 3) International Relations*). Such hopes stemmed from earlier prophetic predictions of the same (see Isa. 56:6-8; Ps. 87; Zech. 8:20-23; 14:16). The Chronicler wanted to insure that these questionable people were included among the highly honored people of Judah after the exile.

More on Ram (3:1-24)

In continuation of the previous genealogy of Ram in 2:10-17 (see figure 6), the Judahite genealogies turn next to the **sons of David** (3:1): David's progeny born in Hebron and Jerusalem (3:1-9), Solomon's descendants up to the exile (3:10-16), and the line of Jeconiah (Jehoiachin) during and after the exile (3:17-24). The steps of this material narrow attention from all of David's children to Zerubbabel who represented the line of David in the early post-exilic period.

First, the Chronicler listed David's sons born in Hebron (3:1-4a) and Jerusalem (3:4b-9), following 2 Sam. 3:2-5; 5:13-16; 13:1. These names appear for completeness and to distinguish the descendants of David in general from the special royal line.

Second, the Chronicler concentrated on **Solomon** (3:10-16), the son of David whom the Lord chose to be king. Unlike the book of Kings, Chronicles never reports the struggle between Solomon and Adonijah for David's throne (see 1 Kgs. 1-2). From the Chronicler's perspective, the move from David to Solomon was a smooth transition perfectly conformed to the plan of God (see comments on 23:1).

Third, the last portion of David's royal line focuses on the **sons of Jeconiah, the captive** (3:17-24). Jeconiah, known also as Jehoiachin (see 3:16), is called **the captive** because he was exiled to Babylon in 597 BC (see 2 Kgs. 24:12). The prophet Jeremiah, whose writings the Chronicler knew (see 2 Chr. 35:25; 36:12,21-22), had announced earlier that God had rejected Jeconiah's family from the royal line (see Jer. 22:28-30). This prophecy may have raised questions about Jeconiah's descendants after the exile. Should some other line of David take the throne? In this genealogy the Chronicler affirmed that God had lifted his curse and re-established Jeconiah's line as the object of Israel's future royal hopes. Jeconiah himself was released from prison in Babylon (see 2 Kgs. 25:27-30). His descendant, Zerubbabel (see 3:19), was the leader of the early post-exilic community (see Ezra 3:1-13). In fact, God declared that Zerubbabel would be like his 'signet ring' (Hag 2:23), directly reversing the curse on Jeconiah (see Jer. 22:24). Zerubbabel never became king, but the Chronicler ended his royal genealogy with a focus on Zerubbabel (see 3:19-24). His line represented the only legitimate royal family for Israel after the exile. Interestingly enough, both Matthew and Luke agreed with the Chronicler and identified Jesus with Zerubbabel's lineage (see Matt. 1:12-13; Luke 3:27).

It should be noted that the Chronicler designated **Pediah** (3:18) as the father of **Zerubbabel** (3:19). Elsewhere, Zerubbabel is called the son of Shealtiel (see Ezra 3:2,8; Neh. 12:1; Hag. 1:12,14; 2:2,23; Matt. 1:12; Luke 3:27). Pediah may have become the head of Zerubbabel's family at Shealtiel's death, adopting Zerubbabel as his own son. Otherwise, Pediah may have married Shealtiel's widow through levirate marriage (see Deut. 25:5-6), making Zerubbabel the legal son of Shealtiel.

Interpreters have disagreed over the number of generations which appear in 3:21b-24. The main point of controversy is the sequence: **of Rephaiah, of Arnan, of Obadiah and of Shecaniah** (3:21). Some interpreters have taken these names as representing more sons of **Hananiah** (3:21; see RSV, NRSV). Others see them as four contemporaries of Zerubbabel (see NIV). It is unclear, therefore, how far this genealogy extends beyond Zerubbabel. In the least, it reaches two generations beyond him: **the sons of Zerubbabel** (3:19b), and **the descendants of Hananiah** (3:21a).

Unless this genealogy was updated at some stage during the transmission of Chronicles (see *Introduction: Translation and Transmission*), this passage indicates that the Chronicler could not have written before the births of Zerubbabel's grandchildren. This limitation, however, does not eliminate the possibility of an early date for composition during Zerubbabel's lifetime so long as we remember that his grandchildren had been born (see *Introduction: Authorship and Date*).

More on Judahite Families (4:1-23)

The Chronicler closed his Judahite genealogies by returning to broad lists of the **sons of Judah** (4:1-23) in balance with 2:3-9 (see figure 6). Personal and clan names are mixed with place names. This material divides between **Perez** (4:1-20) and **Shelah** (4:21-23).

Within his record of Perez's descendants (4:1-20), the Chronicler introduced the first of four brief narratives in his genealogies (4:9-10; see 5:18-22,24-26; 7:21-24). This narrative begins with an authorial comment (4:9) followed by a two step scenario: Jabez prays (4:10a) and God answers (4:10b).

The presence of the name **Jabez** in the line of Perez apparently raised a difficulty for the Chronicler. Perez was the ancestor of David whose lineage the Chronicler wanted to exalt. Nevertheless, the name **Jabez** means 'pain' in Hebrew, hardly a flattering name to include in such an exalted lineage. For this reason, the Chronicler introduced his story with the explanation that **Jabez was more honorable than his brothers** (4:9). His name did not reflect his character. Instead, his mother gave him this name because she bore him **in pain** (4:9). The reputation of the line of Perez remained intact.

To demonstrate how honorable this man was, the Chronicler related a story of prayer (4:10). Jabez prayed that God would **enlarge** [his] **territory**... and **keep** [him] **free from harm** and **pain** (4:10a). The Chronicler closed the episode by simply noting that **God granted his request** (4:10b). God established Jabez's honor by answering his prayer.

Jabez's prayer related directly to the needs of the Chronicler's original readers in at least three ways. First, the Chronicler's readers had experienced much pain during and after the exile. They certainly would have identified with Jabez's desire. Second, Jabez's prayer touched on the issue of expanding the territories of post-exilic Judah. (For the Chronicler's geographical hopes, see 2:42-55.) Third, the Chronicler pointed to Jabez as an example of an appropriate way to gain relief from the problems of suffering and territorial expansion. Jabez prayed, **'Let your hand be with me'** (4:10). In the Chronicler's vocabulary for God to be 'with' someone was for him to aid them in their struggles and to fight for them (see 2 Chr. 13:12; see also *Introduction: 10) Divine Activity*). Sincere prayers to God for his help were essential for the post-exilic community to receive these kinds of blessings (see *Introduction: 17) Prayer*).

The remaining verses of the Judahite genealogies (4:11-23) are fragmentary and difficult to interpret. Yet, two items warrant comment. On the one hand, the passage focuses on trade guilds among Judahites. The **clans of the linen workers** (4:21) and **the potters who... worked for the king** (4:23) probably appear to encourage the post-exilic descendants of these Judahites to take up their ancestors' trades again. On the other hand, these lists mention several locations in and around Judah to encourage the readers once again to expand their territorial hopes. (For the Chronicler's geographical hopes, see 2:42-55.)

As we have seen, the Chronicler set the tribe of Judah at the head of Israel. He pointed out several remarkable people in this line. Yet, his primary concern was to establish the importance of the Davidic throne. The post-exilic people longed for the blessings of God, but in order to receive them, they had to devote themselves to the royal line of David represented by the family of Zerubbabel. Ignoring or rebelling against this divine order would surely bring further ruin. Without David's family at the head of the nation, the Israelites would never receive the glorious kingdom they had been promised.

Tribes Easily Forgotten (4:24-5:26)

Having given Judah first place among God's people (2:3-4:23), the Chronicler turned next to four tribes which could easily have been forgotten in post-exilic times. These four families of Israel were not as important as Judah, Levi, and Benjamin (see figure 7), but they were still to be counted among the people of God.

Structure

This material consists of a variety of lists and genealogies (see figure 6). It divides into two sections marked by the closing words, **to this day** (4:43; 5:26). The first portion focuses on the tribe of Simeon (4:24-43); the second portion deals with the tribes who lived east of the Jordan River: Reuben, Gad, and the half-tribe of Manasseh (5:1-26).

The original readers of Chronicles were prone to exclude these clans from the people of God for at least two reasons. First, few members of the restored community were from these tribes. The returnees primarily included people **from Judah, from Benjamin, and from Ephraim and** [western] **Manasseh** (not the Transjordanian 'half-tribe of Manasseh') (9:3). The tribe of Levi was also well represented (9:10-34). Naturally, the returnees were primarily concerned with themselves and their nearest kinsmen rather than other tribes.

Second, it was easy for the post-exilic community to marginalize Simeon, Reuben, Gad and the half-tribe of Manasseh because they had played relatively minor roles in Israel's history. The four tribes appeared frequently in premonarchical biblical history, but by David's time they were infrequently mentioned (see 1 Sam. 13:7; 2 Sam. 24:5; 2 Kgs. 10:33).

From the Chronicler's perspective, however, those who had returned from exile only represented the initial stages of Israel's restoration. He included these less important tribes in these chapters to encourage his readers to hope, pray, and work for their return as well.

The Tribe of Simeon (4:24-43)

The tribe of Simeon was one of the easiest families of Israel to neglect. From earliest times, Simeon was closely associated with Judah (see Josh. 19:1-9; Judg.

1:3). The land allotted to the tribe was on the southern border of Judah and was even described as 'within the territory of Judah' (Josh. 19:1,9). By the time of David, Simeon had completely lost its identity and was simply counted as one with Judah (see 4:27b). Nevertheless, the Chronicler insisted that Simeon was to regain its original status among the tribes after the exile. His record of Simeon divides into three parts (see figure 6).

Simeonite Genealogy (4:24-27)
Simeon's genealogical record closely follows Num. 26:12-14. Similar accounts also appear in Gen. 46:10 and Exod. 6:15. One interesting feature of this passage is the mention of **Mibsam** and **Mishma** (4:25). These names appear to be Ishmaelite in origin and may reflect the absorption of Ishmaelites from the southern desert regions into the tribe of Simeon. As elsewhere, the Chronicler showed interest in foreigners among the people of God (see *Introduction: 3) International Relations*). He wanted to insure that even the descendants of these foreign converts had a place in the post-exilic community (see 2:55; 9:2).

Simeonite Geographical Notices (4:28-33)
This list of Simeonite settlements stems from Josh. 19:2-8 where it is reported that God gave certain territories to Simeon (see also Josh. 15:26-32). In light of Judah's usurpation of Simeonite property before the exile, it is likely that at least some Judahites claimed these lands of Simeon for themselves after the exile. The Chronicler, however, objected because these territories were only secondarily taken by Judah. He commented directly that **these were their** [Simeonite] **towns until the reign of David** (4:31b). The family of Simeon was to receive its original inheritance upon return to the land.

Simeonite Territorial Expansions (4:34-43)
The Chronicler closed his treatment of Simeon by listing some prominent tribal leaders (4:34-37). He also noted how they grew in number and expanded their territories in several directions (4:38-43). The increase of these families indicated that God had blessed them (see *Introduction: 25) Increase and Decline of Progeny*). Comparisons with Neh. 11:26-29 indicate that some of these locations (**Moladah, Hazar Shual, Beersheba, Ziklag, Ain, Rimmon** ['En Rimmon' in Neh. 11:29]) were resettled soon after the exile. Chronicles draws attention to these cities to secure them and other legal possessions of Simeon. The Chronicler noted these Simeonites experienced **peaceful and quiet** times (4:40). These terms often described his ideal state of blessing (see *Introduction: 23) Victory and Defeat*). Here he noted that the Simeonites experienced a foretaste of what he hoped his readers would soon experience.

The last verses of this section (4:42-43) are particularly telling. They reveal that the Chronicler's interest in Simeon related to his own times. He mentioned that a number of Simeonites had invaded Seir, killed escaping Amalekites, and continued living there **to this day**, i.e. to the Chronicler's own times (4:43).

The expression **to this day** deserves special comment. This phrase and related expressions appear eleven times in Chronicles. Care must be taken to identify the temporal references of these words. At least three possibilities exist:

1) Sometimes these words were merely copied from written sources (e.g. the book of Kings). In these cases, 'to this day' refers to the earlier days of the Chronicler's literary sources, not to the Chronicler's time (see 4:41; 17:5).

2) On other occasions, the expressions appear in sources (e.g. royal annals used by Kings) used by the Chronicler's immediate sources (e.g. Kings). In these examples, the time reference is to the earlier period of a source used by the Chronicler's source (see 13:11; 2 Chr. 5:9; 8:8; 10:19; 21:10).

3) Even so, as in this verse, 'to this day' can also refer to the Chronicler's own time (see 5:26; 2 Chr. 20:26; 35:25).

The Chronicler closed his record of Simeon's family with this reference to his own day in order to draw a connection between Simeon's past and his contemporary audience. The family of Simeon had not been entirely lost. The post-exilic community could identify some Simeonites, who continued to live in the nearby territory of Seir. As a result, his readers needed to include these Simeonites and their relatives among God's people.

The Transjordanian Tribes (5:1-26)

The Chronicler was also concerned that his readers remember the tribes that had settled east of the Jordan River. These families were easily excluded from their minds for several reasons. First, long-term geographical separation was a problem. Reuben, Gad, and the half-tribe of Manasseh had received special permission to settle east of the Jordan River (see Num. 32; Deut. 3:12-20; Josh. 1:12-15; 12:6; 22:1-9). Immediately after Joshua's conquest special arrangements had to be made to insure that they continued to be counted among the tribes of Israel (see Josh. 22:10-34).

Second, the Transjordanian tribes were subjugated to foreign powers very early during the Divided Kingdom. Hazael of Syria overran their lands in c. 837/6 BC (see 2 Kgs. 10:32-33) and the Transjordanians faded even further from participation in national life. Third, the Chronicler mentioned that the Assyrian king Tiglath-Pileser III carried these tribes into exile around 734 BC, twelve years before he did the same to the other northern tribes (see 5:6, 26). Their early exile made it easy to exclude them from the national vision of post-exilic Israel.

The Chronicler focused on several concerns related to the Transjordanian tribes. His material divides into five interconnected sections (see figure 6).

The Tribe of Reuben (5:1-10)

Reuben heads the list of Transjordanian tribes as in many other passages (see Num. 32:1; Deut. 3:12,16; Josh. 1:12; 12:6; 22:1,9-10,13,15,21,25,30-34). This record of the Reubenites includes genealogies (5:1-8a), geographical notes (5:8b-9), and territorial expansion (5:10) much like the preceding Simeonite material.

The genealogical section (5:1-8a) first traces the **sons of Reuben** for one generation (5:1-3). It then mentions the **descendants of Joel** up to the Assyrian exile (5:4-6). Finally, it lists a number of Reubenite chiefs (5:7-8a). Only the immediate sons of Reuben appear elsewhere in Scripture (see Gen. 46:9; Exod. 6:14; Num. 26:5-6).

One of the Chronicler's purposes in these lists becomes evident in the parenthetical comment he inserted into his first genealogy (5:1b-2). Here he explained why the tribe of Reuben had not amounted to much. Reuben was Israel's firstborn. As firstborn son, Reuben was due to receive a double portion of his father's inheritance and should have been the leader of the nation of Israel (see Deut. 33:6). However, he received a relatively small portion of land and only played a minor role. In this passage, the Chronicler provided the only direct explanation of this turn of events. He reasoned that Reuben had **defiled his father's marriage bed** (5:1) and lost the double blessing to Joseph (Ephraim and Manasseh; see Gen. 48:1-22; 49:22-26; Deut. 33:13-17). For the same reason, Reuben also lost his leadership role to Judah from whom **a ruler came**, i.e. David and his family (5:2).

Despite Reuben's loss of privileges, twice this passage calls him **the firstborn of Israel** (5:1, 3). This repetition suggests that the Chronicler still wanted his original readers to honor Reuben. As was the custom in the ancient Near East, the tribes of Israel were to respect Reuben's biological priority. The family of Israel's firstborn should not be forgotten in the post-exilic period.

The Chronicler's record of the **descendants of Joel** (5:4-6) contains an important historical note on the Assyrian King **Tiglath-Pileser** III (745-727 BC) (5:6). His name is spelled 'Tilgath Pilneser' in the Hebrew text of this verse (see NRSV, NASB). Near 734 this Assyrian king took control of the northern kingdom of Israel and deported many Reubenites into exile (see 2 Kgs. 15:29). This humiliating historical fact explained why Reuben may not have seemed important to the Chronicler's readers.

Even so, in the last portion of this material (5:8b-10), the Chronicler balanced Reubenite humiliation with a record of the tribe's territories. He noted their expansion **to the edge of the desert** was **because their livestock had increased** (5:9). The Mosaic covenant identified abundant livestock as a divine blessing for covenant fidelity (see Deut. 28:4,11; 30:9).

Beyond this, the Chronicler also noted that something remarkable happened **during Saul's reign** (5:10a). In the early monarchical period, the Reubenites **occupied the dwellings of the Hagrites** (5:10b). The Hagrites cannot be specifically identified, but they are associated elsewhere with Ishmaelites and Moabites (see Ps. 83:6). The Chronicler mentioned this event to show that the Reubenites had received another special blessing from God. Throughout Chronicles victory for Israelites resulted from divine blessing (see *Introduction: 23) Victory and Defeat*). Reuben found God's favor and accomplished a significant victory against his enemies. For this reason too, Reuben's descendants should be counted among God's people after the exile (see *Introduction: 2) Northern Israel*).

The Tribe of Gad (5:11-17)

The short record of the **Gadites** (5:11-17) begins with geographical notes (5:11-12), moves to lists of families (5:13-15), returns to geography (5:16), and closes with a source notation (5:17). This material is explicitly connected with the preceding Reubenite record by the introductory phrase **next to them** (5:11).

Like Reuben, Gad also had a minor role in the history of Israel after the establishment of David's throne (see 1 Sam. 13:7; 2 Sam. 24:5; 2 Kgs. 10:33; 1 Chr. 2:2; 5:11, 16, 18, 26; 6:63, 80; 12:8, 14, 37; 26:32; see Jer. 49:1; Ezek. 48:27-28, 34). Consequently, the Chronicler sketched the extent of their land to establish the tribe's legitimate territorial claims (5:11-12,16). He also referred to the source of his material as a royal record (5:17). This record was probably a military census written **during the reigns of Jotham ... and Jeroboam** (c. 750 BC). The Chronicler referred to this military record to demonstrate that the tribe of Gad had a significant role in national life at that time. Gad should not, therefore, be overlooked by the Chronicler's post-exilic readers (see *Introduction: 2) Northern Israel*).

Transjordanian Victory (5:18-22)

The Chronicler turned next to the second of four narratives within his genealogies (see 4:9-10; 5:24-26; 7:21-24). This episode focuses on victory in battle for the Transjordanian tribes and stands in sharp contrast with the defeat of Transjordanians later in this chapter (see 5:24-26). These passages illustrate the Chronicler's belief that fidelity will lead to victory (5:18-22) and infidelity to defeat (5:24-26). Similar themes appear time and again in the book of Chronicles (see *Introduction: 23) Victory and Defeat*).

Structure of 5:18-22

This narrative divides into a symmetrical five step pattern (see figure 6). It begins with preparation for battle (5:18) and ends with settlement after war (5:22b). The battle takes place (5:19) and is won (5:21-22a). The turning point of the episode is the prayer and divine intervention (5:20).

Transjordanian Preparations for Battle (5:18)

The Chronicler began this simple narrative with a description of **44,760** warriors in the combined forces of Reuben, Gad, and the half-tribe of Manasseh (5:18). This scene balances with the closing notice of security (5:22b).

Transjordanian Battle Waged (5:19)

The war ensues in 5:19 and the tension of the story rises. Once again, the **Hagrites** are mentioned as Israel's enemies (see 5:10). The Arabian tribes **Jetur, Naphish, and Nodab** appear as well (5:19; see Gen. 25:15). The Chronicler listed these four groups to display the insurmountable odds against the Transjordanian tribes. On many occasions the Chronicler demonstrated that divine favor enabled the people of God to gain victory against enormous odds (see *Introduction: 23) Victory and Defeat*). Later in 5:21 he recalled this theme by mentioning 100,000 captives taken in battle.

Transjordanian Prayer and Divine Intervention (5:20)

The turning point in the story builds suspense momentarily by simply stating **they were helped** (5:20). Who helped the tribes? The next clause specifically identifies **God** as the one who gave the victory. As in many other passages, victory for Israel was the result of divine help for the helpless (see *Introduction: 10) Divine Activity*). The Chronicler then explained why the Transjordanian tribes received God's help. **They cried out to** God (5:20). The Chronicler frequently attributed success in battle to God answering the prayers of his people (see *Introduction: 17) Prayer*; see also *23) Victory and Defeat*). Prayer as opposed to reliance on human ingenuity and effort demonstrated that **they trusted** God (5:20). Divine help often comes to God's people in the book of Chronicles as they trust in him.

Transjordanian Battle Won (5:21-22a)

The tension of the story lessens in 5:21-22a as the Chronicler described the results of battle. The outcome of this conflict was spectacular: **livestock ... one hundred thousand people captive ... and many others fell slain** (5:21-22a). To reinforce his theological perspective of the event, the Chronicler explained once again that victory resulted **because the battle was God's** (5:22a; see *Introduction: 23) Victory and Defeat*; see also *10) Divine Activity*).

Transjordanian Settlement After Battle (5:22b)

The narrative closes as it began, with God's people at peace (5:22b). The Transjordanian tribes lived in the land they had conquered **until the exile** (5:22b). In light of the two references to Tiglath-Pileser III in this context (5:6,26), it is likely that the Chronicler had the year 734 BC in mind when he wrote of **the exile** (5:22b). This temporal reference indicated that a number of years of peace followed for the Transjordanian tribes.

Although the Chronicler frequently attributed victory in battle to prayer, this battle sequence is unique in one way. Every other example concerns military victories for Judah. Taken alone, these stories of Judahite victories could have contributed to exclusivism among the Judahite leaders of the post-exilic community. In this brief narrative, however, the Chronicler reminded his readers that Judah was not the only tribe to experience this remarkable blessing. The tribes east of Jordan had also seen spectacular divine intervention in response to their prayers. They too were the people of God (see *Introduction: 2) Northern Israel*).

The Half-Tribe of Manasseh (5:23-26)

The record of Manasseh is brief. It divides into two sections: an introduction to the clan (5:23) and a narrative of defeat and deportation (5:24-26).

Manassehite Numbers and Territories (5:23)

The Chronicler described the Transjordanian half-tribe of Manasseh very briefly (5:23). He listed no names of Manasseh's descendants, but simply commented that they **were numerous** and gave two geographical references (5:23). Accordingly, his account has two principal concerns.

On the one hand, the Chronicler established that this tribe had been richly blessed by God. The Mosaic Law frequently pointed to numerous descendants as a sign of God's blessing (see Exod. 32:13; Deut. 30:2-6,9-10). The Chronicler himself drew on this belief here and many other places (see *Introduction: 25) Increase and Decline of Progeny*). By this means, he sought to convince the post-exilic community not to forget eastern Manasseh; God had shown favor to this tribe.

On the other hand, the geographical notes indicate once again the Chronicler's concern with expanding the post-exilic vision of Israel's territories. (For the Chronicler's geographical hopes, see comments on 2:42-55.) He established the extent of Transjordanian Manassehite territories so that the restored nation would continue to hope for these lands as well (see *Introduction: 2) Northern Israel*).

Manassehite Deportation Narrative (5:24-26)

In contrast with the earlier episode of victory in Transjordan (see 5:18-22), the final portion of the Chronicler's treatment of the Transjordanians is a brief narrative. This third narrative embedded within these genealogies explains why Tiglath-Pileser III deported these tribes (see also 4:9-10; 5:18-22; 7:21-24).

Structure of 5:24-26

This story displays a simple three step symmetry (see figure 6). The passage begins with a description of famous Manassehite warriors in their allotted land (5:24). By contrast, it ends with the population of Reuben, Gad, and Manasseh deported from their land (5:26). The turning point consists of a report of Manassehite infidelity (5:25).

Manassehite Warriors in the Land (5:24)

The Chronicler described the men of Manasseh as **brave warriors** and **famous men** to indicate the blessings the tribe had experienced before its apostasy (5:24). This blessing made the Manassehite infidelity all the more astounding. On a number of occasions, the Chronicler noted that apostasy occurred after a time of blessing. Infidelity followed blessings during the reigns of Rehoboam (2 Chr. 12:1-4), Jehoshaphat (2 Chr. 18:1), Amaziah (2 Chr. 25:14-15), Uzziah (2 Chr. 26:16), Hezekiah (2 Chr. 32:24-25) and Josiah (2 Chr. 35:20-24). His repeated focus on this scenario warned his post-exilic readers against following a similar pattern in their day.

Manassehite Apostasy (5:25)

The warriors of Manasseh took their prosperity as an occasion for turning away from the Lord (5:25). These events are the Chronicler's summary of 2 Kgs. 15:19, 29; 17:6-23; and 18:11. Tension rises in the story as the Chronicler described them as having been **unfaithful** because they **prostituted themselves** (5:25). The word 'unfaithful' appears frequently in Chronicles to describe flagrant covenant violation (see *Introduction: 21) Unfaithfulness*). They had rejected **the God of their**

fathers and had served **the gods of the peoples of the land** (5:25). The Chronicler used the expression **peoples of the land** in a number of ways. Here he meant the indigenous people of the lands taken by Manasseh (see 2 Chr. 23:13, 20, 21; 26:21; 32:13; 33:25; 36:1). In effect, the Manassehites had denied their own heritage for the abominations of paganism. By this means, the Chronicler made it clear that Manassehite infidelity was serious apostasy.

Manassehite Deportation from the Land (5:26)

In response to this infidelity, **the God of Israel stirred up the spirit of ... Tiglath-Pileser** (5:26a). In accordance with the Mosaic and Davidic covenants, rebellion against God would be met by chastisement from foreign oppressors (see Deut. 1:26-46; Josh. 7:11-12; Judg. 2:10-23; 1 Sam. 12:9-11; Isa. 1:19-20). The Assyrians destroyed and exiled not only the tribe of Manasseh, but the tribes of Reuben and Gad as well.

The Chronicler also noted that the Transjordanian tribes were carried to **Halah, Habor, Hara and the river of Gozan** (5:26b), cities between present day Iran and Iraq. He closed with the note that the tribes are there **to this day**. (For the Chronicler's use of this terminology, see comments on 4:41.) As he had previously identified the location of some Simeonites in Seir (see 4:42), the Chronicler also noted the whereabouts of the Transjordanian tribes in his own time. They had not been utterly destroyed and the Chronicler wanted his readers to hope for their return (see *Introduction: 2) Northern Israel*).

In 4:24-5:26 the Chronicler drew attention to tribes of Israel that were easily overlooked in the post-exilic period. Simeon and the Transjordanian tribes did not play extraordinary roles in the history of Israel. They were not well represented among the first Israelites to return to the promised land. Nevertheless, the Chronicler was determined to have his readers include these tribes within their vision of restoration for God's people. Without these tribes, the nation of Israel would always be incomplete.

Levi in the Center (6:1-81)

As we have already noted, the Chronicler highlighted the importance of the tribe of Levi by placing it in the center of his genealogies (see figure 7). This literary arrangement reflected the symbolic arrangement of the tribes of Israel depicted in Num. 2:1-34. When the tribes encamped during the wilderness march, they arranged themselves on all sides of the tabernacle with the sons of Levi in the center of the camp. The symbolism in the Mosaic period was plain. The worship of the Lord and the servants of that worship were to be the focus of hope for the traveling Israelite community. The Chronicler reflected this symbolism in his model of the post-exilic community by setting the genealogies of Levi in the center of his description of the sons of Israel.

The Chronicler's emphasis on Levi reveals the importance of the temple and its services after the exile. Both kingship and temple were the central institutions in his vision of Israel (see *Introduction: 4-9) King and Temple*). If the returnees were to see God's blessing, then not only the royal family (Judah), but also the temple personnel (Levi) must have their proper place among the tribes.

Structure of 6:1-81

The Chronicler's sketch of the tribe of Levi divides into four large sections (see figure 6). The high priestly families appear first (6:1-15). The duties of various Levites follow (6:16-47). Priestly responsibilities appear (6:48-53) just before the geographical records of the tribe (6:54-81).

The High Priestly Family (6:1-15)

The account of the tribe of Levi begins with a focus on one line of Aaron's descendants, the high priestly family (6:1-15). He set this genealogy at the head of this chapter to symbolize the leading role of the high priests over all other members of the tribe. The Chronicler identified the high priestly family from its origins to the time of exile in two steps (see figure 6).

High Priestly Line Distinguished (6:1-4a)

The Chronicler first distinguished the high priests from other descendants of Levi (6:1-4a). Out of all the sons of Levi (6:1), he focused on **Kohath** (6:2). From all of Kohath's children, he narrowed attention to **Amram** (6:3). **Aaron** (6:3) was Amram's child of special interest. Of Aaron's four sons, only **Eleazar** continued the selected line (6:4a). Out of all of Eleazar's sons, only **Phinehas** represented the high priestly line (6:4b).

This material eliminates a number of families from high priestly service without explanation. The Chronicler relied on his readers' knowledge of Israel's history to supply additional information as it was needed.

High Priestly Line Continued (6:4b-15)

With other branches of Aaron's family eliminated, the Chronicler concentrated on the high priestly descendants of Phinehas (6:4b-15). This material is very similar to Ezra 7:1-5. A number of high priests do not appear in this list: Jehoiada (2 Kgs. 12:2; 2 Chr. 23:8-18; 24:2-3, 6, 12, 14-15, 17, 20, 22, 25), Uriah (2 Kgs. 16:10-16), possibly two other Azariahs (see 2 Chr. 26:17, 20; 31:10-13), as well as the descendants of Ithamar – Eli (see 1 Sam. 1:9; 14:3) and Abiathar (see 2 Sam. 8:17).

Within these verses the Chronicler paused on two occasions to add his own comments (6:10,15). These comments reveal his chief concerns in this section. First, the Chronicler mentioned that **Johanan ... served as priest in the temple Solomon built** (6:10). This comment is significant because the Chronicler viewed Solomonic structures as normative for his post-exilic readers (see: *Introduction: 14) Standards*). The patterns followed in Solomon's temple were to be reinstituted in the new temple after exile. In the Chronicler's day, many families could lay claim to having high priestly ancestors, but only one family of Aaron was the legitimate high priestly line. By referring to Solomon's temple, the Chronicler

responded to any objection that may have been raised against the exaltation of this line of Aaron as the exclusive high priestly family.

Second, the Chronicler also mentioned that **Jehozadak was deported ... by the hand of Nebuchadnezzar** (6:15). This historical note brings the genealogy of high priests to within one generation of the post-exilic community. Jehozadak was the father of Joshua, the high priest of Zerubbabel's reconstruction program. Joshua had returned from exile and displaced other Levites who had led worship in the ruins of the temple. By ending this genealogy of high priests with Jehozadak, the Chronicler settled any question regarding the legitimacy of Joshua's program. God had chosen him; no other son of Levi could function as the high priest.

Duties of Levi's Descendants (6:16-47)

The second section begins with the title **the sons of Levi** (6:16) just as the preceding section (see 6:1). This list, however, focuses on the duties of two kinds of Levites (see figure 6). The Chronicler dealt first with those whom we may call 'Ordinary Levites', those with a variety of responsibilities (6:16-30). He then turned to those whom we may call 'Musical Levites', those in charge of music in worship (6:31-47). These divisions of duties provided guidance for the restoration of proper temple worship after the exile.

Ordinary Levites (6:16-30)

The 'Ordinary Levites' appear in two parallel lists (6:16-19a; 6:19b-30). The former half lists the sons of the second generation of each family (6:16-19a). The latter half traces a number of generations of each family (6:19b-30). Both passages include titles (6:16,19b), Gershonites (6:17,20-21), Kohathites (6:18,22-28), and Merarites (6:19a, 29-30).

The first half of this material reflects traditional records of Levitical descent. Close parallels appear in Exod. 6:16-19 and Num. 3:17-20; 26:57-61. The second half, however, extends for seven generations. The second Kohathite genealogy (6:22-28) is difficult to translate and appears to have suffered corruption through transmission (see *Introduction: Translation and Transmission*). Some reconstructions of this material, however, suggest that it originally extended seven generations as well.

The mention of well-known **Elkanah** (6:25) and **Samuel** (6:27-28) focuses the Kohathite line on the man who anointed David king over Israel (see 1 Sam. 1:20; 16:7,12-13). In 1 Sam. 1:1 Elkanah is identified as 'an Ephraimite', but the Chronicler clarified here that Elkanah and his son Samuel were Levites living among the Ephraimites.

The mention of Samuel suggests that the seven generations of these genealogies reach David's kingdom. If this understanding is correct, the Chronicler brought these genealogies to an end in David's day because he considered David's division of labor among the Levites as normative for his post-exilic readers (see *Introduction: 14) Standards*).

Musical Levites (6:31-47)

This portion of the Chronicler's account of Levi lists **the men David put in charge of the music** (6:31). It points out that these families not only served in David's **tabernacle, the Tent of Meeting** (6:32), but also in Solomon's **temple of the LORD in Jerusalem** (6:32). Thus the orders described here stand on the authority of David and Solomon, the Chronicler's ideal kings (see *Introduction: 14) Standards*).

Musicians were selected from each family of Levi: **Heman, the musician** from the Kohathites (6:33-38), **Heman's associate Asaph ... at his right hand** from the Gershonites (6:39-43), and **at his left hand ... Ethan** from the Merarites (6:44-47).

The Chronicler frequently mentioned musical guilds (see 15:16, 27; 25:1-31; 2 Chr. 29:25-26; see also *Introduction: 8) Music*). His keen interest in this aspect of temple service has led some interpreters to think that the Chronicler himself may have been a Levitical musician. This understanding may be correct, but it is also possible that the Chronicler was simply addressing controversies among Levites in his day (see Neh. 7:43-44; 10:9-13,28-29; 11:15-18; 12:24-47).

Duties of Priests (6:48-53)

The Chronicler turned next to the duties of the Aaronic priests. While the high priesthood was restricted in his day to the Zadokite family, all the descendants of Aaron served as priests. This material divides into two parts (see figure 6).

Priestly Responsibilities (6:48-49)

This section begins with a notice about the Levites (6:48). The Chronicler explained that other Levites took care of **all the other duties** related to the temple (6:48). The sons of Aaron, however, had special responsibilities in the worship of Israel. They **presented ... burnt offering** (see Lev. 1; 6:8-13) and **incense in connection with all that was done in the Most Holy Place** (see Lev. 16:13-16). They also made **atonement for Israel** (6:49) through a variety of services. As was his typical practice, the Chronicler appealed to Mosaic legislation to justify his point of view. His outlook was **in accordance with all that Moses ... had commanded** (6:49; see *Introduction: 14) Standards*).

Priestly Leadership (6:50-53)

With these general Levitical and priestly duties established, the Chronicler noted which families were high priests in charge of all the other sons of Aaron. The Chronicler gave a short genealogy tracing high priests from **Aaron** to **Zadok** and his son **Ahimaaz** (6:50-53). This list extends to the days of David and Solomon like those of the preceding section (see 6:16-30). Joshua, the high priest with Zerubbabel after the exile, descended from this line. Like Ezekiel (see Ezek. 40:46; 43:19; 44:15) and Zechariah (see Zech. 3:1-10), the Chronicler supported the Zadokite priesthood as the only legitimate high priesthood for Israel after the exile.

Lands for Levi's Descendants (6:54-81)
The Chronicler closed this section on the tribe of Levi by listing settlements allotted to various Levites (6:54-81). His description depends heavily on Josh. 21:4-39 and divides into three parts (see figure 6).

The text deals first with Aaronic possessions (6:54-60); then it constructs two parallel lists of land allotments to the Kohathites (6:61, 66-70), Gershonites (6:62, 71-76), and Merarites (6:63,77-81).

The Chronicler had at least two reasons for including these details. First, most of the sites mentioned here were outside the boundaries of the post-exilic province of Judah. They reflected the Chronicler's interest in the territorial expansion of the restored community. He encouraged the sons of Levi to keep the hope of repossessing all the territories they had lost to foreign dominion. (For the Chronicler's geographical hopes, see comments on 2:42-55.)

Second, the Chronicler also instructed all the tribes to remember their responsibilities to Levi. According to Mosaic legislation, the sons of Levi received parcels of land within the boundaries of other tribes (see Lev. 25:32-34; Num. 35:1-5; Josh. 21:1-3). The distribution of these properties came from God through the casting of the **lot** (6:54; for the Chronicler's outlook on casting lots, see comments on 24:5). Moreover, these possessions enabled the Levites to support their families. As **the Israelites gave the Levites ... towns and their pasturelands** (6:64), the post-exilic community was to honor the Levites in these ways (see also 2 Chr. 11:14; 31:4).

Other Tribes Easily Forgotten (7:1-40)
In the seventh chapter of his genealogies, the Chronicler rounded off his list of the tribes of Israel by quickly mentioning six other families easily overlooked.

Structure of 7:1-40
This record divides into six sections (see figure 6). It touches on Issachar (7:1-5), Benjamin (7:6-12), Naphtali (7:13), Manasseh (7:14-19), Ephraim (7:20-29), and Asher (7:30-40). Compared with other portions of his genealogies, this material is characterized by brevity and a paucity of authorial comments. Even so, general features of this chapter reveal the Chronicler's chief concerns.

The Tribe of Issachar (7:1-5)
The record of **the sons of Issachar** (7:1) draws from Gen. 46:13 and Num. 26:23-25, but many of the names do not appear elsewhere in Scripture. This list focuses first on Issachar's four sons (7:1) and narrows attention to the descendants of **Tola** the first born (7:2). The descendants of **Uzzi**, the firstborn of Tola, and his son **Izrahiah** follow (7:3-4). Then the genealogies close with a reference to **the relatives**, other Issacharites not mentioned in the preceding verses (7:5).

By mentioning large numbers of soldiers as well as **many wives and children** (7:4), the Chronicler once again pointed to the blessing of God illustrated in the increase of progeny. The tribe of Issachar had been greatly blessed by God and should not be forgotten in the post-exilic period (see *Introduction: 25) Increase and Decline of Progeny*). 

The most prominent feature of this section is its military focus. Each step of the genealogy closes by citing a number of soldiers: Tola's **fighting men** (7:2), the **men ready for battle** from Izrahiah's sons (7:4), and the **fighting men** from **all the clans of Issachar** (7:5). Previous genealogies mention fighting men on occasion (see 1:10; 2:22-23; 4:38,41-43; 5:24), but this theme does not appear there as prominently as it does here.

The Chronicler's concentration on fighting men drew attention to at least two issues. First, Issachar had offered vital service to the nation of Israel in the past by participating in warfare. In acknowledgment of these contributions, the post-exilic readers were not to exclude this tribe from their vision of restored Israel (see *Introduction: 2) Northern Israel*). 

Second, the post-exilic readers should desire the return of Issachar so that the holy army of Israel could be reconstituted. Earlier prophets had already indicated that warfare against the nations would come after exile. After returning from exile, Israel faced threats from enemies; warfare was a constant menace (see Ezra 4:1-6; 5:3-5; 6:3,6-7,11-12; 7:11,21,24,26; Neh. 2:7,9-10,19; 4:1-23; 6:1-19; 7:3). By concentrating on the military contributions of Issachar, the Chronicler indicated that the return of Issachar would strengthen the post-exilic community against her enemies.

The Tribe of Benjamin (7:6-12)

A brief account of the tribe of **Benjamin** (7:6) appears here prior to the more substantial record in 8:1-40. This material introduces three sons of Benjamin: **Bela, Beker**, and **Jediael** (7:6). It then covers their descendants in the same order (Bela [7:7], Beker [7:8-9], and Jediael [7:10-11]). The section closes with the mention of several other descendants of Benjamin (7:12).

In this passage, the Chronicler did not follow Gen. 46:21 nor Num. 26:38-41 as closely as he did in other places (compare 7:14-19; 7:20-29; 7:30-40; 8:1-40). The uniqueness of this genealogy has been explained in different ways. Some interpreters have suggested that it was originally a record of Zebulun that suffered corruption through transmission (see *Introduction: Translation and Transmission*). However, there is little support for this view. Others have suggested that the Chronicler simply followed a source that was different from other lists. Even if this is correct, we must still ask why the Chronicler chose to present this limited account of Benjamin here and reserve more extensive material for 8:1-40.

Once again, an important clue to the Chronicler's purpose here lies in his emphasis on military matters. The records of Benjamin's three sons end with the numbers of **fighting men** (7:7,9,11). The longer Benjamite genealogy in 8:1-40 occasionally mentions military matters (see 8:13,40), but it provides a much broader picture of Benjamin. This shorter list focuses explicitly on Benjamin's former military might.

It seems likely, therefore, that the military focus of Issachar's preceding genealogy (see 7:1-5) led the Chronicler to add a brief list of another tribe of military importance. The surrounding peoples who threatened the post-exilic community made it essential for more descendants of Benjamite warriors to return to the land and join with the few Benjamites who had already come (see 9:7-9; see also *Introduction: 2) Northern Israel*).

The Tribe of Naphtali (7:13)

One verse covers the **sons of Naphtali**. This genealogy is by far the shortest among the Chronicler's records. The brevity and fragmentary character of this verse have led some interpreters to suggest that a portion of the original text has been lost. It may have been here that the Chronicler originally mentioned Zebulun and Dan (see *Introduction: Translation and Transmission*). This proposal has some merit and could explain the anomalous character of this passage.

As it stands, however, this genealogy offers little information other than the fact that Naphtali was a child of Jacob's concubine **Bilhah** (see Gen. 30:3-8). This comment may have been a response to controversy among the Chronicler's readers. Perhaps some early returnees questioned the legitimacy or importance of Naphtali's descendants because they were children of Bilhah. If this was so, the Chronicler asserted here that the descendants of Naphtali certainly belonged among the people of God (see *Introduction: 2) Northern Israel*).

The Tribe of Manasseh (7:14-19)

The Chronicler himself acknowledged that Manassehites were among the early returnees (see 9:3). Moreover, he already listed some Manassehites who settled east of the Jordan (see 5:18,23). This genealogy, however, deals with families of the tribe who settled west of the Jordan. It draws from Num. 26:29-34 and Josh. 17:1-18, but differs from both sources in several ways. The Hebrew text of this section presents a number of difficulties that have led some interpreters to think it was corrupted through transmission along with the preceding genealogy of Naphtali (see *Introduction: Translation and Transmission*). This possibility cannot be ruled out completely. As it appears, however, Manasseh's record divides into four parts: **Asriel** and **Zelophehad** (7:14-16), **Ulam** (7:17a), **Gilead** (7:17b-18) and **Shemida** (7:19).

The main purpose of this material was to indicate the rightful place of Manassehites among the people of God (see *Introduction: 2) Northern Israel*). One interesting feature of this section is the prominence of women. In these six verses the Chronicler mentioned women five times: the **Aramean concubine** (7:14), Makir's sister **Maacah** (7:15), Zelophehad's **daughters** (7:15b), Makir's wife **Maacah** (7:16), and **Hammoleketh** (7:18).

The well-known stories about Zelophehad's daughters (see Num. 26:33; 27:1-11; 36:1-12; Josh. 17:3-4) deal with the inheritance rights of women in Israel. Zelophehad died leaving only daughters to inherit his land. As a result, Moses made a special ruling affirming that in such situations women should receive their fathers' land so that it would remain a permanent possession of the same tribe.

The Chronicler's mention of Zelophehad's daughters and other women suggests that he used these records to reaffirm the Mosaic legislation regarding the property rights of Israelite women. In the post-exilic period there would undoubtedly be families only represented by women. Questions would arise regarding ownership of family inheritances. The Chronicler appealed to the records of the Manassehites to settle such questions. The restoration of all Israel included the rightful place of women. This focus corresponds to a number of passages in Chronicles which draw attention to children and women (see 2 Chr. 20:13; 21:14, 17; 28:8; 29:9; 31:18; see also *Introduction: 1) All Israel*).

The Tribe of Ephraim (7:20-29)

The tribe of Ephraim was represented among the early returnees (see 9:3), but the Chronicler wanted to encourage his readers to expect much more for the tribe. This material breaks into four sections: the beginning of Joshua's genealogy (7:20-21a), a brief narrative (7:21b-24), the continuation of Joshua's genealogy (7:25-27), and a summary of settlements (7:28-29).

Out of all of **the descendants of Ephraim** (7:20), the Chronicler chose to concentrate on the line leading to **Joshua**, the son of **Nun** (7:27), who led the conquest of the promised land (see Num. 13:8; Josh. 1). The opening genealogical information (7:20-21a) follows Num. 26:35, but the continuation to Joshua (7:25-27) does not appear elsewhere in Scripture.

The Chronicler focused on Joshua because of his interest in military matters. As he called attention to the military accomplishments of Issachar (7:1-5) and Benjamin (7:6-12), the Chronicler reminded his post-exilic readers that Joshua, the famous leader of the conquest, came from the tribe of Ephraim. In a day when Israel's land must be taken again and warfare threatened Israel on every side, having the family of Joshua would be a great asset.

The two remaining portions of Ephraim's record (7:21b-24; 7:28-29) point to locations where various descendants of Ephraim settled. The first section is a brief digression to narrative (see 4:9-10; 5:18-22,24-26). This story divides into four symmetrical steps (see figure 6). It begins with aggression against Gath (7:21) and continues with Ephraim mourning for his sons (7:22). Then this story concludes with the birth of another son **Beriah** (7:23), and Ephraimites settling away from Gath (7:24)

Identifying the character 'Ephraim' in this passage is difficult. He may have been the patriarch of the tribe or an unknown descendant with the same name as the patriarch. The former option would place the aggression in Gath before Israel's sojourn in Egypt. The latter possibility may locate the event after the conquest and settlement. Whatever the case, at some point Ephraimites attempted to move westward toward Gath, but were driven back toward the east. This event provided an explanation for the location of Ephraimite settlements in **Lower and Upper Beth**

Horon and **Uzzen Sheerah** (7:24). Uzzen Sheerah has not been identified, but we should assume from this context that it was east of Gath.

The Chronicler's interest in this event probably resulted from some issue raised in his day. The mention of building settlements points to the blessing of God on the Ephraimites at this time (see *Introduction: 24) Building and Destruction*). Thus the Chronicler highlighted the right of this tribe to be represented among the people of God. Perhaps some of his readers had heard of ancient westward movements of Ephraimites and wondered about the extent of their tribal lands. In this narrative the Chronicler explained where Ephraimites were to settle.

The final list of **lands and settlements** (7:28-29) further established the rightful inheritance of Ephraim. The Chronicler included these materials to inspire his readers to hope for lands beyond the borders of post-exilic Judah. (For the Chronicler's geographical hopes, see comments on 2:42-55.)

The Tribe of Asher (7:30-40)

The Chronicler finalized this portion of his genealogies with **the sons of Asher** (7:30). His record follows Gen. 46:17 for three generations and also reflects Num. 26:44-46 at several points. Apart from these initial names, however, the material here has no parallels in Scripture. The genealogy of Asher divides into three sections: the four sons of Asher (7:30), the line of Beriah (7:31-39), and military information (7:40).

The Chronicler's purpose in this genealogy was at least twofold. First, his exclusive concern with the line of Beriah may have reflected the limitations of his sources, but the Chronicler may also have chosen this strategy because of questions among his readers regarding the descendants of this family.

Second, a more obvious purpose was to inform the post-exilic community of Asher's military contributions in the past. The descendants of Asher listed here included **heads of families, choice men, brave warriors and outstanding leaders** (7:40). After the exile, Israel needed the military power of Asher. This tribe should not be forgotten (see *Introduction: 2) Northern Israel*).

Benjamin in Honor (8:1-40)

The Chronicler's genealogies of Israel close with a second lengthy account of Benjamin (see 7:6-12). The opening of this material (8:1-5) compares with Gen. 46:21 and Num. 26:38-41, but the ending of this material (8:6-40) goes its own way. By closing his genealogies with a long account of Benjamin, the Chronicler raised this tribe to the level of Judah and Levi (see figure 7).

As noted above, this passage is the Chronicler's second record of Benjamin (see 7:6-12). The most likely explanation for this repetition is that the Chronicler distinguished two groups of Benjamites. When the northern tribes broke away from Judah in c. 922 BC, the tribe of Benjamin split its allegiance. Some Benjamites seceded with the North (see 1 Kgs. 11:31-32) while others remained aligned with Judah (see 1 Kgs. 12:21). It is likely that the Chronicler presented the Benjamite genealogy in chapter 7 as representative of those who sided with the North. That list appears among northern tribes (Issachar, Benjamin, Naphtali, Manasseh, Ephraim and Asher [7:1-40]) and has only slight affinities with the second Benjamite genealogy. The second record, however, concentrates on Benjamites who were loyal to Jerusalem. As we will see, it focuses on geographical locations in or near post-exilic Judah. These Benjamites received lengthy attention because they were faithful to the Jerusalem monarch and temple just as Judah and Levi had been.

Structure of 8:1-40

This chapter divides into four sections (see figure 6). The Benjamites in Geba appear first (8:1-7). Those located in several other places follow (8:8-12). The Chronicler then turned to Benjamites in Jerusalem (8:13-28) and closed with others associated with Jerusalem (8:29-40).

Benjamites in Geba (8:1-7)

The first section of this record of **Benjamin** (8:1) narrows quickly to Benjamin's grandson, **Ehud** (8:6) (**Abihud** [8:3] should probably be translated 'father of Ehud' [see NIV text note]). Ehud is the well-known judge who brought victory for Israel over the Moabite king, Eglon (see Judg. 3:12-30). The Chronicler recorded that his descendants lived **in Geba** (8:6), a Levitical city lying on the southern border of Benjamin only six miles north-northeast of Jerusalem (see Josh. 18:24; 21:17; 1 Chr. 6:60). King Asa of Judah fortified Geba during his reign (see 2 Chr. 16:6).

This geographical note was important for the Chronicler's readers because Benjamites repossessed Geba in the early post-exilic period (see Ezra 2:26; Neh. 7:30; 11:31; 12:29). The Chronicler noted that at some point, these families had been **deported to Manahath** (8:6) (probably Malah, three miles southwest of Jerusalem). Yet, the Chronicler affirmed that Geba was the Benjamites' rightful claim. (For the Chronicler's geographical hopes, see comments on 2:42-55.)

Benjamites in Moab, Ono and Lod, Aijalon and Gath (8:8-13)

The second portion of Benjamin's record concentrates on the **Shaharaim** (8:8) and then on **the sons of Elpaal** (8:12). Several locations are mentioned in these verses. Shaharaim lived **in Moab** (8:8), probably during the early years of settlement (see 1 Sam. 22:3f; Ruth 1:1-7). Elpaal's descendants **built Ono and Lod** (8:12). The Chronicler often mentioned successful building projects to indicate the blessing of God (see *Introduction: 24) Building and Destruction*). God was pleased with the people who settled and built in these places. These cities south of Joppa were well-known in the Chronicler's time. A number of returnees in the post-exilic community settled in these regions (see Ezra 2:33; Neh. 7:37; 11:35). Later generations, **Beriah and Shema** (8:13), lived in **Aijalon** and took control of **Gath** (8:13). Both of these cites were located in the post-exilic province of Judah. By mentioning these clans of Benjamites in connection with these locations, the Chronicler addressed issues pertinent to the resettlement of these cites after the exile. In a word, the Benjamites had rights to these places. (For the Chronicler's geographical hopes, see comments on 2:42-55.)

Benjamites in Jerusalem (8:14-28)

The Chronicler next reported a series of genealogical references that end with **all these were heads of families, chiefs ... and they lived in Jerusalem** (8:28). Two comments should be made about this ending.

First, it is difficult to determine to whom the Chronicler specifically referred by the terms **all these** (8:28). He may have had in mind all of the names included in 8:14-27. It is more likely, however, that he had in mind only the last segment of his genealogies (8:26-27).

Second, whatever the extent of the reference, the more important fact is that he placed these descendants of Benjamin **in Jerusalem** (8:28). It would not be surprising that Benjamites faithful to the throne and temple of Jerusalem would have moved there during the divided kingdom. Their territories were often the battlegrounds of wars between the North and South.

The Chronicler noted that these Benjamites lived in Jerusalem to establish their prominence in the post-exilic period. Some families of the tribe had returned to Jerusalem in the early years after exile (see 9:7). They rightfully held an exalted position among the tribes.

More Benjamites associated with Jerusalem (8:29-40)

In this final portion of the Benjamite genealogies, the Chronicler began with references to locations. **Jeiel, the father of Gibeon** (8:29) should be understood as 'Jeiel, the founder of Gibeon'. Many of these Benjamites in Gibeon eventually **lived near their relatives in Jerusalem** (8:32).

In 8:33-34 the Chronicler reported well-known figures such as **Kish** (see 1 Sam. 9:1,3) and **Saul** the first king of Israel (see 1 Sam. 9:18-27). He also mentioned **Jonathan** the close friend of David (see 1 Sam. 18:1,3) and **Merib-Baal** the Saulide protected within David's court (also known as Mephibosheth (2 Sam. 4:4; 9:6-13).

In 8:35-40 a list of several generations ends with the note that some branches of the Benjamite family included **brave warriors** and **many sons and grandsons – 150 in all** (8:40). Once again, the Chronicler noted the military acumen of men in this tribe (see 7:6-12). Moreover, he pointed to the large progeny of this family to indicate God's blessing (see *Introduction: 25) Increase and Decline of Progeny*).

These prominent Benjamites who lived in Jerusalem were ancestors of Benjamites who returned to the land after the exile. The Chronicler was determined to see their descendants receive special honor.

Summation of Tribal Lists (9:1a)

In balance with 1 Chr. 2:1-2 the Chronicler closed his focus on the breadth of God's people with a brief summation (see figure 6). Two aspects of this passage warrant comment. First, by mentioning **the book of the kings of Israel** the Chronicler indicated one of his principal sources for his genealogical information (9:1a). This record authenticated his outlook on Israel's families against any objections that may have been raised.

Second, the Chronicler characterized his lists as containing **all Israel** (9:1a). This terminology indicates that chapters 2-8 represented the breadth of the entire nation of Israel (see *Introduction: 1) All Israel*). Despite the highly selective character of these genealogies and lists, they stood as indications of how broadly the Chronicler wanted his original readers to conceive of the nation. His reason for emphasizing this motif is evident. Until the breadth reflected in these lists was represented among the returnees, the restoration of God's people would be incomplete.

The Continuation of Israel (9:1b-34)

The Chronicler closed his genealogical records by turning attention to the early post-exilic community (see figure 8). Portions of these lists parallel Neh. 11:3-19 in significant ways. It is likely that the Chronicler and the author of Ezra-Nehemiah used a common source for their varying purposes.

The Chronicler reported the names of these returnees to connect his readers with the nation of Israel in the past. Although he mentioned that the returnees went to **their own towns** (9:2), his lists focus only on those who **lived in Jerusalem** (9:3,34). Jerusalem's inhabitants were the center of the restoration effort after the exile.

Structure

This passage divides into three parts:

- Introduction (9:1b-2)
- Laity among the Returnees (9:3-9)
- Priests among the Returnees (9:10-13)
- Levites among the Returnees (9:14-34)
  - Introductory Genealogy (9:14-16)
  - Gatekeepers (9:17-34)

Outline of 1 Chr. 9:1b-34 (figure 8)

This material begins with an historical orientation toward the lists that follow (9:1b-2). Following this introduction, the Chronicler focused on three groups: lay people (9:3-9); priests (9:10-13), and Levites (9:14-34).

Introduction (9:1b-2)

The Chronicler began this portion of his genealogies with the reminder that the people living in **Judah** had been exiled **to Babylon** (9:1b). He referred to the destruction of Jerusalem and the deportation of its population by Nebuchadnezzar in c. 586 BC.

In addition to this historical note, the Chronicler explained why the exile had taken place. The deportation occurred **because of their unfaithfulness** (9:1b). Infidelity appears frequently in Chronicles as a description of flagrant covenant violation, especially in the area of worship (see *Introduction: 21) Unfaithfulness*). The Chronicler made it clear that Judah deserved her punishment because her apostasy was so great. These words anticipate a motif which the Chronicler applied to his readers time and again in later chapters. Put simply, he warned his readers that infidelity to God will not go unpunished (see *Introduction: 10-27) Divine Blessing and Judgment*). If post-exilic Israelites hoped to enjoy the blessings of God, they had to avoid infidelities of the past.

After this historical note, attention shifts to those who were **first to resettle** (9:2). The Chronicler introduced representatives of the early post-exilic community, describing them as **some Israelites, priests, Levites and temple servants** (9:2b). The term **Israelites** refers to lay people not in the tribe of Levi. The **priests** were sons of Aaron and the **Levites** were descendants of Levi outside of the Aaronic family (see *Introduction: Appendix A – The Families of Levi*). Finally, **temple servants** were probably captured foreigners who served as assistants to Levites at the temple (see Num. 31:30; Ezra 8:20). This is the only time the Chronicler mentioned these people by this title. He spoke of other foreigners, however, on a number of occasions (see 2:55; 4:25; see also *Introduction: 3) International Relations*).

The Chronicler also remarked that these early returnees went to **their own property in their own towns** (9:2). Preceding lists and genealogies often referred to the places where the ancestors of these Israelites lived before the exile (see 2:22-23, 42-43; 4:10, 14, 21-23, 28-43; 5:8-10, 11-12, 16, 22, 23; 6:54-81; 7:24, 28-29; 8:6, 8, 12, 13, 28, 29, 32). We have already suggested that the Chronicler mentioned these locations to establish the inheritance rights of families in his own day. (For the Chronicler's geographical hopes, see comments on 2:42-55.) At this point, the Chronicler made his interest in repossession of these tribal properties explicit. The restoration of Israel was incomplete until those original tribal inheritances were possessed once again.

Laity among the Returnees (9:3-9)

The list of returnees begins with a selective account of Israelites **in Jerusalem** who were not associated with the tribe of Levi (9:3).

The Chronicler introduced this material by mentioning **Judah** ... **Benjamin** ... **Ephraim** ... **and Manasseh** (9:3). Ephraim and Manasseh appear only at the head of these lists; no names follow as they do for Judah (9:4-6) and Benjamin (9:7-9). This special attention to Judah and Benjamin parallels the Chronicler's earlier concentrations on these tribes in 2:1-9:1a (see figure 7). The Chronicler gave special place to Judah and Benjamin because they had been relatively loyal to the throne and temple in Jerusalem. Accordingly, in his list of lay returnees the Chronicler only listed specific names and numbers for Judah and Benjamin to highlight their prominence in the post-exilic community. These tribes rightly held roles of leadership in the Chronicler's day.

At the same time, however, the mention of Ephraim and Manasseh reflects the Chronicler's continuing interest in the breadth of God's people. His preceding treatment of Israel's tribes displayed the Chronicler's commitment to encouraging the restoration of every tribe of Israel. Manasseh and Ephraim were prominent within the northern kingdom. Consequently, their appearance here reflected the Chronicler's view that the early restored community represented the entire nation of Israel (see *Introduction: 1) All Israel*). Although Judah, Benjamin and Levi were central, the tribes of the North were not to be forgotten. They too were among the first ones to return (see *Introduction: 2) Northern Israel*).

The verses that follow divide between lists of Judahites (9:4-6) and Benjamites (9:7-9). Judahite returnees appear in association with the three sons of Judah: **Perez** (9:4), Shelah (9:5 [**Shilonites** should probably be translated 'Shelanites', i.e. sons of Shelah.]) and **Zerahites** (9:6). The total of **690** contrasts with 468 in Neh. 11:6. Both texts probably represent loose approximations.

Benjamite returnees (9:7-9) appear in four groups descended from: **Hasenuah** (9:7), **Jehoram**, **Micri**, and **Ibnijah** (9:8). A number of differences appear between this passage and Neh. 11:7-9. Yet, the Chronicler's count of **956** compares favorably with 928 in Neh. 11:8.

In both of these lists the Chronicler revealed his outlook by his numerical references. Although the exile to Babylon had threatened the existence of these tribes, the Chronicler made it clear that a good number of Judahites and Benjamites came back to the land. Just as the Chronicler often mentioned the increase of progeny as a blessing from God, these numbers reflected the blessing received by these tribes (see *Introduction: 25) Increase and Decline of Progeny*).

Priests among the Returnees (9:10-13)

Having established the prominence of Judahites and Benjamites among the returnees, the Chronicler turned to the third tribe which he highlighted earlier, the tribe of Levi (see figure 7). In this passage the Zadokite priesthood is treated separately from the Levites in general. The priests were part of the tribe of Levi, but their role had become so specialized that the Chronicler listed them as a separate group. This list closely parallels Neh. 11:10-14. Many of these names appear elsewhere in Scripture, but several identities are questionable. The importance of this material for the Chronicler appears in at least three aspects of this section. First, the Chronicler made it plain that this line included **the son of Zadok** (9:11). The name **Zadok** was of great importance to the post-exilic community. The high priest Joshua (Jeshua) who served with Zerubbabel represented a controversial re-assertion of Zadokite dominance over other Levitical families after the exile (see *Introduction: Appendix A – The Families of Levi*). By giving this lineage separate treatment here, the Chronicler made explicit his support of Zadokite leadership. Zadok's descendant was **the official in charge of the house of God** (9:11).

Second, the Chronicler also noted that these priests were in control of the central operations of Israel's worship. He mentioned that **Ahitub** served in **the house of God** (9:11). Moreover, he repeated that others in this genealogy were **responsible for ministering in the house of God** (9:13). This repetition indicates that the Chronicler once again emphasized that the Zadokite family was to have exclusive charge of the services of the temple proper (see *Introduction: Appendix A – The Families of Levi*; see also *Appendix B – The Structures, Furnishings and Decorations of Solomon's Temple*).

Third, as the preceding lists of Judahites and Benjamites emphasized their large numbers, the Chronicler also pointed out that the **heads of** priestly **families numbered 1,760** (9:13). This numerical reference approximates the total of priests given in Neh. 11:12-14. The large numbers of returning Zadokites indicated God's blessing and approval of the new temple arrangements. By this means the Chronicler countered any objection to Zadokite leadership.

Levites among the Returnees (9:14-34)
To complete his record of the returnees, the Chronicler gave special attention to the other families of Levi. This material corresponds in many ways with Neh. 11:22-23. It is likely that both passages used a common source. The account divides into four main parts: heading (9:14a), introductory genealogy (9:14b-16), gatekeepers (9:17-33), and a closure (9:34).

Introductory Genealogy (9:14-16)
The Chronicler began his record of returning Levites with a sampling of names representing important divisions of the tribe. After a formal heading (9:14a), these verses touch on the lines of the three chief Levitical families: a **Merarite** (9:14b), descendants of **Asaph** (9:15), and descendants of **Jeduthun** (9:16a). Each of these families appear elsewhere in the Chronicler's history. Here the Chronicler mentioned them to indicate that these prominent families of Levi were represented in the early post-exilic community. They enjoyed the privileges and responsibilities of their ancestors.

In addition to these three major Levitical divisions, the Chronicler also noted Levites **who lived in the villages of the Netophathites** (9:16b). Netophah appears in close association with Bethlehem and Zerubbabel in post-exilic records (2:54; Ezra 2:21-22; Neh. 7:26). It is likely that the Chronicler drew attention to this group of Levites because of his interest in the mutual support of the royal and

Levitical families (see 9:17; see also *Introduction: 4-9) King and Temple*).

Gatekeepers (9:17-34)
The structure of this material is somewhat obscure. It is possible that 9:24-34 touches on duties beyond those of gatekeepers, but this understanding is far from certain. Yet, it seems best to treat the entirety of 9:14-34 as focusing on duties assigned to the gatekeepers.

After a heading (9:17a), the Chronicler drew attention to the family of **Shallum** (9:17b-23). This line was especially blessed because it served at **the King's Gate** (9:18), a royal entrance to the temple which was highly honored after the exile (see Ezek. 46). Once again, the Chronicler drew attention to the close connection between Levitical service and Judah's monarchy (see 9:16; see also *Introduction: 4-*

9) King and Temple). This passage also honors this family of gatekeepers by noting their ancestral heritage. Among their ancestors were the **Korahites** who had guarded **the thresholds of the Tent** as well as **the entrance to the dwelling of the LORD** (9:19). The Chronicler's references are not altogether clear, but it seems likely that he had in mind the tabernacle in the days of Moses or David. Moreover, the Chronicler associated these post-exilic gatekeepers with **Phinehas** and **Zechariah** who were well-known and honored figures (see Num. 25:11; 1 Chr. 26:2,14). To draw attention to the honor of this Levitical heritage, the Chronicler remarked that **the LORD was with** Phinehas (9:20; see *Introduction: 10) Divine Activity*). Once again, the Chronicler's desire to affirm the legitimacy of post-exilic Levitical arrangements is evident.

In 9:22-33 the Chronicler focused on the variety of responsibilities held by the post-exilic gatekeepers. He noted their number as **212** (9:22). He reminded his readers that **David and Samuel** had assigned duties to these men (9:22) in order to indicate the necessity of returning to these arrangements (see *Introduction: 14) Standards*). These duties were not only binding on those living in David's day, but **they and their descendants** were obligated to fulfill their proper roles (9:23).

Having established the permanence of these arrangements, the Chronicler moved to a number of practical considerations. His description looks back at other historical precedence to establish current practices for the Levites. He mentioned that the gatekeepers were to serve **on the four sides** of the temple (9:24). Relatives of the gatekeepers had to come on occasion to **share their duties** (9:25). The four **principal gatekeepers** had to guard **the rooms and treasuries** even during **the night** in addition to opening the **house of God** with **the key ...each morning** (9:26-27). Beyond this, a number of gatekeepers were **in charge of articles used in the temple service** making sure they were brought in and out as needed (9:28). Various groups were also responsible for **furnishings, other articles,** and an assortments of items needed for the proper functioning of the temple (9:29-32). Finally, the Chronicler noted that **those who were musicians stayed in the rooms of the temple** (9:33). Lodging was provided for the musicians and **they were exempt from other duties** performed by Levites because their musical responsibilities kept them busy **day and night** (9:33). Once again, the Chronicler's keen interest in promoting music in Israel's worship is evident (see *Introduction: 8) Music*).

The Chronicler closed his discussion of the Levitical families by noting that they **lived in Jerusalem** (9:34). From time to time during the early post-exilic period, economic and political factors made it unattractive to live in the capital city of Judah (see Neh. 11:1-2). The Chronicler, however, insisted that the proper place of residence for these Levites was the city itself. Just as other prophets saw the repopulation of Jerusalem as an essential element of the restoration of the kingdom of God, the Chronicler knew that only as the proper families remained in the city could the blessings of God come to his people.

Part Two

The Ideal United Kingdom

(1 Chr 9:35–2 Chr 9:31)

Overview of the United Kingdom

Having provided records to identify and establish the privileges and responsibilities of post-exilic Israel (1:1-9:34), the Chronicler shifted attention to the history of Israel's kings. The first segment of this record deals with the United Kingdom (9:35-2 Chr. 9:31) which consists of the reigns of David (9:35-29:30) and Solomon (2 Chr. 1:1-9:31).

A significant change in style takes place as we enter this portion of Chronicles. Up to this point, just a few pages have covered millennia. Less than ten chapters summarize the entire time from Adam to the post-exilic period. By contrast, this material slows considerably and gives much more attention to detail. This change reflects the importance of Israel's royal history to the Chronicler.

Interpreters have a great advantage as they explore the United Kingdom because the Chronicler began to depend heavily on the books of Samuel and Kings. By comparing his record with these books, the Chronicler's unique outlooks emerge (see *Introduction: Historical and Theological Purposes*). In very broad terms, comparisons reveal that he described the United Kingdom as an ideal time. The books of Samuel and Kings present balanced portraits of David and Solomon; both kings received blessings for obedience and curses for disobedience. By and large, however, the Chronicler omitted the failures of David and Solomon (see 13:7-11; 14:3; 21:1-6; 2 Chr. 8:11). Instead, he focused on their positive characteristics and accomplishments to present striking ideals for his post-exilic readers.

As our comments below will demonstrate, David and Solomon were ideals in at least four main ways:

1) both kings displayed outstanding moral character;
2) the nation of Israel united with enthusiastic support for both kings;
3) both kings were fully devoted to proper worship and temple construction;
4) Israel experienced times of joyous celebration under both kings.

These four themes both encouraged and challenged the original Israelite readers. On the one hand, the post-exilic community could gain hope from this ideal period that God would bless them in similar ways. Their national heritage reached back to David and Solomon who received enduring covenant promises from God (see *Introduction: 13) Covenant*). The original readers of Chronicles were heirs of these promises. On the other hand, David and Solomon's reigns also depicted responsibilities for post-exilic Israel. If they wanted to secure divine blessing in their day, they had to imitate the positive accomplishments of these kings. God's favor would appear only as post-exilic Israel followed the patterns of the ideal United Kingdom.

Overview of David's Reign (1 Chr. 9:35-29:30)

Israel's monarchy found its true beginning with David. His anointing marked the beginning of Israel's permanent dynasty. For this reason, David's accomplishments had many implications for the readers of Chronicles.

Comparison of 9:35-29:30 with 2 Sam. 1:1-24:25
2 Samuel conveys David's life in three main sections: his early years of fidelity and blessing (2 Sam. 1-10), his later years of infidelity and curse (2 Sam. 11-20), and a final summation of his reign (2 Sam. 21-24). This evenhanded portrait, however, does not appear in Chronicles.

The Chronicler's outlook on David consisted of four major themes. These emphases become evident in a number of major variations between Samuel and Chronicles (figure 9).

David Becomes King (9:35-12:40)		*David Becomes King (1 Sam 9:1–2 Sam 4:12)*
Saul's Genealogy (9:35-44)	added	———
———	omitted	David Struggles with Saul (1 Sam 9:1-30:31)
Saul Killed by Philistines (10:1-14)	parallel	Saul Killed by Philistines (1 Sam 31:1-13)
David's Family (3:1-4a)	largely omitted	David Struggles with Saulides (2 Sam 1:1-4:12)
David Acknowledged as King (11:1-3)	parallel	David Acknowledged as King (2 Sam 5:1-5)
David Conquers Jerusalem (11:4-9)	parallel	David Conquers Jerusalem (2 Sam 5:6-10)
David's Warriors (11:10-41)	parallel	David's Warriors (2 Sam 23:8-39)
David's Other Supporters (12:1-40)	added	———

Comparison of 1 Chr 9:35-12:40 and 1 Sam and 2 Sam (figure 9)

First, the Chronicler presented David's positive moral character by omitting several significant portions of the book of Samuel.

1) He omitted Michal's reproach of David (2 Sam. 6:20b-23).

2) He also avoided David's troublesome reception of Mephibosheth into the royal court (2 Sam. 9:1-13).

3) Most pointedly, he chose not to repeat the account of David's adultery and ensuing troubles within the royal household (2 Sam. 11:1-21:14). The Chronicler knew that his readers were familiar with David's sins. Yet, he chose not to repeat most of them in his record in order to emphasize the positive moral character of the king.

Second, the Chronicler also highlighted the breadth of David's support. In this history, all the tribes of Israel enthusiastically endorsed David as their king. This motif falls in line with the focus of the lists and genealogies of 1:1-9:34 on all the tribes of Israel. In David's reign a similar theme appears in several additions.

1) With the exception of 1 Chr. 10:1-12 (1 Sam. 31:1-13), the checkered history leading to David's rise is omitted (1 Sam. 1:1-2 Sam. 4:12).

2) The Chronicler added long lists of David's followers from all the tribes of Israel (1 Chr. 12:1-40).

3) He introduced the account of the entry of the ark into Jerusalem with an indication of widespread support (1 Chr. 13:1-4).

4) The same theme also occurs in the repeated use of the terminology 'all Israel' (1 Chr. 11:1,10 // 2 Sam. 5:1; 1 Chr. 11:4 // 2 Sam. 5:6; 1 Chr. 13:6 // 2 Sam. 6:2; 1 Chr. 14:8 // 2 Sam. 5:17). These changes stressed that David reigned with the enthusiastic support of the vast majority of the nation. The Chronicler focused on these matters to encourage his readers to hope and work for the reunification of all Israel under the reign of a son of David in their day as well (see *Introduction: 1) All Israel*).

Third, the most significant dimension of the Chronicler's portrait is David's commitment to the temple. This theme appears in a number of ways.

1) David devoted the spoils of battle for use in the temple (1 Chr. 18:8 // 2 Sam. 8:8).

2) Beyond this, eight chapters not found in Samuel focus exclusively on the king's enthusiastic work in preparation for temple construction (1 Chr. 22:2-29:25).

3) In fact, with the addition of other materials taken from Samuel, more than half of the Chronicler's presentation of David concerns his preparations for temple construction (1 Chr. 13:1-29:25). By focusing on David's enthusiasm for the temple, the Chronicler drew attention to the necessity of similar devotion to the temple in his day.

Fourth, with such a positive presentation of David's reign, it is not surprising that the Chronicler often described times of celebration in David's kingdom (see 12:40; 13:8;15:16,25,29; 16:23-33; 29:9-25). In fact, the end of each major section of the king's reign includes eating in celebration (12:40; 16:3; 29:22). These records of joy were designed to inspire his post-exilic readers to follow the example of David so that they might have similar blessings to his time (see *Introduction: 27) Disappointment and Celebration*).

Structure of 1 Chr. 9:35-29:30

The Chronicler's version of David's reign falls into three main divisions followed by a closure to the reign (see figure 10)

David Becomes King (9:35-12:40)
David Brings the Ark to Jerusalem (13:1-16:43)
David Prepares for Solomon's Temple Construction (17:1-29:25)
Closure of David's Reign (29:26-30)

Outline of 1 Chr. 9:35-29:30 (figure 10)

On a large scale, David's reign forms a threefold crescendo. First, David became the king of Israel (9:35-12:40). Second, he moved his kingdom forward by bringing the ark of God into his capital city (13:1-16:43). Third, David devoted himself to preparing for Solomon to build a permanent temple for God in Jerusalem (17:1-29:25). Each of these sections ends with scenes of joyous celebration and feasting to draw attention to the blessings of God at each stage of David's ideal kingdom.

David's Ideal Reign: Part One
David Becomes King
(1 Chr. 9:35-12:40)

David's reign opens with a focus on how he became the king of Israel. In this material the Chronicler emphasized that David became the powerful ruler over all Israel with the help of God and the support of the entire nation.

Structure of 1 Chronicles 9:35-12:40
This first portion of David's reign divides into two main parts (see figure 11 on pages 106-107).

The first half of this material focuses on Saul's demise as evidence of divine support for David (9:35-10:14). David did not receive royal authority by human schemes but by an act of God. The second half sketches the positive support David received from the nation (11:1-12:40). David's support was not limited to a few tribes of Israel. The entire nation rallied behind his throne.

Divine Transfer from Saul to David (9:35-10:14)
David was not Israel's first king; Saul, the Benjamite had that honor. Consequently, the Chronicler had to give attention to Saul before moving to David. Nevertheless, he only dealt with Saul's demise as a just act by which God gave Saul's throne to David.

Comparison of 9:35-10:14 with 1 Sam. 9-31
By comparison with 1 Sam. 9-31, the Chronicler's record is severely abbreviated. According to the book of Samuel, David's rise to power was difficult and gradual. The Chronicler, however, omitted the history of David's rise and stressed that David became king by divine intervention in the death of Saul and his family.

Structure of 9:35-10:14
This brief account of the transfer of royal authority to David divides into two parts (see figure 11). The text first stresses the blessings bestowed on Saul (9:35-44), but it moves next to explain how this honor led to a severe divine judgment and the transfer of royal power to David (10:1-14).

Divine Blessing on Saul (9:35-44)
The Chronicler repeated this material from his earlier Benjamite genealogy (see 8:29-40). As we have already seen, this list contains Benjamites who once experienced the blessing of living near Jerusalem. This duplicated record drew attention to the fact that Saul, the first king of Israel, belonged to this special group of Benjamites. Having received such remarkable blessings from God, Saul should have lived in grateful fidelity to God. Yet, as the Chronicler pointed out in the next

episode, Saul demonstrated flagrant ingratitude. As a result, his actions led to severe divine judgment.

Divine Judgment Against Saul (10:1-14)

Having reminded his readers of Saul's blessings, the Chronicler moved directly to the judgment that came against Saul. In a single day, God destroyed Saul's family and gave the kingdom to David.

Comparison of 10:1-14 with 1 Sam. 31:1-13

This passage is largely identical with its parallel in 1 Sam. 31:1-13. For the most part, only minor stylistic differences appear. Nevertheless, five significant variations deserve special mention.

First, in 10:6 (//1 Sam. 31:6) the Chronicler added the verb **died** a second time. This repetition intensifies the morbid mood of the passage.

Second, 1 Sam. 31:6 reads 'and all his men' which the Chronicler changed to **and all his house** (10:6). This variation stresses that the death of Saul and his sons was the virtual end of Saul's dynasty.

Third, the Chronicler shifted attention away from the treatment of Saul's body (1 Sam. 31:10) to his decapitation (10:10). This change was probably designed to connect Saul's disgraceful death to the well-known decapitation of Goliath (see 1 Sam. 17:51).

Fourth, the Chronicler simplified the actions of the Gileadites who retrieved the bodies of Saul and his sons (10:12 // 1 Sam. 31:12). He omitted their night-long journey and the cremation of the bodies. These omissions have the effect of drawing attention away from Gileadite heroism and placing more emphasis on the sadness of the events.

Fifth, the Chronicler added the entirety of 10:13-14. These verses explain that the transfer of royal power from Saul to David was the result of God's justice against Saul.

Structure of 10:1-14

These omissions and additions shaped the narrative into two episodes followed by an authorial comment (see figure 11). The story of judgment against Saul begins with an episode of defeat for Israel's army and death for the family of Saul (10:1-7). This episode begins with the Philistine attack (10:1) and closes with the completion of Philistine aggression (10:7). The turning point of this material consists of the death of Saul and his sons (10:2-6). The second episode then presents a twofold scenario: the Philistines defile Saul's body (10:8-10) and the faithful Gileadites bury Saul and his sons in mourning (10:11-12). Finally, the Chronicler added his own comment, explaining why these events occurred (10:13-14).

David Becomes King (9:35-12:40)

- ■Divine Transfer from Saul to David (9:35-10:14)
  - ♦Divine Blessing on Saul (9:35-44)
  - ♦Divine Judgment Against Saul (10:1-14)
    - Saulide Deaths and Israelite Defeat (10:1-7)
      - Israelite Army Flees in Defeat from Philistines (10:1)
        - Saulides Die in Dishonor (10:2-6)
      - Aftermath of Defeat (10:7)
    - Saul's Defilement and Burial (10:8-12)
      - Philistine Defilement of Saul (10:8-10)
      - Gileadite Mourning over Saul (10:11-12)
    - Saul's Death and Defilement Explained (10:13-14)

- ■David's Widespread Support from Israel (11:1-12:40)
  - ♦Anointing at Hebron (and Establishment in Jerusalem) (11:1-9)
    - All Israel Anoints David as King (11:1-3)
      - All Israel Invites David to be King (11:1-2)
        - David Complies with a Covenant with Israel (11:3a)
      - Israel Anoints David (11:3b)
    - All Israel and David Make Jerusalem the Royal Capital (11:4-9)
      - David and Israel March to Destroy Jerusalem (11:4a)
        - Jebusites Challenge David to Enter Jerusalem (4b-5a)
          - David Captures Jerusalem (11:5b)
          - [Historical Note Concerning Joab (11:6)]
        - David Takes Up Residence in Jerusalem (11:7)
      - David and Joab Rebuild Jerusalem (11:8-9)
  - ♦Military Support at Hebron (11:10-47)
    - Introduction to Chiefs of Mighty Men (11:10-11a)
    - Jashobeam (11:11b)
    - Eleazar (11:12-14)
      - Introduction (11:12)
      - Eleazar Gathers with David for Battle (11:13a)
        - Other Troops Flee (11:13b)
        - Eleazar and David Take Stand (11:14a)
      - Eleazar and David Receive Victory (11:14b)

Three Chiefs (11:15-19)
    Introduction (11:15-16)
        David Longs for Water (11:17)
            Three Retrieve Water (11:18a)
        David Refuses Water (11:18b-19a)
    Summation (11:19b)

Abishai (11:20-21)
Benaiah (11:22-25)
List of Mighty Men (11:26-47)

♦Military Support at Ziklag (12:1-7)
    Introduction to Ziklag Supporters (12:1-2)
    List of Ziklag Supporters (12:3-7)
♦Military Support at the Desert Stronghold (12:8-18)
    Gadite Warriors at the Stronghold (12:8-15)
        Descriptive Introduction (12:8)
            List of Ranking Commanders (12:9-13)
        Descriptive Conclusion (12:14-15)
    Benjamite and Judahite Warriors at the Stronghold (12:16-18)
        Men Come to Join David's Band (12:16)
            David Questions Loyalty (12:17)
            Assurance of Loyalty (12:18a)
        Men Join David's Band (12:18b)

♦More Military Support at Ziklag (12:19-22)
    Introduction to Manassehite Supporters (12:19)
        List of Manassehite Supporters (12:20)
    Closing Remarks on Manassehite Supporters (12:21-22)
♦More Military Support at Hebron (12:23-37)
    Introduction to Supporters at Hebron (12:23)
    Lists of Supporters from All Tribes (12:24-37)
♦More on the Anointing at Hebron (12:38-40)
    Widespread Determination to Anoint David (12:38)
    Widespread Celebration of David's Anointing (12:39-40)

Outline of 1 Chr. 9:35-12:40 (figure 11)

Saulide Deaths and Israelite Defeat (10:1-7)

For the most part, this story of transition between Saul and David depends on 1 Sam. 31:1-13. The entire scenario is morbid and brings to light the tremendous loss that occurred under Saul.

Israelite Army Flees in Defeat from Philistines (10:1)

From the outset, this story offers a negative outlook on the reign of Saul in at least two ways. First, in a straightforward manner, the text notes that **the Philistines fought** and immediately adds that **the Israelites fled** (10:1). Absolutely no mention is made of an initial resistance or struggle. The Israelites were overwhelmed by the Philistines and ran for their lives. The theme of fleeing is repeated again in 10:7.

Second, once the story comes to the Israelite resistance at **Mount Gilboa**, the text only mentions that **many** Israelites **fell slain** (10:1b). No record of Philistine losses appears in the episode.

The significance of this unmitigated victory over Israel becomes evident when we remember that the Philistines were the notorious enemies of Israel. Time and again, they had troubled Israel (see Judg. 13:1; 1 Sam. 4:1-10). In the future, David would defeat the Philistines and bring safety from their attacks (see 2 Sam. 5:17-25; 1 Chr. 14:8-17). At this point, however, Saul was entirely incapable of resisting them.

Throughout his history, the Chronicler presented defeat before enemies as evidence of God's judgment (see *Introduction: 23) Victory and Defeat*). When the kings of Israel were faithful to God, they experienced victory. When they were unfaithful, they lost battles. From the very beginning of this passage, the Chronicler made it clear that Saul's reign was one of tremendous defeat for the people of God. This fact alone showed that Saul was under divine judgment.

Saulides Die in Dishonor (10:2-6)

In 10:2-6 the narrative narrows its focus to the experience of Saul and his family. The Philistines did not hesitate in their aggression. They **pressed hard after Saul and his sons** (10:2). Once again, these enemies of Israel were entirely unhindered. They immediately gained a portion of their goal when **they killed** [Saul's] **sons** (10:2).

The action of the narrative slows in 10:3-5 to give a detailed account of Saul's ignoble demise. Step by step the narrative reports that **the fighting grew fierce, the archers overtook** Saul, and **they wounded him** (10:3). The only speech in this episode involves Saul speaking **to his armor-bearer** (10:4). In utter fear that the Philistines **will come and abuse** him, he ordered the armor-bearer to kill him (10:4). The armor-bearer was also **terrified** and refused (10:4). So Saul took his own life (10:4).

Following Samuel, the Chronicler summarized that Saul's **three sons** died (10:6 // 1 Sam. 31:6). Elsewhere we learn that one of Saul's descendants, Esh-Bosheth (Esh-Baal) survived (8:33; 9:39; 2 Sam. 2:8). Nevertheless, the Chronicler added that **all** [of Saul's] **house died together** (10:6). Two aspects of this addition stand out. First, in this context the word **house** has the connotation of 'dynasty', as it does on other occasions (see 17:10 // 2 Sam. 7:11). Although one of Saul's sons survived him, from the Chronicler's perspective this battle sealed the fate of Saul's dynasty. Second, the Chronicler repeated the verb **died** for a second time in this verse. As a result, the same Hebrew term occurs five times in this episode (10:5 [twice], 6 [twice], 7 [once]). The addition of a fifth use of this verb adds to the morbid character of the episode.

Aftermath of Defeat (10:7)

The closing step of this episode focuses on the geographical loss to Israel. Twice the text uses the term **fled**. As in the beginning of this episode (see 10:1), the Israelites demonstrated that they were under God's judgment because they fled from their enemies (see *Introduction: 23) Victory and Defeat*). Moreover, the Philistines **came and occupied** the land without resistance.

At a number of points in the preceding genealogies and lists, the Chronicler drew attention to the land possessed by various groups within Israel. (For the Chronicler's geographical hopes, see comments on 2:42-55.) These geographical references were designed to encourage the post-exilic community to hope for repossession of these lands. At this point, however, the Chronicler pointed out that a portion of this heritage was lost in the days of Saul.

Saul's Defilement and Burial (10:8-12)

The second episode of this section divides into two parts which continue to portray Saul's reign in a negative light. The Philistines abused Saul and his sons, and Israel entered a time of mourning.

Philistine Defilement of Saul (10:8-10)

The brief account of the Philistines handling Saul's dead body divides into two scenes. They found the corpses of Saul and his sons (10:8), and they defiled Saul's corpse (10:9-10).

On the next day the Philistines returned to the battle scene **to strip the dead** and they **found Saul and his sons** (10:8). Saul had committed suicide because he feared how the Philistines would make sport of him (see 10:4); his fear was justified. The Philistines not only **stripped him** (10:9); they also **took his head and his armor** and **sent messengers** to spread the news of their victory over Israel (10:9).

1 Sam. 31:10b reads, 'and fastened his body to the wall of Beth Shan'. The Chronicler shifted attention away from Saul's body and noted that the Philistines **hung up his head** (10:10b). In this way, the Chronicler's account alludes to David's decapitation and public defilement of Goliath (see 1 Sam. 17:48-57). The contest with Goliath had already cast a shadow over Saul's kingship by honoring David over Saul. In the light of this story, however, Saul's disgrace was intensified by the fact that the Philistines dishonored him just as David had disgraced Goliath.

10:9-10 also intensifies the religious dimension of Saul's dishonor. Philistine messengers proclaimed **the news among their idols**, i.e. at their worship centers (10:9). The Philistines placed Saul's armor in **the temple of their gods** (10:10 [1 Sam. 31:10 reads 'the temple of the Ashtoreths']). In addition, the Chronicler noted that Saul's head was displayed **in the temple of Dagon** (10:10). The Philistines celebrated their victory over Saul before their gods because they attributed their success to the powers of their deities. Thus, it was made clear to all that God had utterly forsaken Saul to the power of foreign gods (see Deut. 4:25-28; 28:36,37; Jer. 16:13).

Gileadite Mourning over Saul (10:11-12)

In contrast with these events, some men from Jabesh Gilead retrieved the mutilated bodies of Saul and his sons. This material divides into two parts: the retrieval of the bodies (10:11-12a) and the mourning (10:12b).

Apparently, the men from Jabesh Gilead had not forgotten how Saul defended them against the Ammonites (see 1 Sam. 11:1-15). They risked their own safety to retrieve the corpses. As noted above, the Chronicler omitted some of the details found in 1 Sam. 31:12-13. The writer of Samuel noted that the Gileadites traveled through the night and removed Saul's headless corpse and the bodies of his sons from the wall of Beth-Shan (see 1 Sam. 31:12). They also burned the bodies in defiance of the Philistines (see 1 Sam. 31:12) and buried the bones of their royal family (see 1 Sam. 31:13).

The Chronicler probably omitted these details because of their heroic character. While the record of Samuel emphasizes the courage of the Gileadites, the Chronicler's purpose was to stress the mournful mood of the situation. The Chronicler admitted that these were **valiant men** (10:12), but he downplayed their courageous actions by moving quickly to the final scene where the men of Jabesh **fasted seven days** (10:12). The character of Saul's kingdom was symbolized in this event; he brought only death and mourning to the nation.

Saul's Death and Defilement Explained (10:13-14)

The Chronicler ended this section with an authorial comment. Why had these tragic events taken place? The text boldly urges that **the LORD put him to death** (10:14). The Hebrew of this passage simply reads, 'He put him to death' (see NAS, NRS, NKJ), but the reference to God is clear from the context. On a number of occasions the Chronicler revealed the divine purposes behind the establishment of David's kingdom (see 11:3,9-10,14; 12:18,23;14:2; see also *Introduction: 10) Divine Activity*). Here he pointed out that in the final analysis it was not the Philistines who killed Saul; God himself killed the first king of Israel.

God put Saul to death for three reasons.

1) Saul had been **unfaithful to the LORD** (10:13). The term 'unfaithful' appears a number of times in Chronicles to indicate attitudes and actions which constituted flagrant violations of Israel's covenant with God (see *Introduction: 21) Unfaithfulness*). On the whole, Saul's life was one of serious infidelity.

2) To be more specific, the Chronicler added that Saul had **consulted a medium** (10:13). Saul's consultation with the medium of Endor was a serious violation of Mosaic laws against necromancy (see Lev. 19:31; 20:6,27; Deut. 18:11-12).

3) Saul's encounter with the medium illustrated how he **did not inquire of the Lord** (10:14). The Chronicler frequently spoke of 'inquiring of' or 'seeking' the Lord as expressive of a sincere dependence on God in times of trouble (see *Introduction: 19) Seeking*). From his point of view, Saul's life was characterized by the opposite of such dependence on God.

The Chronicler wasted no time in explaining the purpose for God's judgment. God killed Saul and **turned the kingdom over to David son of Jesse** (10:14). In these words, the Chronicler emphasized that the selection of David as king over Israel was no historical accident, nor did David gain his throne through his own devices. The transfer of royal power from Saul to David was the result of divine intervention.

In the days of David, some Benjamites challenged the right of David's reign on several occasions (see 2 Sam. 2-4). There can be little doubt that challenges against the Davidic throne took place even in the post-exilic period. After all, David's house had brought much trouble to Israel, including the exile to Babylon (see 2 Kgs. 21:11-15). The Chronicler's authorial comment, however, made his point of view evident. David's descendants were the rightful heirs of the throne because David received the throne by a just act of God.

David's Widespread Support from Israel (11:1-12:40)

With God's support for David established through Saul's tragic death, the Chronicler continued to demonstrate the wonder of David's rise to power by turning to his widespread support in Israel. He drew from different periods of the king's life to demonstrate that virtually no opposition arose against David.

Comparison of 11:1-12:40 with 2 Samuel

The following comparison of Samuel and Chronicles reveals several important features of the Chronicler's outlook on David's widespread support in Israel (see figure 12 on next page). A number of small differences between these sections of Samuel and Chronicles will be noted in the comments below. At least three variations are significant on a larger scale.

First, the most obvious difference is the omission of 2 Sam. 1-4. These chapters relate several important interactions between the houses of Saul and David after Saul's death. David heard of Saul's death and lamented (2 Sam. 1); he received a public anointing and struggled with Saul's kinsmen (2 Sam. 2-4). By omitting these chapters, the Chronicler presented the transition from Saul to David as virtually unchallenged.

Second, the Chronicler drew from two different places in Samuel for his record of David's national support. He derived the final anointing of David at Hebron (11:1-3) and David's victory over the Jebusites (11:4-9) from 2 Sam. 5:1-10. Then

1 Chr.		2 Sam.
———	David and Saul (omitted)	
11:1-3	Anointing at Hebron (parallel)	1:1-4:12
———	David Reigns in Hebron (omitted)	5:1-3
11:4-9	Conquering of Jerusalem (parallel)	5:4-5
11:10-47	Support at Hebron (expanded/displaced)	5:6-10
12:1-40	Further Support for David (added)	23:8-39

Comparison of 1 Chr. 11:1-12:40 with 2 Sam. (figure 12)

he drew from a distant passage (11:10-47 // 2 Sam. 23:8-39). As we will see, the Chronicler arranged this material topically rather than in chronological order.

Structure of 11:1-12:40
These two chapters form an extensive symmetrical geographical pattern (see figure 11). With the exception of Jerusalem (11:4-9), each location appears twice. This repetitive geographical structure has the effect of echoing the theme of widespread support for David's kingship time and again.

Beyond this, comparisons with Samuel demonstrate that the Chronicler's outline also follows a twofold chronological pattern. According to Samuel, David's time at the strongholds (see 1 Sam. 22:1-5; 23:14,29) preceded his stay at Ziklag (see 1 Sam. 27:6). His time at Ziklag preceded the anointing at Hebron (see 2 Sam. 5:1-4). In this light we can see that the Chronicler presented a temporal regression followed by temporal progression. He began with the anointing and support at Hebron and then turned to the background of this event at Ziklag and the stronghold. Following these temporal regressions (Hebron > Ziklag > Stronghold), the Chronicler moved forward in time from the stronghold through Ziklag and reached Hebron again (Stronghold > Ziklag > Hebron).

This chronological arrangement makes it appropriate to translate several opening sentences in the pluperfect: '… they … had given his kingship …' (11:10), '… men who had come to David …' (12:1), '… some … had defected …' (12:19), '… who had come …' (12:39).

Anointing at Hebron (and Establishment in Jerusalem) (11:1-9)
The Chronicler moved directly from the collapse of Saul's kingdom to the anointing of David. The book of Samuel reveals that this event was actually David's third

anointing. The first occurred privately (see 1 Sam. 16:1-13); the second was more public at Hebron (see 2 Sam. 2:1-7). This third anointing was unique in that a solemn covenant between Israel and David preceded it (11:3).

Comparison of 11:1-9 with 2 Sam. 5:1-3

The Chronicler varied from Samuel in two important ways in this passage. First, he shifted from 'all the tribes of Israel' (2 Sam. 5:1) to his standard expression **all Israel** (11:1). This change is not substantial in itself, but he also changed 'the king and his men' (2 Sam. 5:6) to **all the Israelites** (11:4). By shifting to this similar terminology twice the Chronicler emphasized that David received support from the entire nation.

Second, the anointing of David closes with the additional phrase **as the LORD had promised through Samuel** (11:3). This line amplifies the fact that David's anointing was ordained by God.

Third, Chronicles omits 2 Sam. 5:4-5, David's seven and a half year reign in Hebron. This omission draws together David's anointing and the establishment of Jerusalem as two closely related episodes. In the Chronicler's viewpoint the years in Hebron were immaterial.

Structure of 11:1-9

This passage consists of two closely related episodes (see figure 11). The first episode divides into three parts. The nation invited David to be king (11:1-2); this invitation balances with the actual anointing of David (11:3b). David's covenant agreement with the nation forms the turning point in the story (11:3a).

The second episode takes the form of five symmetrical steps. David and Israel marched against Jerusalem (11:4a); this attack balances with David's reconstruction of the city (11:8-9). The Jebusites challenged whether David could enter the city (11:4b-5a); this mockery was answered by David taking up residence there (11:7). The story turns decisively toward its end when David captured Jerusalem (11:5b-6).

All Israel Anoints David as King (11:1-3)

The story of David's anointing begins with **all Israel** gathering at Hebron and inviting him to be their king (11:1). The people supported their request with two reasons. First, David had been their military leader even during the reign of Saul (see 1 Sam. 18:5-8; 27-30; 21:11; 23:1-5; 29:5; 30:1-20). Second, David had received the prophecy that he would **shepherd** Israel and become their **ruler** (11:2). We have no record of this particular word from the Lord, but see 11:3.

David responded to Israel's invitation by making a **compact** ('covenant' see NAS, NRS, NKJ) with the people (11:3). It is likely that this covenant was similar to that of Saul in 1 Sam. 10:25. There Samuel wrote on a scroll 'the regulations of the kingship' (1 Sam. 10:25). This written constitutional document defined the role of the king and probably set limits on his privileges along the lines of Deut. 17:14-20. The Law of Moses strictly limited Israelite kingship. David's willingness to enter this covenant exalted him as a model king for the Chronicler's post-exilic readers. Any person ruling on the throne of David must be fully aware of the covenantal restrictions on his leadership (see 2 Chr. 23:1,3,11; see also, *Introduction: 13) Covenant*).

The closing scene of this episode balances with the opening scene. The people invited David to be king (11:1-2); in the end they anointed him as king (11:3b). By adding **as the LORD had promised through Samuel** (11:3b), the Chronicler balanced the earlier reference to prophecy given to David (11:2). Both the beginning and ending of this section emphasize the divine authorization of David's anointing (see 10:13-14; 11:9-10, 11b; 12:18,23; 14:2; see also *Introduction: 10) Divine Activity*).

All Israel and David Make Jerusalem the Royal Capital (11:4-9)

This episode begins with David moving against Jerusalem (11:4a) and ends with him rebuilding the city and becoming **more and more powerful** (11:9). As noted above, the Chronicler drew these events close to David's anointing (see 11:1-3) by omitting his reign in Hebron (see 2 Sam. 5:4-5). This omission demonstrated that David's anointing directly led to his possession and rebuilding of Israel's chief city.

David's possession of Jerusalem was particularly important for the Chronicler and his readers. During the exile, the city had been in ruins, but the returnees were to rebuild Jerusalem as the royal capital of the post-exilic community. David's construction efforts in this episode established the city as the historical seat of royal power. His efforts also explain why the re-establishment of the kingdom after exile must begin in the city of Jerusalem.

A touch of irony appears in the middle portion of the narrative. The Jebusites mocked David saying, **'you will not get in here'** (11:5a). After a parenthetical aside concerning Joab (11:6), the Chronicler boldly ridiculed the Jebusite defiance. He indicated that David not only entered Jerusalem, but **took up residence in the fortress** (11:7). Jerusalem even became known as **the city of David** (11:7).

The final words of the story explain how David won the city. He was victorious **because the LORD Almighty was with him** (11:9). The Hebrew expression translated **LORD Almighty** in NIV may be translated 'LORD of Hosts' (see NRS, NAS, NKJ). This divine appellation portrayed God as the leader of the armies of heaven. The Chronicler used this terminology only two other times in his history (see 17:7,24). Even so, these references resonated with frequent uses of the same terminology by post-exilic prophets Haggai (14 times) and Zechariah (51 times). The image of God as the divine warrior was central to the concerns of Israel after the exile. The nation's only hope for security and blessing was that God would fight for them as he had for David.

David's victory occurred because the Lord of heaven's army was **with him** (11:9). As Abijah's words explained in 2 Chr. 13:12, for God to be 'with' someone in the context of warfare meant that God led into battle and fought on his behalf (see *Introduction: 10) Divine Activity*). David won his battle against the Jebusites because God fought for him.

From the outset of David's reign, the Chronicler drew a sharp contrast between Saul and David. Saul's defeat at the hands of the Philistines was divine judgment against him. In effect, God fought *against* Saul (see 10:14). David, however, was blessed with victory over his enemies because God fought *with* him. This contrast demonstrated divine favor toward David and his dynasty that extended even to the post-exilic period (see *Introduction: 23) Victory and Defeat*).

Military Support at Hebron (11:10-47)

The Chronicler turned next to David's military supporters at Hebron. This passage does not actually mention Hebron. Yet, the similarity in terminology between 11:10 and 12:23 (where Hebron is mentioned) suggests strongly that the Chronicler presented this list of **the chiefs of David's mighty men** (11:10) as those who joined him at Hebron in balance with 12:23-38a (see figure 11). The latter passage completes the description of supporters by focusing on the rank and file. The Chronicler continued his positive portrait of David by drawing attention to the great warriors who supported him at Hebron.

Comparison of 11:10-47 with 2 Sam. 23:8-39

The middle portion of this passage (11:11-41a) closely parallels 2 Sam. 23:8-39. Some minor differences appear, but they are of little significance. Even so, two noteworthy variations occur at the beginning and end of this material where the Chronicler added the opening verse (11:10) and the final six and a half verses (11:41b-47).

First, 11:10 introduces the significance of the lists that follow. The Chronicler made it clear that these were people who supported David as king over all Israel.

Second, 11:41b-47 expands the parallel list in Samuel to include some geographical areas omitted there. 11:11-41a focuses primarily on locations west of the Jordan. 11:41b-47, however, deals primarily with areas east of the Jordan (although some are unknown). These lists demonstrate the breadth of David's support.

Structure of 11:10-47

This passage combines a number of lists and short narratives (see figure 11). Lists of individual warriors appear at the beginning and end of this material (11:11b, 20-47). Near the center, two brief narratives describe scenarios which illustrate the great feats these supporters of David accomplished (11:12-19).

Introduction to Chiefs of Mighty Men (11:10-11a)

In 11:10-11a the Chronicler expanded 2 Sam. 23:8 to provide a more substantial introduction to the **chiefs of David's mighty men** (11:10). Three elements emerge from his expansion.

1) These men **gave his kingship strong support** (11:10). The Chronicler pre-

sented these names because they were leading supporters of David.

2) Their support for David was **together with all Israel** (11:10). These men were not alone; they joined and led the entire nation (see *Introduction: 1) All Israel*).

3) The activities of these men were **as the LORD had promised** (11:10). David's rise to kingship was according to divine, not human design (see 10:13-14; 11:3,14; 12:18,23;14:2; see also *Introduction: 10) Divine Activity*).

The NIV obscures an important portion of 11:10. The Hebrew of this verse reads 'as the LORD had promised *concerning Israel'* (see NAS, NRS, NKJ). This expression reveals an aspect of the Chronicler's outlook that appears time and again. One of God's specific purposes for establishing David's throne was to benefit Israel. The blessing of kingship was not for David and his children alone, but for the whole nation (see *Introduction: 4-9) King and Temple*).

The Chronicler reminded his readers of the benefit of David's throne because David's dynasty was largely responsible for the troubles of exile which Israel endured (see 2 Kgs. 21:10-15). Despite this harsh reality, the Chronicler affirmed the unanimous perspective of Israel's great prophets. The blessing of Israel after exile was inextricably tied to the restoration of the throne of David (see Amos 9:11-15; Isa. 55:3; Ezek. 34:23-24; 37:24-25). God designed David's royal line to benefit the nation. This divine intention established the need for continuing royal hopes in Israel even in the Chronicler's day.

Jashobeam (11:11b)

Jashobeam is perhaps an alternate spelling for Jasho-Baal (Josheb-Basshebeth [2 Sam. 23:8]). He appears also in 12:6; 27:2.

Eleazar (11:12-14)

Information about Eleazar appears in a brief four step episode (see figure 11). After an introduction (11:12), the text notes that Eleazar joined David for battle (11:13a). This scene balances with the closing notice that David and Eleazar were victorious (11:14b) because Eleazar stood by David (11:14a). Eleazar found special notice in these lists because of his remarkable courage.

Three Chiefs (11:15-19)

This brief episode consists of five symmetrical steps (see figure 11). The **three of the thirty chiefs** (one of whom was Eleazar [see 11:12]) are first introduced (11:15-16). This introduction balances with the final summation of the passage (11:19b). The story proper involves three simple actions. David longed for water (11:17); the three mighty men retrieved water for David (11:18a); David humbly refused the water (11:18b-19a).

At least two aspects of this passage were particularly significant for the postexilic community. First, water was retrieved from **Bethlehem** (11:18), the birthplace of David (see 1 Sam. 17:12) while Philistines occupied it (11:16). This scenario certainly had symbolic significance for the Chronicler's readers as they reinhabited Bethlehem and other cities recently held under foreign control. It was the supporters of David who had accomplished this great feat in the past. Supporters of David's line in the post-exilic period could hope to accomplish much as well.

Second, David demonstrated humility and piety in his refusal to drink the water. He refused **because they** (the mighty men) **risked their lives** (11:19). While the three men were courageous, David did not encourage such risks for his personal comfort. Instead, he demonstrated his humility by pouring the water **out before the LORD** (11:18). David's actions highlighted the Chronicler's conviction that David's kingship was for Israel's benefit (see comments on 11:10; see also *Introduction: 4-9) King and Temple*), and encouraged similar self-denial and religious devotion in the leadership of the post-exilic community (see Neh. 5:14-18).

Abishai (11:20-21)

Abishai, Joab's brother, performed Samson-like feats in battle (see Judg. 14:19; 15:15-16). He became the commander of the Three (see 11:15).

Benaiah (11:22-25)

Benaiah showed courage against **Moab's best men** (11:22). Like Samson, he **killed a lion** (11:22; see Judg. 14:5-7). Like David against Goliath, he killed a giant Egyptian warrior whose spear was **like a weaver's rod** (11:23; see 1 Sam. 17:7).

Benaiah remained loyal to Solomon during Adonijah's ill-fated attempt to usurp the throne. His zeal for the protection of the Davidic line was later demonstrated in carrying out King Solomon's orders to put traitors (Joab and Shimei) to death (see 1 Kgs. 1-2). After Joab's death, Solomon named Benaiah as commander of Israel's army (see 1 Kgs. 2:35). **He too was as famous as the three mighty men** (11:24) and probably well-known to the Chronicler's readers. If such a famous man supported David, the post-exilic community should support the Davidic line as well.

List of Mighty Men (11:26-47)

The account of David's leading military supporters at Hebron ends with a long list of names and locations. Although 11:26-41a derives from Samuel, the Chronicler added the final verses (11:41b-47) to emphasize locations outside of Judah. In this way, the list bolstered the Chronicler's insistence that David's reign extended widely (for the Chronicler's geographical hopes see 2:42-55). Moreover, all the tribes of Israel submitted themselves to Davidic rule and should do so in the post-exilic period as well (*Introduction: 1) All Israel*).

Military Support at Ziklag (12:1-7)

Having dealt with events in Hebron and Jerusalem, the Chronicler regressed temporarily to an earlier stage in David's life. He referred to the time when David evaded Saul's persecution by joining with the Philistines. The Philistine king Achish gave David the city of Ziklag (1 Sam. 27:6). There he received support from a variety of Israelites. This passage balances with 12:19-22 (see figure 11).

Comparison of 12:1-7 with Samuel

David's times in Ziklag appear in 1 Sam. 27:6–2 Sam. 1:1. The Chronicler's lists of David's supporters, however, have no direct parallels in the book of Samuel.

Structure of 12:1-7

This brief passage divides into two sections (see figure 11). Several remarkable characteristics of David's supporters at Ziklag come into focus (12:1-2). Then the Chronicler lists the names of some of these remarkable men (12:3-7).

Introduction to Ziklag Supporters (12:1-2)

The introduction to this list describes several noteworthy features of these men.

1) They were skilled warriors, able to shoot **right-handed or left-handed** (12:2a).

2) These supporters of David were **kinsmen of Saul from the tribe of Benjamin** (12:2b). 2 Sam. 2-4 describes how some Benjamites resisted David's claim to royalty. Here, however, the Chronicler listed close relatives of Saul who came to David precisely at the time when David **was banished from the presence of Saul** (12:1). David's support from Israel was so widespread that it even included these prominent Benjamites.

List of Ziklag Supporters (12:3-7)

This list contains names of twenty-three Benjamite warriors who supported David. For other examples of Benjamites in favor of David, see 12:16,23,29. The Chronicler's reason for introducing this material was to encourage all the tribes, perhaps even hesitant Benjamites, to embrace his Davidic ideals for the post-exilic period.

Military Support at the Stronghold (12:8-18)

This passage moves to an even earlier time when David was in his desert stronghold. There he was joined by Gadites, Benjamites, and Judahites. These materials form the centerpiece of the larger context (see figure 11).

Comparison of 12:8-18 with Samuel

The book of Samuel describes this time in some detail (see 1 Sam. 22:3-5; 23:14,29; 24:1), but this material is not paralleled there.

Structure of 12:8-18

The focus on David at his desert stronghold consists of a descriptive list and a brief narrative (see figure 11). The Chronicler's record of David's supporters at Ziklag divides into two main sections. First, a number of Gadite warriors joined David (12:8-15). Second, some Judahites and Benjamites also aligned themselves with him (12:16-18).

Gadite Warriors at the Stronghold (12:8-15)

The record of Gadite warriors joining David overflows with descriptions of their military acumen. They were **brave** (12:8) and skilled in close fighting with **shield and spear** (12:8). They had **the faces of lions** (12:8) and the speed of **gazelles**

(12:8). In biblical times it was common to use zoomorphic language to indicate warriors' ferocity.

Beyond this, no enemies could match these Gadites. In hyperbolic language, the Chronicler wrote that the very least Gadite could handle **a hundred** enemies; the best Gadites could withstand **a thousand** (12:14). In this passage it is evident that the Chronicler intentionally used numerical overstatement to exalt the Gadite warriors. On many occasions he drew attention to the magnificence of Israel's military might by using large numbers. (For the Chronicler's use of large numbers of soldiers, see comments on 12:24-37.) He also magnified Israel's devotion to worship in much the same way (see 1 Chr. 21:25; 22:3-4,14; 29:7; 2 Chr. 1:6; 5:6; 7:5). On two occasions the grandeur of Solomon's kingdom is portrayed in other kinds of numerical hyperbole (see 2 Chr. 1:15; 9:23).

The strength and courage of these Gadite warriors is illustrated further by their crossing the **Jordan in the first month** during spring flooding (see Josh. 3:15) and their defeating **everyone living in the valleys** (12:15). The Chronicler lavished these praises on the Gadites to make it clear to his readers that the very best of this tribe joined David at the stronghold. By doing so, the Chronicler idealized David's supporters and encouraged his own readers to join in support of the Davidic line.

Benjamite and Judahite Warriors at the Stronghold (12:16-18)

The record of men from Benjamin and Judah joining David forms a short but fascinating story. The passage begins with warriors approaching David **in his stronghold** (12:16) and ends with the men not only being received by David, but becoming **leaders of his raiding bands** (12:18). This transition occurred through two intervening steps. First, David asked the men if they were for or against him (12:17). Second, the Holy Spirit inspired Amasai to confirm that the warriors from Benjamin and Judah were on David's side (12:18).

The Chronicler explicitly noted that Amasai's words were the result of **the Spirit** (12:18). The Spirit of God came upon people in various ways in the Old Testament (see Judg. 3:10; 6:34; 11:29; 14:6,19; 15:14; 1 Sam. 10:10; 11:6; 16:13; 19:20,23). In the Chronicler's history, however, the Spirit appears five times and serves one basic function (see 1 Chr. 12:18; 28:12; 2 Chr. 15:1; 20:14; 24:20). In each case the Spirit gave special insight and authorized the words of the person upon whom he came. In one other scenario, a 'lying spirit' also proceeded from heaven and caused prophets to lie (see 2 Chr. 18:21-23). In this passage, the Spirit inspired Amasai to compose a prophetic poem which vindicated the actions of the Benjamite and Judahite defectors. By including this divinely inspired speech, the Chronicler once again noted God's hand behind Israel's history (see 10:13-14; 11:3,9-10,14; 12:23; 14:2; see also *Divine Involvement in History*).

An allusion to this passage appears later in Chronicles. The words of Amasai in support of David stand in sharp contrast with the words of northern Israelites as they rebelled against the house of David in the days of Rehoboam (see 2 Chr. 10:18).

A central concern of Amasai's speech emerges in the threefold repetition of the word **help**. David asked if the men will **help** him (12:17). Amasai responded that **God will help** David, and that **those who help** David will share in his **success** (12:18). Divine help for the Davidic kings and their supporters is a distinctive theme in the book of Chronicles (see 1 Chr. 5:20; 12:18; 15:26; 2 Chr. 14:11; 16:12; 18:31; 20:4; 26:7; 32:8; see also *Introduction: 10) Divine Activity*). The Chronicler's post-exilic readers lived with many political uncertainties. He knew that the only hope for the struggling nation was help from God. Through this episode, he reminded his readers that God's help against enemies was promised to David's family and those who supported it.

More Military Support at Ziklag (12:19-22)
Now moving forward in time, the Chronicler returned to Ziklag. This passage balances with the previous material on Ziklag (12:1-7; see figure 11). In this passage, the Chronicler focused on a group of Manassehites who joined David.

Comparison of 12:19-22 with Samuel
This passage has no parallel in the book of Samuel. The historical circumstances it describes appear in 1 Sam. 27–2 Sam. 1:1.

Structure of 12:19-22
This short section divides into three parts (see figure 11). An introduction (12:19) and final report (12:21-22) enclose the list of Manassehites supporting David (12:20).

Introduction to Manassehite Supporters (12:19)
The Chronicler began this section with an historical note and explanation. These Manassehites joined with David as he fought with the Philistines **against Saul** (12:19). David's association with Philistines raised the possibility of serious misunderstanding. As the prophets before him (see Isa. 30–31; 36–39), the Chronicler frequently warned that military alliances with other nations would result in destruction (see *Introduction: 3) International Relations*). As a result, he noted that David and his band **did not help the Philistines** (12:19). David's time with the Philistines offered no support for post-exilic readers who may have sought inappropriate alliances with foreign powers.

List of Manassehite Supporters (12:20)
The Chronicler listed the names of seven men from Manasseh who **defected to** David (12:20). He stressed the prominence of these men by noting that they were **leaders of units of a thousand** (12:20). This precise numerical designation of the word translated 'thousand' is uncertain and presents problems for the interpretation of many passages. (For the Chronicler's use of large numbers of soldiers, see comments on 12:24-37.) However one understands the numerical designation here, it is evident that these men were significant military leaders in their tribe.

Closing Remarks on Manassehite Supporters (12:21-22)

The closing remarks of this section consist of several reports illustrating the courage of David's Manassehite supporters. **All of them were brave warriors** (12:21). They ranked among the other outstanding men following David (see 11:10-11a, 20-25; 12:1-7). Beyond this, their numbers grew **day after day** during the time at Ziklag (12:22).

Having mentioned the quality and quantity of David's army, the Chronicler reported that by this time David's army had become **like the army of God** (12:22). Throughout the Old Testament, God revealed himself as the leader of an innumerable and invincible army of heaven (see Exod. 15:1-13; Judg. 4:12-24; 1 Sam. 17:26,36; 2 Kgs. 6:17; Isa. 13:4; 26:7-14; Joel 2:11; Zech. 9:14-17; 10:3-5). Undoubtedly, this comparison between David's army and God's army is a hyperbole, designed to indicate that David had an army greater than could be imagined. (For a summary of the Chronicler's use of hyperbole, see comments on 1 Chr. 12:14.) The Chronicler stressed the wonder of David's army to inspire his post-exilic readers to admire the Davidic line and yearn for this kind of army in their day as well.

More Support at Hebron (12:23-37)

In parallel with 11:10-47 (see figure 11) the Chronicler returned to David's supporters at Hebron. In this passage he primarily concerned himself with ordinary soldiers.

Comparison of 12:23-37 with Samuel

Only tangential connections exist between this material and Samuel.

Structure of 12:23-37

This passage consists of two distinguishable parts (see figure 11). A lengthy list (12:24-37) is preceded by an introduction (12:23).

Introduction to Supporters at Hebron (12:23)

The introduction to this list identifies **Hebron** as the place of concern (12:23). It also expresses the Chronicler's conviction that the transfer of power to David was not of human design, but was **as the LORD had said** (see 10:13-14; 11:3,9-10,14; 12:18; 14:2; see *Introduction: Divine Activity*).

Lists of Supporters from All Tribes (12:24-37)

In a fashion common to this portion of his history, the Chronicler described the outstanding features of David's supporters (see 11:10-11a; 11:20-25; 12:1-7). They were **ready for battle** (12:25,35), **brave** (12:26,30), **wise** (12:32), **prepared for battle** (12:33,36), **with undivided loyalty** (12:33), **experienced** (12:36), and bearing **shield and spear** (12:24,34) and **every type of weapon** (12:33,37). These facts were designed to encourage admiration for David's men.

This list of supporters at Hebron is considerably broader than any preceding lists in several ways. First, it includes representatives from all the tribes (acknowledging the distinction between Ephraim and Manasseh). By grouping the Transjordanian tribes (see 12:37), however, the Chronicler maintained the traditional number of twelve tribes.

Second, the breadth of perspective also comes into view in its focus on ordinary fighting men. The material primarily concerns David's supporters among common soldiers.

Third, this passage presents an interpretive problem that appears a number of times in Chronicles. Here the Chronicler indicated the size of David's support by listing the numbers of men involved. Taken at face value, the count seems terribly high for David's initial advocates.

As with similar passages throughout Chronicles, at least three explanations of these large numbers are possible (compare 1 Chr. 21:5; 23:3; 2 Chr. 11:1; 13:3; 14:8,9; 17:14-18; 25:5,11,12; 26:12-13; 28:6,8).

1) The Hebrew word translated **thousand** (12:24) may have been a technical term referring to units considerably less than 1,000. If this were the case in this passage, the numbers would be indefinite. For instance, 12:24 would read, 'men of Judah, carrying shield and spear – six units with 800 armed for battle'.

2) The vowels of the Hebrew term for **thousand** in the traditional Hebrew text may be slightly emended and read 'chiefs'. If so, the numbers are greatly reduced. For example, 12:24 would be translated 'six chiefs with 800 armed for battle'.

3) It is possible that the Chronicler used hyperbole to stress the grandeur of David's support (see 12:22). The Chronicler frequently employed hyperbole. For a summary of the Chronicler's use of hyperbole, see comments on 1 Chr. 12:14.

None of these viewpoints mitigate against the historical reliability of the Chronicler's report. His point was that the number of men with David at Hebron was extremely large. No meager faction of Israelites was involved in the transfer of royal power to David. Mentioning large and skilled armies is one way in which the Chronicler often exalted faithful kings (see 1 Chr. 21:5; 27:1-15; 2 Chr. 13:13; 17:12-19; 25:5-6; 26:13).

Through this broad list of David's supporters at Hebron, the Chronicler displayed his concern for unanimous commitment to the Davidic line in his own day. In the ideal period of David's reign, large numbers from all the tribes joined with the king. All of Israel should support the throne of David after the exile as well (see *Introduction: 1) All Israel*).

More on the Anointing at Hebron (12:38-40)

The Chronicler closed his survey of David's widespread support by returning to the anointing at Hebron. This material balances with 11:1-3 (see figure 11).

Comparison of 12:38-40 with Samuel

The first account of events at Hebron (see 11:1-3) originated in the book of Samuel, but this passage (12:38-40) is entirely from the Chronicler's hand. It ties together a number of themes that characterize this entire account of David's national support.

Structure of 12:38-40

This material divides into a simple two step narrative (see figure 11). The two actions are straightforward. The people plan to anoint David (12:38). Then they celebrate after his anointing (12:39-40). The actual ceremony of anointing recorded in 11:1-3 occurred between these two steps.

Widespread Determination to Anoint David (12:38)

The first portion of this passage highlights Israel's desire to make David their king. The **fighting men** were **firmly determined** to have David as king, not just over a portion of God's people, but **over all Israel** (12:38a; see *Introduction: 1) All Israel*). This desire, however, was not limited to the warriors. **All the rest of the Israelites** agreed to the plan as well (12:38b). Here the Chronicler emphasized the cooperation of the fighting men and the general population. His purpose is evident. Every sector of post-exilic Israel should join in supporting the re-establishment of the Davidic throne in their day.

Widespread Celebration of David's Anointing (12:39-40)

The second step of this short episode concerns the joyful results of David's anointing. The people and David celebrated for **three days** (12:39). This lengthy festival of eating and drinking was possible because **their families** had provided in abundance (12:39). Moreover, people **from as far away as Issachar, Zebulun and Naphtali** also traveled to Hebron with food (12:40). Representatives of the whole nation joined in the celebration by contributing an assortment of foods. The Chronicler highlighted the splendor of the time by mentioning **flour, fig cakes, raisin cakes, wine, oil, cattle and sheep** (12:40). This wonderful celebration took place because **there was joy in Israel** (12:40).

The Chronicler frequently reported events of joy and celebration in his history (see *Introduction: 27) Disappointment and Celebration*). These occasions of national happiness spoke directly to the needs of the Chronicler's post-exilic readers. For the most part, their experiences were far from joyful. Hardship and trouble characterized Israel after returning from Babylon (see Hag. 1:5-11; Ezra 4:1-5:17; Neh. 4:1-6:14). The Chronicler included these scenes of celebration to motivate his readers. If they wanted to enjoy such festivities in their day, they needed to imitate the actions which led to celebration in the past. In this passage, David's anointing brought immeasurable joy to the nation. The restored community should yearn for the re-establishment of David's throne so that such joy could abound again in their day.

David's Ideal Reign: Part Two
David Brings the Ark to Jerusalem
(1 Chr 13:1-16:43)

Overview of 1 Chr. 13:1-16:43

Having established how David rose to kingship with divine authorization and widespread support from the tribes of Israel, the Chronicler turned to David's transfer of the ark to Jerusalem. Although David performed many other acts according to this history, attending to the ark was the first important thing David did as Israel's king. It would be difficult to overemphasize the significance of this connection. The ark of the covenant was the centerpiece of Israel's tabernacle and symbolized the footstool of her divine king (see 13:6; 28:2; Pss. 99:5; 132:7). Jerusalem had already become the seat of the Davidic dynasty (see 11:4-9). At this stage in David's life it also became the city of divine enthronement (see *Introduction: 8)* Divine Kingship). By bringing the ark to his capital city, David moved his kingdom another step toward the Chronicler's ideal for his post-exilic readers, a kingdom in which Jerusalem's king and temple stood at the center of God's people (sec *Introduction: 4-9) King and Temple*).

Comparison of 13:1-16:43 with 2 Sam. 5-6

The strategy of this section becomes clear from a broad comparison with 2 Sam. 5-6. More detailed comparisons will appear in the discussion of each section. Yet, significant rearrangements, additions, and omissions are evident from a large-scale comparison (see figure 13).

1 Chr		2 Sam
13:1-14	Failed Transfer of Ark (parallel/displaced)	6:1-11
14:1-17	David's Distinguishing Blessings (parallel/displaced)	5:11-25
15:1-16:43	Successful Transfer of Ark (expanded)	6:12-20a
15:1-3	David and Israel Assemble (added)	———
15:4-24	David instructs Levites and Priests (added)	———
15:25-16:3	David Moves Ark (parallel)	6:12-19a
16:4-42	David Instructs Levites and Priests (added)	———
16:43	David and Israel Dismiss (parallel)	6:19b-20a

Comparison of 1 Chr 13:1-16:43 with 2 Sam 5:11-6:20 (figure 13)

This large scale comparison reveals two major features. First, the material reverses the actual historical sequence of the first two segments. It depends on 2 Sam. 6:1-11 (// 1 Chr. 13:1-14) and then moves to the events recorded in 2 Sam. 5:11-25 (// 1 Chr. 14:1-17). As we will suggest, the effect of this temporal regression was to demonstrate why David's initial failure to transfer the ark (13:1-14) did not place him on a par with Saul's failed dynasty (14:1-17).

Second, much of the record of David bringing the ark to Jerusalem was the Chronicler's composition (15:1-16:43). His lengthy expansion indicates a number of important elements in his unique outlook on the life of David.

Structure of 13:1-16:43

This record of the ark coming to Jerusalem divides into three parts (see figure 14 on next page).

As this outline suggests, the first and third portions of this material focus specifically on the ark's entry into Jerusalem. David's initial failure (13:1-14) balances with his success (15:1-16:43). A series of blessings from God on the house of David stand in the center (14:1-17). This central material demonstrates that God favored David despite his initial failure.

David's Failed Transfer of the Ark (13:1-14)

The Chronicler postponed attention to God's blessings toward David as they appear in 2 Sam. 5:11-25 (// 1 Chr. 14:1-17) in order to focus on David's first attempt to bring the ark to Jerusalem (1 Chr. 13:1-14 // 2 Sam. 6:1-11). As the record indicates, David tried to transfer the ark, but failed because he did not honor the ark's sanctity.

Comparison of 13:1-14 with 2 Sam. 6:1-19

For the most part, this passage closely follows its parallel in 2 Sam. 6:1-11. A few minor variations appear, but they are of little significance. Several differences, however, should be mentioned.

First, the Chronicler added 13:1-4 as a new beginning for the narrative. His central concerns in this chapter become evident in these verses.

Second, 13:5 depends on 2 Sam. 6:1, but the Chronicler altered 'brought together' to **assembled** (13:5) to heighten the religious nature of the event.

Third, **all the Israelites from the Shihor River in Egypt to Lebo Hamath** (13:5) substitutes for 'thirty thousand in all' (2 Sam. 6:1). This change is in keeping with the Chronicler's concern for Israel's unified support of David.

Structure of 13:1-14

This chapter divides into a five step symmetrical narrative (see figure 14). The story of David's failed attempt to move the ark begins with David speaking and the assembly joining the project (13:1-4). The final step balances with David speaking for a second time and abandoning the project (13:12-14). Initially, the procession moves forward with David full of joy (13:5-8), but it halts with David frustrated

■David's Failed Transfer of the Ark (13:1-14)
  Preparations to Move the Ark to Jerusalem (13:1-4)
    Moving in Celebration (13:5-8)
      Divine Wrath against Uzzah (13:9-11)
    Moving in Fear (13:12-13)
  Ark Remains Outside of Jerusalem (13:14)

■David's Distinguishing Blessings (14:1-17)
  ♦David Acknowledged by Hiram (14:1-2)
    Hiram Honors David (14:1)
    David's Realization (14:2)
  ♦David Blessed with Many Sons (14:3-7)
    David's Family Expands (14:3)
    List of David's Sons (14:4-7)
  ♦David's Victories over the Philistines (14:8-17)
    • David Meets Pursuing Philistines (14:8)
      • First Victory over Philistines (14:9-12)
        Philistines Raid Valley (14:9)
          David Inquires and God Answers (14:10)
            David Defeats Philistines (14:11a)
          David Praises God (14:11b)
        David Finalizes Victory over Philistines (14:12)
      • Second Victory over Philistines (14:13-16)
        Philistines Raid Valley Again (14:13)
          David Inquires (14:14a)
            David Receives God's Response (14:14b-15)
          David Obeys God (14:16a)
        David Defeats Philistines (14:16b)
    • David Secure Against Enemies (14:17)

■David's Successful Transfer of the Ark (15:1-16:43)
  ♦David Forms a New Plan (15:1-2)
  ♦David Instructs Levites and Priests (15:3-24)
    • David Assembles the Levites and Priests (15:3-10)
    • David Consecrates Levites and Priests (15:11-15)
    • David Appoints Levites and Priests (15:16-24)
  ♦David Moves the Ark (15:25-16:3)
    Procession of the Ark (15:25-28)
      Entry of the Ark (15:29)
    Placement of the Ark (16:1-3)
  ♦David Instructs Levites and Priests (16:4-42)
    • David Appoints Levites in Jerusalem (16:4-6)
    • David's Psalm (16:7-36)
      Introduction (16:7)
        Thanksgiving within Israel (16:8-22)
        Praise throughout the World (16:23-33)
        Petition for Greater Praise (16:34-36a)
      Response (16:36b)
    • David Appoints Levites and Priests in Jerusalem and Gibeon (16:37-42)
■David's Plan Completed (16:43)

Outline of 1 Chr. 13:1-16:43 (figure 14)

and angry (13:12-13). The turning point of the narrative is Uzzah's violation and the divine judgment against him (13:9-11).

Preparations to Move the Ark to Jerusalem (13:1-4)

The first step of this passage includes material added by the Chronicler (13:1-4). Consequently, these verses provide a number of insights into the Chronicler's unique viewpoint.

From the outset, the Chronicler made it plain that David's actions were not imposed on the nation. He **conferred** with his nobles before proceeding with his plan (13:1). Moreover, he appealed to the people, **'If it seems good to you** ...' (13:2). The Chronicler also noted that in fact the plan **seemed right to all the people** (13:4). These factors indicated that bringing the ark to Jerusalem was not a royal edict devoid of popular consent. Before making the decision, David won the enthusiastic support of his chiefs and the assembly.

On several occasions, the Chronicler noted that kings sought the support of their nobles and citizens before implementing programs. Here David found agreement and brought the ark to Jerusalem. Jehoshaphat also asked for support (2 Chr. 20:17). Hezekiah appealed for popular consent (2 Chr. 30:2, 4, 12, 23). It is likely that this theme was repeated to instruct the leadership of the post-exilic community in the nature of wise administration.

Moreover, the Chronicler's addition emphasized his 'all Israel' theme. He wrote that David appealed to the **whole assembly** (13:2,4) and invited others **throughout the territories** (13:2) to join in the transfer of the ark. As a result, **all the Israelites** were represented at the event (13:5; see also *Introduction: 1) All Israel*).

The Chronicler also stressed the special religious significance of this event. In the book of Samuel, moving the ark is portrayed as an event primarily involving David's military supporters ('chosen men', 2 Sam. 6:1). The Chronicler's introduction begins in the political realm (13:1), but quickly moves to **the whole assembly** (13:2,4). Similarly, David **assembled** the people (13:5 ['brought together', 2 Sam. 6:1]) to bring the ark to Jerusalem.

The Hebrew root translated here as **assembly** and **assembled** is often used in Chronicles to designate a gathering for worship. The Chronicler was deeply concerned with the restoration of the temple and its services. For this reason, he often spoke of religious assemblies to provide his post-exilic readers with examples of benefits which such gatherings brought to the nation (see *Introduction: 6) Religious Assemblies*). Designating this event as an assembly not only heightened its religious nature, it also set this time in David's life alongside a number of other very important religious assemblies in Israel's history. Along these lines, the Chronicler added that David invited **the priests and Levites** to participate (13:2).

The Chronicler also noted that David purposefully submitted himself to God in this matter. David insisted that he would take up the project only **if it is the will of the LORD our God** (13:2). The king brought the ark to Jerusalem only because it was the desire of God for it to be there.

David's reason for following this course of action also reveals the Chronicler's interests. David reasoned, **'we did not inquire of it** [the ark] **during the reign of Saul'** (13:3). In contrast with Saul's failure to **inquire** (10:14), David desired to bring the ark to his capital city so that Israel would inquire of God (see *Introduction: 19) Seeking*).

Moving in Celebration (13:5-8)

This step of the narrative is an ironic mixture of good and evil. In the first place, this event is portrayed in a positive light. The Chronicler's substitution of **all the Israelites from the Shihor River in Egypt to Lebo Hamath** (13:5) for the reference to 'thirty thousand men' (2 Sam. 6:1) is remarkable. The **Shihor River** should probably be identified with one of the eastern tributaries of the Nile; **Lebo Hamath** is in the land of Lebanon. This is the largest designation of Israelite geography in the Scriptures. (For the Chronicler's geographical hopes, see comments on 2:42-55.) The Chronicler did not claim that David's kingdom officially extended this far. He simply noted that Jewish settlers from these distances joined the company that brought the ark into Jerusalem. As in the days of Solomon (see 2 Chr. 7:8) and Hezekiah (see 2 Chr. 30:1-5), David gathered Israelites from far and wide for this grand event. The Chronicler varied from Samuel in this way to promote Jerusalem as the center of hope even for Israelites still in exile (see *Introduction: 1) All Israel*).

Moreover, David and **all Israel** ('all the house of Israel', 2 Sam. 6:5) celebrated **with all their might before God** (13:8). Their joy abounded in singing with numerous instruments. Although this description originated in Samuel, it fitted well with the Chronicler's emphasis on music in celebrative worship (see *Introduction: 8) Music*). It would appear that the emphasis on music in Chronicles reflected controversies regarding proper musical practices in the post-exilic community. Festivity was certainly appropriate for this occasion in David's life. The footstool of Israel's God was about to enter the capital of the nation. The powerful invocable presence of God was soon to reside in David's city. So the people celebrated with song.

Following the text of 2 Sam. 6:2, the ark of the covenant is described as the place where the Lord **is enthroned between the cherubim** (13:6). The ark symbolized the presence of God with his people in many ways. Here it is depicted as the place of divine enthronement. The ark represented the throne of God, or more precisely his footstool (see 1 Chr. 28:2; Pss. 99:5; 132:7). Bringing the ark to the city was David's way of joining his throne to the throne of God (see *Introduction: 8) Divine Kingship*).

The reason for Israel's joy is also noted in the remark that the ark was also **called by the Name** (13:6). The **Name** of God refers to the nearness of God, divine power accessible through prayer and sacrifice (see *Introduction: 11) Name of God*). The ark was central in the worship of the Lord because it was associated with the Name. It was the place of access to God's throne. The people of Israel were to turn in its direction as they called on the Name of their divine King in hope of his blessing.

Although many aspects of this event were positive, something was dreadfully wrong. The **ark of God** was placed **on a new cart** (13:7). The Mosaic Law specified the divinely ordained manner of transporting the ark. Levites were to carry the ark with poles inserted through rings on either side (see Exod. 25:12-15). Instead of following this procedure, Israel mishandled the ark much like the Philistines had before them (see 1 Sam. 6:7-12). The neglect of this regulation demonstrated a casual attitude toward the sanctity of the divine footstool and for God enthroned above it.

Divine Wrath against Uzzah (13:9-11)

As David's procession moved toward Jerusalem, the oxen stumbled and the ark began to fall to the ground. In reaction, **Uzzah reached out his hand to steady the ark** (13:9). The text offers no indication that Uzzah acted with evil intent. Nevertheless, God became angry and **struck him down** (13:10). The book of Samuel describes Uzzah's actions as 'his irreverent act' (2 Sam. 6:7). The Chronicler specified that God's wrath came upon Uzzah **because he had put his hand on the ark** (13:10). Israel had already demonstrated neglect of the holiness of the divine King of Israel by putting the ark on a cart (see 13:7). Although Moses' Law warned that no human hand was to touch the ark (see Num. 4:15), Uzzah did not restrain himself. As a result, his act so violated the holiness of the divine footstool that God killed him.

This scene dramatically warned the Chronicler's readers against inappropriate worship in their day. The hesitation of the early returnees to re-establish proper worship led to sharp rebukes from Haggai (see Hag. 2:10-14). In the days of Ezra and Nehemiah, impurity in worship rose to new heights (see Ezra 9-10; Neh. 9; 13:15-31). From the example of Uzzah, the Chronicler's readers should have learned that God's patience in these matters was limited. They could not continue to defile his worship with impunity. 

David's response to Uzzah's death was the opposite of his earlier celebration (see 13:8). He **was angry**, or as it may be translated, 'frustrated' (13:11). David had intended this event to be a great blessing for his kingdom (see 13:3), but his plan had failed.

David was angry because God had **broken out against Uzzah** (13:11). He even named the place **Perez Uzzah** which meant 'outbreak against Uzzah' because God's wrath had flooded onto Uzzah. Various forms of the word 'outbreak' occur several times in this and nearby chapters. The first occurrence is very positive. When David first announced his intention to bring the ark to Jerusalem (13:2), he literally said, 'let us send (*break out*) word ...' (13:2). At this point, however, God 'broke out' in judgment. Later in the next chapter, the Chronicler used the term positively again when David exclaimed, **'God has broken out against my enemies'** (14:11).

For the sake of his audience, the Chronicler followed Samuel and noted that the location of this scene was called Perez Uzzah **to this day** (13:11). (For the Chronicler's use of this terminology, see comments on 4:41).

Moving in Fear (13:12-13)

At this point, the narrative shifts attention to the movement of the ark once again. This time, however, the ark is no longer moving toward Jerusalem in celebration. David was **afraid** (13:12) and **did not take the ark to be with him** (13:13).

David abandoned hope of immediately moving the ark into his city because he was **afraid of God** (13:12). His fear was not the sort which the Chronicler often admired (see 1 Chr. 16:25; 2 Chr. 17:10; 19:7,9; 20:29; 26:5). It was not proper worshipful reverence. In this passage, David's fear contrasted with his confidence and celebration. David was afraid in the sense that he feared what God might do at any moment, if the ark were in Jerusalem. As a result, David exclaimed, **'How can I ever bring the ark of God to me?'** (13:12).

To protect himself against the God whom he feared, David sent the ark to the **family of Obed-Edom** (13:13). Obed-Edom is probably to be identified with the man mentioned in two other chapters (see 15:18, 21, 24; 26:4).

The Ark Remains Outside of Jerusalem (13:14)

Following the text of Samuel, our passage notes that the ark remained **with the family of Obed-Edom**. As a result of his proper attention to the ark, **the Lord blessed his household and everything he had**. Despite this positive result for Obed-Edom, David's plan had come to failure. The Chronicler ended this portion of his narrative with the ark outside Jerusalem **for three months**.

The negative ending to this story spoke plainly to the post-exilic readers. Even David was judged when the worship of God was not pursued according to divine regulations. If the plans of David himself were spoiled by neglecting God's holiness, how much more must restored Israel be sure to attend carefully and faithfully to the worship of God.

David's Distinguishing Blessings (14:1-17)

Having ended the previous section with David's failure to bring the ark to Jerusalem, the Chronicler moved quickly to cast positive light on David's kingdom. In all likelihood he recognized that the preceding narrative could raise serious questions among his readers. If David failed so terribly, what made his dynasty different from the cursed line of Saul? Why was David's family not rejected as well? The Chronicler responded to this question by reminding his readers of several blessings David had received. These blessings demonstrated that David's kingship was special in the eyes of God.

Comparison of 14:1-17 with 2 Sam. 5:11-25

In this chapter the Chronicler depended heavily on 2 Sam. 5:11-25 (see figure 14). Several differences, however, should be noted.

First, the most significant variation in Chronicles is a large scale shift of sequence. In the book of Samuel, 2 Sam. 5:11-25 appears before David's first attempt to bring the ark to Jerusalem (2 Sam. 6:1-11). The Chronicler broke with this historical sequence and placed these earlier events after David's failure. For this reason, it would be appropriate to translate the main verbs in this entire section as pluperfects: '... had sent messengers ...' (14:1), '...had taken more wives' (14:3), '...had heard...' (14:8), '...had raided...' (14:13), '...had spread...' (14:17).

Second, several variations in the list of David's progeny result from combining names from 1 Chr. 3:1-9 with 2 Sam. 3:2-5 and 5:13-16. As a result, Chronicles lists thirteen sons, while the book of Samuel lists only eleven.

Third, in 14:8 the Chronicler replaced 'Israel' (2 Sam. 5:17) with his characteristic **all Israel**. This shift continued the Chronicler's focus on the extent of David's ideal reign.

Fourth, the Chronicler changed 'and David and his men carried them [Philistine gods] off' (2 Sam. 5:21) to **and David gave orders to burn them in the fire** (14:12). Some textual witnesses of Samuel read exactly as 1 Chr. 14:12. It is therefore possible that 2 Sam. 5:21 originally read the same as Chronicles (*Introduction: Translation and Transmission*). If this variation came from the Chronicler's hand, it simply specified more clearly that David treated the Philistine gods according to Mosaic Law.

Fifth, the Chronicler's additional comment in 14:17 demonstrated that David's victories (14:8-16) were so great that the nations feared him.

Structure of 14:1-17

This chapter divides into three sections (see figure 14). Simple narratives describe several blessings which David received: international recognition and successful construction (14:1-2), a large progeny (14:3-7), and victories resulting in widespread international fame (14:8-17). As the comments below will demonstrate, these blessings established important contrasts between David and Saul. The first episode ends with the assertion that God had made David king over Israel (14:2). This fact contrasts with the Chronicler's assertion that God killed Saul (see 10:14). The second episode focuses on David's growing progeny (14:3-7). Although Saul's house had died (see 10:6), David's house grew. The third episode concerns David's victories over the Philistines (14:8-17). As we will see, these victories contrasted with Saul's failures in a number of ways.

David Acknowledged by Hiram (14:1-2)

The first contrast between David and Saul built on Hiram's acknowledgment of David. This simple narrative divides into two parts: Hiram's honor (14:1) and David's realization (14:2).

Hiram Honors David (14:1)

Hiram king of Tyre (a Phoenician coastal city) sent men to help with David's palace construction (14:1). Hiram is best known for the similar assistance he gave Solomon in temple construction (see 2 Chr. 2:3-16). By sending his men to David, Hiram demonstrated great respect and affection for the king of Israel.

The mention of David's **palace** construction in a context exalting David fits well with the ancient Near Eastern environment of this book. In the cultures surrounding Israel, successful building projects were often offered as proof of divine favor toward a king. This theme appears many times in the book of Chronicles (see *Introduction: 24) Building and Destruction*).

David's Realization (14:2)

As a result of Hiram's recognition and his own palace construction, **David knew** that **the LORD had established him as king over Israel** (14:2). Although this passage appears in Samuel, it added to the Chronicler's emphasis that God, not human effort, had exalted David (see 10:13-14; 11:3, 9-10, 14; 12:18, 23; see also *Introduction: Divine Involvement in History*).

This passage also repeats the Chronicler's emphasis on the benefit of David's kingship to the nation of Israel (see 11:10; see also *Introduction: 4-9) King and Temple*). God exalted David **for the sake of his people Israel** (14:2). David's line was established to bring blessing to the nation.

Beyond this, David's realization that God had established him as king displayed a marked contrast between David and Saul. The preceding chapter reported how David seriously violated the worship of God and brought divine wrath against Israel (see 13:7-14). This negative event raised the possibility that David's kingship was on the same level as Saul's. For this reason, the Chronicler explained that God did not treat David and Saul in the same manner. God had destroyed the kingdom of Saul (see 10:13-14), but he had established David and his dynasty to benefit the people of Israel.

David Blessed with Many Sons (14:3-7)

The Chronicler moved to another set of blessings which distinguished David from Saul. He first reported that David **took more wives** and had **more sons** (14:3). Following this general statement, the Chronicler listed the names of David's sons (14:4-7). This list is larger than its parallel in 2 Sam. 5:14-16. The Chronicler added the names **Elpelet** and **Nogah** (14:5). Large numbers of descendants frequently appear in Chronicles as an indication of divine favor (see *Introduction: 25) Increase and Decline of Progeny*).

In this case, the dissimilarity with Saul is evident. God had not only killed Saul, but **all his house** (10:6). Thus Saul's family was no longer a viable royal line. David's house, however, increased greatly. His family was to be Israel's royal house in all ages.

David's Victories over Philistines (14:8-17)

Two episodes of warfare with the Philistines close the contrasts between David and Saul. The Chronicler had already reported how the Philistines killed Saul's sons and terrified Saul into suicide. The Philistines won a spectacular victory over Israel and desecrated Saul's body before their gods (see 10:1-10). David's encounters with the Philistines stood in stark contrast with those earlier events.

Structure of 14:8-17

This material consists of two five-step episodes surrounded by a balancing introduction and conclusion (see figure 14). The two episodes of David's battles with the Philistines are enclosed by an introductory report that the Philistines pursued David (14:8) and by a conclusion that David was secure against his enemies (14:17). The intervening episodes are parallel with each other in several important ways.

1) Both passages concern Philistine aggression in the **Valley of Rephaim** (14:9 and **once more** in 14:13).

2) David **inquired of God** in both battles (14:10 and **again** in 14:14).

3) God assured David that divine power would win both conflicts (14:10b, 15).

4) David obeyed the word of the Lord in both situations (14:11a, 16).

5) Tremendous victory came to David both times (14:12,16).

David Meets Pursuing Philistines (14:8)

This story opens with the Philistines coming against David because he **had been anointed king** (14:8). As such, this episode opens with a Philistine challenge directly against David's safety, much like the Philistines had pursued Saul and his family earlier (see 10:1-14). Unlike the days of Saul, however, Israel did not flee from the Philistines. Instead, **David ... went out to meet them** (14:8).

First Victory over the Philistines (14:9-12)

The first battle between David and the Philistines divides into five symmetrical steps (see figure 14). This episode begins with a raid by the Philistines (14:9) and ends with rituals of victory (14:12). The turning point of the story is David's utter defeat of the Philistines (14:11a). Prior to David's victory, he inquired of God and received assurances (14:10). In balance with these assurances, David praised God after the battle (14:11b).

Philistines Raid Valley (14:9)

The initiating event in this and the next episode (see 14:13) is a Philistine raid in the **Valley of Rephaim** (14:9). This act of aggression depicts David as the object of his enemy's pursuit.

David Inquires and God Answers (14:10)

In striking contrast to Saul (see 10:14), David fulfilled one of the Chronicler's highest ideals when he 'sought' or **inquired of God** (14:9-10a; see *Introduction: 19) Seeking*). It was common in Israel's history to consult with God before battle. Often such inquiries were made through prophets (see 2 Chr. 11:1-4; 20:1-30; 25:5-13; 1 Kgs. 20:13-34; 2 Kgs. 3:4-27; 2 Chr. 18:1-34 // 1 Kgs. 22:2-38; 2 Chr. 32:1-22 // 2 Kgs. 18:17-19:37; see *Introduction: 15) Prophets*). David acknowledged that the outcome of battle was in God's hand (14:10a) and God encouraged the king to fight, promising him victory (14:10b).

David Defeats Philistines (14:11a)

The narrative swiftly reports that David **defeated** the Philistines (14:11a). The simplicity of this scene recalls the opposite scenario in the earlier Philistine encounter in Saul's day (see 10:1-14). There the Philistine army defeated Israel with hardly any resistance. In this passage, David conquered these same enemies with ease. By this means, the Chronicler contrasted David and Saul once again.

David Praises God (14:11b)

Not only does this episode idealize David in his inquiry (14:10) and victory (14:11a), it also points out that David appropriately honored God for his victory (14:11b).

David's praise focused on the words **break out**. He called the place of the battle **Baal Perazim** ('Baal of Outbreaks'). In a generic sense, **Baal** merely meant 'master' or 'lord'. Before the worship of Baal became a great problem within Israel, the term was often used as a title for Yahweh. For this reason, David explained his name for the place by saying, **'God has broken out against my enemies'** (14:11). The allusion to the preceding chapter is evident. Although God had broken out against Israel at Uzzah's death (see 13:11), he now came against the Philistines **as waters break out** (14:11). This allusion to the tragedy of Uzzah's death demonstrated that God's anger over David's desecration of the ark had come to an end.

David Finalizes Victory over Philistines (14:12)

Finally, the Philistines fled from David and left behind **their gods** (14:12). David ordered his men **to burn them in the fire** (14:12). The book of Samuel simply reads, 'and his men carried them off' (2 Sam. 5:21). The Chronicler noted more specifically that David obeyed Mosaic legislation for the treatment of foreign gods (see Deut. 7:5,25; 12:3).

The contrast between David and Saul is evident once again. Saul was defeated and his head was taken to the temple of the Philistine gods (see 10:9-10). David, however, defeated the Philistines and destroyed their gods. This event made it plain that Saul and David were not treated equally by God.

Second Victory over Philistines (14:13-16)

The story of David's second victory divides into five symmetrical steps (see figure 14). The opening step of this episode reports that the Philistines attacked David again (14:13). This event is balanced by David's defeat of the Philistines (14:16b). The middle portion of the story divides into David's inquiry before God (14:14a) which balances with David's compliance with the word he received from God (14:16a). The turning point between these events is God's response to David (14:14b-15).

Philistines Raid Valley Again (14:13)

The text explicitly connects this battle with the preceding conflict (see 14:9-10) noting that the Philistines attacked **once more** (14:13). The similarities between these accounts has the effect of echoing the same themes a second time.

David Inquires (14:14a)

David followed his pattern of seeking and receiving divine guidance **again** (14:14a). The repetition of the theme of 'inquiring' or 'seeking' indicates that this kind of action was characteristic of David. Unlike Saul (see 10:14), David demonstrated his loyalty to God by humbly seeking help from him (see *Introduction: 19) Seeking*).

David Receives God's Response (14:14b-15)

God responded to David's inquiry with a particular strategy. David was to **circle around** (14:14b) and wait for **the sound of marching in the tops of the balsam trees** (14:15). The sound of the trees blowing in the wind would demonstrate that **God has gone out in front of** David (14:15). This divine strategy exemplified a point of view that appears throughout the Old Testament. When Israel fought her holy wars, God went before her with the heavenly armies (see Exod. 14:10-31; Num. 21:1-3; Deut. 4:26-36; Josh. 6:1-21; 10:6-15; Judg. 7:1-25; 2 Kgs. 7:6-7; 2 Kgs. 19:35; see also *Introduction: 13) Divine Presence and Help*). Miraculous divine presence was an essential part of all holy war. David's battle with the Philistines was no ordinary conflict; it was a battle in which the Lord and his heavenly armies fought for Israel.

David Obeys God (14:16a)

The text observes in a straightforward manner that David **did as God commanded him** (14:16a). As we expect in this context, David followed the directives of God just as he should have. Once again, David stood in contrast with Saul who **did not keep the word of the Lord** (10:13).

David Defeats Philistines (14:16b)

David's compliance with God's instructions yielded the expected outcome. **He struck down the Philistine army** (14:16b). The grandeur of this victory is highlighted by the notice that the Philistines were destroyed **all the way from Gibeon to Gezer** (14:16b). David's enormous victory stands in stark contrast with Saul's terrible defeat at the hands of the Philistines (10:1-14).

David Secure Against Enemies (14:17)

The Chronicler added an authorial comment to the end of this section. David's **fame spread through every land** so that **all the nations** surrounding Israel would **fear him** (14:17). The Chronicler pointed to several times when foreign nations feared Israel's king and God. These examples of Israel's international security represented a key element in the hopes of post-exilic Israel. So long as Israel remained dependent on God, the nations around her offered no serious threat (see *Introduction: 3) International Relations*). The contrast with Saul is evident for a final time. In Saul's battle, Israel fled in fear from the Philistines (10:1,7); Saul himself feared (10:4). The Chronicler pointed here to the very opposite condition for David; every nation feared him.

Throughout this section of his record, the Chronicler effectively contrasted Saul and David time and again. Although David had failed in his first attempt to transfer the ark, he was not to be set on a par with Saul. On the contrary, David was to be contrasted with Saul as the faithful and blessed king of Israel. For this reason, post-exilic Israel should have viewed David's reign as their model and David's dynasty as their only royal line.

Success in Bringing the Ark to Jerusalem (15:1-16:43)

Having established that David was God's chosen king despite his failure, the Chronicler turned to David's successful transfer of the ark. This material closes with one of the three festive celebrations that mark the main sections of David's reign (see 16:3; compare 12:40 and 29:22). With this positive focus, the Chronicler once again recommended David's reign as an ideal for his post-exilic readers.

Comparison of 15:1-16:43 with 2 Sam. 6:12-19

As we have already noted (see figure 13), the Chronicler added a large amount of his own material (15:1-24; 16:4-42) before and after David's successful procession (15:25-16:3 // 2 Sam. 6:12-19). These additions shape the Chronicler's record into five symmetrical parts (see figure 14).

Structure of 15:1-16:43

The overarching symmetry of this material is evident. It begins with the formation of a plan (15:1-2) and ends with its completion (16:43). On both sides of the center, the passage focuses on the arrangement of priests and Levites in worship (15:3-24; 16:4-42). In the center is the actual transfer of the ark (15:25-16:3).

David Forms a New Plan (15:1-2)

The Chronicler began this portion of his additional material with David experiencing a change of heart. Having failed to bring the ark into Jerusalem (see 13:5-14), David acknowledged the reason for his failure and determined to correct the problem.

The first portion of these verses depicts David preparing his capital city. In 2 Sam. 6:12-13 David received news that the house of Obed-Edom had been blessed by the presence of the ark. Obed-Edom's experience motivated David to make another attempt to bring the ark to Jerusalem. The Chronicler omitted this material from his history and replaced it with 15:1-2. His account emphasizes that David continued to work hard on his building projects and even **prepared a place for the ark** while it remained outside the city (15:1). Because the tabernacle of Moses was in Gibeon (see 16:39), David **pitched a tent** for the ark in Jerusalem (15:1). The Chronicler reported these details to make it clear that David never entirely abandoned his plan to bring the ark to Jerusalem.

Nonetheless, a dramatic change had come over David. David announced, **'No one but the Levites may carry the ark of God, because the LORD chose them to carry the ark'** (15:2). David became newly committed to following the Law of Moses regarding the transport of the ark of the covenant (see Exod. 25:12-15;

Deut. 10:8). David had learned from his error and determined to treat the ark in the appropriate manner (see *Introduction: 14) Standards*).

David Instructs Levites and Priests (15:3-24)

The Chronicler's addition moves directly to the king's efforts to insure that the Levites and priests served their proper role in the second procession. This material divides into three sections (see figure 14) which consist of a report of David's calling an assembly (15:3-10), directing consecrations (15:11-15), and establishing duties (15:16-24) for the Levites and priests.

David Assembles Levites and Priests (15:3-10)

With his new plan in mind, David **assembled** the people (15:3). As before, the Chronicler chose the word **assembled** to indicate the religious character of the event (see *Introduction: 6) Religious Assemblies*). Moreover, he depicted the assembly as comprising **all Israel** (15:3; see *Introduction: 1) All Israel*). Representatives of the entire nation were involved in this second attempt, just as they were when David first tried to bring the ark to his capital (see 13:5).

The Chronicler's record moves to the heart of David's new plan. The main purpose of this assembly was to bring together the **descendants of Aaron and the Levites** (15:4). Here the Chronicler distinguished between the 'priests' (= the descendants of Aaron) and the Levites. Moses originally appointed Aaron and his sons as priests for Israel (see Exod. 28-29); other descendants of Levi came to be known in the Chronicler's day simply as Levites, even though the tribal designation rightly applied to Aaronides as well (see figure 14; see also *Introduction: 5) Royal and Levitical Families*).

15:5-10 lists representatives of the three major Levitical clans: **Kohath** (15:5), **Merari** (15:6), and **Gershon** (15:7). In addition to these leaders, the Chronicler focused on three particular descendants of Kohath: **Elizaphan** (15:8 [Exod. 6:22]), **Hebron** (15:9 [Exod. 6:18]), and **Uzziel** (15:10 [Exod. 6:18]). This sixfold division of Levites has no precedent in Mosaic Law. The Chronicler's particular focus may have been in response to controversies among the Levites in his day.

David Consecrates Levites and Priests (15:11-15)

Following his list of Levites, the Chronicler mentioned that David summoned certain priestly and Levitical leaders (15:11). **Zadok and Abiathar** were both high priests in David's kingdom (15:11; see 2 Sam. 8:17). Zadok served at the Mosaic tabernacle in Gibeon and Abiathar served in Jerusalem (see 18:16; 27:34). Solomon later excluded Abiathar because he supported Adonijah's bid for the throne (see 1 Kgs. 1:19,25; 2:26-27). Only Zadok's descendants continued as high priests after those days (see 6:1-80; 1 Kgs. 2:26-27). The Chronicler also mentioned six other Levites whom David summoned (15:11b).

David then addressed those whom he gathered (15:12-14) and specifically spoke to the **heads of the Levitical families** (15:12). David gave these Levites two instructions.

First, he told them, **'consecrate yourselves'** (15:12). Consecration for involvement in worship required prescribed ritual washings and avoidance of ceremonial defilement (see Exod. 29:1-37; 30:19-21; 40:31-32; Lev. 8:5-35). These rituals presupposed a heart of renewed commitment to the Lord. Rituals of consecration appear frequently in Chronicles as examples of proper worship which the post-exilic readers were to imitate in their day (see *Introduction: 6) Royal Observance of Worship*).

Second, David also ordered these men to **bring up the ark** (15:12). As David expressed at the beginning of this section (see 15:2), God had chosen the Levites to carry the ark.

David explained why he gave the orders for consecration and bearing the ark. He admitted to the Levites that divine wrath had come on Israel because he had failed to have them **bring it up the first time** (15:13 see 13:7-11). Moreover, David confessed that they did **not inquire** of the Lord **to do it in the prescribed way** (15:13). This confession is remarkable because the Chronicler has already condemned Saul for failing to inquire of the Lord (see 10:14) and contrasted David as one who did inquire of him (see 13:3; 14:10,14; see *Introduction: 19) Seeking*). Even so, David had committed the same sin as Saul by failing to seek specific directions from God as he tried to bring the ark to Jerusalem. Now he repented of his error.

In response to David's order, the priests and Levites immediately **consecrated themselves** to **bring up the ark** (15:14). The Chronicler's enthusiasm for this situation caused him to jump ahead chronologically to mention a few aspects of events he will narrate more fully later in the chapter (see 15:25-28). He approvingly reported that these Levites **carried the ark of God with poles on their shoulders as Moses had commanded** (15:15). This time the ark was transported not on a cart (see 13:7), but in compliance with Mosaic Law (see Exod. 25:12-15). Finally, to highlight that David had at last broken with his temporary failure, the Chronicler added that this Mosaic legislation was **in accordance with the word of the LORD** (15:15; see *Introduction: 14) Standards*).

David's renewed commitment and the conformity of the Levites offered impeccable examples of the kind of behavior the Chronicler desired from his post-exilic readers. They were also to forsake their failure to follow the Law of Moses and to devote themselves to the worship of God in accordance with God's Word.

David Appoints Levites and Priests (15:16-24)

The Chronicler returned to the assembly of priests and Levites where David commanded **the leaders of the Levites** to arrange for the music of the procession (15:16). David ordered **joyful songs** and specific musical instruments: **lyres, harps and cymbals** (15:16). These and other instruments were used during both attempts to transfer the ark to Jerusalem (see 13:8; 15:28). On this occasion, however, the text specifies that they were under the direction of the Levites. This arrangement also conformed to Mosaic Law (see Deut. 10:8; Num. 3:31-32).

The Chronicler frequently displayed interest in music. His focus on the subject may have been designed to address controversy among the families of Levi over who was to play particular instruments. Whether or not such controversy existed, his frequent reference to actual performances revealed his delight in musical worship and celebration. Music displayed the joy of Israel under the blessings of God. Through examples of musical celebration, the Chronicler not only instructed his readers on the nature and necessity of music. He also displayed the joy of music which they could experience in their day, if they would follow David's example (see *Introduction: 8) Music*).

In response to David's command, the Levites made a number of appointments to duties (15:17-24). Most of these names appear in other lists in Chronicles (see 6:31-48; 16:5-6; 25:1-26:19). The names **Heman, Asaph** and **Ethan** appear as the chief musicians (15:17). They were followed by assistants and **gatekeepers** (15:18) and **doorkeepers** (15:23,24). Gatekeepers and doorkeepers were associated with singers and musicians because music was often performed at the various gates of the temple complex (see 1 Chr. 23:5; 2 Chr. 35:15; Ezra 2:70; 7:7,24; Neh. 7:1, 73; 10:28; 12:45, 47; 13:5).

The list of Levites in 15:19-21 is divided according to which instruments they played: **bronze cymbals** (15:19), **lyres** (15:20), **harps** (15:21). Beyond this, the Chronicler briefly reflected that **Kenaniah** was **in charge of the singing ... because he was skillful at it** (15:22). In the least, this comment reflected the Chronicler's practical concern that Levitical musical assignments had to be made according to the skills of individual Levites even in his own day.

David Moves the Ark (15:25-16:3)

With priests and Levites consecrated and musical responsibilities properly assigned, the Chronicler returned to the record of Samuel. He proceeded to David's second attempt to transfer the ark to Jerusalem.

Comparison of 15:25-16:3 with 2 Sam. 6:12-19a

In most respects the Chronicler closely followed the record of 2 Sam. 6:12-19a. A number of minor variations may be accounted for as errors in the transmission of Samuel or Chronicles (see *Introduction: Translation and Transmission*). Yet, the Chronicler also intentionally introduced several differences to highlight certain aspects of the event.

First, on two occasions the Chronicler emphasized the large number of people involved. He wrote that **David and the elders of Israel and the commanders of units of a thousand** (15:25) brought the ark – 2 Sam. 6:12 merely mentions 'David'. Moreover, he changed 'the entire house of Israel' (2 Sam. 6:15 // 1 Chr. 15:28) and 'each person in the whole crowd of Israelites' (2 Sam. 6:19 // 1 Chr. 16:3) to **all Israel**, his usual expression for representatives of the entire nation.

Second, the Chronicler drew attention to the importance of the Levites much more than the writer of Samuel.

1) He indicated their divine approval by adding that **God had helped the Levites who were carrying the ark** (15:26 // 2 Sam. 6:13; see 1 Chr. 5:20; 12:18; 15:26; 2 Chr. 14:11; 16:12; 18:31; 20:4; 26:7; 32:8; see also *Introduction: 10) Divine Activity*).

2) He specified that the Levites offered sacrifices. In 15:26, he transformed 'he (David) sacrificed' (2 Sam. 6:13) to 'they (the Levites) sacrificed' (**were sacrificed** [NIV]). Similarly, 'David sacrificed burnt offerings' (2 Sam. 6:17) is changed to **they presented burnt offerings** (16:1).

3) He increased the number of sacrifices made to include **seven bulls and seven rams** (15:26 // 2 Sam. 6:13).

4) The Chronicler also modified 2 Sam. 6:14 (// 15:27) in a way that highlighted the Levites' role. He replaced the report of David dancing (2 Sam. 16:14a) with an explanation that **David was clothed in a robe of fine linen, as were all the Levites who were carrying the ark, and as were the singers, and Kenaniah, who was in charge of the singing of the choirs** (15:27). In so doing, the Chronicler made it clear that David and the Levites were dressed in the same way.

5) He provided more detail on the musical component of the procession by adding **rams horns, cymbals, and the playing of lyres and harps** (15:28) to the material of 2 Sam. 6:15.

Third, the Chronicler treated Michal's reaction to David's procession differently. He followed Samuel in his report of Michal's attitude (15:29 // 2 Sam. 6:16), but omitted her rebuke, as well as the responses of David and the Lord (2 Sam. 6:20-23). The Chronicler replaced Samuel's negative ending with a positive description of the wondrous celebration following the ark's entry into Jerusalem (16:1-3).

Structure of 15:25-16:3

The Chronicler skillfully integrated his own additions with material from Samuel to form a three step narrative of the ark's procession (see figure 14). The movement of the ark took place in three stages: the procession toward the city (15:25-28), the entry into the city (15:29), and the placement within the city (16:1-3). The balance of these episodes is evident in the contrasts of emotional tone. The procession of the ark took place with joy and sacrificing (15:25-28). Similarly, the placement of the ark also ends the sequence with sacrifices and joy (16:1-3). Michal's negative reaction, however, separates these celebrative moods (15:29).

Procession of the Ark (15:25-28)

The first step in the account of David's successful transfer of the ark gives an account of the procession from Obed-Edom's house to Jerusalem. As noted above, the Chronicler added that David was accompanied by **the elders of Israel and the commanders of units of a thousand** (15:25). The explicit mention of these participants fit well with the Chronicler's emphasis on the unified support David received from the nation (see *Introduction: 1) All Israel*).

David and all these men brought the ark to Jerusalem **with rejoicing** (15:25).

David's first attempt to bring the ark had also been joyous at first, but it quickly turned tragic (see 13:9-14). The anxiety which David had at that time was replaced by joyous expectation. This focus on joy touched one of the greatest needs of the post-exilic readers of Chronicles. They longed for the delight of such celebrations and in this passage the Chronicler told them that it could be found in the re-establishment of proper worship (see *Introduction: 27) Disappointment and Celebration*).

Four times in this context the Chronicler described the **ark** as **the ark of the covenant** (15:25, 26, 28, 29). This designation pointed in the first place to the fact that the Law of Moses was contained in the ark (see 2 Chr. 5:10). It also reminded Israel of the Mosaic covenant which ordered the religious life of Israel even in the post-exilic period (see *Introduction: 13) Covenant*).

The Chronicler's description of the actual procession highlights the activity of the Levites (15:25-28). Instead of following 2 Sam. 6:13, the Chronicler noted that **God helped the Levites** (15:26a). The motif of 'help' or assistance from God occurs a number of times in Chronicles to indicate divine approval and blessing against some opposition (see 1 Chr. 5:20; 12:18; 15:26; 2 Chr. 14:11-15; 16:12; 18:31; 20:4; 26:7; 32:8; see also *Introduction: 10) Divine Activity*). Here God's help toward the Levites demonstrated that they were handling the ark properly.

The Chronicler also noted that **seven bulls and seven rams were sacrificed** (15:26). This clause may be translated 'they (the Levites) sacrificed ...' (see NAS, NRS, NKJ), thus emphasizing the active participation of the Levites. Whether or not this alternative translation is followed, the Chronicler increased the number of sacrifices from 'a bull and a fattened calf' (2 Sam. 6:13) to **seven bulls and seven rams** (15:26). By this means, the Chronicler accentuated the sacred and celebrative nature of the event (see 15:25).

Interestingly enough, the Chronicler omitted the reference to David's dancing (2 Sam. 6:14a) and replaced it with a description of David's **robe of fine linen** (15:27). He added that it was the same clothing worn by the Levites in the procession (15:27). Once again, the central role of the Levites is heightened to demonstrate that David had entirely reversed his error in the first procession.

The final verse of this segment draws attention once again to the grand and celebrative nature of the event (15:28). The Chronicler described the crowd as **all Israel** ('the entire house of Israel' [2 Sam. 6:15]) to show that the entire nation was unified in support of David's effort (see *Introduction: 1) All Israel*). Moreover, he also increased the list of instruments in the procession by adding **trumpets, cymbals, lyres** and **harps** (15:28 // 2 Sam. 6:15). The Chronicler frequently showed interest in the details of music. Here the larger list of instruments drew attention to the joy of the event (see *Introduction: 8) Music*).

Entry of the Ark (15:29)

This verse focuses on an incident that took place **as the ark ... was entering the City of David** (15:29). It was derived from 2 Sam. 6:16, but fits well with the

Chronicler's chief concerns in the larger context. As David passed through the streets of Jerusalem toward the designated place for the ark, **Michal daughter of Saul watched from a window** (15:29). The description of Michal as the **daughter of Saul** recalls the sharp contrast the Chronicler had established between David and Saul in the preceding chapters. Once again, the house of Saul stood in opposition to the ways of God. Although all Israel rejoiced with David, Michal **saw David dancing and celebrating** and **despised him in her heart** (15:29). By despising David as he joyously worshipped, Michal displayed the apostasy of her father's house in contrast to the blessed faithfulness of David.

Placement of the Ark (16:1-3)

Following 2 Sam. 6:17-19, the Chronicler closed his account of the second procession with a description of the festivities surrounding the placement of the ark. The ark was brought to **the tent that David had pitched for it**; **burnt offerings and fellowship offerings** were sacrificed as on many other occasions of joyous worship (16:1). David also **blessed the people in the Name of the LORD** (16:2; see *Introduction: 11) Name of God*). He also distributed **a cake of dates and a cake of raisins to each Israelite man and woman** (16:2-3). On three occasions in David's reign, the Chronicler mentioned the eating of food in celebration to mark the highpoints of David's reign (12:39; 16:3; 29:22). The specification that food was distributed to every person displayed the grand scale of the joy that filled Israel when David finally brought the ark to Jerusalem.

The Chronicler portrayed David's second procession of the ark as an example of proper worship resulting in widespread joy. His post-exilic readers were in need of finding this kind of happiness in their own time. The Chronicler's outlook is evident. David's devotion to the worship of God in Jerusalem brought celebration. Post-exilic Israel must follow his example to experience this joy in their lives (see *Introduction: 27) Disappointment and Celebration*).

David Instructs Levites and Priests (16:4-43)

With the ark safely in Jerusalem, the Chronicler turned his attention toward David's further instructions to the Levites and priests. This material balances with the preceding focus on Levites and priests (15:3-24; see figure 14), but concentrates on David's permanent arrangements.

Comparison of 16:4-43 with the Psalms

None of this passage is derived from the book of Samuel. The Chronicler added the narrative portions that set the boundaries of this section (16:4-6, 37-42). The main body of this material, however, stems from several selections from the Psalter.

First, 16:8-22 parallels Psalm 105:1-15. Yet, when David instructed the Levites to sing, he altered the standard form of this psalm in two ways.

1) 16:13a substitutes **Israel** for 'Abraham' (Ps. 105:6). The RSV emends 1 Chr. 16:13 to read 'Abraham', but the Hebrew of this verse shifts to **Israel** (see NIV, NAS, NRS, NKJ).

2) The Hebrew of 16:19a reads 'when *you* were few in number' (see NAS, NKJ), but Psalm 105:12 reads 'when *they* were few in number'. In this case, NIV and NRS emend 1 Chr. 16:19a to match Psalm 105:12 and several ancient witnesses to 1 Chr. 16:19a (see *Introduction: Translation and Transmission*). It would appear, however, that the Chronicler intentionally varied from Psalm 105:12. This change also reflects the Chronicler's desire to have his readers identify themselves more closely with David's psalm.

Second, 16:23-33 depends on the entirety of Psalm 96:1-13 with only a few insignificant stylistic variations.

Third, 16:34-36 follows Psalm 106:1, 47-48. The Chronicler's text adds the directive **cry out** (16:35) which does not appear in Psalm 106:47. This addition also encouraged David's listeners and the Chronicler's readers to adopt the prayer of the psalm as their own.

Structure of 16:4-42

This passage divides into three main sections consisting of a composite psalm framed by two paralleling narratives. The psalm itself breaks into three stanzas (see figure 14).

David Appoints Levites in Jerusalem (16:4-6)

In line with his interest in encouraging proper Levitical arrangements in the post-exilic community, the Chronicler began (16:4-6) and ended (16:39-42) this section with David's Levitical appointments. Unlike the temporary duties assigned during the procession of the ark (see 15:4-24), these designations continued throughout David's reign and established patterns for the post-exilic community.

The worship of Israel was not entirely centralized in Jerusalem at this time. The ark had come to the city, but sacrifices continued in Gibeon (see 16:39). As a result, the Levitical duties **before the ark** in Jerusalem were entirely musical (16:4). There the Levites were to **make petition, to give thanks, and praise the Lord** (16:4). It is likely that these duties correspond to three major types of psalms. Petitioning is most closely associated with Psalms of Lament (see Pss. 13, 22, 44, 80). Giving thanks occurs in Thanksgiving Psalms or Psalms of Narrative Praise (see Pss. 9,18,30,124). **Praise of the Lord** (16:4) refers primarily to Hymns of Praise or Descriptive Praise in the Psalter (see Pss. 29, 33, 100, 150).

Beyond this, the Chronicler listed some of the specific instruments played by different Levites. He mentioned stringed instruments **(lyres, harps)** (16:5), percussion (**cymbals**) (16:5b), and wind instruments (**trumpets**) (16:6). His interest in these details probably reflected his concern that post-exilic worship follow similar practices (see *Introduction: 8) Music*). These duties were to be performed before the **ark of the covenant** (16:6; For the significance of this designation, see *Introduction: 13) Covenant*).

David's Psalm (16:7-36)

The Chronicler introduced David's psalm with a brief note to indicate its historical background. David **first committed** this psalm to **Asaph and his associates** (16:7).

Asaph was the head of the musicians ministering before the ark (see 16:5). In committing the psalm to Asaph, David officially approved the psalm for use in worship.

Furthermore, this introductory note designates the song as a **psalm of thanks to the LORD** (16:7). The expression of joy and thanks was a central aspect of Levitical service (see 16:4). By drawing special attention to this type of song, the Chronicler once again emphasized the link between proper arrangement of worship and the blessing of celebration (see *Introduction: 8) Music*).

David's song is a combination of selections from two psalms (Pss. 105, 106) along with the entirety of Psalm 96. This arrangement may have originated with David. Yet, it may also be the result of the Chronicler reporting only portions of what actually occurred on that day. Whatever the case, David's song not only spoke to the Israelites in David's day, but also had a significant message for the Chronicler's post-exilic readers.

The first portion of David's psalm (16:8-22) stems from Psalm 105:1-15. These verses call the nation of Israel to praise God for national blessings. The Chronicler's belief in the continuing significance of the **covenant … with Abraham … and Jacob** (16:15-17) stands out among these praises. David interpreted the glorious events of his day as fulfillment of these patriarchal covenants (see *Introduction: 13) Covenant*). As mentioned above, the shift from 'O descendants of Abraham' (Ps. 105:6) to **O descendants of Israel** (16:13), as well as the change from 'when *they* were but few' (Ps. 105:12) to 'when *you* were but few' (16:19), indicate the Chronicler's desire to have his readers adopt this psalm as praise for their own circumstances. His readers had been rescued from wandering **from nation to nation**, and **from one kingdom to another** (16:20). David had called Israel to praise the Lord for his mercies in establishing the nation and its worship. The Chronicler reported David's actions to encourage his own readers toward this same end.

The second part of this composite psalm (16:23-33) includes the entirety of Psalm 96. This psalm calls **all the earth** (16:23,30) and nature (16:31-33) to praise the Lord. The psalms frequently express enthusiasm in the praise of God by extending the call to praise to the nations and nature (see Pss. 33:8-12; 47; 67; 68:32-35; 97:1-6). The Chronicler included this material because it revealed the ecstasy of celebration accompanying David's ordering of worship (see *Introduction: 27) Disappointment and Celebration*). It also expressed his hope that the restoration of Israel's worship in the post-exilic period would lead the nations around Israel to honor God (see Ezek. 36:33-36; Isa. 49:6-7,14-26; 52:1-10).

The third portion of David's song (16:34-36) consists of only the beginning and end of Psalm 106 (verses 1, 47-48). The middle portion of this psalm expresses mourning and repentance over Israel's many sins (see verses 2-46). David (or the Chronicler) probably omitted this portion of the psalm because the theme of repentance was deemed inappropriate for this situation of praise and celebration. Psalm 106:1 was included because it recalls the opening line of the composite song (**Give thanks to the LORD** [16:8, 34]). Psalm 106:47-48 (// 16:35-36a) consists of a petition that touches an important theme in Chronicles. The people were to pray, **'Gather us and deliver us from the nations'** (16:35). Throughout his history, the Chronicler emphasized the importance of all the people of Israel returning to the land (see *Introduction: 1) All Israel*). David's psalm drew attention to the manner in which prayer served that purpose (see *Introduction: 17) Prayer*). Finally, the ultimate purpose of Israel's return was that Israel **may give thanks** ... and **glory in** [God's] **praise** (16:35b). On four occasions the text refers to the **Name** of God as the object of praise (16:8, 10, 29, 35). To praise the Name of God was to honor him for his powerful activity in the world (see *Introduction: 11) Name of God*). The honor of God was the final goal of Israel's restoration after exile.

A brief afterword attached to David's song reports that **all the people** enthusiastically endorsed the king's prayer (16:36b). The joys and desires expressed by the king were not his alone. The entire assembly joined with him saying, **'Amen. Praise the LORD'** (16:36b). In much the same way, the Chronicler desired all members of the post-exilic community to share the enthusiasm for the worship of God and the gathering of all Israel (*Introduction: 1) All Israel*).

David Appoints Levites and Priests in Jerusalem and Gibeon (16:37-42)

The Chronicler moved from David's psalm back to his ordering of worship personnel. In balance with the previous focus on these matters (16:4-6; see figure 14), he quickly reviewed the situation in Jerusalem (16:37-38). There the Levites ministered **before the ark of the covenant** (16:37; for the significance of this designation, see *Introduction: 13) Covenant*).

Following this review, attention shifts to **Gibeon** (16:39-42). The priest **Zadok** (see 1 Chr. 6:8,12,53) was placed in charge of daily **burnt offerings to the LORD on the altar of burnt offerings** (16:39-40). The Chronicler was quick to say that worship rites at Gibeon were **in accordance with everything written in the Law of the LORD** (16:40). These words demonstrate that he approved of what had taken place (see *Introduction: 14) Standards*). Beyond this, the Chronicler once again expressed his interest in musical appointments (see *Introduction: 8) Music*). **Heman** and **Jeduthun** were in charge of **trumpets**, **cymbals**, and **other instruments for sacred song** (16:41-42; see also 6:31-48). David's appointments to these positions also provided guidance for worship arrangements in the Chronicler's own day.

David's Plan Completed (16:43)

Having departed from Samuel for 40 verses, the Chronicler returned in 16:43 and quoted 2 Sam. 6:19b-20a. Nevertheless, he skillfully reoriented this material by separating it from its original context. In 2 Samuel 6 these words introduce Michal's rebuke of David (2 Sam. 6:20b-23). The Chronicler omitted Michal's reproach and used the passage for his own purposes. In the context of 1 Chr. 16, these words from Samuel indicate that the transfer of the ark was entirely successful.

The positive mood of 16:43 is apparent. Not only did the people return home, but David left **to bless his family**. David did not return to lament or complain. He intended to share his joy and blessing with his family much as he had with the assembly (see 16:2).

The Chronicler closed this second major portion of David's reign on a note of joy and blessing. Although David had failed, he was still God's chosen king. He succeeded in bringing the ark of the covenant to Jerusalem so that the city was the place of David's throne and the footstool of God. This stage of David's reign spoke plainly to the needs of post-exilic Israel. They should yearn for the day when Jerusalem would once again become the seat of divine presence in the temple as well as the royal capital of David's son.

David's Ideal Reign: Part Three
David Prepares for the Temple
(1 Chr 17:1-29:25)

Overview of 1 Chr. 17:1-29:25

This third major portion of David's reign presents the high point of his life from the Chronicler's perspective. Having already recorded the joy resulting from widespread support for David's dynasty (see 9:35-12:40), as well as celebration over the presence of the ark in Jerusalem (see 13:1-16:43), the Chronicler turned next to the largest and most significant part of David's reign (17:1-29:30). Here David brought indescribable joy to Israel by making preparations for Solomon to build the temple.

Comparison of 17:1-29:25 with Samuel

A number of significant variations occur between 2 Samuel and 1 Chr. 17:1-29:25. More detailed comparisons appear in the discussions below. At this point only a few general comments will be made (see figure 15).

1 Chr		2 Sam
17:1-27	David Accepts Preparatory Role (closely parallel)	7:1-29
18:1-13	David's Victories (closely parallel)	8:1-14
18:14-19	David's Righteous Reign (closely parallel)	8:15-18
———	David Accepts Mephibosheth (omitted)	9:1-13
19:1-20:3	David's Victory over Ammonites (parallel)	10:1-11:1a 12:26,30-31
———	David Sins with Bathsheba (omitted)	11:1b-27
———	David's Rebuke from Nathan (omitted)	12:1-25
———	David's Troubled House (omitted)	13:1-21:14
———	David's Rescue from Philistines (omitted)	21:15-17
20:4-8	David's Victory over Philistines (closely parallel)	21:18-22
———	David's Psalm and Oracle (omitted)	22:1-23:7
21:1-22:1	David's Census (slightly expanded)	24:1-25
22:2-29:25	David's Arrangements for Temple (added)	———

Comparison of 17:1-29:25 with Samuel (figure 15)

First, in broad terms 17:1-22:1 derive from the portions of 2 Sam. 7:1-24:25. As our figure illustrates, the Chronicler omitted a number of segments, but these chapters in Chronicles are at least loosely parallel to Samuel.

Second, this material contains the Chronicler's largest uninterrupted addition to Samuel and Kings (22:2-29:25). As such, it brings to light the Chronicler's chief concern in the reign of David: the king's devotion to preparing for Solomon's temple.

Structure of 17:1-29:25

This portion of David's reign divides into five symmetrical steps (see figure 16).

The overarching symmetry of this material displays its primary concerns. First, David accepted his God-ordained role to prepare for Solomon to build the temple (17:1-27). In balance with this opening, David finished his effort by transferring responsibility for the temple to Solomon (23:1-29:25). In the second step of this section David gathers what was needed for construction (18:1-20:8). In the fourth step, David commissioned that these items be used (22:2-19). The center of this material (21:1-22:1) recollects the preceding theme of David's military accomplishments (18:1-20:8) by reporting David's military census. It also anticipates the commission to build (22:2-19) by indicating how David's military census led to the discovery of the temple site. At the end of these chapters, the Chronicler closed David's reign (29:26-30).

David Accepts Commission to Prepare for Solomon (17:1-27)

In this passage, David began his devotion to the temple by accepting his divinely ordained role. David was not to build the temple, but he was to prepare for its construction.

Comparison of 17:1-27 with 2 Sam. 7:1-29

For the most part, the Chronicler merely copied this material from 2 Sam. 7:1-29. Most differences are minor and stem from stylistic variations or problems in transmission (see *Introduction: Translation and Transmission*). Nevertheless, several variations reveal the Chronicler's intentional changes.

First, the Chronicler omitted 'and the LORD had given him rest from all his enemies around him' (17:1 // 2 Sam. 7:1). In all likelihood, this omission was designed to remove any confusion brought about by the accounts of David's wars in the following chapters (18:1-20:8).

Second, 2 Sam. 7:5 reads, 'Are you the one to build me a house...?' but 1 Chr. 17:4 substitutes, **'You are not the one to build me a house**...' The pronoun **you** is emphatic in the Hebrew text of 17:4. The Chronicler portrayed God prohibiting David specifically from building the temple to make it clear that temple construction itself was not forbidden.

Third, 'I will also give you rest from all your enemies' (2 Sam. 7:11) was changed to **'I will also subdue all your enemies'** (17:10). This variation also anticipated the battles mentioned in the following chapters (18:1-20:8).

Fourth, 2 Sam. 7:16 reads, *'Your [David's] house and your kingdom* will endure

David Prepares for the Temple (17:1-29:25)

- ■David Accepts Commission to Prepare for Solomon (17:1-27)
  - David Expresses His Plan (17:1)
    - Nathan Responds Favorably to David (17:2)
      - God Reveals the Divine Plan to Nathan (17:3-14)
    - Nathan Reports the Divine Plan to David (17:15)
  - David Accepts God's Plan (17:16-27)

- ■David Secures the Nation and Collects Temple Materials (18:1-20:8)
  - ♦David's Victories and Domestic Security (18:1-17)
    - David's Victories in All Directions (18:1-13)
    - David's Resulting National Security (18:14-17)

  - ♦David's Victories against Ammon and Aram (19:1-20:3)
    - • David Insulted by the King of Ammon (19:1-5)
      - David Sends Delegation to Ammonites (19:1-2a)
        - David's Delegation Arrives (19:2b)
          - Ammonite Nobles Advise Rejection (19:3)
        - David's Delegation Rejected (19:4)
      - David Assures Delegation (19:5)

    - • David Destroys Ammonite-Aramean Coalition (19:6-19)
      - Ammonite-Aramean Coalition Formed (19:6-7)

        - Israel's First Victory (19:8-15)
          - Joab Sent to Battle (19:8)
            - Dual Enemy Formations (19:9)
              - Joab's Plan (19:10-13)
            - Dual Formations Destroyed (19:14-15a)
          - Joab Returns from Battle (19:15b)

        - Israel's Second Victory (19:16-19a)
          - Arameans Prepare for War (19:16)
            - David Advances (19:17a)
              - Battle Ensues (19:17b)
            - David Defeats (19:18)
          - Arameans Sue for Peace (19:19a)

      - Ammonite-Aramean Coalition Broken (19:19b)
    - • David Conquers the King of Ammon (20:1-3)
      - Joab Leads Army (20:1a)
        - Joab Destroys Rabbah (20:1b)
        - David Receives Spoils (20:2-3a)
      - David and Army Return (20:3b)

- ♦David's Victories against Philistines (20:4-8)
  - Victory in a Battle with Philistines (20:4)
  - Victory in a Second Battle with Philistines (20:5)
  - Victory in a Third Battle with Philistines (20:6-8)

■David Discovers the Temple Site (21:1-22:1)

- ♦David's Cursed Infidelity (21:1-7a)
  - David Misled by Satan (21:1)
    - David Orders Census (21:2-3)
      - Joab Fulfills Census (21:4)
    - David Receives Census (21:5-6)
  - David Angers God (21:7a)

  - ♦David's Confrontation with God over Israel (21:7b-14)
    - David Punished by God (21:7b)
      - David's Humble Inquiry (21:8)
        - David's Instructions from Gad (21:9-12)
      - David's Humble Compliance (21:13)
    - David Punished by God (21:14)

  - ♦David's Confrontation with God over Jerusalem (21:15-27)
    - David Punished by God (21:15)
      - David's Humble Inquiry (21:16-17)
        - David's Instructions from Gad (21:18)
      - David's Humble Compliance (21:19-26a)
    - David Forgiven by God (21:26b-27)

- ♦David's Blessed Devotion (21:28-22:1)
  - David Offers Sacrifices (21:28)
    - David's Actions Explained (21:29-30)
  - David Declares His Discovery (22:1)

■David Commissions Temple Construction (22:2-19)

- ♦David's Extensive Preparations for Solomon (22:2-5)
- ♦David's Commission of Solomon (22:6-16)
- ♦David's Order for Leaders to Help Solomon (22:17-19)

■David Transfers Power and Responsibility to Solomon (23:1-29:25)
- ♦Title: David Makes Solomon King (23:1)
- ♦Those Whom David Gathered (23:2-27:34)
    - • Introduction (23:2)
    - • Priests and Levites (23:3-26:32)
        - Registry and Divisions of Levites (23:3-5)
        - Levites and Priests Together (23:6-24:31)
            - Levites Divided by Families (23:6-27)
            - Levitical Duties Alongside Priests (23:28-32)
            - Priests Divided (24:1-19)
            - Levites Remaining (24:20-31)
        - Singers (25:1-31)
        - Gatekeepers (26:1-19)
        - Officials and Judges (26:20-32)
    - • Military and Civilian Leaders (27:1-34)
        - Military Leaders (27:1-24)
        - Civilian Leaders (27:25-34)
- ♦David's Final Assembly (28:1-29:25)
    - David Assembles Leaders (28:1)
        - David's First Speeches and Actions (28:2-19)
            - David Addresses Assembly (28:2-7)
            - David Addresses Solomon (28:8-10)
            - Action Following Speeches (28:11-19)
        - David's Second Speeches and Actions (28:20-29:9)
            - David Addresses Solomon (28:20-21)
            - David Addresses Assembly (29:1-5)
            - Action Following Second Speeches (29:6-9)
        - David's Third Speeches and Actions (29:10-25)
            - David Addresses God (29:10-19)
                - Setting (29:10a)
                - Praise of God (29:10b-13)
                - Declaration of Humility (29:14-16)
                - Petitions for the Future (29:17-19)
            - David Addresses Assembly (29:20)
            - Actions Following Speeches (29:21-25)

Closure of David's Reign (29:26-30)

Outline of 1 Chr. 17:1-29:25 (figure 16)

forever before me; *your throne* will be established forever' (italics added). 1 Chr. 17:14 reads, **'I will set *him* [*Solomon*] over *my* [*God's*] *house and my* [*God's*] *kingdom* forever; *his* [*Solomon's*] *throne* will be established forever'** (italics added). These changes diminished the focus on David and emphasized God's kingship as well as the importance of Solomon.

Fifth, the Chronicler omitted 2 Sam. 7:14b: 'When he does wrong, I will punish him with the rod of men, with floggings inflicted by men.' These words refer to the sins of Solomon. They are omitted because they do not fit well with the Chronicler's presentation of Solomon as an ideal king (but compare 28:9).

Sixth, in the Hebrew of the last verse (17:27 // 2 Sam. 7:29) the focus of the verb 'to bless' has shifted. As the variety among English translations indicates, the precise meaning of these variations is difficult to determine (compare NAS, NRS, NKJ).

Structure of 17:1-27

This chapter divides into five symmetrical steps (see figure 16). The uneven sizes of the steps of this material hide its conceptual balance. The alternations of main characters, however, reveals the overarching structure. The sequence consists of David (17:1), Nathan (17:2), God (17:3-14), Nathan (17:15), and David (17:16-27). David wanted to build (17:1) and Nathan agreed (17:2). Yet, because of divine revelation at night (17:3-14), Nathan instructed David not to build (17:15). David joyfully accepted his role as the one who prepared for his son to build (17:16-27).

David Expresses His Plan (17:1)

This narrative begins with a very admirable desire on David's part. Having settled into a palace, he wanted to build a permanent structure for the **ark of the covenant** (17:1; for the significance of this designation see *Introduction: 13) Covenant*). This desire parallels royal ideology in surrounding ancient Near Eastern cultures. The inscriptions of kings and emperors around Israel demonstrate that one way monarchs proved their success was to build temples for their gods. It was expected that all good and powerful kings would build temples. David had reached the point in his life when it was time for him to take this step.

Nathan Responds Favorably to David (17:2)

Nathan's initial response to David was to be expected because it was considered customary for a king to build a temple. It should be noted that there is no indication that Nathan consulted or inquired of the Lord in this matter. His first response was not revelation; it was little more than common sense based on the fact that **God is with** David (17:2). In the Chronicler's vocabulary, for God to be 'with' people meant that God fought for them and gave them victory over struggles (see 2 Chr. 13:12; see also *Introduction: 10) Divine Activity*). Nathan had seen God fighting for David and assumed divine approval of the king's plan.

God Reveals the Divine Plan to Nathan (17:3-14)

Despite Nathan's initial reaction, he received instructions from God to the contrary. David was *not* to build the temple of God.

God revealed himself to Nathan during the night. Revelation at night is common in Scripture (see Gen. 15:12-21; 20:3-7; 26:23-25; 28:10-17; 46:1-4; 1 Sam. 15:10-11; 1 Kgs. 3:5-14; Dan. 2:17-23; 7:1-28; Zech. 1:7-6:15). The Chronicler himself referred to it elsewhere (see 2 Chr. 1:7-12; 7:11-22). Here divine revelation was designed to put a stop to David's plan.

Twice God commanded, **'tell my servant David'** (17:4,7). These words divide Nathan's revelation into two main parts: divine denials (17:4-6) and divine promises (17:7-14).

In 17:4-6 the Lord denied that he ever asked David to build a temple. At first glance, it may appear that God entirely rejected the idea of Israel having a temple. He had been with his people throughout their wanderings and never asked for a **house of cedar** (17:6). As noted above, however, the Chronicler rephrased 17:4 (// 2 Sam. 7:5) to make God's desire as clear as possible. The Chronicler's emphatic Hebrew construction may be translated, 'You, specifically you, are not the one...' (17:4). This construction clarified that the Lord did not entirely reject the idea of a temple. A temple for Israel's God was a central theocratic ideal. God merely revealed that Solomon was to build instead of David. As indicated later, David's involvement in warfare disqualified him from being the one to establish the temple (see 22:8; 28:3). (For the Chronicler's use of the terminology **this day** [17:5], see comments on 4:41.)

The divine promises given to David were numerous (17:7-14); they appear in two groups separated by the expression, **'I declare to you that the LORD will build a house for you'** (17:10b). The first section begins with a brief reminder of past blessings given to David as **ruler over** [God's] **people Israel** (17:7). God promised to **make** [David's] **name like the names of the greatest** (17:8b), **provide a place for** [his] **people** (17:9), **plant them** (17:9), and **subdue all** [of David's] **enemies** (17:10b). God reminded David that he had been **with** him, fighting against David's opponents (17:8; see 2 Chr. 13:12; see also *Introduction: 10) Divine Activity*). Each of these promises focuses on national security against enemies. Their fulfillments appear in the chapters which follow (see 18:1-20:8).

The second set of promises concerned how God **will build a house for** [David] (17:10b). This passage depends on the flexibility of the Hebrew word translated 'house'. The same word appears twice in 17:1 as **palace** ('house' NAS, NKJ, NRS). In these cases, the term referred to David's *palace* of cedar and his proposed *temple* for God. In 17:10c, however, the same term is used to denote David's **house** or *dynasty*.

God made five promises regarding David's dynasty. He would **raise up** [David's] **offspring** (17:11), **establish his throne** (17:12), **be his father** (17:13), **never take** [his] **love away** (17:13), and **set him over** [God's] **house and** [God's] **kingdom forever** (17:14). David received the promise that his dynasty would be the permanent royal family for Israel.

The familial language of this passage (**his father** ... **my son** [17:13]) indicated a special adoption of the Davidic king (see Pss. 2:7; 89:27). Unlike other ancient Near Eastern cultures, Israel did not believe her king was divine or shared in divinity. Israel's kings were brothers of their citizens (see Deut. 17:15). The language of sonship here indicates that the Lord adopted the king of Israel to be his special son among all of his sons and daughters in Israel.

New Testament writers indicate that these words about Solomon foreshadowed Christ, the final Davidic king (see Mark 1:11; Luke 1:32-33; Heb. 1:5). Of course, Christ was not the Son of God simply because he was the son of David. He is the second Person of the Godhead (see John 1:1-18; 17:1), and his humanity was conceived by the Holy Spirit (see Luke 1:35). Jesus is the Son of God like no other. Nevertheless, it is Jesus' special royal sonship rooted in the promise to David that is often in view in the New Testament.

God promised that David's line would be the permanent dynasty over God's people. Unlike Saul's family (see 1 Chr. 10:1-14), God will **never take** [his] **love away** from David's descendants (17:13). 2 Sam. 7:14b indicates that David's descendants would be chastised when they sinned, but God would always raise up another son of David to continue the line. The Chronicler omitted this mention of sin in 1 Chr. 17:13 (compare the same in Heb. 1:5) to sustain his positive outlook on the reign of Solomon. Despite the troubles which the house of David brought on the people of God, the Chronicler asserted that David's house was still the only family with rights to the throne of Israel.

This promise was especially important for the Chronicler's post-exilic community. Post-exilic Israel hoped for national security against her enemies. It was through David and his seed that God promised such security. These promises served the Chronicler's purpose of turning attention to the house of David as the permanent hope for Israel.

As noted above, the Chronicler shifted the wording from *'your [David's]* house and kingdom' (2 Sam. 7:16) to ***'my** [God's]* **house and kingdom'** (17:14). The Chronicler drew a close connection between the human throne of Israel and God's throne because the sons of David ruled as God's vice-regents. In an ultimate sense the kingdom did not belong to David but to God. This aspect of the Chronicler's viewpoint on David's throne provides an essential background for understanding the New Testament teaching on the Kingdom of God (Heaven). With the re-establishment of the Davidic throne in Christ, the reign (Kingdom) of God was re-established (see Matt. 12:22-28; Acts 2:22-36; 7:45-50; see also *Introduction: 8) Divine Kingship*).

Nathan Reports the Divine Plan to David (17:15)

In balance with Nathan's earlier words to David (17:2), the Chronicler reported that Nathan spoke to David once again. According to the command of God (see 17:4,7), Nathan did not keep this revelation to himself. He told David **this entire revelation**.

David Accepts God's Plan (17:16-27)

Following the account of Samuel, the Chronicler set David's prayerful response immediately after God's promises to David. In effect, this prayer reveals that the king was willing to comply with the plan of God. His prayer divides into two parts: praise for blessings (17:16-22) and petitions for blessings (17:23-27).

David began his praise with the admission that neither he nor his family had been worthy of the divine grace shown to them up to that point (17:16). Then he expressed astonishment that God had promised more blessings in the future (17:17). David was left speechless (**'what more can David say'** [17:18]) by the fact that God, knowing David as he did, would bless so richly (17:18-19). David closed his praise by exalting the Lord above all (17:20) and praising him for Israel's great deliverance from Egypt (17:21-22).

David's praise for God's blessings displayed tremendous humility (17:16-22). He began his prayer with a rhetorical question, **'Who am I?'** (17:16). These words appear again in David's later prayer (see 29:14) and Solomon's letter to Hiram (see 2 Chr. 2:6). They indicate the speaker's awareness that he was undeserving of the benevolence he was receiving. As a result, David's opening words set the tone of his entire prayer. He was astounded to receive such great blessings from God.

Contemporary readers often have difficulty appreciating the extent of David's humility because we have little sense of the cultural implications of his prayer. Royal propaganda in the ancient Near East often focused on temple construction as evidence of a king's success. For this reason, the prohibition against David building a temple threatened to bring him great shame. Nevertheless, David humbly submitted to God's pleasure.

The Chronicler included these words from David's prayer to encourage similar attitudes within his readers. The post-exilic community needed to humble itself before God. They too were unworthy of divine grace. Moreover, as they had seen the promises to David fulfilled time and again throughout history, their praise should have been even more exuberant than David's. David praised God for redeeming Israel from Egypt; the Chronicler's readers had much reason to praise God for returning them from captivity in Babylon.

Following his praise, David petitioned the Lord for future blessings (17:23-27). The expression **and now** (17:23) indicates that the king was drawing a conclusion from what had preceded. On the basis of God's goodness toward his people in the past, David determined to pray for the future of his house.

David referred directly to divine promises just given through Nathan in two ways. First, he prayed **that** [God's] **name will be great forever** (17:24). This petition alluded to the earlier divine promise to make David's name great (17:8). David wanted his house to be established, but in the hope that God's Name would be great as well. He desired for all the people to say, **'The LORD Almighty, the God over Israel, is Israel's God!'** (17:24). Second, David also referred to Nathan's prophecy when he said, **'You, my God, have revealed to your servant that you will build a house for him'** (17:25). This phraseology stems from the promise of a permanent dynasty in 17:10-14.

As noted above, at the end of the king's petitions (17:27 // 2 Sam. 7:29), the Chronicler shifted the focus of the verb 'to bless'. The Chronicler substituted the past tense **you ... have blessed it** (17:27) to sum up David's attitude toward the blessings he had received. The final clause – **it will be blessed forever** – may be translated either as an imminent future (NIV, NKJ) or as the present tense (NRS, NAS).

The NIV translation suggests that the Chronicler drew his readers' attention to two similarities between David's situation and their own. They and David had been the recipients of magnificent blessings in the past. At the same time, their past blessings gave them hope for the future. As David anticipated the grace of God, so post-exilic Israel could look forward to a bright future as they followed David's example of prayerful devotion to God and his temple (see *Introduction: 17) Prayer*).

David Secures the Nation and Collects Temple Materials (18:1-20:8)

Having described how David accepted God's commission to prepare for Solomon's temple, the Chronicler turned to David's efforts to provide the security and materials necessary for temple construction.

Comparison of 18:1-20:8 with 2 Sam. 8:1-21:22

The Chronicler's distinctive portrait of these events emerges when his record is compared with Samuel (see figure 17).

1 Chr		2 Sam
18:1-13	David's Victories (closely parallel)	8:1-14
18:14-19	David's Righteous Reign (closely parallel)	8:15-18
———	David Accepts Mephibosheth (omitted)	9:1-13
19:1-20:3	David's Victory over Ammonites (parallel)	10:1-11:1a 12:26,30-31
———	David Sins with Bathsheba (omitted)	11:1b-27
———	David's Rebuke from Nathan (omitted)	12:1-25
———	David's Troubled House (omitted)	13:1-21:14
———	David's Rescue from Philistines (omitted)	21:15-17
20:4-8	David's Victory over Philistines (closely parallel)	21:18-22

Comparison of 1 Chr 18:1-20:8 with 2 Sam 8:1-21:22 (figure 17)

In several portions of this material, the Chronicler followed the book of Samuel rather closely (18:1-19 // 2 Sam. 8:1-18; 19:1-20:3 // 10:1-11:1a; 12:26,30-31; 20:4-8 // 2 Sam. 21:18-22). These passages differ only in small ways which we will discuss in the comments on each segment.

Nevertheless, the Chronicler also omitted several large sections from the book of Samuel. First, he omitted David's acceptance of Mephibosheth into the royal court (2 Sam. 9:1-13). David's action was generous, but it also may have encouraged some Benjamites to hope that the family of Saul would take the throne again (see 2 Sam. 16:1-3; 20:1-2). Apparently, the Chronicler had no time for such considerations.

Second, the Chronicler did not report David's sin with Bathsheba, nor the troubles that followed (2 Sam. 11:2-21:14). This is the largest single portion of Samuel not included in Chronicles. The Chronicler's purpose was to concentrate on those aspects of David's reign which were exemplary for his post-exilic readers. This portion of Samuel did not fit with that purpose.

Third, the Chronicler omitted the story of David's near death at the hands of the Philistines (2 Sam. 21:15-17). This narrative illustrated how David's military might diminished after his fall into sin.

Structure of 18:1-20:8

The Chronicler selected material from 2 Sam. 8:1-22 to form a threefold structure. Each portion of this structure illustrates how David was successful in battle and gathered materials for Solomon's temple project (see figure 16). This threefold division is based on the repeated introductory words **in the course of time** (18:1; 19:1; 20:4). These markers divide the materials into a broad description of David's victories and domestic security (18:1-17) followed by victories against specific enemies (19:1-20:3; 20:4-8).

David's Victories and Domestic Security (18:1-17)

David's collection of materials for the temple began with a series of victories, tributes, and a description of national security under David. This section illustrates how David won battles, gathered plunder, and arranged domestic affairs under God's blessing.

Comparison of 18:1-17 with 2 Sam. 8:1-18

For the most part, the Chronicler followed Samuel closely. A number of minor differences have resulted from errors in textual transmission (see *Introduction: Translation and Transmission*). Nevertheless, four differences deserve comment.

First, the Chronicler did not mention David's harsh treatment of the Moabites (2 Sam. 8:2a). It is possible that this omission occurred by an error in textual transmission (see *Introduction: Translation and Transmission*), but it is also possible that the Chronicler intentionally omitted it to avoid detracting from the positive mood of the passage.

Second, 18:4 reads **seven thousand horsemen**, but 2 Sam. 8:4 reads 'seventeen hundred horsemen' (see NIV margin). It is likely that one or both of these texts has suffered corruption at some point in transmission (see *Introduction: Translation and Transmission*).

Third, 18:8 (// 2 Sam. 8:8) adds the note that **with it Solomon made the bronze Sea and the pillars and the vessels of bronze.** This addition reveals one of the Chronicler's chief concerns in this material. The spoils of David's victories were used in Solomon's temple.

Fourth, it is possible that the omission of 2 Sam. 8:12b-13a occurred accidentally in the transmission of Chronicles (see *Introduction: Translation and Transmission*). Yet, it is also possible that the Chronicler purposefully omitted at least 2 Sam. 8:13a to avoid any negative connotations that may have been associated with 'David [making] a name for himself.'

Structure of 18:1-17

This portion of the Chronicler's record divides into two main parts (see figure 16). David's military accomplishments are quickly surveyed (18:1-13) and the results of national security come to light (18:14-17).

David's Victories in All Directions (18:1-13)

The Chronicler first reported David's victories in a number of geographical settings. The record of victories consists of three sections: David's victories (18:1-6), plunder and tribute (18:7-11), and a final notice of victories (18:12-13).

In the opening verses (18:1-6), the Chronicler mentioned victories against **Philistines** (18:1), **Moabites** (18:2), **Hadadezer king of Zobah** (18:3-4), and the **Arameans** (18:5-6a). Each of these enemies was well-known from Israel's history as notorious opponents (see Num. 22-25; Judg. 3:1-3,7-11,12-31; 13:1-16:31; 1 Sam. 4:1-11). They had troubled the people of God throughout the centuries, but David defeated them all.

The importance of 18:6b can be seen in its duplication in 18:13b. The Chronicler made it clear how David conquered these enemies. He did not win in his own strength; **the LORD gave David victory** (18:6b; see *Introduction: 10) Divine Activity*). In fact, David had victory **everywhere he went** (18:6b).

This catalogue of David's victories encouraged the Chronicler's readers as they faced military dangers in their day. The prophets had promised great victories for the post-exilic community (see Isa. 11:11-16; 49:14-26; 54:1-3; Jer. 30:10-11; Amos 9:11-12). David's successes demonstrated that they could defeat their enemies with the help of the Lord (see *Introduction: 23) Victory and Defeat*).

The second portion of this passage describes how David took much plunder and received tribute (18:7-11). In the first place (18:7-8), David took ceremonial **gold shields** from **Hadadezer** (18:7), whose defeat is mentioned earlier (see 18:3-4). He also took **a great quantity of bronze** (18:8a). The significance of this massive plunder becomes clear in the closing comment in 18:8b. The Chronicler added to 2 Sam. 7:8 that Solomon used this bronze **to make the bronze Sea, the pillars and various bronze articles** (18:8b). These words relate David's victory to the larger overarching purpose of this portion of Chronicles. These wars were part of the king's preparations for the Jerusalem temple.

In the second place (18:9-11), the text mentions the tribute which **Tou king of Hamath** paid to David (18:9). It included **all kinds of articles of gold and silver and bronze** (18:10). Once again, however, the significance of David receiving this grand tribute is made clear in a closing comment. **King David dedicated these articles to the LORD** (18:11a). In other words, this tribute was also used in the temple. To draw even greater attention to this focus, the passage indicates that this was not an unique event. David had given **the silver and gold he had taken from all these nations** to the temple project (18:11b).

The second list of victories (18:12-13) closes this section and balances with 18:1-8 by repeating the explanation of David's successes: **the LORD gave David victory everywhere he went** (18:13b see 18:6b). As noted above, the Chronicler may have omitted the fact that David 'made a name for himself' (2 Sam. 8:13) to avoid any negative connotations that may have been associated with the expression (see Gen. 11:4).

Abishai led David's forces and conquered **eighteen thousand Edomites in the Valley of Salt** (18:12b). In the traditional Hebrew text, 2 Sam. 8:13b reads 'eighteen thousand Syrians' (see NAS, NKJ). The difference between Chronicles and Samuel at this point is due to scribal confusion at some stage in transmission (*Introduction: Translation and Transmission*). In some periods of the Hebrew language, the words 'Syria' and 'Edom' looked very similar and were easily confused. For this reason, some English translations follow a few Hebrew manuscripts and correctly emend 2 Sam. 8:13b to read 'eighteen thousand Edomites' (see NRS, NIV).

In the days of Moses, Israel was to show kindness to the Edomites because they were descendants of Esau and relatives of the Israelites (see Gen. 36:1-43; Deut. 2:1-7; 23:7). Moreover, the Edomites lived outside the land of promise and were not the object of Israel's conquest (see Deut. 20:2-5). Even so, throughout Israel's history the Edomites troubled the people of God and thereby lost their protected status (see Num. 20:14-20; 1 Sam. 14:47). By the Chronicler's day, Edom had come to be a hated enemy of Israel deserving severe punishment. In fact, Amos specifically named Edom as an enemy over whom the post-exilic community would have victory (see Amos 9:11-12). As a result, when the Chronicler reported that **all the Edomites became subject to David** (18:13b), he inspired his readers to hope for their own eventual victory over this archenemy.

David's Resulting National Security (18:14-17)

The Chronicler continued following the account of Samuel with little variation to demonstrate the extent to which David received victory from the Lord (// 2 Sam. 8:15-18). Although these verses mention military leaders (18:15,17), they focus more broadly on David's domestic accomplishments. His positive national achievements resulted from the blessing of military security.

The opening verse reveals the general outlook to be taken on this passage. **David**

reigned over all Israel, doing what was just and right for all his people (18:14). The mention of **all Israel** (18:14) comes from Samuel, but it fits well with the Chronicler's purposes here. It expressed the breadth of David's kingdom which served as an ideal for the Chronicler's readers (see *Introduction: 1) All Israel*). Moreover, David also did **what was just and right for all his people** (18:14). In other words, the entire nation benefitted from David's reign (see *Introduction: 4-9) King and Temple*). It was a kingdom of justice and righteousness for every class of Israelites. This description of the size and quality of David's reign reveals the wonder of his kingdom. His wars were so successful (18:1-13) that he was able to form an ideal kingdom.

The verses that follow (18:15-17) list a number of officials in David's kingdom. Most of these people are well-known from other portions of Scripture. Their appointments provided a secure bureaucracy for Solomon. In this sense, even this aspect of David's efforts prepared the way for temple construction.

The Chronicler incorporated this material into his history to illustrate several ways in which David's kingdom served as an ideal for his post-exilic readers. Just as these aspects of David's reign prepared the way for Solomon's greater achievements, so too the post-exilic kingdom must emulate David to secure further blessings from God.

David's Victory against Ammon and Aram (19:1-20:3)

Having focused on David's general victories, the Chronicler turned next to a specific victory over the Ammonites and their Aramean allies. This passage connects directly to the larger context through 18:11b. There the Ammonites appear among those whose plunder David dedicated to the temple. In this light, we can see that the Chronicler used this account of David's victory over the Ammonites to illustrate further how he prepared for the temple of Solomon.

Comparison of 19:1-20:3 with 2 Sam. 10:1-12:31

In general terms we should be reminded that this portion of the Chronicler's history (19:1-20:3) is selectively based on 2 Sam. 10:1-12:31 (see figure 17). 19:1-20:1a follows 2 Sam. 10:1-11:1a rather closely, but 2 Sam. 11:1b-12:25 (David's sin with Bathsheba and Nathan's rebuke) is omitted. The closing verses of this material (20:1-3) are taken from 2 Sam. 12:26 and 2 Sam. 12:30-31 (see figure 18).

Several minor differences due to style and problems in textual transmission occur (see *Introduction: Translation and Transmission*). Yet, eight variations deserve special mention.

First, on several occasions, the names of some places are updated (see 19:6,7 // 2 Sam. 10:6). These changes indicate the Chronicler's keen sensitivity to his post-exilic readers' knowledge (see 2 Chr. 3:3).

Second, at the end of 19:2 (// 2 Sam. 10:2) the Chronicler added **to express sympathy to him** (Hanun) a second time to emphasize the honorable intentions of David and his delegation.

Third, 19:6 (// 2 Sam. 10:6) adds **a thousand talents of silver to hire chariots**

1 Chr		2 Sam
19:1-19	Ammonite-Aramean Coalition (closely parallel)	10:1-19
20:1a	Introduction (closely parallel)	11:1a
——	David's Adultery and Rebuke (omitted)	11:1b-12:25
20:1b	Joab's Leadership (closely parallel)	12:26
——	Joab Gives Victory to David (omitted)	12:27-29
20:2-3	Plunder from Battle (closely parallel)	12:30-31

Comparison of 1 Chr 20:1-3 with 2 Sam 11:1-12:31 (figure 18)

and charioteers. This additional information focuses on the high quality of the enemy David defeated.

Fourth, 19:7 reads **thirty-two thousand chariots and charioteers** where 2 Sam. 10:6 reads **twenty thousand ... foot soldiers**. This variation also emphasizes the strength of David's enemy.

Fifth, in 19:17 (// 2 Sam. 10:17) the Chronicler increased attention to David's aggressive role by adding that **David** (Hebrew = 'he' [NAS, NRS, NKJ]) **formed his lines to meet the Arameans in battle**.

Sixth, the change from 'seven hundred of their charioteers' (2 Sam. 10:18) to **seven thousand of their charioteers** (19:18) is probably the result of a problem in transmission of one or both texts (see *Introduction: Translation and Transmission*).

Seventh, 19:19 calls more attention to the centrality of David's leadership by shifting the language from 'they made peace with the Israelites and became subject to them' (2 Sam. 10:19) to **they made peace *with David* and became subject to him** (19:19).

Eighth, the Chronicler omitted 2 Sam. 12:27-29. These verses report that David received credit for defeating Rabbah only because Joab was generous enough to include him in the victory. These facts did not fit well with the Chronicler's desire to exalt David for using his military accomplishments to prepare for the building of the Temple.

Structure of 19:1-20:3

The Chronicler's new arrangement of materials from Samuel shaped his account into a three step narrative (see figure 16). This passage begins with the Ammonite king insulting David (19:1-5). David then faced an Ammonite-Aramean coalition (19:6-19). Finally, David conquered and punished the Ammonite king and repaid the initial insult (20:1-3).

David Insulted by the King of Ammon (19:1-5)

This material begins with a story of sincere sympathy, distrust, embarrassment and comfort. David's good intentions were misread and this mistake eventually led to war.

Structure of 19:1-5

The account of David's defeat of the Ammonites begins with a five step symmetrical narrative (see figure 16). This segment opens as David sends a delegation to the Ammonites (19:1-2a) and ends when he comforts them upon their return (19:5). The action rises as the delegation arrives among the Ammonites (19:2b) and falls toward the end as the Ammonites reject the delegation (19:4). The turning point in the narrative is the advice of the nobles against the Israelite delegation (19:3).

The Ammonites were not indigenous to the promised land and so not under the ban of holy war (see Deut. 20:17). Moreover, as Moses recounted in Deuteronomy 2, he reminded Israel of how God prevented them from provoking Ammon because he had given their land as a possession to the sons of Lot (see Deut. 2:19). Joshua gave Gad 'half the land of the sons of Ammon', but they were to stop short of Rabbah (see Josh. 13:25). Therefore, while Joshua had taken some of Ammon, David's conquest of Ammon in 1 Chronicles 19-20 went well beyond Joshua's efforts.

At the beginning of this episode, **Nahash** (an Ammonite king who **showed kindness to** David) had just died (19:1-2a). David extended **kindness to Hanun son of Nahash** (19:1). David was more than eager to continue the peaceful relationship he enjoyed with Hanun's father. For this reason, **David sent a delegation ... to Hanun** (19:2). The Chronicler made David's motivations clear by adding that the king wanted **to express his sympathy to Hanun** a second time (19:2). David had no ulterior motivations for sending his delegation to Hanun.

The tension of this episode grows as David's delegation arrived (19:2b). David's men came before the Ammonite king with every good intention.

The turning point of this episode consists of Hanun's nobles falsely accusing David. They argued that David wanted **to explore and spy out the country and overthrow it** (19:3).

Hanun followed the counsel of his nobles and insulted David. His men shaved the beards of David's delegation and cut their garments short, exposing their **buttocks** (19:4). These insults were not trifling matters (see Ezek. 5:1-4; Isa. 7:20; 50:6; Jer. 13:22,26; Nah. 3:5). They caused profound personal embarrassment for the delegates (see 19:5), and they seriously rebuffed David's attempt to maintain peace with the Ammonites.

This episode ends with David dealing with his delegates (19:5). The king gave them permission to remain outside Jerusalem until their beards grew (19:5). Once again, the passage emphasizes David's sympathetic spirit; it is his chief characteristic in this portion of the narrative. Nevertheless, dramatic tension rises because a question remains. What will David do to the Ammonite king? He showed kindness to the delegates, but how did he respond to Hanun? This portion of the narrative remains unresolved until the closing phase (see 20:1-3).

David Destroys Ammonite-Aramean Coalition (19:6-19)

The second major portion of this material focuses on the formation and destruction of a coalition between the Ammonites and the Arameans. Before David can punish Hanun for his insult, he must destroy the coalition formed to resist him.

Structure of 19:6-19

This section divides into four symmetrical steps (see figure 16). The beginning focuses on the formation of an Ammonite-Aramean coalition (19:6-7) and the ending describes its dissolution (19:19b). The two middle portions (19:8-15, 16-19a) amount to parallel episodes of David's victories over the coalition.

Ammonite-Aramean Coalition Formed (19:6-7)

The first clue of David's attitude toward the Ammonites is indirect. The Ammonites realized they had **become a stench in David's nostrils** (19:6). This expression appears elsewhere in Scripture to indicate a deep disgust and bitter hatred for someone (see 1 Sam. 13:4; 27:12; 2 Sam. 16:21). David was very angry with the Ammonites.

Even so, the Ammonite reaction was not to seek reconciliation with David. Instead they formed an alliance with the Arameans (19:6-7). The Chronicler added descriptions of this coalition to heighten the threat against David. He mentioned the large amounts of money paid for the Arameans (**a thousand talents of silver to hire chariots and charioteers** [19:6 // 2 Sam. 10:6]). He also shifted from attention to foot soldiers to **thirty-two thousand chariots and charioteers** (19:6 // 2 Sam. 10:6). These variations reveal how aggressively the Ammonites came against David. They were not interested merely in defending themselves, but in defeating David. Beyond this, these descriptions of David's enemies highlight a theme that appears many times in Chronicles. As this narrative will show, David conquered a great foe with the help of God (see *Introduction: 23) Victory and Defeat*).

Israel's First Victory (19:8-15)

Israel's first victory (19:8-15) focuses on Joab's successful handling of a battle outside the Ammonite city of Rabbah. It begins with David sending Joab to do battle (19:8). The Ammonite forces stood **at the entrance to their city** and the Aramean forces lined up for battle **in the open country** (19:9). Joab saw that he was in a precarious position with enemies **in front of him and behind him** and sent his troops in both directions (19:10-13). He encouraged **Abishai, his brother** to **be strong** (see 22:13; 28:10,20; 2 Chr. 15:7; 32:7) and to **fight bravely for** [their] **people and the cities of** [their] **God** (19:13). Despite the strength of the coalition, Joab's strategy worked; the Arameans fled and the Ammonites retreated **inside the city** (19:14-15a). The victory was so decisive that Joab returned home to Jerusalem (19:15b).

Israel's Second Victory (19:16-19a)

A second battle immediately followed (19:16-19a). This time the Arameans called for help from other Aramean groups (19:16). In response, **Shophach the commander of Hadadezer's army** (19:16) readied himself for battle. David aggressively advanced against these enemies; he **crossed the Jordan** (19:17a) before they could enter the land of Israel.

The Chronicler focused attention on David's personal involvement in the campaign. He added that **David** (Hebrew = 'he' [NAS, NRS, NKJ]) **formed his lines to meet the Arameans in battle** (19:17). The numbers of the dead indicate how great David's victory was on that day (19:18). He even killed the Aramean commander **Shophach** (19:18). Although various groups of Arameans had joined against David, they sued for peace after this battle. In fact, the Chronicler changed the language of Samuel (//2 Sam. 10:19) to put David in the center of the action once again; he wrote that the Arameans **made peace with David and became subject to him** (19:19a). Here the Chronicler described the blessing of peace in David's day which he hoped the post-exilic community could experience as well (see *Introduction: 23) Victory and Defeat*).

Ammonite-Aramean Coalition Broken (19:19b)

In balance with the formation of an Ammonite-Aramean coalition (19:6-7), 19:19b makes it plain that David utterly destroyed the alliance. Eventually, the Arameans **were not willing to help** (19:19b).

David Conquers King of Ammon (20:1-3)

The record of David's response to the Ammonites remains unresolved until 20:1-3. The Ammonites still remained safe within their city (see 19:15), but in this passage David defeated them.

The record of this battle divides into four balanced steps (see figure 16). Joab leads the army into battle (20:1a) and the army returns (20:3b). The middle portions of the episode balance as Joab destroys Rabbah (20:1b) and David receives the spoils (20:2-3a).

David waited for spring weather before mounting a large offensive strike against **Rabbah**, the capital of the Ammonites (20:1 see Deut. 3:11). The information of 2 Sam. 11:1a is repeated in 1 Chr. 20:1a nearly verbatim, but the new context changes its meaning. 2 Sam. 11:1a introduces the story of David, Bathsheba and Uriah, as well as Nathan's rebuke (see 2 Sam. 11:1b-12:25). The Chronicler omitted this negative material and used 2 Sam. 11:1a to introduce the positive story of David's final victory over the Ammonites (20:1-3).

The positive mood of this portion of Chronicles becomes evident in another omission. In 20:1b the Chronicler picked up the language of 2 Sam. 12:26 only to omit 2 Sam. 12:27-29. In 2 Sam. 12:27-29 David participated in the Ammonite defeat after Joab had nearly won the city without him. David came when Joab warned the king that he had better come if he wished to have any part in the victory.

The Chronicler did not hide Joab's role, but he avoided raising the question of David's ineptitude as it appears in Samuel.

This closing section (20:1-3) brings the readers back to motifs in the opening phase (19:1-5). There the king of the Ammonites insulted David. At this point, David took revenge directly on **their king** (20:2). He took the king's **crown** with its **gold** and **precious stones** and put it on his own head (20:2). By this means, the insult against David was repaid.

The king's crown was of great value, but David also received a **great quantity of plunder** (20:2) and captured laborers (20:3). David's successes were repeated in **all Ammonite towns** (20:3). This stress on David's achievements points once again to the central purpose of this section of Chronicles. David collected much from his battles which he dedicated for use in Solomon's temple (see 18:11).

David's Victories over the Philistines (20:4-8)

The Chronicler filled out his record of David's victories by referring to several battles with the Philistines. He omitted 2 Sam. 13:1-20:26 (see figure 18) to draw this material into close relation with other battles in this context (18:1-20:3 // 2 Sam. 21:15-22). Once again, 18:11 holds the key for understanding why the Chronicler chose to place this passage here. 18:11 specifically mentions the **Philistines** as one of those groups whose plunder was used in temple construction.

Comparison of 20:4-8 with 2 Sam. 13:1-21:22

The following table compares Samuel and Chronicles on a large scale (see figure 19).

1 Chr		2 Sam
——	David's Trouble (omitted)	13:1-20:26
——	Saulides Executed (omitted)	21:1-14
——	David Fights Philistines (omitted)	21:15-17
20:4-8	David Defeats Philistines (abbreviated)	21:18-22

Comparison of 1 Chr 20:4-8 with 2 Sam 13:1-21:22 (figure 19)

As this comparison indicates, the Chronicler omitted large portions of Samuel. He did not repeat the troubles within David's kingdom following his sin with Bathsheba (2 Sam. 13:1-20:26). He also omitted David's severe treatment of Saul's descendants (2 Sam. 21:1-14). These omissions followed his usual practice of focusing on the positive features of David's reign.

The account of Philistine defeats is nearly a third longer in Samuel (see 2 Sam. 21:15-22). The Chronicler left out 2 Sam. 21:15-17 probably because it reflected poorly on David's ability to wage war. There David 'became exhausted' (2 Sam. 21:15) and was rescued by his men (2 Sam. 21:17). In fact, David's own men insisted that he never go to battle again (2 Sam. 21:17). Apparently, the Chronicler did not repeat these verses because they did not fit with his emphasis on David's accomplishments as the great warrior who gained much plunder to be used in the temple.

Several smaller differences deserve comment. First, the Chronicler substituted **Gezer** (20:4) for the lesser known designation 'Gob' (2 Sam. 21:19). This anachronism demonstrates the Chronicler's interest in helping his readers understand. Second, he also added **and the Philistines** (Hebrew = 'they') **were subjugated** (20:4 // 2 Sam. 21:19). This terminology recalls the promise to David in 17:10 that God would subdue his enemies. Third, corruption of Samuel through textual transmission explains the differences between Elhanon killing 'Goliath the Gittite' (2 Sam. 21:19) and **Lahmi the brother of Goliath the Gittite** (20:5) (*Introduction: Translation and Transmission*). Fourth, the Chronicler acknowledged the omission of 2 Sam. 21:15-17 by also omitting the reference to 'four' Philistines in Gath (2 Sam. 21:22 // 20:8).

Structure of 20:4-8

This short passage divides into three sections, each containing a vignette of battle with the Philistines (see figure 16). These battles are marked off by the phrases 'in another battle' (20:5) and 'in still another battle' (20:6).

Victory in a Battle with Philistines (20:4)

In these closing records of David's wars, the Chronicler described three battles in which David was victorious over the Philistines. The first battle took place **at Gezer**, a city located between the hill country of Judah and the Philistine territory. When Joshua was distributing the land, Gezer was given to Ephraim (see 1 Chr. 7:28). Ephraim, however, never succeeded in driving out the Canaanites from the area (see Josh. 16:10). During the early stages of David's conflicts with the Philistines, he drove the Philistines back as far as Gezer (see 1 Chr. 14:16). It is only here that David drove them back beyond Gezer.

Victory in a Second Battle with Philistines (20:5)

The second battle focuses on the death of **the brother of Goliath**. As noted above, this passage is probably corrupted through textual transmission, but it is still clear that the man killed here was a great warrior (see *Introduction: Translation and Transmission*).

Victory in a Third Battle with Philistines (20:6-8)

The third conflict in this series of battles involved another giant warrior. Although this man **taunted Israel** (20:7 compare 1 Sam. 17:10ff; 2 Kgs. 18:19-37; 2 Chr. 32:9-19), David's nephew killed him (20:7). Finally, the **descendants of Rapha in Gath** also appeared among those killed by David and his family (20:8).

These records of David's various victories in war held at least two implications for the Chronicler's readers. First, David secured the land against enemies on all sides. This accomplishment encouraged the post-exilic community to remain faithful to God in hope of military security against their enemies (see *Introduction: 23) Victory and Defeat*). Second, David devoted the spoils of these battles to the temple. The Chronicler's readers should have learned from David's example what priority they had to give to supporting the temple and its service in their day (see *Introduction: 9) Temple Contributions).*

David Discovers the Temple Site (21:1-22:1)

The Chronicler has noted how David accepted his role as one to prepare for the temple (17:1-27); he has also explained how David's wars established security and materials for the temple (see 18:1-20:8). In this chapter the Chronicler recorded how David discovered the location of the temple. This discovery established a particular spot in Jerusalem as the only legitimate place of worship and sacrifice in the future, a vital fact for the post-exilic community.

This passage stands out from the rest of the Chronicler's portrait of David's reign in that it concentrates on David's major sin. For the most part, the Chronicler omitted David's failures in favor of focusing on his exemplary accomplishments (see *Part Two: Overview of the United Kingdom*). As we will see, however, the Chronicler actually emphasized the severity of David's sin in this passage more than the parallel account in Samuel. In the end, however, the Chronicler turned even this event into one of David's positive achievements. The manner in which David handled his circumstances modeled the kind of behavior and attitudes expected of the post-exilic readers as they sought to restore the worship of God in Israel.

Comparison of 21:1-22:1 with 2 Samuel 24:1-25

For the most part, the Chronicler closely followed the account of David's census in 2 Sam. 24:1-25. A number of insignificant variations occur due to minor problems in textual transmission (see *Introduction: Translation and Transmission*). Yet, several differences reveal the Chronicler's unique outlook on this event in David's life.

First, Samuel begins with 'again' (2 Sam. 24:1a) which is omitted in Chronicles (21:1). This introductory word in Samuel related David's census to another parallel passage in Samuel (see 2 Sam. 21:1-14). The Chronicler already omitted this earlier passage and therefore struck 'again' from his text.

Second, Samuel opens the passage with the record that God himself 'incited David' (2 Sam. 24:1a). The Chronicler, however, wrote **Satan rose up against Israel and incited David** (21:1). The Chronicler clarified that God's anger against Israel came through the instrumentality of Satan.

Third, the Chronicler reduced 'Israel and Judah' (2 Sam. 24:2) to **Israel** (21:1). This change reflected his outlook that David reigned over one nation including all the tribes of Israel (see *Introduction: 1) All Israel*).

Fourth, in 21:2 the Chronicler changed 'from Dan to Beersheba' (2 Sam. 24:2) to **from Beersheba to Dan**. The expression 'from Dan to Beersheba' (i.e. from North to South) is found many times in the Old Testament (see Judg. 20:1; 1 Sam. 3:20; 2 Sam. 3:10; 17:11; 24:2,15). The Chronicler, however, reversed the formula to **'from Beersheba to Dan'** (i.e. South to North) in three places (see 2 Chr. 19:4; 30:5). This shift reflected the Chronicler's conviction that Jerusalem and Judah were the center of post-exilic hopes.

Fifth, at least five features of the Chronicler's text heightened attention to David's sin.

1) The Chronicler added to Joab's objection, **'Why should he** (David) **bring guilt on Israel?'** (21:3).

2) In 21:4 the Chronicler omitted 2 Sam. 24:4b-8, thus removing the specific locations of Joab's itinerary. He then changed 'the entire land' (2 Sam. 24:5a) to his usual term **all Israel** to summarize the range of Joab's activity (21:4b). By this means, David's sin is shown to involve the entire nation, not just certain parts of it.

3) The Chronicler added to David's admission of guilt, **'Was it not I who ordered the fighting men to be counted? I am the one who has sinned** ...' (21:17).

4) Some ancient texts of Samuel suggest that 21:6-7a (// 2 Sam. 24:9-10) may have been lost from Samuel through textual transmission (*Introduction: Translation and Transmission*). If so, it should not be considered as an addition by the Chronicler. However, if it was added by the Chronicler, it points once again to the severity of David's sin by more clearly indicating God's displeasure with David's actions.

5) The Chronicler expanded 21:12 (// 2 Sam. 24:13) to emphasize that the **angel of the LORD** [was] **destroying throughout all the territory of Israel**. In so doing, the Chronicler drew more attention to the divine anger in response to David's sin.

Sixth, 21:12 has **three years of famine**, but 2 Sam. 24:13 reads 'seven years of famine' (see NIV marginal note). This variation probably occurred by corruption of Samuel through textual transmission (see *Introduction: Translation and Transmission*).

Seventh, at first glance 21:16,20 appear to be added in Chronicles. Yet, recent discoveries of ancient Hebrew texts of Samuel suggest strongly that the material in Chronicles originally appeared in Samuel but was lost from Samuel through textual transmission (*Introduction: Translation and Transmission*).

Eighth, the differences in the numbers of the census (1.1 million – Israel; 470,000 – Judah [1 Chr. 21:5]; 800,000 – Israel; 500,000 – Judah [2 Sam. 24:9]) probably result from corruption through textual transmission or differences in standards of calculation between the writer of Samuel and the Chronicler (see *Introduction: Translation and Transmission*).

Ninth, 21:25 reads **six hundred shekels of gold** which is significantly more than 'fifty shekels of silver' (2 Sam. 24:24). It is possible that the Chronicler intentionally used hyperbole here. (For the Chronicler's use of hyperbole see comments on 12:14.) Yet, it seems better to suppose that Samuel focuses on payment for 'the threshing floor and the oxen' (2 Sam. 24:24). The Chronicler, however, was probably concerned with a much larger purchase, **the site** (i.e. the entire land required for Solomon's temple which was much larger than the threshing floor). Perhaps David bought the area in several stages and the Chronicler gave the final sum.

Tenth, the most significant difference is the Chronicler's addition at the end of the narrative (21:26b-22:1). Several important elements appear in this addition.

1) David **called on the LORD and the LORD answered him with fire from heaven on the altar of burnt offering** (21:26b). As we will see, this scene confirms God's pleasure with David's discovery.

2) The Chronicler explained why David **sacrificed there** instead of following Mosaic instructions (21:28-30).

3) The most significant factor of this addition is David's explicit expression of discovery (22:1). He had found the place where the temple was to be built. This final element explained the primary way this narrative functions within the Chronicler's record of David's ideal reign.

Structure of 21:1-22:1

This episode divides into four large sections, each of which breaks into a number of smaller units (see figure 16). The drama begins with David's sinful census sparking divine displeasure (21:1-7a) and ends with David discovering the site of Solomon's temple because God showed mercy toward him (21:28-22:1). This movement from judgment to mercy took place through two intervening steps. David reacted to God's punishment against the nation (21:7b-14). Then David reacted to God's punishment against Jerusalem (21:15-27). These central episodes balance with each other in many ways. Both begin with God's judgment (21:7b, 15); David reacted with an inquiry (21:8,16-18); God instructed David (21:9-12,18); David complied (21:13, 19-26a), and received a response from God (21:14, 26b-27).

David's Cursed Infidelity (21:1-7)

This narrative begins with a description of David's sinful census and God's negative response. This portion balances with David's blessed devotion at the end of this chapter (21:28-22:1; see figure 16).

Structure of 21:1-7

The opening portion of this chapter divides into five symmetrical steps (see figure 16). The beginning and ending of this material focuses on heavenly realities which incite (21:1) and react to (21:7a) earthly events. The rising and falling action of the story balance each other. David orders a census (21:2-3) and receives a report of the census (2:5-6). The turning point of this episode is Joab's fulfillment of David's desire (21:4).

David Misled by Satan (21:1)

This remarkable story opens with the statement that **Satan rose up ... and incited David to take a census of Israel** (21:1). The Chronicler varied from 2 Sam. 24:1

('the anger of the LORD') to clarify that God did not directly tempt David to sin; he did this through the instrumentality of **Satan** (21:1).

The name **Satan** appears in the Old Testament in only three passages as a reference to an evil, angelic being (see Job 1:6-2:10; Zech. 3:1). In Hebrew his name means 'the accuser' and indicates one of the special roles this creature played in the heavenly court. Satan brought charges against the people of God. As the story of Job illustrates so clearly, one of his duties as 'accuser' was to tempt and test human beings. Much more attention is given to Satan in the New Testament. For example, the Greek transliteration of 'Satan' occurs 34 times and the word 'devil' appears 36 times. The New Testament makes it clear that Satan had such power over the nations that he was called the 'ruler of this world' (see John 12:31; 14:30). Though he and his demonic cohorts were disarmed by Christ (see Col. 2:15), he is still active and tries to thwart the purposes of God. Thus, he persecutes Christians (see Rev. 2:10), places counterfeit Christians in the church (see Matt. 13:24-30) and abuses Christians who are vulnerable to temptation (see Matt. 26:41; 1 Pet. 5:8-9). Satan hinders (see 1 Thess. 2:18) and buffets believers (see 2 Cor. 12:7). Although God himself tempts no one (see Jas. 1:13), God gives Satan permission to test believers (see Matt. 4:1-10; Luke 22:31-32; Rev. 2:10).

Satan incited David **to take a census of Israel** (21:1 // 2 Sam. 24:1 'Israel and Judah'). The Chronicler noted later that this census only included men older than twenty (27:23). We learn later that David's actions angered Joab (21:6) and God (21:7). It is difficult to know precisely what was wrong with David's census. It is evident that taking a census was not wrong in itself. Moses used a census to collect contributions for the tabernacle (see Ex. 30:11-16). Moses also numbered all of the firstborn of Israel (see Num. 3:40-43). Ezra 2 and Nehemiah 7 contain the numbers of various groups. For other census reported in Chronicles see 1 Chr. 27:23-24 and 2 Chr. 2:17.

David's action was sinful probably because of his motivations. The purpose of his census was to assess military strength. David gave orders to **Joab and the commanders of the troops** (21:2); Joab's report focused on **fighting men** (21:5). David's desire for a military census may have expressed a growing dissatisfaction with reliance on divine power in battle. Like many kings after him, David began to turn from trust in God to trust in his armies.

Later in this passage Joab refused to count the men of Levi (and Benjamin) (21:6); his exception suggests that David may have even ordered the counting of Levi for military purposes. If this was the case, it reveals David's disregard for the Law of Moses (see Num. 1:49) and his disinterest in having the Lord care for his military needs. This evil motivation may explain why Joab objected so strongly.

David Orders Census (21:2-3)

In all events, David ordered Joab to take a census (21:2-3). The king wanted to know the count of all potential fighters **from Beersheba to Dan** (21:2). As noted above, the Chronicler reversed the more common expression in 2 Sam. 24:2 ('from

Dan to Beersheba') as he did elsewhere (see 2 Chr. 30:5; compare 2 Chr. 19:4). By placing the southern region first, he indicated his special focus on the South as the heart of the nation.

Although Joab objected to David's command, he demonstrated his support for David's throne by introducing his objection with a blessing: **May the LORD multiply** [David's] **troops** (21:3). Similarly, no less than three times, Joab addressed David as **my lord** (21:3).

Nevertheless, Joab's response revealed the Chronicler's negative outlook on David's actions. He added that Joab asked, **'Are they not all my lord's servants?'** (21:3) The Lord had already put the entire nation at David's disposal. In much the same way, the Chronicler also added that Joab objected, **'Why should he bring guilt on Israel?'** (21:3).

Joab's charge is enlarged in Chronicles to explain why God reacted so strongly to what may appear to have been a mere peccadillo. From his point of view, failure to trust the Lord in military matters was a serious violation to be avoided by his readers. As they faced military threats all around them, they must not turn to human strength as David did.

Joab Fulfills Census (21:4)

Despite his objections, Joab fulfilled David's order. He **left and ... came back to Jerusalem.** His itineration forms the turning point of this episode.

David Receives Census (21:5-6)

Joab returned with the **number of fighting men** (21:4-5). The numbers in Chronicles (21:5) appear significantly larger than in 2 Sam. 24:9. **One million one hundred thousand ... and four hundred and seventy thousand** are very large for this context (21:5). Several interpretive options are possible. (For the Chronicler's use of large numbers of soldiers, see comments on 12:24-37.) It is possible that the Chronicler intentionally employed hyperbole to depict the enormity of David's military might. (For the Chronicler's use of hyperbole, see comments on 12:14.) Mentioning large and skilled armies is one way in which the Chronicler often exalted faithful kings (see 1 Chr. 12:24-40; 21:5; 27:1-15; 2 Chr. 12:3; 13:3-4,17; 14:9; 17:12-19; 25:5-6; 26:13; 28:6-8). It is also possible, however, that these numbers may have been corrupted through textual transmission (see *Introduction: Translation and Transmission*).

The text gives special attention to the fact that **Joab did not include Levi and Benjamin** (21:6). The Chronicler noted the limits of Joab's census in 27:24a. Mosaic legislation forbade the counting of Levi for military service (see Num. 1:49). The reason for omitting Benjamin, however, is not clear. Joab initially resisted the king's order and made sure not to violate Mosaic Law. For this reason, only David could be blamed for the terrible results that came upon the nation.

David Angers God (21:7a)

The closing scene of this episode introduces the horror with which the rest of this narrative must deal. David's sin was **evil in the sight of God**. Just as this episode began with a glimpse of heavenly realities influencing earthly action (see 21:1), so it ends with a heavenly reaction to earthly action. God strongly disapproved of what David had done.

David's Confrontation with God over Israel (21:7b-14)

The story of David's census moves next to David's encounter with God concerning the entire nation (21:7b-14). This material balances with the king's encounter over Jerusalem (21:15-27; see figure 16).

Structure of 21:7b-14

This portion of the chapter divides into five symmetrical steps (see figure 16). This passage begins and ends with David under God's punishment (21:7b, 14). The turning point is the revelation by Gad (21:9-12). Prior to this revelation, David humbly inquires (21:8); afterwards, he humbly complies (21:13).

David Punished by God (21:7b)

The Chronicler began with the simple note that God **punished Israel** (21:7b). The nature of this punishment is not altogether clear at this point, but the dramatic tension of the passage is evident. The entire nation was suffering divine displeasure because of David's sin. In the Old Testament, kings had a special representative function before God. Their righteous deeds often brought blessings to the nation, but their sins also brought wrath on the entire nation (see 1 Kgs. 18:16-18; 2 Chr. 16:7-9; 1 Kgs. 21:10-15; 2 Kgs. 19:20-36; 20:6).

David's Humble Inquiry (21:8)

In response to divine displeasure against Israel, David confessed, **'I have sinned greatly,'** and asked for forgiveness (21:8). David admitted that he had done **a very foolish thing** (21:8). Although these words come from the parallel account in Samuel, they coincided with the Chronicler's perspective on this event. David's rejection of God as his military security was contrary to wisdom derived from national experiences of the past (see Deut. 2:32-37; 3:1-7; Josh. 6:1-21; 8:1-17; 10:6-15; 10:28-43; 11:1-9; Judg. 7:1-8:12) and from David's own military encounters (see 18:1-20:18).

David's Instructions from Gad (21:9-12)

In response to David's humility, God spoke to **Gad, David's seer** (21:9). Gad appears several times in this chapter and elsewhere in the Chronicler's history. He provided David with prophetic counsel after the king first fled from Saul as a young man (see 1 Sam. 22:5). He advised on the proper arrangement of Levitical music in worship (see 2 Chr. 29:25). He is also credited with having written a record of David's actions (see 1 Chr. 29:29).

The tension of this episode rises as Gad first received the word of God (21:9-10) and then reported it to David (21:11-12). David was offered a choice of three kinds of chastisement: (1) **three years of famine**, (2) **three months ... before your enemies**, or (3) **three days of the sword of the Lord** (21:12).

At first glance, it may seem that the chastisement of lesser time (**three days**) was the lightest sentence, but the severity of this option is revealed in the explanation that follows. It would consist of a **plague in the land**, and **the angel of the Lord ravaging every part of Israel** (21:12). The potential of this option was great. Indeed, 70,000 men fell dead and Jerusalem itself came near utter destruction (see 21:14-15).

David's Humble Compliance (21:13)

Despite its horrible potential, David chose punishment directly from God. His reasoning was remarkable and indicated a significant shift of disposition. When ordering the census, David displayed distrust in God. Now he selected chastisement from God because he believed God's **mercy is very great**. David's trust in God had been renewed.

David Punished by God (21:14)

God's response to David was true to his threat. He **sent a plague** and **seventy thousand men of Israel fell dead**. Despite his repentance, David had to suffer a period of severe consequence for his violation of trust in the Lord. By including this fact in his account, the Chronicler reminded his post-exilic readers that they too had suffered many consequences for rebellion against God (see *Introduction: 10) Divine Activity*).

David's Confrontation with God over Jerusalem (21:15-27)

At this point, the narrative narrows its outlook from the whole nation to Jerusalem. In balance with 21:7b-14, the text repeats a scenario of inquiry and divine response (see figure 16).

Structure of 21:15-27

This portion of the chapter also divides into a five-step symmetrical pattern (see figure 16). At first, David receives punishment (21:15), but this punishment ends with the final step (21:26b-27). Again, the revelation from Gad forms the turning point (21:18). David humbly inquires of God (21:16-17) and humbly complies (21:19-26a).

David Punished by God (21:15)

In this section of the chapter, the spatial framework narrows from the entire countryside to **Jerusalem.** God **sent an angel to destroy Jerusalem**, i.e., to extend the plague to Jerusalem. Yet, just as David had hoped (21:13), at the last moment God was merciful and ordered the angel to **withdraw** (21:15).

The spatial focus of the narrative narrows further when the angel arrives **at the threshing floor of Araunah**. **Araunah** was a Jebusite whose name is spelled 'Ornan' in the Hebrew of Chronicles (see NAS, NRS, NKJ), but is spelled 'Araunah' in Samuel (see 2 Sam. 24:16,18,20,21-24). He owned a threshing floor and its surrounding properties in the vicinity of Jerusalem. This geographical site became the chief concern of the rest of this section.

David's Humble Inquiry (21:16-17)

As God ordered his angel to stop, David saw the angel with **a drawn sword in his hand extended over Jerusalem** (21:16). The angel paused to wait for a final decision from God as to whether Jerusalem would be destroyed. As a result, **David and the elders clothed in sackcloth, fell facedown**. Sackcloth was clothing made from goat or camel hair. It was sometimes worn as a loincloth (see Gen. 37:34) or as an outer garment (see 2 Kgs. 19:1). Sackcloth was also worn during times of sorrow and mourning in grievous conditions (see 2 Sam. 21:10; Esth. 4:1). Similarly, as is evident in this passage, sackcloth was used to express sorrow and repentance because of sin (see Neh. 9:1).

David asked for mercy a second time (21:17-18; see 21:8). This time, however, his heart turned from concern for his own well-being to the interests of the nation. He confessed, **'Was it not I ... ? I am the one** ...' (21:17). David pled with God to treat this matter as his own personal offense. He then asked God to show mercy to the nation and offered himself as a substitute. **'Let your hand fall upon me and my family'** (21:17). Those words revealed the depth of David's contrition.

This portion of the episode spoke to the post-exilic community in a number of ways. Those who led the people of God in the Chronicler's day were to see David's example as a model of attitudes and behaviors they should have in their own day. They had turned from God as David; they had been punished as David. Now they sought to be restored. The way of restoration appeared in David's sincere contrition.

David's Instructions from Gad (21:18)

In response to David's profound repentance, the **angel of the LORD** told **Gad** to have David build an altar **on the threshing floor of Araunah the Jebusite**. Sacrifices had to be made before relief from guilt could come to the nation.

David's Humble Compliance (21:19-26a)

David complied with the directive given **in the name of the LORD** (21:19; see *Introduction: 11) Name of God*) and purchased the threshing floor. Several aspects of this account allude to Abraham's purchase of a burial site for Sarah (see Gen. 23:3-20). Araunah offered to give the land, but David insisted on buying it. The reason for David's insistence is stated explicitly. He argued, **'I will not take for the LORD what is yours'** (21:24). Moreover, as he explained, he would not **'sacrifice a burnt offering that costs** [him] **nothing'** (21:24). Once again, the passage emphasizes David's sincerity and desire to give of himself in payment for his sin.

Once the property was purchased, David **built an altar to the LORD there and**

sacrificed burnt offerings and fellowship offerings (21:26). David took the necessary steps for the return of harmony and peace between himself and God.

In 21:26a, the Chronicler began to diverge significantly from the account of Samuel (// 2 Sam. 24:25). For the most part he added information not found in Samuel. One prominent feature of the Chronicler's addition is that during the sacrificial rituals, David **called on the LORD**, asking for God's forgiveness and help (21:26a).

David's actions in this passage were exemplary for the Chronicler's post-exilic readers. They were to respond appropriately to prophetic instruction, acknowledge their guilt, prepare for proper worship, and invoke God's help. Despite David's failure in this passage, in the end he served as a model of righteousness.

David Forgiven by God (21:26b-27)

The Chronicler also added that in response to David's sacrifices and prayer, God sent **fire from heaven on the altar of burnt offering** (21:26b). The descent of fire onto the altar took place in the Old Testament only three other times (see Lev. 9:24; 1 Kgs. 18:38; 2 Chr. 7:1; see also Judg. 6:21;). On each occasion it displayed extraordinary pleasure from God toward his people. The Chronicler added this element to his account of David's census in order to highlight God's approval of David. The fire from heaven demonstrated that God enthusiastically approved of David's sacrifices.

The Chronicler skillfully balanced the end of this passage with its beginning. In 21:16 the angel stood with sword drawn over Jerusalem. In 21:27, the angel **put his sword back into its sheath**. The Chronicler added this note to make it clear that the chastisement of Israel was over.

As we have seen, 21:7b-14 and 21:15-27 are parallel in many ways (see figure 16), but the end of the episodes are strikingly different. Instead of sending chastisement against Israel a second time, God forgave David. This contrast spoke plainly of the hope of forgiveness for the post-exilic readers. If they emulated David's humility, they too would receive this blessing.

David's Blessed Devotion (21:28-22:1)

The Chronicler's account of David's census ends with more added material. In contrasting balance with the opening of this chapter (see figure 16), these verses draw attention to the most important aspect of this passage. David came upon a great discovery: the place God ordained for the temple.

Structure of 21:28-22:1

This portion of the account divides into three steps (see figure 16). This material actually amounts to two actions: David's sacrifice (21:28) and his discovery (22:1). Between these actions is an explanatory authorial comment (21:29-30).

David Offers Sacrifices (21:28)

Once David saw that God had shown him such favor **on the threshing floor of Araunah**, he **offered sacrifices there**. The concern of this verse is not so much with the fact that David sacrificed, but on the place where he sacrificed. David did something extraordinary. He sacrificed at a place that had not been approved beforehand by God. In fact, a pedantic application of Mosaic Law would have ruled his actions illegitimate. The Chronicler began his description of this new place for sacrifice by noting that it was not until David saw God's grace bestowed at this place that he sacrificed there.

David's Actions Explained (21:29-30)

The Chronicler paused to give an authorial comment explaining further why David had not sacrificed at the tabernacle. This matter was important to him because he normally held both David and the Law of Moses as his standards of righteousness. Now one standard seemed to conflict with the other (see *Introduction: 14) Standards*). Earlier, the Chronicler noted that the Levites serving in Jerusalem away from the Tabernacle only served by playing music. Sacrificial duties were performed in Gibeon (see comments on 16:4-6). The Chronicler admitted that **the tabernacle ... and the altar of burnt offering were at that time in the high place at Gibeon** (21:29). In the strictest sense, David should have made his sacrifices there, but his circumstances were very unusual. As the Chronicler explained, David **was afraid of the sword of the angel of the LORD** (21:30). In other words, David was in an emergency situation and had to appease divine anger as quickly as possible. As in other incidents, the Chronicler showed himself not to be a pedantic legalist. Priorities arising from particular circumstances often led to the approval of unusual and otherwise prohibited behavior (compare 2 Chr. 5:11-12; 30:2).

David Declares His Discovery (22:1)

David drew a conclusion from his encounter with God. He had seen **that the LORD had answered him on the threshing floor** (21:28). Therefore, he concluded, **'The house of the LORD God is to be here, and also the altar of burnt offering for Israel.'** David now understood that the threshing floor of Araunah was to be the site for Solomon's temple.

In these closing words from David, the Chronicler established the central place of worship for Israel even in his own day. Despite the destruction of the temple in Jerusalem, its central role as the place of worship was still in effect in post-exilic times. David's example confirmed the Chronicler's concern with re-establishing the temple in Jerusalem. The site was blessed by God as the place of sacrifice.

David's Commission of Temple Construction (22:2-19)

The Chronicler now came to the fourth major step in David's preparation for the temple (see figure 16). David accepted his commission to prepare for Solomon (17:1-27); he secured the nation and collected much wealth for the temple (18:1-20:8); he also discovered the site of the temple (21:1-22:1). At this point, the Chronicler turned to David's transfer of the temple project to Solomon (22:2-19). This passage balances with 18:1-20:8 as David commissioned the use of the materials he had acquired through war.

Comparison of 22:2-19 with Samuel and Kings

This passage comes entirely from the Chronicler's hand. He may have used other sources, but with the exception of several minor allusions, he did not depend on Samuel, Kings, or other portions of Scripture.

Structure of 22:2-19

David's commission of temple construction divides into three parallel reports (see figure 16). Each of these reports focuses on different aspects of David's commission to build. He explained his preparations (22:2-5), commissioned Solomon (22:6-16), and ordered Israel's leaders to support Solomon (22:17-19). Each of these passages contains a speech by David concerning Solomon as the temple builder (see 22:5a, 7-16, 18-19).

David's Extensive Preparations for Solomon (22:2-5)

The end of this passage reveals the main concerns of this section; David **made extensive preparations before his death** (22:5b). The Chronicler touched on three kinds of provisions: foreign masons (22:2), metals (22:3), and wood (22:4). David recalled this threefold provision in his words to Solomon later in this chapter (see 22:15). It should be noted that David included foreigners among his workers (22:2; see *Introduction: 3) International Relations*). Their presence in David's day set a precedent for the Chronicler's readers.

Several times the quantity of David's provisions comes into focus. **He provided a large amount of iron ... more bronze than could be weighed ... more cedar logs than could be counted ... large numbers of them** (22:3-4). The Chronicler employed these hyperboles to engender wonder and amazement at how much David had done. (For the Chronicler's use of hyperbole, see comments on 12:14.) His temple preparations were not minimal; they were astonishing. In much the same way, the Chronicler's post-exilic readers were to provide astounding supplies for the temple in their day.

David explained why he had made these preparations (22:5a). In all likelihood David said these words before or as he gathered the provisions of 22:4. If this is correct, then the expression **'David said'** (22:5a) should be translated, 'David had said.' The text does not designate to whom David had spoken. Without a clear recipient of speech these words can mean 'to speak to oneself' or 'to think to oneself'. Later David spoke to Solomon (see 22:6-16) and to the leaders of Israel (see 22:17-19). It is possible that David had spoken aloud to the **aliens** he gathered (22:2), but it is also possible that David had merely spoken or thought to himself. If this latter understanding is correct, we have here one of the few times the Chronicler revealed the inner thoughts of a character to his readers (see 1 Chr. 13:12; 14:2; 2 Chr. 32:1).

David reflected that the purpose of his extensive preparations was to aid Solomon. He claimed that **Solomon is young and inexperienced** and the temple is to be **of great magnificence and fame and splendor** (22:5). David was convinced that the task ahead was more than Solomon could handle. He knew that the only way for Solomon to succeed was for materials to be provided for him.

David's actions demonstrated that any temple worthy of the Lord would require extensive preparations. The temple foundation initially built by Zerubbabel disappointed many of the people who saw it because it was not as grand as Solomon's temple (see Ezra 3:12-13). The Chronicler's report of David's words encouraged his readers to continue expanding the temple to the grand scale it deserved despite the enormous efforts required.

David's Commission of Solomon (22:6-16)

The Chronicler turned next to David's commission of Solomon. This speech was one of two in which David spoke directly to his son (see 28:9-16; 20-21). Here the speech is relatively private; the second speech occurred in public ceremony. The record of David's words divides into three parts: heading (22:6), background (22:7-10), and exhortation (22:11-16).

The heading of this section characterizes the speech that follows. Above all, David **charged** [Solomon] **to build a house for the LORD** (22:6). In the background to his charge (22:7-10), David summarized the events of 17:1-14 (// 2 Sam. 7:1-16). He described how he had desired **to build a house for the Name of the LORD** (22:7; see also 22:8,10,19). Like a number of biblical traditions before him, the Chronicler emphasized that the temple was the place of God's Name, his accessible power. He stressed this motif to draw the attention of his post-exilic readers to the source of divine help in their day (see 2 Chr. 6:18-21; see also *Introduction: 11) Name of God*). Even so, David recalled that his personal desire to build was countered by **the word from the LORD** (22:8a).

On several occasions David recalled the words of Nathan as they appear in 17:4-15. God told Nathan that David was prohibited from building the temple (compare 22:8 and 17:4). God also told Nathan that he would raise up one of David's sons (compare 22:9 and 17:11), who would build a temple for the Lord (compare 22:10 and 17:12). Moreover, Nathan spoke of God making David's son his own son (compare 22:10 and 17:13), and he promised to establish his throne forever (compare 22:10 and 17:12,14). Through these allusions the Chronicler demonstrated once again the importance of Nathan's prophecy. Prophetic speech validated David's transfer of power to Solomon much as it had legitimized the transfer from Saul to David (see 11:3; see also *Introduction: 15) Prophets*).

Nevertheless, one element in this passage does not appear in the earlier report of Nathan's revelation. 22:8-9 explains why God did not permit David to build the temple. David had **shed much blood** and **fought many wars** (22:8). As we have already seen, the Chronicler emphasized David's wars as a resource for collecting materials for temple construction (see 18:11). Even so, David's extensive involvement in warfare disqualified him from building the temple.

This divine directive stems from Mosaic legislation. As Deut. 12:8-11 indicates, centralization of worship was to take place only after conquest had ended and the land was occupied in peace. This pattern was reflected in other ancient Near Eastern cultures. Many of Israel's neighbors believed that their gods entered their temples only after they had destroyed their enemies in warfare. Similar associations between peace and temple construction appear in several passages (see 2 Sam. 7:1; 1 Kgs. 5:12). Solomon, whose name is derived from the Hebrew word 'peace', would be **a man of peace and rest**; he would experience the blessing of **peace from all his enemies** (22:9; see also 22:18). David's reign was not sufficiently separated from warfare to permit him to build a place for God's Name on earth.

Perhaps the Chronicler added this material in response to opponents of temple construction and expansion in his own day. If David did not build, then why should they? Here the Chronicler pointed out clearly that the only reason David did not move forward was because God stopped him (see 17:1-27).

David turned next to exhort Solomon (22:11-16). The first portion of this exhortation (22:11-13) alludes to God's word to Joshua at the beginning of the conquest of Canaan (see Josh. 1:1-9). Both Joshua and Solomon were admonished to keep God's Law (compare 22:12-13 and Josh. 1:7-8). In obeying the Law they would be enabled to act wisely (compare 22:12 and Josh. 1:8) and find **success** (compare 22:13 and Josh. 1:8). This outlook on the function of the Law fits well with the Chronicler's overall perspective on the subject. Obedience to God's standards brought blessings to his people (see *Introduction: 14) Standards*). In addition, both Joshua and Solomon were told not to fear or be discouraged, but rather to be **strong and courageous** (22:13; see 19:13; 28:10, 20; 2 Chr. 15:7; 32:7 and Josh. 1:6,7,9). Finally, both men were encouraged to **begin the work** (compare 22:16 and Josh. 1:1) for God was **with** [them] (compare 22:11,16 and Josh. 1:5,9). For God to be 'with' someone meant that God would fight for them and give them success (see 2 Chr. 13:12; see also *Introduction: 10) Divine Activity*). By including these allusions to Joshua, the Chronicler tied Solomon's reign to David as Joshua's leadership was tied to Moses. Even as Moses and Joshua joined together in the one project of claiming the promised land for Israel, David and Solomon joined together in the one project of temple construction.

The last portion of David's exhortation returns to the theme of how much David had provided for Solomon (22:14-16a; see 22:2-5). Once again, the extensive quantity of David's preparations receives emphasis. The amounts of money – **a hundred thousand talents of gold** (about 3,750 tons [3,450 metric tons]), **a million talents of silver** (about 37,500 tons [about 34,500 metric tons]) (22:14) appear enormous. Solomon's annual base revenue was only '666 talents of gold' (1 Kgs. 10:14). That the other metals were described as **too great to be weighed** (22:14) and the craftsmen are said to be **beyond number** (22:16) suggests that all these amounts were intentionally exaggerated to stress how much David provided. (For the Chronicler's use of hyperbole, see comments on 12:14.) Solomon was told he simply had to **add to** what David had done (22:14). Nothing more was needed but for Solomon to **begin the work** (22:16). He would succeed because God was **with him** (22:16), fighting for the king against all opposition (see also *Introduction: 10) Divine Activity*).

David's Order for Leaders to Help Solomon (22:17-19)
The Chronicler closed this section with a scene in which David explained his goals to **all the leaders of Israel** (22:17). The purpose of his speech is summarized as an attempt to get them **to help his son Solomon**. In line with his concern over Solomon's inexperience (see 22:5), David recognized that his son needed the assistance of Israel's leaders. The task was not the exclusive responsibility of the royal family; **all the leaders** were to be involved.

David spoke to the leaders about two matters. First, he reminded them of all he and God had done for them. He said that God had been **'with you'** (22:18; see 22:11,16) because God had fought for Israel against her enemies (see 2 Chr. 13:12; see also *Introduction: 10) Divine Activity*). As a result, God **granted you rest** (22:18; see *Introduction: 23) Victory and Defeat*). But when did these blessings occur? Through what instrument? David made his viewpoint plain. The blessing of God came to the nation when God gave **the inhabitants of the land over to** [David] (22:18). As the Chronicler pointed out a number of times, David's accomplishments as king were the source of great blessings to Israel (see *Introduction: 4-9) King and Temple*).

On the basis of these blessings, David called the leaders of Israel to carry out his plan for temple construction (22:19). David desired no mere outward compliance with his orders. He exhorted the leaders to **devote** [their] **heart and soul to seeking the LORD**. Similar terminology appears many times in Chronicles to indicate a deep seated religious zeal. This devotion is to be from the **heart** and **soul** (see *Introduction: 16) Motivations*) and it is to involve **seeking the LORD** for help and guidance (see *Introduction: 19) Seeking*). Of course, this religious zeal was to show itself in action. The leaders were to **begin to build** so that they might also **bring the ark ... and the sacred articles ... into the temple**.

Once again the Chronicler used traditional language and designated the ark as **the ark of the covenant of the LORD** (22:19). For the significance of this designation in Chronicles see *Introduction: 13) Covenant*.

David mentioned that the temple would be **for the Name of the LORD** (22:19). The Chronicler focused on the presence of God's Name in the temple on a number of occasions. The Name of God was the invocable presence of God. God's people could approach the transcendent God of all creation in the temple (see *Introduction: 11) Name of God*).

The Chronicler undoubtedly reported this address to inspire and direct his post-exilic readers. Support for the temple was not exclusively the responsibility of the royal Davidic family. All the leaders of post-exilic Israel were to help the royal family. Those leaders of Israel who hesitated to support efforts related to the temple opposed the directives of David himself. Moreover, they denied themselves access to the powerful Name of God. The post-exilic readers were called to carry out David's commission just as the leaders in David's day.

David Transfers Power and Responsibility to Solomon (23:1-29:25)
After his commission to build, David gathered the leaders of Israel and publicly appointed Solomon to the throne of Israel so he could take up his role as temple builder. This material balances with 17:1-27 in that it brings to completion the commission David received as the one who would prepare for Solomon (see figure 16).

Comparison of 23:1-29:25 with Samuel and Kings
These chapters make up the Chronicler's largest single addition to Samuel and Kings. 22:1-29:30 amounts to the Chronicler's substitution for 1 Kgs. 1:1-2:9 and 2:13-3:3.

The book of Kings indicates that the transfer of the scepter to Solomon took place amid severe political struggles (see 1 Kgs. 1:1-2:46). Adonijah sought the throne and David's court divided between supporters of Adonijah and Solomon. Once this initial struggle was over, Solomon eliminated his political opponents.

The omission of these events reveals the Chronicler's unique perspective. The political intrigues of Solomon's rise were insignificant to his purposes. Instead of reviewing how Solomon overcame great obstacles to become king, the Chronicler focused on the way in which David had purposed to make Solomon his successor.

Structure of 23:1-29:25
This material divides into two large sections introduced by a title (see figure 16). The opening verse explains that David made Solomon king (23:1). This transfer of power divides into two large segments. First, lists summarize those whom David assembled to make Solomon king (23:2-27:34). Second, the Chronicler recorded what occurred at the assembly (28:1-29:25).

David Makes Solomon King (23:1)
This verse indicates that the Chronicler had arrived at David's last act as the king of Israel. As the rest of this section will demonstrate, David made his son king for the expressed purpose of building the temple.

Those Whom David Gathered (23:2-27:34)
The Chronicler began his record of the transfer of power to Solomon with extensive lists of those whom David gathered for his assembly. The considerable length and details of these lists create an atmosphere of splendid national unity in support of David and Solomon (see *Introduction: 1) All Israel*).

The end of this section indicates that this final assembly of David's reign was the time when Israel acknowledged Solomon as king and Zadok as priest (see 29:22). In all likelihood, the Chronicler had in mind the events of 1 Kings 1:38-53 at which time David publicly acknowledged Solomon as king against the claims of Adonijah. It is apparent, therefore, that the Chronicler saw Adonijah's opposition to Solomon as relatively insignificant (see 1 Kgs. 1:5-11).

Structure of 23:2-27:34

The record of those whom David gathered begins with an introductory summary followed by two lists (see figure 16). The Chronicler's lists first identify the various groups gathered (23:2). Priests and Levites are described in four segments (23:2-26:32). Military and civilian leaders comprise the second grouping (27:1-34). The descriptions of the assembly itself follow (28:1-29:25) and indicate that the preceding lists are only representative (elders/officers of the tribe: 28:1; 29:6,24; military commanders: 28:1; 29:6,24; managers of royal property: 28:1; 29:6; sons of David: 29:24). These four chapters portray the assembly as including the full range of Israel's leadership.

Introduction (23:2)

This lengthy list forms a general introduction which mentions **all the leaders of Israel, as well as the priests and Levites**. The terminology **all** emphasized the theme of unified support for Solomon along the lines of the Chronicler's 'all Israel' theme (see *Introduction: 1) All Israel*). The three categories of **leaders, priests**, and **Levites** appear in the lists that follow but in reverse order: Levites and priests (23:3-26:32) and leaders (27:1-34).

Levites and Priests (23:3-26:32)

The Chronicler first listed the Levites and priests. This material divides into five main parts: the registry and divisions of Levites (23:3-5), Levites and priests who worked closely together (23:6-24:31), Levitical singers (25:1-31), gatekeepers (26:1-19), and officials and judges (26:20-32).

Registries and Divisions of Levites (23:3-5)

These registries and divisions of Levites (23:3-5) include only those Levites who were **thirty years old or more** (23:3). In an effort to guide the practices of his post-exilic readers, however, the Chronicler noted later that **the last instructions of David** were to count **those twenty years old or more** (23:27).

The number of Levites was set at **thirty-eight thousand** (23:3). It is possible to understand these numbers in ways that considerably lower the actual count. (For the Chronicler's use of large numbers of soldiers, see comments on 12:24-37.)

David divided the Levites into four groups presented here in the order of their sizes (23:3-5). Each group is then described in expanded form later in this section (see 23:6-26:32). Comparisons between this summary and the following expanded lists help to identify each group (see figure 20).

The largest group (24,000) were to **supervise the work of the temple** (23:4). This designation is not altogether clear. From 23:6-24:31, however, it seems best to assume that the Chronicler was indicating those Levites who directly assisted the twenty-four divisions of priests. The second group of Levites (6,000) were to be **officials and judges** (23:4). This group is described more fully in 26:20-32. The third group of Levites (4,000) consists of **gatekeepers** (23:5). For duties performed by gatekeepers see comments on 26:1-19. This division appears again in 26:1-32.

Survey of Divisions (23:3-5)	Lists (23:6-26:32)
Supervising (23:4)	Levites with Priests (23:6-24:31)
Officials and Judges (23:4)	Singers (25:1-31)
Gatekeepers (23:5)	Gatekeepers (26:1-19)
Singers (23:5)	Officials and Judges (26:20-32)

Comparison of 1 Chr 23:3-5 with 23:6-26:32 (figure 20)

The fourth group consists of those who **praise the Lord with musical instruments** (23:5); they are the **singers** mentioned in 25:1-31.

Priests and Levites Together (23:6-24:31)

These expanded lists include both Levites and priests (**sons of Aaron** [24:1]). These Levites stand out because they served alongside of the Aaronic priests. As the Chronicler noted several times in this section, they **served in the temple** (23:24), and were **in the service of the temple of the Lord** and performed **other duties at the house of God** (23:28). All of their work was done **for the service of the temple** (23:32).

These lists begin with the three familial divisions of the descendants of Levi (23:6-27); they then turn to the responsibilities of Levites who served in close conjunction with the priests (23:28-32); next the descendants of Aaron (the priests) appear (24:1-19); finally the Chronicler added another list of Levites not mentioned previously (24:20-31).

Levites Divided by Families (23:6-27)

The familial divisions of the tribe of Levi (23:7-27) begin with an introduction (23:6), and mention **Gershonites** (23:7-11), the **sons of Kohath** (23:12-20), and the **sons of Merari** (23:21-23). These divisions are followed by a concluding explanatory note (23:24-27). For a fuller description of the family divisions of the tribe of Levi see *Introduction: Appendix A – The Families of Levi.*

With only a few exceptions, most of the names appearing here do not occur in the Chronicler's earlier genealogies of Levi (see 6:1-80). These differences can be understood when we remember that the terminology **sons of** can mean 'descendants of.' Biblical genealogies frequently skip generations without notice (see *Part One: Overview of Genealogies*). The Chronicler's purpose was not to give a comprehensive lineage, but to show that descendants of all Levitical families oversaw the work of the temple. Moreover, he wanted to point out that representatives of all the Levitical families supported the transfer of power to Solomon.

23:13 reflects the Chronicler's keen interest in the details of David's arrangements. He listed the descendants of Aaron in the next chapter (24:1-19), but paused here to indicate that the Aaronic priests were specially **set apart ... to consecrate ... offer sacrifice ... minister ... and to pronounce blessings in his name forever** (23:13). Like Ezekiel before him (see Ezek. 40:46; 43:19; 44:15-16; 48:11), the Chronicler believed David's order established that only the Zadokite priests had responsibilities for the central operations of temple service. No other family was to usurp that role. Moreover, the Chronicler highlighted once again that these ministries were to be performed **in his name** (23:13). The presence of God's Name in the temple provided accessibility to divine presence and power (see *Introduction: 11) Name of God*). This expansion of the Kohathite genealogy indicated the Chronicler's desire to see the temple service of the post-exilic community follow the Davidic pattern.

The Chronicler also added a notice regarding the **sons of Moses** (23:14-20) and listed the names of members of this family serving in the days of David (23:15-20). Once again, the Chronicler's concern with Solomon's widespread support and for the re-ordering of post-exilic worship is evident.

The familial divisions of Levi close with an explanation (23:24-27). Earlier David only registered **Levites thirty years old or more** (23:3). At this point the text explains that David began to count the Levites from **twenty years old** (23:24). The king changed the minimum registration age once the ark was in Jerusalem and **the Levites no longer need to carry the tabernacle** (23:26). He felt younger Levites could carry on the services in Jerusalem. Apparently, the services in Jerusalem were expanded to the point that more workers were needed. This closing remark also reflected the Chronicler's concern with the age of Levitical service in his own day.

Levitical Duties Alongside Priests (23:28-32)

Following his broad list of Levites serving alongside the Aaronic priests, the Chronicler added a more detailed description of their duties (23:28-32). In general terms, these Levites were **to help Aaron's descendants** (23:28). In other words, they were servants assisting the priests in their many duties. The Chronicler listed eleven specific areas of duties for these Levites: (1) **courtyards** (23:28), (2) **side rooms** (23:28), (3) **purification** (23:28), (4) **other duties** (23:28), (5) **bread set out** (23:29), (6) **flour for the grain offerings** (23:29), (7) **unleavened wafers** (23:29), (8) **baking and mixing** (23:29), (9) **all measurements** (23:29), (10) **to thank and praise** (23:30), (11) **burnt offerings ... on Sabbaths ... New Moon festivals ... and at appointed feasts** (23:31). This extensive list of duties reveals the Chronicler's interest in sketching the appropriate duties of Levites in post-exilic times.

The Chronicler closed this section with the note that all of these duties were to be done **regularly in the proper number and in the prescribed way** (23:31) at the **Tent of Meeting** and **the Holy Place** (23:32). Yet, these Levites were not independent in their work with these things. They were **under their brothers, the descendants of Aaron** (23:32).

The subordination of the Levites to the priests was a critical issue in the post-exilic community. Many of those exiled to Babylon were Aaronic (Zadokite) priests. When they returned from Babylon under the leadership of Joshua the Zadokite high priest, questions rose over who would be in charge of these most sacred duties. The prophet Ezekiel made it clear that the Zadokites were to lead the Levites (see

Ezek. 40:46; 44:10-16; 48:11). The Chronicler took the same stance in his history (see *Introduction: 4) Royal and Levitical Families*).

Priests Divided (24:1-19)

The third segment concerning Levites and priests together focuses on the divisions of the sons of Aaron (24:1-19). The Chronicler introduced the priests of David's day with general background information (24:1-2). He noted the four sons of Aaron: **Nadab, Abihu, Eleazar and Ithamar** (24:1a). He then mentioned that the first two **died before their father did** (24:1b). He referred to divine judgment against Nadab and Abihu for their 'unauthorized fire' described in Leviticus 10:1-3 and Numbers 3:2-4. Only Eleazar and Ithamar had descendants who carried on the priestly line.

Following this general background, the Chronicler recorded how David divided the remaining families of priests (24:3-5). **With the help of Zadok** (24:3), the sole high priest of Solomon's reign, **David separated them into divisions** (24:3). The descendants of Eleazar were twice as numerous as those of Ithamar (24:4). Yet, the various duties of each priest were determined **impartially by drawing lots** (24:5). The Chronicler mentioned the use of lots on a number of occasions to indicate that an action was entirely directed by God. No human prejudice was involved in the division of duties among priestly families (see 6:54; 24:7, 31; 25:8, 9; 26:13, 14, 16; see also Lev. 16:18; Josh. 18:6, 8, 10; 1 Sam. 14:42; Neh. 10:34; 11:1; Job 6:27; Ps. 22:18; Prov. 16:33; Joel 3:3; Obad. 1:11; Jon. 1:7; Nah. 3:10; Luke 1:8-9; Acts 1:26).

The Chronicler closed this material on the priests by noting the record of their divisions (24:6-19). Apparently, some question had been raised in the post-exilic community regarding the division of duties among the priests. For this reason, the Chronicler validated his divisions in three ways. First, he mentioned that this list was made before many witnesses: the **king, officials, Zadok, Abiathar, heads of families of priests and Levites** (24:6). Second, he pointed out that both remaining priestly families were divided equally into twenty-four divisions (24:7-19). Every other assignment was **taken from Eleazar ... and from Ithamar** (24:6). The twenty-four divisions were established to provide for regular rotation of duties among the priestly families (compare Luke 1:8-9). They may also correspond to the registry of twenty-four thousand (or 'divisions') Levites mentioned earlier (23:4). Third, the Chronicler pointed to the authority behind these priestly divisions by noting that they were true to the **regulations** of **Aaron, as the LORD ... had commanded him** (24:19). The Chronicler's attention to these matters reveals his keen interest in presenting David's Levitical order as authoritative for the post-exilic community.

Levites Remaining (24:20-31)

The fourth section of Levites and priests together (24:20-31) consists of lists (24:20b-30) and concluding remarks (24:31). The expression **the rest of the descendants** (24:20) and the repetition of names from the preceding context connects this passage with the Levites who worked closely with the Aaronic priests (23:6-32). In many cases, however, these lists extend the previous passage by one generation. To address issues that must have been relevant in his own day, the Chronicler noted that these Levites also received duties by the casting of **lots** before **King David**, **Zadok**, **Ahimelech**, and Aaronic and Levitical **heads of families** (24:31). For the Chronicler's outlook on the use of lots, see comments on 24:5. Moreover, he noted that **the oldest brother was treated the same as ... the youngest** (24:31). Such details most likely spoke to specific controversies faced as the post-exilic community sought to order the duties of its worship personnel.

Singers (25:1-31)

This lengthy sketch of musicians whom David assembled reveals the Chronicler's special interest in music (for this section, see *Introduction: 8) Music*; 15:16-24). His material divides into two sections: families of singers (25:1-8), and divisions of duties (25:9-31).

This record of the families of singers (25:1-8) begins with an introduction (25:1) which mentions several important facts. First, not only **David**, but **the commanders of the army** also established the order of musicians. As the Chronicler pointed out elsewhere, Levitical music took place both in worship and in war (see 2 Chr. 20:22).

Second, the musical Levites were selected from three families: **Asaph, Heman, and Jeduthun** (25:1). This note follows the normal biblical divisions (see 1 Chr. 6:33, 39; 15:17,19; 16:37-42; 2 Chr. 5:12; 29:12-14; 35:15; Neh. 11:17).

Third, these Levites had responsibility for **prophesying** accompanied by instruments (25:1). From early times in Israel's history, prophets often gave their oracles set to music (see 1 Sam. 10:5; 2 Kgs. 3:15). The Chronicler himself acknowledged this role for Levites on several occasions (see 25:3; 2 Chr. 20:14; 35:15; see *Introduction: 15) Prophets*). Similar prophetic activities for Levites appear in a number of places in Scripture (see Ezek. 1:3; Judg. 18:5; 1 Sam. 1:17; 22:13-15; Jer. 1:1-2).

The lists of singers (25:2-4) follow the pattern established in 25:1: **Asaph** (25:2), **Jeduthun** (25:3), and **Heman** (25:4-5). The first two of these men are said to have **prophesied** (25:2,3). **Heman** is designated as **the king's seer** (25:5), an ancient synonym for 'prophet' (see 1 Sam. 9:9). Many Levites were under the supervision of these heads of Israel's musicians; some of them are listed here by name with their fathers (25:2-5).

The families of singers close with a general description of duties (25:6-8). The instruments listed here (**cymbals, lyres and harps** [25:6]) are but a sampling. Moreover, these men were all **trained and skilled in music for the LORD** (25:7). As in a number of cases, the Chronicler noted that these musicians were well-prepared for their work (see 1 Chr. 15:22; 2 Chr. 34:12). Finally, the Chronicler noted that these Levites were assigned duties like others before them (24:31). They **cast lots for their duties** no matter what age or level of experience (25:8). For the

Chronicler's outlook on the use of lots see comments on 24:5.

Following the record of the families of singers, the Chronicler turned to more specific reflection on duties (25:9-31). Once again, he noted that these Levites received their responsibilities by **lot** to indicate that the design was from God (25:9). For the Chronicler's outlook on the use of lots, see comments on 24:5. Also, the divisions of the musicians number twenty-four. This number of divisions has appeared before (24:7-18), probably indicating an annual rotation pattern. The Chronicler's attention to these details reveals that he believed the proper observance of music rituals was very important.

The Chronicler's attention to these extensive details on the selection, organization, training, and duties of the musicians in David's day was not simply to inform his readers about the past. He set forth patterns that were to be imitated by the postexilic community as it re-established proper worship of God. The restored people of God were to follow the patterns of music established by David in hope of receiving fuller blessings of restoration (see *Introduction: 8) Music*).

Gatekeepers (26:1-19)

The Chronicler's record of the gatekeepers whom David gathered divides into two parts: families of the gatekeepers (26:1-11) and the divisions of duties (26:12-19). Gatekeepers were Levites who had a number of responsibilities. In addition to guarding temple gates (26:16b), they were in charge of equipment (9:23), treasuries (9:26), contributions (2 Kgs. 12:9; 22:4; 2 Chr. 31:14), articles for temple service (9:28), furnishings, oil, spices (9:29), mixing spices (9:30), baking offering bread (9:31), setting bread for Sabbath (9:32), music (9:33), chambers and supply rooms (23:28; 26:20-29), preparation of baked goods (see Exod. 25:30), and supplies and furnishings (see 28:13-18).

The assignment of Levites to these duties was an important goal for the Chronicler. For this reason, he paused to list their families and duties. Only two of the three Levitical families served as gatekeepers (Korahites, and Merarites, but not Gershonites). First, the passage touches on the **Korahites** (26:2-9), and **Meshelemiah** (26:1,2,9). A list of the sons of **Obed-Edom** (26:4) is embedded within the discussion of **Meshelemiah** (26:4-8). The Chronicler's note **(for God had blessed Obed-Edom,** 26:5) alludes to 2 Sam. 6:11 and clarifies that this is the Gittite who cared for the ark of the covenant (see 13:13-14 // 2 Sam. 6:10-11). Second, the sons of Merari come into view in 26:10-11. Select Merarites also served as gatekeepers. The Chronicler had little to say about the Merarites, except that Shimri's **father had appointed him the first** (26:10). Perhaps some of the Chronicler's original readers wondered why the firstborn did not receive a prominent appointment.

The division of duties among gatekeepers (26:12-19) begins with the manner in which divisions were made (26:12-13). The gatekeepers did it **just as their relatives had** (26:12). In other words, **lots were cast for each gate** to insure divine guidance (26:13). For the Chronicler's outlook on the use of lots, see comments on 24:5.

Following this general introduction, the Chronicler listed those families responsible for various gates (26:14-18). He mentioned the **East Gate, North Gate, South Gate**, and **West Gate** (26:14-16). Similar designations appear in Ezekiel's description of the post-exilic temple (see Ezek. 40). These gatekeepers supervised entering and exiting from the temple. They stood **guard ... alongside of guard** (26:16b; i.e. next to each other) in groups of two, four, and six (26:17-18). Once again, the detail which this account offers suggests strongly that the Chronicler was directing his readers in the arrangements for the temple in his own day.

26:19 closes the section of gatekeepers. It simply notes that all of the gatekeepers were from the two families of **Korah and Merari** (see 26:1-11).

Officers and Judges (26:20-32)

After dealing with the Levites who were designated for temple service, the Chronicler turned to other Levites whom David gathered. This passage recalls the Chronicler's previous mention of **officials and judges** (26:29; see 23:9).

This passage presents many difficulties, but the main idea is clear. The family of **Ladan the Gershonite** (26:21) was in charge of **temple treasuries** (26:22). This list extends over 26:21-22. 26:23 indicates other families who had similar tasks. The sons of **Gershom son of Moses** (26:24) were included here (26:24-28). They were in charge of **things dedicated** (26:26) and the **plunder** (26:27) as well as things dedicated by **Samuel the seer** (26:28). Other Kohathites from the **Izrahites** worked **away from the temple** (26:29). Their duties probably included such things as teaching (see Deut. 33:10) and judging (see Deut. 17:9). **Hebronites** (26:30) were divided into those who were **responsible in Israel west of the Jordan** (26:30) and those who worked east of Jordan (26:32). The latter group not only dealt with **every matter pertaining to God**, but also **the affairs of the king** (26:32). For similar divisions of duties, see 2 Chr. 19:11.

In this passage the Chronicler offered his understanding of how widely the Levites served in David's kingdom. They not only worked in the temple, but also handled many worship and social duties throughout the kingdom of Israel. As in other sections of this material, concern with details probably reflected his desire to see such arrangements followed in post-exilic times.

Military and Civilian Leaders (27:1-34)

Having covered the priests and Levites whom David gathered (23:3-26:32), the Chronicler turned next to other leaders who came together for Solomon's coronation (27:1-34). His record divides into two sections: military leadership (27:1-24) and civilian leadership (27:25-34). Many of the names appearing here occur also in 11:11ff, but we cannot be sure which of these names represent the same persons.

One interesting feature of these lists is that each one divides into twelve units: commanders of twelve army divisions (27:1-15), twelve officers over the tribes (27:16-22) and twelve overseers of royal property (27:25-34). This numerical parallel suggests that the Chronicler intended these passages to symbolize that the leadership of all tribes supported the upcoming transfer of royal power to Solomon (see *Introduction: 1) All Israel*).

Military Leaders (27:1-24)

The military leaders appear in two lists: leaders of army divisions (27:1-15) and officers of the tribes (27:16-24). First, the text presents a list of the military divisional officers (27:1-15). These leaders **were on duty month by month throughout the year** (27:1). Here the Chronicler presented a description of David's permanent standing army, not a voluntary militia. This development in David's military organization may shed some light on his motivation for the census of 21:1–22:1. Originally, Israel was to have a militia formed by volunteers as circumstances required. In fact, Mosaic Law looked negatively on the development of large standing armies (see Deut. 17:16). In all events, the leaders of David's army were commanders of twelve divisions which served David one month each year.

Each division is said to have **24,000 men** within it (see 27:1, 2, 4, 5, 7, 8, 9-15). As with other passages where large numbers of men are mentioned, it is possible that the Hebrew word translated 'thousand' may have been a military term indicating a group of less than a thousand men. (For the Chronicler's use of large numbers of soldiers, see comments on 12:24-37.)

Second, the Chronicler listed **the officers of the tribes** (27:16-24). This list is unusual for this context because it does not provide the numbers of men. Instead, this record divides between lists (27:16-22) and an explanation of why no numbers appear (27:23). The precise responsibilities of these officers are not evident. Instead, the focus of these lists is on the extent of those who gathered to make Solomon king. They represented all of the tribes of Israel. The Chronicler emphasized his 'all Israel' theme again (see *Introduction: 1) All Israel*).

27:23-24 explains why the numbers of these men were not available. The Chronicler identified these lists with the census of 21:1-22:1. He noted several details of that event which made it impossible to give statistics.

1) David followed Moses' example and did not number **the men twenty years old or less** (27:23; see Num. 1).

2) Joab did not finish the count (27:24a).

3) The **wrath** of God was so great that **the number was not entered in the book of the annals of King David** (27:24b).

For other examples of census in Chronicles see 2 Chr. 2:17; 14:8; 17:14-19; 25:6.

Despite the lack of numbers, the Chronicler's list made it clear that David gathered widespread support from the officers. They were part of a great assembly for the transfer of power to Solomon.

Civilian Leaders (27:25-34)

The final group of leaders mentioned are **officials in charge of David's property** (27:31). The closing summary of 27:31b indicates that this material divides between twelve representative officials (27:25-31) and a set of remaining leaders (27:32-34).

The first section (27:25-31) lists a number of items managed by these leaders: **storehouses** and **watchtowers** (27:25), **field workers** (27:26), **vineyards** (27:27), **olive and fig groves** (27:28), **olive oil** (27:28), **herds** (27:29), **camels and donkeys** (27:30), and **flocks** (27:31). Kings in the ancient world had many private holdings. David was no exception. Those in charge of these properties also gathered at the assembly.

The final verses of this section (27:32-34) add a number of leaders not accounted for in the previous material. These men also played a variety of important roles in David's kingdom.

The extensive nature of these lists indicates that the Chronicler wanted to impress his readers with the fact that all of Israel supported Solomon as they had David. Moreover, just as support for the temple builder was widespread in David's day, the re-establishment of the temple and its services in the Chronicler's day required extensive support by military and civilian leaders.

David's Final Assembly (28:1-29:25)

Having described the breadth of people David assembled for Solomon's coronation (23:2-27:34), the Chronicler turned to the activities of the assembly itself. This gathering of Israel's leaders finalized the transfer of temple responsibilities and royal power from David to Solomon.

Comparison of 28:1-29:25 with Samuel and Kings

This material does not appear in Samuel or Kings. The Chronicler added this record to highlight the continuity between David and Solomon's reigns and to close David's reign on a crescendo of joy and celebration.

Structure of 28:1-29:25

The account of David's final assembly divides into three main parts (see figure 16). It is introduced by a single verse (28:1). The three following sections reveal several intentional symmetries (28:2-29:25). They all portray David in the dramatic mode of speaking. Then they follow his speeches with straight narration of action. David first focused on the assembly (28:2-7). Then he narrowed attention to Solomon before (28:8-10) and after (28:20-21) giving him the plans for the temple (28:11-19). Third, he returned to a concern with the assembly (29:1-5) and described generous temple donations (29:6-9). The Chronicler then focused on David's joyous address to God (29:10-19) and the assembly (29:20), and closed with the assembly's acknowledgment of Solomon as king (29:21-25).

David Assembles Leaders (28:1)

The Chronicler began this passage by drawing a connection between what follows and what has preceded. Many members of the groups mentioned here also appeared in 23:2-27:34. As we have noted, however, other groups also attended the assembly. They appear at various stages in its actions.

Moreover, David called the people **to assemble**. This designation of the event as a religious assembly sets it on par with similar occurrences in the Chronicler's history. David's assembly here illustrated the importance of such assemblies in the post-exilic period (see *Introduction: 5) Religious Assemblies*).

David's First Speech and Action (28:2-19)

David's first speech has many parallels with his earlier speech in 22:2-19. In that passage David announced his intention to hand the kingdom to Solomon. At this point, he told the assembly it was time to complete the transfer of temple responsibilities and royal power to Solomon. This speech divides into two parts (see figure 16): David's words to the assembly (28:2-7) and his words to Solomon (28:8-10).

David's Speech to the Assembly (28:2-7)

David began his first speech with a strong assertion of humility before the assembly. He addressed those in attendance as **my brothers** (28:2). This designation revealed David's humble attitude toward the nation by alluding to Moses' description of Israel's king (see Deut. 17:20). He considered himself one with the nation in service to God. David also addressed the assembly as **my people** to indicate familial affection for the nation (28:2; see Ruth 1:16; 2 Chr. 2:11; Isa. 40:1).

David first explained what had led to this event. He reminded the assembly how he had wanted to build the temple (28:2). As we noted earlier, David's desire to build a temple for his God was typical for kings in the ancient Near East; successful kings often boasted of their temple construction (see 17:1).

David often called the ark by the traditional terminology, **the ark of the covenant** (28:2). (For the significance of this designation, see *Introduction: 13) Covenant.*) Yet, here he called the ark **the footstool of our God** (28:2). This designation rarely appears explicitly in the Old Testament (Pss. 99:5; 132:7). David conceived of the ark as God's royal footstool which needed a temple-palace in which to rest.

Despite David's desire, God forbade him to construct the temple for his **Name** (see *Introduction: 11) Name of God*) because he was **a warrior** who **shed blood** (28:3). For a second time the Chronicler explained why David did not build the temple (see comments on 22:6-10). According to the Mosaic Law, the permanent placement of the presence of God was to take place only after the conquest of the land was complete. David had spent most of his life fighting enemies within the land. It was inappropriate for God to take residence in his palace so long as warfare was the course of the day. Only when the people of God had peace was the God of the people going to rest in his palace.

David continued to explain that despite the directive not to build, God favored his descendants with the project (28:4-7). He noted that his kingship was divinely ordained. Judah had been chosen out of all the tribes. His family was selected out of all of Judah. He was chosen out of all his father's house.

Moreover, David announced that God had **chosen** [his] **son Solomon to sit on the throne** (28:5). This statement suggests that this assembly took place after 1 Kings

1:15-21, when Bathsheba asked David to announce Solomon's right to the throne. In the Chronicler's presentation, Solomon's right was never seriously challenged.

God had told David, **'I have chosen him to be my son, and I will be his father'** (28:6). This language of royal adoption recalls the earlier promise of God in 17:13. Solomon was a special child of God, but his relationship was not void of conditions. The blessings of David's family were dependent on their fidelity to God's Law (2 Sam. 7:14-16 // 1 Chr. 17:15-17; Pss. 89:30-34; 132:12). God would **establish** (Solomon's) **kingdom forever**, but Solomon's line will succeed only if **he is unswerving** (28:7).

David Addresses Solomon (28:8-10)

After mentioning the conditional nature of the blessings offered to Solomon, David shifted attention away from the assembly to Solomon himself (28:8-10). Before the **assembly of the Lord** representing **all Israel** (28:8), the king gave a number of directives to Solomon. Once again, the term **assembly** heightened the importance of this event as a religious gathering (see *Introduction: 5) Religious Assemblies*). Six imperatives introduce David's directives to Solomon: **be careful** (28:8), **acknowledge** (28:9), **serve** (28:9), **consider** (28:10), **be strong** (28:10), and **do the work** (28:10).

First, David ordered his son to **be careful to follow all the commands** (28:8). These words alluded to God's commission to Joshua after the death of Moses (see Josh. 1:7). The Chronicler pointed to the parallel between Joshua and Solomon earlier (see 22:11-16). Similar allusions to Joshua's commission appear at several points in this material (28:1-10). As Joshua completed Moses' work, so Solomon must complete David's work.

David's call to obey the Mosaic Law was followed by motivational words. Why should the young king Solomon concern himself with the Law? His obedience will determine the quality of his own life (**... you may possess ...**) and future generations (... **and pass it on** ...) (28:8).

Second, David decreed that Solomon should **acknowledge the God of** [his] **father** (28:9). From ancient Near Eastern texts outside of Scripture, we learn that 'knowing' or 'acknowledging' often meant to accept the binding of covenant stipulations as a vassal (compare Amos 3:2; 2 Sam. 7:20 // 1 Chr. 17:18; Hos. 8:2; 13:4-5; Deut. 9:24). Therefore, David told Solomon to devote himself enthusiastically to the covenant stipulations. Just as Jeremiah looked forward to a day when the exiled people would be restored to their covenant fidelity (see Jer. 31:31-34), so the Chronicler reported these words of David to encourage his post-exilic readers to renew themselves in covenant faithfulness (see *Introduction: 13) Covenant*).

Third, David told Solomon to **serve** (28:9). In Chronicles this terminology frequently has overtones of service in worship (see 2 Chr. 24:18; 30:8; 33:16; 34:33; 35:3). It is likely that this command focused primarily on the task of constructing and arranging the temple. Even so, Solomon was not merely to live in external conformity to this decree. He was to serve with **whole hearted devotion** and **willing**

mind (28:9). The requirement of sincere inward devotion from the heart appears frequently in Chronicles (see *Introduction: 16) Motivations*).

The reason for David's insistence on sincere devotion was that God **searches every heart and understands every motive behind the thoughts** (28:9). Divine omniscience served as a reason to obey out of proper motivations (compare Ps. 139:1; 1 Sam. 16:7; Jer. 11:20). In the ancient Near East, kings often boasted of their temple buildings. Propagandistic inscriptions honored kings for these accomplishments. Solomon could easily have constructed a temple in Jerusalem for his own self-aggrandizement. David warned him, however, that God knew his motivations.

To indicate the importance of building with proper motives, David also reminded Solomon of divine blessings and curses (see *Introduction: 10) Divine Activity*). He warned, **'If you seek him, he will be found by you; but if you forsake him, he will reject you forever'** (28:9). Nearly the same words appear in Azaraiah's prophetic instruction to Asa (see 2 Chr. 15:2b). The term **seek** connoted an intense pursuit of God's favor (see *Introduction: 19) Seeking*). To **forsake** is to do the opposite of 'seeking'. To **forsake** God was to violate the covenant by finding help in someone other than the Lord (see *Introduction: 20) Abandoning/Forsaking*). David warned Solomon that failure to serve with sincerity can lead to divine wrath. It was even possible that God would **reject** [him] **forever** (28:9).

Fourth, David told Solomon to **consider** (28:10), or give due thought to a particular facet of his life's work. Solomon was to build **a temple as a sanctuary**, a holy place for God (28:10). Solomon's temple was for the honor of Israel's divine king, and not for her human king. Solomon had to remember this goal as he constructed the temple in Jerusalem.

The fifth and sixth imperatives are closely related and close David's words to his son. **Be strong and do the work** (28:10). David has already acknowledged that temple construction was not an easy task (see 22:5). For this reason, he exhorted Solomon to be diligent. Similar language will appear again the next time David speaks to Solomon (see 28:20). This phraseology is also present in God's encouragement to Joshua after the death of Moses (Josh. 1:6,7,9) and draws attention once again to the similarities between the roles of Joshua and Solomon (see 22:11-16; see also 19:13; 28:20; 2 Chr. 15:7; 32:7).

Actions Following First Speeches (28:11-19)

After his first speech, David gave **the plans** for the temple to Solomon (28:11). The term **plans** recalls Exod. 25:9 where Moses' tabernacle followed a plan (or 'pattern' [NIV]) of the heavenly dwelling of God. Ezekiel had similar 'plans' for the temple of the post-exilic community (see Ezek. 40:45-48; 41:5-14; 43:10). The Chronicler used this term four times (see 28:11, 12, 18b, 19) to indicate the main divisions of this material.

The first portion (28:11) of David's **plans** concerned the actual edifice of the temple proper (28:11). For a fuller discussion of these aspects of the temple plan see *Introduction: Appendix B – Structures, Furnishings and Decorations of Solomon's Temple*.

The second portion (28:12-18a) of David's **plans** related to **the courts of the temple** and the various **treasuries** of the temple complex (28:12). The **courts** and **treasuries** (28:12) were closely associated with the **divisions of the priests and Levites** (28:13) because they did much of their work in these areas. Moreover, the Chronicler noted **articles to be used in various kinds of service** (28:13). David established the weights of the various gold and silver furnishings and instruments to be used by priests and Levites (28:13-18a).

It is instructive to note that although the Chronicler believed that all of David's plans came from God, he specified that **the Spirit had put** these Levitical divisions in David's **mind** (28:12). This special notice of the divine origins of David's plans explained why the Chronicler set the instructions of David alongside the Law of Moses as his principal standards (see *Introduction: 14) Standards*). The Chronicler made this special notice of the Spirit's work to authorize David's plans for his own day. For a summary of the Chronicler's outlook on the Spirit, see comments on 1 Chr. 12:18.

The third portion (28:18b) of David's plan related to **the chariot, that is, ... the ark of the covenant** (28:18b). Once again, the Chronicler used the well-known designation **ark of the covenant** (28:18b), but he also referred to it as God's mobile **chariot** (28:18b). This imagery appears only here in Chronicles and refers to the ark as the place of God's presence in battle; the ark represented the chariot of God on which he went into battle (see Num. 10:33-36; Pss. 18:10; 68:17; 104:3, 4; 132:10-14; Isa. 66:15; Hab. 3:8; Zech. 6:1).

The Chronicler closed this portion of his record by noting David's reflection on his plan. The king said, **'All this, I have in writing from the hand of the LORD upon me'** (28:19). David explicitly attributed his instructions to God, but he also made it clear that God himself had not written the plans. David wrote them by the hand of God on him. This statement is one of the clearest expressions in the Old Testament of the manner in which divine inspiration took place. It lies behind the New Testament conviction that 'all Scripture is God-breathed' (2 Tim. 3:16).

The divine authorization of David's temple plan was vital to the Chronicler's purposes. His post-exilic readers were obligated to follow the Davidic order for the temple because God authorized his plans (see *Introduction: 14) Standards*).

David's Second Speeches and Actions (28:20-29:9)

The second set of speeches and actions parallels the first set in many ways (see figure 16). Once again, David spoke to his son and the assembly. Afterwards, he performed actions appropriate to his speeches.

David Addresses Solomon (28:20-21)

Once again, David exhorted Solomon in a way that alluded to God's words to Joshua (see 22:1-16; 28:1-10; see also Josh. 1:6-10). Solomon was to be **strong and courageous**, not **afraid or discouraged** (28:11). He was to have the same enthusiasm and commitment to his task as Joshua had centuries before him (compare 19:13; 22:13; 2 Chr. 15:7; 32:7).

David explained why Solomon should be strong. In words that recalled Joshua's commission (see Josh. 1:9), he said that **'the Lord God, my God, is with you'** (28:20). The presence of God 'with' Solomon meant that God would fight with Solomon against opponents. He would grant him success (see 2 Chr. 13:12; see also *Introduction: 10) Divine Activity*).

Beyond this, David also assured Solomon that he had made everything ready for him. The **divisions of priests and Levites ... every willing man** who was **skilled**, and **the officials and all the people** were ready to assist Solomon in the construction of the temple (28:21). Solomon enjoyed such widespread support for his temple project that he had no reason to be discouraged.

By noting these words to Solomon, the Chronicler pointed to the reasons for commitment to the temple service in his own day. God was with the post-exilic community, helping them accomplish the goal. Moreover, just as Solomon enjoyed the full support of the nation, the Chronicler's readers must rally behind the temple project of their day.

David Addresses Assembly (29:1-5)

The Chronicler turned next to David's words to **the whole assembly** (29:1). The designation **assembly** raises this event to the level of a number of religious assemblies in Chronicles (see *Introduction: 5) Religious Assemblies*). In this assembly, David's speech focused on the need for financial support for the temple. His words divided into three parts: David's explanation of the need (29:1), his personal example (29:2-5a), and his challenge to the assembly (29:5b).

David introduced his request by explaining why it was necessary to support the temple. Solomon was **young and inexperienced** (29:1). David realized that Solomon himself was not capable of managing the entire responsibility of temple construction. At an earlier point, David explained that Solomon's inabilities caused him to prepare so extensively for the temple (see 22:2-5). A similar motif appears here but with the added request for monetary support from the assembly.

Solomon's inexperience was a factor to be considered **because this palatial structure** [was] **not for man but for the Lord God** (29:1). Again, the perspective is similar to 22:2-5. The Hebrew expression translated **palatial structure** ('temple' NAS, NRS), appears in Chronicles only here and in 29:19 as a designation for the temple. It has the connotations of a royal palace or fortification. In choosing to convey David's speech with this word, the Chronicler highlighted his belief that the temple would be the royal palace of God on earth (see *Introduction: 7) Divine Kingship*).

After explaining the need for support, David described his own commitment to Solomon's temple (29:2-5a). He informed the assembly of two ways he had contributed to Solomon's task: from his official resources (29:2), and from his personal resources (29:3-5a).

David first noted the great quantities he provided **with all** (his) **resources** (29:2). This terminology is not very specific. In the light of 29:3-5a it probably referred to David's use of official state funds for temple construction. As the Chronicler pointed out earlier, David reserved much of his war plunder for use in the temple (see 18:11). This material was probably in view here.

The king elaborated that he gave **gold, silver, bronze, wood, onyx, turquoise,** various **stones** and **marble** (29:2). All of these materials were given **in great quantity**. As the Chronicler pointed out elsewhere, David provided huge quantities for the construction and furnishings of the temple as an example for his post-exilic readers to admire and follow (see 22:3-14).

Beyond this, David informed the assembly that he had also given from another resource (29:3-5a). Out of enthusiastic **devotion to the temple** David gave from his **personal treasures** (29:3). These gifts included **three thousand talents of gold** (about 110 tons [100 metric tons]) of high quality **gold of Ophir** (29:4). He also devoted **seven thousand talents of refined silver** (about 260 tons [240 metric tons]). The possibility of hyperbole cannot be entirely dismissed, but the needs of the temple were great. (For the Chronicler's use of hyperbole, see comments on 12:14.) Once again the large quantities of David's gifts display his enthusiasm and dedication to the temple's construction.

After describing his official and personal contributions, David challenged the assembly (29:5b). He invited them to follow his example, but the manner in which he offered this challenge is instructive. He asked who would **consecrate** themselves **to the Lord**. On several occasions, the Chronicler used the term **consecrate** to connote ritual cleansings in preparation for worship. Rituals of consecration appear frequently in Chronicles as examples of proper worship which the post-exilic readers were to imitate in their day (see *Introduction: 6) Royal Observance of Worship*). In this context, however, giving to the temple was an expression of consecration.

David realized that his request for the assembly's support was to be voluntary. So he asked, **'Who is willing** ...' (29:5b). As the Chronicler himself emphasized in 29:9, these gifts were freely given. Just as David gave beyond mere duty, the assembly was asked to give beyond what was required.

David's challenge to his assembly also challenged the Chronicler's post-exilic readers. They were not to be satisfied with minimal devotion to financial support for the temple in their day. As David invited his assembly, they were to consecrate themselves to God by giving freely and generously (see *Introduction: 9) Temple Contributions*).

Actions Following Second Speeches (29:6-9)

The Chronicler continued his account of David's final assembly by summarizing the assembly's reaction to David's speech. In a word, the leaders of Israel followed David's example and gave freely to Solomon's temple project. The record of these actions divides into two parts: the giving (29:6-8) and the response (29:9).

The Chronicler noted several important facts about these gifts. First, they came from **the leaders of families, the officers of the tribes ... the commanders of thousands ... hundreds** and the **officials** (29:6). These groups of people appear elsewhere in descriptions of assemblies. Here they represent the leadership of the entire nation.

Second, the leaders **gave willingly** (29:6); these gifts were not coerced (see 29:5b). The leaders of Israel responded beyond the requirements of duty.

Third, the quantities of gifts were enormous (29:7-8): **five thousand talents** (about 190 tons [170 metric tons]) and **ten thousand darics** (about 185 pounds [about 84 kilograms]) **of gold, ten thousand talents of silver** (about 375 tons [345 metric tons]), **eighteen thousand talents of bronze** (about 675 tons [610 metric tons]), and **a hundred thousand talents of iron** (about 3,750 tons [3,450 metric tons]). These amounts are very large (with the exception of **ten thousand darics**) and may represent hyperboles (29:7). (For the Chronicler's use of hyperbole, see comments on 12:14.) In all events, the leaders gave tremendous quantities to the temple project.

Fourth, the variety of gifts included **precious stones** in addition to the metals mentioned above (29:8). The Chronicler noted specifically that these stones were put in the charge of **Jehiel** whom he mentioned earlier in connection with temple treasuries (see 26:21).

Much has been made of the term **darics** in 29:7. This description is anachronistic because darics were not minted until the reign of Darius I after whom the currency was named (c.515 BC) Depending on when the Chronicler composed his history (*see Introduction: Authorship and Date*), the term **darics** was either the Chronicler's own attempt to update the currency to his day (compare 2 Chr. 3:3) or it was a later copyist's attempt to update to his day (see *Introduction: Translation and Transmission*).

In all events, the Chronicler's chief concern becomes evident in the manner in which the assembly closed (29:9). Great joy came to the assembly. **The people rejoiced** and **David the king also rejoiced**. Throughout the reign of David, the Chronicler highlighted the joy that resulted from the nation joining in harmony around her king and temple (see *Introduction: 27) Disappointment and Celebration*). In this case, the joy was in response to the fact that the leaders were **willing** and gave **freely**. Moreover, Israel's leaders gave **wholeheartedly**, out of inward devotion to the Lord (see *Introduction: 16) Motivations*).

The exemplary nature of this passage is evident. On the one hand, it presented a model of enthusiasm for the temple. At several stages, the post-exilic returnees were hesitant to give to the support of the temple (see Hag. 1:3-6; Mal. 3:8-12). The Chronicler offered this record to his readers to inspire them toward willing and wholehearted devotion to the temple in their day. On the other hand, this passage conveys an ideal of cooperation among various classes of people. David's appeal for popular support fits well with the Chronicler's ideal that wise kings sought the consent of their people. (For a summary of the Chronicler's view of popular consent, see comments on 1 Chr. 13:2,4.) If the people and the leadership of the post-exilic community would imitate the actions of this assembly, the joy of this assembly could be theirs as well.

David's Third Speeches and Actions (29:10-25)

The third set of speeches and actions in David's final assembly brings this portion of the Chronicler's record to its climax. At this point, David turned his attention to God whose power undergirded his success in temple preparations. As we have noted on a number of occasions, the Chronicler believed strongly that God's power was behind the ideal actions of David (see 10:13-14; 11:3,9-10,14; 12:18,23; 14:2; see also *Introduction: 10) Divine Activity*). Through David's final addresses to God and the assembly the Chronicler brought this perspective to the foreground.

David Addresses God (29:10-19)

David's last praise has a number of thematic connections with his praise in the closure of the previous major section of his reign (see 16:8-36). Both praises call attention to the patriarchs (29:10,18, compare 16:16); they both mention the motif of Israel being **strangers** (29:15, compare 16:19); the kingship of God is celebrated (29:11-12, compare 16:22-23); both praises end with petitions (29:18-19, compare 16:35). The Chronicler established these similarities to connect these closing scenes. 16:8-36 closes David's successful transfer of the ark to Jerusalem; 29:10-19 brings to an end David's preparations for temple construction and the transfer of power to Solomon.

Structure of 29:10-19

This material begins with a brief setting followed by a three part address to God (see figure 16). The progress of thought in this passage is evident. After a description of the situation (29:10a), David began with an elaborate praise of God as the one who rules over all (29:10b-13). He then acknowledged the contrast between his own humble state and divine sufficiency (29:14-16). Finally, David closed this address to his all-sufficient God with a petition for the future of the nation (29:17-19).

Setting (29:10a)

David turned to God **in the presence of the whole assembly** to offer praise for the accomplishments of his life and to ask for divine blessings on future generations. Once again, the Chronicler noted the exemplary character of this event by designating it as an **assembly** (see *Introduction: 5) Religious Assemblies*).

Praise of God (29:10b-13)

David began this speech with a series of praises to God. These praises are divided by four vocatives: (**O LORD** [29:10b], **O LORD** [29:11a], **O LORD** [29:11d], and **our God** [29:13]).

The first portion of this passage acknowledges that God is to be praised **from everlasting to everlasting** (29:10b). David displayed his enthusiasm for what God had done in his life by immediately acknowledging that he deserved eternal praise far beyond that which David was able to give.

Following this initial acknowledgment, David explained why God deserved unending praise (29:11a-c). To him belong **greatness**, **power**, **glory**, **majesty**, and **splendor** (29:11a-b). The piling up of these terms revealed David's enthusiasm. He was impressed by what God had done and proclaimed that **everything in heaven and earth** belongs to God (29:11c). Similar themes appear in the Psalms when the psalmists reached the limits of their expressive powers.

The motif of divine sovereignty continued in the next portion of David's praise (29:11d-e). In this regard, **the kingdom** takes center stage (29:11d). Time and again the Chronicler drew attention to the connection between God's throne and the throne of Israel's kings (see *Introduction: 7) Divine Kingship*). The kings of Israel ruled as God's vice-regents over the land of Israel, but God himself is **head over all** (29:11e); God is the **ruler of all things** (29:12b). As a result, whenever **wealth and honor** (29:12a) come to a nation or king, they **come from** [the Lord] (29:12a). God alone is able **to exalt and give strength** (29:12c-d). Here David's words revealed the Chronicler's perspective that prosperity and strength for faithful Israelites come from God (see *Introduction: 26) Prosperity and Poverty*).

In response to the blessings David had received, he closed his initial praise with an expression of **thanks** to God (29:13a). He praised God's **glorious name** (29:13b), the invocable, active power of God in the world (see *Introduction: 11) Name of God*). David had seen God act on his behalf throughout his life. The Name of God deserved his praise.

Declaration of Humility (29:14-16)

David's amazement with God was also rooted in his recognition of human impotence. In a rhetorical question, he acknowledged that it is only because of God's enablement that he and the nation were **able to give as generously as this** (29:14). Both David and the people had contributed much to the construction of Solomon's temple (see 29:2-9). It would have been natural to take credit for these contributions, but David praised God for them. As he put it, **'everything comes from you, and we have given you only what comes from your hand'** (verse 14). The assembly's generosity toward the temple was merely returning a small portion of what they had received from God.

To highlight this perspective, David described himself and Israel as **aliens and strangers** (29:15). This terminology usually applied to those who were homeless or traveling and who depended entirely on the goodness of others for their sustenance (see Deut. 10:18). Although David and his people had inherited the land of promise by this time, he still considered himself in utter dependence on God. This dependence was not on other people for David was a stranger **'in your** [the Lord's] **sight'**. Despite the security David experienced in the land of Israel, he and his people still depended on God just as much as their **forefathers**, those who first wandered through the land (29:15, see Gen. 12:1-3; Deut. 26:5).

Having acknowledged Israel's utter dependence on God, David once again admitted that the provision made for the **temple for** [God's] **Holy Name comes from** [God's] **hand and all of it belongs to** [God] (29:16; see *Introduction: 11) Name of God*). These words recall the earlier expression of humility before God (29:14b) and the praise of his Name (29:13b).

Petitions for the Future (29:17-19)

The final portion of David's address to God concerned the future of the kingdom, especially future devotion to the temple project. David began with a doctrinal statement acknowledging an important theological conviction. **'I know,'** he affirmed, **'that you test the heart and are pleased with integrity'** (29:17). These words recalled David's earlier charge to Solomon (see 28:9) and brought forward the central concern of his petitions. David wanted the nation and his son to serve God from the heart. God required obedience to his Law that rose out of a wholehearted commitment. Mere outward or reluctant service was not adequate (see *Introduction: 16) Motivations*).

David quickly affirmed that his royal contributions and the donations of the people had been wholehearted. He asserted that he had **given willingly and with honest intent** (29:17). **Honest intent** meant that David supported temple construction precisely for the reasons he stated. He desired for God to have a temple for his Name. No ulterior motives such as self-aggrandizement were behind his actions.

Moreover, as the earlier portion of this chapter demonstrated, David gave far beyond what was required of him (see 29:3), and the assembly had done the same. They gave **with joy** and **willingly** (29:9; see *Introduction: 27) Disappointment and Celebration*). As the Chronicler already noted, the assembly rejoiced because of the **willing** responses of the leaders of the nation (29:9). They saw that the gifts were given **freely and wholeheartedly to the Lord** (29:9; see *Introduction: 16) Motivations*). David therefore affirmed that he and the nation had passed God's test of their hearts (see 29:17d).

David then turned to a series of petitions concerning the future of the nation and her king. First, David asked God to **keep this desire in the hearts** of Israel **forever** (29:18). In other words, David wanted future generations to be enthusiastic about temple support. Mere outward obedience would not be sufficient; joyous wholehearted devotion would be required by a God who tests the hearts of his people (see 29:17). David prayed that the people would **keep their hearts loyal** to God (29:18; see *Introduction: 16) Motivations*).

Second, just as David commented on his own royal integrity, he prayed that Solomon would have **wholehearted devotion** (29:19). Solomon was to observe the Law of God and **to do everything to build the palatial structure** (i.e., the temple, see 29:1). The task ahead of David's son was massive. Only actions rising out of deep inward devotion would be sufficient to carry him through the project.

Undoubtedly, the Chronicler included this aspect of David's prayer to encourage his post-exilic readers to consider their own hearts. They were one of the future generations for which David prayed. In line with their ideal king's desire, they should have been wholeheartedly devoted to the temple in their day. Moreover, in line with their ideal king's practice, they should have devoted themselves to prayerful humility before God (see *Introduction: 17) Prayer*).

David Addresses Assembly (29:20)

The Chronicler briefly noted that David not only praised God himself. He also turned **to the whole assembly** and encouraged them to **praise the Lord**. As a result, the entire assembly **praised the Lord ... bowed low and fell prostrate before the Lord and the king**. All the people in attendance acknowledged the goodness of God toward them and honored David as their national head. The meeting is designated an **assembly** once again (see 29:1,10) to highlight its exemplary quality for the Chronicler's readers (see *Introduction: 5) Religious Assemblies*). This brief scene depicted the entire assembly of Israel in the worship of God and in harmony with the Davidic king. The Chronicler could hardly have imagined a more ideal scene for his post-exilic readers (*see Introduction: 4-9) King and Temple*).

Actions Following Speeches (29:21-25)

With the assembly fully devoted to the task of constructing the temple, David and the people of Israel assembled **the next day** to make Solomon their king. This material divides into two sections: preparations (29:21-22a), and the acknowledgment of Solomon (29:22b-25).

The Chronicler pointed to the religious nature of the transfer of power from David to Solomon by noting joyous sacrificial ceremonies that preceded the actual transfer (29:21-22a). The assembly offered **burnt offerings** which included **a thousand bulls, rams**, and **male lambs** (29:21). In addition to the burnt offerings, **drink offerings** were also made (29:21). Moreover there were **other sacrifices**, probably peace or fellowship offerings, portions of which were eaten by the celebrants (29:21). To emphasize the national unity at this event, the Chronicler noted that these sacrifices were made on behalf of **all Israel** (29:21 see *Introduction: 1) All Israel*). Just as David had found support from the entire nation, the transfer of power to Solomon was now supported by all the people (see 29:25).

Beyond this, the Chronicler also noted that the assembly **ate and drank with great joy** (29:22a). Eating in celebration occurred three times in David's reign: his anointing (12:39-40), the transfer of the ark (16:23-33), and here. By repeating this motif, the Chronicler highlighted the splendor of the event. It was a joyous time for the nation because her new king was about to be acknowledged and all preparations were complete for the construction of the temple.

The Chronicler sought to inspire his post-exilic readers to yearn for the same joy in their day. As they wholeheartedly devoted themselves to setting the royal family and the temple in order, they could also enjoy the celebration of David's day (see *Introduction: 27) Disappointment and Celebration*).

In the end the assembly **acknowledged Solomon ... as king** (29:22b). The traditional Hebrew text of 29:22b reads that at this time Solomon was anointed king **a**

second time. A few textual witnesses omit this phrase and raise the possibility that it was added at some point in the history of transmission (see *Introduction: Translation and Transmission*). If the reading originated with the Chronicler, he probably noted this fact to distinguish the relatively private ceremony (see 1 Kgs. 1:29-31) from this public ceremony (see 1 Kgs. 1:38-42).

The Chronicler noted that the assembly also **acknowledged ... Zadok to be priest** (29:22). Kings reports that Zadok anointed Solomon (see 1 Kgs. 1:39). Zadok's special status was especially important to the Chronicler and his readers. The Zadokite priest, Joshua, joined Zerubbabel in the rebuilding of the temple in the early days of the restoration (see 6:1-81; Ezra 2:2; Hag. 2:2-4). Like Zechariah, the Chronicler insisted that Israel's restoration depended on two figures: the Davidic king and the Zadokite high priest (see Zech. 1-4).

This event closes with the results of Solomon's anointing (29:23-25). It reports three characteristics of Solomon's kingdom.

1) Solomon **prospered** (29:23). The theme of prosperity and wealth appears many times in Chronicles to indicate divine blessing toward a faithful king (see *Introduction: 26) Prosperity and Poverty*).

2) Solomon **was highly exalted** (29:25); exaltation also indicated God's approval of a king.

3) Solomon received **royal splendor such as no king over Israel ever had before** (29:25); this description anticipated Solomon's blessing at Gibeon (see 2 Chr. 1:12).

Beyond this, the ideal quality of Solomon's reign also appears in the broad support he received.

1) The Chronicler specified that **all Israel obeyed him** (29:23) and **all Israel** realized Solomon's exaltation (29:25). The entire nation submitted to Solomon's rule (see *Introduction: 1) All Israel*).

2) **All the officers and mighty men as well as all of King David's sons** swore to support Solomon (29:24). These words stressed the continuity between David and Solomon.

With these words the Chronicler created the expectation in his readers that Solomon's kingdom was as ideal as David's. As the following chapters will indicate, Solomon also served as an ideal for the post-exilic community.

Closure of David's Reign (29:26-30)

The information of 29:26-27 follows 1 Kings 2:10-11 very closely. The remainder of this material comes from the Chronicler's hand.

The Chronicler finalized his record of David's reign in a manner similar to that which he will follow at the end of nearly every other king's reign after this point. He summarized David's reign (29:26-28a), noted his successor (29:28b), and pointed to other records of the king's life (29:29-30).

Above all, in these last comments on David, the Chronicler reminded his readers of his overarching assessment of the king. David ruled **over all Israel** (29:26);

his reign extended to all the tribes (see *Introduction: 1) All Israel*). The Chronicler added that David was blessed by God with **good old age** and **long life** (29:28). In line with earlier biblical traditions David received the blessing of a lengthy reign and life because of his uprightness (see Exod. 20:12; Deut. 6:2; 22:7; 1 Sam. 17:12; 2 Kgs. 20:6; see *Introduction: 28) Healing and Long Life / Sickness and Death*). Other righteous kings share this blessing as well (see 2 Chr. 24:15; 32:24-26; 33:1; but compare 33:21). David is also said to have died with **wealth and honor** (29:28). David's prosperity exalted him as an ideal for the post-exilic readers to follow (*see Introduction: 26) Prosperity and Poverty*).

Finally, the Chronicler noted several sources he used for the history of David besides the canonical book of Samuel (see *Introduction: Historical and Theological Purposes*). He mentioned **the records of Samuel the seer** (not to be confused with the canonical book of Samuel), **Nathan**, and **Gad** (29:29). These prophetic books no longer exist, but they contained many **details of his reign and power** as well as other **circumstances** in **Israel and the kingdoms of other lands** (29:30). The Chronicler's reference to these prophetic sources indicated the important role the prophetic word played in his evaluation of Israel's history (see *Introduction: 15) Prophets*).

The Reign of Solomon
2 Chronicles 1:1-9:31

Overview of 2 Chronicles 1:1-9:31

The Chronicler's record of Solomon is closely connected to his account of David's life. Both kings served as ideals for the post-exilic community. To understand how Solomon functioned as such an ideal, it is necessary to gain an awareness of the broad contours of the Chronicler's portrait of his reign. At this point, we will sketch a general comparison between Chronicles and Kings as well as an overarching outline of this material.

Comparison of 2 Chr. 1:1-9:31 and 1 Kgs. 1:1-11:43

A number of significant features in the Chronicler's portrait of Solomon become clear from a large scale comparison with the record in Kings (see figure 21).

2 Chr.		1 Kgs.
———	Solomon's Struggle for Throne	1:1-2:46a
1:1	Solomon's Establishment	2:46b
———	Solomon's Egyptian Wife	3:1-3
1:2-13	Solomon's Promises	3:4-15
———	Solomon's Political Wisdom	3:16-4:34
1:14-17	Solomon's Construction Wisdom	10:26-29
2:1-18	Solomon's Help From Hiram	5:1-18
3:1-14	Solomon's Construction of Temple	6:1-38
———	Solomon's Construction of Palace	7:1-12
3:15-5:1	Solomon's Construction of Temple	7:13-51
5:2-7:10	Solomon's Dedication of Temple	8:1-66
7:11-22	Solomon's Response from God	9:1-9
8:1-9:28	Solomon's Wisdom and Wealth	9:10-10:29
———	Solomon's Apostasy and Decline	11:1-40
9:29-31	Solomon's Death	11:41-43

Comparison of 2 Chr. 1:1-9:31 and 1 Kgs. 1:1-11:43 (figure 21)

The book of Kings presents a balanced picture of Solomon's life. It begins with his struggle for the throne (1 Kgs. 1:1-2:46a) and ends with Solomon's apostasy and decline (1 Kgs. 11:1-40). The middle portion of the record of Kings focuses primarily on his positive accomplishments (1 Kgs. 3:1-10:29).

By contrast, the Chronicler's desire to present Solomon as an ideal for his post-exilic readers caused him to omit the problematic rise of Solomon (1 Kgs. 1:1-2:46a) and his decline (1 Kgs. 11:1-40). Beyond this, the Chronicler also omitted several portions of the middle section in Kings (3:1-10:29). He dropped the account of Solomon's Egyptian wife (3:1-3) because of the moral implications of the marriage. He also omitted the account of Solomon's political wisdom (3:16-4:34) and the record of Solomon's palace (7:1-12) to focus exclusively on the king's building projects, especially the temple.

The result of these changes was that Solomon's reign reflects the four major motifs that appear in David's reign. First, Solomon is portrayed as a king of high moral character. Two major omissions from Kings reflect this motif.

1) The book of Kings describes Solomon's struggles and his ruthless treatment of political opponents (1 Kgs. 1:1-2:46a). Solomon's actions are defended by the writer of Kings, but opposition from within the Davidic court and Solomon's treatment of his political opponents were probably considered too controversial for the Chronicler to maintain in his history. In all events, omitting this material removed any question about Solomon's rise.

2) Beyond this, the Chronicler also omitted Solomon's foreign wives and the syncretism they introduced into his kingdom (1 Kgs. 11:1-25). Solomon's Egyptian wife is mentioned once, but only inadvertently (2 Chr. 8:11).

Second, the Chronicler was also very interested in the extent of Solomon's support. Although this motif is not as prominent in the Solomonic material as it is in the Davidic record, it is evident in at least two places that Solomon reigned over all of Israel and Judah.

1) In 1 Chr. 29:22b-25 Solomon was publicly recognized **by all Israel** (1 Chr. 29:23) as the successor to David. The scene gives a clear indication that the entire nation recognized Solomon as King.

2) The Chronicler added an introduction to the story of Solomon's dream at Gibeon (1:1-6). In this material the Chronicler noted that Solomon gave decrees to **all Israel** (1:2). This passage makes it clear that even early in his reign Solomon was in the company of supporters representing the entire nation.

Third, a number of additions emphasized Solomon's interest in the temple. The location and time at which Solomon began to build the temple appear (3:1-2). Specific aspects of the edifice are described (4:7-9). The presence of Yahweh came to Solomon's temple in dramatic display (7:1b-3,6). The practice of sacrifice and temple order also appears in the account (8:12-16). In these ways, the Chronicler presented Solomon as a monarch fully devoted to the proper establishment and operation of the temple.

Fourth, because Solomon's reign was presented as an ideal for the post-exilic community, special note is taken of the times of joy and celebration in his kingdom. Some of these events already appeared in Kings, but the Chronicler included them because they fit with his interests (2 Chr. 5:2-3 // 1 Kgs. 8:2; 2 Chr. 7:8-10 // 1 Kgs. 8:65-66; 2 Chr. 9:7 // 1 Kgs. 10:8). Moreover, Chronicles expands and adds times of joy (see 5:11-13; 7:1-3). These scenes of joy and happiness were designed to offer the Chronicler's readers a portrait of what their experience could be, if they would follow Solomon's example.

Structural Overview of Solomon's Reign

Solomon's reign divides into eight symmetrical steps followed by a standard closure (see figure 22).

Solomon's Great Wisdom and Wealth (1:1-17)
  Solomon's International Assistance (2:1-18)
    Solomon's Temple Building Project (3:1-5:1)
      Solomon's Assembly to Dedicate the Temple (5:2-7:10)
      Solomon's Response from God (7:11-22)
    More on Solomon's Building Projects (8:1-15)
  More on Solomon's International Relations (8:16-9:21)
More on Solomon's Great Wisdom and Wealth (9:22-28)
Closure of Solomon's Reign (9:29-31)

Outline of Solomon's Reign (figure 22)

This symmetrical structure creates a resonance between corresponding elements that gives insight into their prominent concerns. All of Solomon's reign is enclosed by the theme of his wisdom (1:1-17; 9:13-28). Solomon's international recognition demonstrates the extent of his wisdom (2:1-18; 8:17-9:12). At the heart of the king's reign, however, is his devotion to construction projects (3:1-5:1; 8:1-15) and especially the ceremony of the temple's dedication (5:2-7:22).

With this overarching structural pattern in mind, the smaller units of Solomon's reign fall into place (see figure 23).

- ■ Solomon's Great Wisdom and Wealth (1:1-17)
  - ♦ Solomon Receives Divine Promises (1:1-13)
    - Solomon Reigns over Israel (1:1)
      - Solomon Goes to Gibeon to Worship (1:2-6)
        - Solomon and God Dialogue (1:7-12)
          - God Speaks (1:7)
            - Solomon Responds (1:8-10)
          - God Speaks (1:11-12)
        - Solomon Returns to Jerusalem (1:13a)
      - Solomon Reigns over Israel (1:13b)
  - ♦ Solomon Experiences Divine Promises (1:14-17)
    - Military Strength (1:14)
    - Domestic Prosperity (1:15)
    - International Trade (1:16-17)

- ■ Solomon's International Assistance (2:1-18)
  - Solomon's Conscripted Laborers (2:1-2)
  - Solomon and Hiram Correspond (2:3-16)
    - Solomon's Letter (2:3-10)
    - Hiram's Letter (2:11-16)
  - More on Solomon's Conscripted Laborers (2:17-18)

- ■ Solomon's Temple Building Project (3:1-5:1)
  - ♦ Solomon Begins Construction (3:1-2)
    - Solomon's Temple Building (3:3-17)
      - Overview of the Temple (3:3-4)
      - Divisions of the Temple (3:5-17)
        - Main Hall (3:5-7)
        - Most Holy Place (3:8-14)
        - Portico (3:15-17)
    - Solomon's Temple Furnishings (4:1-10)
      - In the Priestly Court (4:1-6)
      - In the Main Hall (4:7-8)
      - In the Priestly Court (4:9-10)
    - Reiteration and Elaboration (4:11-22)
      - Hiram's Help (4:11-18)
      - Solomon's Furnishings and Decorations (4:19-22)
  - ♦ Solomon Completes Construction (5:1)

- ■ Solomon's Assembly to Dedicate the Temple (5:2-7:10)
  - ♦ Solomon's Assembly Gathers (5:2-3)
    - • Solomon's Initial Celebration of the Temple (5:4-6:2)
      - Celebrative Worship Outside the Most Holy Place (5:4-6)
        - Placing the Ark in the Most Holy Place (5:7-10)
      - Celebrative Worship Outside the Most Holy Place (5:11-6:2)
      - • Solomon's Praise for the Past (6:3-11)
        - Transitional Introduction (6:3)
        - Praise for Fulfillment of the Promise to David (6:4-6)
          - Explanation of Solomon's Role (6:7-9)
        - Praise for Keeping the Promise to David (6:10-11)
      - • Solomon's Prayer for the Future (6:12-42)
        - Introduction to the Prayer (6:12-13)
        - Solomon's Dedicatory Prayer (6:14-42)
          - Praise and Petitions for the Monarchy (6:14-17)
            - Praise (6:14-15)
            - Petitions (6:16-17)
          - Praise and Petitions for the Temple (6:18-39)
            - Praise (6:18)
            - Petitions (6:19-39)
              - In General (6:19-21)
              - Regarding Oaths (6:22-23)
              - Regarding Defeat (6:24-25)
              - Regarding Drought (6:26-27)
              - Regarding Assorted Disasters (6:28-31)
              - Regarding Foreigners (6:32-33)
              - Regarding Foreign Wars (6:34-35)
              - Regarding National Exile (6:36-39)
          - Petitions for the Temple and Monarchy (6:40-42)
    - • Solomon's Concluding Sacrifices and Celebration (7:1-7)
      - Divine Fire and Glory (7:1-3)
      - Numerous Sacrifices (7:4-7)
  - ♦ Solomon's Assembly Dismisses (7:8-10)

- Solomon's Response from God (7:11-22)
  - Introduction (7:11-12a)
  - Divine Approval of the Temple (7:12b)
  - Divine Instructions and Assurances to the Nation (7:13-16)
  - Divine Instructions and Warnings to the Monarchy (7:17-22)

- More on Solomon's Building Projects (8:1-15)
  - Solomon's Widespread Construction Projects (8:1-6)
  - Solomon's Extensive Labor Force (8:7-10)
  - Solomon's Temple Construction (8:11-15)

- More on Solomon's International Relations (8:16-9:21)
  - Introduction (8:16)
  - ♦ Solomon and Hiram in Maritime Trade (8:17-18)
    - Solomon Begins the Venture (8:17)
      - Hiram Sends Ships (8:18a)
    - Solomon Receives Goods from the Venture (8:18b)
  - ♦ Solomon and Arabian Reactions (9:1-14)
    - • Queen of Sheba Honors Solomon (9:1-12)
      - Queen Comes to Solomon (9:1)
        - Solomon Answers the Queen's Questions (9:2)
          - The Queen Admires Solomon (9:3-9)
          - [Note on Solomon's Wealth (9:10-11)]
        - Solomon Responds to the Queen's Admiration (9:12a)
      - Queen Departs from Solomon (9:12b)
    - • Arabian Kings Acknowledge Solomon (9:13-14)
  - ♦ Solomon and Hiram in Maritime Trade (9:15-21)

- More on Solomon's Great Wisdom and Wealth (9:22-28)
  - Introduction (9:22)
  - Solomon's Worldwide Recognition (9:23-24)
  - Solomon's Worldwide Imports (9:25-28)

- Closure of Solomon's Reign (9:29-31)

Outline of 2 Chr. 1:1-9:31 (figure 23)

Solomon's Great Wisdom and Wealth (1:1-17)

The Chronicler began his account with a focus on how Solomon gained wisdom and wealth. Omitting the struggles Solomon had in his early career (see 1 Kgs. 1:1-2:46a) set the stage for his glorious portrait of the king. This portion of Solomon's reign balances with the closing verses which also focus on his wealth and wisdom (9:13-28; see figure 22).

Structure of 1:1-17

This material divides into two sections consisting of a narrative and a series of reports (see figure 23). The first episode (1:1-13) depicts Solomon calling a religious assembly and obtaining divine promises for wealth and wisdom. The second portion (1:14-17) consists of an assortment of reports which illustrate some of the ways these divine promises became realities.

Solomon Receives Divine Promises (1:1-13)

The Chronicler began his record of Solomon's reign with the king's authority in full swing. He showed no concern with the gradual acquisition of power, but moved directly to the king's first momentous act, an assembly of all Israel at which Solomon received the gift of wisdom from God.

Comparison with 1 Kings 2:46b-3:15

A number of variations between Kings and Chronicles occur in this passage. Some variations result from problems in textual transmission (see *Introduction: Translation and Transmission*). At times, Chronicles simply paraphrases Kings for stylistic reasons. Nevertheless, several significant differences deserve special mention.

First, the Chronicler exalted Solomon with additions and omissions.

1) He omitted the record of Solomon's marriage to Pharaoh's daughter (1 Kgs. 3:1-2) and replaced it with the notice that **the LORD his God was with him and made him exceedingly great** (1:1b).

2) 1 Kgs. 3:3 is omitted because it mentions that Solomon worshipped at 'high places'. The text admits that Solomon worshipped at the one **high place** of Gibeon (1:3 // 1 Kgs. 3:4), but carefully explains Solomon's actions (1:3b-6). It refers once again to Gibeon as a **high place** (1:13), but immediately comments that the **Tent of Meeting** was there (1:13).

3) The Chronicler diverged from Kings to turn attention away from David to Solomon. He eliminated the extensive description of David's uprightness (1 Kgs. 3:6b). Moreover, he shortened 1 Kgs. 3:7-8, omitting the reference to Solomon's youth and naiveté (but compare 1 Chr. 22:5; 29:1 and 2 Chr. 13:7).

4) The Chronicler omitted the warning of 1 Kgs. 3:14 (// 1:12), which focused on the conditionality of Solomon's kingship (see also 1 Kgs. 11:26-40).

5) The report of Solomon's sacrifices at Jerusalem (1 Kgs. 3:15b) does not appear because it raised questions about Solomon's fidelity to the Law of Moses. Earlier in the chapter (see 1:3-6) the Chronicler justified Solomon's sacrifices at Gibeon. For this reason, this material is omitted.

Second, Solomon's time at Gibeon is described as a nationwide religious assembly. He detailed the participants as **all Israel** ... **commanders** ... **judges** ... **all the leaders in Israel** ... **heads of families** ... **Solomon and the whole assembly** ... (1:2-6 // 1 Kgs. 3:4).

Third, as mentioned above, the Chronicler admitted that Solomon sacrificed at Gibeon (1:3 // 1 Kgs. 3:4). This admission apparently raised questions about the appropriateness of Solomon's act for readers living after the establishment of the temple in Jerusalem. As a result, the text adds a significant explanation of why Solomon performed sacrifices at Gibeon (1:3b-6).

Fourth, the addition of **and he reigned over Israel** (1:13b) balances with the opening verse of this section and forms an inclusio which closes this section of Solomon's reign.

Structure of 1:1-13

These variations formed a symmetrical five step narrative (see figure 23). This story opens and closes with the notice that Solomon had become **exceedingly great** (1:1; 1:13b). Solomon went to Gibeon to worship at the bronze altar (1:2-6). This movement balances with his return to Jerusalem (1:13a). The turning point of the story is Solomon's dialogue with God in Gibeon (1:7-12).

Solomon Reigns over Israel (1:1)

The Chronicler quickly summarized the early phases of the king's reign. The terminology **established himself** (1:1) and similar expressions occur many times in Chronicles (see 2 Chr. 12:13; 13:21; 15:8; 17:1; 21:4; 23:1; 25:11; 27:6). They refer to such accomplishments as building fortifications (see 17:1-2; 27:6; 32:5), forming an army (see 17:1-2; 23:1; 25:11), reforming the nation (see 15:8), and securing the throne against opponents (see 12:13; 13:21; 27:6). Solomon accomplished much at the beginning of his reign.

The great accomplishments at this stage receive emphasis in the explanation added to this verse. To counter any charge of wrongdoing (see 10:4,11), the Chronicler made explicit the reason for Solomon's greatness. Solomon's successes occurred **for the Lord his God was with him and made him exceedingly great** (1:1). When God was 'with' someone in the book of Chronicles, he gave help in various struggles (see 13:12; see also *Introduction: 10) Divine Activity*). The Chronicler often emphasized divine help behind the accomplishments of David. At this point, he applied the same perspective to Solomon. His successes were not the result of human schemes or tyranny. They resulted from God's blessing.

Solomon Goes to Gibeon to Worship (1:2-6)

The core of this material derives from 1 Kgs. 3:3-15. Yet, the Chronicler's record differs in several ways. He omitted the reference to Solomon's marriage to Pharaoh's daughter (1 Kgs. 3:1-2) and his worship at the high places (1 Kgs. 3:3,4) to avoid detracting from Solomon as his ideal.

Beyond this, Solomon invited **all Israel** (1:2), the Chronicler's favorite designation for groups representing the entire nation and groups of national leaders (1:2; see also *Introduction: 1) All Israel*). The organization of these leaders follows patterns already established in David's reign. Solomon included **commanders of thousands** (see 1 Chr. 13:1; 29:6), **commanders of hundreds** (see 1 Chr. 13:1; 29:6), **judges** (see 17:8,10), **all the leaders in Israel** (see 1 Chr. 11:3; 17:6), and **heads of families** (see 1 Chr. 15:12; 23:9,24; 24:6,31; 26:21).

Moreover, the Chronicler also designated these supporters as **the whole assembly** (1:3). The term **assembly** (see also 1:5) has the connotation of a religious gathering designed especially for worship. Expanding the record of Kings in this way drew a parallel between this initial event in Solomon's reign and the assemblies of David's reign. Like David before him, the highpoints of Solomon's reign involved assembling the whole nation in times of worship. These assemblies conveyed the importance of the temple and its services for the post-exilic readers (see *Introduction: 5) Religious Assemblies*).

The Chronicler's desire to exalt Solomon as an ideal for his readers led him to add a defense of Solomon's worship at Gibeon (1:3b-6). The entire history of Chronicles emphasized the centrality of Jerusalem worship. This message was vital for the Chronicler's post-exilic readers. For this reason, he explained that **God's Tent of Meeting was there** in Gibeon (1:3b). This **Tent of Meeting** was none other than the one **Moses ... had made in the desert** (1:3b; see Exod. 40:17-19). When David **brought up the ark** to Jerusalem, he **pitched** [another] **tent for** [the ark] **in Jerusalem** (1:4), but **the bronze altar** for sacrifices (see Exod. 31:1-5; 35:30-36:7) remained **in Gibeon** (1:5a). For this reason, it was perfectly acceptable that **Solomon and the assembly inquired ... there** (1:5b).

It is noteworthy that the king and people **inquired of him** at Gibeon (1:5b). The Hebrew of this clause is ambiguous. It may be that Solomon 'inquired of it' (i.e. the bronze altar [NAS, NEB]) or 'inquired of him' (i.e. the Lord [NIV, NKJ, NRS]). Whatever the case, the Chronicler drew a connection at this point between Solomon and David. Several times he contrasted David with Saul precisely because David inquired of God and Saul did not (see 1 Chr. 10:14; 13:3; 14:10,14; see *Introduction: 19) Seeking*). This emphasis appears at the beginning of David's reign (see 1 Chr. 10:14) much as it does here at the beginning of Solomon's reign.

The text also adds that the bronze altar had been made by **Bezalel** (1:5). **Bezalel** appears only in Exodus and Chronicles (see Exod. 31:2; 35:30; 36:1,2; 37:1; 38:22; 1 Chr. 2:20; 2 Chr. 1:5). He was the chief artisan of Moses' tabernacle. This attention to Bezalel suggests that a subtle typological connection supported the Chronicler's portrait of Solomon. Bezalel fulfilled Moses' plans for the tabernacle much like Solomon fulfilled David's plans for the temple. Bezalel and Solomon were both from the tribe of Judah and endowed with special wisdom for the task of building (see Exod. 31:1-3; 35:30-35; 2 Chr. 1:5). While the writer of Kings spoke of Solomon's wisdom in general terms (see 1 Kgs. 3:16-20), the Chronicler focused on Solomon's wisdom in the building project. Furthermore, the writer of

Kings noted Hiram's tribute to Solomon as 'a wise son over this great people' (1 Kgs. 5:7). In Chronicles, Hiram's compliment included the notice that Solomon is the **son who will build** (2:11-12). These portions of the narrative continue to highlight Solomon as the temple builder.

The Chronicler also followed the account of Kings by noting that **a thousand burnt offerings** were offered on the bronze altar at Gibeon (1:6 // 1 Kgs. 3:4). The large number of sacrifices may be a hyperbole (for the Chronicler's use of hyperbole see comments on 1 Chr. 12:14), but depicts Solomon's enthusiasm for the worship of God (see 1:6; 5:6; 7:4-5; 24:14; 29:32-35; 35:8-9). The Chronicler's readers must be a people who have the same enthusiasm for worship (see *Introduction: 6) Royal Observance of Worship*).

Solomon and God Dialogue (1:7-12)

Following 1 Kgs. 3:5-15 the text describes Solomon's nocturnal revelation in Gibeon. The basic structure of his account is threefold: God speaks (1:7), Solomon responds (1:8-10), and God speaks again (1:11-12).

God initiated the dialogue with Solomon after sacrifices (1:7). Chronicles twice omits the explicit remark that this event was a dream (see 1 Kgs. 3:5,15), but the expression **that night** served as the equivalent (1:7). God's offer to Solomon was without qualification: **'Ask for whatever you want'** (1:7b). Apparently God was very pleased with Solomon and the assembly's worship at Gibeon.

Solomon's well-known response to the divine offer follows Kings for the most part (1:8-10 // 1 Kgs. 3:6-9), but two important differences emerge. First, Chronicles omits the reference to David's outstanding life (1 Kgs. 3:6b). Apparently, the Chronicler did not consider this the appropriate time to focus on David. Solomon's exemplary qualities are his concern here. Second, a similar explanation holds for the omission of Solomon's self-deprecation in Kings, 'But I am only a little child' (1 Kgs. 3:7).

Solomon asked for **wisdom and knowledge that** [he] **may lead** (1:10 // 1 Kgs. 3:7,9). Wisdom and the ability to lead are connected elsewhere in Scripture (see Prov. 8:15). Solomon's concern was to attain those necessary qualities that would allow him to reign effectively. The terminology **that I may lead** ('to go out and come in' [NAS, NRS, NKJ]) may allude to Num. 27:17 where Moses made the same request for Joshua. If so, the Chronicler compared David and Solomon to Moses and Joshua once again (see 1 Chr. 22:11-16; 28:20-21). By doing so, the Chronicler also endorsed Solomon as the rightful heir of David's kingdom and the one who brought David's vision to fruition.

Beyond this, Solomon described the nation as **this great people of yours** [God] (1:10 // 1 Kgs. 3:9). Although this expression is based on the parallel in Kings, it alluded to the emphasis elsewhere on the connection between divine kingship and the human throne of Israel (see *Introduction: 8) Divine Kingship*). Solomon sought only to represent, not usurp divine authority over Israel.

God's response to Solomon in Chronicles is similar to the account of Kings

(1:11-12 // 1 Kgs. 3:10-14). The Chronicler maintained that Solomon would be incomparable with regard to **wisdom and knowledge ... wealth, riches and honor** (1:12), but he omitted any reference to the conditions of these promises (1 Kgs. 3:14) as he had done earlier (see 1 Chr. 17:14 // 2 Sam. 7:14b). The idea that conditions applied to Solomon was in line with the Chronicler's doctrine of divine judgment and blessing (see *Introduction: 10) Divine Activity*), but he downplayed this matter, as well as Solomon's failures, to highlight the king's ideal character. In so doing, Solomon was an example of the kind of king who received prosperity from God (see *Introduction: 26) Prosperity and Poverty*).

In line with this concern, God's response to Solomon instructed the Chronicler's post-exilic readers about their motivations. Solomon's **heart desire** was not **wealth, riches or honor, nor for the death of** [his] **enemies**, nor **for a long life** (1:11). Therefore, he would be greatly rewarded. These words drew attention to Solomon's **heart's desire** or inward motivation (see *Introduction: 16) Motivations*). Those who had returned from exile faced the temptation to treat religion as a means of gaining these kinds of things for themselves. Their motivations for re-establishing the kingdom of Israel were not to be their own gain, but the honor of divine kingship in Israel. Only then could they hope to receive the other benefits of security and prosperity that they needed so desperately.

Solomon Returns to Jerusalem (1:13a)

The Chronicler abbreviates the Kings account at this point. Kings demonstrates Solomon's wisdom by reporting his establishment of Jerusalem as the place of worship (// 1 Kgs. 3:15). The Chronicler, however, had already gone to great lengths to justify Solomon's worship at Gibeon (see 1:3-6) and waited until later to describe Solomon's shift to Jerusalem (see 3:1ff). To balance the travel to Gibeon (1:2-6), he simply noted that **Solomon came from ... Gibeon ... to Jerusalem** (1:13a).

Solomon Reigns over Israel (1:13b)

To close the story as it began (see 1:1) the text adds the note that Solomon **reigned over Israel** (1:13b). By repeating this motif, the Chronicler highlighted his chief concern in this passage. Solomon began his reign over the people of God with a religious assembly including all of Israel and brought enormous blessings to the nation.

Solomon Experiences Divine Promises (1:14-17)

Having established the origins of Solomon's blessed kingdom, the Chronicler reported some of the ways these blessings appeared. A shorter version of this material is repeated in 2 Chr. 9:25, 27-28 to balance this passage in the overarching symmetrical structure of Solomon's reign (see figure 22). This account illustrated the kinds of divine benevolences that were available to the post-exilic kingdom, if they would follow Solomon's example.

Comparison with 1 Kings 10:26-29

For the most part, these verses derive from 1 Kings 10:26-29. Two minor differences appear between these passages. First, in 1:15 Chronicles reads **and gold**, but the absence of this expression in 1 Kgs. 10:27 probably resulted from corruption in textual transmission of Kings (see *Introduction: Translation and Transmission*).

Second, Chronicles reads **they** for 'the king's traders' (1:17 // 1 Kgs. 1:29), but this reflects the Chronicler's style, not a substantive change.

Third, the most important point of comparison is the transposition of this entire passage to this context in Chronicles. 1 Kgs. 10:26-29 summarizes how much Solomon had gained at the zenith of his kingdom. The Chronicler, however, placed this material immediately after God's promises to Solomon in order to emphasize that these promises were realized as a result of Solomon's devotion to God.

Structure of 1:14-17

This record of Solomon's wealth divides into three segments. Each portion amounts to a brief report (see figure 23). This brief summary of Solomon's wealth presented him as the incomparable king of Israel. God blessed him richly in military strength (1:14), civilian matters (1:15), and international trade (1:16-17).

Military Strength (1:14)

Solomon introduced the use of **chariots** in Israel's military arsenal. He not only accumulated many **chariots ... and horses**, but also housed them in **chariot cities** and **in Jerusalem**. Although no certain identifications of Solomonic stables have been established, archaeological finds in Megiddo, Hazor and Lachish suggest that such stables were plentiful at various times. These stables were broadly distributed to ensure rapid response in times of crisis. The sophistication of Solomon's achievements in this regard is remarkable. Israel had come to the verge of equaling the military strength of some of her more powerful neighboring empires. The Chronicler repeatedly presented military strength as a blessing from God. It was only when Israel's kings relied on their own might that military strength became problematic. In later years, reliance on military might led to apostasy in Israel (see Mic. 1:3-7; Amos 2:6-9,14), but at this time Solomon's chariots and horses were a display of divine blessing.

Domestic Prosperity (1:15)

The domestic economic benefits of Solomon's reign appear in two far reaching hyperboles. **Silver and gold** are said to have been **as common in Jerusalem as stones** (1:15). This description of Solomon's ideal Jerusalem may lie in the distant background of New Testament descriptions of the New Jerusalem (see Rev. 21:15-21). Moreover, **cedars** became **as plentiful as sycamore trees** (1:15). Sycamore trees grew in such abundance in the foothills that they were considered of little value (see 1 Chr. 27:28; Isa. 9:10). Cedars were valued much more highly and were usually imported (see 1 Chr. 17:1; Isa. 2:13; Ezek. 27:5). Needless to say, the purpose of the Chronicler's exaggerations was to emphasize that Solomon's economic benefit to Israel was incredible. (For the Chronicler's use of hyperbole, see comments on 1 Chr. 12:14.)

International Trade (1:16-17)

One of the signs of Solomon's greatness was the degree to which he entered the arena of international trade. Other descriptions of this aspect of his kingdom appear elsewhere (see 1 Kgs. 9:26-28; 10:1-13). Here the text mentions some of Solomon's more impressive trading partners: **Egypt ... Kue ... Hittites ... and Arameans** (1:16-17). Israel's central location among the great empires of the middle east made it subject to repeated conquests. During Solomon's reign, however, his kingdom was so strong that he used his geographical position to become an international trader.

Solomon's involvement with other nations offered important guidance to the Chronicler's readers. On several occasions, Chronicles touches on the theme of Israel's economic involvement with foreign nations (see *Introduction: 3) International Relations*). These examples of positive international relations encouraged the post-exilic community to seek such economic successes again.

Solomon's International Assistance (2:1-18)

The mention of Solomon's international trade (1:16-17) led the Chronicler to focus next on the international assistance he received in building the temple. This portion of Solomon's reign balances with 8:17-9:21 where Solomon receives international recognition for his accomplishments (see figure 22).

Comparison with 1 Kgs. 5:1-16; 7:13-14

This material derives primarily from two portions of the book of Kings. Nevertheless, the Chronicler added, omitted, and rearranged sections of these passages for his own purposes. In addition to insignificant variations due to stylistic changes and textual transmission, five items deserve comment.

First, the most important variation is the omission of 1 Kgs. 3:16-4:34. In these chapters the book of Kings illustrates Solomon's wisdom in his judicial decisions and governmental bureaucracy. None of this material ran counter to the Chronicler's purposes, but he probably streamlined events in Solomon's life so that the temple project moved quickly into view.

Second, several variations have the effect of enhancing Solomon's role in these events.

1) 2 Chr. 2:1 replaces 1 Kgs. 5:1. 1 Kgs. 5:1 begins with Hiram initiating contact with Solomon. The Chronicler had no reason to deny this fact, but he removed the verse in Kings to emphasize Solomon as solely responsible for the events described here.

2) 2 Chr. 2:2 is a displaced summary of 1 Kgs. 5:15 which also appears in 2 Chr. 2:18. The Chronicler repeated the same information in 2 Chr. 2:2 and 2:18 to

construct the passage into a symmetrical unit. Moreover, the repetition of the large numbers of workers at Solomon's disposal enhanced his importance.

3) The Chronicler omitted Solomon's offer to let Hiram set the wages for his workers (2:8 // 1 Kgs. 5:6) and added a record of Solomon's pledge to pay large sums for Hiram's laborers (2:10). By this means, Solomon remained in complete control of the affair.

4) The Chronicler expanded Hiram's praise of Solomon (2:11-12 // 1 Kgs. 5:7). His adulations focus on Solomon's **discretion and understanding** (2:12) in ways that allude to the Queen of Sheba's words in the balancing portion of Solomon's reign (see 9:5-8). Hiram's elaborate adulations included the Chronicler's belief that the Davidic throne showed that **the LORD loves his people** (2:11).

Third, in two places the Chronicler omitted references to David.

1) As we have seen before (see 1:1-13), the Chronicler turned his attention away from David to Solomon in this material. 1 Kgs. 5:3-4 explains why David did not build the temple. The Chronicler omitted these verses; apparently he felt he had sufficiently dealt with this issue earlier (see 1 Chr. 17:15).

2) The reference to David choosing Solomon is probably omitted for the same reason (1 Kgs. 5:5b).

Fourth, 2:13-14 alludes to 1 Kgs. 7:13-14. A number of affinities in terminology appear between these passages. In 2:13-14 the Chronicler reported Hiram's plan to send the skilled man **Huram-Abi** (not to be confused with King Hiram) to Solomon. He did not, however, report the actual sending of the **Huram-Abi**.

Fifth, Chronicles abbreviates 1 Kgs. 5:14-18 (// 2:15-18) to focus on the numbers of conscripted laborers. This variation probably resulted from his desire to parallel the concerns of the corresponding section of 2:2.

Structure of 2:1-18

The Chronicler's interaction with Kings resulted in three symmetrical segments (see figure 23). Very closely parallel passages report the numbers of conscripted laborers at the beginning and end (2:1-2; 2:17-18). These portions frame Solomon's correspondence with Hiram (2:3-16) which also divides into Solomon's letter (2:3-10) and Hiram's response (2:11-16).

Solomon's Conscripted Laborers (2:1-2)

At this point Chronicles turns to Solomon's construction of the temple. This shift is indicated by the simple assertion that Solomon gave **orders to build a temple** (2:1). Throughout Chronicles, successful building projects appear as signs of divine blessing (see *Introduction: 24) Building and Destruction*). As mentioned above, this verse replaces 1 Kgs. 5:1 which indicates that Hiram the king of Tyre contacted Solomon first. The Chronicler did not deny this fact, but did not want to distract from his portrait of Solomon as the indisputable leader of temple construction.

The Chronicler noted that Solomon not only called for **a temple for ... the LORD,** but also a **royal palace for himself**. Solomon's splendid palace comes into focus a number of times (see 2:12; 7:11; 8:1; 9:3, 11), but the details of its construction (1 Kgs. 7:1-12) are omitted. The Chronicler may have viewed the amount of time spent on Solomon's palace relative to the temple as a flaw in the king's character (see 1 Kgs. 6:38; 7:1). In all events, Chronicles concentrates attention on the surpassingly more important palace (temple) for God.

As in other passages, Solomon said the **temple** would be **for the Name of the LORD** (2:1). The Name of the Lord refers to the immanent presence of God on earth. The invocable powerful presence of God would dwell in Solomon's temple so that Israel could have access to the transcendent God through prayer in and toward the temple. This Name theology focused attention on the importance of the temple not only in Solomon's day but also in the Chronicler's time (see *Introduction: 11) Name of God*).

The Chronicler moved to a description of the conscripted laborers used in temple construction. He briefly drew upon 1 Kgs. 5:15 which he repeated again in 2:18. In the ancient Near East, it was customary for kings to have many forced laborers for large building projects. The writer of Kings made it clear that Solomon did not make Israelites his slaves (see 1 Kgs. 9:20-22). Yet, the complaints of Northerners against Rehoboam and Solomon imply that Israelites may have been compelled to be supervisors of the workers (see 10:1-4; see also 1 Kgs. 5:13-18). 1 Kings 11:28 indicates that Solomon gave Jeroboam charge of the laborers. Along these lines, the **foremen** in 2:2,18 may refer to this arrangement as well. The laborers themselves, however, were **aliens who were in Israel** (2:17).

Mosaic Law prohibited the enslavement of Israelites except for temporary and voluntary indentured service (see Lev. 25:39,42). Moses permitted the enslavement of foreigners living in the land (see Lev. 25:39-55) as well as prisoners of war (see Deut. 20:14; Lev. 25:46). Yet, slaves were protected by Mosaic Law far more than in many cultures surrounding Israel. A slave was emancipated if physical harm was done to him and the master was punished if the slave died from a beating (see Exod. 21:20,26). Even foreign slaves celebrated the Sabbath with their masters (see Exod. 20:10; Deut. 5:14). As progressive as Old Testament Law may have been for its time, it still fell short of the divine ideal. The teaching of the New Testament on the subject of slavery (see 1 Cor. 7:21; Phil. 16) makes it clear that these Mosaic regulations were concessions to the 'hardness of heart' (Matt. 19:8) because 'it was not so from the beginning' (Matt. 19:8).

The large numbers of workers show how Solomon put his national resources to the task of building the temple. Solomon's enthusiastic pursuit of temple construction formed a vital aspect of the Chronicler's ideal portrait. The post-exilic readers were to imitate Solomon's devotion as they supported the temple and its services in their day.

Solomon and Hiram Correspond (2:3-16)

Building the temple required materials and skilled workers beyond those available in Israel. For this reason Solomon turned to **Hiram king of Tyre** (An alternative spelling 'Huram' appears in the Hebrew of Chronicles [see NRS, NKJ, NAS]). Tyre was a seaport along the Phoenician coast. From biblical records we know that Hiram was a prominent trader in the ancient world with access to rare goods and skilled workers (see 1 Kgs. 5:1,12; 1 Chr. 14:1; 2 Chr. 2:11,12; 9:21).

The Chronicler's record of contact between Hiram and Solomon divides into two parts: Solomon's letter (2:3-10) and Hiram's response (2:11-16). These materials are similar to the account of 1 Kgs. 5:2-12 and 7:13-14, but several variations reveal a distinctive outlook.

Solomon's letter to Hiram (2:3-10) consisted of three requests. Solomon asked for: (1) a supply of **cedar logs** (2:3b-4); (2) a **man skilled** (2:5-7); (3) **cedar, pine, and algum logs from Lebanon** (2:8-10). Only the third request closely parallels the book of Kings (2:8a // 1 Kgs. 5:6a). Consequently, this record of Solomon's requests came from the Chronicler's hand and reflected his chief concerns.

In the first request for **cedar logs** Solomon appealed to Hiram's relationship with **David** (2:3; see 1 Chr. 14:1). Just as David had to depend on Solomon to fulfill his plans (see 1 Chr. 22:7-10; 29:1), now Solomon depended on David's previous relation with Hiram. This interdependence between David and Solomon was an important dimension of the Chronicler's viewpoint on the United Kingdom. Each of them represented aspects of one ideal which the Chronicler set before his post-exilic readers.

The explanation for his first request (2:4) is part of the largest addition the Chronicler made to Solomon's letter. This temple was for **the Name of the LORD** [his] **God** (2:4; see *Introduction: 11) Name of God*). Solomon wrote that this temple would be **dedicated** to God for three particular purposes: **incense** (see Exod. 25:6; 30:7-8), **consecrated bread,** and **burnt offerings** (see Num. 28:3; see Lev. 1; 6:8-13) **every morning and evening on Sabbaths** (see Num. 28:9-10), **New Moons** (see Num. 10:10) and **feasts** (see Num. 10:10). Many of these elements of worship have already been highlighted in other ideal assemblies (see 1 Chr. 16:1; 21:26; 29:21; 2 Chr. 1:6; 7:7; 8:12).

The reason for the Chronicler's emphasis on these worship activities appears in words that follow: **this is a lasting ordinance for Israel** (2:4b). Most translations of this verse treat these words as part of Solomon's letter. It is possible, however, that they are the Chronicler's own authorial comment. Whatever the case, the effect is the same. Solomon's plan to observe these elements of worship was not just for his day. The Chronicler stated explicitly that his worship arrangements had been decreed for Israel throughout the Old Testament period, including the Chronicler's post-exilic era (see *Introduction: 14) Standards*).

The second portion of Solomon's letter (2:5-7) is the Chronicler's addition to the text of Kings. It consists of an explanation (2:5-6) and a request (2:7). In his explanation, Solomon expressed his plan for the building itself. It **will be great** (i.e. both **large and magnificent** [2:9]) because **our God is greater than all other gods** (2:5). The temple must reflect the supremacy of Israel's God (see Exod. 18:11; Ps. 135:5).

Beyond this, Solomon acknowledged that no one is **able to build a temple** that is splendid enough **for him**, because the **highest heavens ... cannot contain him** (2:6). No matter how great the temple may be, it would not be magnificent enough to match the grandeur of Israel's God. Solomon drew on these concepts again at the dedication of the temple (see 6:18; see also Ps. 139:7-10; Isa. 66:1; Jer. 23:24; Acts 7:48,49).

It is no wonder that Solomon closed his explanation with an allusion to the humble words of David, **'But who am I?'** Solomon recognized that he was unworthy of this honor. Moreover, he knew he was unable to do anything more than make **a place to burn sacrifices before** God (2:6). The temple could be nothing more than a place to perform earthly sacrifices to honor Israel's transcendent God.

For these reasons, Solomon made a second request. He asked for **a skilled man** (an artisan) who knew how to work with **gold, silver, bronze, iron, purple crimson, blue yarn**, and **engraving** (2:7). As later descriptions of the temple illustrate, these skills were needed for the various furnishings and decorations of the temple. Hiram's **skilled man** was not to work alone; he was to supervise the **skilled craftsmen** whom **David provided** (2:7).

Solomon's third request was for trees **from Lebanon** (2:8). The forests of Lebanon were renowned for producing trees of strength and beauty (see Pss. 29:5; 104:16; Song. 5:15; Isa. 37:24). While this request has a rough parallel in 1 Kgs. 5:6a, Solomon's motivation is largely without parallel in Kings. He said that **the temple ... must be large and magnificent** (2:9). To insure Hiram's positive response, Solomon promised to pay the **woodsmen** well for their work (2:10). Once again, expense was not an issue for Solomon. He was willing to spend whatever it took to build an appropriately splendid temple for God. The Chronicler's post-exilic readers must be ready to do the same in their day.

Hiram's Letter (2:11-16)

Hiram sent a letter to Solomon agreeing to meet his requests. His letter divides into three parts: praise of Solomon (2:11-12), report of sending Huram-Abi (2:13-14), and the request for payment (2:15-16). The first and last portions roughly parallel Kings (2:11-12 // 1 Kgs. 5:7-8; 2:15-16 // 1 Kgs. 5:9). The middle portion (2:13-14) has no direct parallel in 1 Kgs. 5, but corresponds to the account of Hiram's fulfillment of his promise in 1 Kgs. 7:13-14.

Hiram began his response to Solomon with extensive praises for the king (2:11-12). Both Kings and Chronicles report how Hiram wrote that God had **given David a wise son** (2:12 // 1 Kgs. 5:7). In addition to this, however, more elaborate praises were heaped on Solomon.

First, Hiram claimed that Solomon was king **because the LORD loves his people** (2:11). On several occasions, the Chronicler emphasized that the Davidic line was God's gift of love to Israel (see *Introduction: 5) Royal and Levitical Families*). To counter any misgivings about the legitimacy and necessity of re-establishing David's royal line, the Chronicler seized another opportunity to remind his post-exilic readers that the Davidic line was their divine blessing.

Second, after expanding the praise of God to include **who made heaven and earth** (2:12a // 1 Kgs. 5:7), the Chronicler's details of Hiram's letter resumed praise of Solomon. He added to Kings that Solomon has received **intelligence and discernment** (2:12b). He also urged that Solomon would build **a temple for the LORD and a palace for himself** (2:12c). This last addition recalls 2:1 and demonstrates Hiram's agreement with all that Solomon planned to do. Moreover, it also anticipates the praise which the Queen of Sheba gave to Solomon (see 9:5-8). The Chronicler revealed his own attitude toward Solomon in Hiram's words. Solomon was wise and accomplished much that benefited Israel.

The second portion of Hiram's letter describes how he sent **Huram-Abi** to oversee the artisans working on the temple (2:13-14). As we have seen, a number of correspondences exist between this section and 1 Kgs. 7:13. 1 Kgs. 7:13 calls this man 'Huram', but the Chronicler used the longer form of the name ('Huram-Abi').

The third portion of Hiram's letter requests that Solomon pay for his services (2:15-16). This portion roughly parallels 1 Kgs. 5:9, but has been adapted to match the language of Solomon's promised payment in 2:8-10. This modification also made it clear to the Chronicler's readers that Solomon received full cooperation from Hiram (see 2:1-2).

This correspondence between Solomon and Hiram contributed a significant element to the Chronicler's portrait of relations between Israel and other nations. In later portions of his history, the Chronicler demonstrated the dire consequences of reliance on foreign powers (see 16:1-9; 28:16-21; see also *Introduction: 3) International Relations*). Solomon's actions, however, make it clear that the Chronicler did not prohibit all contact with foreigners. In fact, he honored Solomon for using the help of other nations even in temple construction. The Chronicler may have focused on this feature of Solomon's activity to counter radical exclusivism in the post-exilic community. So long as Israel's cooperative efforts with other nations were in the service of God's purposes and under its supervision, such cooperation was not forbidden.

More on Solomon's Conscripted Laborers (2:17-18)

In balance with the opening of this section (see 2:2), the Chronicler gave additional information on Solomon's conscripted laborers. The first portion roughly parallels 1 Kgs. 5:13-17 and reports that Solomon **took a census of all the aliens who were in the land** (2:17). As mentioned above (see 2:2), Solomon did not conscript Israelites as laborers. He numbered the aliens who had survived the conquest (see 8:8) and employed them for work on the temple much as **David his father** had done (2:17; see 1 Chr. 22:2). For other examples of census in Chronicles see 1 Chr. 21; 27:23-24; 2 Chr. 2:17; 14:8; 17:14-19.

The second portion of this material (2:18) is nearly a perfect repetition of 2:2. The expression **with 3,600 foremen over them to keep the people working** is somewhat ambiguous. It may be understood that the 3,600 were from among the laborers (NRS, NAS, NKJ), or it may be taken as a reference to another group (perhaps Israelites) who served over the conscripted laborers (NIV). The latter approach seems best in the light of the fact that David did not conscript Israelites as laborers (see 8:9).

In all events, by repeating this information, the Chronicler highlighted Solomon's exemplary devotion of national resources to the temple project. The Chronicler's post-exilic readers also had to be ready to dedicate the resources of the nation to the temple in their own day.

Solomon's Temple Building Project (3:1-5:1)

The Chronicler moved directly from Solomon preparing to build the temple (2:1-18) to the construction itself (3:1-5:1). This material balances with his further discussion of the actual construction in 8:1-16 (see figure 22). These chapters focus on various structures, furnishings, and decorations in Solomon's temple. A summary of the temple and its contents may be found in the Introduction to this commentary (see *Introduction: Appendix B - The Structures, Furnishings and Decorations of Solomon's Temple*).

Comparison with 1 Kings 6:1-7:51

The Chronicler depended to varying degrees on 1 Kgs. 6:1-7:51 as he described the buildings and furnishings of the temple complex. A detailed analysis is beyond the scope of this commentary, but a number of large scale comparisons will reveal the distinctive emphases of the Chronicler's record.

The following comparison traces the contours of the relationship with Kings (see figure 24 on next page). As the comparison indicates, the texts of Chronicles and Kings relate in four ways. First, most of the Chronicler's text amounts to rough parallels with sections from Kings. In these portions, small differences appear, but the Chronicler's dependence on Kings is still evident. Particular differences in these sections will be addressed in the comments that follow.

Second, some portions of these chapters very closely parallel the book of Kings. They too will be noted in the comments that follow.

Third, the Chronicler omitted large portions of Kings.

1) He did not refer to 1 Kgs. 6:4-20. Apparently, some of the details of the temple did not interest him (1 Kgs. 6:4-10, 14-20). Moreover, he did not repeat the conditional promise of divine presence in the temple (1 Kgs. 6:11-13). Although the Chronicler mentioned conditionality in David's speech to Solomon (see 1 Chr. 28:9), here he omitted the conditions associated with God's promises to Solomon as he had beforehand (see 2 Sam. 7:14b // 1 Chr. 17:13; 1 Kgs. 3:10-14 // 2 Chr. 1:11-12).

2) 1 Kgs. 6:28-7:14 also do not appear in Chronicles. Once again, for some unknown reasons certain details do not seem to have interested the Chronicler (1 Kgs. 6:28-38; 7:9-14). He also omitted the record of Solomon's palace (1 Kgs. 7:1-

2 Chr.		1 Kgs.
3:1-2	Introduction (loosely parallel)	6:1
	Buildings (3:3-17)	
3:3-4	- Overview of Temple (loosely parallel)	6:2-3
———	- Details and Solomon's Conditional Promise (omitted)	6:4-20
3:5-7	- Main Hall (loosely parallel)	6:21-22
	- Most Holy Place	
3:8-9	Details(added)	———
3:10-13	Cherubim (loosely parallel)	6:23-27
3:14	Huram-Abi (added)	———
———	- Details and Solomon's Palace (omitted)	6:28-7:14
3:15-17	- Portico (loosely parallel)	7:15-22
	Furnishings (4:1-10)	
	- In the Priestly Court	
4:1	Bronze altar (added)	———
4:2-5	Metal Sea (closely parallel)	7:23-26
———	- Details on Ten Moveable Stands (omitted)	7:27-37
4:6	(roughly parallel)	7:38-39a
4:7-8	- In the Main Hall (added)	———
	- In the Priestly Court	
4:9	Courts Distinguished (added)	———
4:10	Location of Sea (loosely parallel)	7:39b
4:11-22	Appendix (closely parallel)	7:40-50
5:1	Closing (closely parallel)	7:51

Comparison of 2 Chr. 3:1-5:1 and 1 Kgs. 6:1-7:51 (figure 24)

8). His focus was on the temple instead. Moreover, he may have interpreted the contrast of 'seven years' construction for the temple (1 Kgs. 6:38) with 'thirteen years' construction for the palace (1 Kgs. 7:1) as a blemish on Solomon's record.

3) Details regarding 'the ten movable stands of bronze' (1 Kgs. 7:27-37) are omitted. The Chronicler was less concerned with the detailed descriptions of the stands and more interested in explaining their function (see 4:6,14).

Fourth, new material is added to the account of Kings in four places.

1) 3:8-9 adds information about the Most Holy Place. Gold overlay and **nails** in the room are of particular interest.

2) 3:14 adds information about the skills of Huram-Abi.

3) The Chronicler added a brief note about the **bronze altar** (4:1) to the record of furnishings in the priestly court (4:1-6).

4) Similarly, he added information regarding the distinction between the **courtyard of the priests** and **the large court** (4:9). The reasons for these additions are not clear. In all likelihood, however, they were motivated by questions related to the reconstruction of the temple in post-exilic times.

Structure of 3:1-5:1

This passage divides into five symmetrical sections (see figure 23). 3:1-2 and 5:1 form a frame for this passage by describing the beginning and ending of Solomon's construction effort. The king's work divides into three parts: the building itself (3:2-17), the furnishings (4:1-10), and an addendum which reiterates and elaborates on the preceding material (4:11-22).

Solomon Begins Construction (3:1-2)

The opening words of this section set this material on par with the first two steps of Solomon's reign, in which he **established himself** (1:1) and **gave orders to build a temple** (2:1). In the third step of his kingdom he **began to build the temple** (3:1). Moreover, this verse also balances with 5:1 where it is said that **all the work ... done for the temple ... was finished**.

3:1-2 differs from its parallel in 1 Kgs. 6:1-3 in several important ways. On the one hand, Kings dates this event from the exodus from Egypt. The Chronicler simply noted the day within Solomon's reign (3:2). On the other hand, the Chronicler informed his readers of a fact not presented anywhere else in Scripture. He noted that **the temple of the Lord** was build on **Mount Moriah** which was **the threshing floor of Ornan the Jebusite** (3:1). The Chronicler stressed the holiness of the place of temple construction by identifying it with the site where God had shown mercy to Abraham and to David. Abraham prepared to offer Isaac and received a substitute for Isaac on **Mount Moriah** (see Gen. 22:1-19). **The threshing floor of Ornan** (3:1) was the **place David had appointed** (3:1). God demonstrated great mercy to David at this threshing floor by forgiving David of his sins and healing the land (see 1 Chr. 21:1-22:1). As a result, the Chronicler established that Solomon's temple was located at the place where his readers could find mercy from God as well.

Solomon's Temple Buildings (3:3-17)

The first concern of this material is the central architectural structure of the temple complex. Following the account of 1 Kgs. 6:2-3, the Chronicler began with a brief overview of the central building (3:3-4). His record focuses on the dimensions of **the temple** (3:3) (which included the Main Hall and the Most Holy Place) and the **portico** (3:4). Contrary to the NIV, 3:4b should be kept with the first half of the verse (compare NAS, NKJ, NRS). The Chronicler added the fact that the interior of the portico was overlaid with gold.

An unusual insight into the Chronicler's motivations appears in 3:3. Unlike the parallel in 1 Kgs. 6:2-3, the Chronicler explained that the measurements he gave were **using the cubit of the old standard** (3:3). The standard size of a cubit in the

Chronicler's day was larger than 'the old standard' (see Ezek. 40:5; 43:13). Here the Chronicler openly revealed his concern to communicate clearly to his post-exilic readers (compare 1 Chr. 29:7).

After his quick overview of the central building of the temple complex, the Chronicler narrowed his focus to describe details of its three main sections (3:5-17): the **Main Hall** (3:5-7), the **Most Holy Place** (3:8-14), and the **portico** (3:15-17). His concern with some specific items may seem pedantic to contemporary readers, but they provided his readers with essential knowledge of the splendor of Solomon's temple. These visual images inspired them to reach for this glorious ideal in their own day.

First, the Chronicler dealt with the **Main Hall** (3:5-7 // 1 Kgs. 6:21-22). He focused on its glory in two ways. He added that Solomon **paneled the main hall with pine** (3:5). He also added that this paneling was decorated with **precious stones** (3:5). Moreover, rather than simply stating that Solomon 'overlaid the whole interior in gold' (1 Kgs. 6:22), he specified that gold was overlaid on **the ceiling beams, doorframes, walls, and doors ... and the carved cherubim on the walls** (3:7). Only a few choice people had ever seen the Main Hall of the temple. The Chronicler's detailed description gave his readers a spectacular vision of the room.

Second, the Chronicler turned to **the Most Holy Place** (3:8-14). The last verses of this section parallel Kings (3:10-14 // 1 Kgs. 6:23-27), but the opening verses are additional (3:8-9). Once again, the addition focuses on the splendor of the decorations. The text mentions **six hundred talents of fine gold** on the walls (about 23 tons or 21 metric tons), **gold nails** (or 'hooks' as it may be translated) each weighing **fifty shekels** (about 1.25 pounds or 0.6 kilograms) and **gold** on **the upper parts** (3:8-9).

Abbreviating the record of Kings (3:10-14 // 1 Kgs. 6:23-27), the Chronicler described the **pair of sculptured cherubim ... overlaid ... with gold** (3:10). The combined wing span of the cherubs extending from one end of the room to the other was **twenty cubits** (about 30 feet or 18 meters) (3:11,13). These cherubs represented the angelic beings worshipping and ministering around the throne of God in heaven (see Ezek. 1:4-28; 10:1-22; Isa. 6:2-3; Rev. 4:8-9; 5:8-14).

The Chronicler closed his description of the Most Holy Place by adding 3:14. He mentioned a colorfully decorated **curtain** separating the Most Holy Place from the Main Hall. Kings describes doors at this location (see 1 Kgs. 6:31-32; 7:50). A curtain hung at this place in the tabernacle (see Exod. 26:31; 36:35). Apparently both doors and a curtain separated the two rooms in Solomon's temple.

Third, the Chronicler skipped a large portion of Kings (1 Kgs. 6:28-7:14) to place his discussion of the **portico** next to the other sections of the central temple building (3:15-17 // 7:15-22). His main concern here was the two **pillars** that stood at the top of the stairs leading to the portico. He abbreviated the record of Kings and mentioned the decorative **chains** and **pomegranates** (3:16). His primary concern, however, was the symbolic names of the **pillars** (3:17). The pillar to the left **(south)** was named **Jakin** which means, 'He (God) establishes.' The pillar to the right (**north**) was called **Boaz** which means 'Strength is in him (God)'. The pillars were doxological displays of what went on within the walls of the temple. The nation of Israel found strength and was established by the divine presence there.

By mentioning this symbolism, the Chronicler inspired his post-exilic readers to give due attention to the temple in their own day. The pillars of the portico reminded them that the divine presence in the temple was their only hope for safety and victory.

Solomon's Temple Furnishings (4:1-10)

The record of the furnishings for various parts of the temple complex divides into three sections. Notes appear on the priestly court (4:1-6), the Main Hall (4:7-8), and the priestly court for a second time (4:9-10).

First, the Chronicler turned to the priestly court (4:1-6). These verses do not explicitly identify the priestly court as the location, but a comparison of the items here with those of 4:8-10 makes the connection clear. The Chronicler's description consists of an addition of his own (4:1), a closely parallel middle portion (4:2-5 // 1 Kgs. 7:23-26), and an omission of 1 Kgs. 7:27-37 which allowed him to place the material of 4:6 (// 1 Kgs. 7:38-39a) adjacent to this section.

The **bronze altar** mentioned in the Chronicler's addition (4:1) is well-known in Kings and Chronicles. In line with his focus on the colossal dimensions of the temple, the Chronicler mentioned that it was **twenty cubits long**, **wide**, and **ten cubits high** (approximately 30 x 30 x 15 feet [or 9 x 9 x 4.5 meters]).

A description of the **Sea** appears next (4:2-5); its use is described later (4:6b). The **Sea** was about 15 feet (2.3 meters) in diameter with about a 44 feet (13.3 meters) circumference (1 Chr. 18:8; 2 Chr. 4:6,10,15). It held approximately 17,500 gallons (66 kiloliters) of water. The book of Kings mentions 'gourds' under the rim of the Sea (1 Kgs. 7:24). The Chronicler called them **figures of bulls** (4:3a) or as it may be translated 'figures like bulls' (see NAS, NKJ). His words probably reflect his impression of the gourds' appearance. These **twelve bulls** on which it stood (4:3-4) faced in all directions and probably represented the twelve tribes of Israel who came to the temple from all directions.

The last items within the priestly court were the **ten basins for washing** (4:6). The mention of these items caused the Chronicler to add an explanation of their function. The **Sea** was for the **priests for washing** while the **basins** were for **the things** (utensils) **to be used in burnt offerings** (4:6b).

Second, the Chronicler turned to the furnishings of the **Main Hall** in a short addition to the record of Kings (4:7-8). He mentioned **ten gold lampstands** (4:7,20; 13:11; 1 Kgs. 7:49) corresponding to the one lampstand of Moses' tabernacle (see Exod. 25:31-39; 37:17-24; 40:4). **Ten tables** were in the room (4:8,19; 13:11; 29:18) corresponding to the one table in the tabernacle (see Exod. 25:23-30; 37:10-16; 40:4,22). In addition to these furnishings, Solomon made one hundred **gold sprinkling bowls** (4:8,11,22). The large number of these bowls is known only from Chronicles. Again, the grandeur of Solomon's temple comes to the foreground.

Third, this section ends by returning to the furnishings of the priestly court (4:9-10; compare 4:1-6). A distinction is made between **the courtyard of the priests and the large court** (4:9). Kings reports that there were courts surrounding the temple (see 1 Kgs. 6:36; 7:12), but the Chronicler distinguished these two courts along the lines of Ezekiel's descriptions of the post-exilic temple (see Ezek. 40-48). The **large court** was for the laity involved in worship; the **courtyard of the priests** was for the priests and Levites only (4:9). His purpose in adding this note was to locate the **Sea** in the priestly courtyard at the **southeast corner** of the temple (4:10).

Reiteration and Elaboration (4:11-22)

This passage breaks the overarching symmetry of this section (see figure 23) and follows the book of Kings closely (// 1 Kgs. 7:40-50). Some interpreters have concluded that these verses may have been inserted into Chronicles after its original composition during the centuries of textual transmission (see *Introduction: Translation and Transmission*). It is more likely, however, that the Chronicler simply copied from Kings at this point as an addendum to his main discussion. This material divides into two sections: work attributed to Huram-Abi (4:11-18) and Solomon's furnishings and decorations (4:19-22).

Only a few comments are necessary for this passage. First, it should be noted that the NIV omits the name Hiram(-Abi) from 4:11a. The Hebrew reads, 'Hiram also made ...' The entirety of 4:11 deals with Hiram(-Abi)'s work. Second, many of the items mentioned here have already been described in much greater detail, but some have not appeared before now. Third, the Chronicler may have included these lists which record item after item in order to illustrate further the glory of the temple, revealing it as a place containing things of wonder beyond number (see 4:18).

Solomon Completes Construction (5:1)

The Chronicler closed his account of Solomon's temple construction by quoting 1 Kgs. 7:51. This verse balances with the opening verses of this section. There **Solomon began to build the temple of the LORD** (3:1-2); now he **finished the temple of the LORD** (5:1).

Upon completion of the construction, Solomon **brought in the things his father David had dedicated** (5:1). Chronicles reports David's wars (1 Chr. 18:1-20:8) and explains that David had devoted the spoils of battle to **the treasuries of God's temple** (see 1 Chr. 18:8,10; 22:3,14,16; 26:26; 29:29). By alluding to this connection between David and Solomon's temple, the Chronicler once again tied the two kings together around their central concern, the temple project. As two sides of this one project, both David and Solomon served as models for post-exilic Israel.

Solomon's Assembly to Dedicate the Temple (5:2-7:10)

In this section of Solomon's reign we come to the fourth and greatest act Solomon performed, the dedication of the temple. He **established himself** as king (1:1),

gave orders to build a temple (2:1), **began to build the temple** (3:1), and now **summoned** an assembly **to Jerusalem** (5:2). This assembly is the topic of the Chronicler's record until Solomon **sent the people to their homes** (7:10).

Comparison with 1 Kgs. 8:1-66 and Ps. 132

In this passage, the Chronicler followed two main texts: 1 Kgs. 8:1-66 and Ps. 132. His record diverges in small ways on occasion. These differences will be addressed in the discussions that follow. On a large scale, however, a number of comments deserve attention.

First, the Chronicler added 5:11-13a. These verses draw attention to details related to the priests and Levitical musicians present at the assembly. In his usual fashion, the Chronicler showed himself much more interested in the priests and Levites than the book of Kings (see *Introduction: 4-9) King and Temple*).

Second, at first glance it appears that Chronicles adds 6:5b-6a, but this is probably not the case. An analysis of 1 Kgs. 8:16 suggests that it is more likely that these sentences were originally in Kings and lost through the textual transmission of Kings (see *Introduction: Translation and Transmission*). The repetition of the word 'there' in 6:5b-6a triggered the loss.

Third, 6:13 also appears to be added to the record of Kings (// 1 Kgs. 8:22). It is more likely, however, that this verse was also lost from the book of Kings through a scribal error (see *Introduction: Translation and Transmission*). The repetition of 'spread out his hands' (6:12-13) probably caused a scribe to skip the intervening material.

Fourth, in 6:40-42 the Chronicler replaced 1 Kgs. 8:50-53 with portions of Ps. 132:1, 8-10. In Kings, Solomon's prayer ends with an appeal to God's redeeming work in the Exodus from Egypt. The Chronicler dropped this theme (see 3:2 // 1 Kgs. 6:1; also 6:11 // 1 Kgs. 8:21) in order to heighten the importance of the promise to David. This focus fit well with the Chronicler's emphasis on the vital connections between David and Solomon's reigns.

Fifth, the Chronicler diverged from Kings in a small manner in 6:14. 1 Kgs. 8:25 reads 'walks before me'. The Chronicler specified the meaning of this expression by shifting to **walks in my law** (6:14). This change fit well with his emphasis on the Mosaic Law as the standard for Israel (see *Introduction: 14) Standards*).

Sixth, in 7:1b-3 the Chronicler shifted from Solomon's blessing toward the assembly in 1 Kgs. 8:54-61 to God's display of approval for Solomon's prayer. He then followed 1 Kgs. 8:62-64 closely (// 7:4-5,7) with the exception of an elaboration on the performances of priests and Levites (7:6).

Seventh, in 7:9 the Chronicler replaced the latter half of 1 Kgs. 8:65 with an explanation of the connection between the festival of the temple and the feast of Tabernacles. This change may be another indication of his special interest in re-establishing proper worship patterns in the post-exilic community.

Structure of 5:2-7:10

The Chronicler's version of these events divides into six parts which form a symmetrical pattern (see figure 23). This section begins with Solomon calling an assembly (5:2-3) and ends with its dismissal (7:8-10). The assembly opens with sacrifices and musical celebration (5:4-6:2); it closes in much the same way (7:1-7). In the assembly, Solomon speaks twice. He praises God for past blessings (6:3-11); then he prays to God for the future (6:12-42).

Solomon's Assembly Gathers (5:2-3)

The gathering of Solomon's temple assembly is a brief episode dividing into two parts: the king's summons (5:2) and the response (5:3). In 5:2 the Chronicler followed Kings closely, but the language of the opening verse draws attention to several similarities between Solomon and David.

1) Solomon called for a religious assembly. Although the NIV simply says **summoned to Jerusalem** (5:2), the expression translated 'summoned' is the same word translated 'assembled' elsewhere (see NRS, NAS, NKJ; also compare 1 Chr. 13:5; 15:3 [but see **summoned to assemble** in 1 Chr. 28:1]). For the Chronicler, this wording was often technical terminology for a religious assembly (see *Introduction: 5) Religious Assemblies*). Like David before him, Solomon's reign involved a number of assemblies which served to inspire the Chronicler's readers to proper worship observances in their day. The purpose of this assembly was **to bring up the ark of the LORD's covenant** (5:2; for the significance of this designation, see *Introduction: 13) Covenant*).

2) Beyond this, the groups of people in attendance at Solomon's assembly recollect the assemblies of David. He gathered **elders** (5:2; see 1 Chr. 11:3; 15:25), **heads of the tribes** (5:2; see 1 Chr. 28:1), and **chiefs** (5:2).

3) Another connection with David appears in the response to Solomon's summons (5:3). The Chronicler followed the language of Kings here (1 Kgs. 8:2), but the terminology fit his purposes well. Although the leaders of the nation had been specifically identified as the recipients of Solomon's call, the Chronicler summed up the attendees as **all the men of Israel** (5:3). Thus Solomon's assembly is representative of the entire nation much as David's assemblies before him (1 Chr. 11:1 // 2 Sam. 5:1,3; 1 Chr. 13:5 // 2 Sam. 6:1; 1 Chr. 22:2; 28:1). The Chronicler's theme of 'all Israel' united under David and Solomon is apparent (see *Introduction: 1) All Israel*).

The Israelites gathered **at the time of the festival in the seventh month** (5:2). The occasion was the annual feast of Tabernacles (see Lev. 23:33-43; Num. 29:12-39; Deut. 16:13-17) which was celebrated the 15th day of the seventh month (i.e. mid-October). The book of Kings notes that the temple was actually completed in the eighth month (see 1 Kgs. 6:38). In all likelihood, therefore, this celebration and dedication of the temple took place one month before the final touches on the temple were completed in order to coincide the dedication with the annual feast of Tabernacles.

Solomon's Initial Celebration of the Temple (5:4-6:2)
The Chronicler followed the book of Kings and reported aspects of Solomon's celebration. His record is very much like 1 Kgs. 8:1-13 with the exception of the additional information on the priests and Levites, especially their musical responsibilities (5:11-13a; see *Introduction: 8) Music*). The heart of this passage is 5:7-10 where the ark is placed in the Most Holy Place. On either side are accounts of celebrative worship moving toward the Most Holy Place (5:4-6) and moving away from it (5:11-6:2; see figure 23). At least two aspects of the passage support this outline. First, locations are mentioned explicitly. The celebrants are on the way (5:4-6); they reach their destination of the Most Holy Place (5:7-10); they come out (5:11-6:2). Second, both the first and last portions focus on **priests** (5:5, 11) along with **Solomon** (5:6; 6:1).

Celebrative Worship Outside the Most Holy Place (5:4-6)
This passage first attends to the procession toward the Most Holy Place. The procession involved **all the elders** (5:4), the **Levites** (5:4), **priests** (5:5), **King Solomon** (5:6) and **the entire assembly of Israel** (5:6). It was a grand event, much like David's earlier procession of the ark (see 1 Chr. 15:25-16:3). The Chronicler's use of the term **assembly** (5:6) raised this event to a prominent place on par with a number of other exemplary religious assemblies (see *Introduction: 5) Religious Assemblies*).

The enormous crowd brought up **the ark and the Tent of Meeting and all the sacred furnishings in it** (5:4). David had already retrieved the **ark** (see 15:25-16:3), but the **Tent of Meeting** and its various **furnishings** had been left in Gibeon (see 1 Chr. 16:39; 2 Chr. 1:3). Solomon, therefore, completed the centralization of worship in Jerusalem. No longer would worship be split between Jerusalem and Gibeon as it had been in David's reign and in Solomon's early years (see 1 Chr. 16:37-42; 2 Chr. 1:4-5).

Moreover, when the tabernacle of Moses came to rest in Solomon's temple (presumably in some storage chamber), it reflected the covenantal continuity between Solomon's structure and that of Moses (see 5:10). The temple was not a replacement of the tabernacle. It was larger and more splendid, but the temple incorporated and furthered the worship ideology of the Mosaic period. The chief change was that the tabernacle was mobile and that the temple was a permanent structure. This development corresponded to Israel's change from a moving people to a stable empire. In a word, Solomon's temple brought Moses' tabernacle to greater heights.

This passage focuses on the procession **from Zion, the City of David** (5:2) to **the Most Holy Place** (5:7). We do not know when Solomon brought the **Tent of Meeting** and its **furnishings** (5:5) to Jerusalem, but we are told here what happened on its short journey within the city.

The rather vivid portrait focuses on three aspects of the procession. First, the **priests** carried the items from the Tent of Meeting (5:5b). Second, **Solomon and**

the entire assembly of Israel walked before **the ark** (5:6). Third, as the ark moved, the king and assembly sacrificed **so many sheep and cattle that they could not be recorded or counted** (5:6).

These descriptions also allude to similarities between this event and David's earlier retrieval of the ark. David's procession also involved Levites carrying the holy items (see 1 Chr. 15:2,12-15,26) and sacrifices surrounded the event (see 1 Chr. 15:26; 16:1-2). For other parallels between David's and Solomon's processions, see comments on 5:2-3. The Chronicler's hyperbole regarding the number of Solomon's sacrifices raises this event beyond David's earlier procession (5:6b; for the Chronicler's use of hyperbole, see comments on 1 Chr. 12:14). Large numbers of sacrifices are frequently mentioned to inspire the post-exilic readers to enthusiasm for temple worship (see 1:6; 5:6; 7:4-5; 24:14; 29:32-35; 35:8-9; see also *Introduction: 6) Royal Observance of Worship*). By maintaining the text of Kings as he did, the Chronicler not only drew attention once again to the close connections between David and Solomon, but also portrayed Solomon as taking Israel's worship beyond David.

Placing the Ark in the Most Holy Place (5:7-10)

The centerpiece of this section is the placement of the **ark of the covenant** (for the significance of this designation, see *Introduction: 13) Covenant*) in **the inner sanctuary**, or **the Most Holy Place** (5:7). Once again, the Chronicler followed the account of Kings very closely. He repeated the visual details of the **wings of the cherubim** (5:7) near the ark of the covenant (see 3:10-13). He noted that they **spread their wings** not only over the ark but also over **its carrying poles** (5:8). Poles were inserted through rings on either side of the ark; they were always to remain in place (see Exod. 25:15). To add to the splendor of the scene the Chronicler repeated from Kings that the **poles were so long** ... that they **could be seen from in front of the inner sanctuary** (5:9). In other words, they could be seen from the Main Hall or **Holy Place** (5:10). The carrying poles of the ark probably extended parallel to the rear wall of the Most Holy Place. Yet, their size made them visible from outside the room.

The text comments that these poles **are still there today** (5:9 // 1 Kgs. 8:8). Of course, by the time of the writing of Chronicles the temple of Solomon had been destroyed and the ark had long disappeared (see *Introduction: Authorship and Date*). This was the case with the book of Kings as well.

Two explanations are feasible. 1) This statement, **still there today**, may be an idiomatic way of saying, 'from then on' or 'in perpetuity'. If so, it simply means that as long as the temple stood, the poles continued to be visible from the Main Hall. 2) The Chronicler (following the writer of Kings) may simply have copied from an earlier record which was composed while the temple actually stood. Whatever the case, it is clear that the Chronicler was not saying that the poles of the ark were present in his own day. For a fuller discussion of the Chronicler's use of this terminology, see comments on 1 Chr. 4:41.

The passage closes with a brief reminder that this **ark of the covenant** was none other than the one from the days of Moses (5:10). It contained **the two tablets**, but the gold jar of manna (see Exod. 16:32-34) and Aaron's staff (see Num. 17:10-11) which were apparently inside the ark at one time (see Heb. 9:4) may have been lost while the Philistines had the ark (see 1 Sam. 4:10-11; 5:1-6:12). Despite these losses, the text once again makes clear the continuity between Solomon's temple and Moses' tabernacle (see comments on 5:4-6).

Celebrative Worship Outside the Most Holy Place (5:11-6:2)

Having placed the ark of the covenant in the Most Holy Place the priests withdrew to the Main Hall. As noted above, the Chronicler added 5:11b-13 and focused attention on the activities of the priests and Levites. His addition highlighted several considerations that drew even more attention to the splendor of the event.

First, the Chronicler pointed to the number of people involved. For instance, the number of priests present was unusually large because **all the priests who were there had consecrated themselves regardless of their divisions** (5:11). Rituals of consecration appear frequently in Chronicles as examples of proper worship which the post-exilic readers were to imitate in their day (see *Introduction: 6) Royal Observance of Worship*). Normally, the priests served according to the divisions David established (see 1 Chr. 24:1-19). Here the Chronicler noted that the normal procedures were set aside for this special event. Similarly, **all the Levites who were musicians ... stood on the east side of the altar** (5:12). Once again, the normal divisional rotation was not observed (compare 1 Chr. 21:28-22:1; 2 Chr. 30:2-3). All the musicians attended worship that day standing directly in front of the bronze altar. Moreover, **120 priests** accompanied the Levite musicians with **trumpets** (5:12).

Second, the quality of the worship stands out. All who played and sang did so **in unison, as with one voice** (5:13). Rather than a variety of songs playing here and there (as was often the case in the daily affairs of the temple), the massive company standing before the altar was entirely unified.

Third, exhilarating doxology characterized the event. The Chronicler piled phrase upon phrase to depict the thrilling time. The worshippers gave **praise and thanks to the LORD ... they raised their voices in praise to the LORD** (5:13). He even went so far as to give a snippet of the well-known words they used in praise, **'He is good; his love endures forever'** (see 1 Chr. 16:34; 2 Chr. 7:3; Ezra 3:11; Pss. 100:5; 106:1; 107:1; 118:1,29; 136:1; Jer. 33:11).

Fourth, to close off this scene of praise and celebration, the Chronicler returned to the book of Kings (5:13b-6:2 // 1 Kgs. 8:10b-13). He noted that the presence of God came into the temple in the form of **a cloud** (5:13b). The **dark cloud** (6:1) is identified as **the glory of the Lord** (5:13b). This glory cloud is none other than the cloud that had appeared at Sinai (see Exod. 20:21; Deut. 4:11; 5:22). It is alternatively described as dark and fiery (see Exod. 14:19-20; Deut. 4:11; 5:22). Apparently, its thick, dark underside veiled the brilliant fiery light of God's glory. In all events, the cloud so filled the Main Hall that the priests could no longer **perform their service** (5:14).

As a result, Solomon praised God for the entry of his presence. He noted that God promised **he would dwell in a dark cloud** (6:1) and connected the blessing on his temple with the great events of Moses' day (see Exod. 19:19). Then Solomon concluded with words that reflect the commission he received from his father David. He acknowledged that the purpose of the **magnificent temple** was not for his own glory but for God's permanent dwelling on earth (6:2). The transfer of the ark was complete when the divine presence inhabited the temple just as Solomon, and David before him, had always hoped.

The Chronicler expanded the description of Solomon's grand worship to inspire his post-exilic readers. When Solomon first set the temple in proper order, the worshipful celebration resulted in large numbers, magnificent music, and dramatic divine presence. By this means the Chronicler sought to motivate his readers to imitate Solomon's devotion to the temple (see *Introduction: 27) Disappointment and Celebration*).

Solomon's Praise for the Past (6:3-11)

With the presence of God established in the temple, the Chronicler continued to follow the account of Kings very closely (6:3-11 // 1 Kgs. 8:14-21). In this passage, Solomon addressed the people gathered at the temple complex (see figure 23). This passage begins with a transitional note indicating that Solomon had turned toward the people and blessed them (6:3). His speech (6:4-11) divides into three parts. The first and last paragraphs frame the entire speech with reflections on God's faithfulness to the promises given to David (6:4-6, 10-11). The middle paragraph is Solomon's public explanation of his own role in fulfilling the promises to David (6:7-9).

Transitional Introduction (6:3)

Following the account in Kings (// 1 Kgs. 8:14) the Chronicler portrayed the setting of Solomon's praise. The king turned away from the temple and toward the people as he blessed them.

Praise for Fulfillment of the Promise to David (6:4-6)

The focus of this portion of Solomon's praise is that God **fulfilled what he promised ... to ... David** (6:4). Solomon alluded to the promises made to David in 1 Chr. 17:4-14. The content of this praise is familiar from previous chapters in Chronicles. Yet, three motifs deserve special attention.

First, this passage enhanced the Chronicler's repeated efforts to connect Solomon and David's actions. Solomon was not acting on his own; he merely served to bring about the divine promise given to David.

Second, Solomon praised God for his involvement from beginning to end. Solomon knew that the promise came to David through Nathan the prophet (see 1 Chr. 17:3-4), but he acknowledged God's involvement by saying that God gave the promise **with his mouth** (6:4; see also 6:15; 1 Chr. 16:12; 2 Chr. 35:22). David and Solomon worked hard on the temple project, but the king insisted that God brought it about **with his hands** (6:4; see also 6:15; 1 Chr. 21:13; 28:19; 29:12,14,16; 2 Chr. 6:32; 20:6; 30:12). As the rest of his speech indicated, Solomon did not deny the human instruments involved. Nevertheless, in the final analysis the work resulted from divine action, not human plans or efforts (see *Introduction: 10) Divine Activity*).

Third, the temple was to be the place of God's Name. Here the expression **my Name** occurs two times (6:5,6 [six times in 6:3-11]). The Name of the Lord was his immanent divine presence on earth; it was his power accessible to the people of God through calling on his Name in prayer (see *Introduction: 11) Name of God*). The temple was not a mere symbol; it was the place where God's invocable presence was given to Israel. The centrality of this theme in Solomon's temple speeches will be evident throughout this chapter.

Explanation of Solomon's Role (6:7-9)

Solomon paused from offering his praise to explain why David himself had not built the temple. This explanation has already appeared in Chronicles several times. Nevertheless, we learn here that God told David **you did well to have this in your heart** (6:8). The idea of building a temple for God was appropriate (see comments on 1 Chr. 17:12) and God approved of his heart motivations (see *Introduction: 16) Motivations*). Yet, David was a man of war and the temple was to be built only after Israel had gained control of her land in peace (see 1 Chr. 22:8-10; 28:3). The Chronicler's post-exilic readers had no reason to think that the temple was somehow a mistake or David's failed project.

Beyond this, we should note that the three main themes of Solomon's speech appear again in this paragraph.

1) The connection between Solomon and David is established in the use of **my father David** twice here (6:7,8 see also 6:4) and in the divine word calling Solomon **your own flesh and blood** (6:9).

2) Solomon noted that the Lord intervened and said that David was not to build (6:9); divine involvement was made evident again (see *Introduction: 10) Divine Activity*).

3) The temple was said to be for the **Name** in each verse (6:7, 8, 9).

Praise for Keeping the Promise to David (6:10-11)

Solomon turned back to praise once again. He indicated his amazement at all that God had accomplished. The three main themes of Solomon's praise stand out again. First, Solomon was drawn into close relation with David in at least two ways. 1) He called David **my father** again (6:10). 2) He also declared that he sat **on the throne of Israel** (6:10); Solomon saw his reign as the continuation of David's kingdom.

Second, divine approval is enhanced again as Solomon mentioned the promise of God twice (6:10).

Third, the concept of the temple as the place of the **Name of the LORD** also appears (6:10). The temple was important because the divine presence was attainable there (see *Introduction: 11) Name of God*).

One additional theme also appears at the end of Solomon's praise. He mentioned the placement of **the ark** in the temple (6:11), but said that the ark contained **the covenant of the Lord that he made with the people of Israel**. The parallel in Kings also adds, 'when he brought them out of Egypt' (1 Kgs. 8:21). The reason for the Chronicler's abbreviation is not clear. Whatever the case, the connection between Solomon's temple and Moses' tabernacle is evident again. Solomon saw his edifice as the continuation of the Mosaic covenant, not its replacement (see *Introduction: 13) Covenant*).

Solomon's Prayer for the Future (6:12-42)

Still following the book of Kings closely, the Chronicler moved from Solomon's praise for blessings in the past to his prayer for Israel's future. This prayer gives the fullest expression of Israel's temple theology found in Scripture. It focuses on the hopes which Solomon attached to the presence of God's Name in the temple.

This material divides in the following manner (see figure 23). Solomon's dedicatory prayer follows an intricate introduction (6:12-13). The prayer itself divides into three main parts. Solomon expressed concern for the future of the monarchy (6:14-17) and the future of the temple (6:18-39). Finally, he combined petitions for the temple and monarchy (6:40-42).

Introduction to the Prayer (6:12-13)

Solomon's dedicatory prayer is introduced by a rather elaborate visual depiction of the scene (compare 6:3). As noted above, these details do not appear in the traditional text of 1 Kgs. 8:22, but they were probably lost through textual transmission. Solomon first stood **before the** (bronze) **altar** and then moved to **a bronze platform** measuring approximately 7.5 feet (2.3 meters) long and wide and 4.5 (1.3 meters) high (6:12-13). Before the platform, Solomon **stood ... and spread out his hands** (6:12); on the platform **he stood ... knelt down ... and spread out his hands** (6:13). Standing and kneeling in prayer is common in the Old Testament (kneeling: 1 Kgs. 18:42; Ezra 9:5; Ps. 95:6; Dan. 6:10; standing: Gen. 18:22; Lev. 9:5; 1 Sam. 1:26; 2 Chr. 20:5,13,19; Neh. 9:2,4; Jer. 18:20); spreading the hands is also a normal gesture of praise and pleading in Scripture (see Exod. 9:29, 33; 1 Kgs. 8:54; Ezra 9:5; Job 11:13; Ps. 44:20). All of these actions occurred **in front of the whole assembly ... in the center of the outer court** (6:12-13). The Chronicler already distinguished between the courtyard of the priests and the court of the laity (see 4:9). Here he used the term **outer court** which probably referred to the court of the laity (6:13). These details of Solomon's ritual created an atmosphere of liturgical grandeur and solemnity for the prayer that follows. The use of the term **assembly** (6:12) to describe this gathering placed this event among a number of religious assemblies which the Chronicler set forth as exemplary for his readers (see *Introduction: 5) Religious Assemblies*).

Praise and Petitions for the Monarchy (6:14-17)

These verses are tied together by the repetition of the words **Lord, God of Israel** (6:14,16,17). After this portion of the prayer, Solomon addressed God differently as **O Lord, my God** (6:19), **my God** (6:40), and **O Lord God** (6:41 [twice], 42).

Solomon began his praise and petitions on behalf of the monarchy. The praise of God (6:14-15) expressed Solomon's confidence that **there is no God like you in heaven or on earth** (6:14). Assurance of the incomparability of God over all other supernatural forces often occurs in Scripture after God has demonstrated his supremacy in history (see Exod. 8:10; 9:14; 15:11; Deut. 4:35,39; Isa. 45:5-6). Solomon viewed the completion of the temple as proof that Israel's God was supreme.

The king focused more specifically on God's covenant fidelity. He addressed God as **'you who keep your covenant of love'** (6:14). That God keeps his covenants is expressed throughout the Old Testament (see Lev. 26:9; Deut. 7:9,12; Judg. 2:1; Neh. 1:5; 9:31; Ps. 111:5; Dan. 9:4). This praise mentions one qualification. God keeps covenant **with** [his] **servants who continue wholeheartedly in** [his] **way** (6:14). Conditions applied to each of the major biblical covenants (see Hos. 6:7; Gen. 9:4-7; 17:10-14; Exod. 19:5-6; 20:2-17). The Chronicler included these words from Kings (// 1 Kgs. 8:22) because they fit his purposes so well. He wanted his post-exilic readers to keep covenant in their day so they could receive the blessings of God (see *Introduction: 13) Covenant*).

Solomon narrowed his focus even further by remarking that God's covenant fidelity had been demonstrated in his keeping his **promise** to **David** (6:15). In language reminiscent of his preceding praise (6:3), the king said that God himself spoke and fulfilled his word on that very day (6:15b).

On the basis of what God had already done for David's dynasty, Solomon turned his attention to the future (6:16-17). He asked God to continue fulfilling the promises to David (6:16). In particular, Solomon was concerned with the promise, **'You shall never fail to have a man to sit before me on the throne of Israel'** (6:16). These words allude to the dynastic promises given to David in several places in Scripture (see 2 Sam. 7:1-17 // 1 Chr. 17:1-15; Pss. 89,132). The Davidic line was established as Israel's permanent dynasty. Yet, conditions applied to the individual kings in the family of David. They enjoyed the benefits of this promise only if they **walk before** [God] **according to** [his] **law** (6:16). Here the Chronicler varied from the text of 1 Kgs. 8:25 ('walk before me') to specify that walking before God meant obedience to the Law of Moses.

Solomon noted that the sons of David must walk **as** (David has) **done** (6:16). David had his share of flaws, even in the Chronicler's idealized portrait. Perfection was not required of Israel's kings. However, basic covenant fidelity of the heart was required of all who sat on the throne of Israel. As the Chronicler's own history illustrated so vividly, kings who forsook covenant loyalty received the curses of the covenant (see *Introduction: 13) Covenant*).

Praise and Petitions for the Temple (6:18-39)
Having praised and petitioned on behalf of the Davidic dynasty, Solomon turned to the second central institution in Israel, the temple. This portion of his prayer divides into two major parts, the second of which consists of eight sections (see figure 23). Beginning with praise (6:18) as he did in the preceding section with praise (6:14-15), Solomon proceeded to a series of petitions on behalf of the temple (6:19-39). He first asked in general terms for the temple to be a place for effective prayers (6:19-21). He then cited seven circumstances in which he hoped prayers in and toward the temple would be heard from heaven (6:22-39). These last seven petitions are marked by the formulaic expression **then hear from heaven**... (6:23, 25, 27, 30, 33, 35, 39).

Praise (6:18)
Solomon's prayer on behalf of the temple began with a brief word of praise. His doxology acknowledged the transcendence of God and the inadequacy of the temple to contain him. These words recalled Solomon's correspondence with Hiram (see 2:4-6). There he concluded that divine transcendence implied that his temple could only be **a place to burn sacrifices before him** (2:6). In this passage, Solomon dealt with these issues in a slightly different way. It cannot **contain** God, even **the highest heavens cannot** do that (6:18). What then is the value of having the temple? As we will see in the verses that follow, it will serve as a place of prayer in times of trouble.

Petitions in General (6:19-21)
Solomon first offered a general petition for the temple. Despite the fact that the temple cannot provide God a place to dwell, Solomon asked God to do something for him and his temple.

Solomon's emotional state stands out in his petition. In humility he called himself **your servant** four times (6:19 [twice], 20,21). By this terminology the king acknowledged himself to be a submissive vassal under the imperial rule of the divine King. Along with humility, however, Solomon's intensity is evident. He spoke of his requests as **the cry** ... **the prayer which your servant is praying** ... **the prayer** ... and **the supplications** (6:19-21). This intensity becomes even more evident in the rapid succession of petitions in short order. He asks God to **give attention** ... **hear** ... **may your eyes be open** ... **may you hear** ... **hear** ... **hear** ... **forgive** (6:19-21).

For what did Solomon pray so fervently? Put simply, Solomon asked for the temple to serve as a place for effective prayer. This request was stated in several ways. He asked, **'May your eyes be open toward this temple day and night'** (6:20). In other words, Solomon asked that God watch what happens in the temple all the time (see 6:20; 6:40 // 1 Kgs. 8:52; 2 Kgs. 19:16; Neh. 1:6; Ps. 34:15; Dan. 9:18). He then expounded this theme by saying, **'Hear the prayer your servant prays toward this place'** (6:20) as well as **'the supplications of your servant**

and of your people Israel' (6:21). Solomon earnestly desired that God pay attention both to the kings and people as they pray in and toward the temple.

The basis of these requests appears in 6:20b. Solomon reminded God, **'You said you would put your Name there.'** From the days of Moses God had assured his people that they would one day find the place of his Name (see Deut. 12:5, 11, 21; 14:23, 24; 16:2, 6, 11; 26:2). Solomon relied on that promise as the basis for God answering prayers in and toward the temple. Instead of God himself dwelling in the temple, Solomon asserted that the temple would only house the **Name** of God (6:20b). As we have seen elsewhere, the Name of God is his invocable power, his accessible presence (see *Introduction: 11) Name of God*). In other words, Solomon saw the temple as the place of access to divine attention. God himself would still **hear from heaven** (6:21), but his approachable, immanent Name would reside in the temple and could be invoked there.

As a result of this divine accessibility, the temple became the heart of Israelite religion. No matter where they were, faithful Israelites in all times and places could turn toward the place of the Name (see Ps. 5:7; Dan. 6:10; Jon. 2:4). The centrality of the temple in Solomon's day gave rise to the Chronicler's conviction that the temple must be reinstated to its central role in the post-exilic community. Only there could the restored people gain access to their transcendent God in heaven.

Petition Regarding Oaths (6:22-23)

Solomon's first specific petition was that God pay attention to the times **when a man wrongs his neighbor and is required to take an oath** (6:22). This procedure is well documented as part of the service of the tabernacle (see Lev. 6:3-6; also Amos 8:14). Oaths were required in cases of default (see Exod. 22:7-15), adultery (see Num. 5:11-31) and theft (see Lev. 6:3-5). Taking an oath was a sacred act involving the potential of divine curse for fraud or violation (see Lev. 19:12; Judg. 17:1-4; Ezek. 17:13-19; Ps. 15:4).

Petition Regarding Defeat (6:24-25)

Solomon's second petition concerned situations when the Israelites **have been defeated by an enemy because they have sinned** (6:24). The explicit qualification **because they have sinned** (6:24) suggests that not all military failures result from sin (see 16:1; 25:13; 32:1). Even so, defeat and captivity by an enemy is frequently mentioned in Mosaic literature as a covenant curse for national rebellion against God (see Deut. 28:36-37,64; Lev. 26:17). The prophets also reflect the same perspective (see Isa. 8:5-8; Jer. 5:10-17; Hab. 1:2-11). The Chronicler frequently pointed to military defeat as a judgment for sin, especially in the Divided Monarchy (see 2 Chr. 12:5-8; 21:12-17; 24:20, 23-24; 25:20; 28:1-7; 33:10-11; see also *Introduction: 23) Victory and Defeat*).

When defeat came because of sin, Solomon prayed that God would hear the people once **they turn back** (see *Introduction: 22) Repentance*) **and confess** [his] **name** (6:24; see *Introduction: 11) Name of God*). At such a time he hoped that God would **bring them back to the land** (6:25). Solomon's hope of return was based on earlier biblical traditions. The Mosaic covenant explicitly assured that repentance would lead to restoration to the land (see Deut. 4:29; 30:1-3). The Chronicler records two times when temporary exile occurred. Northern Israelites exiled Judahites during the reign of Ahaz. No mention of prayer appears in that account (see 28:6-15). Nevertheless, the Chronicler's version of Manasseh's life illustrates Solomon's petition in action. He was exiled and brought back because of his repentance and prayer (see 33:10-13).

Solomon's petition for return to the land was particularly poignant for the Chronicler's post-exilic readers. They had been exiled and returned to the land. Solomon's desire for the temple had been fulfilled in their lives (see 36:23). How much more should they now support the temple and its services?

Petition Regarding Drought (6:26-27)

In his third petition Solomon addressed those times **when the heavens are shut up and there is no rain** (6:26). Once again, he qualified the phenomenon by adding **because they have sinned against you** (6:26 see 6:24). Throughout the Old Testament rain is considered a divine blessing and drought a covenant curse (see Lev. 26:3-4; Deut. 11:13-14; 28:23-24; Prov. 16:15; Jer. 3:3; 5:24; Hos. 6:3; Joel 2:23; Amos 4:6-8).

Here Solomon acknowledged that in such circumstances God must teach Israel **the right way to live** before he once again gives **rain** (6:27). For this reason, he not only asked God to hear **when they pray and confess** [his] **name** (6:26; see *Introduction: 11) Name of God*). He also insisted that such prayer and confession must take place as the people **turn from their sin** (6:26; see *Introduction: 22) Repentance*).

Although the Chronicler mentioned no specific examples of this covenant curse in his history, his expansion of 7:14 included drought. The early post-exilic community had suffered from drought because of their inattention to the temple (see Hag. 1:11). To enjoy fructifying rains they had to give due attention to the temple where their prayers would be heard.

Petition Regarding Assorted Disasters (6:28-31)

Solomon's fourth petition lists a number of disasters: **famine, plague, blight, mildew, locusts, grasshoppers**, or **when enemies besiege them** (6:28). He enlarged the list to include **whatever disaster or disease may come** (6:28).

Each of these disasters ranks among the various biblical lists of covenant curses.

1) **Famine** comes through natural causes, warfare and siege (see Gen. 12:10; 26:1; 41:1-57; Lev. 26:25-26; Judg. 6:3-6; Ruth 1:1; 2 Sam. 21:1; 24:13 // 1 Chr. 21:12; 1 Kgs. 18:1-2; 2 Kgs. 6:24-25; 25:1-3; 2 Chr. 32:11; Job 5:20-22; Ps. 33:18-19; Isa. 51:19; Jer. 14:11-18; 16:4; 21:7-9; 42:13-22; 52:6).

2) The term **plague** refers primarily to diseases of animals (see Exod. 9:3; Ps. 78:48-50) and people (see Lev. 26:25-26; Num. 14:12; 2 Sam. 24:13 // 1 Chr. 21:12; Ezek. 5:12; 7:15).

3) The word **blight** ordinarily refers to a natural disaster or an expression of divine punishment for covenant disobedience (see Deut. 28:22; Amos 4:9; Hag. 2:17). It is often an effect of the very hot, dry wind which can blow destructively over Palestine from the desert and bring severe agricultural hardship.

4) The term **mildew** is often associated with blight arising out of covenant cursing (see Deut. 28:22; Amos 4:9; Hag. 2:17). If it refers to people (compare the Septuagint of this passage), it speaks of paleness due to fear or a jaundiced condition (see Jer. 30:6). If the term is agricultural, it speaks of any variety of fungi.

5) The Hebrew term **locusts** generally refers to locusts that are fully developed and can therefore fly (see Exod. 10:4; Deut. 28:38; Joel 2:25). The term translated **grasshopper** may refer to locusts at an earlier stage of development, making hopping their primary means of movement (see Isa. 33:4; Joel 1:4). At times, they are used as metaphors for invading armies (see Judg. 6:5; Isa. 33:4; Jer. 46:22-23; 51:27; Joel 2:1-27; Nah. 3:15).

6) **Enemies besiege** Israelite cities many times in biblical history. The Chronicler himself noted the siege on Jerusalem in Rehoboam's day (see 12:2), Joash's reign (see 24:23), Amaziah's reign (see 25:23), and Hezekiah's reign (see 32:1-2).

7) **Disease** also appears in a number of situations in the Chronicler's history (see 16:12; 21:15,18-19; 26:19-21; 30:18-20; 32:24). Sometimes these diseases are healed through prayer; at other times, they are not.

Solomon asked God to deal with each individual **since you know his heart (for you alone know the hearts of men)** (6:30). Mercy was to be shown not according to some outward standard, but according to the inward standard of the heart (see Ps. 7:9; 1 Sam. 16:7; Jer. 11:20; 17:10; 20:12; see also *Introduction: 16) Motivations*). The result of this individual treatment would be that the people would **fear** [God] **and walk in** [his] **ways** (6:31).

Petition Regarding Foreigners (6:32-33)

The fifth specific petition regarded **the foreigner who ... has come ... and prays toward this temple** (6:32). At various times in the Old Testament Gentiles converted to the faith of Israel (see Ruth 1:16; 2 Kgs. 5:15; Josh. 2:9-13). Solomon himself was in a position of influence among the Gentiles (see 1 Kgs. 4:21,24 // 2 Chr. 9:26; 1 Kgs. 4:34 // 2 Chr. 9:22-24; 1 Kgs. 9:26-10:29 // 2 Chr. 8:17-9:28). Moreover, the Chronicler's readers knew that the prophets expected many Gentiles would come to Jerusalem after the exile to worship the Lord (see Amos 9:11-12; Isa. 56:6-8; Ps. 87; Zech. 8:20-23; 14:16-21).

In this passage, Solomon elaborated on his concept of the Name of God in the temple. He said that foreigners may come **because of your** [God's] **great name** (6:32). Then he expanded his focus to God's **mighty hand and** [his] **outstretched arm** (6:32). These expressions appear many places in the Old Testament to indicate displays of divine power in dramatic events (see Exod. 6:6; Deut. 4:34; 5:15; 6:21; 7:8, 19; Jer. 21:5; 27:5; Ezek. 20:33-34). The Name of God, therefore, is closely associated with the power of God intervening in human history. This power is accessible through prayer in and toward the temple (see *Introduction: 11) Name of God*).

Solomon asked that the sincere prayers of foreigners be answered so that **all the peoples of the earth may know your name and fear you ... and may know that this house I have built bears your Name** (6:33). Israel's relationship to other nations was a longstanding motif of biblical history. She was blessed to bless others (see Gen. 12:1-3). Solomon hoped that this destiny would be fulfilled in part through prayers offered in the temple. As the Chronicler's readers dealt with foreigners all around them, they too could hope that their faith would spread among the nations (see Zech. 8:23). But this hope could be realized only if they, like Solomon, gave proper attention to the temple (see *Introduction: 3) International Relations*).

Petition Regarding War (6:34-35)

Solomon's prayer moved next to **when** [God's] **people go to war** (6:34). Military actions took place for many reasons in the Old Testament. Here Solomon had in mind those times **'when you send them'** (6:34). In other words, these are not battles faced as punishment for sin (see 6:24-25), but aggressive warfare ordered by God. Even in these circumstances, the armies of Israel were expected to **pray toward this city** ... **and the temple** (6:34). Then God would **uphold their cause** (6:35 see 6:39); he would come to their aid and lead them to victory. The Chronicler recorded a number of battles where prayer of this sort led to victory (see *Introduction: 17) Prayer*; see also *23) Victory and Defeat*). The post-exilic readers faced the prospect of warfare in their day. Their only hope for victory was prayer toward **the temple ... built for** [God's] **Name** (6:34; see *Introduction: 11) Name of God*).

Petition Regarding National Exile (6:36-39)

The seventh petition touched on the potential of exile **to a land far away or near** (6:36). Solomon had already addressed aspects of this topic (6:24-25). He admitted that exile is a potential for the nation in every generation **for there is no one who does not sin** (6:36). Prophets who rejected the possibility of exile were false prophets (see Jer. 28:1-17). Yet, Solomon's chief concern here was to focus more thoroughly – even programmatically – on what the exiled people were to do.

Building on the basic Mosaic covenantal structures (see Deut. 4:29; 30:1-3), Solomon set down conditions upon which he hoped God would return his people from exile.

1) They must have **a change of heart** (6:37). A deep seated change of affections and loyalties must take place (see *Introduction: 16) Motivations*; see also 1 Kgs. 8:48; 2 Chr. 7:14; 12:6, 12; 30:11; 33:12, 19, 23; 34:27; Jer. 24:7; 29:13).

2) They must **repent** or turn away from their sins (Deut. 4:30; 30:2; Isa. 19:22; see *Introduction: 22) Repentance*).

3) They must **plead**, that is, ask sincerely and earnestly.

4) These inward changes must be expressed in prayer. **'We have sinned, we**

have done wrong and acted wickedly' (6:37). The piling up of confessional language reveals the intensity required in these prayers.

5) They must **turn back to** [God] **with all their heart and soul** (6:38). No insincerity was acceptable (see *Introduction: 16) Motivations*).

6) This sincerity must be expressed by praying **toward the land** ... **toward the city** ... **toward the temple** (6:38). The physical act of turning toward Jerusalem in prayer (see Jon. 2:4,7; Dan. 6:10) expressed a reorientation of life toward the only source of deliverance, invoking the Name of God (see *Introduction: 11) Name of God*).

The results of this kind of repentance were as expected. God would **hear their prayer, uphold their cause**, and **forgive** (6:39).

Petitions for the Temple and the Monarchy (6:40-42)

At this point the Chronicler diverged from 1 Kings 8:50. In the Kings account, Solomon also asked that the captors may 'show mercy' to their captives. In all likelihood the writer of Kings had in mind the release of Jehoiachin (see 2 Kgs. 25:27-30) as an example of God answering this prayer. The Chronicler did not include this event in Jehoiachin's life and omitted this portion of Solomon's petition. Instead, he moved the focus of the petition more toward the experience of his readers. They had received more than good treatment by their captors. They had been released from exile and returned to the land (see 36:22-23). Having seen the power of prayer toward the land and the city, they now needed to see the power of the Name in the reconstructed temple.

The Chronicler's account of Solomon's prayer closed differently from Kings in another way (see 1 Kgs. 8:50b-53). In Kings, Solomon offered the deliverance of Israel out of Egypt as the basis of his requests. The Chronicler dropped this material and replaced it with a summary request (6:40) and a free citation of Ps. 132:1, 8-10 (6:41-42).

It is difficult to determine precisely how the Chronicler expected his readers to understand this change. On the one hand, it is possible that he added the words of Psalm 132 as a report of what Solomon actually said. He may have known this information from some source other than Kings. The beginning of 7:1 (**when Solomon finished praying**) offers support for this understanding.

On the other hand, it is possible that the Chronicler added 6:40 to bring Solomon's actual prayer to an end. The opening word of this verse (**now**) often introduces a conclusion to a speech or prayer. If this is correct, the citations from Psalm 132 may have been intended as the Chronicler's own authorial prayer for the temple in his day.

Whatever the case, the passage turns to a combined concern for the temple and the monarchy. Here we find the Chronicler's conviction that the throne and worship center were the central institutions necessary for the full restoration of blessing to post-exilic Israel.

The Chronicler selected pertinent portions of Psalm 132. The psalm itself begins with the request that God remember David's devotion to finding a home for the ark (verses 1-5). It then recalls the call to travel to the dwelling place of the ark (verses 6-9). The remainder of the psalm enjoins God to remember his covenant oath to David and rejoices in the blessings that will come to Zion and the king (verses 10-18). The Chronicler began his selection with the priests processing with the ark to Jerusalem (6:41 // Ps. 132:8-9). He then closed by enjoining God to remember both his oath and David's faithfulness (6:42 // Ps. 132:1a, 10).

In so doing, this ending combines the hopes Solomon had for his temple and the Davidic throne. The psalm asks that God would **come to** [his] **resting place** (6:40). With the **ark of** [his] **might** in the temple, the power of the Name would be accessible to the people. It also requests that the **priests** and **saints** (probably the sanctified laity [see Pss. 16:3; 30:4; 31:23; 34:9; 116:15; 149:1, 5]) attend to the temple with great joy. Then as a basis for these requests, the Chronicler selected the psalmist's appeal to God's promises to David (6:42 // Ps. 132:11). In effect, the fulfillment of the temple ideal was the fulfillment of the Davidic covenant. Without the presence of God in the temple, the Davidic hope is in vain.

Needless to say, the Chronicler's addition in 6:40-42 spoke directly to his hopes for post-exilic Israel. His message focused on the full establishment of the temple with the priests and people in joyous worship. These concerns were central in his design for the restored nation (see *Introduction: 4-9) King and Temple*).

Solomon's Concluding Sacrifices and Celebration (7:1-7)

Having finished with Solomon's prayer of dedication, the Chronicler continued to follow the account of Kings and recorded further celebration (// 1 Kgs. 8:62-66). As noted above, the Chronicler omitted Solomon's blessing of the people (1 Kgs. 8:54b-61) and replaced it with God's dramatic acceptance of the prayer and burnt offerings (7:1b-3). He then followed 1 Kgs. 8:62-64 (// 7:4-5,7) and added 7:6. These changes were probably motivated by a desire to form a balancing section for the earlier celebration before Solomon's praise and petitions (see 5:4-6:2; see figure 23). The parallels between these passages have led some interpreters to hold that we have here a second account of the same events described in 5:4-6:2. The correspondences are remarkable, but the introductory word, **when Solomon finished praying** (7:1) mitigates against such an interpretation. It seems best to take these verses as reporting an increase of celebration that took place after Solomon's prayer.

The Chronicler's account of these events divides into two vignettes of the wonder of that day (see figure 23). 7:1-3 depicts the response of fire from heaven. 7:4-7 draws attention to the number of sacrifices made.

Divine Fire and Glory (7:1-3)

The Chronicler's first vignette involves three aspects of God's powerful display. First, attention is given to God's blessing toward Solomon. **Fire came down from heaven** and **consumed the burnt offering** which the king offered (7:1). The descent of fire upon a sacrifice appears elsewhere as a miraculous display of divine approval (see 1 Chr. 21:26; Exod. 40:34-38; 1 Kgs. 18:38; Judg. 6:20-22). In this passage the supernatural event demonstrated God's acceptance of Solomon's temple, prayers, and sacrifices.

Second, **the priests** come into focus (7:2). Alongside the descent of fire, **the glory of the LORD filled** the temple (7:2). This glory recalls the smoke that previously halted priestly services inside the Main Hall (see 5:11-6:2). Perhaps the glory had subsided slightly during Solomon's prayers and the priests tried to proceed with their responsibilities. At this point, however, the priests **could not enter the temple** (7:2).

Third, notice is taken of **all the Israelites** in the assembly (7:3). They saw the **fire** consuming Solomon's sacrifice; they also observed the **glory** inside the temple rising **above the temple** (7:3). In response, the assembly **knelt, worshipped**, and **gave thanks** (7:3). Earlier the priests sang, **'He is good; his love endures forever'** (see 5:13). Now the entire assembly adds its voice to the song (7:3).

This series of expanding notices – **Solomon** (7:1), **priests** (7:2), and **all the Israelites** (7:3) – creates an ever widening circle of wonder and joy. The Chronicler reported how God's response to Solomon's prayer overwhelmed all who were there in order to inspire his readers toward re-establishing the temple and its services in their day (see *Introduction: 27) Disappointment and Celebration*).

Numerous Sacrifices (7:4-7)

The second vignette concentrates on sacrifices and divides into three parts. First, **the king and all the people offered sacrifices** (7:4-5). Before Solomon's prayer innumerable sacrifices were made (see 5:6). Here the numbers appear, but they are astounding: **twenty-two thousand ... and a hundred and twenty thousand** (7:5). In all likelihood these numbers are hyperbolic. 144,000 sacrifices in the period of fourteen days (7:8-9) would require at least seven sacrifices every minute, every day, around the clock. Moreover, grain offerings were made as well (7:7). The purpose of the hyperbole was to indicate that the number of sacrifices was absolutely incredible. (For the Chronicler's use of hyperbole, see comments on 1 Chr. 12:14.) On a number of occasions Chronicles points to large numbers of sacrifices in order to inspire the post-exilic readers to observe worship with enthusiasm in their day (see 2 Chr. 1:6; 5:6; 7:4-5; 24:14; 29:32-35; 35:8-9; see also *Introduction: 6) Royal Observance of Worship*).

Second, attention shifts to **the priests** and **Levites** (7:6). They accompanied the sacrifices with **the LORD's musical instruments which King David had made** (see 1 Chr. 15:24). They too sang, **'His love endures forever'** (7:6).

Third, a quick note expands the outlook of this report to include the whole assembly as in the preceding vignette (see 7:3). As the music continued **all the Israelites were standing** (7:6). The entire assembly rose to its feet in honor of the Lord.

To heighten the grandeur of the event even further, the text provides an addendum explaining how so many sacrifices could be made. Solomon **consecrated the**

middle part of the courtyard for sacrifice (7:7). Temporary altars were erected because the bronze altar **could not hold the burnt offerings, the grain offerings and the fat portions** (7:7). Rituals of consecration appear frequently in Chronicles as examples of proper worship which the post-exilic readers were to imitate in their day (see *Introduction: 6) Royal Observance of Worship*).

The grandeur of this festival surely inspired the Chronicler's readers to wish for similar experiences. They wanted to exchange their hardships for such joy. Yet, such splendid festivity could occur only if they followed Solomon's example and gave due attention to the temple (see *Introduction: 27) Disappointment and Celebration*).

Solomon's Assembly Dismisses (7:8-10)

The Chronicler's account of Solomon's temple assembly closes with its dismissal. The text mirrors the order of events in 5:1-2 (see figure 23). It sums up the size and length of celebration (7:8-9 compare 5:2) and then reports the king's dismissal of the assembly (7:10 compare 5:1). For the most part, this material follows 1 Kgs. 8:65-66. Several comments should be made.

First, in 7:10 the Chronicler added to 1 Kgs. 8:66 that the assembly for temple dedication was connected with the Feast of Tabernacles. This information probably reflected an interest in the patterns of worship to be followed in the post-exilic community.

Second, although the Chronicler derived 7:8 from 1 Kgs. 8:65, the passage still emphasizes that **all Israel** attended Solomon's assembly (see *Introduction: 1) All Israel*). It was **a vast assembly** (7:8; see also 7:9) and therefore stood among a number of religious assemblies which the Chronicler saw as exemplary for his readers (see *Introduction: 5) Religious Assemblies*). The people came from **Hamath to the Wadi of Egypt** (7:8). These geographical notes represent the ideal boundaries of Israel (see Gen. 15:18; Num. 34:5,8; Josh. 15:4,47; 2 Kgs. 14:25; 24:7; Isa. 27:12; Ezek. 47:15,19; 48:1) and reflected the Chronicler's hope for his readers.

Third, the emotional quality of the entire event appears plainly. The people returned home **joyful and glad in heart** (7:10 // 1 Kgs. 8:66), an appealing state of affairs for the post-exilic community (see *Introduction: 27) Disappointment and Celebration*).

Fourth, the text connects the reigns of David and Solomon once again. The traditional Hebrew text of Kings reads 'to David his servant and to Israel his people' (1 Kgs. 8:66). The traditional Hebrew text of Chronicles reads, **for David and Solomon and for his people Israel** (7:10). It is possible that Kings originally had the reference to Solomon, but this is not altogether certain (see *Introduction: Translation and Transmission*). In all events, the Chronicler's text certainly sees Solomon's success as a divine blessing to David and to Solomon together. Moreover, this blessing toward the two ideal monarchs was not for them alone. It was a blessing to the nation as well. As we have seen before, the reigns of Israel's ideal kings were blessings for the nation as a whole (see *Introduction: 4-9) King and Temple*).

This final qualification pointed plainly to the way of blessing for the Chronicler's post-exilic readers. The monarchy and temple must be established together.

Solomon's Response from God (7:11-22)

Having given an account of Solomon's splendid temple assembly, the Chronicler followed the record of Kings (// 1 Kgs. 9:1-9) and described God's response to Solomon. Although this section is shorter than others, the opening words indicate that we have come upon another major section in Solomon's life (see figure 22). Solomon **established himself** (1:1), **gave orders to build a temple** (2:1), **began to build** (3:1), and **summoned to Jerusalem** (5:2). At this point, the Chronicler indicated that Solomon **had finished the temple ... and the royal palace** (7:11). Solomon's success in building established him as God's favored king (see *Introduction: 24) Building and Destruction*). With Solomon's building projects completed, this passage looks into Israel's future and speaks directly to the circumstances faced by the Chronicler's post-exilic readers.

Comparison with 1 Kgs. 9:1-9

Several insignificant variations appear in 7:11-12a (// 1 Kgs. 9:1-2), but three very important differences can be found in 7:12b-19.

First, the Chronicler roughly followed 1 Kgs. 9:3 (// 7:12), but added the expression **and have chosen this place for myself as a temple for sacrifices**. This addition alluded to words of David (see 1 Chr. 22:1) and Solomon (see 2:6). It made it clear that God approved of the hopes David and Solomon had placed in the temple.

Second, the Chronicler added 7:13-15. These verses describe situations in which prayers in and toward the temple will bring about the restoration of God's blessing. They give clear expression to the Chronicler's doctrine of divine judgment and blessing (see *Introduction: 10-27) Divine Blessing and Judgment*).

Third, the Chronicler paraphrased 1 Kgs. 9:6 in 2 Chr. 7:19 and employed his frequently used term, **forsake** (see *Introduction: 22) Abandoning/Forsaking*). The Chronicler did not repeat the qualification 'you and your sons' found in 1 Kgs. 9:6.

Structure of 7:11-22

This material divides into four main sections (see figure 23). An historical setting introduces the revelation to Solomon (7:11-12a). Then the divine word appears in three segments. God indicated his acceptance of Solomon's temple (7:12b). Then he explained the implications of this approval of the temple for the nation (7:13-16) and for the Davidic dynasty (7:17-22).

Introduction (7:11-12a)

In these opening verses the Chronicler's variations are slight and have little bearing on interpretation. God's response to Solomon took place after **Solomon had finished the temple** and **palace** (7:11). We learn from 1 Kgs. 7:1 and 9:10 that the palace was not completed until 13 years after the dedication of the temple. Thus God responded to Solomon's dedicatory prayer at least 13 years after the temple was built. Despite this historical distance, both Kings and Chronicles place this event in literary proximity to Solomon's dedicatory prayer. As we will see, God agreed to Solomon's requests on behalf of the temple, but this approval led to significant responsibilities for Solomon and Israel.

Divine Approval of the Temple (7:12b)

Although Solomon's palace has just been mentioned twice (7:11), it now disappears from consideration. God's response to Solomon only concerned the temple. Solomon had asked for many blessings to come to the royal family and the nation through the temple. He looked to the temple as the source of divine help whenever the people strayed or faced hardships (see 6:14-42). At this point, God responded to these requests.

God's response to Solomon was straightforward. He announced to the king he had heard his prayers and had **chosen this place ... as a temple for sacrifices** (7:12b). The Chronicler added this element to the divine response (// 1 Kgs. 9:3). It alludes to Solomon's remark to Hiram that because the temple could not contain God, it would have to be **a place to burn sacrifices before him** (2:6). A similar motif appears when David discovered the location of the temple (see 1 Chr. 22:1). By alluding to these events God affirmed the Davidic-Solomonic conception of the temple. God would not be bound to the structure; it could not contain him. Yet, it would be the place where acceptable sacrifices (as symbolic of the whole of worship) could be offered.

With these words from God the Chronicler added vital support for the temple in his own day. God himself ordained it as the place where he was to be approached by his people. This was no mere human belief; it was God's own perspective.

Divine Instructions and Assurances to the Nation (7:13-16)

Having established the acceptance of the temple in principle, God elaborated on how the temple was to serve the nation of Israel. As noted above, 7:13-15 is unique to the Chronicler's record. While Kings focuses entirely on the responsibilities of the king and his descendants toward the temple, this material gives attention to the responsibilities of the people in general. More than any other portion of this section, these verses spoke directly to the post-exilic community.

God began with specific instructions to the nation as it faced future hardships (7:13-14). There will be times of **no rain, locusts**, and **plague** (7:13). In his prayer, Solomon anticipated that **drought** (6:26-27), **locusts** (6:28-31), and **plague** (6:28-31) along with other difficulties would come upon Israel. Here God portrayed himself as the active agent of these national trials (**'I shut ... command'** [7:13]).

What were the Israelites to do when God chastised them? They were to turn to the invocable power of God in the temple (7:14a). The specific terms of this human responsibility deserve comment.

First, the identity of the nation is emphasized. Israel is called **my people** (7:14a). This terminology recalled Solomon's repeated use of **'your people'** in his dedicatory prayer (6:14-42). Throughout the Old Testament this terminology reflected the special covenantal bond between God and Israel (see Exod. 3:7,10; Lev. 26:12; 1 Chr. 17:6,7,9,10; Jer. 31:33; Hos. 1:9; 2:23). The nation is also **called by my name** (7:14a). Once again, the covenantal character of the language is evident (see Isa. 43:7; Jer. 14:9; Dan. 9:18-19). These instructions were not for the nations of the earth, but for those who were joined by covenant to God. All modern uses of this passage must recognize this limitation.

Second, these instructions employ four terms to indicate the intensity and sincerity with which the covenant people must yearn for help from God. Reliance on external performances of temple rituals had led the nation of Israel into false confidence (see Isa. 1:10-15; Jer. 7:1-15; Amos 5:21-24; Mic. 3:9-12). These instructions make it clear that the people must go far beyond outward ritualism in four ways.

1) The people must **humble themselves** (7:14a). For the Chronicler this meant they were to recognize sin and acknowledge their utter dependence on God (see *Introduction: 18) Humility*).

2) The wayward were to **pray** (7:14). This generic term is often associated as it is here with calling on God for help in times of need (see *Introduction: 17) Prayer*)

3) The people of Israel were to **'seek my face'** (7:14). The Chronicler used the expression 'to seek' many times with the connotations of worship and pursuit of God's favor (see *Introduction: 19) Seeking*).

4) The covenant people must **turn from their wicked ways** (7:14b). Devotion to God must demonstrate itself in changed lives. The Chronicler referred to the concept of repentance or 'turning' from sin and toward God on a number of occasions (see *Introduction: 22) Repentance*).

The response from God to such sincere devotion would be as expected. He promised that he would **hear from heaven and will forgive** (7:14b). This language recalls similar repeated phrases in Solomon's prayer (see 6:14-42). Moreover, God promised to **heal their land** (7:14). In situations where the sins of the people brought disaster to the land and its natural inhabitants, sincere repentance would bring healing.

These instructions and assurances spoke plainly to the Chronicler's post-exilic readers. They found themselves in difficult circumstances and in need of divine favor. God's instructions here showed them the way to national blessing.

After the instructions and assurances (7:13-14) the Chronicler added a more generalized commitment from God (7:15). The word **now** (7:15) often introduces a conclusion or summary. God repeated that he had **chosen** the temple and **consecrated** or devoted it to special use (7:16; see 7:12b). Rituals of consecration appear frequently in Chronicles as examples of proper worship which the post-exilic readers were to imitate in their day (see *Introduction: 6) Royal Observance of Worship*). This special use of the temple was designated in language already familiar to the Chronicler's readers. The temple would be the place where God's **Name may be there forever** (7:16). In a remarkable aside, God explained himself more fully. The presence of the Name in the temple meant that God's **eyes** (see 6:20,40) and his **heart** (see Ps. 33:11; Jer. 31:20; 32:41; Hos. 11:8) would be in the temple. It would be the place of his attention and compassion (see *Introduction: 11) Name of God*).

Divine Instructions and Warnings to the Monarchy (7:17-22)
The divine address to the nation was followed by an address to Solomon and his descendants. It is evident that Solomon is addressed in 7:17-18. The passage begins with the contrastive **as for you** (7:17). This pronoun is singular in Hebrew and referred to the recipient of the dream, namely Solomon. As mentioned above, the Chronicler paraphrased 1 Kgs. 9:6 (// 7:19) and omitted 'you and your children' (1 Kgs. 9:6). In 7:19, however, the pronoun **you** is plural in Hebrew. Therefore, the meaning here is the same as in Kings. Solomon was addressed in 7:17-18, but he and his descendants were the focus of 7:19-22. In his dedicatory prayer, Solomon prayed on behalf of the temple as a source of help for the nation (see 2 Chr. 6:24, 25). Moreover, he prayed for the future of the Davidic dynasty (see 6:16,17). At this point God addressed the latter requests from Solomon.

These observations suggest that this portion of God's response to Solomon divides into two parts: instructions and assurances to Solomon (7:17-18) and warnings to the dynasty (7:19-22).

God assured Solomon that his dynasty would be established in the future, but under certain conditions (7:17). The expression, **'if you walk before me as your father David'** appears elsewhere in Chronicles (7:17; see 17:3; 28:1; 29:2; 34:2) and surfaces many other places (see 1 Kgs. 3:14; 9:4; 11:4,6,12; Pss. 89:30-45; 132:12). The covenant with David was never properly conceived of as unconditional. Unfortunately, false prophets in Israel often neglected these conditions, but they were always in effect (see Jer. 14:13-14; Ezek. 13:1-23). Once again, the standard of devotion is David, a man well-known for his failures, but also a man whose heart was committed to his God. Loyalty, not perfection, was the condition of the covenant (see *Introduction: 13) Covenant*; see also *16) Motivations*).

If Solomon kept the covenant, he could be assured of something (7:18). Here, the Chronicler diverged from 1 Kings 9:5 in two significant ways. He substituted the word **I covenanted** for 'I spoke'. The specific language of covenant heightened the status of the word to David. It was an inviolable covenantal guarantee. But what was guaranteed? 1 Kings 9:5 reads, 'you shall never fail to have a man on the throne of Israel'. Apparently, the Chronicler wanted to clarify that this promise did not mean Israel's kings would never lose their thrones. The Chronicler substituted the more generic expression, **'you shall never fail to have a man to rule over Israel'** (7:18b; see Mic. 5:1-5). These words guaranteed that despite the fact that a king may not always sit on the throne of Jerusalem (as in the post-exilic period), the nation should look for the rightful heir of David and follow his leadership. In the

Chronicler's day this man was none other than Zerubbabel and/or his descendants (see 1 Chr. 3:19-24; Ezra 2:2; 3:2,8).

The guarantee for the continuation of the Davidic line raised the question of the responsibilities of future generations (7:19-22). The conditionality of the covenant took center stage and the severe consequences of apostasy were set forth. The focus here was on descendants of Solomon who may **serve other gods and worship them** (7:19). The results of such flagrant apostasy will be astonishing.

First, God will **uproot Israel** from his land (7:20). Exile will be their punishment (see 2 Chr. 6:24,25).

Second, not even the temple will protect the people from the wrath of their God. It may be the place of God's **Name** (7:20; see *Introduction: 11) Name of God*), but God declared he **will reject this temple** (7:20). Although false prophets and popular opinion were to the contrary generations later (see Jer. 7:4,8-10; Mic. 3:11), God's intention was clear. The temple may have been **imposing** in Solomon's day (7:21), but flagrant apostasy could turn it into **a byword and an object of ridicule among all peoples** (7:20). This passage alludes to Deut. 28:37 (see Jer. 24:9) where the people will be scorned as they are taken to exile.

Against whom will the ridicule come? God declared that he would be exalted by the surrounding nations as they recognize that his wrath brought Israel's disaster. All will know that exile occurred **because they have forsaken the LORD ... who brought them out of Egypt** (7:22). Israel owed its very existence to her God. To turn from him to other gods violated their sacred debt of gratitude and made exile just (see *Introduction: 22) Abandoning/Forsaking*).

Unfortunately, as the Chronicler's history will illustrate, God's warning did not keep the nation from turning from him. Exile and scorn came to Israel just as God had warned. Nevertheless, the Chronicler's post-exilic readers were in a fresh situation in which this warning needed to be heard again. Even in their day, the threat of divine punishment could only be avoided through fidelity to God.

More on Solomon's Building Projects (8:1-15)

Following the overall pattern of Kings (1 Kgs. 9:10-28) the Chronicler gave more information on Solomon's building projects. This portion of his history marks another major step in Solomon's career. Solomon had **established himself** (1:1), **gave orders to build a temple** (2:1), **began to build** (3:1), **summoned to Jerusalem** (5:2), **had finished the temple ... and the royal palace** (7:11). Now we learn that **at the end of twenty years ... Solomon rebuilt** (8:1).

Moreover, it helps to note that this portion of his record balances with 3:1-5:1 in a number of ways (see figure 22). Both passages deal with construction (compare 8:1-6 and 3:1-4:22); both focus on Solomon's provisions for the temple (compare 8:12-15 and 4:1-5:1). These similarities indicate that the Chronicler included this portion of Solomon's reign as a thematic parallel with 3:1–5:1.

Comparison with 1 Kgs. 9:10-28
In addition to several insignificant stylistic changes, the Chronicler made some notable omissions and additions. Four of these variations deserve comment.

First, the Chronicler only roughly followed 1 Kgs. 9:10-14. He omitted Hiram's displeasure with the cities Solomon had given him and spoke instead of Solomon rebuilding the cities once Hiram had returned them. The Chronicler's account does not contradict Kings; it simply supplements it.

Second, the Chronicler entirely omitted 1 Kgs. 9:15-17a. The record of forced labor and Pharaoh's gift did not interest him at this point. He moved to related topics later in the chapter (see 8:7-11).

Third, the Chronicler expanded the report on Pharaoh's daughter (8:11 // 1 Kgs. 9:24). Both accounts speak of Solomon moving her **to the palace he had built for her**. The Chronicler, however, added an explanation of Solomon's motives which extol his concern for the sanctity of the temple. The king said that his wife could not live **in the house of David ... because the places the ark of the LORD ... has entered are holy** (8:11b). This change fit well with the Chronicler's desire to treat Solomon as Israel's ideal king.

Fourth, the Chronicler slightly modified 1 Kgs. 9:25 (// 8:12) to draw attention to the bronze altar. Then he added three verses (8:13-15) describing what Solomon ordained to be done in its vicinity. These changes were designed to instruct the Chronicler's readers in worship practices for their own day.

Structure of 8:1-15
The changes which the Chronicler made to the record of Kings formed his account into a series of interrelated reports (see figure 23). The Chronicler first described a series of Solomon's successes throughout the land (8:1-6). He then qualified the nature of his forced labor (8:7-10), and supplemented Solomon's provisions for the temple (8:11-15).

Solomon's Widespread Construction Projects (8:1-6)
This part of the chapter focuses on how Solomon was successful in building **whatever he desired to build in Jerusalem, in Lebanon and throughout all the territory he ruled** (8:6). In the ancient Near East, kings were often praised for their extensive building projects. The Chronicler frequently described royal building projects to illustrate divine blessings on Judah's kings (see *Introduction: 24) Building and Destruction*). Solomon is his greatest example of such blessing.

8:1-2 reports Solomon's rebuilding of cities returned to him by Hiram. As we have seen above, 8:1-2 only roughly parallels the record of 1 Kgs. 9:10-17a. The Chronicler omitted that Solomon first gave these cities to Hiram and that Hiram was displeased with them (see 1 Kgs. 9:10-14). Instead, Chronicles simply reports what Solomon did with these cities after Hiram returned them. Undoubtedly, the Chronicler's readers knew the other details from the history of Kings. The Chronicler drew attention to Solomon's improvements of the sites.

Moreover, the Chronicler added that Solomon **settled Israelites in them** (8:2). By shifting the attention of his account in this manner, he upheld Solomon as an ideal for his post-exilic readers. He was concerned with rebuilding and repopulating the land of Israel in his day. (For the Chronicler's geographical hopes, see comments on 1 Chr. 2:42-55.) Solomon showed what could be done in this regard when the kingdom's central institutions (temple and monarchy) were in proper order.

The Chronicler also omitted 1 Kgs. 9:15-17a in order to list other building projects. Solomon took **Hamath**, **Zobah** (8:3); he **built up Tadmor**, and constructed **store cities in Hamath** (8:4). These northern districts established Solomon's control over the major trade routes to the north. Moreover, he also **rebuilt Upper Beth Horon** and **Lower Beth Horon as fortified cities** (8:5). These cities guarded the main route from Jerusalem to the coast. They were vital for the trade and defense of the capital city. In addition to these sites, Solomon also built **his store cities** and places to house his **chariots** and **horses** (8:6). This list was intended as a mere sample of all that Solomon had accomplished. It illustrated well that Solomon was a successful builder. His successes made him an exemplary king for the Chronicler's post-exilic community as it longed to rebuild the nation.

Solomon's Extensive Labor Force (8:7-10)

The Chronicler returned to follow the book of Kings closely (// 1 Kgs. 9:20-23) and gave additional information on the labor forces Solomon employed in his building projects. This topic has come up before in the reign of Solomon (see 2:2,17-18), but the earlier report left some questions unanswered. Here the Chronicler presented an explanation that he thought was important for his post-exilic readers.

The discussion of Solomon's laborers divides into two parts. 8:7-8 reports that Solomon conscripted many different groups of people from those who remained in the land after the conquest. Beyond this, the text makes it clear that Israelites did not serve as conscripted laborers. They held positions of authority such as **fighting men, commanders of ... captains, chariots, charioteers** and **chief officials** (8:9-10). Apparently these Israelites and others had responsibilities in **supervising the men** of the labor force (8:10; see 2:1-2). For the Chronicler's use of the terminology **to this day**, see comments on 5:7-10 and 1 Chr. 4:41.

This information was important for the Chronicler's day. It made at least two things clear to the post-exilic community as it contemplated the enormous task of rebuilding the nation. Foreign assistance in the projects was acceptable. Yet, the people of Israel themselves were not to become slaves in the work. Their status as free citizens was to be maintained despite the needs of the nation (see *Introduction: 3) International Relations*).

Solomon's Temple Construction (8:11-15)

As the Chronicler continued to follow the book of Kings (// 1 Kgs. 9:24-25), he offered more information related to Solomon's work on the temple. His lengthier discussion of these matters appears in 3:1-5:1,10. Here he considered two items brought up by Kings, but he expounded on both themes.

The first portion of these verses reports Solomon's treatment of Pharaoh's daughter (8:11 // 1 Kgs. 9:24). Solomon moved Pharaoh's daughter away from the temple complex **to a house he had built for her**. The Chronicler then added an explanation of Solomon's motivations. The king knew that **the places the ark of the LORD has entered are holy**. Solomon's precise thinking is not clear. He was obviously concerned to have the ark surrounded only by what was holy. Yet, it is not evident whether the problem with his wife was that she was a woman or that she was a Gentile. Women were restricted from full access to the temple in the Old Testament period. Even so, the preceding context concerns Gentiles laboring for Solomon and the separation of Israelites from them (8:7-10). In this light, Solomon's concern here may have been that Pharaoh's daughter was not converted to the religion of Israel (see 1 Kgs. 11:1-5). This well-known fact may have motivated the Chronicler to demonstrate that Solomon recognized the threat his Gentile wife posed to the holiness of the temple.

The final portion of this section looks more directly at the temple (8:12-15). The opening verse parallels the record of Kings (8:12 // 1 Kgs. 9:25), but omits the reference to 'burning incense' (1 Kgs. 9:25) in order to focus attention on the **altar ... that he had built in front of the portico** (8:12). The architectural elements of the temple take center stage.

The Chronicler added a lengthy description of the ceremonies surrounding the bronze altar which Solomon had built (8:13-15). This report of activities ordained by Solomon falls into two sections.

First, many activities were **commanded by Moses** (8:13), namely the **daily requirement** (see Exod. 29:38) for **Sabbaths** (see Num. 28:9), **New Moons** (see Num. 10:10), and **annual feasts** (see Exod. 12:17; Num. 28:16-25; Exod. 23:16; Num. 29:12-38). By this means, the Chronicler approved of Solomon's many ordinances for worship.

Second, the **divisions of the priests ... Levites** and **gatekeepers** were **in keeping with the ordinance of his father David** (8:14). They were what **David the man of God had ordered** (8:14; see 1 Chr. 23:6; 24:1; 25:1). Solomon insured that **they did not deviate** (8:15) from David's instructions. The emphasis of this additional information is evident. Solomon did all things in the proper manner. At this highpoint in Israel's history, the temple and its services functioned according to Mosaic and Davidic instructions. The Chronicler made it clear that this was to be the policy in his own day (see *Introduction: 14) Standards*).

More on Solomon's International Relations (8:16-9:21)

With the building projects of Solomon finished (8:1-15), the Chronicler continued to follow the account of Kings (// 1 Kgs. 9:26-10:22). He added a new beginning to this material in 8:16 to identify another major division. Solomon had **established himself** (1:1), **gave orders to build a temple** (2:1), **began to build** (3:1), **summoned to Jerusalem** (5:2), **had finished the temple ... and the royal palace**

(7:11), **at the end of twenty years... Solomon built** (8:1). At this point, the Chronicler added that **all of Solomon's work was carried out ... So the temple ... was finished** (8:16).

This section continues the Chronicler's large scale chiasm for Solomon's reign by returning to the theme of the king's international relations (see figure 22). From beginning to end, this passage deals with Solomon's southern maritime trade through the ports at Ezion Geber and Elath on the Red Sea (8:17). The balance between this passage and 2:1-18 is evident. It deals repeatedly with the recognition and assistance Solomon received from other nations. Moreover, Hiram is present throughout the material (8:18; 9:10,21) as he was in 2:1-18. By juxtaposing these elements in Solomon's reign, the Chronicler drew attention to another aspect of the ideal Solomon represented for the post-exilic Israelites as they struggled with the international environment of their day (see *Introduction: 3) International Relations*).

Comparison with 1 Kgs. 9:26-10:22

For the most part the Chronicler's text closely parallels Kings. At times it is difficult to know if small differences between Chronicles and Kings reflect the Chronicler's intentions or merely represent stylistic variations or problems in textual transmission. Nevertheless, four dissimilarities deserve special mention.

First, the Chronicler added a new beginning to this section (8:16). By this means he separated these events from Solomon's earlier accomplishments and indicated the beginning of a major portion of Solomon's reign.

Second, the Chronicler changed the language of 1 Kgs. 10:9 ('on the throne of Israel') to **on his** [God's] **throne as king to rule for the LORD your God** (9:8). This variation fit well with his repeated emphasis that the king of Israel was God's vice-regent (see *Introduction: 8) Divine Kingship*).

Third, on two occasions the Chronicler added a role for Solomon and his men in conjunction with Hiram's sailors in order to highlight Solomon's leading role in international relations (8:17 // 1 Kgs. 9:26; 9:10 // 1 Kgs. 10:11).

Fourth, the Chronicler varied from 1 Kgs. 10:13 ('besides what he had given her out of his royal bounty') to **more than she had brought to him** (9:12a). This change exalted Solomon as the dominant party in the relationship with the Queen of Sheba.

Structure of 8:16-9:21

After an introductory note (8:16), the entire section divides into three parts including reports, a brief narrative and one fully developed narrative (see figure 23). This portion of Solomon's reign begins and ends with records of Hiram helping Solomon establish a successful maritime operation (8:17-18; 9:15-21). This frame establishes the main concern of the text. The pivotal middle portion focuses on Arabian reactions to Solomon's successful foreign trade (9:1-14).

Transitional Introduction (8:16)

The Chronicler added this verse to provide a temporal setting for the events that followed. This brief introduction repeats the same motif twice. First, the Chronicler noted that **all Solomon's work was carried out ... until** [the temple's] **completion**. Then he added that **the temple of the LORD was finished** (8:16). Although this portion of Solomon's reign deals with Solomon's international trade, it was vital to the Chronicler's ideal portrait of Solomon to establish that the king gave himself fully to developing international trade only after he had first accomplished his most important task, the building of the temple. The implications for the Chronicler's readers are evident. Their priorities must be the same: the temple and its services first, then international trade and national prosperity (see *Introduction: 3) International Relations*).

Solomon and Hiram Open Maritime Trade (8:17-18)

Following the parallel material in Kings rather closely (// 1 Kgs. 9:26-27), the Chronicler presented a brief narrative recording the initiation of Solomon's maritime trade on the Red Sea. The account divides into three parts (see figure 23).

The opening of this brief account mentions Solomon as the initiator of a new trade venture. **Ezion Geber and Elath** were Edomite ports on the northwestern portion of the Red Sea (8:17). 1 Kgs. 9:26 reads, 'Solomon also built ships', but the Chronicler varied slightly and wrote **Solomon went** (8:17). By doing so, he emphasized Solomon's personal responsibility for the successful maritime effort.

These ports of Edom were Israel's nearest access to the Red Sea and lucrative maritime trade with Africa and India. Until this time, Israel depended primarily on Arabian caravans to bring goods from these regions across the Arabian desert. Now Israel had direct access to this commerce.

Solomon was not ready to accomplish this task on his own. Israel had little experience in sea travel. As a result, **Hiram**, king of the Mediterranean port at Tyre, assisted Solomon. He **sent him ships commanded by his own officers, men who knew the seas** (8:18a). The mention of Hiram recalls Hiram's earlier help with Solomon's building projects (see 2:3-16). This lifelong ally was also instrumental in Solomon's international trade.

The initial success of Solomon's venture stands out quickly. **Solomon's men** and Hiram's experienced sailors travel to **Ophir** (8:18b). The location of Ophir is not certain; it could have been in Northwestern Africa (in the region of modern Somalia), on the South Arabian coast, or further east. The reference to the 'three year journey' (see 9:21) suggests that it may have been at a far distance. In all events, Ophir was known for its fine gold and other rare goods (see Job 28:16; Ps. 45:9; Isa. 13:12).

More than this, the success of Solomon's effort becomes evident in the amount of goods the seamen brought back. They returned with **four hundred and fifty talents of gold**, about 17 (16 metric) tons (18:18).

Solomon's success in this international commercial venture offered the Chronicler's readers an important perspective on their own lives. When Israel's king and temple are in proper order, there are hardly any limits on the prosperity that may come to the nation through lucrative international trade (see *Introduction: 3) International Relations*).

Solomon's and Arabian Reactions (9:1-14)

At the time Solomon was extending his trade routes with Hiram's help, a number of Arabian states thrived because of trade with Africa and the Far East. Their Southern coastal cities served as convenient ports for desert caravans which transferred exotic goods inland. It would have been natural for these Arabians to be hostile toward Solomon. Nevertheless, their response was just the opposite. As the Chronicler's text reports, the Arabians were so impressed with Solomon's success that they sought to please him.

The account of Arabian reactions divides into two parts (see figure 23): the reaction of the Queen of Sheba (9:1-12) and the reactions of other Arabian monarchs (9:13-14).

The Queen of Sheba Honors Solomon (9:1-12)

Following the text of Kings (//1 Kgs. 10:1-13) with only a few stylistic changes, the Chronicler first recorded the reaction of the **Queen of Sheba** (9:1). This full scale narrative divides into five steps (see figure 23). The Queen of Sheba came to Solomon (9:1) and returned home (9:12b). Solomon answered her questions (9:2), gained her admiration (9:3-9), and responded favorably to her (9:12a). Interrupting this story is a note on Hiram's fleet and how it benefited Solomon with the kinds of goods that gained the Queen's admiration (9:10-11).

The Queen Comes to Solomon (9:1)

The **Queen of Sheba heard of Solomon's fame** because of his new ventures into her commercial arena (9:1). Archaeological research strongly suggests that Sheba was a commercial sea port located along the coast of southwest Arabia. As such, the Queen had heard reports from those who traded with Solomon's fleet sailing from Ezion-Geber and Elath (see 8:17-18). She doubted the reports of Solomon's wisdom (see 9:6) and came **to test him with hard questions** (9:1). She spoke **with him about all she had on her mind** including economic matters (9:1). She came with **a very great caravan** to establish good relations with the King of Israel (9:1).

Solomon Answers the Queen's Questions (9:2)

Solomon passed the Queen's test. He answered **all her questions** without difficulty. Her best efforts to expose his shortcomings were unsuccessful; **nothing was too hard for him** (9:2). This feature of the story fits well with the view that Solomon was the wisest of all kings (see 1:11-12; 9:23; see also 1 Kgs. 3:12; 4:29-31; 5:12; 10:23).

The Queen Admires Solomon (9:3-9)

The Chronicler continued following the account of Kings by reporting the Queen's reaction to Solomon (// 1 Kgs. 10:4-10). At this point the pace of the story slows tremendously to allow the readers time to ponder the Queen's reaction to Solomon. Her response divides into three parts: her experience in Solomon's court (9:3-4), her praise for Solomon (9:5-8), and her gift to Solomon (9:9).

The passage first reports the Queen's experience in Solomon's court (9:3-4). In a word, **she was overwhelmed** (literally, 'she was breathless' [see NRS and NKJ]) (9:4). Her reaction was not simply to Solomon's answers to her riddles. She saw **the wisdom of Solomon**, but was also impressed with his **palace** ... **food** ... **his officials** ... **attending servants** ... **cupbearers** and **burnt offerings** (perhaps 'his stairway' NAS [9:3]).

As a result of seeing Solomon's court, the Queen offered extensive praise (9:5-8). Her words of admiration began with a focus on Solomon himself (9:5-7) and then turned to Solomon's God (9:8). She first admitted that the report she received **in** [her] **own country** ... was **true** (9:5). She also admitted that she **did not believe what they said** until she saw **with** [her] **own eyes** (9:6). Having witnessed Solomon's greatness herself, she concluded that reality **far exceeded the report** (9:6). Then she extolled Solomon by expressing her envy of those who **continually stand before** [him] **and hear** [his] **wisdom** (9:7).

These words of exuberant praise for Solomon offer significant confirmation for the Chronicler's perspective. He had repeatedly asserted Solomon's incomparability, but now confirmation came from the lips of a skeptical foreign queen. Solomon's greatness was not an Israelite exaggeration; it was an internationally recognized fact.

To highlight the Queen's reaction even more, the passage reports how she offered praise to Solomon's God (9:8). This event falls in line with Solomon's desire for foreigners to recognize his God (see 6:32-33). Apparently, Solomon not only exposed the Queen to his political successes, but to his religion as well (see *Introduction: 3) International Relations*). Her language of praise indicates a deep awareness of Israel's concept of the relation of divine and human kingship. The Chronicler shifted the language of 1 Kings 10:9 ('on the throne of Israel') to **on his** [God's] **throne as king to rule for the LORD your God** (9:8). The idea that the Davidic throne was the throne of God appears several times in Chronicles (see *Introduction: 8) Divine Kingship*). The Queen also recognized Solomon's throne as a benevolence to the nation. God made Solomon king **because of the love of** ... **God for Israel and his desire to uphold them forever** (9:8). This theme also appears a number of times in Chronicles (see *Introduction: 4-9) King and Temple*). Finally, the Queen mentioned that the divine purpose for Solomon's throne was to **maintain justice and righteousness**, a motif often associated with the Davidic line (see 2 Sam. 8:15; 23:3-5; 1 Chr. 18:14; 1 Kgs. 3:11,28; 10:9; Ps. 72:1-2; Isa. 9:6-7; 16:5).

By maintaining this passage from Kings in his history, the Chronicler once again supported points of view presented elsewhere in his history. Solomon's wisdom was so great that it convinced even a foreigner of the divine purpose of kingship in Israel. If one outside of Israel understood these things, surely the post-exilic Israelites to whom he wrote should acknowledge the importance of the Davidic line for their day.

Gifts to Solomon (9:9)
As was the custom in the ancient Near East, the Queen of Sheba gave wonderful gifts to Solomon. She delivered **120 talents of gold** (about 4.5 tons [4 metric tons]). Moreover she gave him **large quantities of spices** the likes of which **had never been** in Israel (9:9). No doubt, these spices came from the Far East and were very rare in the Mediterranean world. The exotic quality of the Queen's gifts not only revealed the wealth she had, they also enhanced the wonder of Solomon's ideal kingdom in the eyes of the Chronicler's readers.

A Note on Solomon's Wealth from Hiram's Fleet (9:10-11)
At this point the Chronicler followed the book of Kings (// 1 Kgs. 10:11-12) and added a tangential note. Perhaps he felt a need to explain why the Arabian queen was so impressed with Solomon. Whatever the case, the text mentions items procured by Hiram's fleet. The Chronicler changed 'Hiram's ships' (1 Kgs. 10:11) to **the men of Hiram and the men of Solomon** (9:10 // 1 Kgs. 10:11) to emphasize Solomon's involvement. The list of items remains the same: **gold from Ophir** (see 8:18), **algumwood and precious stones** (9:10). Mentioned also are the uses to which Solomon put the algumwood: **steps for the temple** and **harps and lyres for the musicians** (9:11). These items were beyond compare **in Judah** (9:11).

Solomon Responds to the Queen's Admiration (9:12a)
In response to the Queen's words and actions, Solomon gave her **all she desired and asked** (9:12a). As noted above, the Chronicler shifts the language of 1 Kgs. 10:13 ('besides what he had given her out of his royal bounty') to **more than she had brought to him** (9:12a). This change was designed to exalt Solomon beyond the generosity demonstrated by the Queen of Sheba. This shift was important to the Chronicler's readers. Although Solomon benefited from his relations with others, he was always the dominant partner. Nothing less was the ideal for the post-exilic community (see *Introduction: 3) International Relations*).

The Queen Departs from Solomon (9:12b)
To close off the story, the text reports that the Queen of Sheba returned home **with her retinue** (9:12b). She left richer than when she came. Solomon had received blessing from her, but he in turn was a blessing to her. This theme recalls the patriarchal promise to the same effect (see Gen. 12:1-3).

Arabian Kings Acknowledge Solomon (9:13-14)
These verses are repeated with little changed from 1 Kgs. 10:14-16. They first offer a summation of Solomon's riches. The wealth received by Solomon is counted at

666 talents of **gold** (about 25 tons [23 metric tons]) (9:13). Mention is then made of the **gold and silver** brought by **all the kings of Arabia and the governors** (9:14). The connection with the preceding narrative of the Queen of Sheba is evident. These were Solomon's competitors in trade, but like the Queen of Sheba, they acknowledged Solomon as their superior.

Solomon and Hiram in Maritime Trade (9:15-21)

Continuing his dependence on Kings (// 1 Kgs. 10:16-22), the Chronicler listed a number of items Solomon made from his vast wealth. The emphasis of this material appears in the repetition of the word **made** (9:11,15,17,19).

First, Solomon made numerous items of **gold** (9:15 [twice], 16 [twice]). He made **large shields** (9:15) and **small shields** of **hammered gold** (9:16). These smaller shields were carried off by Shishak after his attack on Jerusalem in Rehoboam's day (see 12:1-12). Solomon placed these **in the Palace of the Forest of Lebanon** (9:16). The palace received this name because of four rows of large cedar pillars that gave the impression of a forest (see 1 Kgs. 7:2).

Second, Solomon decorated his throne elaborately (9:17-19). It was **inlaid with ivory and overlaid with pure gold** (9:17). **Six steps** led up to **a footstool of gold** (9:18). The images of royal **lions** decorated the **armrests** and **steps** (9:18-19). The purpose of these details is explicitly stated. They exalted Solomon's glory for **nothing like it had been made for any other kingdom** (9:19).

Third, the **goblets** and **household articles** in the palace were all made of **pure gold ... because silver was considered of little value in Solomon's day** (9:20). Once again, Solomon's kingdom is exalted as ideal.

To connect this material to its context, the text notes the source of much of these riches. **Once every three years** the **trading fleet manned by Hiram's men** brought back great treasures (9:21). This reference to Hiram frames the assorted material in 8:17-9:21. Solomon's interaction with other nations is not limited to this passage and its earlier parallel (2:1-18), but the concern with Hiram pervades the material.

Solomon's relation with Hiram illustrated for the post-exilic readers the kind of positive benefits that came to Solomon from this relationship. In a day when the economic conditions of Israel were in need of much improvement, Solomon's willingness to engage in international trade provided guidance for those who had returned to the land (see *Introduction: 3) International Relations*).

More on Solomon's Great Wisdom and Wealth (9:22-28)

At this point, the Chronicler's division of his material is obscured by the fact that he continued to follow the book of Kings (// 1 Kgs. 10:23-29). Nevertheless, it seems best in light of his broad chiastic structure to see this portion as a move to another section (see figure 22). These verses are held together by the repeated expression **all the kings** (9:22,23,26) which the Chronicler introduced each time into this passage.

Comparison with 1 Kgs. 10:23-29

Two observations are important for understanding the Chronicler's use of this passage. First, these verses result from a combination of different portions of the record of Kings. The Chronicler followed 1 Kgs. 10:23-25 (// 9:23-24) to which he attached his version of 1 Kgs. 10:26-29 (// 9:25,27-28). This latter portion, however, is interrupted at 9:26 by an insertion from 1 Kgs. 4:21.

Second, three changes reflect the panoramic perspective that the Chronicler emphasized in this material. He changed 'the whole world' (1 Kgs. 10:24) to **all the kings of the earth** (9:23). He shifted from 'over all the kingdoms' (1 Kgs. 4:21) to **all the kings** (9:26). These changes correspond to **all the other kings of the earth** (9:22) which he copied from 1 Kgs. 10:23. A third change occurs in the last sentence of this section. 'From Egypt and from Kue' (1 Kgs. 10:28) is changed to **from Egypt and from all other countries** (9:28) to emphasize the grandeur of Solomon's exaltation.

Structure of 9:22-28

This short passage divides into three parts (see figure 23). It begins with an introductory title indicating Solomon's superiority over all other kings (9:22). It then moves to two illustrations of that superiority: the recognition of his wisdom by other kings (9:23-24) and his worldwide imports (9:25-28).

Introduction (9:22)

The Chronicler adopted 1 Kgs. 10:23 as a title for this section. Solomon was superior in **riches and wisdom** to **all the other kings of the earth** (9:22). God had promised Solomon would receive **wealth, riches and honor** beyond any king before and after him (1:12). As he introduced his finale to Solomon's reign, the Chronicler wanted his readers to know that God had kept his promise to Solomon. He expressed this by means of a hyperbole making Solomon richer than any other king before or after him. (For the Chronicler's use of hyperbole, see comments on 1 Chr. 12:14.) Solomon's wealth demonstrates that his kingdom was blessed by God and rightly served as a model for the post-exilic readers (see *Introduction: 26) Prosperity and Poverty*).

Solomon's Worldwide Recognition (9:23-24)

The Chronicler supported his perspective on Solomon by focusing on his international recognition. The Queen of Sheba was not alone in her desire to visit Solomon. In an extreme hyperbole, the Chronicler wrote that **all the kings of the earth sought audience** (9:23). (For the Chronicler's use of hyperbole, see comments on 1 Chr. 12:14.) They all wanted to hear for themselves this **wisdom God had put in his heart** (9:23). Again, the allusion to 1:1-12 is evident. God's fulfillment of his promise to Solomon was recognized by the whole world. In addition to acknowledging Solomon's wisdom, every king also contributed to Solomon's wealth **year after year** (9:24).

Solomon's Worldwide Imports (9:25-28)

The second support given to the idea that Solomon received incomparable wisdom and riches (see 9:22) was his international trade. In these four verses, the Chronicler drew together materials from 1 Kgs. 10:26 (// 9:25), 1 Kgs. 4:21 (// 9:26), and 1 Kgs. 10:27-28 (// 9:27-28). The materials of 9:25,27-28 are duplicated from 1:14-17. They are repeated here to point to the balance this passage has with the opening of Solomon's reign.

The insertion of 9:26 (// 1 Kgs. 4:21) explains how Solomon managed to reach this height of glory. Solomon's riches were immense because he **ruled over all the kings from the River to the land of the Philistines, as far as the border of Egypt** (9:26). Solomon had enormous numbers of **horses and chariots** (9:25) and brought prosperity to Jerusalem (9:27). In the last verse of this section, the Chronicler varied 'from Egypt and Kue' (1 Kgs. 10:28 and 2 Chr. 1:16) to **from Egypt and from all other countries** (9:28). The purpose of this change is apparent. Solomon's supremacy over the vast territories mentioned in 9:26 was the source of his incomparable riches.

Solomon's worldwide imports spoke directly to the needs of the post-exilic readers. As they struggled with economic hardship, the memory of Solomon's territorial and commercial successes inspired them to hope for the same. The Chronicler's message to them was straightforward. Only if they followed the example of Solomon, could they see the same results of riches and blessings in their day.

Closure of Solomon's Reign (9:29-31)

The Chronicler ended his account of Solomon's reign by indicating the honor afforded to Solomon in his death and burial. He also noted his literary sources.

Comparison with 1 Kgs. 11:41-43

The Chronicler relied on Kings for the basic format of this material. Two aspects of his account should be noted.

First, it is important to point out that the Chronicler omitted a large segment of Kings (1 Kgs. 11:1-40; see figure 21). This portion of Kings reports Solomon's failures and the resulting trouble in his kingdom. The Chronicler's purpose in omitting these materials was not to deny Solomon's failures, but to create an ideal model for his post-exilic readers. For this reason, Chronicles moves directly from Solomon's worldwide fame to the notice of his death.

Second, the Chronicler added references to a number of the literary sources he used beyond those mentioned in the book of Kings (9:29). He mentioned **the records of Nathan ... Ahijah ... and the visions of Iddo** (9:29). Nathan's records were mentioned earlier (1 Chr. 29:29). **Ahijah** is the prophet who condemned Solomon for his failures (see 1 Kgs. 11:29-39). **Iddo** appears in 12:15; 13:22. These books are no longer extant, but probably contained stories and prophecies much like the biblical prophetic books. The Chronicler's reliance on these sources demonstrated his affinities toward the office of prophet (see *Introduction: 15) Prophets*).

To close out his record of Solomon, the Chronicler mentioned two facts. First, Solomon reigned forty years over **all Israel** (9:30). Although these words appear in 1 Kings 11:42, they reiterate the Chronicler's interest in the unity of the nation under Solomon (see *Introduction: 1) All Israel*). Second, in typical fashion, the Chronicler revealed his overarching assessment of Solomon's reign. His burial report mentions that Solomon was buried in the city of David (9:31). Thus, Solomon was honored as one of Israel's greatest kings (see *Introduction: 28) Healing and Long Life/Sickness and Death*). From beginning to end, the Chronicler presented Solomon as a royal ideal.

Part Three

Judah During the Divided Kingdom (2 Chr 10:1-28:27)

Overview of the Divided Kingdom

As the Chronicler entered the Divided Kingdom he left behind the reigns of his ideal kings. Although a number of kings during this period accomplished some remarkably positive achievements, this material is much more balanced between positive and negative events. Instead of providing the post-exilic community with extended models of faithful living, the kings of the Divided Kingdom offered contrasting scenarios of obedience and disobedience which led to divine blessing and judgment.

Comparison of 10:1–28:27 with 1 Kgs. 12:1–2 Kgs. 17:41

Detailed comparisons of each portion of the Divided Kingdom in Chronicles and Kings appear under the discussion of each reign. At this point it is important simply to note that the greatest difference between the two records is that Chronicles omits all materials dealing exclusively with northern Israel. Events in the North appear only as they touched on life in Judah. As a result, this material nearly exclusively focuses on conditions within Judah during the Divided Kingdom. This orientation reflected the Chronicler's keen interest in Jerusalem and Judah as the center of the post-exilic restoration. From his point of view, his readers needed to concentrate their attention on events in the South so that they could learn how to further the restoration of the Kingdom in their day.

Structure of 10:1-28:27

The structure of this portion of the history is not immediately apparent. Yet, it is evident that divisions between times of blessing and judgment shape much of the material. Moreover, it is possible to identify three groupings of Judahite reigns in which particular themes come to the foreground (see figure 25).

Judgments and Increasing Blessings in Judah (10:1-21:3)
- Rehoboam (10:1-12:16)
- Abijah (13:1-14:1)
- Asa (14:2-16:14)
- Jehoshaphat (17:1-21:3)

Northern Corruption in Judah (21:4-24:27)
- Jehoram (21:4-21:20)
- Ahaziah (22:1-9)
- Athaliah (22:10-23:21)
- Joash (24:1-27)

Half-Hearted Obedience in Judah (25:1-28:27)
- Amaziah (25:1-28)
- Uzziah (26:1-23)
- Jotham (27:1-9)
- Ahaz (28:1-27)

Outline of 2 Chr. 10:1-28:27 (figure 25)

The features which characterize each portion of the Divided Kingdom will be discussed at the beginning of each section. It should be noted, however, that the motifs of each segment are much more complex than this outline suggests. The Chronicler wove countless topics throughout this material. Nevertheless, the themes of increasing blessing (10:1-21:3), northern corruption (21:4-24:27), and half-hearted obedience leading to judgment (25:1-28:27) tie these materials together into these three groupings.

Judgments and Increasing Blessings in Judah (10:1-21:3)

The first phase of the Divided Kingdom includes the reigns of Rehoboam (10:1-12:16) Abijah (13:1-14:1), Asa (14:2-16:14), and Jehoshaphat (17:1-21:3). These chapters present a variety of situations in which God responded to his people in judgment and blessing. Several motifs run through these reigns and distinguish them from the rest of the history.

First, every reign has at least one episode concerning Judah's involvement with northern Israel. In each case Judah remains distinct from her northern neighbor. Rehoboam suffered the rebellion of the northern tribes and nearly went to war against them (10:1-11:4). Abijah distinguished Judah from Israel in a speech before battle and subsequently defeated Israel (13:1-20). Asa failed to trust God in the face of Northern aggression, but nevertheless remained separate from them (16:1-10). Although Jehoshaphat joined in alliance with Ahab (18:1-19:3) and Ahaziah (20:35-37), he was sharply distinguished from the North (17:4; 19:1-3).

The focus on separation of Judah from Israel differs from the second phase when Judah is deeply corrupted by the northern queen Athaliah (21:4-24:27). It also differs with the third phase when Judah gradually falls into the state of becoming like the Northern kingdom (25:1-28:27).

Second, each record includes at least one battle narrative. Episodes of warfare are not in themselves unusual, but these battles all have a common element. In at least one battle in each reign, Judahites called out to God in the face of powerful foes and God responded positively to their prayers. Rehoboam was delivered from total defeat at the hands of a superior Egyptian army (12:6). Abijah received victory over northern Israel despite their greater numbers (13:14). God gave Asa a similar victory over the Cushites (14:8-15). Jehoshaphat had two battles in which he called for and received help from God against great foes (18:31; 20:5-12). These parallels tie the first four reigns of the divided period together in distinction from the material that follows.

Third, reactions to announcements of God's word also determined the outcome of blessings and judgment in each reign. Rehoboam reacted appropriately two times to the prophet Shemaiah (11:2-4; 12:5-8). Abijah announced God's word before battle, but northern Israel ignored him to their defeat (13:4-12). Asa was blessed for obeying the prophetic word (15:1-8), but he was cursed for rejecting the same word later in life (16:7-9). Jehoshaphat interacted positively with two prophets (18:1-19:3); he also received God's word from a Levite (20:14-19) which led to a great victory from God.

Fourth, a crescendo of blessings occurs in these materials as well. As one indication of this dimension of the record, the Chronicler noted how many soldiers were in Judah's army during each reign. The blessing of God is evident in that the number of soldiers increased steadily from Rehoboam to Jehoshaphat. Rehoboam had 180,000 soldiers (11:1); Abijah's army numbered 400,000 (13:3); Asa had 580,000 (14:8); Jehoshaphat mustered 1,160,000 men (17:14-19), the greatest army during the Divided Kingdom. Similar statistics do not appear again until Amaziah (25:5) and Uzziah (26:11-15). This feature unites this early portion of the Divided Kingdom as a time of increasing blessing alongside of appropriate judgments.

The Reign of Rehoboam (10:1-12:16)

The Chronicler's presentation of Rehoboam's reign (931-913 BC) introduced his readers to themes that will appear time and again in this period of the divided monarchy. He shaped his record to present Rehoboam as a king who failed twice, but received blessings from God on both occasions because of his appropriate response to the prophetic word.

Comparison of 10:1–12:16 with 1 Kgs. 12:1–14:31

The following comparison indicates large scale similarities and differences between Chronicles and Kings (see figure 26). Detailed comparisons follow at the beginning of each section.

2 Chr.		1 Kgs.
10:1-19	Rehoboam's Loss of Northern Support (closely parallel)	12:1-20
11:1-4	Rehoboam's Refrain from Attack (closely parallel)	12:21-24
——	Jeroboam's Enterprises (omitted)	12:25-33
11:5-12	Rehoboam's Fortifications (added)	——
11:13-17	Rehoboam's Support (added)	——
11:18-23	Rehoboam's Progeny (added)	——
——	Jeroboam's Altar (omitted)	13:1-34
——	Jeroboam's House (omitted)	14:1-20
12:1-12	Rehoboam's Battle with Shishak (expanded)	14:25-28
12:13-14	Rehoboam's Reign Summarized (abbreviated)	14:21-24
12:15-16	Closure of Reign (closely parallel)	14:29-31

Comparison of 2 Chr. 10:1-12:16 with 1 Kgs. 12:1-14:31 (figure 26)

The Chronicler's account of Rehoboam's reign relates to Kings in several ways. First, in his usual fashion the Chronicler focused exclusively on the southern kingdom of Rehoboam by omitting several sections that dealt with Jeroboam (1 Kgs. 12:25-33; 13:1-24; 14:1-20). Second, the Chronicler's account adds several elements not found in Kings. These additions primarily include several blessings Rehoboam received (11:5-12, 13-17, 18-23). Third, various portions derived from Kings are closely parallel (10:1-19; 11:1-4; 12:15-16), expanded (12:1-12), and abbreviated (12:13-14).

Structure of 10:1-12:16

The Chronicler shaped his account of Rehoboam into two parallel sequences followed by the closure of the king's reign (see figure 27).

The disproportionate sizes of the two parts of Rehoboam's reign obscure their thematic parallels. As this outline suggests, however, both parts reflect each other in three ways.

1) They begin with Rehoboam committing sin. He foolishly followed the advice of his peers and threatened the northern tribes (10:1-19); he forsook God's law (12:1).

2) Both sections record Rehoboam's submission to the prophetic word. He did not attack the North (11:1-4); he humbled himself in repentance (12:5-8).

3) Both passages report blessings Rehoboam received as a result of his response to the prophet. An assortment of positive developments took place (11:5-23) and Rehoboam was spared from utter destruction (12:9-12). These similarities create a literary resonance within Rehoboam's reign which draws attention to the dangers of rebellion against God and value of submitting to the prophetic word.

Rehoboam's Early Sin, Prophetic Encounter, and Blessing (10:1-11:22)

The reign of Rehoboam begins with an account of northern Israel's rebellion against Judah. The Chronicler arranged this portion of his record so that it focused on sin, submission to a prophet, and divine blessing.

Comparison of 10:1-11:22 with 1 Kgs. 12:1-24

This passage closely parallels 1 Kgs. 12:1-24, but a number of significant variations appear. First, in two places the Chronicler diverged from Kings to employ his standard phrase **all Israel** (see *Introduction: 1) All Israel*). Chronicles shifts from 'the whole assembly of Israel' (1 Kgs. 12:3 // 2 Chr. 10:3) and 'Israel' (1 Kgs. 12:16d // 2 Chr. 10:16d) to **all Israel**.

Second, in 10:7 the Chronicler softened the demands of the northern Israelites. 1 Kgs. 12:7 reads, 'If today you will be a servant to these people and serve them...' 2 Chr. 10:7 reads, **'If you will be kind to these people and please them**...' This change made it clear that the requirements of the northern tribes were not unreasonable.

Third, a few Hebrew texts of 10:14 read as the NIV ('My father made your yoke

Rehoboam's Early Sin, Prophetic Encounter, and Blessing (10:1-11:22)

Rehoboam's Sin and Israel's Rebellion (10:1-19)
Rehoboam's Foolish Treatment of the North (10:1-17)
All Israel Gathers to Make Rehoboam King (10:1)
Rehoboam and Northern Israel Discuss Terms (10:2-5)
Rehoboam Chooses a Foolish Response (10:6-11)
Rehoboam and Northern Israelites Discuss Terms (10:12-16a)
Northern Israelites Return Home (10:16b-17)

Rehoboam's Failure to Subjugate Northern Israel (10:18)
Rehoboam Sends Representative (10:18a)
Rehoboam's Representative is Killed (10:18b)
Rehoboam Flees to Jerusalem (10:18c)
Authorial Comment (10:19)

Rehoboam's Compliance and Blessing (11:1-23)
Rehoboam's Compliance with the Prophetic Word (11:1-4)
Rehoboam Prepares for Battle (11:1)
Rehoboam Receives a Prophetic Word (11:2-4a)
Rehoboam Turns Back from Battle (11:4b)

Rehoboam's Blessings for Compliance (11:5-23)
Rehoboam's Successful Fortifications (11:5-12)
Rehoboam's Support from Faithful Northerners (11:13-17)
Rehoboam's Support from Priests and Levites (11:13-15)
Rehoboam's Support from Other Northerners (11:16)
Rehoboam's Resulting Benefits (11:17)
Rehoboam's Enlarged Family (11:18-23)

Rehoboam's Later Sin, Prophetic Encounter, and Blessing (12:1-12)

Rehoboam's Strength Leading to Apostasy (12:1)
Shishak's Attack against Judah and Jerusalem (12:2-4)
Rehoboam's Response to the Prophetic Warning (12:5-8)
Shishak's Limited Victory over Jerusalem (12:9)
Rehoboam's Resulting Weakness (12:10-11)
Authorial Comment (12:12)

Closure of Rehoboam's Reign (12:13-16)

Outline of 2 Chr. 10:1-12:16 (figure 27)

heavy.') which conforms to 1 Kgs. 12:14. Other Hebrew texts of 10:14 shift to 'I have made your yoke heavy' (see NAS margin). The latter reading is probably original to the Chronicler and indicates his attempt to shift blame for the division away from Solomon to Rehoboam (see *Introduction: Translation and Transmission*).

Fourth, the Chronicler omitted the reference to Jeroboam's kingship (10:19 // 1 Kgs. 12:20). This omission conforms to the focus on Judah in this portion of the history.

Fifth, the most significant difference between Chronicles and Kings is the Chronicler's addition of 11:5-23. These reports of divine blessing close this section on a positive note and shape the account into a parallel for the latter half of Rehoboam's reign.

Structure of 10:1-11:22

The first segment of Rehoboam's reign divides into two main parts consisting of several narratives and a series of reports (see figure 27). The text first describes the rebellion of northern Israel against Rehoboam (10:1-19). It then depicts Rehoboam's compliance with the prophetic word and his resulting blessings (11:1-23).

Rehoboam's Sin and Israel's Rebellion (10:1-19)

Rehoboam's reign begins with an account of the division of the nation. In his attempt to present Solomon as a model for his readers, the Chronicler omitted the prophetic rebuke against Solomon which laid much blame for the division of the nation on Solomon (see 1 Kgs. 11:9-13). As a result, in the Chronicler's history the responsibility for national division fell squarely on Rehoboam's shoulders.

Structure of 10:1-19

The record of Rehoboam's sin against the North closely parallels the account of 1 Kgs. 12:1-19. It divides into two episodes followed by an authorial comment (see figure 27). Geographical orientations frame this material. It begins with Rehoboam leaving Jerusalem for Shechem (10:1) and ends with him returning to Jerusalem (10:18c). Within this framework two episodes appear. The first and longer episode concerns the king's foolish decision to oppress the northern tribes (10:1-17); the second and shorter episode reports Rehoboam's failure to suppress the rebellion of the northern tribes (10:18a-c). The section then closes with an authorial comment (10:19).

Rehoboam's Foolish Treatment of the North (10:1-17)

The reign of Rehoboam does not begin in the usual manner. Instead of opening with general characteristics of the king's reign as he often did, the Chronicler moved directly to Rehoboam's first sinful act. At the time of his coronation, Rehoboam foolishly mistreated the northern tribes.

Structure of 10:1-17

The account of Rehoboam's mistreatment of the North forms a five step symmetrical narrative (see figure 27). It begins with the Israelites coming to Shechem (10:1) and ends with them leaving for their homes (10:16b-17). Rehoboam and the northerners negotiate the terms of their relationship (10:2-5; 10:12-16a). These steps balance each other because both contain speeches by the king (10:5,14) and representatives of the tribes (10:3-4, 16). Moreover, the repetition of the reference to **three days** (10:5, 12 [twice]) also points to the symmetry between these portions of the story. Finally, the turning point of the episode focuses on Rehoboam's decision to respond harshly to the proposal of the northerners (10:6-11). This step itself divides into two movements: consultation with elders (10:6-7), and consultation with young men (10:8-9).

All Israel Gathers to Make Rehoboam King (10:1)

Rehoboam traveled **to Shechem** in the territory of Manasseh to obtain the support of the northern tribes. **All Israel had gone there** to make him king (10:1). In this passage **all Israel** refers to representatives of the northern tribes (see 10:3,16). Shechem is well-known as a place of many important events in biblical history (see Gen. 12:6-7; 33:18-20; 37:12-14; Josh. 21:21; 24:32; Judg. 9:1-57). Its central location served as a reasonable meeting place for all the parties involved. Even so, the fact that the northern tribes did not come to Jerusalem to offer their support implied from the outset that relations between these tribes and David's house were already strained.

Rehoboam and Northern Israel Discuss Terms (10:2-5)

The text offers some background information for these events. **Jeroboam** had fled from Solomon to **Egypt** (10:2). The Chronicler omitted the fuller record of this event in an effort to present Solomon as a model (see 1 Kgs. 11:1-40). Yet, here he acknowledged that Jeroboam had fled from Solomon, and later joined **all Israel** to negotiate with Rehoboam (10:2).

As noted above, the Chronicler mollified Jeroboam's proposal. The account of Kings calls Rehoboam to be a 'servant' of the tribes (1 Kgs. 12:7). The Chronicler, however, clarified that Jeroboam's intention was merely to ask Rehoboam to **lighten the harsh labor** because Solomon had already inflicted a **heavy yoke** on northern Israel (10:4). No Israelites were actually conscripted as slaves (see 2:17). In all likelihood the complaint focused on heavy taxation and the requirement that men from these tribes serve as supervisors of the forced labor. In all events, the northern tribes only asked for good treatment and vowed, **'We will serve you'** (10:4).

The Chronicler softened the demands of the North in order to encourage his post-exilic readers toward an irenic outlook toward northern Israel. As they sought to re-establish the kingdom of God, it was necessary to heal the breech between the North and South stemming from Rehoboam's actions. One aspect of this healing was to acknowledge many legitimate efforts put forth by the North in the days of Rehoboam (see *Introduction: 2) Northern Israel*).

Apparently, Rehoboam needed time to consider this difficult decision. The economic repercussions of changing labor policies would be complex, but he also needed the support of these tribes. As a result, Rehoboam asked Jeroboam and Israel to **come back** ... **in three days** (10:5).

Rehoboam Chooses a Foolish Response (10:6-11)

The middle portion of this narrative summarizes Rehoboam's deliberations during the three day period. This material divides into two scenes: Rehoboam's consultation with **the elders** (10:6-7) and his meeting with **the young men** (10:8-11).

Rehoboam turned first to his older advisors (10:6-7). The text honors these men as experienced and wise. They **served his father Solomon**, the wisest king of Israel (10:6). The king asked for their direction and they responded soberly. They advised that Rehoboam should **be kind to these people and please them** (10:7). If he did, he would be assured of the North's abiding loyalty.

Unfortunately, the king did not heed the advice of the older men, but turned to **the young men** (10:8). These advisors were his peers who **had grown up with him** (10:8). By this time, Rehoboam was forty one years old (see 12:13). It is likely therefore, that the term **young men** had pejorative connotations, suggesting sarcastically that Rehoboam's peers thought and acted with youthful folly.

Rehoboam's friends encouraged a harsh response. They arrogantly advised Rehoboam to do more than simply reject the offer. They suggested that he say, **'My little finger is thicker than my father's waist'** (10:10). Beyond this, Rehoboam was to add that Solomon may have **scourged** ... **with whips**, but he would **scourge** ... **with scorpions** (10:11). In effect, the young men counseled the king to threaten even greater hardships.

Rehoboam and Northern Israelites Discuss Terms (10:12-16a)

As instructed earlier, **Jeroboam and all the people** met again with the king **three days later** (10:12). The description of the scene begins abruptly with Rehoboam's response. As noted above, there is some question whether the original reading of Chronicles was 'I have made your yoke heavy' or **'my father made your yoke heavy'** (10:14; see *Introduction: Translation and Transmission*). The former may be correct because it shifts attention away from Solomon's culpability. Even so, the Chronicler did not deny Solomon's oppressive actions (see 10:4). Whatever the case, the text recalls again that Rehoboam followed the foolishness of **the young men** (10:14) and it repeats some of the words they encouraged (10:14). These repetitions were designed to highlight the folly of Rehoboam's actions.

As if to explain why Rehoboam would do such a foolish thing, the text comments that **this turn of events was from God** (10:15). Although this comment appears in Kings (// 1 Kgs. 12:15), it fit well with the Chronicler's theological outlooks. He often explained that divine providence was behind remarkable events (see *Introduction: 11) Divine Blessing and Judgment*). Rehoboam's actions precipitated the succession of the northern tribes **to fulfill the word of the LORD** ...

through Ahijah the Shilonite (10:15). The Chronicler had previously omitted this prophecy because it reflected negatively on Solomon (see 1 Kgs. 11:26-40). Nevertheless, his maintenance of the reference indicates that he expected his readers to know the prophecy. Rehoboam had foolishly driven the Northerners to rebellion, but this event was still under the sovereign control of the God of Israel.

In response to Rehoboam's words, **all Israel** (i.e. the representatives of the northern tribes) refused to submit to the king (10:16). Their words form a striking contrast to the earlier support offered to David (see 1 Chr. 12:18; also 1 Sam. 25:10; 2 Sam. 20:1). The antithetical sentiments are evident in the following comparison with 1 Chr. 12:18 (see figure 28)

1 Chr. 12:18	2 Chr. 10:18
We are yours, O David! We are with you, O son of Jesse! Success, success to you, and success to those who help you, for your God will help you.	What share do we have in David, What part in Jesse's son? To your tents, O Israel! Look after your own house, O David!

Comparison of 1 Chr. 12:18 and 2 Chr. 10:18 (figure 28)

In 1 Chr. 12:18 Benjamites affirmed that they belong to David's kingdom; here the northern tribes rejected that relationship. The former passage wished good for David and those who helped him; the latter called Israelites to mobilize for conflict. The former hoped for divine help for David; the latter condemned David's house to its own devices. As such, Rehoboam experienced a reversal of David's blessing. David received support from all the tribes, but Rehoboam lost the unified support of the nation.

Northern Israelites Return Home (10:16b-17)

The end of this episode mentions that the Northerners returned home from Shechem. The Chronicler shifted from 'Israel' (1 Kgs. 12:17) to **all Israel** to indicate the great loss to Rehoboam (10:16b). The ideal of the United Kingdom had vanished. In an aside, the passage notes that only those Northerners **who were living in the towns of Judah** remained under Rehoboam's authority (10:17; see *Introduction: 2) Northern Israel*). The harm to the kingdom was enormous. Only a minority of displaced Northerners remained loyal.

Rehoboam's Failed Attempt to Oppress Northern Israel (10:18-19)

The Chronicler continued following the record of Kings (// 1 Kgs. 12:18-19) to show that Rehoboam's kingdom deteriorated even further. This episode divides into three simple steps (see figure 27). The king sends his representative to the North (10:18a); the representative is assassinated (10:18b); Rehoboam flees to Jerusalem in fear (10:18c).

Rehoboam Sends Representative (10:18a)
Despite the rebellion that had taken place, the king began to carry through with his plan to oppress the North even more than Solomon. He sent **Adoniram who was in charge of the forced labor** (10:18a).

Rehoboam's Representative is Killed (10:18b)
When Adoniram arrived to enforce Rehoboam's plan, the northern Israelites **stoned him to death** (10:18b). The ease with which Adoniram was killed suggests that Rehoboam had entirely misread the situation. Apparently, he thought his royal authority would be recognized in the end. Not surprisingly, however, Adoniram was treated as a criminal and executed (see Lev. 20:2, 27; 24:14, 16, 23; Num. 15:35; Deut. 13:10; 17:5).

Rehoboam Flees to Jerusalem (10:18c)
With rebellion now in full swing, Rehoboam feared for his own safety and barely escaped with his life. He ran from Shechem for the safety of Jerusalem. The portrait of Rehoboam at this point is an ironic reversal of his earlier arrogant assertions. Before he felt invincible; here he ran for his life.

Authorial Comment (10:19)
A brief authorial comment closes these two episodes. As a result of what happened during this time **Israel has been in rebellion ... to this day** (10:19). In this passage, it is likely that the Chronicler adopted this phrase from 1 Kings 12:19 as a reference to his own day. (For a discussion of the expression **to this day**, see 1 Chr. 4:41.) Distrust and animosity between Judah and the northern tribes was a major concern for the Chronicler. In this note, the Chronicler placed responsibility for centuries of conflict between the North and South at the feet of Rehoboam (see *Introduction: 2) Northern Israel*).

The Chronicler's somber recollection of these events stands in sharp contrast with his repeated national celebrations during the reigns of David and Solomon (see *Introduction: 27) Disappointment and Celebration*). His history had now entered a new phase when Israel was far from ideal. Yet, in many ways Rehoboam's reign resembled the realities Israel faced in the post-exilic period. The tribes were divided; the throne of David was stripped of its glory. The next section of Rehoboam's reign illustrated the proper way to respond to this kind of situation.

Rehoboam's Compliance with the Prophetic Word (11:1-4)
Rehoboam mounted an effort to subjugate the northern rebels. Yet, as he was about to move against his fellow Israelites, a prophet warned against the action and Rehoboam complied. This episode begins a reversal of fortunes for the king.

Comparison of 11:1-4 with 1 Kgs. 12:21-24
Several minor stylistic changes exist between the parallel accounts of 11:1-4 and 1 Kgs. 12:21-24, but most of these are of little significance. The only important variant

occurs in 11:3 (// 1 Kgs. 12:23). Kings reads 'and to all the house of Judah and Benjamin', but the Chronicler shifted to **and to all Israel in Judah and Benjamin**. This change emphasized the connection between the southern tribes and their northern kinsmen whom he called **all Israel** earlier in this chapter (see 10:1; see *Introduction: 2) Northern Israel*; see also *1) All Israel*).

Structure of 11:1-4

This episode consists of a three step symmetrical narrative (see figure 27). It begins with Rehoboam preparing to attack the North (11:1). The ending balances the opening with Rehoboam turning away from battle (11:4b). The turning point of the passage is a revelation given to Rehoboam through Shemaiah the prophet (11:2-4a).

Rehoboam Prepares for Battle (11:1)

Rehoboam planned to suppress the rebellion of the northern tribes with troops from **Judah and Benjamin** (11:1). A number of Benjamites remained loyal to the Jerusalem throne during the Divided Kingdom (see 14:8; 15:2,9; 17:17). As we have seen, the Chronicler gave them special notice in his genealogies (see 1 Chr. 7:6-12; 8:1-40). This passage also informs us that Rehoboam gathered **a hundred and eighty thousand** soldiers from these two tribes (11:1). These numbers appear rather large. As in other similar passages, several explanations are possible. For the Chronicler's use of large numbers, see comments on 1 Chr. 12:24-37.

To display the blessing of God toward Judah during the early divided monarchy, the Chronicler noted that the number of soldiers increased over the first four reigns of the divided monarchy. Rehoboam had 180,000 soldiers (11:1); Abijah's army numbered 400,000 (13:3); Asa had 580,000 (14:8); Jehoshaphat mustered 1,160,000 men (17:14-19). Later in the history, Amaziah had 400,000 (25:5) and Uzziah counted 307,000 soldiers (26:11-15).

The purpose of the king's actions is stated explicitly. He prepared to **make war with Israel** (11:1). Rehoboam still acted imprudently. He continued to violate the model of David and Solomon who wisely kept the nation united. Nevertheless, the Chronicler called the meeting an **assembly** (11:1). This terminology focused on the religious nature of the meeting and set it alongside a number of other religious assemblies (see *Introduction: 5) Religious Assemblies*). As the following verses explain, during this religious gathering the Lord spoke to Rehoboam.

Rehoboam Receives a Prophetic Word (11:2-4a)

As Rehoboam prepared for battle, the prophet Shemaiah appeared and spoke to him. Several elements combine in this verse to establish Shemaiah's authority. The text speaks first of his message as the **word of the Lord** (11:2; see also 11:4b). The prophet's perspective on these events was not his personal opinion; he spoke with divine authority. Moreover, the technical term **man of God** is attached to the prophet's name (11:2). This title also acknowledged the authority of the prophetic word (see 1 Chr. 23:14; 2 Chr. 8:14; 11:2; 25:7-9; 30:16; Deut. 33:1; 1 Sam. 2:27).

Finally, Shemaiah's own words reinforce the origin of his oracle. In a manner common to biblical prophets (see Isa. 40:1; 1 Chr. 17:4; 21:11; 2 Chr. 34:23), he introduced his speech with a messenger formula which referred to the divine source of his speech (11:4). By repeatedly drawing attention to Shemaiah's divine authority, the Chronicler eliminated any question about the authority of the prophetic perspective.

Shemaiah made explicit what the opening verse of this episode merely hinted. Rehoboam was wrong to attack the northern tribes. As noted above, the Chronicler varied the description of those whom Shemaiah addressed from 'the whole house of Judah and Benjamin' (1 Kgs. 12:23) to **all the Israelites in Judah and Benjamin** (11:3). This shift drew attention to the heart of the matter. Rehoboam's attack involved Israelite against Israelite. Shemaiah told Rehoboam not to fight **'against** [his] **brothers'** (11:4; compare 19:10; 28:11; 28:15; 35:5, 6). The familial ties that unified the tribes made it inappropriate for Rehoboam to attack.

Beyond this, Rehoboam was wrong to attack because the northern rebellion was from the hand of God (see 10:15). God affirmed, **'this is my doing'** (11:4; see *Introduction: 10) Divine Activity*). In effect, the divine approval removed all support from those who looked despairingly on their northern neighbors for their initial rebellion. It also encouraged the Chronicler's readers to remember Judah's responsibility in the division (see *Introduction: 2) Northern Israel*).

Rehoboam Turns Back from Battle (11:4b)

At last, Rehoboam acted with prudence. He **obeyed the words of the LORD** and returned home (11:4b). As the following verses reveal, Rehoboam received many blessings for this response to Shemaiah.

Obedience to the prophetic word is the source of blessing on a number of occasions in Chronicles (see 1 Chr. 12:1-8; 21:19; 2 Chr. 14:4; 31:21; see *Introduction: 15) Prophets*). This motif was important for the Chronicler and his readers because a number of prophets appeared at different times during the post-exilic period. These prophets revealed the word of God to the post-exilic community and their response to him should be like that of Rehoboam.

Rehoboam's Blessings for Compliance (11:5-23)

An emphasis on the consequences of sin and obedience comes into play at this point (see *Introduction: 10-28) Divine Blessing and Judgment*). In chapter 10 Rehoboam reaped the results of his foolishness. In 11:1-4, however, the king listened to God's word and received blessings (11:5-23).

Comparison of 11:5-23 with Kings

11:5-23 has no parallel in Kings. Some features of this passage suggest that the Chronicler depended on official court records. Whatever the case, the Chronicler added this material to illustrate the grand benefits which submission to God's prophets can bring.

Structure of 11:5-23

This material divides into three reports which are joined together by the common thread of divine blessing toward the king (see figure 27). Rehoboam built fortifications (11:5-12), received many defectors from the North (11:13-17), and saw his family enlarged (11:18-23).

Rehoboam's Successful Fortifications (11:5-12)

In this passage, the Chronicler reported how Rehoboam **built up** cities **for defense** (11:5). As a result of his actions, **Judah and Benjamin were his** (11:12). Rehoboam secured his control over these territories.

To understand the significance of this report, we must remember that ancient Near Eastern royal propaganda in the cultures surrounding Israel often demonstrated the success of kings by enumerating their building projects. These building projects usually included temple construction (as in the case of Solomon), as well as fortifications of cities (as in this passage). This motif was so common in the ancient world that the Chronicler felt no need to state the implication that Rehoboam's fortifications demonstrated the blessing of God (see *Introduction: 24) Building and Destruction*).

It is not possible to settle precisely when these fortifications occurred. The list of cities does not focus on Rehoboam's northern border and may therefore reflect a time early in his reign before troubles with the north began again (see 1 Kgs. 14:30). Even so, it is possible that these fortifications took place throughout Rehoboam's reign. The last portion of this section (11:18-23) certainly covers events throughout Rehoboam's life. In all events, the proximity of this report to Rehoboam's reaction to the prophetic word (11:1-4) indicates that the Chronicler attributed the king's successful fortifications to his submission to Shemaiah.

This report certainly would have piqued the interest of the Chronicler's post-exilic readers. Their military vulnerability must have led many to wonder how they could find security in their day. The example of Rehoboam made this path plain. Fortification of Judah will come if they submit to the prophetic word.

Rehoboam's Support from Faithful Northerners (11:13-17)

The second illustration of God's blessing for Rehoboam's response to the prophet is the support he received from northern defectors. On several occasions the Chronicler reported that faithful northern Israelites gave their support to the kings of Jerusalem (see 13:8-11; 15:9; 20:10-20). The political division of the nation did not utterly destroy connections between the South and North. As these examples demonstrate, religious affections of many Northerners led them to shift their political loyalties as well.

Structure of 11:13-17

This passage divides into three parts (see figure 27). The defection of Northerners began with priests and Levites (11:13-15), but their example quickly led others to join Rehoboam (11:16). These defections resulted in tremendous benefits for Rehoboam (11:17).

Rehoboam's Support from Priests and Levites (11:13-15)

The Chronicler did not estimate the numbers of **priests and Levites** that **sided with** Rehoboam, but he mentioned that they came from **all their districts throughout Israel** (11:13). The NIV obscures the Hebrew of this verse. The original language reads, 'priests and Levites *in all Israel'* sided with Rehoboam (see NAS, NRS, NKJ). The Chronicler used the term 'all Israel' to convey that these Levitical defectors represented all the northern tribes (see *Introduction: 1) All Israel*). From Mosaic times, the Levitical families lived without a distinct tribal territory, but they received portions of land throughout the tribes. The Chronicler noted the level of commitment from these defectors by mentioning that they **even abandoned their pasture lands and property** to join with Rehoboam (11:14). It was at great cost that these priests and Levites moved to Jerusalem. (For the Chronicler's interest in Levitical lands, see comments on 1 Chr. 6:64.)

The reason for this defection is also noted. The priests and Levites were displaced from their services in the North when **Jeroboam and his sons rejected them as priests** (11:14). Jeroboam had **appointed his own priests** (11:15). The Chronicler omitted the portion of Kings that reports Jeroboam's worship centers in Dan and Bethel. As 1 Kings 12:26-27 explains, Jeroboam feared that permitting his people to worship in Jerusalem would eventually lead to a political reunification of the nation.

Chronicles simply mentions that Jeroboam had erected **goat and calf idols** and that this idolatry was unacceptable to the priests and Levites who defected (11:15). The book of Kings reports the golden calves erected at Dan and Bethel (see 1 Kgs. 12:28-29) and the similarity to Israel's severe apostasy in the wilderness is apparent (see Exod. 32:1-33:6). The imagery of strong bulls representing divinity was common in the cultures surrounding Israel. It was an image of distinction and honor. Even so, the Chronicler associated Jeroboam's calves with **goats** (11:15). It is possible to translate this portion of 11:15, 'goats, even calf idols'. If this translation is correct, it suggests that the Chronicler disparaged Jeroboam's golden calves by equating them with the 'goat idols' so strongly condemned in Lev. 17:7.

In all events, it is clear that those who defected to Rehoboam did so for religious, not political reasons. As we have seen, in many respects the northern tribes were justified in their rebellion against Rehoboam's tyranny (see 10:1-19; see also *Introduction: 2) Northern Israel*). They were not free, however, to turn from the true worship of God at the temple in Jerusalem. Like the post-exilic readers of Chronicles, they were obligated to proper worship despite their circumstances.

Rehoboam's Support from Other Northerners (11:16)

The Chronicler broadened his view for a moment and mentioned that the priests and Levites were not alone. People **from every tribe of Israel** followed their example and came **to Jerusalem to offer sacrifices** (11:16). As in 11:13, the NIV obscures the Chronicler's special terminology. These people came from 'all the tribes of Israel' (NAS, NRS, NKJ); like the priests and Levites before them, these worshippers represented 'all Israel' (see *Introduction: 1) All Israel*).

To highlight the character of these defectors the Chronicler mentioned that they came to worship **the LORD, the God of their fathers** (11:16). This traditional terminology (see 1 Chr. 29:20; 2 Chr. 7:22; 11:16; 13:12,18; 14:4; 15:12; 19:4; 21:10; 24:18,24; 28;6,9,25; 29:5; 30:7,19,22; 34:33; 36:15; Deut. 6:3; 26:7; 29:25; Exod. 3:15; Ezra 10:11; Josh. 18:3) characterized their worship as true and acceptable in contrast with the false worship begun by Jeroboam (see 13:8-11). Moreover, the Chronicler noted that these people had **set their hearts on seeking the LORD** (11:16). In the Chronicler's vocabulary 'seeking' God meant eagerly to search for his blessing. The programmatic promise to Solomon (7:14) established seeking God as the proper way to respond to trouble (see *Introduction: 19) Seeking*). Moreover, the Chronicler's focus on the **hearts** of these defectors made it plain that their actions were sincere (see *Introduction: 16) Motivations*). These defectors were the faithful Israelites whose hearts were devoted to pursuing the worship of God as he had ordained it.

Rehoboam's Benefits (11:17)

The Chronicler closed with an explicit statement of his main purpose in this section. He first noted that the defectors **strengthened the kingdom of Judah** and **supported Rehoboam** (11:17). The event was a great blessing to all of Judah. This historical fact certainly encouraged the post-exilic readers to reflect on what benefits would come to them as they responded appropriately to the prophetic word and welcomed the faithful from the North in their day (see *Introduction: 2) Northern Israel*).

The defectors benefited Rehoboam **for three years** so long as he was **walking in the ways of David and Solomon** (11:17). In 12:1 Rehoboam's situation will change for the worse. At this time, however, Rehoboam imitated the ideal kings David and Solomon and tasted widespread national support similar to that of the United Kingdom.

The lesson for the readers was plain enough. David and Solomon served as ideals for his readers to follow (see *Introduction: 14) Standards*). If the leaders of God's people imitated the ideal practices of David and Solomon, as Rehoboam did, the nation would receive the blessing of political stability and strength.

Rehoboam's Enlarged Family (11:18-23)

The Chronicler added yet a third illustration of the blessings Rehoboam received because of his submission to the prophet. At this point, he focused on the increase of Rehoboam's family. Two of Rehoboam's wives are mentioned by name: **Mahalath** (11:18) and **Maacah** ... the one **Rehoboam loved more** (11:20-21). Their sons are named as well (11:18-21). Then the Chronicler computed sums.

Rehoboam had **eighteen wives ... sixty concubines ... twenty-eight sons and sixty daughters** (11:21). These large numbers of children were signs of God's favor toward Rehoboam. The Chronicler frequently depicted large progeny as divine blessing (see *Introduction: 25) Increase and Decline of Progeny*).

To close off this section (11:22-23), Chronicles also adds the note that Rehoboam **acted wisely** with regard to his sons (11:23). In contrast to the opening episode of the king's reign, he is now characterized as a wise king (see 10:8). His wisdom is illustrated in his appointment of **Abijah** as successor to the throne (11:22) and the distribution of territories to his other sons (11:23). By making these arrangements Rehoboam spared the next generation from the turmoil often associated with the transfer of power.

The increase of Rehoboam's family and the security he provided the next generation spoke directly to the needs of the post-exilic readers. They lived in a day of many uncertainties. If the nation would adhere to prophetic instruction, it would enjoy the kind of prosperity and security that Rehoboam experienced at this time.

Rehoboam's Later Sin, Humility, and Blessing (12:1-12)

Rehoboam lived with God's blessing **for three years** (11:17), but troubles began **in the fifth year of King Rehoboam** (12:2). The difficulties of the fifth year became an opportunity for the Chronicler to illustrate the basic pattern of disobedience, response to the prophetic word, and blessing for a second time.

Comparison of 12:1-12 with 1 Kgs. 14:25-28

This passage displays one of the more creative uses the Chronicler made of materials found in Kings. The parallel of 1 Kgs. 14:25-28 is merely a brief report. The Chronicler expanded these four verses into a full scale narrative of twelve verses. The following figure identifies the additions he made to Kings (see figure 29).

2 Chr.	1 Kgs.
12:1	———
12:2a	———
12:2b	14:25b
12:2c	14:25a
12:3-9a	———
12:9b-11	14:26-28
12:12-13	———

Comparison of 2 Chr. 12:1-13 with 1 Kgs. 14:25-28 (figure 29)

As this comparison illustrates, the account of Chronicles is greatly expanded beyond Kings. The writer of Kings simply noted that Shishak attacked Jerusalem in the fifth year of Rehoboam (1 Kgs. 14:25a,b). He mentioned that Shishak took from the royal and temple treasuries including Solomon's gold shields (1 Kgs. 14:26). He also reported Rehoboam's substitution of bronze shields (1 Kgs. 14:27) and the king's special attention to their safekeeping (1 Kgs. 14:28).

The Chronicler included this material from Kings, but added much more information. He explained the background of these events (12:1) and the date of the attacks (12:2b). The heart of this material is added (12:3-9a) and a new ending appears in the Chronicler's version (12:12-13).

Structure of 12:1-12

The Chronicler's additions to Shishak's invasion formed his account into a full scale narrative with five symmetrical steps followed by an authorial comment (see figure 27). The story begins with Rehoboam's failure to remain faithful while he experienced God's blessing (12:1). It ends with his kingdom in a weakened condition, but secure and blessed (12:10-11). Shishak attacked Rehoboam (12:2-4), but Shishak's attack is balanced by his failure to gain a full victory (12:9). The turning point in this episode involves Shemaiah's prophecies and the humble response of Judah's leadership (12:5-8). An authorial comment also appears at the end of this passage (12:12).

This narrative presents both positive and negative motifs. The emotional tension displayed leaves the reader yearning for a resolution that does not occur. Rehoboam was **established** and **strong**, but he **abandoned the law of the LORD** (12:1). Shemaiah the prophet condemned Jerusalem to utter abandonment by God (12:5), only to mollify his threat (12:7). Rehoboam kept his throne, but he had to replace **the gold shields Solomon had made** with **bronze shields** (12:10). He feared for his life (12:11), but was **not totally destroyed** (12:12).

The ambivalence of Rehoboam's situation reveals the Chronicler's perspective on the event. The utter destruction that comes from turning away from the Law of God may be averted through humility, but severe and repeated infidelity will have lasting consequences. This message readily applied to the Chronicler's post-exilic readers as they faced similar complexities in their day.

Rehoboam's Strength Leading to Apostasy (12:1)

The Chronicler began this account with an additional scene. Rehoboam **was established** and **strong** (12:1). The Chronicler had already noted that Rehoboam's reign was **strengthened** by northern defectors (11:17). The terminology **established** indicates that no significant opposition to Rehoboam's kingship continued. (For the significance of this terminology, see 2 Chr. 1:1.) On the heels of the previous chapter, it seems at first glance that Rehoboam had reached a time of positive blessings. Yet, the Chronicler quickly revealed that Rehoboam's reign was in trouble.

Rehoboam's prosperity led him to turn away from God. On a number of occasions, kings responded to God's blessing with infidelity. For the Chronicler's warning against permitting blessings to lead to infidelity see comments on 1 Chr. 5:24. In this situation, the king and people **abandoned the law of the LORD** (12:1). The term **abandoned** ('forsake' [NAS, NRS, NKJ]) is one of the standard expressions the Chronicler used to describe flagrant violations of Israel's covenant relationship with God (see *Introduction: 22) Abandoning/Forsaking*). Moreover, the text adds that **all Israel** joined in the king's apostasy (12:1) to indicate how far the apostasy had spread (see *Introduction: 1) All Israel*).

Shishak's Attack against Judah and Jerusalem (12:2-4)

Having established that Judah was in serious rebellion against the Lord, the narrative moves to the divine judgment that came upon the nation through the invasion of the Egyptian Shishak. As noted above, only 12:2a,c parallel the record of Kings (// 1 Kgs. 14:25a,b). The rest of 12:2-4 comes from the Chronicler's hand. 1 Kings 14:25 simply notes that the invasion took place in Rehoboam's fifth year.

Several important additions occur in Chronicles. In the first place, this record inserts the reason for Shishak's attack. It was **because they had been unfaithful to the LORD** (12:2a). Here the Chronicler used another of his usual terms for serious rebellion against God. To be **unfaithful** was much worse than falling into day to day peccadilloes; it meant to violate the fundamental loyalty required in covenant with God (see *Introduction: 21) Unfaithfulness*). By adding this clause, the text eliminates any question as to why this misfortune had come on Judah.

In the second place, the Chronicler elaborated further on Shishak's invasion to increase the dramatic tension (12:3-5). Although 1 Kgs. 14:25b (// 12:2c) simply states that the attack took place, this account makes it clear that divine judgment against Judah was severe. A description of the force under the Egyptian's command appears. Rehoboam faced **twelve hundred chariots and sixty thousand horsemen** (12:3). Moreover, **innumerable troops** from other nations also fought for Shishak (12:3). On a number of occasions, the superiority of Judah's enemies is noted to stress that divine power was the source of victory (see *Introduction: 23) Victory and Defeat*). As we will see, Rehoboam's ability to withstand Shishak to some measure was the result of God's intervention.

The Chronicler also added that Shishak's enormous army **captured the fortified cities of Judah and came as far as Jerusalem** (12:4). Rehoboam's earlier reinforcement of fortified cities in Judah was a sign of God's blessing (see 11:5-12), but now the king's sin had caused a direct reversal. His fortified cities had been conquered and Jerusalem stood alone.

Rehoboam's Response to the Prophetic Warning (12:5-8)

As the destruction of Jerusalem seemed imminent, **the prophet Shemaiah** spoke once again to **Rehoboam and to the leaders of Judah** (12:5 see 11:2-4). At first the prophet announced, **'You have abandoned me; therefore, I now abandon you to Shishak'** (12:5). The word **abandoned** (see *Introduction: 22) Abandoning/*

Forsaking) alludes to the opening scene in this episode (12:1). The impending judgment against Jerusalem was recompense for Judah's abandonment of the Law of God. For God to **abandon** his people was tantamount to placing them under the covenant curses (see Deut. 31:17; 2 Chr. 15:2; 24:20; Isa. 54:7; see also Jer. 12:7; 25:38; Ezek. 8:12; 9:9). Judah was now the object of divine wrath.

Although Shemaiah did not explicitly offer any hope of reprieve, **the leaders of Israel and the king humbled themselves** (12:6). Their response indicated that prophecies of judgment were not utter condemnations, but threats that could be averted by repentance and humility. A tacit condition was to be assumed with this prophecy as with most others (see Jon. 3:10; Joel 2:1-16; Jer. 18:1-10). The leaders of Judah did not resign themselves to destruction; instead, they humbly sought God's favor. As the following verses indicate, Rehoboam's response to the prophetic word was paradigmatic for the Chronicler's readers. As they heard the prophetic word, they should react as Rehoboam and his nobles reacted (see *Introduction: 15) Prophets*).

Rehoboam and the leaders were **humble** before the Lord (12:6 see also 12:7). This state of affairs connected this passage with God's promise to Solomon in 7:14 where blessings are promised to those who humble themselves. Humility is an attitude of submission and utter dependence on God (see *Introduction: 18) Humility*). The king and leaders expressed their humility in a simple prayer, **'The LORD is just'** (12:6). These words acknowledged God's justice in his judgment and cast the fate of the nation solely on the mercies of God (see *Introduction: 17) Prayer*). Other prayers during and after the exile follow a similar pattern (see Dan 9:4-19; Ezra 9:5-15).

This expression of humility led to a positive end (12:7-8). A change of divine disposition resulted **when the LORD saw that they humbled themselves** (12:7). The prophet announced that God **will not destroy them, but will soon give them deliverance** (12:7).

Nevertheless, God did not completely reverse his previous threat. Rehoboam and his leaders needed a vivid demonstration that their violations were serious. As a result, the prophet declared that Judah would still **become subject** to Shishak (12:8). Judah would become a vassal of Egypt, subject to taxation and other mistreatments. The purpose of this subjection was to teach Rehoboam and Judah **the difference between serving** [God] **and serving the kings of other lands** (12:8). Here God spoke as Israel's great Emperor whose benevolence had been ignored. Now perhaps the nation would see how much better it was to have God as their King rather than foreign human oppressors. However restrictive the Law of God may have seemed to Judah (see 12:1), they would soon understand that its burden was light compared to the yoke of foreign dominion. The Chronicler's readers also faced the temptation to turn from God's Law. Yet, the experience of exile had taught them the lesson Rehoboam was about to learn.

Shishak's Limited Victory over Jerusalem (12:9)

Shishak **attacked Jerusalem** and won the victory (12:9). It is likely that Rehoboam sued for terms of peace, agreeing to pay a heavy tribute for **the king of Egypt ... carried off the treasures of the temple of the LORD** and **the royal palace** (12:9). The Chronicler had drawn attention earlier to the wealth David and Solomon collected in the temple treasuries (see 1 Chr. 29:1-9; 2 Chr. 2:1-5:1); he also mentioned the wealth of the royal treasuries (see 2 Chr. 9:13-28). The riches obtained by David and Solomon were important aspects of the Chronicler's ideal portrait of these kings. Now that glory of Israel had been taken by a foreign king. The Chronicler summarized the extent of the harm by adding that Shishak **took everything,** even the **gold shields** of **Solomon** (12:9; see 9:16).

Rehoboam's Resulting Weakness (12:10-11)

The mention of Solomon's golden shields in 12:9 opens the way for a wonderfully symbolic scene. Rehoboam made **bronze shields to replace** the shields of gold (12:10). The exchange of bronze for gold nicely symbolized the changes in Rehoboam's kingdom. He had not lost everything, but he had lost the glory inherited from Solomon.

Along with his economic reduction, Rehoboam no longer felt secure. He put **the commanders of the guard ... at the entrance to the royal palace** in charge of the bronze shields (12:10). The shields were given over to the best of Rehoboam's soldiers. More than this, when Rehoboam left his palace to go **to the LORD's temple** (12:11) his **guards went with him, bearing the shields** (12:11). Apparently, Rehoboam wanted to keep what little he had close by. When he returned to the palace, the shields were safely locked away in **the guardroom** (12:11). This scene of timidity stands in sharp contrast with the opening of this story. The record of Rehoboam began with him **established** and **strong** (11:1); at this point he barely held onto his kingdom.

Authorial Comment (12:12)

The Chronicler added a comment to the end of this narrative to explain his understanding of the Shishak invasion. **Rehoboam** escaped total destruction from **the anger of the LORD ... because he humbled himself.** The king's sincere contrition averted a horrible fate. **He was not totally destroyed**. In fact, **some good** could be found **in Judah** despite the Egyptian victory. The Chronicler was deeply concerned that his readers take to heart the effect of Rehoboam's humble response to the prophetic word. Humility before God and his prophet led to forgiveness and blessing.

Moreover, Shishak's invasion pointed the Chronicler's readers in at least two other directions. On the one hand, it explained why the post-exilic community still had not fully recovered from the exile. They still needed to learn the difference between serving God and human kings (see 12:1-2,5). On the other hand, this passage warned them not to permit their experiences of success and blessing to lead them astray. The consequences of such rebellion against God could last for a very long time.

Closure of Rehoboam's Reign (12:13-16)
The Chronicler closed his record of Rehoboam's reign with a summary and notice of the king's death. He left his readers with a few final thoughts about the king and his significance for their lives.

In addition to a few stylistic variations, the Chronicler made a number of additions to Kings. First, the Chronicler summarized the content of 1 Kgs. 14:21-24 in 12:13-14. These verses give a summary evaluation of Rehoboam's reign which emphasizes some central theological concerns.

Second, the Chronicler cited his source for his additional information about Shemaiah's encounter with Rehoboam during the Shishak invasion (see *Introduction: Historical and Theological Purposes*). He replaced 'the annals of the kings of Judah' (1 Kgs. 14:29) with **the records of Shemaiah the prophet and of Iddo the seer** (12:15).

Several other details are also added. First, **Rehoboam established himself firmly** and **reigned seventeen years** (12:13 // 1 Kgs. 14:21). Rehoboam's submission to the prophetic word (12:5-8, 12), eventually led to a measure of security and success. On the whole, the Chronicler left his readers with a positive assessment.

The description of Jerusalem as **the city the LORD had chosen out of all the tribes of Israel in which to put his Name** (12:13) points out that Rehoboam's ability to seek and find the mercy of God was due to having the temple as the place of the **Name**. Here the Chronicler reminded his readers that Rehoboam's life, especially the episode with Shishak, exemplified the role which prayer in and toward the temple was to have in national life. The accessible divine presence dwelling in the temple was the only hope for relief from hardship caused by sin (see 6:1-7; see also *Introduction: 11) Name of God*). If the power of the invocable **Name** did so much for Rehoboam, surely the post-exilic readers of this book could see how much they needed to attend to the temple and its services in their day.

The Chronicler then closed with an evaluation that served as a subtle warning to his readers. Rehoboam fell into **evil** that brought much trouble to the nation **because he had not set his heart on seeking the LORD** (12:14). In contrast to those who defected to Rehoboam (see 11:17), Rehoboam failed to serve God sincerely from his **heart** (12:14; see *Introduction: 16) Motivations*) and was not **seeking the LORD** (12:14). Once again, the text alludes to God's programmatic response to Solomon's prayer (see 7:14 see also *Introduction: 19) Seeking*). The way for the post-exilic readers to avoid Rehoboam's trials was to avoid his failure to seek God from his heart.

For the most part, 12:15-16 are derived from 1 Kgs. 14:29-31. For some unknown reason, the Chronicler transferred the reference to **Naamah** to 12:13 (// 1 Kgs. 14:31). He also added a reference to the **records of Shemaiah ... and Iddo** (12:15) to indicate where he found some of the earlier information he added to Rehoboam's reign. Once again his keen interest in the prophetic office for his post-exilic readers led him to mention these sources (see *Introduction: 15) Prophets*).

It is interesting to note that Rehoboam **rested with his fathers and was buried**

in the city of David (12:16). Despite his obvious and serious failures, Rehoboam found the way of forgiveness and blessing. These final words extended hope to the original readers. Whatever failures or problems they continued to experience, the reign of Rehoboam exemplified the way to find the honor of God's blessing.

The Reign of Abijah (13:1-14:1)

Abijah succeeded his father as king of Judah (913-911 BC). The record of his reign in Chronicles points to the blessings which result from faithfulness.

Comparison of 13:1-14:1 with 1 Kgs. 15:1-8

The reign of Abijah appears in Kings as well as Chronicles. Portions of these records are similar, but the Chronicler also diverged from Kings in remarkable ways (see figure 30).

2 Chr.		1 Kgs.
13:1-2a	Opening of Abijah's Reign (closely parallel)	15:1-2
———	Summary and Evaluation of Abijah (omitted)	15:3-6
13:2b-21	Abijah's War with Jeroboam (greatly expanded)	15:7b
13:22-14:1	Closure of Abijah's Reign	15:7a-8

Comparison of 2 Chr. 13:1-14:1 with 1 Kgs. 15:1-8 (figure 30)

At least four variations should be noted. First, the Chronicler's version is approximately three times larger than Kings. He devoted 23 verses to Abijah, whereas the writer of Kings only gave 8 verses.

Second, only the opening and closing of this account depends on Kings. 13:1-2a stems from 1 Kgs. 15:1-2 and 13:22-14:1 depends on 1 Kgs. 15:7a,8. A few minor variations occur in these parallel materials.

Third, a striking contrast appears in the main body of Abijah's reign. Kings dismisses Abijah as evil and explains that he reigned only because of God's promise to David (1 Kgs. 15:3-6). The Chronicler, however, omitted this material in order to portray the positive side of Abijah's reign. He greatly expanded 1 Kings 15:7b into a full-scale account of a battle between Abijah and Jeroboam (13:2b-21). In this battle, Abijah received a tremendous victory because of his fidelity to God.

Fourth, it should be noted that the NIV obscures one difference between Kings and Chronicles. The Hebrew text of Kings spells the name of this king 'Abijam'

('My father is Yam.') referring to the West Semitic god of the sea. Apparently, the writer of Kings had no problem with using the name because he viewed Abijah (Abijam) negatively. The Chronicler, however, focused on the positive side of the king's reign and therefore called him Abijah ('My father is Yah[weh].'), referring to the Lord of Israel.

Structure of 13:1-14:1
The Chronicler's changes to the account of Kings resulted in a simple threefold pattern (see figure 31).

■Opening of Abijah's Reign (13:1-2a)

Abijah's Victory Over Jeroboam (13:2b-21)
- ♦ Battle between Abijah and Jeroboam (13:2b-18)
  - • Abijah Faces Numerically Superior Jeroboam (13:2b-3)
    [Abijah Delivers Speech to Jeroboam (13:4-12)]
    - • Abijah Attacked by Jeroboam (13:13)
      - • Abijah's Reaction and Divine Intervention (13:14-15)
    - • Abijah Defeats Jeroboam (13:16)
  - • Abijah Inflicts Great Losses on Jeroboam (13:17)
    [Authorial Comment (13:18)]
- ♦ Aftermath of Abijah's Battle (13:19-21)
  Jeroboam's Curses (13:19-20)
  Abijah's Blessings (13:21).

■Closure of Abijah's Reign (13:22-14:1)

Outline of 2 Chr. 13:1-14:1 (figure 31)

This record of Abijah's reign focuses on one key event, a battle between Abijah and Jeroboam (13:2b-21). This central element is enclosed within an historical framework that opens (13:1-2a) and closes (13:22-14:1) the king's reign.

Opening of Abijah's Reign (13:1-2a)
The Chronicler began his account of Abijah's reign with a brief historical note largely taken from 1 Kings 15:1-2. The Chronicler recognized the king's mother. He does the same many times in his history (see 15:16; 22:2; 24:1; 25:1; 26:3; 27:1; 29:1). Yet, from Manasseh until the end of his book, the Chronicler omitted all such references to the royal mother (see 33:1// 2 Kgs. 21:1; 33:21 // 2 Kgs. 21:19; 34:1 // 2 Kgs. 22:1; 36:2 // 2 Kgs. 23:31; 36:5 // 2 Kgs. 23:36; 36:9 // 2 Kgs. 24:8; 36:11 // 2 Kgs. 24:18).

13:1 includes **in the eighteenth year ... of Jeroboam** from 1 Kgs. 15:1 to synchronize the history of Judah and northern Israel. Coordinating northern and southern kings occurs frequently in Kings, but this is the only time the Chronicler included such a note in his history (see *Introduction: 2) Northern Israel*). This exception probably resulted from the fact that this entire record focuses on a battle between Abijah and the northern army of Jeroboam.

Abijah's Victory Over Jeroboam (13:2b-21)

The central concern of the Chronicler's record is Abijah's battle with Jeroboam. This battle illustrates several principles that govern the Chronicler's assessments of the Divided Kingdom.

Structure of 13:2b-18

The account of this battle divides into two episodes (see figure 31). The first segment deals with a battle between Abijah and Jeroboam (13:2b-18). The second segment focuses on the twofold aftermath of the battle (13:19-21).

Battle between Abijah and Jeroboam (13:2b-18)

The Chronicler's account of battle between Abijah and Jeroboam is a complex narrative in which the Chronicler's interests stand out on a number of occasions.

Structure of 13:2b-21

This material is comprised of a basic story line to which the Chronicler added some special features. The basic story line forms a symmetrical presentation (see figure 31). The action begins with Abijah facing an Israelite army twice his size (13:2b-3); it closes with Abijah reducing Israel's army to fewer men than his own (13:17). Jeroboam's attack from the front and rear (13:13) balances with Jeroboam fleeing from Abijah (13:16). The turning point of the story is Abijah's cry to God and God's intervention on his behalf (13:14-15).

The Chronicler added two features to the basic framework of this story that serve as interpretive focal points. On the one hand, he included a lengthy speech by Abijah (13:4-12). This speech halts the main action of the story long enough to provide Abijah's (and the Chronicler's) theological assessment of the events. On the other hand, an authorial comment appears at the end of the story which explains the outcome of the battle (13:18).

Abijah Faces Numerically Superior Jeroboam (13:2b-3)

The story of battle begins with a description of the numbers of men facing each other. The opening words of 13:2b derive from 1 Kgs. 15:6. In Kings this information summarizes the reign of Abijah. In Chronicles, however, it serves as a title for this episode. Abijah's forces numbered **four hundred thousand** and Jeroboam's army included **eight hundred thousand** men (13:3). These numbers appear very high; a number of explanations are possible. For the Chronicler's use of large numbers of soldiers see comments on 1 Chr. 12:24-37. Even so, Abijah was blessed with an army greater than Rehoboam. As he did on a number of other occasions, the Chronicler noted that Jeroboam had twice as many soldiers as Abijah (see *Introduction: 23) Victory and Defeat*). This detail insured that the Chronicler's readers would recognize the miraculous character of the victory that followed.

Abijah Delivers Speech to Jeroboam (13:4-12)

Facing an army twice the size of his own, Abijah made a speech. This speech halts the battle narrative for nine verses and provides an indispensable theological analysis of the events about to take place.

Structure of 13:4-12

Abijah's speech divides into an introduction followed by two main segments (see figure 31). It begins and ends with direct addresses to the Israelite recipients: **Jeroboam and all Israel** (13:4b) and **men of Israel** (13:12b). These addresses frame the speech. The concentration of related terms reveals that the speech divides into two parts. The first half focuses on the monarchy in Jerusalem: **kingship** (13:5), **David and his descendants** (13:5), **Solomon son of David** (13:6), **Rehoboam son of Solomon** (13:7), **kingdom** (13:8a), and **David's descendants** (13:8a). The second half concentrates on the temple in Jerusalem: **gods** (13:8b, 9), **priests** (13:9,10,12), **sons of Aaron** (13:9,10), and **Levites** (13:9,10). This twofold concentration reflects the Chronicler's concern with the institutions of monarch and temple in his own day (see *Introduction: 4-9) King and Temple*).

Introduction to the Speech (13:4a)

Abijah stood on **Mount Zemaraim**, a site identified elsewhere with Benjamin (see Josh. 18:22), but here with **Ephraim**. The precise location is not known, but it seems most likely that these events took place somewhere along the northern border of Benjamin adjacent to the territories claimed by the northern tribes.

In the ancient world, it was not uncommon for a king, prophet, or priest to make a proclamation just before battle (see Deut. 20:1-4; 2 Chr. 20:5-17). Abijah's purpose was twofold. He discouraged the North from attacking, but he also assured the Judahites of victory.

Exhortation Based on David's Throne (13:4b-8a)

Abijah first exhorted Jeroboam not to attack Judah because of God's choice of the Davidic line. He addressed the northern tribes as **all Israel** (13:4b). Through this terminology Abijah extended a hand of peace to the tribes of the North (*Introduction: 1) All Israel*).

Abijah's argument regarding David's throne divided into three parts. First, he reminded the northern Israelites that God had made a **covenant of salt** with **David and his descendants** (13:5). The precise meaning of the expression **covenant of salt** is not certain; it appears nowhere else in association with David. A close parallel appears in Numbers 18:19 where Levites receive assurance that their share of sacrifices is 'an everlasting covenant of salt' (see also Lev. 2:13). The association with salt spoke of the enduring quality of David's covenant, perhaps because salt was widely used as a preservative. The covenant God made with David was of vital importance to the Chronicler (see 2 Sam. 7; // 1 Chr. 17; Pss. 89; 132). It assured the family of David a permanent right to the dynasty of Israel even in the post-exilic period (see *Introduction: 13) Covenant*).

Second, Abijah focused on Israel's initial rebellion against Judah. **Jeroboam ... rebelled against his master** (13:6). Rehoboam was rightly Jeroboam's **master**, one against whom rebellion should not take place lightly.

If this statement were all that Abijah said, then we might think his words contradict the Chronicler's perspective that the rebellion of the North was in some measure justified (see 10:1-19). Nevertheless, Abijah qualified his reference to Israel's initial rebellion by commenting on Rehoboam's condition at the time of the crisis (13:7).

Much controversy surrounds this passage because of an ambiguity in the clause **'worthless scoundrels gathered around him'** (13:7). The question is whether the word **him** refers to Jeroboam or Rehoboam. At least two observations point in favor of Rehoboam. 1) The Chronicler recorded men counseling Rehoboam foolishly; nothing of this sort is reported about Jeroboam (see 10:2-4). 2) The Chronicler never condemned the North for its initial rebellion against Rehoboam because it was appropriate in the light of Rehoboam's foolish response. For these reasons, it seems best to understand Rehoboam as the antecedent of **him** in 13:7d. If this view is correct, the verse would read in this manner: 'Some worthless scoundrels gathered around him (Rehoboam) and he (Jeroboam) rebelled against Rehoboam son of Solomon when he (Rehoboam) was young and indecisive and not strong enough to resist them.' Abijah's point was that Jeroboam resisted the throne of Judah when it was understandable for him to do so. Rehoboam was **young and indecisive** at the time (13:7) and did not follow the advice of the elders.

Third, Abijah's exhortation turned to the very day on which he spoke. The opening phrase **and now** (13:8) may be translated 'but now', drawing the contrast between the initial succession of the North and current events. Although Jeroboam's initial rebellion was understandable, the northern tribes were violating the will of God by continuing to resist Judah (see *Introduction: 2) Northern Israel*).

Abijah proclaimed his view forcefully. This war is an attack on **the kingdom of the LORD ... in the hands of David's descendants** (13:8). David and his sons were nothing less than vice regents of God. On several occasions the Chronicler described the throne of Jerusalem as the throne of God (see *Introduction: 8) Divine Kingship*). In his view, the kingdom of David and his sons was an earthly expression of the divine heavenly reign. Therefore, to continue resisting David's house was to resist God himself.

Exhortation Based on Temple Service (13:8b-12)

The second portion of Abijah's speech turned attention toward the Jerusalem temple and the security it provided for Judah. This material divides into three steps.

First, Abijah acknowledged the reasons why the northern tribes had confidence as they entered battle. He noted that Jeroboam had **a vast army** (13:8b see 13:3). Moreover, he remarked on his **golden calves** (13:8b). The Chronicler had already mentioned the idols at the northern worship centers in Dan and Bethel (see 11:15). Perhaps the army had brought some of these idols with them into the battle. In all events, Abijah cleverly took up the perspective of his northern opponents. He let them know that he is aware that their hope for victory was in their army and their idols.

Second, Abijah followed his acknowledgment with another accusation. As Jeroboam formed his distinctive religious practices, he removed **the priests of the LORD, the sons of Aaron, and the Levites** from their rightful places of duty (13:9). The legitimate leaders of Israel's worship were replaced with **'priests of your own ... like other people of other lands'** (13:9 see 1 Kgs. 12:31; 2 Chr. 11:14-15). These new priests were not ordained by God. They bought their way into service, and serve idols which **are not gods** (13:9; see Hos. 8:6).

In effect, Abijah warned the northern Israelites that they had violated their relationship with God. The northern tribes had spurned divinely ordained leaders of worship and served idols instead of the living God. Therefore, God would not come to their aid in this battle.

Third, Abijah boldly contrasted Judah with Israel in this regard (13:10-12a). He began with the declaration, **'the LORD is our God, and we have not forsaken him'** (13:10). Abijah did not claim that Judah had no failures; the reign of his father Rehoboam proved otherwise (see 2 Chr. 12:1-12). Instead, he insisted that Judah had temple personnel in order and services took place according to **the requirements of the LORD** (13:11). The northern Israelites, however, had **forsaken him** (13:11). The term 'forsake' appears frequently in the Chronicler's history to denote a serious violation of the covenant relationship (see *Introduction: 22) Abandoning/ Forsaking*). In the Chronicler's vocabulary, when God's people forsake him, God forsakes them.

As a result, Abijah boldly announced, **'God is with us; he is our leader'** (13:12). With these words, Abijah explained that the presence of God with his people ('God with us') meant that God would lead them into battle. Similar meaning applies to other uses of the expression throughout the Old Testament (see *Introduction: 10) Divine Activity*).

Abijah elaborated on this concept by describing the rituals of battle: [God's] **priests with their trumpets will sound the battle cry against** northern Israel (13:12). Following the Mosaic instructions for the placement of priests in battle (see Num. 10:8-9), Abijah's army was to be led by the music of the priesthood (see 1 Chr. 25:1; 2 Chr. 20:22; 13:14). Elsewhere in the Old Testament the appearance of God as Israel's divine Warrior occurred at the blast of trumpets. The priests' trumpets announced that Israel fought with the help of her God. (For a discussion of music in warfare, see comments on 2 Chr. 20:21; see also *Introduction: 8) Music*).

This royal speech closes as it began with a direct address to the northern army. He began his speech to **Jeroboam and all Israel** (13:4b). Now he turned to the people themselves, **men of Israel** (13:12b). Abijah warned northern Israel not to fight because they would be fighting **against the LORD, the God of your fathers** (13:12b). God was with Judah and the Israelite army would be opposing him in their battle. The expression **God of your fathers** represented a final challenge to the confidence of the northern tribes. Twice the king referred to the Lord as **our** (Judah's) **God** (13:10,11), a designation that no longer applied to the northern tribes. The Lord was only the God of their **fathers** (13:12b). Now that they had become the enemies of God, Abijah warned them that they would **not succeed** (13:12b).

Abijah Attacked by Jeroboam (13:13)

With Abijah's speech completed, the Chronicler moved back to the main action of his battle narrative. Perhaps while Abijah delivered his speech, Jeroboam attacked. Jeroboam divided his men and surrounded the Judahite army. His plan was to attack from the front and drive Abijah into a rear ambush. With twice as many soldiers at his command (see 13:3), Jeroboam seemed to have victory well in hand.

Abijah's Reaction and Divine Intervention (13:14-15)

The turning point of this episode is Abijah's reaction and God's intervention. These verses involve a series of rapid actions. The Judahite army realized they were surrounded **front and rear** (13:14a); **they cried out to the LORD** (13:14b); the **priests blew the trumpets** (13:15a); the soldiers **raised the battle cry** (13:15a). God then responded to the cry of Judah and **routed Jeroboam and all Israel** (13:15b).

The Chronicler already supplied the theological framework in terms of which these events were to be understood. On the one hand, this divine intervention recalled the prayer of Solomon (see 6:34-35; see *Introduction: 17) Prayer*). Like Rehoboam before him (12:6), and Asa and Jehoshaphat after him (14:11; 20:6-12), Abijah depended on Solomonic hopes and received God's deliverance from his enemies through prayer (see *Introduction: 23) Victory and Defeat*). On the other hand, Abijah's preceding speech explained what happened. Abijah claimed that the Lord would help Judah (see 13:12). The reference to the **trumpets** of the priests and the **battle cry** (13:14) directly corresponds to Abijah's prediction of victory (see 13:12; for a discussion of music in warfare, see comments on 2 Chr. 20:21). God's intervention on Abijah's behalf illustrated the kind of response to be expected by those who faithfully relied on God and called on him (see *Introduction: 17) Prayer*).

Abijah Defeats Jeroboam (13:16)

In direct contrast with Jeroboam's earlier aggression (13:13), he and his army **fled before Judah** (13:16). The presence of God in battle had been predicted (see 13:12) and the Chronicler noted that **God delivered them into their hands** (13:16).

Abijah Inflicts Great Losses on Jeroboam (13:17)

The main action of this battle narrative closes with a description of Judah's victory over Israel. The Chronicler focused on the number of losses inflicted on the northern army to balance the numerical notices at the beginning of the story (see 13:3).

While Jeroboam began with 800,000 compared to Judah's 400,000, the battle reduced Jeroboam's army to 300,000. These numbers revealed that the battle was a decisive victory for Judah.

Authorial Comment (13:18)

In order to make his assessment of this event perfectly clear, the Chronicler added an authorial comment. Judah won the battle **because they relied on the LORD, the God of their fathers**. The Chronicler used the term 'rely' on several occasions to describe trust and conscious dependence on God (see 14:11; 16:7, 8). Abijah's reliance and trust in God were demonstrated in his courageous speech (see 13:4-12) and in his prayer (see 13:14).

Abijah's victory illustrated a vital principle for the Chronicler's readers. If they hoped to have victory in the conflicts they faced, they must follow Abijah's example. If they joined commitment to the Davidic monarchy and temple to reliance on God through prayers in and toward the temple, God would fight for them as well (see *Introduction: 23) Victory and Defeat*).

Aftermath of Abijah's Battle (13:19-21)

In the preceding authorial comment the Chronicler described the fate of both Israel and Judah. These verses contain reports which elaborate on this distinction.

Structure of 13:19-21

The aftermath of battle divides into two parts (see figure 31). The Chronicler first summarized what came of Jeroboam (13:19-20) and then reported Abijah's contrasting experience (13:21).

Jeroboam's Curses (13:19-20)

In a word, Jeroboam's defeat in battle was only the beginning of his losses. Abijah did not refrain from pursuing Jeroboam until he **took from him** a number of cities, including **Bethel** (13:19). These cities remained under Judahite control **during the time of Abijah** (13:20).

The Chronicler emphasized the final severity of God's judgment against Jeroboam's aggression by stating that **the LORD struck him down and he died** (13:20). Jeroboam actually outlived Abijah (see 1 Kgs. 15:6-10), but from the Chronicler's point of view, nothing else significant happened in Jeroboam's reign. Moreover, he made it clear that Jeroboam's death was not from natural causes. The language of 'striking down' demonstrates that it was by divine intervention (see 1 Sam. 25:38; 26:10; 2 Sam. 12:15; 2 Chr. 13:15; 14:12; 21:14, 18). 1 Kgs. 14:19-20 does not characterize Jeroboam's death as an act of God. The Chronicler, however, saw it as an extension of the divine judgment begun at his defeat before Abijah (see 13:4-18).

Abijah's Blessings (13:21)

The contrast between Abijah and Jeroboam could hardly be greater. Jeroboam lost territories and died by God's hand, but Abijah enjoyed God's blessings. The Chronicler mentioned two great blessings.

First, Abijah **grew in strength** (13:21). This terminology indicated that Abijah defeated his foes and enjoyed relative peace and prosperity. Instead of losing territories, Abijah expanded and consolidated his kingdom.

Second, in contrast with Jeroboam who died under God's curse, Abijah had **fourteen wives, twenty-two sons and sixteen daughters** (13:21). As he did on several occasions the Chronicler reported numerous progeny as a demonstration of divine blessing (see *Introduction: 25) Increase and Decline of Progeny).*

The Chronicler ended his expansion of the reign of Abijah with these contrasts between Jeroboam and Abijah to encourage his post-exilic readers. He and his readers wanted to strengthen the nation and to receive more blessings from God. The Chronicler made their choices very clear. To be like Jeroboam meant loss and death, but to be like Abijah meant tremendous blessing.

Closure of Abijah's Reign (13:22-14:1a)

The Chronicler returned to Kings to close out the reign of Abijah (13:22-14:1 // 1 Kgs. 15:7-8). His record differs, however, by mentioning his source of **the story of the prophet Iddo** (13:22). This source appears two other times (see 9:29; 12:15). The Chronicler's repeated references indicate the influence of this prophet on his theology (see *Introduction: 15) Prophets*).

The Reign of Asa (14:1b-16:14)

The Chronicler continued his account by turning to the reign of Asa (911/10-870/69 BC). His record of Asa focuses on two contrasting actions and their equally contrasting results. Asa served God faithfully and received the blessings of peace and prosperity. Yet, war, trouble, and death came to him when he turned from God. As such, the reign of Asa gave a clear picture of the options which the post-exilic community faced.

Comparison of 14:1b-16:14 with 1 Kgs. 15:9-24

The Chronicler's record of Asa differs significantly from its parallel in Kings. This difference is evident in that Chronicles increases the 16 verses of Kings into 47 verses. At this point, it will help to compare the two accounts on a large scale (see figure 32 on next page). More detailed analyses for each section will follow.

As this large scale comparison indicates, the account of Kings is much simpler than the record of Chronicles. Kings introduces Asa (1 Kgs. 15:9-11), describes his reforms (1 Kgs. 15:12-15), records his war with Baasha (1 Kgs. 15:16-22), and closes his reign (1 Kgs. 15:23-24a). The Chronicler omitted the synchronization with the north (1 Kgs.. 15:9-10) and the notice of cultic prostitution (1 Kgs. 15:12) as he usually did in his history. Nevertheless, after an introduction (14:1b-2) he

2 Chr		1 Kgs
———	Synchronization with North (omitted)	15:9-10
14:1b-2	General Evaluation (slightly expanded)	15:9-11
———	Prostitution and Idols Eliminated (omitted)	15:12
14:3-8	Reforms and Prosperity (added)	———
14:9-15	War with Zerah (added)	———
15:1-15	Prophecy and Response (added)	———
15:16-19	Further Reforms (parallel)	15:13-15
16:1-6	War with Baasha (parallel)	15:16-22
16:7-10	Prophecy and Response (added)	———
16:11-14	Closure of Reign (expanded)	15:23-24a

Comparison of 2 Chr 14:1b-16:14 and 1 Kgs 15:9-24 (figure 32)

added a record of Asa's reforms and resulting prosperity (14:3-8). He then added a lengthy section dealing with war and prophecy (14:9-15:15). After this addition, the Chronicler returned to following Kings in his description of reforms (15:16-19 // 1 Kgs. 15:13-15), and another battle (16:1-6 // 1 Kgs. 15:16-22). He then added a second prophecy (16:7-10), and closed his account with a slightly expanded summation and notice of death (16:11-14). As in the reign of Rehoboam (see 10:1-12:16), the book of Kings is oriented toward only one battle in Asa's reign, but Chronicles focuses on two conflicts. These two battles permit the Chronicler to draw striking contrasts between the earlier and later years of Asa.

Structure of 14:1b-16:14

The Chronicler's expansion from one to two battles shaped his record of Asa into two symmetrical sections. These halves mirror each other in a number of ways (see figure 33).

After the opening of Asa's reign (14:1b) which is balanced by its closure (16:13-14), the record divides into the early years under the blessings of God (14:2-15:19) and the later years under divine judgment (16:1-12).

Chronological notices appear throughout this material to separate these two sections. The Chronicler mentioned Asa's first **ten years** of **peace** (14:1b). He also noted an **assembly** of celebration in Jerusalem during his **fifteenth year** (15:10). The first half closes with a report that Asa's peace extended **until the thirty-fifth year** of his reign (15:19). The second half begins, however, with war **in the thirty-**

- ■ Opening of Asa's Reign (14:1b)
  - ♦ Asa Under Divine Blessing (14:2-15:19)
    - • Asa's Early Years of Reform and Blessings (14:2-7)
      - Asa's Reforms (14:2-5a)
      - Asa's Blessings (14:5b-7)
    - • Asa's Victory, Prophetic Approval and Obedience (14:8-15:19)
      - – Asa's Victory in Conflict (14:8-15)
        - Asa's Standing Army (14:8)
          - Asa and Zerah Draw Battle Lines (14:9-10)
            - Asa Invokes Divine Intervention (14:11)
          - Asa Defeats Zerah in Battle (14:12-15a)
        - Asa's Army Returns to Jerusalem (14:15b)
      - – Asa's Prophetic Approval and Obedience (15:1-19)
        - Prophetic Approval (15:1-7)
          - Introductory Setting (15:1-2a)
          - Doctrinal Principle (15:2b)
          - Historical Illustrations (15:3-6)
          - Contemporary Application (15:7)
        - Asa's Response (15:8-19)
          - Asa's Worship Reforms (15:8)
          - Asa's Assembly for Reform (15:9-15)
            - Assembly Called (15:9-10)
              - Assembly Opening Ceremonies (15:11)
                - Assembly Oaths (15:12-13)
              - Assembly Closing Ceremonies (15:14)
            - Assembly Results (15:15)
          - Asa's Other Reforms (15:16-19)
  - ♦ Asa Under Divine Judgment (16:1-12)
    - • Asa's Failure, Prophetic Disapproval and Disobedience (16:1-10)
      - – Asa's Failure in Conflict (16:1-6)
        - Asa Threatened (16:1)
          - Asa Appeals to Syria for Help (16:2-3)
          - Syria Attacks Israel (16:4)
        - Asa No Longer Threatened (16:5-6)
      - – Asa's Prophetic Rebuke and Disobedience (16:7-10)
        - Prophetic Disapproval (16:7-9)
          - Accusation and Result (16:7)
          - Contrast with Earlier Conflict (16:8-9a)
          - Accusation and Sentencing (16:9b)
        - Asa's Response (16:10)
    - • Asa's Final Years of Judgment (16:11-12)
- ■ Closure of Asa's Reign (16:13-14)

Outline of 2 Chr. 14:1b-16:14 (figure 33)

sixth year (16:1), followed by his disease **in the thirty-ninth year** (16:12) and his death **in the forty-first year** (16:13).

These two sections mirror each other structurally. The first half opens with reforms and prosperity (14:2-7); the second half closes with failure and disease (16:11-12). The first portion reports a sequence of victory, prophetic approval, and Asa's positive response (14:8-15:19); the second portion reports a sequence of failure in battle, prophetic disapproval, and Asa's negative response (16:1-10).

Opening of Asa's Reign (14:1b)

Although he omitted any notice of the northern kingdom (see 1 Kgs. 15:9-11), the Chronicler expanded the notice of Asa's rise to include the comment that **the land had rest for ten years** (14:1b). 'Rest' appears as God's blessing in a number of places in Chronicles (see *Introduction: 23) Victory and Defeat*). It often describes the condition of peace and prosperity given to kings as they were faithful to God. This positive outlook on Asa sets positive mood for the reign which is confirmed by the burial notice (16:14; see *Introduction: 28) Healing and Long Life/Sickness and Death*).

Asa Under Divine Blessing (14:2-15:19)

The account begins with the first thirty-five years of blessing in Asa's reign (see 15:19). Asa's positive achievements and the resulting prosperity during this time come to the foreground.

Comparison of 14:2-15:19 with 1 Kgs.. 15:9-15

Although Chronicles depends on Kings for some material in this section (14:1b-2 / / 1 Kgs. 15:11 and 15:16-19 // 1 Kgs. 15:13-15), it also omits and adds information. Some of these variations amount to insignificant matters of style, but other shifts reveal important perspectives on Asa's early years.

First, in his usual fashion the Chronicler omitted the synchronization of Asa's reign with the northern kingdom (1 Kgs. 15:9). The Chronicler omitted references to events in the North except in connection with the history of Judah (see *Introduction: 2) Northern Israel*).

Second, enthusiasm for Asa is evident in the expansion of 'he did what was good' (1 Kgs. 15:11) to … **he did what was good and right** (14:2a). Nevertheless, Kings says that Asa was 'like David his father' (1 Kgs. 15:11), but Chronicles omits these words (14:2). It is likely that the Chronicler did not want to compare Asa with David because of his idealization of David and his emphasis on Asa's sins in the second half of his reign (see 16:1-14).

Third, the reference to Asa removing 'the male shrine prostitutes' and 'all of the idols his fathers had made' (1 Kgs. 15:12) are omitted. The presence of male prostitutes in Judah's past was probably irrelevant to the needs of the post-exilic community. The Chronicler omitted every mention of this practice in the book of Kings (see 1 Kgs. 14:24; 15:12; 22:46; 2 Kgs. 23:7).

Fourth, in the place of 1 Kgs. 15:12 the Chronicler lists a number of reforms Asa implemented (14:3-5). These reforms are described in ways that spoke to specific needs of the post-exilic readers.

Fifth, an additional account of war and prophetic approval appears (14:6-15:15). This material illustrates Asa's positive acts and contrasts them with the later battle sequence (see 16:1-6).

Sixth, summary and chronological notices are added in 15:19. This information provides a temporal framework for the Chronicler's division of Asa's reign into good and bad years.

Structure of 14:2-15:19

The record of Asa's positive years divides into two main sections. This first half of Asa's reign focuses on his reforms and blessings (14:2-7) and on his victory (14:8-15:19). These two segments themselves divide into two smaller units each (see figure 33).

Asa's Early Years of Reform and Blessing (14:2-7)

At first, the reign of Asa was a time of extensive reforms and prosperity. This material contrasts with 16:12-14, a time of trouble and sickness for Asa (see figure 33). This portion of Asa's reign divides into his reforms (14:2-5a) and the resulting blessings (14:5b-7; see figure 33).

Asa's Reforms (14:2-5a)

The Chronicler began his record with a general characterization of Asa as one who did **good and right in the eyes of the LORD** (14:2 // 1 Kgs. 15:11). Although the Chronicler omitted the comparison with David (see 1 Kgs. 15:11), he added that Asa did good **and right** (14:2 //1 Kgs. 15:11). This expansion indicated his enthusiasm for this period of Asa's life.

The Chronicler's record of Asa's reforms (14:3-5) replaced the report of male shrine prostitution (see 1 Kgs. 15:12) with the notice that Asa destroyed pagan worship centers (14:3). The **foreign altars** may have been those altars Solomon erected for his foreign wives (see 1 Kgs. 11:7-8). Asa also razed the **high places**, worship centers in Judah other than the temple in Jerusalem (14:3). Moreover, he crushed **sacred stones**, pillars erected next to pagan altars as representations of the deities or as phallic symbols. Such stones were strictly forbidden in Mosaic Law (see Exod. 23:24; Lev. 26:1; Deut. 16:21-22). **Asherah poles** were probably wooden representations of the divine consort of Baal (see Judg. 3:7; 2 Kgs. 23:4) or another kind of phallic symbol associated with the goddess. They were also demolished in Asa's reforms. The description of Asa's efforts closely follows the instructions of Deut. 12:1-3. The Chronicler cast the king's reforms in this traditional language to present him as an example of what Judah's kings were always to do.

The Chronicler also summarized the instructions Asa delivered to Judah during his reform efforts. First, the king ordered his people **to seek the LORD** (14:4). This terminology alludes to the programmatic promise given to Solomon at the dedication of the temple (7:14). 'Seeking' God in sincere prayer and worship was the way to the favor of God (see *Introduction: 19) Seeking*). Moreover, the use of this terminology early in Asa's reign anticipates the dominance of the theme of seeking God throughout this account. The term occurs no less than eleven times in his reign (14:4, 7 [twice]; 15:2 [thrice], 4, 12, 13, 15; 16:12).

Second, the king commanded his people to submit to God's **laws and commandments** (14:4). The importance of obedience to the Law of God appears throughout Chronicles. The standard the Chronicler held for his post-exilic readers was the same Asa held for his community (see *Introduction: 14) Standards*).

The Chronicler's initial record of Asa's reforms closes with another reference to **high places** and the mention of **incense altars** (14:5; see 14:3). The meaning of the latter term is not altogether certain. It has been translated 'sun pillar', but modern research points in the direction of the NIV translation. Whatever the specific meaning, the term is associated with pagan worship in several places (see Lev. 26:30; 2 Chr. 30:14; 34:4,7; Isa. 17:8; 27:9; Ezek. 6:4,6).

The Chronicler noted here that Asa destroyed the **high places ... in every town in Judah** (14:5). Some interpreters have seen this statement as a contradiction of 15:17 (// 1 Kgs. 15:14) where it is reported that Asa did *not* remove the high places. A similar juxtaposition occurs in the reign of Jehoshaphat (see 17:6 and 20:33). There is no reason for finding a contradiction here. 14:5 refers to Asa's practices during his early years of blessing; 15:17 is limited to his later years of disobedience and judgment. Moreover, 14:5 explicitly mentions **Judah** and 15:17 speaks of **Israel**. It is possible that the Chronicler distinguished here between what Asa did early in Judah itself and what he did not do in the territories of northern Israel which he conquered during his lifetime.

Asa's Blessings (14:5b-7)

In 14:5b the Chronicler shifted attention away from Asa's reforms to the blessings he received. Traditional versification and the NIV obscures this change of topic, but the shift is apparent. In fact, 14:5b forms an introduction to 14:6-7 much like 14:2 introduced the actions of 14:3-5a. At this point, the text is concerned with how **the kingdom** experienced a time of **peace** as a result of Asa's reforms (14:5b).

Peace is an important goal the Chronicler set before his readers. As elsewhere in the Old Testament, it connoted not only the absence of war, but economic prosperity and social well being. In this positive half of Asa's reign the Chronicler mentioned the theme of peace four times (see 14:1,5,6; 15:5). This portion of Asa's reign depicts the benefits of fidelity for God's people; it brings them peace (see *Introduction: 23) Victory and Defeat*).

The Chronicler's record of Asa's early prosperity divides into straight narration of his actions (14:6), royal decree (14:7a-c), and a straight narration of further actions (14:7d). The chief focus of the material stands out in the repetition of the concept of 'building' (14:6,7 [twice]).

Asa **built up fortified cities** (14:6). In line with common ancient Near Eastern beliefs, the Chronicler saw the king's success in building as a demonstration that God had blessed him. Asa was able to concentrate on his fortifications **since the land was at peace** (14:6; see *Introduction: 23) Victory and Defeat*). This note was important to the Chronicler's evaluation of Asa's fortifications. If a king built fortifications as a result of peace given by God, the Chronicler approved the projects as God's blessing. If a king built in response to the threat of an enemy, the fortification demonstrated a lack of trust in God (see *Introduction: 24) Building and Destruction*).

Beyond this, the Chronicler also described this time of Asa's kingdom as a period of **rest** (14:6). The term **rest** appears three times in this portion of Asa's reign (14:6b,7; 15:15). The association of rest and peace in this material suggests that the Chronicler drew a line of contact between these years of Asa's reign and David and Solomon. He used both of these terms to describe the splendor of the ideal reigns of David and Solomon (see *Introduction: 23) Victory and Defeat*). Although Asa fell short of reaching the full stature of the ideal monarchs, this portion of his reign reflected the goodness experienced in those days.

Perhaps the Chronicler's readers wondered if the blessings afforded David and Solomon were far beyond their grasp. The Chronicler's description of Asa's reign demonstrated that Judah can enjoy the blessings of peace and rest at any time if she responds faithfully to God.

The Chronicler paused to make his theological perspective on these events plain. Why did Asa enjoy this period of peace? **The LORD gave** him these blessings (14:6). Many times the Chronicler pointed to divine activity as the ultimate cause of events in Israel's history (see *Introduction: 10) Divine Activity*). This period of prosperity was not the result of human effort; it was divine response to Asa's fidelity.

The account of Asa's blessing turns to a summary of his speech that inspired the building projects (14:7). Asa ordered the people to **build** because **'the land is still ours'** (14:7). God had kept Judah safe in her land. Asa's words made it clear, however, why this divine protection had come. It was **'because we sought the LORD ... we sought him'** (14:7). These words recall the earlier account of Asa's reforms (14:4). He and the nation had fulfilled the requirement of 'seeking' help from God (see *Introduction: 19) Seeking*). Consequently, God gave **rest on every side** (see *Introduction: 23) Victory and Defeat*).

To close off this section of his account, the Chronicler pointed out that the nation **built and prospered** (14:7). Once again, the blessing of building comes to the foreground (see *Introduction: 24) Building and Destruction*). The terminology of 'prosperity' appears many times in Chronicles as a description of a time of economic well being resulting from obedience blessed by God (see *Introduction: 26) Prosperity and Poverty*). The result of Asa's reforms was grand prosperity for the entire nation of Judah.

As the Chronicler's readers heard these descriptions of Asa's time, they were to yearn to see the same blessings in their own day. Rebuilding and prosperity were among their goals as well. The Chronicler left no room for misunderstanding the way that would lead to these results. Seeking the Lord as Asa did was the key to their desires.

Asa's Victory, Prophetic Approval, and Obedience (14:8-15:19)
The next section of Asa's reign covers several closely related events. These materials also demonstrate that Asa was under divine blessing during this portion of his reign.

Structure of 14:8-15:19
This material divides into two main sections. First, Asa won a victory in battle against Zerah (14:8-15). Second, the battle is followed by two more closely related events: a prophetic encouragement to the king (15:1-7), and the king's positive response to the prophet (15:8-19). With the exception of 15:16-18 (// 1 Kgs. 15:13-15), all of this material came from the Chronicler's hand (see figure 32). On a large scale, these verses balance with 16:1-10 (see figure 33).

Asa's Victory in Conflict (14:8-15)
This first battle of Asa's reign ended with a resounding victory for Judah. As such, it contrasts with the second battle of defeat in 16:2-6. Here Asa fought in an exemplary manner, demonstrating full reliance on God.

Structure of 14:8-15
The episode divides into five symmetrical parts (see figure 33). The opening describes the size and quality of the king's standing army in Jerusalem (14:8). The end of the story notes that this army returned to its original position in Jerusalem (14:15b). The tension rises as Zerah approaches with a huge army and Asa goes out to meet him (14:9-10), but the drama begins to resolve as Asa defeats Zerah's army (14:12-15a). The turning point in the narrative is Asa's prayer for divine assistance (14:11).

Asa's Standing Army (14:8)
In many respects this verse bridges the gap between the preceding context of Asa's blessing and this battle. The size and quality of the king's army is another example of Asa's prosperity. His standing army (presumably housed in Jerusalem [see 17:13]) consisted of **three hundred thousand men from Judah** and **two hundred and eighty thousand from Benjamin** (14:8). For comparisons with other records of Judah's army, see 11:1. The total of 580,000 soldiers seems very large. As with other passages where high numbers occur, several explanations are possible. (For the Chronicler's use of large numbers of soldiers, see comments on 1 Chr. 12:24-37.) However one handles these numbers, the point is that Asa's army is extraordinarily large. The text makes it plain that Asa's army was of fine quality as well. His soldiers were **brave fighting men** equipped with **large shields**, **spears**, **small shields**, and **bows** (14:8).

Asa and Zerah Draw Battle Lines (14:9-10)

Despite the size and quality of Asa's army, his enemy was even greater. **Zerah the Cushite** came against Judah **with a vast army** (14:9). At this time, Cush (Ethiopia) was under Egyptian rule, and Zerah was probably acting on behalf of the Egyptian Osorkon I. Literally, the Hebrew text describes Zerah's soldiers as 'a thousand thousands' (i.e. one million). Again, there are several options for interpreting this extremely large number. (For the Chronicler's use of large numbers of soldiers, see comments on 1 Chr. 12:24-37.) However one handles this calculation, Asa was greatly outnumbered. As in Abijah's conflict with Jeroboam (see 13:1-20) the enemy of Judah is nearly twice his size. Moreover, Zerah had **three hundred chariots** at his command (14:9). The motif of Judah facing an enemy with a larger army appears a number of times in Chronicles. In each case, the apparent inadequacy of Judah's army demonstrated that divine intervention was the cause of victory (see *Introduction: 23) Victory and Defeat*).

Asa took his army **to meet Zerah** in **the Valley of Zephthah near Mareshah** (14:10), one of Rehoboam's fortified cities (see 11:8). The tension of the narrative builds as the battle ensues against formidable odds.

Asa Invokes Divine Intervention (14:11)

Asa prepared for battle against his sizable foe by calling for help from God. His actions recall the similar responses of Rehoboam (12:6) and Abijah (13:14), and anticipate the prayers of Jehoshaphat (18:31; 20:6-12; see *Introduction: 17) Prayer*; see also *23) Victory and Defeat*).

Asa's prayer was straightforward. First, he declared his confidence in the supremacy of God as a helper of the weak: **'There is no one like you to help the powerless'** (14:11). The acknowledgment of Judah's weakness appears again in Jehoshaphat's prayer (see 20:12). Asa confessed his inability to withstand the attack of Zerah's army in his own strength.

Second, Asa asked God to **help** (14:11). In the Chronicler's vocabulary, God helps his people by furthering their causes (see *Introduction: 10) Divine Activity*). Why should God help? Asa declared, **'for we rely on you'** (14:11). The Chronicler mentioned reliance on God four times in his history (see 13:18; 14:11; 16:7,8). In each case relying on God amounted to seeking his help in times of military struggle. Such reliance on God always resulted in victory for God's people. At this point in his life, Asa depended on God instead of himself or any human ally (see 13:18; 16:7,8).

Asa specified that he trusted **'in** [God's] **name'** (14:11). Here Asa recalled the theological perspective that the temple was the place of God's Name, his invocable powerful presence (see *Introduction: 11) Name of God*). Solomon's prayer at the dedication of the temple described a situation like that which Asa faced (see 6:34-35).

Third, Asa concluded that God should help him instead of letting **man prevail against** [him] (14:11). Once divine assistance had been sincerely invoked, the battle was no longer Asa's. It became God's battle. As a result, defeat for Judah would amount to defeat for God. This belief was also confirmed by the close connection established between God's throne and the throne of David (see *Introduction: 8) Divine Kingship*).

Asa's prayer served well as an instrument of the Chronicler's message to his post-exilic readers. As they faced various international threats, Asa's appeal for divine help was exemplary of the sort of actions and attitudes they should follow. They should acknowledge God as their only hope by relying on him and calling on his Name (see *Introduction: 23) Victory and Defeat*).

Asa Defeats Zerah in Battle (14:12-15a)

The Cushites were severely defeated. Judahites chased them southward **as far as Gerar** (14:13). Gerar was a southern city bordering the Negeb that served as an Egyptian outpost at the time. The Cushites and Egyptians had occupied many villages in the region, but the Judahites **destroyed all the villages around Gerar ... and plundered ... much booty** (14:14).

The Chronicler's outlook on this event becomes evident in the role God plays in these scenes. Asa called on God's name (14:11) and for the first time God becomes a major character in the story: **the LORD struck ... before Asa and Judah** (14:12). Three times the Chronicler mentioned that it was God's effort that brought defeat to the Cushites (14:12, 13, 14). It is not altogether clear what the Chronicler had in mind when he mentioned **the LORD and his forces** defeated the Egyptians (14:13). The reference could be to the army of Judah, the heavenly army, or both. The third option seems likely in the light of the Chronicler's comparison of the army of Israel with the army of God (see 1 Chr. 12:22) and the connection he drew between the throne of Judah and the divine throne (see *Introduction: 8) Divine Kingship*). In all events, the emphasis of this passage is on the fact that **the terror of the LORD** – not Asa – **had fallen upon them** (14:14). This was a miraculous victory, the kind of victory the post-exilic readers of Chronicles hoped for in their own day (see Hag. 2:6-9).

Asa's Army Returns to Jerusalem (14:15b)

Having shown the miraculous victory brought about through prayer and reliance on God, the Chronicler closed his story with a simple note. Asa and his army returned to their standing position in **Jerusalem** (14:15b). This note signaled the end of the episode.

Asa's Prophetic Approval and Obedience (15:1-19)

Having described Asa's victorious battle against Zerah, the Chronicler added another series of positive events to Asa's reign. He focused on the approving words of the prophet Azariah and Asa's reforms that followed. These events balance with contrasting events in the second half of Asa's reign (16:7-10; see figure 33).

Structure of 15:1-19

This portion of the Chronicler's addition to Kings divides into two main parts (see figure 33). These two elements form a closely connected passage. The first portion deals with the prophet speaking to Asa (15:1-7); the second portion records what Asa did in response to the prophetic word (15:8-19). In these passages, the Chronicler continued his depiction of Asa's early years as a time under God's blessing.

Prophetic Approval (15:1-7)

After Asa returned from battle, he encountered the prophet Azariah. The Chronicler conveyed his own understanding of these events through the prophetic speech.

Structure of 15:1-7

Azariah's speech is introduced with a description of the setting (15:1-2a). The speech itself divides into three main points (see figure 33). A basic doctrinal position is expressed (15:2b); historical illustration of the principle follows (15:3-6); an application is made to the contemporary circumstances (15:7). This basic pattern has been dubbed a 'Levitical Speech' and appears in a number of passages. For instance, David's instructions to the leaders of Israel in 1 Chr. 22:17-19 included a principle (verse 17), historical illustration (verse 18), and an application (verse 19). A similar pattern appears in 1 Chr. 28:2-10: verses 2-3 are the basic principle; the historical illustration follows (verses 4-7); an application closes the speech (verses 8-10).

Introductory Setting (15:1-2a)

To avoid any misunderstanding regarding the reliability of Azariah, the Chronicler introduced his speech by noting that **the Spirit of God came upon** him (15:1). This unusual introduction to Azariah's speech may have been necessary because he spoke so approvingly of Asa. In the Old Testament positive words toward a king are often associated with false prophets (see 2 Chr. 18:4-7; Jer. 5:12-13; 6:14; 14:13; 23:17; Ezek. 13:10; Mic. 3:5-12; cf. 1 Kgs. 22:5-8). Moreover, Azariah insisted on certain forms of social and religious reforms that would have challenged the post-exilic readers of Chronicles. Therefore, the prophet's divine inspiration would have legitimized efforts to apply the prophet's instructions after the exile. For a summary of the Chronicler's outlook on the Spirit, see comments on 1 Chr. 12:18.

Doctrinal Principle (15:2b)

In the case of this speech, the prophetic doctrinal principle appears in language familiar to readers of Chronicles (15:2b). First, Azariah affirmed that God is **with you when you are with him** (15:2b). When the Lord was 'with' his people, he led them into battle and secured their victory (see *Introduction: 10) Divine Activity*). Nevertheless, God's joining his people in battle depended on a condition. It occurred **when** [they] **are with him** (15:2b). God allied himself with Israel only when Israel allied itself with him.

Second, Azariah stated, **'if you seek him, he will be found by you'** (15:2b).

During the period of the divided monarchy the Chronicler frequently referred to 'seeking' God as an allusion to the programmatic promise given to Solomon (see 7:14). God promised that seeking him through humble prayer and devotion would result in blessing. Asa's prayer in the preceding passage (see 14:11), illustrated this principle in action. Here Azariah stated this principle in a forthright doctrinal affirmation (see *Introduction: 19) Seeking*).

Third, the prophet warned against forsaking God because **he will forsake** (15:2b) those who do so. Once again the prophet uses terminology appearing frequently in Chronicles. 'Forsaking' God was to violate flagrantly Israel's covenant requirements; to be forsaken by God was to come under the covenant curses (see *Introduction: 22) Abandoning/Forsaking*).

The Chronicler believed Asa was meeting the requirements of these covenant principles at this stage of his reign. He had fought his enemies and gained victory because he sought and relied on God (see 14:11). The prophet's words explicitly explained why Asa experienced God's blessings at this point in his life.

Historical Illustrations (15:3-6)

After his doctrinal focus, the prophet's speech turned to historical illustrations of the principle (15:3-6). The prophet reminded Asa of conditions during the period of the judges. During that time Israel **was without the true God, without a priest to teach and without the law** (15:3). Widespread apostasy characterized this period. Priests and Levites who were supposed to teach the Law (see Lev. 10:11; Deut. 33:10; Jer. 18:18; Hos. 4:6-7; Mal. 2:7) had themselves become corrupt (see Judg. 17:1-21:25). The Law was forsaken and 'everyone did as he saw fit' (Judg. 17:6; 18:1; 21:25).

Despite the extreme conditions of that time, the doctrinal principle of 15:2 still applied to Asa's reign. To draw the connection plainly, Azariah used terminology he had employed before. When trouble came in the days of the judges, the people **returned to the LORD** ... (see *Introduction: 22) Repentance*), **sought him and he was found by them** (15:5 see 15:2; see also *Introduction: 19) Seeking*). The terrible conditions were overcome (however temporarily) by the nation's humility and dependence on God (see Judg. 3:9, 15; 4:3; 6:6, 7; 10:10, 12; 15:18; 21:2-3).

In order to strengthen his argument, the prophet described the distress of the period of the Judges (15:5b-6). It was a time of **great turmoil** ... for **the lands** (15:5b; i.e. the various districts of the promised land or nearby nations). Nations surrounding Israel were in constant war (15:6a). Nevertheless, God heard and answered the prayers of his people (see *Introduction: 17) Prayer*).

The final clause of the prophet's historical illustrations provided an interesting clue to his intentions. Why was the period of Judges such a terrible time? The book of Judges emphasized the sins of Israel as the cause of trouble. Azariah would not have disagreed with this assessment. Yet, the emphasis here was on divine involvement once again (see *Introduction: 10) Divine Activity*). The troubles came **because God was troubling them with every kind of distress** (15:6). The active role that God played in the period of the Judges brought those events into contact with the experience of the Chronicler's readers. They had seen times of distress due to apostasy and had felt the effects of God **troubling ... with every kind of distress** (15:6). Of course, the implication for the Chronicler's post-exilic readers was evident. The principle affirmed by Azariah applied to them. Their exilic circumstances had been reversed and their current situation could be improved only as they sought the Lord and were found by him.

Contemporary Application (15:7)

The prophet's immediate concern in this passage becomes clear in his application to Asa (15:7). With the doctrinal principle and historical illustration established, he called on Asa to **be strong** and not to **give up** (15:7). Similar exhortations occur elsewhere in Chronicles (see 32:7; 1 Chr. 19:13; 22:13; 28:10,20). Azariah did not rebuke Asa, but encouraged him to continue with the full assurance that his **work will be rewarded** (15:7). At this stage in Asa's reign, he was a faithful king. Yet, more needed to be done. As the verses that follow explain, idolatry had spread through the land and the temple had been neglected (see 15:8). Azariah encouraged Asa to go further. If he did, even more blessings would come his way.

The prophet's positive words to Asa easily applied to the Chronicler's readers. Like Asa, they had received deliverance from their enemies. Yet, much remained to be done. The prophetic word to Asa encouraged post-exilic readers to move forward in their restoration efforts. Initial successes were not sufficient. They had to continue in the way of fidelity as they hoped for more blessings from God.

Asa's Response (15:8-19)

The Chronicler's record of Asa's early years continues with a series of reports on Asa's response to the prophet. He explicitly connected these materials with the prophet's announcement by repeating terminology found there. **When Asa heard ... Azariah ... he took courage** (15:8 see 15:7). All of Judah vowed **to seek the Lord** (15:12; compare 15:2). Moreover, **they sought God eagerly and he was found by them** (15:15 see 15:2). The emphasis on the theme of 'seeking' is apparent. The Chronicler saw this characteristic of Asa's early years as the reason for his great blessing (see *Introduction: 19) Seeking*). Asa's actions were direct responses to the instructions of the prophet. They illustrate how the king took his words to heart.

Structure of 15:8-19

Asa's response to the prophet divides into a series of three reports (see figure 33). The text describes Asa's worship reforms (15:8), Asa's assembly for reform (15:9-15), and Asa's other reforms (15:16-19). As noted above (see figure 32), the first two sections of this material come from the Chronicler's hand. They were his additions to King's account of Asa's reign. The final section, however, stems for the most part from 1 Kgs. 15:13-15; only 2 Chr. 15:19 is additional.

Asa's Worship Reforms (15:8)

When Asa put the prophet's instructions into action he first reformed Judah's worship practices. Similar reforms took place in other portions of the history (see *Introduction: 6) Royal Observance of Worship*). He destroyed **detestable idols from the whole land of Judah and Benjamin** (15:8). While the Chronicler presented Rehoboam and Abijah positively, these actions make it clear that neither of them stopped all idolatry. At this time, however, Asa rid **the whole land** of idols, including areas of **Ephraim** which he had taken from Baasha, king of Israel (15:8).

Asa's efforts were not only destructive, but constructive as well. He **repaired the altar**, the bronze altar Solomon had erected **in front of the portico of the LORD's temple** (15:8). Apparently, during the very first years of Asa's reign temple maintenance had been neglected.

The presence of idols and the disrepair of the bronze altar explain why Azariah exhorted the king to go further in righteousness (see 15:1-7). Many changes had to be accomplished and the work began with correcting the worship of Judah. Once again, Asa's actions were exemplary for the Chronicler's post-exilic readers. As a number of kings' actions illustrated, worship was the place for them to begin their reforms as well.

Asa's Assembly for Reform (15:9-15)

The report of Asa's response to the prophetic encouragement continues with an account of a national assembly. This assembly extended Asa's reform efforts.

Structure of 15:9-15

These materials divide into a five step balanced narrative (see figure 33). Asa's assembly begins with a detailed description of those who came to Jerusalem (15:9-10) and closes with the benefits the assembly brought to the nation (15:15). Opening sacrificial ceremonies (15:11) balance with the ceremonies closing the assembly (15:14). In the center of the story is a report of the oath sworn at the assembly (15:12-13).

Assembly Called (15:9-10)

This passage begins with the notice that Asa **assembled all Judah** (15:9). This terminology (see also 15:10) sets this event alongside a number of religious assemblies in the Chronicler's history (see *Introduction: 5) Religious Assemblies*). As in other such assemblies, the actions taken here are paradigmatic for the post-exilic community. Asa led Judah in covenant renewal; the Chronicler's readers should learn to do the same in their day (see *Introduction: 13) Covenant*).

These verses emphasize the extent of the tribes represented in the assembly. **All Judah and Benjamin** came to Jerusalem, but along with them were representatives of **Ephraim, Manasseh and Simeon** (15:9). The Chronicler added the notice that the northerners were from among those **who had settled among them** (15:9). As in the days of Rehoboam (see 11:5-17), **large numbers had come ... from Israel** (15:9). The inclusion of Simeon among the northern tribes is problematic because the territory of Simeon is actually located south of Judah. It is feasible that some historical event not known from biblical records led to migrations from Simeon's traditional territory to a more northern location. Perhaps, Edomite incursions in the southern regions after the reign of Solomon explain their movements. Whatever the case, the Chronicler mentioned migrations from the North on several occasions (see *Introduction: 3) Northern Israel*).

This defection from the North took place when **they saw that the Lord his God was with him** (15:9). The fact that **God was with him** recalls the previous section of Asa's victory over Zerah (see 14:11-15). There victory resulted from God fighting on Judah's side (see 13:12; see also *Introduction: 10) Divine Activity*).

This and other migrations from the North were very important to the Chronicler. They were foretastes of the Chronicler's ideal of reunification of all Israel under the reign of the Davidic family (see *Introduction: 2) Northern Israel*).

Assembly Opening Ceremonies (15:11)

In recognition of the solemnity of this occasion, the Chronicler described the sacrifices offered at the beginning of the assembly. Asa and those who had joined him sacrificed **seven hundred head of cattle and seven thousand sheep and goats**. These numbers compare favorably with other similar events (see 1 Chr. 15:26; 2 Chr. 5:6; 7:5; 29:27-33). This assembly was attended by representatives of many tribes and included grand sacrificial ceremonies.

Assembly Oaths (15:12-13)

The Chronicler's chief interest in Asa's assembly also formed the turning point of the narrative. On this occasion the people **entered into a covenant to seek the Lord** (verse 12). This ceremony of covenant renewal was probably concurrent with the annual Feast of Weeks or Pentecost (see Exod. 23:16; 34:22; Lev. 23:15-21; Num. 28:26-31; Deut. 16:9-10). The Chronicler mentioned several events of covenant renewal to inspire his post-exilic readers to reaffirm their covenant commitments before God as well (see *Introduction: 13) Covenant*).

From other portions of Scripture, we may surmise that a covenant renewal ceremony of this sort would include a number of elements. For instance, four movements emerge within the proceedings of Josh. 24:1-25. The ceremonies began with the recollection of God's acts in Israel's history (24:1-13). The restating of the covenant privileges and responsibilities followed (24:14-15). The covenant people respond with repentance and commitment (24:16-18). Laws, promises, and terms of agreement are recorded (24:25). Like Joshua before him, Asa led the nation in renewal of commitments to the Lord (see Deut. 29:1; Josh. 8:30-35; 1 Sam. 11:14).

The Chronicler explicitly tied Asa's covenant renewal to the preceding context. First, he described the assembly's oath as 'seeking' (15:12; see 15:2; see also *Introduction: 19) Seeking*). Similarly, he described the sacrifices offered in conjunction with this covenant renewal as **plunder they had brought back** from victory over Zerah (15:11; see 14:9-15). These two elements in this story demonstrate that the Chronicler saw Asa's assembly as the climax of Asa's response to the prophet.

A remarkable note appears at the end of this covenant renewal. **All who would not seek the LORD ... were to be put to death** (15:13). The practice of executing flagrant covenant violators was established by Mosaic Law (see Exod. 22:20; Deut. 17:2-7;13:6-10). As with all Mosaic instructions on capital punishment, the motivation behind this Law was to rid Israel of evildoers who would lead others from fidelity to the covenant. In the Old Testament period, religious and national policies were nearly inseparable. The judgments of the state of Israel in compliance with the Law of God were the judgments of God himself. As a result, one dimension of national covenant renewal was the purification of the nation. These executions are comparable to the New Testament practice of excommunication which is itself a purification of the believing community (see Matt. 18:17; 1 Cor. 5:1-13; 1 Tim. 1:18-20; 2 Thess. 3:14).

Assembly Closing Ceremonies (15:14)

In balance with the opening ceremonies of sacrifice (see 15:11), the Chronicler turned to the ceremonies following covenant renewal. The people delighted in the event with **shouting and with trumpets and horns**. Once again, the Chronicler's interest in connecting music and joy is apparent (see *Introduction: 8) Music*). As in similar passages throughout his book, the Chronicler emphasized the joy and splendor of this event to motivate his readers toward imitation (see *Introduction: 27) Disappointment and Celebration*). Instead of threats of judgment, this scene of celebration offered positive incentive for covenant renewal. The wonder of Asa's joyous celebration could be theirs, if they would follow the example of Asa's covenant fidelity.

Assembly Results (15:15)

The description of the results of Asa's assembly closes with a continuing focus on the emotions of the event: **All Judah rejoiced**. Representatives of the entire population were excited about the renewal of the covenant. Moreover, they swore **wholeheartedly**. Wholehearted devotion was one of the Chronicler's most repeated themes (see *Introduction: 16) Motivations*). At this time Judah went far beyond external religious requirements and offered their souls to God. Moreover, the Chronicler added that because Asa and the assembly **sought the LORD eagerly ... he was found by them**. Wholehearted, eager pursuit of covenant renewal is once again expressed in terms of 'seeking' (see 14:4; 15:2,12,13; 16:12; also see *Introduction: 19) Seeking*). Finally, the result of the assembly's joyous and sincere devotion was that **the LORD gave them rest on every side**. In language that recalls the ideal reign of David (see 1 Chr. 22:18; 23:25) as well as Asa (see 14:6,7) and anticipates Jehoshaphat (see 20:30), the Chronicler pointed out that Asa's covenant loyalty led to protection from enemies (see *Introduction: 23) Victory and Defeat*).

The encouragement to the Chronicler's readers is evident. The delightful experiences of this assembly should have motivated them to eager pursuit of covenant renewal in their day. They had to go far beyond mere external conformity to wholehearted devotion. Only then would the joy exhibited in this passage be theirs.

Asa's Other Reforms (15:16-19)

The Chronicler rounded off his record of Asa's reforms by returning to the book of Kings (15:16-19 // 1 Kgs. 15:13-15). This material forms an inclusion with 15:8 that frames the story of Asa's assembly (see figure 33).

Several items come into the picture at this point. First, Asa **deposed** ... **Maacah** ... **as queen mother** (15:16). The **queen mother** was nearly an official status afforded to the mother or grandmother of a king (see 1 Kgs. 2:19; 15:13; 2 Kgs. 10:13; 24:12,15). These royal matriarchs often had much influence over the affairs of state. Asa's **grandmother Maacah** (see 13:2) had erected an **Asherah pole** (15:16). Apparently she was not fully committed to Asa's reforms. Not only did Asa destroy her idol, but deposed her as well. Even the king's own family was not exempt from his reform efforts. (For an explanation of the Asherah pole, see 2 Chr. 14:3-5.)

Second, the Chronicler repeated from 1 Kings 15:14 that Asa **did not remove the high places from Israel** (15:17). This admission is not contradictory of 14:5. There the Chronicler asserted only that Asa removed high places **from Judah** (14:5). Here it would appear that the Chronicler understood the book of Kings as referring to those lands of Ephraim which Asa possessed (see 15:8; 17:2). Despite this failure on Asa's part, the Chronicler also included from Kings that **Asa's heart was fully committed** ... **all his life** (15:17). Although the Chronicler turned next to Asa's years of infidelity, he noted that deep within this king was a heart devoted to the Lord. Once again, the Chronicler stressed wholehearted devotion but acknowledged that it did not imply perfect behavior (see *Introduction: 16) Motivations*).

Third, the text refers to Asa's dedication of **silver and gold** ... and other **articles** to **the temple of God** (15:18). This exemplary action recalls the similar actions of David and Solomon (see 1 Chr. 29:3; 2 Chr. 5:1). Once again, this part of Asa's reign was subtly compared to these ideal monarchs.

Fourth, the Chronicler added a final note to this portion of his record (15:19). He had already mentioned the nation's **rest on every side** (15:15; see *Introduction: 23) Victory and Defeat*). At this point, he emphasized that **there was no more war** (15:19). Asa was free of major conflicts **until the thirty-fifth year** of his reign (15:19). The allusion to the ideal reign of Solomon is evident (see 2 Chr. 9:30).

With these closing reports the Chronicler presented the depth of Asa's reforms and the longlasting blessing of peace he received. For the post-exilic readers these features of the king's reign were enviable. They could experience the same peace, if they would imitate Asa's reforms in their day.

Asa Under Divine Judgment (16:1-12)

Having dealt with the earlier years of Asa's reign under divine blessing, the Chronicler turned to the time of divine judgment against the king. His depiction of this portion of Asa's life stands in sharp contrast to the preceding material.

Comparison of 16:1-12 with 1 Kgs. 15:16-24

Chronicles depends on 1 Kgs. 15:16-24 for much of this material (see figure 32). In several portions slight differences appear due to changes in style and corruptions through textual transmission. Yet, a number of variations are due to the Chronicler's unique outlook on these events.

First, several times the Chronicler varied from Kings to display his chronological division of Asa's reign.

1) 1 Kings 15:16 generalizes that war took place between Asa and Baasha of northern Israel 'throughout their reigns'. The Chronicler, however, had already specified that there was peace during Asa's early years (14:6). For this reason he replaced the reference in Kings with a note of war taking place **in the thirty-sixth year** (16:1).

2) 1 Kings 15:23 reads, 'in his old age', but the Chronicler shifted to **in the thirty-ninth year of his reign** (16:12).

3) He also added the information that Asa died **in the forty-first year of his reign** to the parallel material in 1 Kgs. 15:24. Each of these shifts were designed to shape the record of Asa into well-defined temporal units that supported his division of the king's reign into a time of blessing and judgment.

Second, the largest addition which was made to this part of Asa's reign appears in 16:7-10. This story of Hanani the prophet was added to contrast and balance with the previous story of the prophet Azariah (see 15:1-7).

Third, the Chronicler expanded the reference to sources from the book 'of the kings of Judah' (1 Kgs. 15:23) to the book of **the kings of Judah and Israel** (16:11).

Fourth, the simple notice that 'his feet became diseased' (1 Kgs. 15:23) is expanded to indicate that the king responded inappropriately to his illness by failing to seek God (16:12). The purpose of this expansion was to contrast Asa's behavior in this circumstance with the actions of his earlier years (see 15:8-18).

Structure of 16:1-12

The Chronicler's record divides into two main sections (see figure 33). The first portion describes Asa's failure in battle and the subsequent prophetic rebuke and royal reaction (16:1-10). This material is followed by a description of Asa's resulting disease (16:11-12).

Asa's Failure, Prophetic Disapproval and Disobedience (16:1-10)

The first half of Asa's reign involved fidelity, victory, prophetic approval and obedience. This portion contrasts with infidelity, failure, prophetic rebuke, and disobedience (see figure 33). At this point the Chronicler followed a scenario he presented on a number of occasions. A time of blessing was followed by a time of infidelity. (For the Chronicler's warning against permitting blessings to lead to infidelity, see comments on 1 Chr. 5:24.) The contrasts between these two periods could hardly be more striking.

Structure of 16:1-10

This material divides into two segments (see figure 33). It begins with a narrative describing the king's failure in battle (16:1-6) which is followed by a prophetic encounter and the king's reaction (16:7-10).

Asa's Failure in Conflict (16:1-6)

To contrast Asa's remarkable victory over Zerah (14:12), the Chronicler followed the book of Kings (// 1 Kgs. 15:16-22) and recorded one of Asa's encounters with Baasha, king of northern Israel. This battle was not a total defeat for Asa. In fact, in purely political terms it was only a slight setback. Yet, from the Chronicler's point of view it represented a serious violation of Asa's loyalty to God and it brought God's judgment against the king.

Structure of 16:1-6

The account of this battle divides into four symmetrical steps (see figure 33). It begins with an economic threat against Judah (16:1) and ends with its removal (16:5-6). In this regard, Asa appears to be blessed once again. The key to understanding this event, however, is the manner by which Asa resolved his problem. As the middle portions of the story indicate, Asa appealed to Syria for help (16:2-3) and the Syrians fought against northern Israel in alliance with Asa (16:4). Asa's alliance with Syria curtailed his dominance over the region.

Asa Threatened (16:1)

This episode begins with the information that **Baasha king of Israel** began aggression against Judah. He **fortified Ramah**, a site six miles north of Jerusalem, to cut off a major trade route from the east toward Jerusalem. This aggression was one in a long series of skirmishes and conflicts between Asa and Baasha (see 1 Kgs. 15:16).

The opening chronological reference to **the thirty-sixth year of Asa's reign** is problematic (16:1). Similarly, the mention of the **thirty-fifth year** in 15:19 raises difficulties in harmonizing Kings and Chronicles. 1 Kings 15:33 and 16:8 indicate that Elah succeeded Baasha in the twenty-sixth year of Asa's reign, but Chronicles speaks of Baasha making war in the **thirty-sixth year** (16:1). Two resolutions have been proposed. On the one hand, some interpreters hold that 15:19 and 16:1 date these events from the time of the schism of the North and South. If this were so, it would bring Kings and Chronicles into harmony. Nevertheless, this would be the only time the Chronicler oriented his dating in this direction. On the other hand, it is possible that the numbers 'thirty' and 'twenty' were confused at some point in the history of transmission (see *Introduction: Translation and Transmission*). This confusion would not be impossible in Hebrew script of some periods. The latter proposal seems more likely than the former. Yet, further research may point toward a better solution in the future.

Asa Appeals to Syria for Help (16:2-3)

Contrary to his appeal for divine help in his battle with Zerah (see 14:11), Asa turned to human power to remove the threat of Baasha's fortification. He appealed to **Ben-Hadad king of Aram** (16:2). Asa sought an alliance with Israel's Syrian neighbor.

The text clearly indicates that Asa's move was inappropriate in the way it describes his appeal. Not only did the king send treasures from **his own palace**, he also **took the silver and gold out of the treasuries of the Lord's temple** ... **and sent it to Ben-Hadad** (16:2). Near the end of his account of Asa's positive years, the Chronicler praised Asa because he **brought** ... **silver and gold** to the temple (15:18). At this point, Asa did just the opposite. He took from God in order to establish an alliance with a foreign power. The text emphasizes this contrast by repeating a reference to **silver and gold** in Asa's speech to Ben-Hadad (16:3). As we will see, this pursuit of foreign alliance was Asa's serious error (see 16:7-9).

Asa appealed to Ben-Hadad to establish **a treaty** with him (16:3). This arrangement was a parity treaty. Ben-Hadad and Asa functioned as peers, but Asa had to buy Ben-Hadad's loyalty because the latter would have to break his treaty with northern Israel (16:3). The terms of the treaty were simple. Syria would attack northern Israel so that Baasha would have to withdraw from Judah (16:3).

Although the Chronicler said nothing explicit at this point about the religious dimensions of Asa's plan, he later exposed this treaty as rebellion against God. Treaties and cooperation with foreign powers were not entirely forbidden to Israel (see Deut. 20:10-15). Yet, when these treaties were established in lieu of dependence on God for military security, they were strongly condemned. The Chronicler condemned another such alliance in the days of Ahaz (see 28:16-21). Such events were important to him because his post-exilic readers were tempted to find their security in similar ways, rather than rely on God for protection (see *Introduction: 3) International Relations*).

Beyond this, it is important to note that in this situation Asa not only allied himself with a foreign power, but he did so against northern Israel. This fact may also have inspired the Chronicler's condemnation. Although the northern tribes were in apostasy (see 13:4-12) and were aggressive against Judah, conspiring with foreign nations against them was outrageous. The northern tribes troubled the early post-exilic community (see Ezra 4:1-5), but here the Chronicler instructed his readers not to make war against them, especially by means of an alliance with foreign powers (see *Introduction: 2) Northern Israel*).

Syria Attacks Israel (16:4)

In balance with the treaty established between Asa and Syria (see 16:2-3), this portion of the story reports that Ben-Hadad attacked **the towns of Israel** (16:4). The towns listed – **Ijon, Dan, Abel Maim, Naphtali** – were in the northern regions of Israel's territories.

Asa No Longer Threatened (16:5-6)
Just as Asa had hoped, **Baasha stopped building Ramah and abandoned his work** (verse 5). The threat to Judah's security was halted. Moreover, Baasha was so distracted by troubles with Syria that **Asa** and **all Judah** went to Ramah, took Baasha's **stones and timber** and used them to fortify **Geba and Mizpah** (verse 6). The Chronicler reported these events to convey the enormous success of Asa's strategy.

To the unsuspecting reader, this whole series of events looks like a great victory for Asa. His plan worked out splendidly. Only subtle hints of religious failure appear up to this point. The Chronicler used this quality of the record of Kings to prepare his readers for a surprise. Although this event seemed to honor Asa for his diplomatic and military skills, it will soon be seen for what it really was, an act of rebellion against God.

Asa's Prophetic Rebuke and Disobedience (16:7-10)
Asa's second battle was in need of evaluation. The Chronicler immediately offered an explicit judgment of what the king had done.

Structure of 16:7-10
This material divides into two reports (see figure 33). The first consists of a prophetic rebuke (16:7-9). The second confirms this evaluation by noting the king's response to the prophet (16:10). This material balances with the previous announcement by Azariah and the king's positive response at that time (see 15:1-19).

Prophetic Disapproval (16:7-9)
The Chronicler added a second prophetic word from **Hanani the seer** (16:7) to balance with the previous announcement from Azariah the prophet (see 15:1). The earlier prophetic word was entirely positive, encouraging Asa to go further in his reforms. This prophetic speech, however, condemned Asa's actions.

Structure of 16:7-9
Hanani's speech divides into three parts (see figure 33). This prophetic speech follows a pattern of a judgment oracle (accusation and sentencing) that occurs frequently in the prophetic literature of the Old Testament. It begins with an accusation (16:7), a reminder of past blessings (16:8-9a), and an accusation and sentencing (16:9b).

Accusation and Result (16:7)
In his usual fashion the Chronicler reported that God's prophet warned of judgment to come (see *Introduction: 15) Prophets*). He surprised his readers, however, with the opening words of the prophet. Instead of congratulating the king for his clever diplomacy, the prophet accused him of sin. Asa was accused of having **relied on the king of Aram**. In the Chronicler's theological vocabulary, the only one

upon whom Israel should 'rely' was God himself (see 13:18; 16:7, 8). In his struggle with Zerah, Asa specifically affirmed that he **relied** on God (14:11). The Chronicler consistently condemned reliance on anyone but God, especially foreign nations (see *Introduction: 3) International Relations*).

The prophet continued his accusation by pointing to the results of Asa's reliance on foreign power. He announced, '**Aram has escaped from your hand**.' Some ancient texts emend this clause to read 'Israel has escaped...' This emendation is probably a later attempt to clarify the prophet's message (see *Introduction: Translation and Transmission*). The meaning of the traditional Hebrew text, however, is that Asa lost not only victory over Israel (Baasha), but also over Syria (Ben-Hadad) because of his failure to rely on God (see *Introduction: 23) Victory and Defeat*).

Contrast with Earlier Conflict (16:8-9a)

To highlight the folly of Asa's actions, the prophet continued to contrast this situation with the previous conflict in Asa's reign. The **Cushites and Libyans** attacked **with great numbers**, but Asa defeated them because he **relied on the LORD** (16:8 see 14:8-15).

To support his claim, the prophet appealed to a doctrinal belief. He asserted that **the eyes of the LORD** were watching (16:9). The Chronicler referred several times to the eyes of God as his ability to know all things (see 2 Chr. 6:20, 40; 7:15, 16). Here God looks inside human motivations to see whose **hearts are fully committed to him** (16:9). Once again, the Chronicler drew attention to the need for sincere heart devotion to God (see *Introduction: 16) Motivations*). Moreover, the prophet explained that God intervenes **to strengthen** (16:9) those who have hearts devoted to him. In the first part of Asa's reign, it was the whole-hearted commitment of the king and the people of Judah that won the Chronicler's praise. Now that the king had turned from such loyalty, the **eyes of the LORD** became a cause of fear (16:9).

Accusation and Sentencing (16:9b)

The prophet closed his speech by returning to accusation. Asa had done **a foolish thing**. As a result, Asa would suffer severely for his sin. The prophet sentenced him to **war** ... **from now on**. In sharp contrast with the blessing of peace during the earlier period in Asa's reign (see 15:15,19), his kingdom would be troubled with warfare.

The Chronicler dramatically condemned the actions of Asa by drawing these deliberate contrasts with earlier times in the king's life. The message to the Chronicler's audience is not difficult to discern. They longed to avoid war with their neighbors. Only reliance on God would bring them such rest from conflict.

Asa's Response (16:10)

The Chronicler's addition to Kings continues with Asa's reaction to the prophetic word. This portion parallels the king's response to the earlier word from Azariah, but it sharply contrasts with that event (see 15:8). In the early years of his reign, Asa responded with obedience to the prophet's encouragement. At this point, he reacted negatively to the second prophet's accusation.

Asa reacted in two ways. First, he **was angry with the seer** instead of repenting of the infidelity exposed by the prophet. Moreover, he put the prophet Hanani **in prison**, much as Zedekiah imprisoned Jeremiah at a later time (see Jer. 32:3). When prophets rebuked the people and predicted negative consequences, they often suffered severe punishment. Once again, the Chronicler's keen concern with the prophetic office is evident (see *Introduction: 15) Prophets*).

Second, Asa not only imprisoned the prophet, but also **brutally oppressed some of the people**. These people apparently sympathized with the prophet Hanani. The gravity of this action becomes clear when we remember how the Chronicler argued strongly that the Davidic line was ordained for the benefit of the people of Judah and Israel (see *Introduction: 4-9) King and Temple*). Asa's later years of rebellion against God led to a violation of one of his fundamental purposes as king.

Asa's Final Years of Judgment (16:11-12)

The Chronicler returned to the record of Kings (// 1 Kgs. 15:23) to close off Asa's reign. He first followed Kings closely and noted other sources (16:11a // 1 Kgs. 15:23a). Yet, the note that 'his feet became diseased' (1 Kgs. 15:23b) caused him to pause and add other new information.

First, the Chronicler added a chronological note that the foot disease took place **in the thirty-ninth year of his reign** (16:11). The text gives no clues as to the precise nature of the disease, but it is evident that the Chronicler considered it a curse.

Second, he added a theological explanation. Asa's disease was severe, but **he did not seek help from the LORD, but only from the physicians** (16:12). The theme of 'seeking' God is repeated time and again in the Chronicler's version of Asa's reign (see 14:4; 15:2,12,13; 16:12; see also *Introduction: 19) Seeking*). In addition, Asa forgot that effective **help** only comes from God. The Chronicler repeatedly illustrated that God intervened to help his people in their struggles (see *Introduction: 10) Divine Activity*). The Chronicler pointed out here that Asa did just the opposite of what he did in the earlier years of his reign. It should be noted that the Chronicler did not forbid Asa from receiving help from **the physicians**. The Old Testament shows no hesitation about taking advantage of medical care (see 2 Kgs. 20:5-8; Jer. 8:22; 46:11; 51:8). Yet, using ordinary means was never to be divorced from seeking divine assistance. Asa's sin here was similar to his sin in conflict with Baasha (16:1). He relied on human power rather than divine help. As a result, Asa found no relief from his disease.

Closure of Asa's Reign (16:13-14)

With one more additional chronological note (**the forty-first year of his reign** [16:13]), the Chronicler moved to Asa's death and burial. The Chronicler expanded the record of his burial in a way that brought honor to the king (compare 16:14 and 1 Kgs. 15:24). He mentioned details of the burial ceremony which included **spices and various perfumes** (16:14). Moreover, the Judahites **made a huge fire in his honor** (16:14; see Jer. 34:5). Asa's burial contrasts with that of Jehoram whose disgraceful burial had no honorary fire (see 21:19). The Chronicler included this information on Asa's burial to express his belief that Asa was on the whole a good king. Despite his failures, Asa was to be honored by the post-exilic community as the Judahites of Asa's day honored the king (see *Introduction: 28) Healing and Long Life/Sickness and Death*).

The Reign of Jehoshaphat (17:1-21:3)

The next king of Judah was Jehoshaphat (872-848 BC). In general terms, the Chronicler presented this king as one whose fidelity resulted in tremendous blessing. Nevertheless, on two occasions Jehoshaphat involved himself with the sinful northern Israelite kingdom. Jehoshaphat's reign therefore illustrated the blessings derived from fidelity and warned of troubles that come to anyone who compromised with the unfaithful.

Comparison of 17:1-21:3 with 1 Kgs. 22:1-50

The Chronicler's point of view on Jehoshaphat becomes evident when his record is compared with Kings. Detailed notes will follow in the comments on each section, but an overarching comparison provides a helpful orientation to the Chronicler's presentation (see figure 34).

2 Chr		1 Kgs.
17:1-2	Opening of Jehoshaphat's Reign (expanded)	15:24c
17:3-19	Jehoshaphat's Earlier Fidelity (added)	———
———	Events in Northern Israel (omitted)	15:25-21:29
18:1-34	Jehoshaphat's Earlier Battle (loosely parallel)	22:1-40
19:1-11	Jehoshaphat's Later Fidelity (added)	———
20:1-30	Jehoshaphat's Later Battle (added)	———
20:31-21:3	Closure of Jehoshaphat's Reign (expanded)	22:41-50

Comparison of 2 Chr 17:1-21:3 and 1 Kgs 15:25-22:50 (figure 34)

Although the Chronicler (as he usually did) omitted events in northern Israel found in 1 Kgs. 15:25-21:29, he more than doubled the size of material devoted to Jehoshaphat (50 verses in Kings and 104 verses in Chronicles). 17:1-19 greatly expands 1 Kings 15:24c and gives examples of blessings which Jehoshaphat received during reforms in the first years of his reign. The Chronicler then followed Kings in its description of a battle with Syria (18:1-34 // 1 Kgs. 22:1-40). The Chronicler added a second record of Jehoshaphat's reforms and blessings (19:1-11) as well as another battle he faced (20:1-30). Near the end, Chronicles returns to material in Kings to close Jehoshaphat's reign (20:31-21:3 // 1 Kgs. 22:41-50).

Structure of 17:1-21:3

Jehoshaphat's reign divides into four main sections (see figure 35). Its opening (17:1-2) and closure (20:31-21:3); the body of the reign separating into the king's early years (17:3-19:3); and his later years (19:4-20:30).

After brief opening remarks (17:1-2), the account deals first with Jehoshaphat's earlier years (17:3,7; 18:2). This first period consists of a time of blessing followed by battle (17:1-19:3). Jehoshaphat's later years also include a record of blessing followed by battle (19:4-20:30). As we will see in the comments that follow, this symmetry was designed to draw attention to similarities and contrasts between the earlier and later years of the king's reign. Jehoshaphat's reign closes with an unusually complex ending (20:31-21:3).

Opening of Jehoshaphat's Reign (17:1-2)

In his usual fashion, the Chronicler began with a brief description of Jehoshaphat's rise to power. The Chronicler included the information of 1 Kgs. 15:24c (// 17:1). He also expanded this notice with an additional verse (17:2).

Jehoshaphat first **strengthened himself** (17:1). In the Chronicler's vocabulary, for a king to 'strengthen himself' meant that he consolidated power so that opponents offered no genuine threat (for the significance of this expression, see 1:1). In this case, the Chronicler specified that Jehoshaphat was secure **against Israel** (17:1). Conflict between Judah and northern Israel originated with Rehoboam (see 2 Chr. 11:1-4) and extended through the reigns of Abijah (see 13:19) and Asa (see 15:8). Jehoshaphat, however, secured his borders against northern aggression. He not only **stationed troops** in **Judah** but also in **the towns of Ephraim** that Abijah (see 13:19) and Asa (see 15:8) had taken before him (17:2).

By describing Jehoshaphat's security as **against Israel** (17:1), the Chronicler immediately prepared his readers for relating this material to the next section of Jehoshaphat's early years, namely his alliance with Israel against Syria (see 18:1-19:3). The Chronicler made it clear that the king had nothing to fear from his northern kinsmen, but he nevertheless entered an alliance in which he helped northern Israel against a common foe.

Jehoshaphat's Earlier Years (17:3-19:3)

The Chronicler's record of Jehoshaphat's early years focuses in two directions. It first deals with the king's acts of obedience and the blessings he received (17:3-19). It then describes his mixed experience in battle against the Syrians (18:1-34).

■ Opening of Jehoshaphat's Reign (17:1-2)

♦ Jehoshaphat's Earlier Years (17:3-19:3)
• Jehoshaphat's Earlier Fidelity (17:3-19)
Jehoshaphat's Strength Explained (17:3-9)
Jehoshaphat's International Blessings (17:10-11)
Jehoshaphat's Strength Elaborated (17:12-19)

• Jehoshaphat's Earlier Battle (18:1-19:3)
Jehoshaphat Visits Ahab (18:1-2a)
Jehoshaphat Agrees to Fight with Ahab (18:2b-27)
Synopsis of Royal Deliberations (18:2b-3)
First Prophetic Inquiry (18:4-5)
Second Prophetic Inquiry (18:6-27)
Jehoshaphat Fights with Ahab (18:28-34)
Ahab's Twofold Plan (18:28-29a)
Ahab Enters Battle (18:29b)
Twofold Results of Ahab's Plan (18:30-34)
Jehoshaphat Returns to Jerusalem (19:1-3)

♦ Jehoshaphat's Later Years (19:4-20:30)
• Jehoshaphat's Later Fidelity (19:4-11)
Title: Jehoshaphat's Extensive Reforms (19:4)
Judicial Reforms Outside Jerusalem (19:5-7)
Appointments Outside Jerusalem (19:5)
Instructions Outside Jerusalem (19:6-7)
Judicial Reforms Within Jerusalem (19:8-11)
Appointments Within Jerusalem (19:8)
Instructions Within Jerusalem (19:9-11)

• Jehoshaphat's Later Battle (20:1-30)
- Jehoshaphat's Enemies Attack (20:1)
- Jehoshaphat Holds an Assembly in Jerusalem (20:2-19)
Calling of the Assembly (20:2-4)
Jehoshaphat Learns of Attack (20:2)
Jehoshaphat Calls Judah to Assemble (20:3)
Judah Assembles (20:4)
Ceremony of the Assembly (20:5-19)
Assembly Prays for Help (20:5-13)
Assembly Receives Response (20:14-17)
Assembly Responds with Praise (20:18-19)
- Jehoshaphat's Army Marches to Battle (20:20-21)
- God Intervenes for Jehoshaphat (20:22-23)
- Jehoshaphat's Army Gathers Plunder (20:24-26)
- Jehoshaphat Returns and Holds an Assembly (20:27-28)
- Jehoshaphat Has Peace and Rest (20:29-30)

■ Closure of Jehoshaphat's Reign (20:31-21:3)
Summary of Jehoshaphat's Reign (20:31-34)
Jehoshaphat's Maritime Alliance (20:35-37)
Jehoshaphat Builds Ships with Ahaziah (20:35-36a)
Prophetic Condemnation (20:36b-37a)
Jehoshaphat's Ships are Destroyed 20:37b).
Jehoshaphat's Death, Burial, and Successor (21:1-3)

Outline of 2 Chr. 17:1-21:3 (figure 35)

Jehoshaphat's Earlier Fidelity (17:3-19)
Jehoshaphat's reign begins with a record of the king's early fidelity and blessing which appears only in Chronicles. This expansion of Kings reflects the Chronicler's typical style and vocabulary on many occasions.

Structure of 17:3-19
The record of Jehoshaphat's early fidelity divides into three parts (see figure 35). His strength is described (17:3-9), his international blessings appear (17:10-11), and then an elaboration closes the section (17:12-19). The Chronicler formed these reports to explain and illustrate how Jehoshaphat was able to consolidate his strength in such a remarkable way.

Jehoshaphat's Strength Explained (17:3-9)
The Chronicler explained the king's success by reporting his domestic blessings (17:3-9). The Chronicler first explained that **the LORD was with Jehoshaphat** (17:3). The concept of God being 'with' a king usually bore the connotation that God was acting as his military leader (see *Introduction: 10) Divine Activity*). The context here is also one of military success. Jehoshaphat's successful positioning of his troops against the North was evidence that God was on the side of Judah **in his early years** (17:3).

The reason for this divine favor is stated explicitly. It was **because** Jehoshaphat **walked in the ways his father David had followed** (17:3). Comparing kings to David was a common technique in the book of Kings (see 1 Kgs. 3:14; 9:4; 11:4-6; 14:8; 15:3,11; 2 Kgs. 14:3; 16:2; 18:3; 22:2), but the Chronicler used this device less frequently (28:1; 29:2; 34:2; see *Introduction: 14) Standards*). It is noteworthy, therefore, that Jehoshaphat's early years were comparable to the ideal king David.

The text catalogs a number of specific actions that made Jehoshaphat comparable to David. First, he **sought the God of his father** rather than **the Baals** (17:3). The Chronicler noted a number of times that David sought God (1 Chr. 16:11; 22:19; 28:8-9). 'Seeking' God for direction and help was one of the Chronicler's highest ideals (see *Introduction: 19) Seeking*). The rejection of **the Baals** contrasts Jehoshaphat with the syncretism taking place in the North under the influence of Jezebel (see 1 Kgs. 16:31-33; 18:4).

Second, the king's **heart was devoted** to God (17:6). Whole-hearted commitment to the Lord frequently appears in Chronicles as a sincere service that is blessed by God (see *Introduction: 16) Motivations*). In this way as well, Jehoshaphat was likened to David whose sincere heart is highlighted a number of times (see 1 Chr. 22:7,9; 28:2,9; 29:17-19).

Third, Jehoshaphat **removed the high places ... and the Asherah poles from Judah** (17:6). Just as David had been devoted to centralizing worship in Jerusalem, Jehoshaphat destroyed the high places. The destruction of pagan worship sites and objects appears frequently in Chronicles as a sign of devotion to God (14:3-5;

17:6; 29:16; 31:1; 33:15; 34:3-7; see *Introduction: 6) Royal Observance of Worship*). For an explanation of Asherah poles see comments on 2 Chr. 14:3-5. As 20:33 indicates, however, Jehoshaphat did not continue with this level of devotion throughout his reign.

As a result of the king's zeal, **the LORD established the kingdom** (17:5). Judah was strengthened because of Jehoshaphat's fidelity and he was blessed with **great wealth and honor** by gifts from **all Judah**. **Wealth and honor** are mentioned in connection only with a few kings. The use of this terminology here pointed out that Jehoshaphat's early years reached a level of prosperity enjoyed by few (see *Introduction: 26) Prosperity and Poverty*). Moreover, the fact that this **wealth and honor** came from **all Judah** is another way the Chronicler exalted the king. The entire southern kingdom honored Jehoshaphat (*Introduction: 1) All Israel*).

After listing a number of ways in which Jehoshaphat had shown himself to be faithful like David, the Chronicler paused to point out the king's most remarkable act of devotion (17:7-9). **In the third year** (17:7), probably the king's first year to reign after his father's death, he sent **officials ... to teach in the towns of Judah** (17:7). A number of **Levites** and **priests** accompanied these political leaders (17:8). Levites and priests were designated as teachers of the people in the Law of Moses (see Deut. 24:8; 27:14-26; 31:9-13). Under the king's direction, they took **the Book of the Law** (probably the Pentateuch) and **taught the people** (17:9). A similar event took place later in Jehoshaphat's reign as well (see 19:4-12).

The Chronicler's keen interest in the mutual support of king and temple personnel becomes evident here. The ideal kings David and Solomon concentrated on establishing the priests and Levites in their proper roles (see 1 Chr. 15:11-24; 16:4-6,37-42; 23:1-26:32; 2 Chr. 8:14-15); Hezekiah also gave much attention to the temple personnel (see 29:1-36; 30:15-17,21-27; 31:2-21) as did Josiah (see 34:8-13; 35:1-19). Here Jehoshaphat established the priests and Levites in their rightful place as teachers of the Law (see *Introduction: 4-9) King and Temple*).

The Chronicler used the example of Jehoshaphat to illustrate the means by which security and wealth could come to the people of God. His post-exilic readers desired these blessings, but they needed to be reminded of the kinds of actions that would lead to such positive results. Devotion to purity in worship and instruction in the Law were to be high priorities in their day.

Jehoshaphat's International Blessings (17:10-11)

In addition to domestic blessings that secured Judah against Israel, Jehoshaphat's fidelity was also rewarded on the broader international front. **The LORD was with Jehoshaphat** (17:3) to fight on his behalf (see *Introduction: 10) Divine Activity*). As a result, **the fear of the LORD fell on all the kingdoms** (17:10). The dread of God upon foreign nations is mentioned several times in Chronicles as a way of exalting certain kings (see 14:14; 17:10; 20:29). The motif appears elsewhere in Scripture as an ideal for which Israel should hope (see Exod. 15:16; 23:27; Deut. 2:25; 11:25; Josh. 2:9-11). The nations feared because God was fighting for Jehoshaphat and giving him great victories (see *Introduction: 3) International Relations*). In fact, the presence of God with Jehoshaphat was so evident in his military strength that the nations around him **did not make war** with him (17:10). Instead, they brought **gifts and silver as tribute** ... **rams** and **goats** (17:11).

This paragraph explains another reason why Jehoshaphat was able to fortify himself so strongly against northern Israel (see 17:1-2); he had no other enemies to worry him. All the nations, especially the **Philistines** to the west and the **Arabs** to the east (17:11), were pacified by their fear of Jehoshaphat's God.

Jehoshaphat's Strength Elaborated (17:12-19)

After explaining how Jehoshaphat became so strong, the Chronicler returned to the subject of the king's military strength (17:12-19; compare 17:1-2). He mentioned the construction of **forts and store cities** (17:12). Successful building projects frequently exhibited divine blessing in Chronicles (see *Introduction: 24) Building and Destruction*). **Large supplies** also indicated his readiness for battle (17:13a).

The Chronicler then described the king's army (17:13b-19). He listed men from **Judah** and **Benjamin** (17:14,17). The number of **experienced fighting men** (17:13b) totaled 1,160,000. This is the largest number recorded for Judah's army (see comments on 2 Chr. 11:1). This and other large numbers may be understood in several ways. For the Chronicler's use of large numbers of soldiers, see comments on 1 Chr. 12:24-37. However one deals with the number itself, it is evident that Jehoshaphat's army was very large. The Chronicler stressed the size of his army in 17:19 by noting that this number was in addition to those he mentioned in 17:2.

The Chronicler introduced the reign of Jehoshaphat in a positive light to draw attention to the significance of the king's failure that followed (18:29; 19:1-3). God had secured Judah against northern Israel because Jehoshaphat had been faithful to teach and enforce the Law of Moses. These blessings only made his later alliance with the North that much more difficult to justify.

The message of this section to the post-exilic readers was at least twofold. On the one hand, this chapter demonstrated how Judah could find divine support against enemies. Through faithful service to God expressed by obedience and reform, the province of Judah could hope to be strong against her enemies once again. On the other hand, however, strength gained from trust in God made all attempts to find security elsewhere an abrupt affront to God.

Jehoshaphat's Earlier Battle (18:1-19:3)

The first battle of Jehoshaphat's reign is an intricate account which reveals a complex portrait of the king. On the one hand, Jehoshaphat seems pious and devoted to the Lord (18:6; 18:31). On the other hand, he appears foolish and is rebuked for his folly (18:29; 19:2-3).

In many respects this episode mirrors the Chronicler's earlier account of Asa's battle against northern Israel. At least three points of contact appear.

1) In both records, the kings of Judah made alliances with other kings. Asa

relied on Syria against Israel (16:1-6); Jehoshaphat allied himself with Israel in opposition to Syria (18:1-19:3).

2) In each story a prophet of God was imprisoned. Asa jailed Hanani (16:10); Ahab imprisoned Micaiah (18:25-26).

3) In both passages, the Chronicler reserved explicit judgment on the events until after the battles had taken place. Hanani rebuked Asa (16:7-9); Jehu, son of Hanani rebuked Jehoshaphat (19:1-3). The common element of both rebukes was that the king of Judah should not have formed an alliance with another human power.

Comparison of 18:1-19:3 with 1 Kgs. 22:1-40

For the most part, the Chronicler copied this material from 1 Kgs. 22:1-40. A few stylistic differences occur here and there. Also, problems in textual transmission lie behind some minor differences. Nevertheless, the Chronicler himself made several omissions and additions that reveal his outlook on these events.

First, the Chronicler modified the beginning of the narrative (18:1 // 1 Kgs. 22:1). This new opening connected this story with the preceding focus on Jehoshaphat's wealth and security.

Second, the Chronicler added 18:2 to highlight Ahab's extensive effort to gain Jehoshaphat's cooperation.

Third, 18:31 (// 1 Kgs. 22:33) presents a special textual problem (see *Introduction: Translation and Transmission*). The traditional Hebrew text of 1 Kings 22:33 does not mention the Lord responding to Jehoshaphat's cry. At first glance, Chronicles seems to add ... **and the LORD helped him. God drew them away from him** ... (18:31). Yet, some ancient manuscripts of 1 Kings 22:33 suggest that these words may have been original to the book of Kings and therefore simply copied by the Chronicler. Whatever the case, the concept of God answering Jehoshaphat's prayer fit well with the repeated theme of divine judgment and blessing found elsewhere in Chronicles.

Fourth, the Chronicler substituted his own ending for the finale in Kings. 1 Kings 22:35b-40 ends the record in Kings with the announcement that the prophetic judgment against Ahab had been fulfilled. 19:1-3, however, replaces this ending with a scene depicting Jehoshaphat's return to Jerusalem and the prophetic rebuke he received. This final prophetic rebuke of Jehoshaphat unveiled the Chronicler's chief concern in this narrative.

Structure of 18:1-19:3

Jehoshaphat's battle in alliance with northern Israel divides into four symmetrical parts (see figure 35). The chapter begins with Jehoshaphat visiting his ally, King Ahab of Northern Israel (18:1-2a). While visiting Ahab, Jehoshaphat agreed to join in battle against Syria after consulting with prophets (18:2b-27). Jehoshaphat then traveled to Ramath-Gilead and carried out Ahab's battle plan (18:28-34). In balance with the beginning of the story, Jehoshaphat returned to Jerusalem to encounter another prophet who rebuked him for his alliance with Ahab (19:1-3).

Jehoshaphat Visits Ahab (18:1-2a)
The Chronicler replaced the opening of this story in Kings (1 Kgs. 22:1-2) with his own beginning to provide a different setting for the events that follow. 1 Kings 22:1-2 simply notes that war began between Syria and northern Israel. The Chronicler, however, paused to give more extensive historical background.

The background information of 18:1 reports two important facts. First, these events took place at a time when **Jehoshaphat had great wealth and honor** (18:1). These words repeat the language of 17:5 and draw a connection between this narrative and the entire preceding chapter. As we have already seen, the Chronicler added the preceding chapter to demonstrate that Jehoshaphat was blessed during his early years for his loyalty to God (see *Introduction: 26) Prosperity and Poverty*). As the Chronicler pointed out on a number of occasions, it was precisely when some kings enjoyed great blessings from God that they turned away from him. For the Chronicler's warning against infidelity after blessings, see comments on 1 Chr. 5:24.

Second, the Chronicler added that Jehoshaphat had entered an alliance **by marriage** with Ahab (18:1). This marriage was between Jehoshaphat's son Jehoram and Ahab's daughter Athaliah (see 21:6; 22:2). In the ancient Near East, marriage was typically viewed as more than the union of two individuals; it was a bond between two families. In the case of royal families, such marriages also formed political alliances between nations. Though this practice was common, God had prohibited his people from intermarrying with idolaters because they would inevitably lead his people into apostasy (see Deut. 7:3-4; Josh. 23:11-13; Neh. 13:23-27; see also *Introduction: 3) International Relations*). Jehoshaphat's marriage proved to be a serious problem for Judah in later generations. Athaliah led Jehoram into the sins of Ahab (see 21:5-6), and led Ahaziah into the same sins (see 22:2-3). Moreover, Athaliah usurped the throne by killing nearly all of the royal offspring of Judah (see 22:10-12). At this point, however, the Chronicler introduced the marriage alliance to explain why Jehoshaphat gave his support to northern Israel.

Jehoshaphat **went down to visit Ahab in Samaria** (18:2). The Chronicler did not explain Jehoshaphat's motivations for this journey. His interest was primarily in what Ahab did once Jehoshaphat arrived.

Jehoshaphat Agrees to Fight with Ahab (18:2b-27)
Jehoshaphat and Ahab deliberated extensively before waging war against Syria. These deliberations create a mixed characterization of Jehoshaphat.

Structure of 18:2b-27
This lengthy portion of the narrative divides into three main sections (see figure 35). The first verses of this material (18:2b-3) summarize the negotiations between the kings. This summation is followed by two rounds of prophetic inquiries (18:4-5, 6-27), both of which were initiated at Jehoshaphat's insistence (18:4,6).

Synopsis of Royal Deliberations (18:2b-3)

At the meeting of the kings, Ahab went to great lengths to have Jehoshaphat join him in battle. He **slaughtered many sheep and cattle** for a great feast to honor Jehoshaphat and his men (18:2b). Moreover, he **urged** Jehoshaphat **to attack Ramath Gilead** (18:2b).

The term translated **urged** sometimes occurs with the connotation of 'entice' or 'seduce' (see 1 Chr. 21:1; 2 Chr. 32:11,15). It is likely to have this meaning here (see NAS, NRS). By opening this portion of the story in this manner, the Chronicler subtly gave his own evaluation of the events taking place. Jehoshaphat was about to be enticed into something evil.

The long process of establishing an agreement (see 18:4-27) is reduced to a simple request and response in 18:3. Ahab asked, **'Will you go with me ...?'** and Jehoshaphat replied, **'We will join you in the war.'** As the verses that follow make clear, Jehoshaphat did not immediately agree to join Ahab. Lengthy deliberations took place, but in the end the king of Judah agreed to fight.

First Prophetic Inquiry (18:4-5)

After the synopsis of negotiations between Ahab and Jehoshaphat, the text describes the process by which this agreement came about. The Chronicler followed 1 Kgs. 22:5 and reported that Jehoshaphat complicated matters by insisting that Ahab **first seek the counsel of the LORD** (18:4 see also 18:6). This insistence revealed Jehoshaphat as one still committed to 'seeking' God. He was a man who desired the wisdom and blessing of God (see *Introduction: 19) Seeking*). At the end of this narrative the Chronicler's addition praises Jehoshaphat for his abiding devotion (see 19:3). Ironically, however, as this chapter progresses Jehoshaphat did not take to heart the prophetic word that his seeking evoked. He disregarded the warning of the prophet (18:18-22,28).

In response to Jehoshaphat's insistence, Ahab **brought together the prophets** (18:5 // 1 Kgs. 22:6). It was customary in the ancient Near East for kings to surround themselves with professional prophets when they prepared for warfare. The practice is also well attested in the Old Testament (see 1 Kgs. 12:21-24 // 2 Chr. 11:1-4; 1 Kgs. 20:13, 28; 2 Kgs. 3:11-19; 6:12-22; 7:1-7; 13:14-20; 2 Chr. 20:14-19; Isa. 7:3-25; Jer. 21; see also *Introduction: 15) Prophets*). Ahab asked these professional prophets if he should go to war and the prophets answered in the affirmative.

Second Prophetic Inquiry (18:6-27)

Although Ahab's prophets had promised victory, Jehoshaphat was not convinced. He asked specifically for **a prophet of the LORD** (18:6 // 1 Kgs. 22:7). The prophets that gathered by Ahab very likely claimed to be the prophets of Israel's God. Note that they use the Lord's name in their prophecies (see 18:10-11 // 1 Kgs. 22:11-12). It is not altogether clear why Jehoshaphat did not accept Ahab's professional prophets as 'of the Lord'. It is possible that he was asking for a prophet who remained faithful to the throne and temple of Jerusalem. From Jehoshaphat's Judahite outlook only such prophets would have been legitimate. Moreover, the positive response of the prophets may also have raised doubts in Jehoshaphat's mind. Frequently in the Old Testament, false prophets were characterized as only giving positive oracles in favor of the king (see 36:16; 2 Kgs. 17:13-15; Neh. 9:26; Jer. 25:4; 26:4-5; 28; 29:24-32). The fact that these prophets spoke so enthusiastically in favor of royal plans caused Jehoshaphat to be suspicious. So, in effect he asked for a prophet not on Ahab's payroll.

Ahab admitted that a there was one man **'through whom we can inquire of the LORD ... Micaiah son of Imlah'** (18:7 // 1 Kgs. 22:8). Micaiah appears nowhere else in Scripture but here and in the parallel section of Kings. Yet, he was well-known to Ahab. As Ahab complained, **'he never prophesies anything good about me'** (18:7 // 1 Kgs. 22:8). Micaiah served as God's spokesperson and said only what God commanded. Ahab blurted out, **'I hate him**,' but Jehoshaphat rebuked him for his insolence (18:7). As a result, Ahab conceded to Jehoshaphat's wishes and ordered that Micaiah be brought before them (18:8 // 1 Kgs. 22:9).

In 18:9-11 (// 1 Kgs. 22:10-12) the text turns momentarily from the main action of the narrative to elaborate on the earlier scene of false prophets before the kings (see 18:5). All the verbs in this section should therefore be translated as previous events (e.g. '...had been sitting...' [18:9]). These verses provide a striking counterpoint to Micaiah's upcoming prophecy (see 18:18-22). The two kings had been sitting **on their thrones ... by the gate of Samaria** and **all the prophets** (400 of them [18:5]) had been **prophesying before them** (18:9). To enhance the scene even further, the passage focuses on one prophet, **Zedekiah** who **had made iron horns** and had announced that Ahab would **gore the Arameans** (18:10). Such symbolic acts are well-known from the rest of the Old Testament. Prophets often accompanied their prophecies with symbolic displays (see Jer. 27:2; 28:1-17; Ezek. 4:1-17; 5:1-17; 12:1-7). This dramatic scene ends with the words of **all the other prophets** in unanimous agreement that Ahab and Jehoshaphat would be **victorious** (18:11). Without exception, the professional prophets had urged war and had promised success.

The main action of the story continues with a **messenger** of the royal court looking for Micaiah and instructing him to agree with the false prophets (18:12). Micaiah, however, answered with an oath that reflected his character as a true prophet. He swore only to say what **God says** (18:13 // 1 Kgs. 22:14).

The scene of Micaiah before Ahab and Jehoshaphat (18:14-27 // 1 Kgs. 22:15-28) consists of interactions among four main characters: Ahab, Jehoshaphat, Zedekiah and Micaiah. The sequence of action may be summarized as follows:

1) Ahab invited Micaiah to prophesy (verse 14).
2) Micaiah agreed with the false prophets (verse 14).
3) Ahab challenged Micaiah to speak truth **in the name of the LORD** (verse 15; see *Introduction: 11) Name of God*).

4) Micaiah reversed himself and predicted disaster (verse 16).
5) Ahab complained to Jehoshaphat (verse 17).
6) Micaiah explained his reversal (verses 18-22).
7) Zedekiah, the false prophet, rebuked Micaiah (verse 23).
8) Micaiah responded to Zedekiah (verse 24).
9) Ahab ordered Micaiah's imprisonment (verses 25-26).
10) Micaiah responded to Ahab (verse 27).

The most perplexing aspect of these interactions is how a true prophet of the Lord could first predict victory (verse 14) and then disaster (verse 16). Micaiah himself explained his actions in his description of a heavenly vision (verses 18-22). Although Micaiah's description of the heavenly court scene is unusually detailed, it is a common Old Testament theme that prophets viewed and participated in the activities of the court of God. They later reported the deliberations of the divine assembly to people on earth (see Isa. 6:1-13; Dan. 7:9ff.; Amos 7:1,4,7).

In effect, Micaiah explained his actions on the basis of divine purposes behind these events. The Chronicler frequently appealed to divine intentions to explain earthly events (see *Introduction: 10) Divine Activity*). This passage reveals heavenly purposes in great detail. Micaiah had seen the Lord ask for a volunteer from the **host of heaven** (verse 18) to **lure** Ahab to his death (verse 19). An unnamed **spirit** had agreed to do so by becoming **a lying spirit in the mouths of all** [of Ahab's] **prophets** (verses 20-21). God had agreed to the plan and guaranteed success (verse 21). Simply put, Micaiah gave his first message of success to Ahab in order to comply with the divine desire to see the king lured into death. His second message of judgment was actually the expected outcome of the battle.

Micaiah's two oracles were designed to seal Ahab's fate. While prophets usually warned to encourage repentance, occasionally their role was to insure destruction (see Isa. 6:9-13). Jesus spoke in parables for a similar reason (see Luke 8:9-10). Although the Chronicler omitted the record of Ahab's apostasy in 1 Kgs. 16:29-22:40, Ahab's rebellion against God led him into a terrible condition. Ahab had turned so far from God that prophecy became a means of confusing him and luring him to his death.

After Micaiah delivered his message to Ahab, the king ordered that he be put **in prison** (18:26). The Chronicler mentioned a similar reaction from Asa (see 16:10). The prophet was to be incarcerated until the king returned in safety. Micaiah remarked that if Ahab returned safely it would prove that his prophesy was not from God. Then he turned to the crowd and defiantly shouted, **'Mark my words, all you people'** (18:27). Of course, as events soon proved, Micaiah's words were from God (see 18:33-34).

Jehoshaphat Fights with Ahab (18:28-34)

With deliberations out of the way, the story proceeds to the actual battle at Ramath Gilead. As expected, events unfolded as Micaiah predicted.

Structure of 18:28-34

This segment of the narrative divides into three symmetrical steps (see figure 35). The passage begins with Ahab's two-sided plan (18:28-29a), then the battle ensues (18:29b), and a twofold outcome occurs (18:30-34).

Ahab's Twofold Plan (18:28-29a)

Ahab and Jehoshaphat **went up to Ramoth Gilead** to make war against the Syrians (18:28 // 1 Kgs. 22:29). No record is given of the entire battle strategy; just one aspect of the plan is reported. Ahab proposed that he enter battle **in disguise** while Jehoshaphat wore his normal **royal robes** (18:28 // 1 Kgs. 22:30).

The reasoning behind Ahab's plan is not altogether clear. He may have anticipated the plan of the king of Syria (see 18:30). Or like Josiah (see 35:22), he may have tried to foil the prophecy of Micaiah by hiding himself in the crowd. Whatever his intentions, Ahab's plan did not succeed.

Ahab Enters Battle (18:29b)

Just as he had planned, Ahab entered the battle only after he **disguised himself** (18:29b // 1 Kgs. 22:30b). No explicit mention is made of Jehoshaphat's actions because he simply remained clothed as usual.

Twofold Results of Ahab's Plan (18:30-34)

This episode of battle closes with two scenarios depicting the outcomes of Ahab's plan. The first outcome focuses on Jehoshaphat (18:30-32); the second concerns Ahab (18:33-34).

The result for Jehoshaphat was great danger and deliverance (18:30-32 // 1 Kgs. 22:31-33). A central goal of Syria's strategy in this battle was to kill Ahab. As a result, the **chariot commanders** were ordered to concern themselves with no one **except the king of Israel** (18:30). Nevertheless, Jehoshaphat was mistaken for the king of northern Israel and the chariots **turned to attack him** (18:31).

In response to this threat, **Jehoshaphat cried out and the LORD helped** (18:31). As mentioned above, the traditional Hebrew text of the parallel verse in 1 Kgs. 22:32 simply reads 'Jehoshaphat cried out' (see *Introduction: Translation and Transmission*). The terminology **cried out** is somewhat ambiguous in itself. It can mean that Jehoshaphat merely shouted from fear (see 1 Sam. 4:13; 5:10; 28:12; Esth. 4:1) or it can mean that he prayed with intensity (see Judg. 3:9; 6:6; 10:10; Pss. 107:13, 19; 142:1; Jon. 1:5). The expressions **and the LORD helped him** and **God drew them away from him** (18:31) clarified this ambiguity. The language of the traditional Hebrew text of Chronicles makes it clear that Jehoshaphat prayed and God **helped** by intervening on his behalf (see *Introduction: 10) Divine Activity*). Once again, the Chronicler presented an event in the divided monarchy that fulfilled the hopes of Solomon's temple prayer (see 6:34-35; 7:14; see also *Introduction: 17) Prayer*). Jehoshaphat's alliance with Ahab had brought him to a dreadful situation of military defeat. Yet, he turned to God in prayer and received a merciful deliverance (see *Introduction: 23) Victory and Defeat*).

While the king of Judah was rescued from death by divine intervention, Ahab did not fare so well (18:33-34 // 1 Kgs. 22:34-35). He had done his best to protect himself (see 18:29), but his plan was ineffective. The text describes an ironic occurrence. **Someone drew his bow at random** (18:33). An unnamed archer shot an arrow into the crowd and it struck Ahab **between the sections of his armor** (18:33). Had the arrow fallen slightly to the right or left, it would have caused no harm. But the arrow struck Ahab and **at sunset he died** (18:34). The implication is plain; the random arrow striking a precise target was an act of God which fulfilled the prophecy of Micaiah (see 18:22, 27; see *Introduction: 10) Divine Activity*). Just as Jehoshaphat was shown mercy, Ahab suffered divine judgment.

Jehoshaphat Returns to Jerusalem (19:1-3)

The Chronicler added a new ending to the story of Jehoshaphat's alliance with Ahab. These verses balance with the opening scene in which Jehoshaphat traveled to Samaria (18:1-2a) (see figure 35). He now returns to Jerusalem.

Besides this, the Chronicler added this ending to give his theological interpretation of the event. As with Asa's battle in alliance with Syria against Israel (see 16:1-10), a prophet confronted the king of Judah after battle. Without this prophetic reflection, readers may have the impression that this narrative depicts Jehoshaphat in a positive light. Up to this point, the text has not clearly denounced Jehoshaphat for his actions. Moreover, his prayer and deliverance sharply contrasted with the fate of Ahab. Yet, the Chronicler closed his record with an interpretative prophetic word to clarify matters.

Jehoshaphat **returned safely to his palace** (19:1). All seemed well until **Jehu the seer, the son of Hanani** approached him (19:2). As in other passages, a prophet stepped forward to warn of judgment (see *Introduction: 15) Prophets*). The mention of **Hanani** alludes to the parallel scene where Hanani rebuked Asa upon his return from Ramah (see 16:7-9).

Jehu first accused Jehoshaphat (19:2a). His accusation was similar and dissimilar to his father's words to Asa (see 16:7-9). Both prophets condemned the alliance of Judah with another power, but their reasons were not the same. Jehu challenged Jehoshaphat with two questions. He asked if the king of Judah should **help the wicked** or **love those who hate the LORD** (19:2). The term **help** often appears in Chronicles to describe God's assistance to those whom he favored (see *Introduction: 10) Divine Activity*). It also appears as a description of what sinful kings hope to get from sources other than God himself (see 2 Chr. 28:16,21,23). Here, however, we see the one time the Chronicler used the term to denote the assistance a king of Judah gave to someone else. Jehu not only accused Jehoshaphat of offering **help**, but also **love** (19:2). The term **love** frequently occurs in the ancient Near East to indicate a political loyalty. Jehu rebuked the king for what he had given to Ahab.

The Chronicler frequently encouraged an irenic outlook toward the northern kingdom. Here, however, the prophet denounced them as **wicked** and **those who**

hate the LORD (19:2). Just as **love** often connoted political loyalties, **hate** suggested political or covenantal disloyalty. As the record of Kings indicates clearly, Ahab led northern Israel into severe apostasy (see 1 Kgs. 20-21). The northern kingdom was in flagrant rebellion against God. Jehu therefore reproved Jehoshaphat for aiding them in their rebellion. The implication for the Chronicler's readers was plain. While they were to work toward the ideal of a unified Israel, this goal was not to be pursued at the cost of aiding those who were in flagrant violation of Israel's covenant with God (see *Introduction: 2) Northern Israel*).

Following his accusation, the prophet announced Jehoshaphat's sentence (19:2b-3). He first said that **the wrath of the LORD** was upon the king (19:2b). In other words, disasters would come to Jehoshaphat's kingdom. Yet, this harsh condemnation was mollified by the words that followed. God recognized **some good** in Jehoshaphat (19:3). A similar expression occurs in 12:12 where **some good** remained in Rehoboam's kingdom after Shishak's invasion (see also 10:7). The king of Judah was not a flagrant covenant breaker like his northern counterpart. For this reason, God's anger was not in full force against Judah.

This **good** in Jehoshaphat is described in two ways. First, he **rid the land of Asherah poles** (19:3). Here the Chronicler alluded to 17:6 where the king's devotion showed itself in extensive reforms. For the meaning of Asherah poles, see 2 Chr. 14:3-5. Second, Jehoshaphat had given his **heart to seeking God** (19:3). These words touch on two of the Chronicler's central concerns. Jehoshaphat served God from his **heart**. His devotion was not merely outward; it stemmed from deep within (see *Introduction: 16) Motivations*). Moreover, Jehoshaphat was **seeking God**. 'Seeking' God's help occurs five times in Jehoshaphat's reign (see 17:4; 18:4,6; 19:3; 20:3). As one who sought God from his heart, the king could expect to receive divine blessings even though troubles would come his way (see *Introduction: 19) Seeking*).

This event in Jehoshaphat's life had many implications for the post-exilic readers of Chronicles. Perhaps one of the most important lessons to be learned was its counterbalance to the Chronicler's encouragement toward an irenic attitude toward the North. Despite the need for the post-exilic community to expand its vision of Israel to include northern tribes, Jehoshaphat's experience taught that reunion must not be done in a manner that supports the wickedness of Judah's northern neighbors. Unity at the expense of covenant loyalty to God was unacceptable (see *Introduction: 2) Northern Israel*).

Beyond this, these events also provided a word of hope for those who had failed to remain faithful. Jehoshaphat was delivered from the consequences of serious failure by seeking God through prayer. The Chronicler's readers could take hope in their own experiences of failure that seeking God would deliver them from trouble as well.

Jehoshaphat's Later Years (19:4-20:30)
At this point the Chronicler turned to the second half of his record of Jehoshaphat's reign. His record includes other acts of fidelity (19:4-11) and a second battle (20:1-30).

Comparison of 19:4-20:30 with Kings
This entire section is without parallel in the book of Kings. The Chronicler added this material to balance the first half of Jehoshaphat's reign (see figure 35).

Later Fidelity (19:4-11)
The Chronicler began this portion with another record of the king's reforms. These changes also extended throughout his kingdom.

Structure of 19:4-11
This account divides into a title followed by two main sections (see figure 35). The Chronicler first gave a summary for the section (19:4). He then offered reports on Jehoshaphat's work outside Jerusalem (19:5-7) and within the vicinity of Jerusalem (19:8-11).

Jehoshaphat's Extensive Reforms (19:4)
Jehoshaphat began these reforms by going out **again among the people** (19:4). This expression does not necessarily imply that the king personally went about the country. In fact, the term **again** suggests that the Chronicler meant that the king sent representatives throughout the land as he had done beforehand (see 17:7).

The emphasis of this verse is on the extent of Jehoshaphat's influence. His efforts reached **from Beersheba to the hill country of Ephraim** (19:4). In his usual style, the Chronicler's geographical notice moved from the South to the North (see comments on 1 Chr. 21:2). The northward limits of this geographical designation fell far short of the traditional 'Dan' because Jehoshaphat only controlled those northern territories which were conquered earlier (see 13:4; 15:8). Nevertheless, the king's reforms extended to the limits of his kingdom including the northern territories (see *Introduction: 2) Northern Israel*).

The Chronicler reported that Jehoshaphat **turned** [his citizens] **back to the LORD** (19:4). Popular religious practices continued to be less than ideal during Jehoshaphat's reign (see 20:33), but at this point the king attempted to bring the entire population into conformity with the Law of God. Similar widespread reforms took place at other times (see *Introduction: 6) Royal Observance of Worship*).

Judicial Reforms Outside Jerusalem (19:5-7)
Having established the general topic of this section, the Chronicler proceeded to illustrate how Jehoshaphat tried to bring about reform. He dealt first with the king's actions **in each of the fortified cities of Judah** (19:5). This record deals first with the king's appointments (19:5) and then with his instructions (19:6-7).

Appointments Outside Jerusalem (19:5)
Jehoshaphat **appointed judges** throughout his kingdom (19:5). In patriarchal times, the heads of families and tribal elders performed the functions of judges. Under Moses' leadership, judges were selected from the tribes to make rulings in less complicated cases while leaving more difficult cases for Moses himself (see Exod. 18:13-26). In the days of the Judges, local authorities ruled in disputes (e.g. Deborah, Gideon). David and Solomon established local courts to hear cases (see 1 Chr. 23:4; 26:29). Jehoshaphat reordered the court system of Judah so the Law could be more effectively enforced in his times.

Instructions Outside Jerusalem (19:6-7)
The appointment of judges did not insure justice in Judah's courts. Bribery and deceit constantly plagued the judicial system of Judah and Israel. For this reason the Old Testament frequently warned judges and kings against accepting bribes and favoring the rich (see Exod. 23:6-8; Deut. 1:17; 16:18-20; Ps. 15:5; Prov. 17:23; Mic. 3:11; 7:3). Jehoshaphat was aware of this difficulty and appropriately charged his judges.

The king's instructions amount to two commands followed by explanations. First, the judges were to **consider carefully** their duties (19:6). The reason for this care is that they were not working **for man but for the LORD** (19:6). Jehoshaphat made it clear that these judges worked neither for him, nor for the nation. Moreover, God intended to be **with** them (19:6), giving them strength against all opposition (see *Introduction: 10) Divine Activity*). Their duty was a sacred service to God. For this reason, the king warned them that they must **fear the LORD** (19:7a).

Second, Jehoshaphat commanded his appointees to **judge carefully** (19:7b). His explanation of this order rested on the character of the God whom these judges served. God allowed **no injustice, partiality or bribery** in his judgments (19:7c). Here the king depended on long-standing Old Testament beliefs about the justice of the divine Judge (see Gen. 18:25; Exod. 18:16; Deut. 1:17; 10:17; Job 8:3; Pss. 9:16; 11:7; 89:14; 99:4). Jehoshaphat's judges were to reflect the character of the heavenly Judge whom they represented.

Judicial Reforms Within Jerusalem (19:8-11)
Having reported Jehoshaphat's national judicial reforms, the Chronicler narrowed his view to Jehoshaphat's reform efforts **in Jerusalem** (19:8). This material also contains judicial appointments followed by instructions.

Appointments Within Jerusalem (19:8)
The Chronicler noted that the king established **Levites, priests and heads of Israelite families** to serve as judges (19:8). It is likely that the same groups of appointees were to be understood in the preceding passage (see 19:5-7). Whatever the case, the parallel between these events and those of Jehoshaphat's earlier acts of obedience is evident (see 17:8-9). David and Solomon had both ordained Levitical

family members to serve as judges (see 1 Chr. 23:4; 2 Chr. 1:2). Jehoshaphat followed well-established precedents (see also Ezek. 44:24).

Instructions Within Jerusalem (19:9-11)

Once again, Jehoshaphat instructed his newly appointed judges. His instructions fell into four main categories. First, these men were to fulfill their tasks **faithfully and wholeheartedly in the fear of the LORD** (19:9). The Chronicler's ideal of sincerity and devotion from the heart was to characterize these men (see *Introduction: 16) Motivations*). Moreover, reverence for God is mentioned again as a central feature of the judges' service (see 19:7).

Second, in all their activities the judges were to warn the people **not to sin** (19:8). Upholding the Law of God was their principle task. Jehoshaphat explained that without the judges' instruction in the Law, **'wrath will come on you and your brothers'** (19:8). The king knew that only obedience to the Law would bring divine blessing. For this reason, he insisted that the Law be taught.

Third, Jehoshaphat established a hierarchy among the judges. **Amariah the chief priest** would have charge of **any matter concerning the LORD** (19:11). **Zebadiah ... the leader of the tribe of Judah** would have charge over **any matter concerning the king** (19:11). The Chronicler reported similar distinctions in one other place (see 1 Chr. 26:30,32). The precise differences between matters of the king and the Lord are not altogether clear. They do not correspond precisely to church/state divisions in contemporary nation-states because both spheres of authority were regarded as under the rule of Israel's religious beliefs. The difference appears to be between those matters related more directly to the temple and its services as opposed to matters more closely connected to Israel's statecraft. The fact that the Chronicler focused on this difference suggests that such matters may have been somewhat controversial in his day. In his view, both royal and priestly interests were to be maintained within legal arrangements of the post-exilic community.

Fourth, the king closed his instructions with an encouragement. He exhorted the judges to **act with courage** (19:11). Enforcing the Law of God would not be an easy task among a people prone to injustice and sin. He also hoped for blessings on those judges **who do well** (19:11). Divine rewards were in store for the judges who performed their tasks as they should.

Jehoshaphat's judicial reforms had many implications for the post-exilic readers of Chronicles. As they sought to rebuild the kingdom of Israel, Jehoshaphat's actions demonstrated the importance of re-establishing a judiciary throughout the land. Along these lines, Ezra was commissioned to return to Jerusalem precisely because he was an expert in the Law (Ezra 7:6,10). Jehoshaphat's actions exemplified the importance of the Law's enforcement in post-exilic Israel (see *Introduction: 14) Standards*).

Jehoshaphat's Later Battle (20:1-30)

The Chronicler added a second battle in the reign of Jehoshaphat which contrasts with his previous battle in 18:1-19:3 (see figure 35). Instead of forming an alliance to help the wicked (18:1-19:3), Jehoshaphat faced the challenge of war with complete fidelity to God.

Comparison of 20:1-30 with Kings

The Chronicler continued to add material which had no parallel in the book of Kings. These verses display a number of motifs characteristic of the Chronicler's theology.

Structure of 20:1-30

The story of Jehoshaphat's later battle forms a symmetrical seven step narrative (see figure 35). This passage begins with enemies attacking Jehoshaphat (20:1). In the end, however, the king enjoyed peace and rest (20:29-30). In response to the threat of enemies, Jehoshaphat held an assembly in Jerusalem (20:2-19); this material balances with the king's return to the city and the worshipful praise at that time (20:27-28). Judah's army marched into battle (20:20-21); the army collected plunder after battle (20:24-26). The turning point of the drama is God's intervention on Jehoshaphat's behalf (20:22-23).

Jehoshaphat's Enemies Attack (20:1)

This episode opens with a list of Jehoshaphat's enemies. They consisted of **Moabites**, **Ammonites**, and **Meunites** (20:1). The first two groups of people are well-known from Scripture and archaeology. The identity of the **Meunites**, however, is problematic. In the first place, the traditional Hebrew text of 2 Chr. 20:1 does not read 'Meunites'. Instead, it repeats 'Ammonites' twice. The reading of **Meunites** in the NIV is probably correct, but it stems from the Septuagint, the ancient Greek version of the Old Testament (see *Introduction: Translation and Transmission*). Later in this passage, these **Meunites** are identified as people **from Mount Seir** (20:23), a southwestern mountain range traditionally associated with the Edomites (see Gen. 36:8,9; Num. 24:18; Judg. 5:4; Ezek. 25:8; 35:15). Another related difficulty is the reading of the traditional Hebrew text in 20:2. There the attacking armies are said to come 'from Aram' (NAS, NKJ). Some modern translations assume that this reading is an error that entered through textual transmission and emend to read **Edom** (NRS, NIV). The words 'Edom' and 'Aram' look very similar at several stages in the development of Hebrew script (see *Introduction: Translation and Transmission*). In favor of the NIV emendation is the fact that Aram (Syria) is in the north, but these armies were from the southern regions of **Mount Seir** (20:23). Therefore, it is likely that the Chronicler's text originally read **Edom** (20:2). The Chronicler mentioned the **Meunites** two other times in his history, always in association with the southern regions near Edom (see 1 Chr. 4:41; 2 Chr. 26:7). It would appear, therefore, that Jehoshaphat was attacked by a coalition originating in the south and east.

Jehoshaphat Holds an Assembly in Jerusalem (20:2-19)
The Chronicler turned next to Jehoshaphat's actions in Jerusalem. In the overarching structure of this chapter, these verses balance with the king's return to Jerusalem and the assembly of praise (see 20:27-28; see figure 35).

Structure of 20:2-19
This section divides into two parts, each of which divides into three symmetrical steps (see figure 35). This portion of Jehoshaphat's fidelity in battle focuses on two events. First, Jehoshaphat called an assembly in response to the threat of his enemies (20:2-4). Second, the text reports the ceremony of the assembly (20:5-19). The Chronicler gave much attention to detail, showing how very interested he was in the specific actions taken by Jehoshaphat and the people of Judah.

Calling of the Assembly (20:2-4)
These verses describe the calling of Judahites to Jerusalem. In 20:5,14,26 this gathering is called an **assembly**. This terminology was the Chronicler's way of noting the sacred character of the meeting. Throughout his history he pointed to such religious assemblies as particularly important events. Each incident of an assembly displayed activities that the post-exilic community should have followed in its day (see *Introduction: 5) Religious Assemblies*).

Structure of 20:2-4
This material divides into three steps (see figure 35). Jehoshaphat realized his problem (20:2), called for an assembly (20:3), and the assembly convened to deal with the problem (20:4).

This assembly was initiated because Jehoshaphat heard about his enemies. His men told him that **a vast army** was approaching (20:2). In his usual fashion, the Chronicler prepared his readers for a great victory of God by describing the enormous size of Judah's enemies (see *Introduction: 23) Victory and Defeat*). In this chapter the enemies are described as a **vast army** four times (see 20:2,12,15,24). This massive army had come from beyond **the Sea** (i.e. the Dead Sea) and had reached **En Gedi**, a location halfway along the western shore of the Dead Sea (20:2). This route of approach was somewhat unusual and may have taken Jehoshaphat by surprise. Thus the Chronicler enhanced the emotional tension of the story.

The second step of this segment describes how Jehoshaphat was **alarmed** by his enemy's approach (20:3). To have such a large army so near by (approximately 25 miles southeast of Jerusalem) threatened Jehoshaphat. As a result, he **resolved to inquire of the LORD** (20:3). The Chronicler emphasized 'inquiring of' or 'seeking' God as necessary for those who wished to receive God's blessing (see *Introduction: 19) Seeking*). Jehoshaphat is praised a number of times for seeking God (see 17:4; 18:4,6; 19:3; 20:3). In this difficult situation Jehoshaphat did precisely what Solomon hoped his own readers would do in their troubles (see 7:14). He sought help from God.

Jehoshaphat **proclaimed a fast for all Judah** (20:3). The biblical record reports many fasts in connection with a time of war or other trouble (see 1 Sam. 7:6; Ezra 8:23; Neh. 1:4; Esth. 4:16; Isa. 58:6; Jer. 36:6; Dan. 9:3; Joel 1:14). Even so, Jehoshaphat is the only king in Chronicles who called a national fast. The Chronicler exalted Jehoshaphat by reporting his extraordinary religious devotion.

The third step of this segment was Judah's response to the king's call. The Chronicler already reported that the king invited **all Judah** to the fast (see 20:3). At this point, he made it very clear that the **people of Judah ... from every town** joined the king (20:4). This description fit well with the Chronicler's ideal of the unity of all Israel (see *Introduction: 1) All Israel*).

Beyond this, the Chronicler reported that the people came with a clear motivation. They assembled **to seek help from the LORD ... to seek him** (20:4). Not only did the Chronicler point to his frequent theme of divine help (see *Introduction: 10) Divine Activity*), he also repeated the motif of 'seeking'. Repeating this theme so near the similar description of Jehoshaphat (see 20:3) highlighted the exemplary character of this event. Jehoshaphat's assembly conformed to the conditions for blessing set forth to Solomon (see 7:14; see also *Introduction: 19) Seeking*).

Judah's response to Jehoshaphat modeled the kind of actions which were incumbent upon the post-exilic readers of Chronicles. As they faced hardships, they too should have joined together in fasting and seeking God.

Ceremony of the Assembly (20:5-19)

Having elucidated how Jehoshaphat called an assembly, the Chronicler continued with a focus on the ceremonies performed at the gathering (20:5-19).

Structure of 20:5-19

As the outline above indicates (see figure 35), this material divides into three parts: the prayer (20:5-13), the divine response (20:14-17), and the praise (20:18-19). The opening and closing sections of this material balance each other. The opening prayer (20:5-13) begins with the note that **Jehoshaphat stood up** (20:5); it ends with the fact that all the people attending also **stood there before the LORD** (20:13). The closing praise (20:18-19), however, notes that **Jehoshaphat bowed ... and all the people ... fell down in worship before the LORD** (20:18). The juxtaposition is evident and sets the boundaries for this material.

This passage reflects a common pattern in Israel's worship known as a liturgy of lament. It opens with a prayer of lament followed by a priestly/prophetic announcement of deliverance, and closes with a response of praise. This basic pattern appears many times in the Old Testament (see 1 Sam. 1:3-20; Joel 2) and lies behind a number of Psalms of lament (see Pss. 22, 44, 60, 74, 79, 83, 89).

Assembly Prays for Help (20:5-13)

The first step consists of Jehoshaphat's prayer (20:5-13). The king's prayer is introduced (20:5) and a closing remark follows it (20:13). The prayer itself contains the elements typical of laments. It divides into a recital of past blessings (20:6-7), a statement of innocence and trust (20:8-9), a complaint about trouble (20:10-11), and a petition (20:12).

Jehoshaphat's prayer took place **at the temple in front of the new courtyard** (20:5). This description oriented the readers to the prayer as an example of the temple's significance in the life of Israel. As Solomon prayed (see 6:14-42) and God promised (see 7:12-22), the temple served as the place of prayer in this time of trouble (see *Introduction: 17) Prayer*). This is the only appearance of the designation **the new courtyard** and its referent is not altogether clear. It is likely, however, that the Chronicler had in mind 'the large court' as opposed to the inner court of the priests (see 4:9; see also *Introduction: Appendix B – The Structures, Furnishings and Decorations of Solomon's Temple*).

Jehoshaphat began with praise for God's blessings in the past. His praise first affirmed that God was **'the God of our fathers'** (20:6). The king then immediately moved to a more general descriptive praise of God. He praised God because he is **in heaven** and therefore rules **over all the kingdoms of the nations** (20:6). God has such **power and might** that **no one can withstand** him (20:6). Jehoshaphat's words were very similar to the prayer of David (see 1 Chr. 29:11-12). Both prayers exalt God by focusing on his power over all kingdoms.

After a general description of God's supremacy, Jehoshaphat's praise narrowed to a particular demonstration of divine power that was relevant to his situation. He mentioned the conquest of Canaan (20:7). God used his power on behalf of his people at that time, and Jehoshaphat was about to call on him to do the same in his day. Moreover, the king urged that God gave the land of Canaan **forever to the descendants of Abraham** (20:7). Jehoshaphat's reference to the permanent bestowal of the land to Israel fit well with his situation. The approaching armies threatened Judah's possession of the land, but God had given it to them **forever**. The king intensified his perspective by describing Abraham as **your** (God's) **friend** (20:7). Only Isa. 41:8 refers to Abraham in this manner (see also Jas. 2:23). The intimate relationship between God and Abraham pointed to the importance of God protecting Judah's rights to the land of promise.

Jehoshaphat's praise not only suited his situation, but the post-exilic readers' circumstances as well. Just as Jehoshaphat hoped for deliverance because God had power over the kingdoms of the earth, the post-exilic community had to rely on divine power over the nations for security in its day. Moreover, the Chronicler held firmly that the patriarchal promise of the land applied to his day as well (For the Chronicler's geographical hopes, see comments on 1 Chr. 2:42-55.)

As is typical for prayers of lament, Jehoshaphat's opening praise was followed by a declaration of fidelity and trust (20:8-9). He mentioned that Israel had built **a sanctuary for** [God's] **Name** (20:8). The king referred to Solomon's construction of the temple. As Solomon declared in his dedicatory prayer (see 2 Chr. 6:18-20, 34, 38), the temple was built not for God himself, but for his **Name**. The Name of God is his accessibility, his invocable presence on earth (see *Introduction: 11)*

Name of God). Solomon built the temple in hope that God would bless the building as the place at which Israel could find help from God in the generations to come.

To draw this connection to Solomon more explicitly, Jehoshaphat paraphrased Solomon's dedicatory prayer in 20:9. Solomon demonstrated trust in God by asking God to hear prayers offered in the temple. Jehoshaphat alluded to 6:28,34, but he shaped his summary of Solomon's words to suit his own circumstances. Judah now faced the threat of war and appealed to Solomon's hopes in the temple as a basis for his petition.

Jehoshaphat's declaration of fidelity led to his complaint (20:10-11). In the Psalms of lament petitioners often complain about their personal suffering, their opponents, and their God. Here Jehoshaphat complained about the approaching armies. His complaint consisted of two main thoughts. First, he recalled how God did not **allow Israel to invade** the lands of **Ammon, Moab, and Mount Seir** in the days of Moses and Joshua (20:10; see 20:7). The armies of Israel **did not destroy them** as they could have (20:10). Jehoshaphat referred to the well-known events recorded in Num. 20:14-21 and Deut. 2:4-6,9,18-19.

Second, Jehoshaphat reflected on the fact that the people spared by God and Israel were **now repaying** [them] **by coming to drive** [them] **out** (20:11). Instead of reciprocating Israel's kindness, the Ammonites, Moabites, and Meunites attacked. They intended to drive Israel out of her **inheritance** (20:11). The terminology of **inheritance** is derived from Mosaic legal language which indicated a permanent bestowal of land from God (see Lev. 25:23-24; Deut. 11:8-12; 1 Kgs. 21:3; 1 Chr. 28:8). As Israel's King, God gave the land of Canaan to his people in perpetuity. (For the Chronicler's geographical hopes, see comments on 1 Chr. 2:42-55.) For this reason, when these enemies attacked Israel, they defied God himself. Jehoshaphat's complaint was not only designed to express his own frustration with the ingratitude of these nations, but also to incite divine wrath against them.

Jehoshaphat's prayer reached its high point in 20:12. Here he offered his petition and support for his request. Simply put, the king asked God to **judge them** (20:12). His request was in the form of a question fully expecting a positive response: **'Will you not judge?'** (20:12). Jehoshaphat felt he had every reason to believe God would destroy his enemies. He explained that his confidence rested on the fact that Israel had **no power to face this vast army** (20:12). As we have already seen, this battle narrative emphasizes the inadequacy of Judah's army (see 20:2). The superiority of Judah's enemies is a repeated theme in several of the Chronicler's battle narratives (see *Introduction: 23) Victory and Defeat*). In this case, however, the motif not only points to divine power as the source of victory. It also expresses Jehoshaphat's humble dependence on God. He and the Judahites did **not know what to do** except to **turn** [their] **eyes upon** God (20:12).

Just as the Chronicler described the setting of Jehoshaphat's prayer (20:5), he also closed the prayer with another look at the scene (20:13). This passage does not focus on the king, but on the people involved in the assembly. **All the men of Judah** stood with Jehoshaphat as he prayed (20:13). This fact highlighted another exemplary aspect of this event. All the people joined Jehoshaphat in prayer (see 20:3,4). The text states explicitly that **wives and children and little ones** were present as well (20:13). On a number of occasions the Chronicler mentioned the participation of women and children. His repeated references suggest that these segments of society were important aspects of his concept of the people of God. Although we can be sure that not every individual Judahite came to Jerusalem, the vast majority of the citizens of Judah attended the assembly (see *Introduction: 1) All Israel*).

Jehoshaphat's prayer was reported so that it spoke directly to the needs of the Chronicler's post-exilic readers. As we have already seen, this story portrays Jehoshaphat as a positive example. His prayer of lament was exemplary as well. His humility and dependence on God was precisely what the first readers of Chronicles needed to imitate. The attendance of all of Judah, including women and children, encouraged unity and widespread participation in such humility.

Assembly Receives Response (20:14-17)

As often happened in liturgies of lament, God responded to his people through an oracle. In this case, the response came through a Levite in the assembly. The Chronicler first described the scene of the oracle (20:14) and then summarized the message (20:15-17).

The messenger of God was **Jahaziel ... a Levite** (20:14). A number of times, the Chronicler mentioned that Levites served a prophetic function. (For the Chronicler's outlook on Levitical prophecy, see comments on 1 Chr. 25:1; see also *Introduction: 15) Prophets*.) **Jahaziel** stood in the assembly and **the Spirit of the LORD came upon** him (20:14). We do not know precisely how the special descent of the Spirit effected the human recipient. Perhaps some kind of ecstatic experience took place (see 1 Sam. 10:5-6, 9-10). In all cases where the Spirit of God came on people, his inspiration authorized their outlooks. Jahaziel did not speak on his own, but under the power of the Holy Spirit. (For a summary of the Chronicler's outlook on the Spirit, see comments on 1 Chr. 12:18.)

Jahaziel's message is typical of prophetic oracles of salvation given in response to laments (see Jer. 28:2-4; Isa. 43:1-4; 44:1-5). Even so, it is clear that the Chronicler reported Jahaziel's speech in such a way as to connect it closely with Deut. 20:2-4. In this passage, Moses ordered that priests were to assure the people of victory as they prepared to fight in the conquest of the land. Moses himself had done the same at the Red Sea (see Exod. 14:13-14). The Chronicler had already connected this battle with Israel's earlier conquest (see 20:7,10). By modeling Jahaziel's speech after Moses and his instructions, the Chronicler demonstrated that the battle in Jehoshaphat's day followed the pattern of the earlier ideal holy war battles of Israel.

Jahaziel's speech divides into three parts. After an introductory address (20:15a), he spoke a word of encouragement (20:15b). He then instructed Jehoshaphat and Judah on the battle plan (20:16-17a). This instruction is framed in by another encouragement (20:17b) which is very similar to the openings words (20:15b).

Jahaziel addressed **King Jehoshaphat and all who live in Judah and Jerusalem**

(20:15a). The word that followed was not just for the king's hearing. It was to be received by the assembly representing the entire nation of Judah (see 20:3,4,13; see *Introduction: 1) All Israel*).

Jahaziel began his speech with an exhortation for Judah not to be **afraid or discouraged** (20:15b). Similar language appears in the Mosaic passages of preparation for battle (see Exod. 14:13-14; Deut. 3:22; 7:17-19; 20:1-4; 31:6, 8; see also Josh. 1:9; 1 Chr. 22:13; 28:20; 2 Chr. 32:7). These words assured the listeners that they had nothing to fear.

The Levite continued with a reason for confidence: **'for the battle is not yours, but God's'** (20:15b). This motif points once again to the connection with Moses and his instructions for priests (see Exod. 14:13-14; Deut. 7:19-22; 20:2-4; see also 1 Sam. 17:47). In these passages as well, the reason for confidence is that God will fight on behalf of his people. The Chronicler expressed this theme on several other occasions (see *Introduction: 10) Divine Activity*). From his point of view, when God fought on behalf of Judah, victory was inevitable.

Instructions for Jehoshaphat and Judah followed the initial encouragement (20:16-17a). Judah's army must **march down against** the approaching enemies (20:16), but they **will not have to fight this battle** (20:17a). To one degree or another, every exemplary holy war battle in the Bible downplays the human factor and exalts the action of God. In this case, however, the passivity of the army of Judah is emphasized beyond normal. All Judah had to do was to **take up ... position** and **stand firm and see** (20:17a). Jehoshaphat and his army did not need to fight at all. The allusion to the crossing of the Red Sea is evident (see Exod. 14:13). There Israel simply watched God destroy the Egyptian army. In this battle, the army of Judah would do much the same (see 20:24).

Jahaziel closed his speech as he began it (see 20:15b). He exhorted the people not to be **afraid** or **discouraged** (20:17b). He supported his exhortation once again. This time, however, he simply said **'the LORD will be with you'** (20:17b). That God was 'with' his people was the same as saying he would lead them into battle (see *Introduction: 10) Divine Activity*).

Assembly Responds with Praise (20:18-19)

The Chronicler's account of Jehoshaphat's assembly closes with the reaction to Jahaziel's oracle (20:18-19). In effect, two things happen. First, there is humble bowing before God. The king **bowed with his face to the ground and all the people fell down** (20:18). Note once again that the participation included **all the people** (see *Introduction: 1) All Israel*). The act of bowing demonstrated the humility of the king and the entire assembly in response to the kindness of God.

Second, as with most laments in the Old Testament (for exceptions see Pss. 44 and 88), the oracle of salvation led to joyous praise. The people of Judah prepared to march into battle full of confidence and grateful praise to God. The Chronicler noted that some **Kohathites and Korahites stood up and praised the LORD** (20:19). The Chronicler identified these divisions of Levites a number of times in his history (see 1 Chr. 6:22-23, 33-38, 54-61, 66-70; 9:19, 31-32; 12:6; 15:5; 23:12-20; 26:1-19; 2 Chr. 29:12-14; 34:12-13). They honored God **with a very loud voice** (20:19). The enthusiasm of the musicians reflected the joyous celebration in the hearts of all who attended the assembly (see *Introduction: 8) Music*).

This scene of overwhelming joy expressed in song recalls a number of similar scenes throughout the Chronicler's history. The description of celebration before God was designed to inspire the post-exilic readers to emulate the attitudes and actions that led to these joyous results (see *Introduction: 27) Disappointment and Celebration*).

Jehoshaphat's Army Marches to Battle (20:20-21)

The next day Jehoshaphat led his army to meet the enemies (20:20-21). This report of departure divides into three simple scenes: the departure (20:20a), the exhortation (20:20b), and the marching order (20:21).

The Chronicler began this section by noting that the departure was **early in the morning** (20:20a). This temporal reference indicates that Jehoshaphat did precisely as he was commanded. Jahaziel had ordered him to leave **tomorrow** (20:16). As soon as tomorrow came, Jehoshaphat left for battle. Once again, Jehoshaphat's behavior was presented as exemplary (see Josh. 6:12; 8:10; 1 Sam. 17:20).

After noting when the army left, the Chronicler turned to Jehoshaphat's exhortation (20:20b). The king exhorted his army **as they set out** (20:20b). Speeches before battles take place on several occasions in Chronicles (see 1 Chr. 19:12-13; 2 Chr. 13:4-12; 25:7-9; 32:7-8). Jehoshaphat's speech divides into three parts noted by three imperatives: **listen ... have faith ... have faith** (20:20b).

Jehoshaphat gave these final instructions because the outcome of battle was still uncertain. As with many prophecies in the Old Testament, implicit conditions applied to the prophecy of victory. In this case, the Levite's instructions for battle formed an implicit condition which Judah still had to meet (see 20:16-17).

The language of the first sentence in Jehoshaphat's exhortation alludes to the speech of Jahaziel in 20:15-17. The Levite addressed the king and **all who live in Judah and Jerusalem** (20:15). Jehoshaphat spoke to **Judah and the people of Jerusalem** (20:20b). As he sent his people into battle, Jehoshaphat addressed the same people as the Levite before him.

The second sentence exhorts the people to **have faith in the LORD** (20:20b). Unlike Asa before him (see 16:1-9), Jehoshaphat relied entirely on God to give him this victory. As the king and his army went out to battle, Jehoshaphat wanted to make sure that his army met the condition of trusting God to fight for them. If they trusted God, they would **be upheld** (20:20b).

In much the same way, the third sentence of Jehoshaphat's exhortation tells the people to **have faith in his prophets** (20:20b). In all likelihood, the use of the plural referred not simply to Jahaziel who had just prophesied the day before (see 20:15-17), but to all of the Levites who confirmed the message of Jahaziel with their music and praise (see 20:19). They would soon lead the army into battle (see

20:21). Jehoshaphat insisted that his army follow the directions of the Levitical prophet(s). If they did so, they would **be successful** (20:20b).

Jehoshaphat's call to listen to the prophets fit with a motif that appears many times in Chronicles. On a number of occasions blessings and judgments occur as a result of reaction to prophets (see *Introduction: 15) Prophets*). Undoubtedly, this theme encouraged post-exilic Israelites to pay attention to the prophetic word in their day.

After exhorting the people, Jehoshaphat arranged the army in marching formation (20:21). The Chronicler noted, however, that Jehoshaphat did not act until **after consulting with the people** (20:21). By doing so, the Chronicler drew attention to the importance of leadership making decisions with the consensus of the people. (For the Chronicler's use of this motif, see comments on 1 Chr. 13:1.) The Chronicler's repetition of this theme may have been motivated by political realities in his day.

Jehoshaphat then **appointed men to sing to the LORD** (20:21). It seems most likely that these appointments were from within the Levitical musical clans. They sang a psalm that the Chronicler elsewhere attributed to the Levitical singers (see 5:13). These Levitical musicians went forward **at the head of the army** (20:21). In yet another way, the Chronicler emphasized Jehoshaphat's exemplary actions. Here he made it clear that the king followed the marching directives of Moses by putting Levites at the head of the army (see Num. 10:33-35).

Levitical music played an important role in the holy wars of Israel (see *Introduction: 8) Music*). Priests and Levites often led into battle with music (e.g. Josh. 6:4-20; 2 Chr. 13:11-12). This feature of Israelite warfare should be understood in light of its symbolic nature. Israel's army was only an earthly reflection of the great army of heaven led by God himself (see Deut. 33:2-5, 26-29; Josh. 5:13-15; Judg. 5; Ps. 68:8-13; 2 Kgs. 6:15-19; 7:6; Isa. 13:1-13; Joel 3:9-12; Hab. 3). As such, the work of Israel's musicians corresponded to the spiritual, heavenly music that accompanied the appearance of God in battle. His march into battle was marked by the blast of a heavenly trumpet (see Exod. 19:16,19; Isa. 18:3; 27:13; Amos 2:2; Zeph. 1:14-16; Zech. 9:14; Matt. 24:31; 1 Cor. 15:52; Rev. 8–9; 10:7; 11:15). The music of Israel's earthly army symbolised that heavenly reality.

God Intervenes for Jehoshaphat

With Judah moving toward her approaching enemies, the Chronicler came to the turning point of his story: divine intervention (20:22-23). The record consists of a summary of the event (verse 22) which is followed by more details (verse 23).

The Chronicler set the time for divine intervention as the beginning of singing (20:22). This chronological reference indicated that the defeat of Judah's enemies occurred before Jehoshaphat even reached the site. By this means the Chronicler stressed the supernatural character of the event.

The Chronicler simply stated that **the LORD set ambushes** (20:22). The chronological reference at the beginning of the verse rules out a Judean ambush. For this reason, some interpreters have suggested that the Chronicler meant that a small contingent from one of the opposing armies began setting ambushes. This point of view cannot be ruled out (see 20:23). On the other hand, the Chronicler may have meant that the heavenly army of God ambushed the enemies of Judah. Elsewhere in the Old Testament the army of heaven moves ahead of the army of Israel (see 2 Sam. 5:24; 2 Kgs. 7:5-7; 19:35; Isa. 13:4; Ezek. 1:24). The Chronicler's understanding of this event was probably along these lines (see *Introduction: 10) Divine Activity*). In all events, the enemies of Judah **were defeated** by God (20:22).

After attributing the defeat of Jehoshaphat's enemies to God's intervention, the Chronicler explained how the defeat took place in two steps (20:23). The armies of **Ammon and Moab rose up** against the Meunites (verse 23a). Then, **after slaughtering the men of Seir** (the Meunites), the Ammonites and the Moabites turned on each other (verse 23b). God caused confusion among the enemies of his people so that they actually destroy themselves. An enemy's self-defeat appears frequently in the Old Testament and depicts one way in which supernatural intervention is recognized (see Judg. 7:22; 1 Sam. 14:20; 2 Kgs. 3:23; Ezek. 38:21; Hag. 2:22; Zech. 14:13). When enemies become so confused that they destroy themselves, it demonstrates that God was behind their defeat. The Chronicler described these events in this manner to make it clear to his readers that God had intervened on behalf of Jehoshaphat (see *Introduction: 10) Divine Activity*).

In a political environment that held threats on every side, post-exilic Israel needed God to intervene for them as well. Through Jehoshaphat's example, the Chronicler taught his readers how this kind of divine help was possible in their day.

Jehoshaphat's Army Gathers Plunder (20:24-26)

In balance with the marching of Judah's army into battle (20:20-21; see figure 35), the Chronicler described the aftermath of divine intervention (20:24-26). This portion divides into three scenes: the arrival of the army (verse 24), the collection of plunder (verse 25), and praise on the battlefield (verse 26).

Once again, the Chronicler stressed the passivity of Judah's army (20:24). When the army came to the place of battle, they looked toward **the vast army** (20:2,12,15). Yet, the preceding divine intervention was so complete that **they saw only dead bodies**; ... **no one had escaped** (20:24). The Chronicler recorded a number of battles in which the people of God were victorious (see *Introduction: 23) Victory and Defeat*). Yet, at no other place did he depict the defeat of Israel's enemies in such categorical terms. Not only did Judah's army have nothing to do with the battle; the entire opposing force was destroyed.

Moreover, the Chronicler increased his readers' astonishment at Judah's victory by describing the plunder of battle (20:25). The army of Judah found **a great amount** ... **more than they could take away**. In fact, **it took three days to collect it** (20:25). The plunder of this battle is greater than any other battle in Chronicles. The Chronicler wanted his post-exilic readers to look with amazement at Jehoshaphat's victory.

After three days of collecting plunder, the Judahites assembled and **praised the LORD** (20:26). The place of this praise was **the Valley of Beracah** (20:26). **Beracah** derives from a Hebrew word often translated 'praise'. The Judahites had no doubt as to who deserved credit for the defeat of these enemies. God had won a great victory for his people.

The Chronicler also added the note that the name of **Beracah** was used even **to this day** (20:26). Here he referred to the days of his post-exilic readers to draw a connection between these events and their own times. For a fuller discussion of his use of this terminology see the comments on 1 Chr. 4:41.

The spectacular victory experienced in Jehoshaphat's day certainly encouraged the Chronicler's readers to take Jehoshaphat's example to heart. Tremendous victories could be theirs as well.

Jehoshaphat Returns and Holds an Assembly (20:27-28)

In balance with Jehoshaphat's earlier assembly of fasting (20:2-19; see figure 35), the Chronicler depicted another assembly in Jerusalem (20:27-28). In this case, however, the mood is very positive; here the Chronicler continued his focus on the joy resulting from Judah's victory. Although the term 'assembly' does not appear in this passage, it is clear that this gathering was a religious assembly because it took place at **the temple of the LORD** (20:28). As such, the actions here also contribute to the Chronicler's emphasis on the importance of religious assemblies in Israel's history (see *Introduction: 5) Religious Assemblies*).

Jehoshaphat led the army back to Jerusalem. They **returned joyfully ... for the LORD had given them cause to rejoice** (20:27). Instead of fear which characterized the initiation of Jehoshaphat's first assembly (20:2-3), the Judahites were full of joy because of God's intervention (see *Introduction: 27) Disappointment and Celebration*). Their victory parade reached Jerusalem and **went to the temple of the LORD with harps and lutes and trumpets** (20:28). This passage demonstrates the Chronicler's continuing interest in the music of worship (see *Introduction: 8) Music*). As in many other passages, the splendor of Judah's joyful experience is described as a time of playing many musical instruments. The music of this scene recalls the musical response to the oracle of Jahaziel (see 20:19). Liturgically, it may be seen as an extension of that earlier praise. Now that victory had come, the people of Judah returned to the temple to honor God for fighting on their behalf. A number of psalms probably represent the kind of songs employed at times of victory celebration (see Pss. 24, 68, 118, 136). In these psalms, God was celebrated as the incomparable Divine Warrior.

The Chronicler filled this story with the wonder of Judah's praise not only to instruct his readers, but to give them positive motivation for imitating the ways of Jehoshaphat in this narrative. If they desired to experience this kind of joy, they had to follow the example of Jehoshaphat (see *Introduction: 27) Disappointment and Celebration*).

Jehoshaphat Has Peace and Rest (20:29-30)

Jehoshaphat's second battle closes with a hopeful report. In contrast to the beginning of this story (20:1; see figure 35), Judah was no longer threatened by foreign powers. The nations around Judah **heard how the LORD had fought against the enemies of Israel**. Word spread far and wide that Judah had victory over her innumerable foes. As a result, **the fear of God came upon all the kingdoms** (20:29). The Chronicler spoke of the nations fearing God and Judah on several occasions (see *Introduction: 3) International Relations*).

In this passage, the fear of God over the nations resulted in **peace** and **rest on every side** (20:30). The terms rest and peace imply military security and economic prosperity. A number of times Chronicles indicates that the people of God received these blessings from God as reward for their fidelity (see *Introduction: 23) Victory and Defeat*).

The Chronicler's outlook becomes clear when we remember that the same motif appears earlier in Jehoshaphat's reign. Because of Jehoshaphat's fidelity to God, the nations feared God and they did not make war with Judah (see 17:10). By ending this narrative with the same motif, the Chronicler held out a great hope to his post-exilic readers. Jehoshaphat had failed to be loyal to God in his alliance with Ahab and was condemned to the wrath of God (see 19:2). Nevertheless, all was not lost for Jehoshaphat. After his failure, he served God faithfully (see 19:4-11) and was exemplary in battle (see 20:1-30). As a result, he received another portion of peace and rest later in his reign. The Chronicler's readers could take hope from this series of events. Although they had failed God, all hope was not lost for them.

Closure of Jehoshaphat's Reign (20:31-21:3)

The Chronicler closed his record of Jehoshaphat's reign with a summary of his life, a brief narrative, and reports of his death and successor. This material reminds the readers that Jehoshaphat's reign was a mixture of infidelity and fidelity.

Comparison of 20:31-21:3 with 1 Kgs. 22:41-50

Much of this material stems from the book of Kings. The following comparison indicates a number of variations (see figure 36).

As the comparison above indicates, a number of typical changes are evident. First, the Chronicler omitted the synchronization with the North as he normally did (20:31a // 1 Kgs. 22:41). Second, he shifted attention to the prophetic records of Jehoshaphat's reign as he did elsewhere (20:34 // 1 Kgs. 22:45; see *Introduction: 15) Prophets*). Third, once again the mention of male cultic prostitution is omitted (1 Kgs. 22:46).

An important shift takes place in the notice that 'the people continued to offer sacrifices and burn incense' (1 Kgs. 22:43). The Chronicler turned attention away from the acts themselves to indicate the source of the problem: **the people still had not set their hearts on the God of their fathers** (20:33).

2 Chr.		1 Kgs.
20:31a	Synchronization with North (abbreviated)	22:41
20:31b-33	Summation (closely parallel)	22:42-43
20:34	Records of Jehoshaphat (loosely parallel)	22:45
———	Male Prostitution (omitted)	22:46
20:35-37	Maritime Venture (expanded)	22:44,48-49
21:1	Closure of Reign (closely parallel)	22:50
21:2-3	Jehoram's Brothers (added)	———

Comparison of 2 Chr. 20:31-21:3 with 1 Kgs. 22:41-50 (figure 36)

The most significant variation in this passage appears in the expansion of Jehoshaphat's maritime venture (20:35-37 // 1 Kgs. 22:44, 48-49). The Chronicler added that Jehoshaphat entered an alliance with the Israelite king Ahaziah (20:35). He also added a prophetic rebuke directed toward Jehoshaphat because of his alliance and indicated divine judgment destroyed the king's ships (20:37). These themes fit well with the Chronicler's opposition to alliances with the North (see *Introduction: 2) Northern Israel*) and with the important role prophets played in his history (see *Introduction: 15) Prophets*).

Structure of 20:31-21:3

As a result of his changes, the Chronicler's ending to Jehoshaphat's reign divides into three parts (see figure 35). A summation of Jehoshaphat's reign (20:31-34) is followed by an expanded record of the king's maritime alliance (20:35-37). It is difficult to understand why the Chronicler chose to introduce this story among the final notices of Jehoshaphat's life. It may be that he wanted to leave the symmetry of the main portion of the king's reign intact. Whatever the motivation, this story forms an afterword to the main account of Jehoshaphat's reign. The third element in this section is a typical record of the king's death and burial (21:1-3).

Summary of Jehoshaphat's Reign (20:31-34)

In his usual fashion, the Chronicler summarized Jehoshaphat's reign by noting a number of facts about the king. He recorded that the king ruled **twenty-five years** (20:31). The book of Kings reports 'twenty-two years' (2 Kgs. 3:1; 8:16). In all likelihood, the Chronicler included three years of co-regency with Asa during his severe foot disease (16:10-14).

The Chronicler's summary of Jehoshaphat's reign compares him with Asa (20:32-33). Both kings **did what was right in the eyes of the LORD** (20:32 // 1

Kgs. 22:43). The Chronicler's record of the king includes times of obedience and disobedience. Positive evaluations were not withheld from kings who had serious failings. On the whole the Chronicler wanted his readers to evaluate both kings positively.

20:33, however, raises two negative considerations. The Chronicler noted that **the high places, however, were not removed**. Like Asa (see 14:3, 5; 15:17), Jehoshaphat both removed and did not remove high places (17:6; 20:33). Apparently, Jehoshaphat was not entirely consistent in this matter throughout his reign. Nevertheless, the Chronicler also indicated that the resilience of worship at the high places was not due to the king himself, but to the people. As we have seen, the book of Kings reads at this point that 'the people continued to offer sacrifices and burn incense there' (1 Kgs. 22:43). The Chronicler substituted his own characteristic concern with wholehearted devotion. He noted that **the people still had not set their hearts on the God of their fathers** (20:33). Although Jehoshaphat served God from his heart (see 19:3), the lack of inward devotion among the people caused trouble in the future. Here the Chronicler focused on the heart motivations of the people as he did in many other passages (see *Introduction: 16) Motivations*).

The Chronicler closed his summary of Jehoshaphat's reign by adding that more information appeared in **the annals of Jehu son of Hanani** which are themselves in the larger work of **the book of the kings of Israel** (20:34). The reference here is not to the canonical book of Kings. Jehu only appears in 1 Kgs. 16:1, 7, 12 which hardly constitute **annals of Jehu** (20:34). In his typical fashion, the Chronicler indicates his keen interest in the prophetic records of Judah's kings (see *Introduction: 15) Prophets*).

Jehoshaphat's Maritime Alliance (20:35-37)

As noted above, the record of 1 Kgs. 22:47-50 has been transformed into a story of alliance with the North. This change drew attention to a theme already mentioned in the king's reign. Earlier Jehoshaphat allied himself with Ahab and received a sharp prophetic rebuke (19:1-3). At this point, the text indicates that Jehoshaphat fell into the same problem again.

Structure of 20:35-37

This brief narrative divides into three steps (see figure 35). Jehoshaphat began to build with Ahaziah (20:35-36a). A prophet condemned the action (20:36b-37a). Jehoshaphat's plans were spoiled in fulfillment of the prophetic word (20:37b).

Jehoshaphat Builds Ships with Ahaziah (20:35-36a)

The first step of this episode describes how Jehoshaphat constructed **a fleet of trading ships** (20:36a). This action in itself was acceptable, if not admirable. The ideal king Solomon had established an extensive maritime trade system (see 8:17-18).

Nevertheless, he accomplished this end by making **an alliance with Ahaziah king of Israel** (20:35). Solomon had cooperated with Hiram in his ventures into sea trade (see 8:17-18). It would appear that the Chronicler did not consider cooperation with other nations in such efforts as infidelity (see *Introduction: 3) International Relations*). Jehoshaphat's error was that he allied himself with a Northern Israelite king **who was guilty of wickedness** (20:35). A similar rebuke came to Jehoshaphat earlier for his alliance with Ahab (see 19:1-3). Northern Israel was in rebellion against God and consequently alliances were forbidden (see *Introduction: 2) Northern Israel*).

Prophetic Condemnation (20:36b-37a)
As it happened earlier in Jehoshaphat's reign (see 19:1-3), a prophet appeared to rebuke the king for his infidelity. **Eliezer son of Dodavahu** is otherwise unknown (20:37a), but his message followed the standard form of an oracle of judgment. He first brought an accusation: the king had **made an alliance with Ahaziah** (20:37a). As the reigns following Jehoshaphat will illustrate, this practice proved to have severe consequences for Judah in future generations (see 21:1–24:27; see also *Introduction: 2) Northern Israel*). The prophet then followed his accusation with a sentencing: **the LORD will destroy what you have made** (20:37a). The judgment was appropriate for the sin.

Jehoshaphat's Ships are Destroyed (20:37b)
In contrasting balance with the king's initial plan, the Chronicler ended this scenario by adding that the prophetic word was fulfilled. Jehoshaphat's ships **were wrecked and were not able to set sail to trade** (20:37b). The king's dependence on the wicked instead of God proved to have serious consequences. The implications for the post-exilic readers were evident. Disaster comes to those who turn to the wicked of the North for help. Trust in God is the way of success for Judah.

Jehoshaphat's Death, Burial, and Successor (21:1-3)
Having finished his version of Jehoshaphat's failed attempt to establish sea trade, the Chronicler returned to following the text of 1 Kgs. 22:50 very closely. He noted that Jehoshaphat was succeeded by his son Jehoram.

Following this straightforward notice of succession, the Chronicler added an historical report explaining how Jehoshaphat had prepared the way for his son. Jehoshaphat had treated all of his sons well. He **had given them many gifts** … **as well as fortified cities** (21:3). Yet, Jehoram received **the kingdom** … **because he was the firstborn son** (21:3). It is difficult to determine if the Chronicler praised Jehoshaphat for his actions. They certainly provided for a smooth transition of power. Yet, it may also have been the case that the choice of Jehoram was simply due to his firstborn status. In other words, Jehoshaphat may not have considered the character of sons as he made his choice of successor. As we will see, Jehoram proved to be the cause of many troubles for Judah. The Chronicler may have been suggesting that Jehoshaphat's choice was the cause of this turn for the worse. In all events, Jehoshaphat's reign came to an end and his son Jehoram took the throne of Judah.

Corruption through Northern Influence (21:4-24:27)

The second portion of the Divided Kingdom covers the reigns of Jehoram (21:4-21:20), Ahaziah (22:1-9), Athaliah (22:10-23:21), and Joash (24:1-27). Each of these records displays a variety of motifs which the Chronicler designed to direct his readers toward the restoration of the kingdom in the post-exilic period. Yet, this material primarily holds together around the central theme of the northern Israelite corruption of Judah. Jehoshaphat's reign has already anticipated the problem of close association with wicked Northerners (see 19:1-3; 20;35-37). At this point, however, this motif dominates the history. Jehoram **walked in the ways of the kings of Israel, as the house of Ahab had done, for he married a daughter of Ahab** (21:6). This **daughter of Ahab** was none other than Athaliah whose presence is felt throughout this section. Ahaziah **too walked in the ways of the house of Ahab, for his mother encouraged him in doing wrong** (22:3). The record then moves to Athaliah herself and the trouble she caused the house of David, including her opposition to king Joash whose reign ends in corruption (22:10-24:27). Put simply, the Chronicler focused in this material on the corruption that came to Judah because of alliance with wicked persons from northern Israel. By doing so, he warned his post-exilic readers against the dangers of compromising fidelity to the Lord for relationship with those among the northern tribes who rebelled against God even in his own day (see *Introduction: 2) Northern Israel*).

The Reign of Jehoram (21:4-22:1)

The Chronicler continued his account of the kings of Judah with an expanded record of Jehoram's reign (853-841 BC). The Chronicler presented a one-sided outlook on the king. Without exception, Jehoram behaved in ways that brought the judgment of God against him. As such, he illustrated what outcome lies ahead for those who relentlessly turned away from God.

Comparison of 21:4-22:1 with 2 Kgs. 8:17-25

The Chronicler's account of Jehoram's life loosely parallels the record of Kings (see figure 37).

2 Chr.		1-2 Kgs.
——	Events in Northern Israel (omitted)	1 Kgs. 22:51-2 Kgs. 8:16
21:4-11	Jehoram's Sins (slightly expanded)	8:17-22
21:12-17	Jehoram's Condemnation (added)	——
21:18-22:1	Jehoram's Sickness and Death (greatly expanded)	8:23-25

Comparison of 2 Chr. 21:4-22:1 and 1 Kgs. 22:51-2 Kgs. 8:25 (figure 37)

A number of other changes appear, but are of little significance. For instance, Kings consistently uses the name 'Joram'. An alternative form of 'Jehoram' appears in Chronicles. In addition to this, a number of more specific variations deserve comment.

First, the most obvious contrast between Kings and Chronicles is the large omissions of 1 Kgs. 22:51–2 Kgs. 8:16. For the most part, this material was not important to the Chronicler because it focuses on events in the northern kingdom. The Chronicler typically focused on the southern kingdom of Judah and touched on the North only when events there were closely tied to events in the South (see *Introduction: 2) Northern Israel*).

Second, at the end of Jehoshaphat's reign the Chronicler added a list of Jehoshaphat's many children to exalt him as one blessed by God (see 21:2-3). At the beginning of Jehoram's reign, the Chronicler reported that Jehoram murdered his brothers to secure his power over the kingdom of Judah (21:4). This beginning for the king's reign replaces the innocuous report in 2 Kgs. 8:16 and immediately cast the king's entire reign in a negative light.

Third, the Chronicler slightly shifted the language of 2 Kgs. 8:19 (// 21:7). 2 Kings 8:19 reads that God 'was not willing to destroy Judah'. The Chronicler, however, wrote that God **was not willing to destroy the house of David** (21:7). This variation focuses on God's commitment to the continuation of the Davidic line, one of the Chronicler's central themes.

Fourth, 21:10 (// 2 Kgs. 8:22) adds an explanatory clause that Libnah rebelled **because Jehoram had forsaken the LORD, the God of his fathers**. By this means the Chronicler pointed to one manner in which Jehoram's reign illustrated his views on divine judgment and blessing.

Fifth, the Chronicler inserted 21:11-20 into the reign of Jehoram. This material mentions a number of the king's serious sins, Elijah's letter to him, further rebellion, and the king's severe suffering and death. This addition contributed significantly to the negative assessment of Jehoram.

Sixth, Chronicles omits the reference in Kings to literary sources for the king's activities (2 Kgs. 8:23). This omission was probably designed to disparage the king by ignoring his official records (see *Introduction: Historical and Theological Purposes*).

Seventh, the book of Kings refers to the fact that Jehoram 'slept with his fathers and was buried with his fathers' (2 Kgs. 8:24). The Chronicler simply noted that **they buried him** (21:20). Moreover, he commented that Jehoram's burial was **not in the tombs of the kings** (21:20). Once again, the Chronicler's negative outlook is evident.

Eighth, 2 Kgs. 8:24b-25 notes the succession of Ahaziah in very simple terms. The Chronicler, however, explained a number of details related to his succession. 1) **The people of Jerusalem**, not Jehoram, appointed Ahaziah as king (22:1). Jehoram's kingdom was in such disarray that the people had to resolve the matter. 2) The Chronicler reminded his readers why Ahaziah succeeded Jehoram. It was because **the raiders, who came with the Arabs had killed all the older sons** (22:1b). The allusion to 22:17 is evident. In a word, Judah made Ahaziah king because there was no other choice. These additions continue the focus on divine judgment against Jehoram.

Structure of 21:4-22:1

The Chronicler's version of Jehoram's reign forms a symmetrical pattern of five sections (see figure 38).

■ Opening of Jehoram's Reign (21:4-7)
 ♦ Rebellion against Jehoram (21:8-11)
  • Rebellion of Edom (21:8-10a)
   Edom Begins Rebellion (21:8)
    Jehoram Attacks (21:9a)
     Edom Surrounds Jehoram (21:9b)
    Jehoram Escapes (21:9:c)
   Edom Remains in Rebellion (21:10a)

  • Rebellion of Libnah (21:10b-11)
   Libnah Begins Rebellion (21:10b)
   Explanation of Rebellion (21:11)

    ♦ Elijah's Condemnation of Jehoram (21:12-15)

 ♦ More Rebellions against Jehoram (21:16-17)
  Rebellions Stir (21:16)
   Rebels Attack Judah (21:17a)
  Rebellions End (21:17b)
■ Closure of Jehoram's Reign (21:18-21:1)

Outline of 2 Chr. 21:4-22:1 (figure 38)

The symmetry of this passage is apparent. First, the opening (21:4-7) and closing (21:18-22:1) sections are drawn together by the repetition of a chronological note. Both 21:5 and 21:20 mention the age of the king when he began to reign and the length of his enthronement. Second, the rebellions of Edom and Libnah (21:8-11) are balanced by the rebellions of Philistines and Arabs (21:16-17). Third, Elijah's letter to Jehoram (21:12-15) forms a turning point in the reign because it looks back to the king's preceding sins (21:12-13) and anticipates the punishment that will come against the king (21:14-15).

Opening of Jehoram's Reign (21:4-7)

The Chronicler began his record of Jehoram's reign with his own addition to Kings. He focused on the time when Jehoram **established himself** (21:4). Consolidating strength was an important goal for every king. It marked control and power over opponents. The Chronicler used similar terminology a number of times. For the significance of this terminology, see 1 Chr. 1:1.

When Jehoram **established himself** it was not during a period of fidelity. Jehoram rose to power by putting **all his brothers to the sword along with some of the princes of Israel** (21:4). According to 21:2, Jehoram was the firstborn of six brothers. The Chronicler did not explain why Jehoram killed his brothers. In light of the divine condemnation that follows, it is unlikely that his actions were justifiable. It seems much more likely that he ruthlessly murdered his brothers to eliminate any competition for the throne (see Judg. 9:56; 2 Kgs. 10:11). In many respects, this report of Jehoram's fratricide seems to be out of place. It would appear much more in line with the Chronicler's usual approach first to provide a chronological framework (21:5-7) and then move to Jehoram's crimes (21:4). Nevertheless, with this unusually abrupt opening, he immediately led his readers to conclude that Jehoram was a terribly wicked king.

The Chronicler turned to the record of Kings to give a more general description of Jehoram's reign (21:5-7 // 2 Kgs. 8:17-19). He first noted the king's age and the length of his time on the throne (21:5). These facts appear again at the end of the Chronicler's account (see 21:20). From other chronological notices related to Jehoram (see 2 Kgs. 1:17; 3:1; 8:16), it seems best to conclude that Jehoram was coregent with Jehoshaphat for at least four years.

This chronological framework leads to an evaluation of the king's reign which is also largely taken from Kings (21:6-7 // 2 Kgs. 8:18-19). The text compares Jehoram with **the kings of Israel** and specifically with **the house of Ahab** (21:6). The books of Kings and Chronicles compare other kings of Judah with northern Israelite kings (see 2 Kgs. 16:3) and with Ahab specifically (see 2 Kgs. 8:27; 21:3) to indicate how evil some Judahite kings had become (see 2 Chr. 21:6,13; 22:4; 28:2-4; see also *Introduction: 2) Northern Israel*). The point of comparison here and elsewhere is primarily religious syncretism. The connection with Ahab is made even more direct because Jehoram **married a daughter of Ahab** (21:6). Jehoram sought a marriage alliance with the North like his father Jehoshaphat (see 18:1). We learn later that the name of Ahab's daughter was Athaliah. She influenced Jehoram toward evil as she did her son (see 22:3).

The Chronicler summarized Jehoram's activities as **evil in the eyes of the LORD** (21:6b). Nevertheless, God did not destroy Judah as would be expected from the Chronicler's doctrine of blessing and judgment (see *Introduction: 10-28) Divine Blessing and Judgment*). As noted above, 2 Kgs. 8:19 reads that God 'was not willing to destroy Judah'. The Chronicler, however, explained that God **was not willing to destroy the house of David** (21:7). This shift drew attention to the Chronicler's insistence that the dynasty of David was an essential part of the kingdom of Israel, even in the post-exilic period (see *Introduction: 4-9) King and Temple*). The reason for God's actions is plainly stated. God refused to destroy the Davidic line **because of the covenant the LORD had made with David** (21:7). The Davidic covenant established David's family as the permanent dynasty over Israel (see 2 Sam. 7; Pss. 89; 132).

The promise to David is described as God's determination **to maintain a lamp for him and his descendants forever** (21:7). These words recall God's word to David in 1 Chr. 17:4-14 (// 2 Sam. 7:5-16). There David received assurances from the prophet Nathan that no matter how sinful his descendants became, God would not utterly destroy his royal line. Instead, God promised to keep a **lamp** for David (21:7). The translation of the word **lamp** is problematic. The Hebrew term is normally translated in this manner, but it is possible in this case to render it as 'fief' or 'dominion'. 1 Kgs. 11:36 supports this interpretation. Moreover, the immediately following context also supports this translation as it focuses on territorial losses for the house of David (see 21:8-11, 16-17). In the least, **lamp** is a metaphor for the continuing hope that the house of David would not lose all of its land.

From the Chronicler's perspective the only reason the throne of Judah was not utterly destroyed during Jehoram's reign was divine favor toward David. In other words, Jehoram did nothing to forestall the anger of God. He deserved severe punishment, but God's love for David mollified the divine response to his sins.

Rebellions against Jehoram (21:8-11)

Having established Jehoram as unfaithful and disobedient, the Chronicler reported two rebellions that took place during the reign of Jehoram. For the most part, this material comes from 2 Kgs. 8:20-22.

Structure of 21:8-11

This portion of Jehoram's reign divides into two episodes which describe rebellions against Jehoram (see figure 38). The rebellion of Edom falls into a five step symmetrical narrative (21:8-10a). The rebellion of Libnah amounts to a simple report (21:10b) followed by a brief explanation (21:11).

Rebellion of Edom (21:8-10a)

The rebellion of Edom began when Edom **set up its own king** (21:8). For a summary of Judah's involvement with Edom see comments on 2 Chr. 25:5a.

The middle portion of this story moves quickly. Jehoram sent **all his chariots** (verse 9a). In response, the Edomites **surrounded him and his chariot commanders** (verse 9b). Jehoram barely escaped with his life **by night** (verse 9c). As a result, Jehoram was unable to overcome the rebellion of Edom (verse 10a).

The Chronicler closed with the observation that the Edomites remained separated from Judah **to this day** (verse 10a). The meaning of the expression 'to this day' varies from passage to passage in Chronicles. (For the Chronicler's use of this terminology, see 1 Chr. 4:41.) In this passage, the Chronicler adopted the language of Kings (// 2 Kgs. 8:22) and extended the significance of **this day** to reach to the post-exilic period. This passage explained why Judah continued to be weak in relation to her neighboring Edomites. Jehoram's infidelity led to enduring results.

Rebellion of Libnah (21:10b-11)

The Chronicler followed 2 Kgs. 8:22b and reported that **Libnah revolted at the same time** (verse 10b). Libnah was probably located westward in the Philistine plain. If this geographical identification is correct, then Jehoram faced enemies on the east (Edom) and west (Libnah). Conflicts on both fronts demonstrated how severely God judged Jehoram.

As noted above, the Chronicler explained the reason for this punishment (verses 10b-11). It was **because Jehoram had forsaken the LORD** (verse 10b). These words do not appear in 2 Kgs. 8:22 and express the Chronicler's repeated concept of 'forsaking' covenant fidelity. Jehoram had seriously violated the Law of God and deserved God's judgment (see *Introduction: 22) Abandoning/Forsaking*).

The Chronicler continued his addition by specifying Jehoram's sins. He **built high places** (21:11). Contrary to his fathers who tore down high places (see 14:3, 5; 17:6; but see 15:17; 20:33), Jehoram erected these syncretistic worship sites (see 28:25; 33:3). Moreover, Jehoram also **caused the people of Jerusalem to prostitute themselves ... and led Judah astray** (21:11). The terminology of prostitution refers to the practice of idolatry (see 1 Chr. 5:25; also 2 Chr. 21:13). The metaphor stemmed from the practice of fertility prostitution in Canaanite worship (see Jer. 3:1; Ezek. 16:35f.) and the belief that Israel was the bride of God (see Hos. 1:2-7).

Elijah's Condemnation of Jehoram (21:12-15)

The turning point of the Chronicler's account consists of a prophetic warning of judgment. This warning is unique in the Chronicler's history because it consists of a letter from the prophet Elijah. This letter recollected events already mentioned (21:12-13) and anticipated events to follow (21:14-15). The letter itself follows an introduction (verse 12a) and takes the form of a typical prophetic oracle of judgment: messenger formula (verse 12b), accusation (verse 13), and sentencing (verses 14-15).

The Chronicler explicitly identified the author of this letter as **Elijah the prophet** (verse 12a). This well-known prophet appears in 1 Kgs. 17-19 but nowhere else in Chronicles. 2 Kgs. 2-3 suggests that Elijah went to heaven during the reign of Jehoshaphat. So, it is likely that Elijah lived only during the years when Jehoram was co-regent with Jehoshaphat. Elijah's letter indicates that he knew of Jehoram's fratricide which took place very early in his reign (verse 13).

The prophet's accusation against Jehoram was threefold. First, the king did not **walk in the ways of ... Jehoshaphat or of Asa** (verse 12b). As we have seen, the Chronicler did not hide the faults of these kings. Yet, Jehoram's reign did not even measure up to these reigns.

Second, instead of following the examples of his father and grandfather, Jehoram was like **the kings of Israel** (verse 13). The Chronicler made the same accusation earlier (see 21:6). Jehoram followed the example of the northern kings by leading his people **to prostitute themselves** (verse 13a; see also verse 11).

Third, Elijah accused Jehoram of fratricide (verse 13b). As the Chronicler himself just reported (see 21:4), Jehoram killed his brothers to take Judah's throne. Elijah heightened this accusation by saying that those whom Jehoram killed **were better than** Jehoram (verse 13b).

As a result of Jehoram's guilt, Elijah proclaimed divine judgment against the king (verses 14-15). The king's punishment would be twofold. First, Elijah wrote that God will **'strike your people, your sons, your wives and everything that is yours'** (21:14). In contrast with the blessing of increased progeny, the Chronicler indicates that Jehoram's progeny will be harmed (see *Introduction: 25) Increase and Decline of Progeny*). The fulfillment of this threat appears in 21:16-17.

Second, God will make Jehoram himself **very ill** (verse 15). This illness will be **a lingering disease** that will cause his **bowels to come out**. The precise identity of this disease is uncertain; interpreters have suggested colitis, chronic diarrhea, or dysentery. Whatever the case, it is apparent that Elijah predicted a terrible manner of death for the king. This judgment was fulfilled in 21:18-19.

The Chronicler's record gives no indication that Jehoram responded to the prophet's words with humility. Unlike Rehoboam (see 11:4; 12:6), Asa (see 15:8), and Jehoshaphat (see 18:6ff), Jehoram did not submit to the prophetic word. Instead, he continued in his disobedience. His contumacy led directly to the realization of divine judgment (see *Introduction: 15) Prophets*).

By reporting Elijah's harsh letter to Jehoram, the Chronicler pointed out once again that judgment comes against those who turn away from God (see *Introduction: 10-27) Divine Blessing and Judgment*). The Chronicler's readers must resist all temptations to fall into Jehoram's infidelities and remain strongly committed to the ways of Judah's honorable kings.

More Rebellions against Jehoram (21:16-17)

The Chronicler continued his addition to Jehoram's reign by illustrating how Elijah's prediction was fulfilled.

Structure of 21:16-17

This material amounts to a simple three step episode (see figure 38). It begins with the stirrings of rebellion (verse 16) and ends with the aftermath (verse 17b). The actual attacks form the turning point (verse 17a).

Rebellions Stir (21:16)

In the previous section dealing with rebellion, Edom and Libnah are the active agents (21:8, 10; see figure 38). Here the active agent is God: **the LORD aroused** ... **the Philistines** and **the Arabs**. On a number of occasions, the Chronicler pointed to God as the power behind important events (see *Introduction: 10) Divine Activity*). In fulfillment of Elijah's prophecy, God caused these subjugated kingdoms to rebel against the king of Judah.

Rebels Attack Judah (21:17a)

The rebellion stirred by God brought great trouble to Jehoram. The Philistines and Arabs **attacked** and **invaded**. It is likely that these attacks came from the west (Philistines) and the south or southeast (Arabs). Once again, troubles came to Jehoram from many directions.

Rebellions End (21:17b)
These rebellions proved to be devastating to Jehoram's kingdom. The enemies took **all the goods** of the palace as well as Jehoram's **sons and wives.** In contrast with the blessing of increased progeny (see *Introduction: 25) Increase and Decline of Progeny*), only one son, **Ahaziah**, was left to Jehoram.

Elijah's prediction proved to be true in great detail because Jehoram did not heed his warning. The Chronicler's outlook is evident. Continuing in sin and resisting prophetic warnings insure divine judgment (see *Introduction: 15) Prophets*).

Closure of Jehoram's Reign (21:18-22:1)
The Chronicler closed Jehoram's reign with another allusion to Elijah's prophecy. Elijah had predicted that Jehoram would suffer a terminal illness (see 21:15). The Chronicler's addition to Jehoram's reign ends with the fulfillment of this prophecy. The Chronicler described Jehoram's disease in several ways to depict its severity. It was **an incurable disease** (verse 18); it lasted to the **end of the second year** (verse 19). Jehoram's **bowels came out** and the king **died in great pain.**

The Chronicler also focused on the shame of Jehoram's death. **His people made no fire in his honor** (verse 19). Honorific fires occurred at Asa's death (16:14), but Jehoram received no such honor. Besides this, when Jehoram died it was **to no one's regret** (verse 19). The disintegration of Judah's kingdom had become so severe that the people did not care that the king died. Finally, the Chronicler added the observation that Jehoram was **not** buried **in the tombs of the kings**, a special site in Jerusalem set aside for the royal family (21:20b). Jehoram was excluded from the site; similar fates awaited Joash (see 24:25) and Uzziah (see 26:23; see also *Introduction: 28) Healing and Long Life/Sickness and Death*).

Following 2 Kgs. 8:24-25, the Chronicler closed the reign of Jehoram with a notice of succession (22:1). As noted above, the Chronicler added much to this material. He reported that **the people of Jerusalem** made Ahaziah king. In other words, Jehoram's kingdom was in such disarray that he was unable to appoint a successor. For similar situations, see 23:20-21; 26:1; 33:25; 36:1. The Chronicler's addition makes it plain why these events took place. It was because **the Arabs had killed all the older sons** (22:1; see 21:16). In effect, Ahaziah was the only option left for Judah. The significance of this turn of events will become evident as the character of Ahaziah is exposed in the verses that follow (22:1-2). Simply put, Ahaziah was no better a king than his father Jehoram. He too turned from God and brought trouble to Judah.

These descriptions make it clear that the Chronicler wanted to impress his post-exilic readers with the severity and shame of Jehoram's punishment. In contrast with the preceding kings of the divided period, this son of David was so corrupted by the wicked of northern Israel that he suffered terribly for his violations. The message for post-exilic Judah is evident. They should do all they can to avoid the severe punishment that comes against those who flagrantly violate their covenant with God in this manner.

The Reign of Ahaziah (22:2-9)

The Chronicler summarized the reign of Ahaziah (841 BC) in only eight verses. The brevity of his account may be due in part to the fact that Ahaziah reigned less than one year. It may also result from the lack of sources of information. Whatever the case, Ahaziah's reign represents another poignant example of divine judgment against a king who was unduly influenced by the wicked of northern Israel.

Comparison of 22:2-9 with 2 Kgs. 8:25-9:29

The Chronicler's account followed the basic pattern of Kings, but reduced Ahaziah's reign to a much shorter record (see figure 39).

2 Chr.		2 Kgs.
———	Synchronization with the North (omitted)	8:25
22:2	Ahaziah's Reign Begins (parallel)	8:26
22:3-6	Ahaziah's Wickedness (slightly expanded)	8:27-29
22:7-9	Ahaziah and Jehu (greatly abbreviated)	9:1-10:36

Comparison of 2 Chr. 22:2-9 and 2 Kgs. 8:25-10:36 (figure 39)

At first glance, it becomes apparent that the Chronicler's material on Ahaziah is much shorter than the account in Kings. By and large this variance is due to the fact that the writer of Kings set Ahaziah's reign within the context of events in the North. The Chronicler omitted the synchronization with the northern kingdom (22:1 // 2 Kgs. 8:25) as he did in every case except 13:1 (see *Introduction: 2) Northern Israel*). Moreover, the material dealing with Jehu's actions (2 Kgs. 9:1-10:36) is severely abbreviated in 22:7-9.

Beyond this, however, the Chronicler made several small additions that reveal his central concerns. First, the Chronicler identified those persons responsible for Ahaziah's evil actions. 1) The king walked in the ways of the North **for his mother encouraged him in doing wrong** (22:3). Athaliah influenced Ahaziah toward evil. 2) In much the same way, the Chronicler added that the house of Ahab influenced him. He followed their ways **for after his father's death they became his advisers, to his undoing** (22:4b). These additions confirm the Chronicler's focus on corruption from the North.

Second, the Chronicler's account emphasized the role of God in these events. 1) He noted that **through Ahaziah's visit to Joram, God brought about Ahaz-**

iah's downfall (22:7a). 2) Similarly, 22:7b adds that Jehu was the **son of Nimshi, whom the Lord had anointed to destroy the house of Ahab**.

Third, the Chronicler's account of Ahaziah's death (22:9) includes information not found in Kings that displays his evaluation of Ahaziah.

1) He mentioned that Ahaziah was captured **while he was hiding in Samaria** (22:9). The portrait of Judah's king hiding in Samaria indicates his affinities for the North and displays the great shame of the king.

2) The Chronicler explained that the only reason Ahaziah was buried with some measure of honor was because he was **a son of Jehoshaphat, who sought the LORD with all his heart** (22:9). By this addition, the Chronicler made it evident that Ahaziah himself did not have enough positive qualities to warrant an honorable burial.

3) Instead of the normal notice of a successor, the Chronicler added that **there was no one in the house of Ahaziah powerful enough to retain the kingdom** (22:9). Like Jehoram before him (see 22:1), Ahaziah had not successfully appointed a son to rule after him. His house was under the curse of God.

Fourth, a small variation occurs in 22:2 (// 2 Kgs. 8:26). Kings reads that Ahaziah was 'twenty-two' when he took the throne. The traditional Hebrew text of 2 Chr. 22:2 reads 'forty-two'. NIV correctly adjusts the number to match the reading of Kings, but note NKJ and NRS. It is very likely that the text of Chronicles was corrupted at some stage in transmission (see *Introduction: Translation and Transmission*).

Structure of 22:2-9

The reign of Ahaziah follows a simple outline of three main steps (see figure 40).

■Opening of Ahaziah's Reign (22:2)
- ■Ahaziah's Wicked Actions (22:3-6a)
  - Reports of Wickedness (22:3-4)
  - Narrative of Wickedness (22:5-6a)

■Closure of Ahaziah's Reign (22:6b-9)
- Ahaziah Meets Jehu with Joram (22:6b-7)
  - Ahaziah's Family Killed by Jehu (22:8)
    - Ahaziah is Sought and Captured (22:9a)
  - Ahaziah Killed by Jehu (22:9b)
- Ahaziah Buried without Successor (22:9c)

Outline of 2 Chr. 22:2-9 (figure 40)

The King's reign begins and ends as expected (22:2, 6b-9). The middle portion of the account depicts Ahaziah's wickedness (22:3-6a).

Opening of Ahaziah's Reign (22:2)
Chronicles closely follows 2 Kgs. 8:26 at this point. **Ahaziah's mother Athaliah** is of northern royal descent, **a granddaughter of Omri** who married Jehoram (21:6). She influenced her son's actions for the worse (see 22:3), just as she had misled her husband (see 21:6). Athaliah will play an even more central role with the next generation (see 22:10ff). For further discussion of the royal mother motif, see comments on 2 Chr. 13:2.

Ahaziah's Wicked Actions (22:3-6a)
The center of Ahaziah's record contains nothing positive. He is portrayed as corrupt from beginning to end.

Structure of 22:3-6a
The Chronicler summarized the actions of Ahaziah in two reports (22:3,4) and a brief narrative (22:5-6a).

Reports of Wickedness (22:3-4)
The initial words of each portion repeat similar motifs. Ahaziah **walked in the ways of the house of Ahab** (verse 3); **he did evil in the eyes of the LORD, as the house of Ahab had done** (verse 4); **he went with Joram son of Ahab ... to war against Hazael** (verse 5). These facts are all contained in the record of 2 Kgs. 8:27-28. The Chronicler followed the outlook of Kings and noted how Ahaziah's close relation with the North resulted in the corruption of Judah. This motif appears a number of times in Chronicles and contributed significantly to the Chronicler's outlooks on the relationship between the northern tribes and the post-exilic community (see *Introduction: 2) Northern Israel*).

The Chronicler's additions tie these events together. Ahaziah sinned **for his mother encouraged him in doing wrong** (verse 3); he did evil because members of Ahab's house **became his advisers, to his undoing** (verse 4). He even went to war as an ally of the North because he **followed their counsel** (verse 5). In each verse the Chronicler explained that Ahaziah's trouble came because he was influenced by wicked northern Israelites.

The Chronicler followed 2 Kgs. 8:27 when he noted that Ahaziah **too** (i.e. like Jehoram) lived **in the ways of the house of Ahab** (verse 3). He repeated the same Hebrew word when he added to the account of Kings that Ahaziah **also** listened to the counsel of the northerners (verse 5). This repetition emphasized the connection between Ahaziah and Jehoram. Both of the kings followed the ways of Ahab's house and violated their loyalty to God (see 21:6, 13).

Although the Chronicler hoped for the eventual expansion of the post-exilic community to include all the tribes and their original territories, the Chronicler insisted that his readers not compromise righteousness under the influence of wickedness from the North. Jehoram (21:12-15), and Ahaziah (22:4) were soundly condemned for their involvement with the wicked of the North (compare also Jehoshaphat 19:1-2; 20:35). Athaliah corrupted Judah and such corruption was to be avoided in post-exilic times (see also 2 Kgs. 8:26; 11:1-3, 13-14, 20; 1 Chr. 8:26; 2 Chr. 21:6; 22:2, 10-12; 23:12-13, 21; 24:7; see also *Introduction: 2) Northern Israel*).

Narrative of Wickedness (22:5-6a)

The extent of Ahaziah's involvement with the northern kingdom becomes particularly clear in the brief narrative of 22:5-6a. This brief four step episode comes from the book of Kings (// 2 Kgs. 8:28-29). It tells how Ahaziah joined the Northern king **Joram son of Ahab** in battle against Syria (verse 5a). In the battle, the Syrians **wounded Joram** (verse 5b) and Joram **returned to Jezreel to recover** (verse 6a). The Chronicler consistently condemned military alliances with the North (see *Introduction: 2) Northern Israel*). From his perspective, these events illustrated the fact that Ahaziah was too involved with the wicked family of Ahab.

Closure of Ahaziah's Reign (22:6b-9)

The Chronicler closed his account of Ahaziah's reign with a narrative of his death. This material was added to finalize his perspective on the king. The narrative of 22:6b-9 sets forth how God brought about Ahaziah's downfall.

Structure of 22:6b-9

This part of the Chronicler's addition divides into five steps (see figure 40). This passage reports the movement from Ahaziah meeting with Jehu and Joram (verses 6b-7) to his death (verse 9c). In the middle portion, Jehu kills Ahaziah's family (verse 8); pursues Ahaziah (verse 9a), and kills Ahaziah (verse 9b).

Ahaziah Meets Jehu with Joram (22:6b-9)

The first step of this story (verses 6b-7) describes Ahaziah visiting the wounded northern king Joram. As the story begins, Ahaziah was apparently unaware of any danger. He visited Joram at Jezreel, a summer palace of the kings of Israel (see 1 Kgs. 18:45-46; 21:1; 2 Kgs. 9:30) and joined Joram to meet Jehu.

The Hebrew grammar of 22:7a suggests that this sentence was intended as a parenthetical note. The Chronicler explained that God had a secret purpose for Ahaziah's visit to Joram. It was the means by which **God brought about Ahaziah's downfall** (verse 7a). In fact, the Chronicler also noted that Jehu **had been anointed to destroy the house of Ahab** (22:7b). As he did on many occasions, the Chronicler pointed to the hidden ways of God behind otherwise ordinary events (see *Introduction: 10) Divine Activity*).

The book of Kings provides the historical background for the story of Ahaziah's death (2 Kgs. 10:18-36). Elijah had appointed Jehu to destroy the house of Ahab because its wickedness was so great. Even so, Jehu's coup also involved an attack on Ahaziah and his house as they visited Joram at Jezreel.

Ahaziah's Family Killed by Jehu (22:8)

As the tension of this story rises, Jehu also came upon **the princes of Judah and the sons of Ahaziah's relatives** who were in the North and **killed them**.

Ahaziah is Sought and Captured (22:9a)
The turning point of the story portrays a terrified Ahaziah **hiding in Samaria**. Not only does this scene reveal the king's shameful state; it also reveals his loyalties as he opted to hide in Samaria rather than Jerusalem.

Ahaziah Killed by Jehu (22:9b)
After a search, Jehu's men find Ahaziah. In balance with the execution of Ahaziah's sons and relatives (see 22:8), Jehu also had Ahaziah **put to death**.

Ahaziah Buried without Successor (22:9c)
This event leads to the closing of this episode. Jehu and his men were strongly committed to the ways of God. Ahaziah was so disgraced that he was buried with some measure of honor for one reason alone: **he was a son of Jehoshaphat, who sought the Lord with all his heart** (verse 9b; see also *Introduction: 28) Healing and Long Life/Sickness and Death*). In his characteristic manner, the Chronicler praised Jehoshaphat as one who sought God (see *Introduction: 19) Seeking*). Ahaziah sought his strength in alliance with the northern kingdom, and he received divine judgment because he never turned from this disloyalty to God. The severity of God's judgment against Ahaziah is evident in the last sentence of this episode. Ahaziah had no clearly appointed successor. No one was **powerful enough to retain the kingdom**.

The Chronicler's message to his post-exilic readers was straightforward. Compromise with the wickedness of the northern kingdom would lead to serious consequences. God's judgment against a wayward Judah may come in the most unusual and unexpected ways, but it will come. Although Ahaziah prospered for a while, his compromise with the wicked ways of the house of Ahab eventually led to his destruction. The post-exilic readers of Chronicles were to learn from these events that the judgment which Ahaziah experienced could be theirs as well.

The Reign of Joash (22:10-24:27)
The Chronicler's record of Joash's reign (835-796 BC) is unusual in that it devotes a whole chapter to Joash's rise to power. The judgment of God against Ahaziah (22:7) left the royal line of David near extinction. For a period of six years Judah had no king. Ahaziah's mother, Athaliah, reigned as queen. For this reason, the Chronicler first dealt with the transition of power from Athaliah to Joash instead of turning directly to the king's reign. Whereas other transfers of power usually take place in the space of a verse or two, the Chronicler spent an entire chapter explaining what happened when a wicked northern Israelite queen ruled Judah.

Comparison of 22:10-24:27 with 2 Kgs. 11:1-12:21
In light of the complexity of this portion of the divided monarchy, it is helpful to compare Kings and Chronicles on a large scale. More detailed analyses will be given under each section (see figure 41).

2 Chr.		2 Kgs.
22:10-23:21	Joash's Rise to Power (parallel)	11:1-20
24:1-14	Joash's Fidelity (loosely parallel)	11:21-12:16
24:15-16	Jehoiada's Death (added)	———
24:17-22	Joash's Infidelity (added)	———
24:23-27	Joash's Defeat and Death (loosely parallel)	12:17-21

Comparison of 2 Chr. 22:10-24:27 and 2 Kgs. 10:15-12:21 (figure 41)

As this comparison indicates, the Chronicler depended on the record of Kings for the account of Athaliah's overthrow (22:10-23:21 // 2 Kgs. 11:1-20) and Joash's early years of fidelity (24:1-14 // 2 Kgs. 11:21-12:16). He then added materials on the death of Jehoiada (24:15-16) and Joash's years of infidelity (24:17-22). After this additional material, he returned to the text of Kings for Joash's defeat and death (24:23-27 // 2 Kgs. 12:17-21).

Structure of 22:10-24:27

The Chronicler's version of Joash's reign divides into two main sections followed by normal closing remarks. Each of the main portions consist of complex inner structures (see figure 42).

Joash's Rise over Athaliah (22:10-23:21)

The Chronicler's first concern was to establish how the influence of Northern Israel was broken. Athaliah, daughter of Ahab (22:2) had taken the throne of Judah. Joash could become king only when she had been removed.

Comparison of 22:10-23:21 with 2 Kgs. 11:1-20

The Chronicler depended heavily on 2 Kgs. 11:1-20 for his record of the coup leading to Joash's enthronement. At some points, he varied from the book of Kings simply for stylistic reasons. For example, the Chronicler consistently shortened the king's name from Jehoash to Joash. The name Jehosheba in Kings is lengthened to Jehoshabeath in the Hebrew of Chronicles (NIV simply renders Jehosheba both in Kings and Chronicles). These changes are insignificant, but on several occasions the Chronicler added and omitted significant materials that revealed his outlook on these events.

First, in many places the Chronicler highlighted the role of the priests and Levites in the overthrow of Athaliah.

- ■ Joash's Rise over Athaliah (22:10-23:21)
  - ♦ Athaliah's Evil Reign Over Judah (22:10-12)
    - Covenant with the King (23:1-3a)
      - Jehoiada's Plan and Its Implementation (23:3b-10)
        - Joash's Coronation (23:11)
        - Athaliah's Reaction to Coronation (23:12-13)
      - Jehoiada's Plan and Its Implementation (23:14-15)
    - Covenant with God (23:16-19)
  - ♦ Joash's Peaceful Reign Over Judah (23:20-21)

- ■ Joash's Kingship (24:1-27)
  - ♦ Opening of Joash's Reign (24:1-3)
    - ♦ Joash's Early Years of Fidelity (24:4-14)
      - Joash Begins Temple Restoration (24:4)
        - Joash's Failed Collection (24:5)
          - Joash and Jehoiada Compromise (24:6-7)
        - Joash's Successful Collection (24:8-11)
      - Joash Completes Temple Restoration (24:12-14)
      - ♦ Jehoiada's Death (24:15-16)
    - ♦ Joash's Later Years of Infidelity (24:17-26)
      - Joash and Leaders Provoke God (24:17-18)
        - Zechariah Prophesies against Joash (24:19-20)
          - Joash Orders Zechariah's Death (24:21-22)
        - Zechariah's Prophecy Fulfilled (24:23-24)
      - Joash Assassinated by Leaders (24:25-26)
  - ♦ Closure of Joash's Reign (24:27)

Outline of 2 Chr. 22:10-24:27 (figure 42)

1) In 22:11 (// 2 Kgs. 11:2) he added the information that Jehosheba was not only the daughter of King Jehoram and sister of Ahaziah (see 2 Kgs. 11:2), but was also wife of the priest Jehoiada. Thus the Chronicler explicitly attributed the rescue of Joash to the priestly families.

2) In addition to a list of commanders, the Chronicler added that the Levites were among those gathered for the coup (23:1-2 // 2 Kgs. 11:4).

3) In 2 Kgs. 11:5 the text reads 'You who ... are going on duty ...' The Chronicler, however, specified **you priests and Levites who are going on duty** ... (23:4) to draw attention to their central role.

4) The Levites are explicitly mentioned again in 23:7 (// 2 Kgs. 11:8).

5) 2 Kgs. 11:8 leaves unspecified the people who were to surround the king. The Chronicler added that this special group of bodyguards was to be the **Levites** (23:7).

6) Kings reads that 'the commanders' did as they were told (2 Kgs. 11:9); the Chronicler substituted the **Levites** for 'the commanders' (23:8).

7) The Chronicler also specified that **Jehoiada and his sons** anointed Joash, whereas Kings merely attributes the action to the whole assembly (23:11 // 2 Kgs. 11:12).

8) The Chronicler added that **singers with musical instruments were leading the praises** (23:13 // 2 Kgs. 11:14).

9) The Chronicler also added 23:18b-19 to describe the function of the priests and Levites in the new temple order established by Jehoiada. All of these changes illustrate the Chronicler's special interest in the temple and its functionaries.

Second, the Chronicler also emphasized the breadth of those involved in the coup. This emphasis fell in line with his concern for the unity of God's people in support of the Davidic line (see *Introduction: 1) All Israel*). His concern with popular support of the coup resembles other times when the Chronicler emphasized unanimity between the people and their leaders. (For a summary of the Chronicler's view of popular consent, see comments on 1 Chr. 13:2,4.) This outlook becomes evident in a number of ways.

1) He added that Jehoiada gathered **the heads of Israelite families from all the towns** (23:2 // 2 Kgs. 11:4).

2) Kings reads that Jehoiada made a covenant with the king (2 Kgs. 11:4); the Chronicler specified that the **whole assembly made the covenant** (23:3).

3) In Kings, instructions are given only to the leaders; the Chronicler included that **all the other men are to be in the courtyards** (23:5 // 2 Kgs. 11:7).

4) While Kings reads that 'the commanders' did as they were instructed, Chronicles reads that **all the men of Judah did just as Jehoiada the priest ordered** (23:8 // 2 Kgs. 11:9).

5) Kings mentions only that 'the guards' stood ready (2 Kgs. 11:11); Chronicles says he set **all the men, each with his weapon in his hand, around the king** (23:10).

6) Finally, the Chronicler added that **Athaliah heard the noise of the people running and cheering the king** (23:12 // 2 Kgs. 11:13).

Third, the Chronicler demonstrated a concern for the sanctity of the temple not found in Kings. He noted specific instructions on entry to the temple for different groups (23:6 // 2 Kgs. 11:7). This coup was set forth as an ideal event; the temple was not violated in the least (see *Introduction: 4-9) King and Temple*).

Fourth, the Chronicler added a direct quotation which reminded his readers that Joash's claim to the throne rested on the covenant God made with David (23:3 // 2 Kgs. 11:4). This addition fit well with his emphasis on the Davidic covenant (see *Introduction: 13) Covenant*).

Structure of 22:10-23:21

This passage displays a rather complex structural symmetry. It divides into eight main parts that balance each other (see figure 42). The story of Joash's rise to power begins with the years of Athaliah's dreadful reign (22:10-12), but it ends with the peaceful reign of Joash (23:20-21). Jehoiada led the people of Judah to make a covenant with Joash as their king (23:1-3a); this event is balanced by Jehoiada leading the people to make covenant with their divine King (23:16-19). Twice Jehoiada gave instructions which were carried out (23:3b-10; 23:14-15). The center of the story balances between the coronation of Joash (23:11) and Athaliah's reaction to his coronation (23:12-13).

Athaliah's Evil Reign Over Judah (22:10-12)

The Chronicler began this section with a brief look at the trouble caused by Athaliah. He followed the basic plot as it appears in the book of Kings (// 2 Kgs. 11:1-3). Athaliah saw that her son Ahaziah was dead and began to murder **the whole royal family** (22:10). She wished to rid the kingdom of all male heirs of the throne.

Jehosheba spoiled Athaliah's plans. In a dramatic act of courage, she rescued Joash and hid him with a wet nurse just as the **royal princes ... were about to be murdered** (22:11). As indicated above, the Chronicler added to the information on Jehosheba found in Kings. He noted that she was the wife of the priest Jehoiada (22:11). This identification heightened the role of the priesthood in the coup. Not only did Jehoiada lead the coup itself; his wife was responsible for Joash's initial rescue. Beyond this, the identity of Jehosheba also explains how Jehosheba hid Joash at the temple of God (22:12). As a member of a priestly family she had access to the inner circles of the temple personnel. Perhaps Joash hid among other priests' children or among young temple servants who were dedicated to temple work.

Joash remained safely hidden for six years (22:12). It was in his seventh year of age that the coup occurred (see 23:1; 24:1). Until that time Athaliah ruled the land (22:12).

Covenant with the King (23:1-3a)

Jehoiada determined to make his move in Joash's seventh year (23:1). He first made a covenant with the commanders (23:1). The Chronicler added a list of the names of these commanders (23:1).

Beyond this, the Chronicler stressed the exemplary unity of the nation in these events. He noted that these commanders went throughout Judah for the purpose of gathering **Levites and the heads of Israelite families from all the towns** (23:2). This action involved representatives of the entire kingdom of Judah. In much the same way, this segment of the story ends with a similar variation between Kings and Chronicles. 2 Kgs. 11:4 simply states that Jehoiada made a covenant with Joash. 2 Chr. 23:3, however, states that **the whole assembly made a covenant.** This information fit well with the Chronicler's interest in the times when Israel gathered in religious assemblies in the past. Here the whole nation assembled to support the son of David in covenant renewal (see *Introduction: 5) Religious Assemblies*). From the Chronicler's perspective, covenant renewal with a son of David also needed to take place among the post-exilic readers to whom he wrote.

The **covenant** with Joash probably involved the terms under which his rule would be accepted by the nation (23:3a). Joash was only seven years of age; special provisions had to be made for his kingship. Similar covenant arrangements between the people and the king occurred in David's day (see 1 Chr. 11:3). Apparently, one condition of this covenant was that Jehoiada was to act as regent for the young king. A written copy of this covenant was probably given later to the king (see 23:11). These arrangements may have provided a background for the subsequent conflict between Jehoiada and Joash (see 24:4-12).

The Chronicler's record pointed to several aspects of these events that were relevant to the post-exilic Israelites. Jehoiada's actions modeled the proper way the priesthood was to relate to the monarchy. Jehoiada served the throne of David. A similar relationship existed between Zerubbabel and Joshua in the post-exilic community (see Zech. 3-4). Beyond this, the Chronicler stressed the broad national support for Joash. This event modeled the unity of purpose the Chronicler encouraged among his readers (see *Introduction: 1) All Israel*). Finally, by pointing to the covenant made between Judah and Joash, the Chronicler made it clear that Judah's monarchs were not to rule without restraint. Their right to rule had to be balanced with the rights of the nation.

Jehoiada's Plan and Its Implementation (23:3b-10)

After their initial agreement with the young king, the gathering planned and enacted the coup. The Chronicler's record of these events divides into two parts: Jehoiada's instructions (23:4-7), and the implementation of the instructions (23:8-10). This sequence balances with Jehoiada's later instructions and their implementation (23:14-15; see figure 42).

Jehoiada's instructions divided into four points. First, the Chronicler added a theological justification for the coup that was about to take place (23:3a // 2 Kgs. 11:4). In the Chronicler's account, Jehoiada insisted that the dynastic promise to David (see 1 Chr. 17:7-14) required that **the king's son shall reign, as the Lord promised concerning the descendants of David** (23:3b). The fact that the Chronicler added these words to his record indicates how important this issue was for him (see *Introduction: 13) Covenant*). When a Davidide did not sit on the throne of Judah, it was the responsibility of the priest and the nation to rectify the situation. The dynastic promise to David was valid for all times, even during the post-exilic period.

Second, the Chronicler varied from 2 Kgs. 11:5 and specified that Jehoiada addressed the **priests and Levites ... going on duty on the Sabbath** (23:4). As we have seen above, the Chronicler gave the priests and Levites a more central role in this event. The element of surprise in Jehoiada's strategy is evident. The day of his coup was the Sabbath, a time when few would have expected trouble. Moreover, the coup was to occur as a new shift of priests and Levites entered the temple. As one division replaced another, there was much movement in the temple precinct and fewer suspicions would be raised by the actions of large groups. Jehoiada divided the priests and Levites into thirds. They were to station themselves **at the doors** (23:4), the **royal palace** (23:5), and **the Foundation Gate** (23:5).

Third, because the Chronicler applied the first portion of these instructions to the priests and Levites, he added instructions for the other participants. **All the other men**, military personnel and civilians, were to go to the **courtyards of the temple** (23:5 // 2 Kgs. 11:7). The Chronicler also noted that only **the priests and Levites on duty ... may enter the temple itself** (23:6). This policy was based on the fact that the priests and Levites were **consecrated** for service in the temple (23:6). Rituals of consecration appear frequently in Chronicles as examples of proper worship which the post-exilic readers were to imitate in their day (see *Introduction: 6) Royal Observance of Worship*). The Chronicler made it clear that Jehoiada's coup did not defile the temple.

Fourth, the Chronicler once again specified a special role for the **Levites** in 23:7. The account of Kings makes it plain that military personnel supported Jehoiada's coup, but the Chronicler focused on the Levites as the central figures of the action. From the days of Moses the Levites served to enforce God's ways in times of special need (e.g. Exod. 32:26-29). 2 Kgs. 11:8 simply orders some people to 'station [themselves] around the king'. The Chronicler, however, informed his readers that these men were a select group of **Levites** (23:7). Each Levite was to have **weapons in his hand** and anyone else who came into the temple **must be put to death**.

Having presented Jehoiada's instructions, the text moves to the implementation of his plan (23:8-10). The participants did **just as Jehoiada the priest ordered** (23:8). In his characteristic fashion the Chronicler shifted the designation of the participants from 'the commanders of units of a hundred' (2 Kgs. 11:9) to **the Levites and all the men of Judah** (23:8). Not only did this variation highlight the role of the Levites once again, it also indicated the breadth of participation. The people involved represented the entire tribe of Judah. As such, this event reinforced the Chronicler's concern for unanimous support for the Davidic throne (see *Introduction: 1) All Israel*).

From 23:4 it would appear that only those priests and Levites going on duty participated in the coup. 23:8, however, clarifies that all the priests and Levites participated. The Chronicler made this fact plain by adding that **Jehoiada the priest had not released any of the divisions** (23:8). Weapons that had **belonged to King David** which were stored **in the temple** were distributed (23:9). Special bodyguards also took their places **around the king** (23:10).

Joash's Coronation (23:11)

With the temple and its courts secured, the revolutionaries crowned Joash. Once again, the Chronicler emphasized the role of the priests by adding that **Jehoiada and his sons** performed the ceremony (23:11 // 2 Kgs. 11:12). They put the **crown on him** and **anointed him**. Moreover, they presented him **a copy of the covenant**. In all likelihood this covenant was a copy of the arrangements established in 23:3. It is possible, however, that it was a copy of the Mosaic Law (see Deut. 17:18; see also *Introduction: 13) Covenant*). In all events, the scene ends with a shout from the priests, **'Long live the king!'** This shout contrasts with Athaliah's screams of treason in the next step of the story (23:13).

This scene represented a high ideal for the Chronicler in many ways. The priesthood anointed and crowned the Davidic king. The bonds of covenant were established and the temple was filled with shouts of joy (see *Introduction: 27) Disappointment and Celebration*). In Jehoiada's day the throne of David had been empty for years, but in this scene all was set aright. The Chronicler and his readers had seen the throne of David deserted for an even longer period of time. Their hope for blessings could be realized only as the temple and King were in proper order (see *Introduction: 4-9) King and Temple*).

Athaliah's Reaction to Coronation (23:12-13)

This portion of the Chronicler's account compares with the preceding scene in at least three ways (see figure 42). Both segments occur in the temple. Both scenes involve shouting, first by the crowd (23:11) and then by Athaliah (23:12). The action of this segment is in reaction to the preceding verse. In these ways, this portion of the story balances with the scene of coronation (23:11).

Although this scene appears in 2 Kgs. 11:13-14, the Chronicler intensified the action with two additions. First, he added that the people were **running and cheering the king** (23:12) to convey the excitement of the event. Second, the Chronicler followed 2 Kgs. 11:14 (// 2 Chr. 23:13) and mentioned that **the people of the land were rejoicing and blowing trumpets**. In other words, the common people were involved in the ceremonies. (For the Chronicler's use of 'people of the land', see 1 Chr. 5:25; 2 Chr. 23:20,21; 26:21; 33:25; 36:1.) Even so, he also added that **singers with musical instruments were leading the praises** (2 Chr. 23:13). Thus he highlighted the role of the Levite singers as he did in other portions of this narrativ The music and excitement of the situation was greatly enhanced in the Chronicler's version (see *Introduction: 8) Music*).

When Athaliah heard the noise (23:12), she came to the temple and saw the rejoicing. Realizing what had happened, she tore her robes and shouted, **'Treason! Treason!'** (23:13). One cannot help but notice the irony of one who had taken the throne violently now protesting indignantly the violence taken against her.

Jehoiada's Plan and Its Implementation (23:14-15)

The story focuses a second time on Jehoiada's instructions (verse 14) and the implementation of his orders (verse 15). As such, it balances with the earlier section devoted to similar material (see 23:3b-10; see figure 42). In this portion of the narrative, the Chronicler followed the account of Kings (// 2 Kgs. 11:15-16) without significant additions or omissions.

Jehoiada ordered Athaliah's execution, but he revealed his concern for the sanctity of the temple. He insisted, **'Do not put her to death at the temple of the Lord'** (verse 14). Once again, the priest showed his concern for the sacred house of God even during the emergency of the coup (see 23:6).

Just as the priest ordered, **the commanders** took Athaliah away from the temple (verse 14). They brought her to the palace grounds and there **they put her to death** (verse 15). The Chronicler did not include a typical summary and burial notice for Athaliah. In his perspective Athaliah was not a legitimate monarch. She deserved no formal regnal summary.

Covenant with God (23:16-19)

This portion of the narrative records the second time Jehoiada established a covenant (see figure 42). Earlier Jehoiada supervised a covenant between **the assembly** and **the king** (23:3). Now the priest established a covenant that **he and the people and the king would be the Lord's people** (verse 16). In this way, Jehoiada acknowledged the ideal authority structure for Judah. The priest mediated a covenant between himself, the people, the Davidic king and the Divine King. The nation repented of sins during the years of Athaliah's reign and committed their loyalties exclusively to the Lord. The Chronicler presented these events in part to inspire his readers to do the same (see *Introduction: 13) Covenant*).

The covenant renewal under Jehoiada's leadership had a negative and positive side. Negatively, **all the people went to the temple of Baal and tore it down** (23:17). The widespread support of Jehoiada's reforms fits well with the Chronicler's desire to see all Israel participate in the renewal of the post-exilic community (see *Introduction: 1) All Israel*). Beyond this, the people turned against the worship of Baal. Athaliah had introduced the worship of Baal in Jerusalem, following the syncretistic practices of her father Ahab. The first act of reform according to Jehoiada's covenant renewal was to rid the city of its Baal temple. The Chronicler took this opportunity to stress another reform of worship in Judah. Syncretism was unacceptable (see *Introduction: 6) Royal Observance of Worship*).

Positively, Jehoiada reorganized the worship of the Lord (verses 18-19). The Chronicler's account of Jehoiada's restoration of temple service is greatly expanded over Kings. He added that Jehoiada arranged the Levites just as David had made assignments and just as it was written in the Law of Moses (23:18; see *Introduction: 14) Standards*). They also were **rejoicing and singing as David had ordered** (23:18). The restoration of worship brought great joy to God's people (see *Introduction: 8) Music*; see also *Introduction: 27) Disappointment and Celebration).*

The Chronicler added this information to make it clear that Jehoiada's reforms were enacted just as they should have been. He approved of Jehoiada and exalted him as ideal. Jehoiada had done just as David and Moses ordered. In much the same way, the Chronicler also added the note that Jehoiada once again protected the temple from defilement (see 23:14). He **stationed doorkeepers at the gates so that no one who was in any way unclean might enter** (verse 19).

In these verses the Chronicler established Jehoiada's actions as exemplary of the kind of devotion to the temple expected of post-exilic Judah. They were in need of renewing their commitments to the temple. Jehoiada's reforms demonstrated many important aspects of this renewal.

Joash's Peaceful Reign Over Judah (23:20-21)

The Chronicler returned to the record of Kings to finish his account of Joash's rise to power (23:20-21 // 2 Kgs. 11:11-12). The text briefly describes Jehoiada bringing the leaders and **the people of the land** (i.e. the common people; see 1 Chr. 5:25; 2 Chr. 23:13, 21; 26:21; 33:25; 36:1) to the temple along with King Joash. In this public ceremony seven year old Joash sat on the royal throne at the **Upper Gate** (verse 20).

As a result of the events of this narrative, **the people of the land rejoiced** (verse 21). Celebration came to all the people (see *Introduction: 27) Disappointment and Celebration*). Moreover, **the city was quiet** (23:21). The Chronicler associated the term 'quiet' with the blessing of peace and security for the faithful (see *Introduction: 23) Victory and Defeat*). This blessing for the nation came **because Athaliah had been slain** (23:21). With these words the text balances the end of this story with the beginning (22:10-12; see figure 42). Athaliah's reign of terror was over. With Joash on the throne and Jehoiada at his side a period of quiet had come.

The Chronicler's message to post-exilic Judah was plain. The readers of Chronicles could expect the blessing of God only as they avoided involvement with the wicked and turned to the ways of renewed loyalty to God. The priests were to lead the way and all the people were to serve the Davidic king faithfully. If they did, the land of Judah would experience quiet once again.

Joash's Kingship (24:1-27)

The Chronicler's record of Joash's reign presents the king as faithful in his early years and unfaithful in his later years. As such Joash represented the two options facing the Chronicler's readers. They could either serve God and receive blessings, or they could rebel against God and receive his judgment (see *Introduction: 10-27) Divine Blessing and Judgment*). A central concern in this material continues to be the relationship of the king and priesthood. As the preceding episode has already demonstrated, Jehoiada strongly supported the Davidic line. By contrast, however, Joash's regard for the priesthood and the proper worship of God did not extend throughout his life.

Comparison of 24:1-27 with 2 Kgs. 11:21-12:21
At times, the Chronicler's version is so different from Kings that some interpreters have suggested he relied on a completely different version of Joash's reign. While this viewpoint is not impossible, sufficient similarities exist between Kings and Chronicles at this point to assume the Chronicler's dependence on Kings.

Many variations between these texts result from the Chronicler's normal practices and style. Even so, four variations reveal the Chronicler's unique outlook on these events.

First, the Chronicler shaped his account to divide Joash's reign into two distinct periods, early years of obedience and later years of disobedience.

1) 2 Kgs. 12:3 reports that high places were not removed from Judah and that the people sacrificed there during Joash's early years. The Chronicler omitted this information so as not to tarnish his portrait of Joash's early obedience.

2) The Chronicler added 24:17-24 as an introduction to Joash's war with Syria (24:23-27 // 2 Kgs. 12:17-21). These verses explain that the war resulted from divine retribution for Joash's infidelity in the second half of his reign.

3) The Chronicler replaced 2 Kgs. 12:18 with 24:23b-24 to depict the severity of divine judgment against Joash. He pointed out that Judah lost her battle despite her superior numbers. In this manner he made it clear that the king was judged by God in the second half of his reign.

4) The Chronicler added that Joash was not buried in the tombs of the kings (24:25b). In so doing, the Chronicler indicated again that Joash's latter years were under divine curse (see *Introduction: 28) Healing and Long Life/Sickness and Death*).

Second, the Chronicler's interest in the mutual support of priesthood and kingship during the post-exilic period led him to draw attention to Jehoiada in a number of ways.

1) In 24:3 he added that Jehoiada was blessed with wives and children.

2) 24:7 adds that Athaliah and her Baal priests had misused the instruments of the temple. In all likelihood, the Chronicler added this information to clarify that Jehoiada had not neglected the temple.

3) 2 Kgs. 12:11 reads 'they gave', but the Chronicler substituted **the king and Jehoiada gave** (24:12) to emphasize the priest's leadership role and his cooperation with King Joash.

4) The Chronicler substituted 24:14 for 2 Kgs. 12:14. He noted Jehoiada's central role in the proper functioning of the temple in Joash's early years.

5) The addition in 24:17-22 focuses on the central role that Jehoiada and his son Zechariah played in Joash's reign.

6) The Chronicler added the account of Jehoiada's death in 24:15-16. This addition served as the turning point in his account of the king's reign which made it

clear that once the priest died, Joash turned away from the Lord.

7) The Chronicler added an explanation of why Joash's servants killed him. They conspired against him **for murdering the son of Jehoiada the priest** (24:25 // 2 Kgs. 12:20).

Third, on three occasions the Chronicler drew attention to the role which the Levites played in these events.

1) In 24:5 he added that Joash called together **the priests and Levites** whereas 2 Kgs. 12:4 simply mentions 'the priests'.

2) 2 Kgs. 12:6 says that for twenty-three years nothing was done to repair the temple. To avoid the negative light this long interval of time cast on the Levites, the Chronicler merely said that **the Levites did not act at once** (24:5b).

3) The Chronicler also added the important role of the Levites in gathering money for the temple in (24:6).

4) Similarly, 24:11 (// 2 Kgs. 12:10) adds the detail that the Levites helped to carry the chest used to collect money for the temple.

Fourth, several verses demonstrate much more interest in the details of Judah's worship.

1) Joash's plan for supporting the temple is identified with the Mosaic tabernacle practices (24:6, 9-10).

2) A notice of the musical instruments used in the temple is added (24:14 // 2 Kgs. 12:13). The Chronicler's interest in these details is characteristic of the kinds of attention to music and worship that he often demonstrated.

Structure of 24:1-27

The main body of Joash's reign divides into five main sections consisting of a number of reports and full narratives. The Chronicler arranged these sections so that they displayed a balanced account of the king's activities (see figure 41). The Chronicler divided the reign of Joash into two periods by adding a notice of Jehoiada's death in the center of his account (24:15-16). Balancing segments stand on either side of this central scene. The king's years of fidelity balance with his years of infidelity (24:4-14, 17-26). The beginning of his reign corresponds to the notice of the end of his reign (24:1-3, 27).

Opening of Joash's Reign (24:1-3)

The Chronicler began his record by following the general description in 2 Kgs. 11:21-12:3. He omitted the synchronization with northern Israel as he usually did (12:1a; see *Introduction: 2) Northern Israel*). He noted that the king was **seven years old when he became king** (24:1). Moreover, he **reigned in Jerusalem forty years** (24:1). After mentioning his mother **Zibiah** (for further discussion of royal mothers in Chronicles, see comments on 2 Chr. 13:2), the Chronicler characterized the king as one who **did what was right in the eyes of the LORD** (24:2). The Chronicler described a number of kings as doing **right in the eyes of the LORD** (see 14:2; 20:32; 24:2; 25:2; 26:4; 27:2; 29:2; 34:2). He also characterized other kings as having done **evil in the eyes of the LORD** (21:6; 22:4; 28:1; 29:6; 33:2, 6, 22; 36:5; 36:9, 12). These depictions must be taken as general, not categorical. This text explains that Joash was exemplary only during **the years of Jehoiada the priest** (24:2). This information from 2 Kgs. 12:2 led the Chronicler to his sharp division of the king's reign into the earlier and latter years. The earlier years of obedience were due to Jehoiada's influence.

2 Kgs. 12:3 mentions that the people continued to worship at 'the high places' during the early years of Joash. The Chronicler, however, omitted this report to avoid tarnishing his presentation of Joash as a good king in these years. Instead, he substituted a report of Jehoiada's **two wives** and **sons and daughters** (24:3) to illustrate God's blessing on the king. The Chronicler frequently mentioned progeny as a demonstration of divine favor (see *Introduction: 25) Increase and Decline of Progeny*).

Joash's Early Years of Fidelity (24:4-14)

Having hinted at his perspective on Joash's early years, the Chronicler continued to follow the general order of 2 Kgs. 12:3-16. His version of these events, however, shows many of his special interests.

Structure of 24:4-14

This material divides into five steps (see figure 42). The Chronicler focused his record of Joash's positive years on the king's restoration of the temple. Joash determined to restore the temple (24:4) and succeeded (24:12-14). In the process, however, the collection effort failed because of conflict with Jehoiada (24:5). The two leaders resolved their differences (24:6-7) and the collection of funds proceeded along lines acceptable both to the king and the high priest (24:8-11).

Joash Begins Temple Restoration (24:4)

While the book of Kings records many of Joash's actions in restoring the temple, it does not contain a parallel to this verse. The Chronicler added that at an undetermined time, Joash decided it was time **to restore the temple of the LORD** (24:4). Similar efforts to reform the worship of Judah took place at other times as well (see *Introduction: 6) Royal Observance of Worship*). From the outset the Chronicler made clear the central focus of this episode. He was interested in conveying how Joash restored the temple to its rightful order. During the six years of Athaliah's reign the temple had been defiled and neglected (see 22:10-12). Joash was about to correct this situation.

The implications for the post-exilic situation are evident. One of the Chronicler's chief concerns for the post-exilic community was that they bring about the full restoration and operation of the temple.

Joash's Failed Collection (24:5)

Joash's first attempt to raise money for temple restoration failed. At first glance, it seems odd that the Chronicler would record the king's failure in his period of fidelity and blessing. The details of this failure explain why he included this material in his record.

The Chronicler's account reveals a conflict between Joash and the Levites. Joash wanted to restore the temple, but he also wanted to pay for the repairs with money collected by the Levites. In 2 Kgs. 12:4-5 Joash proposed three specific sources of revenue: a half a shekel tax on twenty year old males (see Exod. 30:11-16; 38:25-26), money from individual vows (see Lev. 27:1-25), and voluntary offerings (see Lev. 22:18-23; Deut. 16:10). The Chronicler focused only on the first of these proposed sources of revenue. In his record, Joash ordered **the Levites to go to the towns of Judah and collect the money** (24:5). Bearing the responsibility and expense of gathering this money was more than the Levites were willing to do. 2 Kgs. 12:6 says the Levites delayed following Joash's order for twenty-three years. The Chronicler mollified the Levitical resistance and simply said that they **did not act at once** (24:5b). The restoration of the temple was delayed because of this conflict between the king and the temple personnel.

This portion of the Chronicler's record was particularly important to the post-exilic readers. It illustrated a conflict between the royal and temple personnel over the funding of the temple. It is likely that similar conflicts occurred between the temple personnel and political leaders during the post-exilic period. We may be sure that the potential for disharmony over these matters always existed. The Chronicler presented this narrative to address these potential conflicts.

Joash and Jehoiada Compromise (24:6-7)

In the turning point of this narrative Joash held Jehoiada responsible for the delay of the temple restoration. Very little is said in this scene. Joash asked Jehoiada why he had not **required the Levites to bring in ... the tax imposed by Moses** (24:6). The Chronicler's interest in the standard of Mosaic legislation is evident (see *Introduction: 14) Standards*; see also *Introduction: 9) Temple Contributions*). The Chronicler also mentioned that Jehoiada's duty was also confirmed by the will of **the assembly of Israel** (24:6). Apparently, the desire to see the temple put back in proper order also rose from the enthusiasm of the people in a solemn assembly (see 23:21; see also *Introduction: 5) Religious Assemblies*). The assembly of God's people demonstrated that the king's orders had popular support. For the Chronicler's outlook on popular consent, see comments on 1 Chr. 13:2.

The record of Kings also mentions that the Levites refused to cooperate with the king (see 2 Kgs. 12:8). The Chronicler, however, substituted a parenthetical remark explaining that the temple was in need of repair entirely because **that wicked woman Athaliah had broken into the temple of God and used even its sacred objects for the Baals** (24:7). In other words, the Levites had not neglected the temple; its disrepair was due to the reign of Athaliah alone.

Both Kings and Chronicles abbreviated their records of the meeting between Joash and Jehoiada. Neither book tells us Jehoiada's reaction. We must infer what happened from the verses that follow.

Successful Collection (24:8-11)

From all appearances Joash and Jehoiada reached a compromise. Instead of sending the Levites out to collect money (see 24:5), **a chest** was made and **placed outside at the gate of the temple** (24:8). The Chronicler shifted attention from Jehoiada setting up this chest (see 2 Kgs. 12:9) to the fact that this occurred **at the king's command** (24:8). He mentioned this fact to highlight the renewed cooperation between the king and the priest.

2 Kgs. 12:9 sets the chest beside the altar. The Chronicler, however, set it at the gate of the temple of the LORD (24:8). From this variation we must suppose that 'the altar' of 2 Kgs. 12:9 was not the bronze altar of the inner court, but a smaller altar somewhere near the gate of the temple complex (see *Introduction: Appendix B – The Structures, Furnishings and Decorations of Solomon's Temple).*

The Chronicler added 24:9-11a, 11c to the account of Kings. In this material he emphasized several concepts that were important for his post-exilic readers.

First, a proclamation was **issued in Judah and Jerusalem** reminding the people of their responsibility to fulfill the Mosaic tax (24:9). The breadth of this proclamation exemplified the Chronicler's concern for all the people of God to support the temple and its program in the post-exilic period (see *Introduction: 1) All Israel*).

Second, the Chronicler noted the emotions with which the contributors gave to temple renovation. They **brought their contributions gladly** ... **until** [the chest] **was full** (24:10). Rather than merely fulfilling a duty, the people were enthusiastic in their support for the temple. These comments provide another example of the Chronicler's concern that the post-exilic readers have zeal and joy in contributing to the temple in their day (see *Introduction: 16) Motivations*).

Third, the offerings amounted to **a large amount of money** (24:11a); the officials regularly collected from the chest **a great amount of money** (24:11c). In this exemplary event, the contributions to the temple were plentiful (see *Introduction: 9) Temple Contributions*).

These three additions spoke directly to the needs of the original readers of Chronicles. They should have evaluated their own involvement with the temple in the light of the enthusiastic support of Joash's day.

Joash Completes Temple Restoration (24:12-14)

This segment of Joash's early years of fidelity closes with a report of the various workers hired for temple renovation. The Chronicler's account depends loosely on 2 Kgs. 12:11-16. He specified that **the king and Jehoiada** hired workers (24:12) to highlight once again the spirit of cooperation between the royal family and the priesthood. Following the record of Kings, the Chronicler noted that no aspect of temple repair was neglected. They employed **masons, carpenters**, and **workers in iron and bronze** (24:12). Moreover, the Chronicler added that the supervisors of the work were **diligent** (24:13). They succeeded in bringing the temple back **to its original design and reinforced it** (24:13). In contrast with 2 Kgs. 12:13, the Chronicler added that **when they had finished** the main work, various worship accouterments were produced as well (24:14). Finally, the Chronicler mentioned that **as long as Jehoiada lived, burnt offerings were presented continually** (24:14). The Chronicler's variations from Kings demonstrate again that he described these events to direct his post-exilic readers regarding their own responsibilities toward the temple in their day. They should not have been satisfied with their efforts until they were as extensive as those of Joash and Jehoiada (see *Introduction: 6) Royal Observance of Worship*).

Jehoiada's Death (24:15-16)

The Chronicler added a report of Jehoiada's death to separate the two periods of Joash's reign (see figure 42). He honored the priest by noting that he was **old and full of years**, living to be **a hundred and thirty** years old (24:15). This notice of age falls in line with the longstanding biblical tradition that long life is the demonstration of divine favor (see *Introduction: 28) Healing and Long Life/Sickness and Death*). The Chronicler also honored Jehoiada by mentioning that he was **buried with the kings ... because of the good he had done in Israel for God and his temple** (24:16; see 1 Chr. 23:1). The close association between the priest Jehoiada and the Davidic line is established even in his death and burial. Even so, with Jehoiada gone, it is not long before Joash turned from his early fidelity to disobedience.

Joash's Later Years of Infidelity (24:17-26)

The text turns immediately to a series of events that depicted Joash as unfaithful to God in the later years of his reign. As we have seen in the comparison above, this material loosely parallels 2 Kgs. 12:17-21. Even so, the Chronicler omitted and added information to stress his own perspectives.

Structure of 24:17-26

This record divides into a five step narrative illustrating how Joash was unfaithful to God, ungrateful to Jehoiada, and unable to maintain control of his kingdom (see figure 42). The leaders of Judah affirm their allegiance to the king as they rebel against God (24:17-18). This beginning balances with the ironic scenes of Joash's death at the hands of these leaders (24:25-26). Zechariah, the son of Jehoiada, declared that God had abandoned Joash (24:19-20). This prophecy was fulfilled in the corresponding section which describes the victory of Syria over Judah (24:23-24). The turning point in this narrative is the murder of Zechariah at Joash's command (24:21-22).

Joash and Leaders Provoke God (24:17-18)

The Chronicler began this portion of his record with a three step scenario which he added to the account of Kings. First, after the death of Jehoiada leaders **paid homage** to Joash and the king **listened to them** (24:17). Apparently, Jehoiada's influential role in the royal court was now fulfilled by these officials. 24:25-26 suggests that some of these new advisors may have been foreigners. These new advisors turned Joash away from God. Like other kings, Joash proved to be unfaithful once his kingdom was secure. For the Chronicler's warning against permitting blessings to lead to infidelity, see comments on 1 Chr. 5:24.

Second, Joash and these officials **abandoned the temple ... and worshipped Asherah poles and idols** (24:18). The Chronicler described this infidelity with one of his important theological terms: **abandoned** (see *Introduction: 22) Abandoning/Forsaking*). He repeated this same word (**forsaken** [NIV]) later in this story (24:20,24) with the meaning that Joash and the officials had flagrantly violated their covenant loyalty to God. This violation was illustrated by the fact that Joash now did just the opposite of what he had done earlier in his life (see 24:4-14). The king who had restored the temple now abandoned it.

Third, as a result of their rebellion, **God's anger came upon Judah and Jerusalem** (24:18b). It is not altogether clear whether the Chronicler meant that God began to punish Joash with specific covenant curses, or if he merely meant that divine wrath was stirred against the king. In all events, Joash and his leaders had provoked God against them. The king's path was leading to judgment.

The Chronicler shifted abruptly in his depiction of Joash. A greater contrast could hardly be imagined. He followed this course to illustrate the striking difference between obedience leading to divine blessing and disobedience leading to divine judgment (see *Introduction: 10-27) Divine Blessing and Judgment*).

Zechariah Prophesies against Joash (24:19-20)

As it often happens in the Chronicler's history, God sent prophets to warn the rebellious nation of impending judgment (see *Introduction: 15) Prophets*). This portion of the Chronicler's addition to the life of Joash first notes that God sent a number of **prophets to the people to bring them** (i.e. cause them to turn) **back to him** (24:19). As in many cases, the purpose of the prophetic ministry was not to condemn, but to call for repentance leading to renewal of covenant ties with God (see *Introduction: 22) Repentance*). Even so, the people **would not listen** (24:19). Similar refusals to accept prophetic warnings take place elsewhere in the Chronicler's history (see 2 Chr. 16:7-10; 25:14-16; 36:12; see also *Introduction: 15) Prophets*) and in many other portions of Scripture.

Having given this overview of rebellion against prophetic warnings, the Chronicler focused on the example of **Zechariah, the son of Jehoiada** (24:20). As in other portions of Chronicles, a temple functionary served in the role of a prophet (see *Introduction: 15) Prophets*). **The Spirit of God came upon Zechariah** much as he had on Azariah (24:20; see 15:1). (For a summary of the Chronicler's view of the Spirit, see comments on 1 Chr. 12:18.)

Zechariah's speech followed the pattern of oracles of judgment found frequently in the prophetic Scriptures. He first raised his accusation in the form of a rhetorical question. **'Why do you disobey the LORD's commands?'** (24:20a). This accusation was followed by two sentencings.

First, he declared, **'you will not prosper'** (24:20a). The term 'prosper' frequently appears in Chronicles as a notice of divine blessing. Zechariah stated an important principle in the Chronicler's theology. He warned that if Judah continued in the way of rebellion, covenant blessings would not come (see *Introduction: 26) Prosperity and Poverty*).

Second, the prophetic priest announced, **'Because you have forsaken the Lord, he has forsaken you'** (24:20). The Hebrew word translated **forsaken** in this verse is the same as that translated **abandoned** in 24:18 (see *Introduction: 22) Abandoning/Forsaking*). Zechariah declared that Judah had violated her covenant with God. As a result, divine abandonment followed.

This dramatic warning depicted how the Chronicler believed God reacted to the abandonment of his temple. He hoped that his post-exilic readers would see the dire consequences of neglecting the temple and give it their full support.

Joash Orders Zechariah's Death (24:21-22)

The Chronicler continued to add to the record of Kings by describing Joash's reaction to the oracle of judgment. Humility and repentance were the appropriate response to a prophet's warning. Nevertheless, Joash ordered the death of **Zechariah** (24:21). Jesus mentioned the death of Zechariah when he referred to the prophetic tradition in the Old Testament (see Matt. 23:35). He spoke of 'Abel' and 'Zechariah' who appear in the first (Genesis) and last (Chronicles) books in the Hebrew Bible.

The Chronicler drew attention to the heinous character of Joash's crime by reminding his readers of the debt Joash owed to Jehoiada. He did not remember **the kindness Zechariah's father Jehoiada had shown him** (24:22). Joash owed his life and kingdom to Jehoiada (see 24:1-16), but he had lost all regard for his former mentor. In this dramatic scene, the Chronicler noted that as Zechariah died, his final words were, **'May the Lord see this and call you to account'** (24:22). The verses that follow demonstrate that God heard Zechariah's dying wish.

Zechariah's Prophecy Fulfilled (24:23-24)

The Chronicler returned to the account of Kings for a moment (compare 24:23 and 2 Kgs. 12:17), but he quickly departed from Kings once again (compare 24:24 and 2 Kgs. 12:18). Zechariah had prophesied that God would forsake Judah. This prophecy was fulfilled in Syria's victory over Joash. The Chronicler's account of this fulfillment divides into a three step scenario (24:23) with an additional authorial comment (24:24).

The army of Aram (Syria) **marched** against Judah (24:23a). This invasion resulted in the deaths of **all the leaders of the people** (24:23b), and the plunder of Judah was sent back **to their king in Damascus** (24:23). The rapidity with which the Chronicler recounted the defeat of Judah reflected the ease with which their victory was achieved. It was a swift victory for Syria.

Typically, the Chronicler's accounts of war involved Judah defeating armies much larger than their own (*see Introduction: 23) Victory and Defeat*). Here, however, he reversed the scenario. Judah had a much larger army than Syria; the Syrians had **only a few men** (24:24). Nevertheless, they were victorious over Judah because **the LORD delivered** (Judah) **into their hands** (24:24).

Once again, the Chronicler explained that God was behind an important event in Israel's history (*Introduction: 10) Divine Activity*). To insure that his readers understood the reason for Judah's defeat, the Chronicler added that it was **because Judah had forsaken the LORD, the God of their fathers**. The use of the term **forsaken** recalls the previous references to Judah's apostasy in this narrative (see 24:18,20,24-25; see also *Introduction: 22) Abandoning/Forsaking*). Judah's covenant infidelity resulted in a remarkable defeat before the Syrians. The Chronicler's analysis of the event demonstrated that their own military strength could not secure them against an enemy. Military security was found only in the power of God (see *Introduction: 23) Victory and Defeat*).

Joash Assassinated by Leaders (24:25-26)

In contrast with the opening of this section (see figure 42), the leaders of Judah did not honor Joash. Instead, they conspired against him. This event is described in 2 Kgs. 12:20, but the Chronicler added a few details that highlight Joash's dishonor. The officials **conspired against Joash for murdering the son of Jehoiada** (24:25). Ironically, these men probably were the ones who first convinced Joash to follow the path that led to Zechariah's death (see 24:21-22). Moreover, Joash's death occurred while he was lying helplessly **in his bed** suffering from wounds inflicted by the Syrians (24:25). Finally, while 2 Kgs. 12:21 reports that 'he was buried with his fathers in the City of David', the Chronicler added **but not in the tombs of the kings** (24:25). Joash's infidelity resulted in a disgraceful death and burial (see *Introduction: 28) Healing and Long Life/Sickness and Death*).

Having established the disgrace of Joash's death and burial, the Chronicler added a note indicating who was responsible for the king's assassination (24:26). His list differs from that of 2 Kgs. 12:21 in that it emphasizes the role of foreigners in the event. Perhaps the Chronicler added this aspect of the narrative to explain Joash's worship of foreign gods (see 24:18). In all events, the assassination of Judah's king by the hands of an Ammonite and a Moabite demonstrated the severity of God's judgment against Joash (see *Introduction: 3) International Relations*).

Closure of Joash's Reign (24:27)

The Chronicler added a brief notice of additional records for Joash's life. He then merely followed the text of 2 Kgs. 12:21d and noted that **Amaziah his son succeeded him as king**. Joash's reign ends with no praise or positive evaluation. His latter years of disobedience brought him to his grave in disgrace.

Deterioration Through Half-Hearted Obedience (25:1-28:27)

The final phase of the Divided Kingdom reports on the reigns of Amaziah (25:1-28), Uzziah (26:1-23), Jotham (27:1-9), and Ahaz (28:1-27). As with the first and second phases of this material, the Chronicler's text is complex and presents a number of motifs. Nevertheless, this material falls together principally by explicit comparisons among the various kings. This major motif comes to the foreground in the description of Amaziah as one who **did what was right in the eyes of the LORD, but not wholeheartedly** (25:2). Half-hearted obedience is a central theme in each reign that follows. Uzziah **did what was right in the eyes of the LORD, just as his father Amaziah had done** (26:4). His half-hearted commitment is evident in the second half of his reign (26:16-23). Jotham also **did what was right in the eyes of the LORD, just as his father Uzziah had done** (27:2). Although the Chronicler made it clear that Jotham himself avoided the inconsistencies of his father (27:2b), he also noted that **the people, however, continued their corrupt practices** (27:2b). At the end of this series of comparisons between fathers and their sons, the Chronicler closed this section by drawing a connection between Amaziah and Ahaz. Both of these kings were defeated by northern Israelite armies because Judah had become so corrupt (25:14-24; 28:6-15). As we will see in the comments below, at the end of this phase of the divided period, Judah had become as corrupt as her northern neighbor. This leveling of North and South set the stage for Hezekiah's Reunited Kingdom.

The Reign of Amaziah (25:1-26)

The reign of Amaziah (796-767 BC) presents another example of divine blessing and cursing based on fidelity and infidelity. In this case, Amaziah was initially spared severe consequences for his inconsistency, but God's patience led him to further infidelity and curses. As such, his reign encouraged the post-exilic readers of Chronicles not to allow divine mercy to lead to further infidelities.

Comparison of 25:1-26 with 2 Kgs. 14:1-20

The Chronicler's account of Amaziah depends heavily on the record of Kings (// 2 Kgs. 14:1-20), but the former is eight verses longer than the latter (see figure 43).

2 Chr.		2 Kgs.
———	Events in the North (omitted)	13:1-14:1
25:1-2	Opening of Amaziah's Reign (slightly abbreviated)	14:2-4
25:3-13	Amaziah's Half-hearted Fidelity (greatly expanded)	14:5-7
25:14-24	Amaziah's Infidelity and Trouble (greatly expanded)	14:8-14
25:25-28	Closure of Amaziah's Reign (abbreviated)	14:15-28

Comparison of 2 Chr. 25:1-28 with 2 Kgs. 13:1-14:28 (figure 43)

A number of variations should be noted. First, the Chronicler omitted several passages focusing on events in the North.

1) He did not include 2 Kgs. 13:1-25. His interest in the divided period is exclusively in the southern kingdom unless events in the North have a bearing on events in the South (see *Introduction: 2) Northern Israel*).

2) True to his ordinary practice, the Chronicler also omitted the opening synchronization with the northern kingdom (see 2 Kgs. 14:1).

3) The notice of Jehoash's death (2 Kgs. 14:15-16) is also omitted for the same reason.

Second, the Chronicler replaced the comparison between Amaziah and David (2 Kgs. 14:3b) with the notice that Amaziah obeyed God **but not wholeheartedly** (25:2). The Chronicler's characteristic concern with heart devotion and inward sincerity is evident.

Third, Chronicles omits the mention of Amaziah's failure to remove high places (2 Kgs. 14:4). This omission shapes the record of Amaziah into a presentation of years of relative fidelity followed by infidelity.

Fourth, the note of victory over Edom (2 Kgs 14:7) has been expanded into a full scale narrative (25:5-13). This additional material contains a number of typical themes in Chronicles. It touches on the dangers of alliances with northern Israelites, prophetic warnings, and the benefit of submission to the prophetic word.

Fifth, a second encounter between Amaziah and a prophet appears (25:14-16). This meeting is introduced by the king's syncretism, and depicts the king as rejecting the prophetic warning. This expansion gives shape to the second half of the record as one of a period of Amaziah's infidelity.

Sixth, Chronicles adds an explanation of why Amaziah did not heed the warnings of Jehoash of northern Israel. It notes that Amaziah foolishly spurned his enemies' offer of peace **for God so worked that he might hand them over to Jehoash because they sought the gods of Edom** (25:20b // 2 Kgs. 14:11). The Chronicler explained that the terrible defeat of Judah was the result of divine retribution.

Seventh, the Chronicler explicitly noted his division of Amaziah's reign into years of fidelity and infidelity by adding a small comment in 25:27 (// 2 Kgs. 14:19). He noted that the conspiracy against the king began **from the time that Amaziah turned away from following the LORD**.

Structure of 25:1-26

The additions and omissions appearing in this passage form a fivefold symmetrical account (see figure 44).

This chapter begins with the rise of Amaziah (25:1-2) and ends with the closure of his reign (25:25-28). The king's reign divides into acts of half-hearted fidelity (25:3-12) and a balancing account of infidelity (25:14-24). In the center of this structure is a brief note which serves as a report of the negative results of Amaziah's half-hearted fidelity and initiates his acts of infidelity (25:13).

- Opening of Amaziah's Reign (25:1-2)
  - Amaziah's Half-hearted Fidelity (25:3-12)
    - Execution of Assassins (25:3-4)
      - Report of Executions (25:3)
      - Qualification and Evaluation (25:4)
    - Half-hearted Fidelity in Battle (25:5-12)
      - Amaziah Enrolls the People for War (25:5a)
        - Amaziah Conscripts and Hires Soldiers (25:5b-6)
          - Amaziah Encounters Prophetic Rebuke (25:7-9)
        - Amaziah Releases Hired Soldiers (25:10)
      - Amaziah Gains Victory (25:11-12)
    - Amaziah's Trouble from Israel (25:13)
  - Amaziah's Infidelity (25:14-24)
    - Amaziah Worships Edomite Gods (25:14)
      - Amaziah Encounters Prophetic Rebuke (25:15-16)
    - Amaziah Receives Punishment for Infidelity (25:17-24)
      - Amaziah Challenges Jehoash to Battle (25:17-19)
        - Amaziah Refuses Jehoash's Warnings (25:20)
      - Amaziah Loses Battle to Jehoash (25:21-24)
- Closure of Amaziah's Reign (25:25-28)

Outline of 2 Chr. 25:1-28 (figure 44)

Opening of Amaziah's Reign (25:1-2)

The reign of Amaziah notes a few historical details of his rise to power. The name of the king's mother appears. For the significance of royal mothers, see comments on 13:2. As we have seen in the comparison above, synchronization with the Northern kingdom is omitted (see 2 Kgs. 14:1) and the text remarks that the king was **twenty-five years old** when he ascended to the throne (25:1). A number of chronological notes in Kings (e.g. 2 Kgs. 14:2, 23; 15:1) suggest that as many as twenty-four years of Amaziah's twenty-nine year reign was a co-regency with Uzziah. Amaziah's capture by Jehoash of Israel also suggests this historical reconstruction (see 25:23).

The Chronicler evaluated Amaziah's reign as a mixture of good and evil. **He did what was right ... but not wholeheartedly** (25:2). In this regard, the Chronicler varied from 2 Kgs 14:3 which compares Amaziah with David and Joash. Instead, he focused on the condition of Amaziah's heart. Heart motivation is a chief concern in Chronicles. The history often focused on the need for obedience to rise out of a sincere heart (see *Introduction: 16) Motivations*). Amaziah, however, was only mediocre in his devotion to God.

By describing Amaziah in this manner, the Chronicler provided his post-exilic readers with a framework for evaluating the materials that followed. He warned them not to expect striking contrasts between blessing and cursing in the king's life. Instead, they would find here the results that come to those who obey, but with half-hearted devotion.

Amaziah's Half-hearted Fidelity (25:3-12)
The Chronicler followed the book of Kings (// 2 Kgs. 14:3-7) and focused first on the relatively positive side of Amaziah's reign.

Structure of 25:3-12
This portion of his record divides into two main parts (see figure 44). The Chronicler's account consists of an evaluative report (25:3-4) and a full narrative (25:5-12). The opening report is entirely positive, but the full narrative illustrates a mixture of obedience and disobedience.

Execution of Assassins (25:3-4)
Following the account of Kings very closely, Chronicles reports that Amaziah's first action after consolidating his power was to execute **the officials who had murdered his father** (25:3). A list of these officials appears in the preceding chapter (see 24:26). Although the dishonorable death of Amaziah's father resulted from the judgment of God against him, those who performed the deed were still held responsible for their actions. The text does not spell out Amaziah's motivations for these executions. The fact that some of these men were sons of Ammonite and Moabite women made their loyalty to Amaziah questionable (see 24:26). He may have executed them for this reason.

Whatever the case, the records of Kings and Chronicles honor Amaziah for his restraint. He did not **put their sons to death ... in accordance with what is written in the Law ... of Moses** (25:4). The fear of reprisals from the sons of those executed did not dissuade Amaziah from following the Law of Moses. Remarkably, the text actually quotes the particular Law in question (see Deut. 24:16). The principle of the Law was that **each is to die for his own sins** (25:4). This principle fit well with the Chronicler's emphasis on divine blessing and cursing in the post-exilic period. Chronicles focuses on how each generation of Judah suffered for its own sins and benefited from its own obedience (see *Introduction: 10-27) Divine Blessing and Judgment*). Amaziah's restraint illustrated this principle at work.

The Chronicler's concern with individual responsibility before the Law is similar to several portions of Scripture stemming from the exilic period. Jeremiah (see Jer. 31:29-30) and Ezekiel (see Ezek. 18:1-2,19-24) stressed the idea that the exiles were not simply suffering because of the sins of their forebears. The recipients of their prophecies were themselves continuing in the practices of their ancestors and therefore suffered the consequences of their sins. On occasion in Scripture children were punished along with their fathers (see Josh. 7:24; 2 Kgs. 9:26; 1 Chr. 10:14). Although these passages do not explicitly comment on the guilt of the children, we may assume from the Mosaic legislation that these children were sufficiently involved in the sins of their fathers or in sins of their own that they deserved to die as well. The Mosaic Law included the threat of curses on future generations (see Exod. 20:5-6; Deut. 5:9), but the wrath belonging to forebears is not transferred to later generations. The later generations themselves also prove disloyal and deserving of punishment. In all events, the Chronicler honored Amaziah for observing this principle of Mosaic Law (see *Introduction: 14) Standards*).

Half-hearted Fidelity in Battle (25:5-12)

At this point the Chronicler expanded the notice of one verse in Kings (2 Kgs. 14:7) into a full narrative of nine verses (25:5-13).

Structure of 25:5-12

This material elaborates on the events that led to Amaziah's victory over the Edomites in five symmetrical steps (see figure 44).

Amaziah Enrolls the People for War (25:5a)

Amaziah gathered **the people of Judah** and **assigned them to commanders** (25:5a). Amaziah was preparing for war. We learn later that this war was against the Edomites (see 25:11). David had conquered the Edomites (see 1 Chr. 18:11-13) and Solomon used their territories to establish maritime trade to the east (see 8:17-18). As an expression of divine judgment, however, the Edomites rebelled against Jehoram (see 21:8-10). Amaziah was attempting to exert Judahite control over these Southern regions again. In the end, his son Uzziah was able to rebuild the Edomite port city of Elath (see 26:2).

Amaziah took a count of his military men much like David (see 1 Chr. 21; 27:23-24), Solomon (see 2:17), Asa (see 14:8), and Jehoshaphat (see 17:14-19). This army included men from **all Judah and Benjamin** (25:5a). It was not a professional standing army, but an army raised for a particular occasion much as Moses had ordered (see Exod. 30:14; 38:26; Lev. 27:3-5; Num. 1; 1 Chr. 27:23; 23:24; 2 Chr. 31:17).

The dramatic effect of this scene must not be overlooked. The Chronicler had just exalted Amaziah for his obedience to the Mosaic Law (25:4). At this point he portrayed the king as preparing for battle with the same Law in mind. The expectation raised for the original readers is that this will be a grand battle of victory. But the Chronicler had also noted that Amaziah was not devoted to the Lord wholeheartedly (see 25:2). The next step in this story reveals why he made this evaluation.

Amaziah Conscripts and Hires Soldiers (25:5b-6)

Amaziah continued to follow the standards of the Mosaic Law in the first portion of this step (25:5b). He **mustered those twenty years old or more** from Judah and Benjamin just as Moses had commanded (25:5b; see Exod. 30:14). When these conscripts came together, Amaziah had **three hundred thousand men ready for military service** (25:5b). Mentioning large and skilled armies is one way in which the Chronicler often exalted faithful kings (see 1 Chr. 12:24-40; 21:5; 27:1-15; 2

Chr. 13:3; 17:12-19; 26:13). As with many references to the numbers of fighting men, this large number may be understood in several ways. (For the Chronicler's use of large numbers of soldiers, see comments on 1 Chr. 12:24-37.) The number of Amaziah's soldiers does not represent the greatest army of Judah, but it is still very large and may be a hyperbole. (For the Chronicler's use of hyperbole, see comments on 1 Chr. 12:14.) Moreover, these soldiers were **able to handle the spear and shield** (25:5b). Although they were not professional soldiers, these men were extraordinarily well prepared for fighting. Once again, the Chronicler raised the expectations of victory.

The first hint of something going wrong appears in 25:6. The Chronicler added the note that Amaziah **also hired a hundred thousand fighting men from Israel** (25:6). No words of condemnation appear immediately, but the history of Chronicles has already provided ample information to cause hesitation at Amaziah's move. The Chronicler already strongly condemned involvement with northern military power. With this brief note, he began to show how Amaziah was half-hearted in his loyalty to God (see *Introduction: 2) Northern Israel*).

Amaziah Encounters Prophetic Rebuke (25:7-9)

The turning point in this narrative consists of a dialogue between an unnamed prophet and Amaziah. This scene depicts the prophet speaking to the king (25:7-8), the king's question (25:9a), and the prophet's response (25:9b). In these verses, the Chronicler made his evaluation of Amaziah's actions explicit.

The **man of God** (i.e. the prophet) warned Amaziah that **these troops from Israel must not march with** [Amaziah] (25:7). Once again the Chronicler demonstrated his keen interest in prophets (see *Introduction: 15) Prophets*). In no uncertain terms, the prophet insisted that **the LORD is not with Israel** (25:7). This entire speech is reminiscent of Abijah's speech to the northern tribes (see 13:4-12). In the Chronicler's terminology, when God was 'with' an army it meant that he would lead and fight for the army (see *Introduction: 10) Divine Activity*). The prophet warned the king that he would be defeated by his enemies **'even if you go and fight courageously in battle'** (25:8). Although Amaziah had a strong army (see 25:5-6), he was sure to lose if he opposed the command of God **for God has the power to help or to overthrow** (25:8).

In these words the Chronicler revealed his own caution regarding northern Israel. Although he held out hope for reunification with the faithful of the North, this event and a number of similar occurrences demonstrate that military alliances with evil people in the northern kingdom were forbidden (see *Introduction: 2) Northern Israel*).

Amaziah responded to the prophetic warning with a trifling objection which revealed the priorities of his heart. He wondered what to do about **the hundred talents** he paid for the soldiers from Israel (25:9a). His concern over his monetary investment revealed that Amaziah was more worried about his money than the word of his God.

In response to the king's objection, the prophet said what should have been obvious. God could give much more to Amaziah than the money he might lose if he were obedient to God (25:9b). Time and again the Chronicler had already illustrated how fidelity to God resulted in riches and prosperity for Judah (see *Introduction: 26) Prosperity and Poverty*). In this way, the Chronicler portrayed Amaziah as lacking a wholehearted devotion to God.

Amaziah Releases Hired Soldiers (25:10)

In balance with the hiring of northern mercenaries (25:5b-6), Amaziah **dismissed the troops ... from Ephraim and sent them home**. The king acted in accordance with the prophetic word, but the Chronicler did not present the king's compliance as a complete turn toward divine blessings. Instead he foreshadowed future trouble for Amaziah by noting that the northern soldiers **were furious with Judah and left for home in a great rage**. This fact will appear again (see 25:13) and contribute to the troubles Amaziah experiences then (see 25:17-24). As in Rehoboam's reign (see 12:7,8), the Chronicler's message here was plain enough. Infidelity often had enduring consequences despite repentance (see *Introduction: 10-27) Divine Blessing and Judgment*).

Amaziah Gains Victory (25:11-12)

In spite of the foreshadowing of trouble to come, the Chronicler recorded that Amaziah had a great victory. He **killed ten thousand men of Seir** in battle (25:11). The army also **captured ten thousand men alive** and executed them by throwing them over a cliff (25:12). Although this form of mass execution seems inhumane by modern standards, it stands as only one example of the horrors of ancient warfare (see Josh. 11:7-11; 1 Sam. 4:10). Once again, these large numbers may be understood in a number of ways. (For the Chronicler's use of large numbers of soldiers, see comments on 1 Chr. 12:24-37.) In all events, Amaziah gained the victory because he removed the northern Israelite soldiers from his ranks. This victory in battle ranked among other similar victories as a demonstration of divine favor (see *Introduction: 23) Victory and Defeat*).

Amaziah's Trouble from Israel (25:13)

In the center of Amaziah's reign the Chronicler added a relatively disconnected report of trouble from the northern Israelites (see figure 44). The soldiers whom the king sent home **in a great rage** (25:10b) wreaked havoc in Judah while Amaziah battled with the Edomites. It is difficult to understand how these mercenaries plundered **from Samaria to Beth Horon**, unless they were dismissed from duty as they readied themselves in Samaria. Whatever the case, the raids of these troops were extensive. They killed **three thousand people and carried off great quantities of plunder**.

This brief report forms a pivotal event between the two accounts of battle in Amaziah's reign (see figure 44). It resulted from the king's intended alliance with the North against Edom (see 25:6), and led to his provocation of war against the

North (see 25:17). By structuring his account in this manner, the Chronicler demonstrated that the king's initial disloyalty eventually led to defeat and death.

Amaziah's Infidelity (25:14-24)
Having reported Amaziah's victory over the Edomites and the incursion of angry northern mercenaries into Judah, the Chronicler demonstrated how victory over the Edomites led to a failed attempt to redress the atrocities of the Israelite mercenaries.

Structure of 25:14-24
The Chronicler's account of these matters divides into three major steps, the last of which is a self-contained narrative in its own right (see figure 44). Amaziah adopts Edomite gods (25:14). He is rebuked by a prophet (25:15-16). Finally, Amaziah receives the punishment appropriate for his infidelity (25:17-24).

Amaziah Worships Edomite Gods (25:14)
The Chronicler added 25:14 to the account of Kings. Amaziah **brought back the gods of the people of Seir** (25:14). At first glance it may seem incongruous that Amaziah would worship the gods of a defeated people. Nevertheless, it was customary in the ancient Near East for a conquering people to carry the gods of their defeated enemies back to their own temples (see 1 Sam. 5:1-2). Records from nations surrounding Israel explain that victors in battle often worshipped captured idols to thank them for betraying their own people to defeat. Amaziah probably **bowed down to them** for similar reasons. Whatever his precise motivations, Amaziah's actions proved to be a flagrant violation of his loyalty to God and led to serious trouble in his kingdom. His actions followed a common scenario in Chronicles; an experience of blessing from God led to infidelity. (For the Chronicler's warning against permitting blessings to lead to infidelity, see comments on 1 Chr. 5:24.)

Amaziah Encounters Prophetic Rebuke (25:15-16)
The Chronicler continued to add his own material to the reign of Amaziah and immediately explained that Amaziah's act of disloyalty stirred **the anger of the LORD** (25:15). In his usual fashion, the Chronicler presented **a prophet** who came to warn the king (25:15; see *Introduction: 15) Prophets*). As in Amaziah's previous encounter with a prophet (see 25:7-9), a dialogue occurred in which the prophet spoke (25:15), the king responded with a question (25:16a), and the prophet replied (25:16b).

In the first place, the prophet asked, **'Why do you consult** ...' the Edomite gods (25:15). The Hebrew word translated **consult** in this passage is one of the Chronicler's favorite terms often translated 'inquire' or 'seek' (see *Introduction: 19) Seeking*). By expressing the prophet's message in this manner, the Chronicler revealed that Amaziah's worship of the Edomite gods was earnest and a serious act of infidelity. The prophet demonstrated the folly of Amaziah's actions by pointing out how impotent these gods were. They were unable to **save their own people** (25:15). Such gods were not worthy of worship.

Second, the Chronicler reported Amaziah's answer to this harsh prophetic rebuke (25:16a). The king interrupted the prophet and asked, **'Have we appointed you an adviser to the king?'** (25:16a). Amaziah hired prophets to serve in his court much as Ahab had in the northern kingdom (see 18:8). He gathered around himself prophets who gave the kinds of prophecies he desired. Once on the royal payroll, it was difficult for a prophet to speak words of condemnation. This unnamed prophet was not a member of the royal court. Like Amos of Tekoa, he was not a professional prophet, nor the son (student) of a professional prophet (see Amos 7:14). He spoke as a free agent and therefore brought a very negative warning. So, Amaziah told him not to speak or he would be **struck down** (25:16a).

Amaziah's disposition toward the prophet was mixed, demonstrating his half-hearted devotion to God once again. On the one hand, he did not want to see the prophet of God harmed. On the other hand, he considered himself in control of the prophets and rejected the prophetic word. This event contrasted with the king's earlier compliance with the warning of another prophet (see 25:7-10). The Chronicler's mixed assessment of Amaziah (see 25:2b) held true in these scenes as well.

Third, **the prophet stopped but said** a final word of warning (25:16b). The prophetic speech followed the form of an oracle of judgment. First, he sentenced Amaziah to a difficult future. **God has determined to destroy** the king (26:16b). Then, two accusations provided the basis for this harsh sentence. The king had **done this** (i.e. worshipped the Edomite gods) and had **not listened** to the advice of the prophet (26:16b).

In these few words the Chronicler repeated a theme he mentioned a number of times in his history. To ignore the words of God's prophets was to fall subject to the judgment of God (see *Introduction: 15) Prophets*). The Chronicler was convinced that paying attention to the prophetic word was one of his readers' most urgent needs. To avoid divine judgment, they must reject the example of Amaziah.

Amaziah Receives Judgment for Infidelity (25:17-24)

In 25:17-24 the Chronicler returned to his source in 2 Kgs. 14:8-14 (but see 25:20). His dependence on Kings at this point leads to a somewhat awkward structural transition, but his intention is clear. The Chronicler introduced Amaziah's syncretism and rejection of the prophet as the explanation for the defeat of Judah recorded in these verses. In an unusually positive portrait of the northern kingdom, the Israelites defeated Amaziah in fulfillment of the prophetic word (25:16b).

Structure of 25:17-24

The account of battle between Amaziah and Jehoash of northern Israel divides into a three step narrative (see figure 44). This story begins with Amaziah challenging Jehoash to battle (25:17-19). This challenge is balanced by Jehoash defeating Amaziah in battle (25:21-24). The turning point in the drama is Amaziah's refusal to heed Jehoash's warning of certain defeat (25:20).

Amaziah Challenges Jehoash to Battle (25:17-19)
From the preceding context it seems likely that Amaziah challenged Jehoash because of the earlier incursion of Israelite mercenaries (see 25:13). 2 Kgs. 14:8 simply says that 'Amaziah sent messengers to Jehoash'. The Chronicler expanded this verse by mentioning that Amaziah first **consulted his advisors** (25:17). This additional detail drew a sharp contrast between Amaziah's reaction to the prophet and his favored court advisors. The king had earlier rejected the man of God, declaring that he had no right to be **an advisor** to the king (25:16). Now he readily listened to the advice of those whom he paid. Amaziah compounded his sin by this act.

Amaziah challenged Jehoash to meet **face to face** (25:17). Later in the story Jehoash and Amaziah **faced each other** (25:21), but not immediately. Instead, the story highlights Amaziah's folly by recording Jehoash's warning (25:18-19). In an ironic twist, the text depicts the king of northern Israel rightly rebuking Amaziah for pursuing war.

In the first place, Jehoash spoke a parable about **a thistle in Lebanon** (i.e. Judah) that asked for the daughter of **a cedar** (i.e. Edom). Meanwhile, **a wild beast** (i.e. northern Israel) came along and **trampled the thistle underfoot** (25:18).

Second, Jehoash interpreted his parable. The record of 2 Kgs. 14:10 simply says that Amaziah was 'arrogant'. The Chronicler expanded the description by adding that Amaziah was **arrogant and proud** (25:19). Similar language indicating pride and arrogance appears a number of times in the Old Testament as a cause of disloyalty to God (see 1 Sam. 2:3; 2 Kgs. 19:28; Prov. 8:13; 11:2; 16:18; 21:24; 29:23; Isa. 2:17; 37:29; Hos. 5:5; Amos 6:8; Zeph. 2:10). The Chronicler mentioned the subject three other times (see 26:16; 32:25, 26). Like the thistle who would dare to ask for the daughter of a cedar, Amaziah had ventured arrogantly into matters too great for him.

Third, Jehoash asked why Amaziah wanted to cause his own **downfall and that of Judah also** (25:19). Jehoash warned Amaziah that his arrogance had caused him to be unaware that battle with northern Israel would be like a lion trampling a thistle. Judah would be destroyed. The text does not explain why Jehoash was so confident about the outcome of battle. Perhaps his army far outnumbered Amaziah's forces. Whatever the case, the rest of this story demonstrates that Amaziah should have listened to him (see 25:21-24).

Amaziah Refuses Jehoash's Warnings (25:20)
The turning point of this account amounts to Amaziah's foolish refusal of Jehoash's advice. Although Jehoash had given him fair warning, Amaziah **would not listen** (25:20). This act led directly to one of Judah's worst defeats.

The Chronicler expanded the record of Kings (// 2 Kgs 14:11) to give the reason for Amaziah's foolish refusal. He added that **God so worked that he might hand them over to Jehoash because they sought the gods of Edom** (25:20). As in a number of other passages divine purposes undergird this extraordinary event (see *Introduction: 10) Divine Activity*). God had determined that Judah would be defeated for the sin of turning to Edomite gods (see 25:14-15).

By this expansion, the Chronicler made it explicit that the misfortune soon to come on Judah was the direct result of divine judgment. His message to the original post-exilic readers was evident. Pride resulting from ill-gotten successes would be avenged by God. Only success in the context of humble service to God would lead to further blessing.

Amaziah Loses Battle to Jehoash (25:21-24)

Chronicles returns to following the account of 2 Kgs. 14:11b-14 and describes the manner in which divine judgment came against Amaziah. The scenes move with great speed, displaying the utter defeat of Judah. Jehoash struck first (25:21). **Every man** of Judah **fled home** (25:22). Jehoash **captured Amaziah** (25:23). He **broke down the wall of Jerusalem ... a section about six hundred feet long** (25:23). He took **all the gold and silver and all the articles found in the temple** as well as **the palace treasures and the hostages** (25:24). Jehoash inflicted tremendous destruction on the city of David and **returned to Samaria** in safety (25:24).

The extensive details of these events makes the Chronicler's outlook very clear. Never before had Jerusalem suffered such a defeat. Amaziah's half-hearted devotion to God (see 25:2) may have brought some good to the nation, but in the end it led to a horrible outcome for him and all of Judah. The Chronicler's post-exilic readers could expect the same in their day, if they refused to serve the Lord wholeheartedly.

Closure of Amaziah's Reign (25:25-28)

The Chronicler closed his account of Amaziah's reign in his usual manner. After omitting the record of Jehoash's death in 2 Kgs 14:15-16, he depended on 2 Kgs. 14:17-20 to bring Amaziah's kingdom to an end. This ending amounts to two reports on his death and burial (25:25, 27-28) which frame a reference to other sources (25:26).

The most significant aspect of these verses is the Chronicler's addition in 25:27 (// 2 Kgs. 14:19). He added that the conspiracy leading to Amaziah's death began **from the time that Amaziah turned away from following the LORD** (25:27). Much like his father Joash, Amaziah's apostasy was the cause of a conspiracy that eventually led to his death (see 24:25). By adding these words, the Chronicler made it clear that Amaziah's ignoble death was also the result of divine judgment. After the death of Jehoash (24:25), Amaziah fled for his life to Lachish, but divine judgment was sure and murderers **killed him there** (25:27). Nevertheless, true to his historical records and his earlier assessment of the king (see 25:2), the Chronicler admitted that Amaziah was **buried with his fathers in the city of Judah** (25:28), an honor withheld from Joash his father (see *Introduction: 28) Healing and Long Life/Sickness and Death*).

The Reign of Uzziah (26:1-23)

The Chronicler moved next to Uzziah son of Amaziah (792/91–740/39 BC). Uzziah's reign provided his readers with another example of a Judean king whose life, like Amaziah before him, was divided into years of blessing and judgment because of half-hearted devotion.

Comparison of 26:1-23 with 2 Kgs. 14:21-15:7

The Chronicler included most of the reign of Uzziah in Kings within his account (see figure 45). A number of insignificant stylistic differences appear, but the Chronicler also varied his account in major ways to conform to his doctrine of divine blessing and judgment (see *Introduction: 10-27) Divine Blessing and Judgment*).

2 Chr.		2 Kgs.
26:1-2	Opening of Uzziah's Reign (A) (closely parallel)	14:21-22
———	Events in the North (omitted)	14:23-15:1
26:3-4	Opening of Uzziah's Reign (B) (closely parallel)	15:2-3
26:5-15	Uzziah's Fidelity and Blessings (added)	———
26:16-21	Uzziah's Infidelity and Curse (greatly expanded)	15:4-5
26:22-23	Closure of Uzziah's Reign (parallel)	15:6-7

Comparison of 26:1-23 with 2 Kgs. 14:21-15:7 (Figure 45)

First, the most obvious difference between Kings and Chronicles on a large scale is the omission of 2 Kgs 14:23-15:1. In his usual fashion, the Chronicler omitted this material because it focused on events in northern Israel. Here as elsewhere he only touched on the northern kingdom as it came into contact with Judah.

Second, a word should be said about the name of this king. The Hebrew text of Kings calls him 'Azariah' (see 2 Kgs. 15:1, 6, 7, 8, 17, 23, 27). The Chronicler designated him **Uzziah** throughout this chapter. 'Uzziah' appears here and in Isa. 1:1; 6:1; Hos. 1:1; Amos 1:1; Zech. 14:5; 2 Kgs. 15:13, 30, 32, 34. Nevertheless, the Chronicler himself used the name **Azariah** in 1 Chr. 3:12. It is likely that one name was given to the king at birth and the other at the time of his enthronement. Moreover, the Chronicler may have used **Uzziah** consistently in this chapter to distinguish him from the priest **Azariah** who also appears in this chapter (see 26:17,20).

Third, the Chronicler added much material to the account of Kings. Kings gives only nine verses to Uzziah's life (2 Kgs. 14:21-22; 15:1-7). The Chronicler's record consists of twenty three verses. Two large additions appear. 1) The Chronicler added 26:5-15 to illustrate how Uzziah received divine blessings during his early years. 2) He expanded 2 Kgs. 15:5 // 26:21 to reveal the king's failure that led to his severe skin disease (26:16-20). Both of these major additions were necessary to shape Uzziah's reign into years of blessing and judgment.

Fourth, the Chronicler omitted the notice of high places remaining in Uzziah's early years to enhance his division of the king's reign into a period of fidelity and infidelity (2 Kgs. 15:4).

Fifth, the Chronicler shifted from royal sources (2 Kgs. 15:6) to a prophetic source (26:22). In all likelihood, this was his primary source for the materials he added to Uzziah's reign.

Structure of 26:1-23

The Chronicler shaped his account so that it divided into four symmetrical sections (see figure 46).

Opening of Uzziah's Reign (26:1-5)

- Uzziah's Fidelity and Blessing (26:6-15)
  - Uzziah's Military Victories (26:6-8)
    - Uzziah's Domestic Successes (26:9-10)
  - Uzziah's Military Strength (26:11-15)

- Uzziah's Infidelity and Curse (26:16-21)
  - Powerful Uzziah Enters Temple (26:16)
    - Priests Follow Uzziah into Temple (26:17)
      - Confrontation Between Priests and Uzziah (26:18-19)
    - Priests Escort Uzziah Out of Temple (26:20)
  - Powerless Uzziah is Barred from Temple (26:21)

Closure of Uzziah's Reign (26:22-23)

Outline of 2 Chr. 26:1-23 (figure 46)

Uzziah's reign begins with a summary of how he came to power and some general comments about his reign (26:1-5). This material balances by striking contrast with the closing notices about his last days (26:22-23). The body of the Chronicler's record divides into two contrasting sections as well. Reports of Uzziah's successes due to fidelity (26:6-15) are followed by an event of flagrant infidelity and divine curse (26:16-21).

Opening of Uzziah's Reign (26:1-5)

The Chronicler began his record with introductory notes on the king's rise to power and general information about his kingdom. His opening follows 2 Kgs. 14:21-22 and 15:2-3 closely, but omits 2 Kgs. 14:23-15:1 which deals with events in the North. This type of omission is normal for the Chronicler (see *Introduction: 2) Northern Israel*), but here it caused the Chronicler to mention twice in close proximity that Uzziah was sixteen years old when he rose to power (26:1,3).

The opening words **all the people of Judah took Uzziah** (26:1) is an unusual way to describe the rise of a king. It may indicate that popular demand brought Uzziah to power while his father was in captivity in Samaria (see 25:23-24). For other situations where similar transitions of power took place see 22:1; 23:20-21; 33:25; 36:1. Whatever the case, Uzziah shared power with Amaziah from 792/1 to 767 BC. He then reigned as sole regent until his son Jotham ruled alongside him for the last ten years of his life (750-740/39).

The opening notes on Uzziah's reign highlight several positive features.

1) He **rebuilt Elath ... after Amaziah rested** (26:2). Elath was an important port city in Edomite territory which Solomon had taken for his kingdom (see 8:17-18 // 1 Kgs. 9:26-28) and Jehoram had lost (see 21:8-10). Amaziah subdued the Edomites (see 25:11-12), but Uzziah rebuilt the port. The opening of this sea port was a very positive dimension of Uzziah's reign. For a summary of Judah's involvement with Edom see comments on 25:5a.

2) Uzziah enjoyed one of the longest reigns of Judah's kings, **fifty-two years** (26:3; compare Manasseh in 33:1).

3) In general terms, Uzziah is noted as one who **did right in the eyes of the LORD** (26:4). This description appears in the introductory notes on a number of kings (see 14:2; 20:32; 24:2; 25:2; 26:4; 27:2; 29:2; 34:2). The Chronicler also characterized other kings as having done **evil in the eyes of the LORD** (21:6; 22:4; 28:1; 29:6; 33:2, 6, 22; 36:5; 36:9, 12).

These depictions must be taken as general, not categorical. In this case, however, the Chronicler also copied from Kings the qualification that Uzziah did right **just as his father Amaziah had done** (26:4 // 2 Kgs. 15:3). This qualification is easily understood in the book of Kings for the writer of Kings hardly mentioned the sins of Amaziah and Uzziah. The Chronicler, however, insisted that Amaziah did what was right, **but not wholeheartedly** (25:2). In this light, the comparison of Uzziah with Amaziah in Chronicles implied that the former gave similar half-hearted devotion as well. This evaluation of Uzziah is supported by the verse that follows. (For the significance of the king's royal mother, see comments on 2 Chr. 13:2.)

The Chronicler began his first addition to Uzziah's reign with an explanation of his comparison with Amaziah. Uzziah **sought God** (26:5). In the Chronicler's theology, this terminology referred to one of the most important demonstrations of faith. 'Seeking' the Lord was to devote oneself to finding God's blessing, especially to finding counsel and help in times of trouble (see *Introduction: 19) Seeking*). Nevertheless, the Chronicler was also quick to say that Uzziah sought God only during the life of **Zechariah who instructed him in the fear of God**. The identity of this **Zechariah** is uncertain. It is possible that he was a witness of the prophet Isaiah (see Isa. 8:2), but this identification cannot be firmly established. Whatever the case, the parallel to Jehoiada's influence over Joash must not be missed (see 24:2). Uzziah **sought the LORD** only under Zechariah's tutelage. This allusion to Joash's reign prepared the Chronicler's readers to expect Uzziah to be much like Joash. His fidelity was followed by severe infidelity.

In these opening verses the Chronicler foreshadowed his purpose in recording the reign of Uzziah. Uzziah was righteous only under the sway of another. Thus the Chronicler drew his readers' attention to the need for enduring fidelity stemming from wholehearted devotion, rather than mere temporary obedience brought about by external influences.

Uzziah's Fidelity and Blessing (26:6-15)
Having introduced his readers to Uzziah, the Chronicler made a substantial addition focusing on the king's fidelity and resulting blessings. Despite his qualification of Uzziah's faithfulness, the Chronicler reported benefits that came to the king during the years of Zechariah's influence.

Structure of 26:6-15
This account divides into three parts (see figure 46). The first and last sections (26:6-8, 11-15) form an inclusion that frames this material. Both portions deal with the subject of military strength and similar terminology appears in both portions. The king's victories came about because **God helped him** (26:7) and the result was that **his fame spread** (26:8). Similarly, Uzziah's military strength made **his fame spread** because **he was greatly helped** by God (26:15). Beyond this, 26:8 states that the king had **become very powerful** and 26:15 mentions that he **became very powerful**. The middle section (26:9-10) focuses on the domestic improvements Uzziah made during this time.

Uzziah's Military Victories (26:6-8)
The first report of Uzziah's blessings concerns victories over enemies. The Chronicler frequently referred to the defeat of enemies as demonstration of divine favor (see *Introduction: 23) Victory and Defeat*). Here he described Uzziah's successes in ways that stressed the magnificence of this blessing. He mentioned victory over **Philistines, Arabs, Meunites** and **Ammonites** (26:6-7). Each of these groups appear elsewhere in Chronicles as enemies of Judah (see 1 Chr. 10:7-9; 2 Chr. 26:6-8). Uzziah's military aggression was limited to the west, south, and southeast because Jeroboam II of northern Israel was very strong at this time.

The Chronicler made it clear that Uzziah's accomplishments were not by human power. He was successful because **God helped him** (26:7). This terminology occurs a number of times in Chronicles where an intervention by God is in view. Unusual success and extraordinary accomplishments are often attributed to the **help** of God (see 1 Chr. 5:20; 12:18; 15:26; 2 Chr. 14:11; 16:12; 18:31; 20:4; 26:7; 32:8; see also *Introduction: 10) Divine Activity*). God extended such favor to Uzziah that **his fame spread as far as the border of Egypt** (26:8). News of his victories spread great distances (see *Introduction: 3) International Relations*).

Finally, Uzziah's victories were not isolated occurrences. They demonstrated that he **had become very powerful** (26:8). Although the Chronicler had already made it clear that this period of fidelity will be short lived (see 26:5), Uzziah benefited greatly from the blessings of God.

Israel's prophets had announced that those who returned from exile would be given military superiority over their enemies (see Isa. 11:11-16; 29:18-23; 49:14-26; 54:1-3; Jer. 30:10-11; Ezek. 38-39; Amos 9:11-12). Uzziah experienced a foretaste of this supremacy. This promise, however, would never come in its fullness so long as the post-exilic community did not learn the lesson of Uzziah's early years. Fidelity to God alone leads Judah to military victory.

Uzziah's Domestic Successes (26:9-10)

The Chronicler frequently pointed to building projects and economic growth as demonstrations of God's blessing (see *Introduction: 24) Building and Destruction*; see also *26) Prosperity and Poverty*). Here he added a description of Uzziah that focuses on these kinds of domestic successes during his early years of faithfulness. This report mentions three areas of Uzziah's kingdom.

First, Uzziah completed building projects **in Jerusalem** (26:9). The Chronicler specifically mentioned the fortification of the city with **towers** at key places in the city wall.

Second, Uzziah **had much livestock in the foothills and in the plain**. For this reason he built **towers in the desert**, outposts that provided for storage, as well as protection for royal workers. He also constructed **cisterns** for water retention (26:10).

Third, in an unusual moment of insight into Uzziah's personality, the Chronicler wrote that Uzziah **loved the soil**; he had a keen interest in the agricultural development of Judah. As a result, he had **people working** in agricultural efforts throughout the land (26:10).

This list of domestic successes had a direct bearing on the lives of the Chronicler's post-exilic readers. They had hopes of seeing the land of promise developed in the ways Uzziah took the nation in his day. Military fortification, livestock and agricultural development were high priorities for the restored community. The Chronicler's purpose in these reports is evident. Uzziah received these blessings because he was loyal to his God; they too would see these blessings when they devoted themselves to their God.

Uzziah's Military Strength (26:11-15)

The Chronicler closed this portion of Uzziah's reign by returning to the topic of military strength. In the preceding passage on the subject, he focused on the actual victories in Uzziah's day (see 26:6-8). At this point, his attention turned to a more general description of Uzziah's continuing military strength. His report divides into four items.

First, Uzziah's military strength is introduced in general terms. He had **a well-trained army, ready to go out** (26:11). Uzziah had a sophisticated military organization headed by a series of officers. This was no rag-tag militia.

Second, Uzziah's army was very large (26:12-13). The total given here is 310,100. These large numbers may be handled in a number of ways. (For the Chronicler's use of large numbers of soldiers, see comments on 1 Chr. 12:24-37.) In all events,

Uzziah's army was large and **a powerful force** (26:13). Mentioning large and skilled armies is one way in which the Chronicler often exalted faithful kings (see 1 Chr. 12:24-40; 21:5; 27:1-15; 2 Chr. 13:3; 17:12-19; 25:5-6; 26:13).

Third, Uzziah made significant provisions for his army (26:14). His soldiers were not expected to provide their own arms as often occurred in biblical times (see Judg. 20:8-17; 1 Sam. 13:19-22; 1 Chr. 12:2, 8, 24, 33). Instead, the king distributed equipment of different sorts **for the entire army** (26:14). Not only did this fact enhance the portrait of Uzziah's military strength; it also pointed to his economic success.

Besides this, Uzziah's military was supplied with **machines designed by skillful men** (26:15a). The precise nature of these **machines** is not clear. Much debate has surrounded the matter. Some interpreters hold that the Chronicler spoke of some kind of catapult. Yet, little archaeological evidence supports the idea that catapults were used at this time in Judah. Other interpreters believe that Uzziah's men designed a defensive (perhaps mobile) structure on the walls and towers of cities that provided archers and throwers protection as they performed their duties. Whatever the case, the Chronicler's point is clear. Uzziah's army was a well-equipped professional army.

Fourth, the Chronicler concluded by mentioning that Uzziah's **fame spread far and wide** (26:15b). Everyone knew that God had **greatly helped** him (25:15b; see *Introduction: 10) Divine Activity*). Uzziah's celebrity continued until **he became powerful** (25:15b). These last descriptions of Uzziah repeat ideas mentioned in the opening of this section (see 26:7) and form an inclusio around this portion of Uzziah's reign. The Chronicler made his analysis of this period in Uzziah's life evident. He received divine assistance, became famous as one blessed of God, and received much power.

By framing his reports in this manner, the Chronicler extended a word of hope to his post-exilic readers. They too could find the help of God, fame, and power, if they would only serve the Lord faithfully.

Although the themes of divine help, Uzziah's fame, and power are repeated in 26:8 and 26:15, a slight change occurred in the way the Chronicler handled the third of these motifs. In 26:8 the Chronicler merely mentioned that Uzziah had **become very powerful**. In 26:13, however, he said that Uzziah received divine help **until he became powerful**. In other words, divine assistance came to Uzziah up to the time he gained much power. By this turn of the phrase, the Chronicler foreshadowed the events that follow. Uzziah's power brought an end to the period of his blessing from God. In the final analysis, his success was the occasion of his downfall.

Uzziah's Infidelity and Curse (26:16-21)

At this point in his record, the Chronicler turned from the period of Uzziah's blessing to the time of divine judgment due to his infidelity.

Structure of 26:16-21

In this section the Chronicler expanded a simple report of Uzziah's leprosy (2 Kgs. 15:5 // 2 Chr. 26:21) into a full scale narrative which explained how and why this terrible fate befell the king. This material divides into a five step narrative (see figure 46). It begins with Uzziah at the zenith of his power entering the temple (26:16). By contrast, it ends with him having lost all his royal power and being prohibited from entering the temple for life (26:21). The turning point of this narrative is the scene in which the courageous priests confronted Uzziah within the temple and Uzziah resisted their warning to his own destruction (26:18-19). On either side of this turning point are scenes of the priests entering (26:17) and leaving (26:20) the temple. In effect, this narrative explained that Uzziah contracted a skin disease and lost his power because he defiled the sanctuary of the Lord despite priestly warnings.

Powerful Uzziah Enters the Temple (26:16)

The Chronicler began this portion of his record by recalling the preceding sentence. Uzziah was helped by God **until he became powerful** (26:15), **but after Uzziah became powerful** (26:16) trouble began. With success and power in his hand, the king became the victim of **his pride**. On a number of occasions the Chronicler recorded that blessings preceded a king's downfall. (For the Chronicler's warning against permitting blessings to lead to infidelity, see comments on 1 Chr. 5:24.) In this case, he focused specifically on the motive of **pride**. Uzziah's **pride led to his downfall**. Pride was a sin to which the Chronicler pointed on several occasions (see 25:19; 32:25, 26). The principle that pride destroys is well established in biblical traditions (Prov. 11:2; 16:18; 29:23).

The motif of pride leading to destruction suggests strongly that the Chronicler at least feared his post-exilic readers would face a similar temptation. Perhaps he was concerned that various successes (construction, organization, reforms, etc.) leading to a measure of blessing would result in self-assurance and infidelity. Whatever the specific issue may have been, it would appear that he was sensitive to this possibility for his readers. The results of Uzziah's pride would have warned his readers of the dire consequences sure to befall them, if they fell into the same trap.

The Chronicler described Uzziah as becoming **unfaithful** (26:16). This terminology also appears frequently in Chronicles as a description of serious disregard for the sanctions of Israel's covenant life with God. To be **unfaithful**, especially in the realm of worship, was to insure harsh judgment from God (see *Introduction: 21) Unfaithfulness*).

Uzziah's infidelity expressed itself in a particular way that was of special interest to the Chronicler. The king **entered the temple ... to burn incense on the altar of incense** (26:16). According to the Mosaic Law, burning incense was the exclusive privilege of the priests of Israel (see Exod. 30:1-10; Num. 16:40; 18:1-7). Uzziah's pride led him to feel no constraint to follow the restrictions of Mosaic Law. Having been favored by God in many ways (26:6-15), he apparently thought himself above such restrictions.

The Chronicler frequently pointed to the importance of observing the rules of worship given by Moses (see *Introduction: 14) Standards*). To violate the Mosaic regulations of worship was to disregard the manner in which Israel's divine King desired to be attended in his holy sanctuary. Violating worship order was to be unfaithful to God himself and was sure to lead to destruction. This motif was particularly important to the post-exilic readers of Chronicles as they struggled through the process of re-establishing the temple and its worship.

Priests Follow Uzziah into Temple (26:17)
The tension of this episode rises as the Chronicler reported the reactions of the priests. **Azariah** and **eighty other priests** did not approve of Uzziah's usurpation of their duties. So they **followed him**. It is no wonder then that the Chronicler described these men as **courageous priests**. They moved against the king at great risk. At this time, Uzziah was very powerful (see 26:8, 15, 16). In his powerful position, Uzziah could easily have had these priests executed for their actions. Yet, their zeal for Moses' Law gave them courage to face the powerful king. This complementary portrayal of the priests encouraged the Chronicler's readers to the same courage in resisting those who disregarded the Law of God, especially the regulations of the temple.

Confrontation Between Priests and Uzziah (26:18-19)
At this point, the narrative turns to events within the temple. The courageous priests confronted Uzziah as he was about to offer incense. This step in the story divides into three elements: 1) The priests' rebuke and threat (26:18), 2) Uzziah's angry response (26:19a), and 3) the fulfillment of the priests' threat (26:19b).

The priests (perhaps Azariah on behalf of the group) **confronted** Uzziah (26:18). The Hebrew term translated **confronted** (NIV) may also be rendered 'opposed' or 'withstood' (see NRS, NKJ, NAS). The priests did not humbly appeal to the king or entreat him. They boldly resisted him by directly addressing him as **'you, Uzziah'** (26:18).

Their speech is similar to the pattern of an oracle of judgment which accuses and then sentences. In no uncertain terms, the priests told Uzziah, **'It is not right for** [you] **to offer incense'** (26:18). They insisted that this duty was **for the priests, the descendants of Aaron** (26:18). Their reason was plain; the priests **have been consecrated** (26:18) for that role. Rituals of consecration appear frequently in Chronicles as examples of proper worship which the post-exilic readers were to imitate in their day (see *Introduction: 6) Royal Observance of Worship*). Having rightly accused the king, the priests sentenced him to **leave the sanctuary** because he had **been unfaithful** (26:18; see *Introduction: 21) Unfaithfulness*). Moreover, they predicted that Uzziah would **not be honored by the Lord God** (26:18).

In a number of earlier passages, the Chronicler had already demonstrated what a faithful king should do in such circumstances. He should repent and humble himself before God in hopes of receiving mercy (see *Introduction: 15) Prophets*).

To do otherwise was to insure that the threat of dishonor from God would be realized.

Uzziah's pride kept him from repentance (see 26:16). Instead, as he stood **with a censer in his hand**, he **became angry** (26:19a). The king even began **raging at the priests** (26:19b). Uzziah refused to listen to the Word of God and turned in anger toward those who spoke on God's behalf. In earlier accounts, the Chronicler made it evident that this kind of response to a messenger from God led inevitably to divine judgment (see *Introduction: 15) Prophets*). The same would prove true for Uzziah.

Once the king responded inappropriately to the warning of the priests, their prediction was fulfilled. **Leprosy broke out on his forehead** (29:19). Like Asa and Jehoram, and perhaps Hezekiah (see 16:12-13; 21:12-19; 32:24), the Chronicler viewed disease as the judgment of God against Uzziah. It is difficult to know precisely what disease Uzziah contracted; the Hebrew term translated **leprosy** referred to a broad range of skin diseases. In fact, there is some evidence against identifying this disease with modern leprosy. It may be better simply to translate the term 'skin disease'. In all events, Uzziah's dermatological illness visibly demonstrated that he was under the judgment of God.

Priests Escort Uzziah Out of Temple (26:20)

When Azariah and the priests noticed what happened to Uzziah, **they hurried him out** (26:20). The disease rendered the king ceremonially unclean according to the Law of Moses and made it impossible for him to stay in the temple complex and to perform his normal royal duties (see Lev. 13:46; Num. 5:1-4; 12:15; 2 Kgs. 7:3). Moreover, the Chronicler noted that Uzziah himself did not resist the efforts of the priests. **He himself was eager to leave**, perhaps for fear of an even worse judgment (26:20). In a striking contrast to earlier scenes where the king and priests enter the temple, they now leave as fast as possible. The priests had been vindicated by God; Uzziah had been judged. The Chronicler dramatically displayed to his post-exilic readers the consequences of allowing power and pride to lead to infidelity.

Powerless Uzziah Barred from Temple (26:21)

In this verse the Chronicler followed closely 2 Kgs. 14:5, the passage that gave rise to his expansion on Uzziah's infidelity. This last step of the narrative contrasts sharply with the opening verses (see figure 46). At the beginning of the story (26:16), Uzziah was politically powerful and fully intending to exert himself in the sanctuary of the temple. As the story closes, the king was **excluded from the temple of the LORD** (26:21). His skin disease had made it impossible for him even to attend to his ordinary role in worship. Moreover, Uzziah lived **in a separate house**. Upon contracting his disease, **Jotham his son** ruled as co-regent with Uzziah. Uzziah was utterly powerless both in the affairs **of the palace** and in matters concerning **people of the land.** (For the Chronicler's use of this terminology, see 1 Chr. 5:25; 2 Chr. 23:13, 20, 21; 33:25; 36:1.) This was the state of Uzziah's kingship **until the day he died** (26:21).

Thus, in a striking manner the Chronicler distinguished these years of Uzziah's reign from the earlier years of blessing. Uzziah's devotion to God led to great political successes and prosperity. His pride led to the judgment of God. The lesson for post-exilic Israel could not have been more obvious.

Closure of Uzziah's Reign (26:22-23)
The Chronicler continued to rely on information in Kings (// 2 Kgs. 15:6-7) to close out the reign of Uzziah. He mentioned his prophetic source for the king's activities (26:22; see *Introduction: 15) Prophets*). He also reported the king's death, burial (26:23a), and successor (26:23b).

The most significant variation in this passage is the Chronicler's description of Uzziah's burial. 2 Kgs. 15:7 merely states that Uzziah was 'buried near' his fathers. The Chronicler, however, pointed to the king's dishonorable burial. He added that Uzziah was buried **in a field for burial that belonged to the kings** (26:23). Uzziah rested in royal land, but not in the tombs of his fathers. The reason for this dishonor is also explicitly stated. **People said, 'He had leprosy.'** Even in death, Uzziah did not lose the shame of the skin disease which he received as a result of his infidelity (see *Introduction: 28) Healing and Long Life/ Sickness and Death*).

The Reign of Jotham (27:1-9)
With the reign of Jotham the Chronicler broke the pattern he established over the last three reigns. Instead of dividing this king's years between times of fidelity and infidelity, he presented Jotham in an entirely positive light. As we will see, the Chronicler patterned his account of Jotham after the early years of Uzziah his father. Jotham accomplished much, but unlike Uzziah he did not lose his kingdom because of infidelity. After the tremendous dishonor that came upon his father Uzziah, Jotham's life offered a portrait of fidelity and blessing for the Chronicler's post-exilic readers.

Comparison of 27:1-9 with 2 Kgs. 15:8-38
The Chronicler depended heavily on the record of 2 Kgs. 15:32-38 for his account of Jotham's reign (see figure 47).

2 Chr.		2 Kgs.
———	Events in the North (omitted)	15:8-32
27:1-2	Opening of Jotham's Reign (parallel)	15:33-35a
27:3-6	Jotham's Accomplishments (greatly expanded)	15:35b
27:7-9	Closure of Jotham's Reign (loosely parallel)	15:36-38

Comparison of 2 Chr. 27:1-9 with 2 Kgs. 15:8-38 (figure 47)

First, the Chronicler omitted 2 Kgs. 15:8-32 which concerns the last kings of northern Israel and the synchronization of Jotham's reign with the northern kingdom. In his usual fashion, the Chronicler focused only on materials concerned with the kingdom of Judah (see *Introduction: 2) Northern Israel*).

Second, the Chronicler replaced the reference to high places in 2 Kgs. 15:35a with his own statement of contrast between Jotham and Uzziah. He noted that Jotham did right like his father **but unlike him he did not enter the temple of the Lord** (27:2). This change fit with the Chronicler's desire to present Jotham as a righteous king.

Third, the Chronicler enlarged the accomplishments of Jotham. 2 Kgs. 15:35b reports that he rebuilt the upper gate of the temple. The Chronicler kept this information, but added other construction efforts and accomplishments in battle (27:3-6).

Fourth, 2 Kgs. 15:37 mentions the attacks of the northern Israelite-Syrian coalition against Jotham. The Chronicler omitted this reference to avoid detracting from the king's blessings and to associate the attacks of the coalition primarily with the infidelity of Ahaz.

Fifth, the Chronicler repeated information about Jotham's age and the length of his reign at the end of his account (compare 27:1 and 27:8). This repetition contributes to the overarching symmetry of the presentation by balancing the beginning and ending of the king's reign.

Structure 27:1-9

The Chronicler's omissions and additions form his record of Jotham's reign into a simple threefold structure (see figure 48).

Opening of Jotham's Reign (27:1-2)
    Jotham's Positive Accomplishments (27:3-6)
Closure of Jotham's Reign (27:7-9)

Outline of 2 Chr. 27:1-9 (figure 48)

The opening and closing sections of this material form an inclusio. Both sections mention his age and the length of his reign (27:1, 8). This symmetry frames the central reports of Jotham's accomplishments (27:3-6).

Opening of Jotham's Reign (27:1-2)

The Chronicler opened the reign of Jotham in his usual fashion with some general information. Following 2 Kgs. 15:33, he mentioned that the young king was only **twenty-five years old** when he rose to be co-regent with his father Uzziah (27:1). As we have seen (see comments on 26:21) the evidence of various biblical passages suggests that Jotham shared royal power with his ill father for ten years. The Chronicler also mentioned the name of the king's mother as he did with other kings (see comments on 2 Chr. 13:2).

Following these historical facts, the text of Chronicles and Kings offers an evaluation of the king's reign. He **did what was right in the eyes of the LORD** (27:2). As with other kings who receive similar evaluations Jotham was not absolutely perfect. These words characterized the king in general terms. For the Chronicler's use of this evaluative terminology see comments on 24:2.

The unique element in this description of Jotham is that he is said to have done **just like his father Uzziah had done**. The appearance of these words in 2 Kgs 15:34 is not surprising. The writer of Kings did not mention Uzziah's failures. Yet, the Chronicler's account of Uzziah gave much attention to his infidelity (see 26:16-21). For this reason the Chronicler added a qualification to the comparison between Jotham and his father. Jotham was like Uzziah **but unlike him he did not enter the temple of the LORD**. In other words, Chronicles distances Jotham from Uzziah's great failure. Indeed, the whole account of Jotham's reign records none of his sins. The only slight shadow on this presentation is that **the people ... continued their corrupt practices**. The parallel passage in Kings (2 Kgs. 15:35) mentions high places and the sacrifices made there. The Chronicler shortened the matter and merely acknowledged that Jotham's piety was not shared by all the people.

The similarity and contrast drawn between Jotham and Uzziah reveals one of the Chronicler's central interests in this material. Jotham's reign illustrated for the post-exilic readers the blessings available for those who avoided the failures of Uzziah and imitated the fidelity of his son.

Jotham's Positive Accomplishments (27:3-6)

What were the blessings that came to Jotham's kingdom? The Chronicler focused in two directions as he had in Uzziah's reign: building projects (27:3-4) and military accomplishments (27:5). First, in material which he largely added (with the exception of 27:3 // 2 Kgs 15:35b), the Chronicler mentioned the king's building projects. Jotham **rebuilt the Upper Gate of the temple** (27:3), like Uzziah who rebuilt the Corner Gate and Valley Gate (see 26:9). The restoration of the temple and its worship was of chief importance to this exemplary king as with other idealized kings in Judah (see *Introduction: 4-9) King and Temple*).

Jotham also had more widespread building projects. He fortified **Ophel** (27:3), a site mentioned elsewhere (see 33:14; Neh. 3:27; 11:21), but whose precise location is not known. He also **built towns ... forts and towers** throughout Judah (27:4; see *Introduction: 24) Building and Destruction*). These activities also paralleled Uzziah's building projects in various parts of Judah (see 26:10).

Second, Jotham also had success in military conflicts much like his father Uzziah. Jotham received tribute from the **Ammonites** (27:5), as Uzziah had done before him (see 26:8). Once again, the Chronicler drew a close parallel between Uzziah and his son in order to show what can be done by a king who imitates Uzziah's early years (27:2).

The addition of 27:6 draws attention to the results of Jotham's military strength. Jotham grew **powerful** like his father (see 26:8, 13, 15, 16; see also comments on

1:1). This parallel surely raised questions in the minds of the original readers. Power led to pride and infidelity in Uzziah's reign. Would the same happen to Jotham? The Chronicler quickly answered this question. Jotham continued with great power to the end of his days. The reason for this contrast is evident. Jotham **walked steadfastly before the LORD his God**. The disappointing end of Uzziah's kingdom would not be repeated in Jotham's day. His reign ended on a crescendo of blessing and power.

The Chronicler's message to his post-exilic readers is evident. Uzziah's accomplishments during his years of fidelity occurred again in the reign of Jotham. Yet, Jotham was able to keep his powerful position because he remained faithful to God. In a similar way, post-exilic Israel was not bound to the pattern of sin and judgment characterized by previous generations. They too could be faithful to God and hope to receive blessings.

Closure of Jotham's Reign (27:7-9)

The Chronicler closed his record of Jotham with information derived from 2 Kgs. 15:36-38, but he replaced the report of the Israelite-Syrian coalition (verse 37) with a repetition of information from the beginning of Jotham's reign (27:8). This replacement maintained the positive outlook on Jotham and created an effect of balance with the beginning of his reign.

The remainder of the Chronicler's account includes several usual items. The text refers to sources of information (27:7). It balances with the opening of the reign by mentioning the age of the king and the length of his reign (27:8). It then closes with a notice of his death, burial, and successor (27:9). Like Uzziah before him, Jotham **rested with his fathers** (26:23; 27:9). The two kings are contrasted, however, in that Uzziah was only buried **near them** in a separate field (26:23). Jotham was buried as other honorable kings of Judah because he remained faithful (see *Introduction: 28) Healing and Long Life/Sickness and Death*).

The Chronicler's idealized portrait of Jotham offered hope to his post-exilic readers. Although Uzziah had lost all through infidelity, it was not necessary for the blessings of God to be temporary. Each generation had the opportunity to be faithful to the end and could pass their blessings to the next generation.

The Reign of Ahaz (28:1-27)

The Chronicler's record of Ahaz's reign (735–716/15 BC) presents a mirror image of Jotham's ideal kingdom (27:1-9). In the book of Chronicles, Ahaz represented the worst of Judah's kings. His life conveyed to the original post-exilic readers the results of a life of disloyalty to God, even on the heels of a time greatly blessed by God.

Comparison of 28:1-27 with 2 Kgs. 16:1-20

The relationship between the account of Ahaz in Kings and Chronicles is complex. A number of insignificant stylistic and text critical issues appear, but several important differences occur as well (see figure 49).

2 Chr.		2 Kgs.
———	Synchronization with North (omitted)	16:1
28:1-5	Opening of Ahaz's Reign (expanded)	16:2-5
28:6-15	Northern Fidelity to God (added)	———
28:16-25	Ahaz's Infidelity to God (loosely parallel)	16:6-18
28:26-27	Closure of Ahaz's Reign (parallel)	16:19-20

Comparison of 2 Chr. 28:1-27 with 2 Kgs. 16:1-20 (figure 49)

First, in his usual fashion the Chronicler omitted 2 Kgs. 16:1, a synchronization with the northern kingdom (see *Introduction: 2) Northern Israel*).

Second, several additional materials and expansions illustrate the flagrant character of Ahaz's apostasy.

1) 28:2b-3 mentions images of Baals and Ahaz's worship of them.

2) In 28:5 the Chronicler expanded the parallel in 2 Kgs. 16:5 to attribute these events to divine purposes. He added that the victory of Syria over Judah occurred because **the Lord his God handed him over to the king of Aram** (28:5). Moreover, he stated that Ahaz **was given into the hands of the king of Israel** (i.e. by God) (28:5). The Chronicler frequently attributed dramatic events to the action of God (see *Introduction: 10) Divine Activity*). Moreover, in this verse the Chronicler also shifted attention away from the failed Syrian-Israelite attempt to capture Jerusalem (2 Kgs. 16:5) to note that both Syria and Israel inflicted terrible losses on Judah (28:5).

3) Chronicles also adds a description of conflict between Ahaz and the northern Israelites (28:6-15). These expansions depicted the severity of divine judgment against Ahaz and portrayed northern Israelites as more righteous than Ahaz.

4) The record of Edom's victory against Judah at Elath is expanded to depict this event as the cause of Ahaz's humiliation and his motivation for seeking help from Assyria. As such, it forms another illustration of severe divine judgment against Ahaz's apostasy (28:16-21 // 2 Kgs. 16:6-8).

5) The Chronicler abbreviated the episode in 2 Kgs. 16:10-18 which focused on the cooperation between Ahaz and Uriah the priest in bringing Assyrian religious practices to Jerusalem. Instead, his shorter version of the events places responsibility entirely upon Ahaz (28:22-23). This change also fits the event into a series of acts in which Ahaz sought help from someone other than his God.

6) The Chronicler added a report of Ahaz's total cessation from the worship of the Lord (28:24-25). In this section he also added that this apostasy **provoked the Lord, the God of his fathers, to anger** (28:25).

Third, in order to dishonor Ahaz, the Chronicler omitted the notice of 2 Kgs. 16:20 that Ahaz was buried 'with his fathers'. Instead, he clarified that this did not mean that Ahaz enjoyed an honorable burial in the royal tombs. He added that **he was not placed in the tombs of the kings of Israel** (28:27). This change was consistent with the Chronicler's negative assessment of Ahaz's reign.

Structure of 28:1-27

The Chronicler's variations from the account of Kings shapes his record into four main sections. These portions of Ahaz's reign give a striking portrait of the king's apostasy (see figure 50).

■ Opening of Ahaz's Reign (28:1-5)

◆ Northern Israel's Fidelity to God (28:6-15)
Victorious Israel Takes Plunder and Prisoners (28:6-8)
Israel Receives Prophetic Rebuke (28:9-11)
Israel Responds to Prophetic Rebuke (28:12-13)
Victorious Israel Returns Plunder and Prisoners (28:14-15)

◆ Ahaz's Infidelity to God (28:16-25)

• Ahaz Fails to Receive Help from Assyria (28:16-21)
Ahaz's Initial Appeal to Assyria (28:16-20)
Ahaz Seeks Assyrian Help (28:16)
[Explanation of Ahaz's Actions (28:17-19)]
Ahaz Receives Negative Response (28:20)
Ahaz's Further Appeal to Assyria (28:21)
Ahaz Intensely Seeks Assyrian Help (28:21a)
Ahaz Receives Further Negative Responses (28:21b)

• Ahaz Fails to Receive Help from Syrian Gods (28:22-25)
Ahaz's Increasing Infidelity (28:22)
Ahaz's Worship of Syrian Gods (28:23a)
Ahaz's Downfall Explained (28:23b)
Ahaz's Further Worship of Other Gods (28:24-25a)
Ahaz's Judgment (28:25b)

■ Closure of Ahaz's Reign (28:26-27)

Outline of 2 Chr. 28:1-27 (figure 50)

The Chronicler's portrait of Ahaz is straightforward. He opened the reign with an overview of the king's sinful practices (28:1-5) and closed with a summation of his dishonorable end (28:26-27). The main body of the record divides between a story illustrating not only Ahaz's defeat, but also the relative piety of northern Israelites (28:6-15). This episode is followed by another narrative which depicts the utter apostasy of the Judean king Ahaz (28:16-25). By this means, the Chronicler portrayed Ahaz as the worst of Judah's kings during the divided period.

Opening of Ahaz's Reign (28:1-5)

As noted above, the Chronicler expanded the record of 2 Kgs. 16:2-4 in a number of ways in 28:1-5. This material consists of notices and reports that characterize the entire reign of Ahaz.

The initial notice seems ordinary enough at first glance. Ahaz was **twenty** at the time of his accession **and he reigned ... sixteen years** (28:1). Nevertheless, this information is difficult to reconcile with the notice that the son of Ahaz, Hezekiah, was twenty-five when he came to the throne at the end of Ahaz's sixteen year reign (see 29:1). If these numbers are taken at face value, it would mean that Ahaz became a father at eleven years old. While such an early paternity is not absolutely impossible, it would be unique in the biblical record. Surprisingly, however, no special comment is offered in Kings or Chronicles to explain the matter. The lack of comment suggests the possibility that the ages and/or lengths of reigns have been corrupted in one way or another at some stage(s) of textual transmission (see *Introduction: Translation and Transmission*). In all events, the reconstruction of precise dating for the reigns of Jotham, Ahaz, and Hezekiah presents one of the most difficult problems of biblical chronology.

The text wastes no time in giving the reader an evaluation of Ahaz. In terminology appearing frequently in Kings and Chronicles, we are told that Ahaz **did not do what was right in the eyes of the Lord** (28:1 // 2 Kgs. 16:2). For the Chronicler's use of this evaluative terminology see comments on 2 Chr. 24:2.

In addition to this normal way of evaluating a king, the text also adds that Ahaz was **unlike David his father**. This is the only example of the Chronicler negatively comparing a Judean king with David (compare 2 Chr. 17:3; 29:2; 34:2). As such, this passage set Ahaz in direct opposition to the Chronicler's ideal king David (see *Introduction: 14) Standards*). As we will see, Ahaz represented the very opposite of what a king of Judah should be.

The striking contrast between Ahaz and David is supported by the words that follow. Ahaz **walked in the ways of the kings of Israel** (28:2). In Chronicles as in the book of Kings, this comparison is a harsh condemnation. As we have seen a number of times, the Chronicler held out hope for the northern kingdom, but he also characterized northern Israel as apostate. To associate Ahaz with these kings was to portray him in very strong, negative terms (see *Introduction: 2) Northern Israel*).

To illustrate what he meant, the Chronicler provided a catalogue of Ahaz's terrible disobedience. First, he added to the record of Kings that Ahaz **made cast idols for worshipping the Baals** (28:2b) and offered **sacrifices in the Valley of Ben Hinnom** (28:3a).

Second, he followed Kings and reported that Ahaz **sacrificed his sons** (28:3b). The traditional Hebrew text of 28:3b reads 'his sons', and the traditional Hebrew text of 2 Kgs. 16:3b reads 'his son'. Yet, this difference is probably a problem in textual transmission and not the Chronicler's intentional change (see *Introduction: Translation and Transmission*).

Child sacrifice was strongly forbidden by Mosaic Law (see Lev. 18:21; 20:2-4; Deut. 12:31). This sin is described as **the detestable ways of the nations the LORD had driven out before the Israelites** (28:3b). The Chronicler compared the people of God to the Canaanites a number of times. For the Chronicler's use of this comparison, see comments on 33:2-9. Ahaz had become as evil as the Canaanites of long ago whose evil practices had brought the divine judgment of Israel's conquest against them (see Gen. 15:18-21; Deut. 18:9-12).

Third, Ahaz also involved himself in a vast array of pagan worship practices. He **sacrificed and burned incense at the high places ... hilltops ... and spreading trees** (28:4). Such practices were strongly condemned by Israel's prophets and represent serious violations of Ahaz' fidelity to his God. In the Chronicler's history Ahaz was the worst of Judah's apostate kings.

The Chronicler followed his catalogue of Ahaz's sins with brief reports of Judah's defeats before Syria and northern Israel (28:5). In the last years of Jotham and during the reign of Ahaz, Judah was troubled by enemies from the north. King Rezin of Syria and King Pekah of northern Israel joined forces against Assyria. To secure their position against the stronger army of Assyria, Syria and Israel pressured Judah to join their coalition (see 2 Kgs 16:5-7; Isa. 7:1-6). Under the influence of the prophet Isaiah (see Isa. 7:1-6), Ahaz refused to join the Syrian-Israelite coalition. Contrary to the advice of Isaiah, however, Ahaz sought help from Assyria and became a vassal of the Assyrian emperor. This action demonstrated his refusal to rely on the Lord for help against his enemies and eventually brought great trouble to Judah. In the meanwhile, Syria and Israel attacked Judah a number of times in an attempt to force Ahaz into submission.

The Chronicler's record of Ahaz's defeats before Syria and northern Israel is shaped to convey his theological perspective. 2 Kgs. 16:5 merely notes that the attacks occurred. The Chronicler, however, added that Syria was victorious because **the LORD his God handed him over to the king of Aram** (28:5a). Similarly, he noted that Ahaz **was also given into the hands of the king of Israel** (28:5b). These additions make it clear that the Chronicler saw these events as another example of divine judgment against Ahaz for the preceding catalogue of sins (see 28:2-4; see also *Introduction: 23) Victory and Defeat*).

Moreover, just as the Chronicler highlighted the severity of Ahaz's infidelity (28:2), he also added that the defeats of Judah were severe. 2 Kgs. 16:5 merely reports that the kings of Syria and Israel tried to conquer Jerusalem. The Chronicler, however, drew attention away from the sparing of Jerusalem itself to severe losses elsewhere. He noted that the **Arameans defeated him and took many of his people as prisoners ... to Damascus** (28:5a). He also pointed out that the king of northern Israel **inflicted heavy casualties** on Ahaz (28:5b). In effect, Judah experienced a small exile during Ahaz's reign. This fact comes into view once again in Hezekiah's reign (see 29:9).

The purpose of these variations from the book of Kings is evident. The Chronicler wanted his post-exilic readers to understand that Ahaz's sins had not gone unpunished. His troubles were the result of divine judgment. After the tremendous blessings given to Jotham for his unwavering fidelity, the judgment against the apostate Ahaz should have struck fear in the hearts of the Chronicler's readers. Blessings in the past were no assurance of blessings in the future. Each generation stood responsible for its own actions (see *Introduction: 10-27) Divine Blessing and Judgment*).

Northern Israel's Fidelity to God (28:6-15)

Having already touched on the war between Ahaz and the Syrian-Israelite coalition as a demonstration of divine judgment (28:5), the Chronicler added a story focusing on one of Judah's defeats. This narrative came from the Chronicler's hand and revealed an ironic turn of events. While Ahaz had taken his nation into apostasy, northern Israelites listened to the prophet of God and humbly obeyed his instructions.

Structure of 28:6-15

The passage divides into four main parts (see figure 50). The balance of this narrative is straightforward. It begins with plunder and prisoners being taken from Judah (28:6-8). Their return forms the ending of the episode (28:14-15). The middle portion of the material consists of a prophetic rebuke (28:9-11) and the response to the rebuke (28:12-13).

Victorious Israel Takes Plunder and Prisoners (28:6-8)

Instead of reporting Israel's failed attempt to take Jerusalem (see 2 Kgs. 16:5), the Chronicler wrote about Ahaz's terrible defeat. As in a number of passages, the Chronicler reported Israel and Judah in conflict. This time, however, the northern kingdom will demonstrate more righteousness than Judah (see *Introduction: 2) Northern Israel*). Given the general characterization of Ahaz in the opening verses of his reign, it was no wonder from the Chronicler's perspective that the army of northern Israel had a great victory over him (see *Introduction: 23) Victory and Defeat*). The Chronicler stated explicitly that Judah's defeat was **because Judah had forsaken the LORD, the God of their fathers** (28:6). The concept of 'forsaking' appears frequently in Chronicles to describe serious violations of the covenant established between God and his people (see *Introduction: 22) Abandoning/Forsaking*). Those who forsake God are in line for God to forsake them (13:10-12; also see 12:5). On many occasions, this divine judgment against Judah resulted in defeat in battle (see 21:16-17; 22:5; 24:23-25; 28:5-8; 33:10-11; 36:6-7, 9-10,15-21; see also *Introduction: 23) Victory and Defeat*).

The severity of this defeat is highlighted in several ways.

1) A **hundred and twenty thousand soldiers** in the Judahite army died at the hand of the northern Israelites **in one day** (28:6). This large number may be under-

stood as other large numbers in Chronicles. (For the Chronicler's use of large numbers of soldiers, see comments on 1 Chr. 12:24-37.) It is clear, however, that Ahaz's defeat was astounding.

2) Certain prominent figures died in battle against the North: **the king's son** ... **the officer in charge of the palace** ... and the man **second to the king** (28:7). The deaths of these important people recalled the deaths of Saul and his sons (see 1 Chr. 10:7). It displayed the critical nature of the defeat.

3) The Israelites also took **two hundred thousand wives, sons and daughters** (28:8). Once again, the large numbers may be understood in a number of ways, but they indicate that northern Israel's victory was tremendous.

4) The victors also **took a great deal of plunder** (28:8). Without a doubt, the Chronicler added these details to make it clear that Ahaz suffered terribly for his sins.

The relevance of this material for post-exilic Judah must not be overlooked. The returnees were troubled on all sides by potential enemies, including those living in the vicinity of northern Israel (see Ezra 4:1-5; Neh. 4; 6). At this point in the story, the Chronicler emphasized that Judah was not necessarily protected from northern aggression. In fact, when Judah proved unfaithful to God, God used Israel as an instrument of judgment. The same possibility held true for the post-exilic community.

Israel Receives Prophetic Rebuke (28:9-11)

The army of northern Israel returned to the capital of Samaria with captives and plunder (28:8). Along the way, however, **a prophet of the LORD named Oded** met them (28:9a). This prophet is mentioned only here. The Chronicler made it clear, however, that he was a true **prophet of the LORD**. As in many other passages in Chronicles, the prophet presented a warning from God and the fate of those who heard was determined by their response (see *Introduction: 15) Prophets*). The prophet of God delivered a call to repentance to the Israelite army. His speech divides into the two main parts of a judgment oracle: an accusation of sin (28:9b-10) and a call to repent (28:11).

First, the prophet accused the Northerners of two sins. On the one hand, he said they went much too far in killing so many Judahites. He admitted that God gave Israel victory **because the LORD ... was angry with Judah** (28:9b; see 28:15a). Yet, the Israelites did not show appropriate restraint. They **slaughtered them in a rage that reaches to heaven** (28:9b). The expression **reaches to heaven** probably had two connotations in this context. It meant that their rage was very great and that it had gained the attention of heaven (see Ezra 9:6). The Chronicler already indicated the large numbers of Judeans who lost their lives; the prophet announced that this excess had not gone unnoticed (see Zech. 1:15; Isa. 10:12; 40:2).

On the other hand, the prophet's accusation focused on what the army was planning to do. Not only did they kill too many in Judah, now they intended **to make the men and women of Judah and Jerusalem ... slaves** (28:10a). Enslaving fellow Israelites was forbidden in Mosaic Law (see Lev. 25:39-55; Exod. 21:8;

Neh. 5:8). This accusation was particularly poignant in light of Northerners' resistance to the labor policies of Solomon and Rehoboam (see 11:4).

Second, Oded called the northern army to repentance. He first reminded them of their own condition. They were **also guilty of sins against the Lord** (28:10b). They had no reason to feel superior to the Judahites whom they attacked. For this reason, he ordered the army, **'Send back your fellow countrymen'** (28:11; see 28:15). In a manner that fit well with the Chronicler's theology, the prophet demanded the return of the Judahite prisoners because they are **fellow countrymen** or 'brothers' as the term may be translated (see NAS). This appeal to the kinship of North and South recalls prophetic words to Rehoboam as he prepared to attack the northern tribes (see 11:4). Even at this late date, the ideal of unity among all the tribes had not been forgotten by the prophet of God. He appealed to this bond as the basis for not enslaving the Judahites. Finally, the prophet warned the northern Israelite army of the danger that lies ahead for them. They must repent of their sin against Judah **for the LORD's fierce anger rests on** [them] (28:11).

The Chronicler's description of this scene touched several motifs which were particularly important to his post-exilic readers. The accusation of excess and the appeal for good treatment for the Judahites would have fit well with Judahite self-interests. Moreover, the threat of judgment against Judah's enemies would also have sounded a responsive chord.

Israel Responds to Prophetic Rebuke (28:12-13)

After the prophetic warning, **some of the leaders in Ephraim** confronted the approaching army (28:12). This third step of the story consists primarily of a speech that corresponds in several ways to the preceding prophetic speech. The leaders of Israel insisted that the prisoners not be brought to Samaria (28:13a). Having realized that they had violated the will of God by excessive force during battle (see 28:9), the leaders of Israel asked if the army intended to increase Israel's **sin and guilt** (28:13c). The leaders openly agreed with the prophet that their **guilt is already great**; they also agreed that God's **fierce anger rests on Israel** (28:13d).

This record of Israelite reaction to the prophetic warning provided a perspective on the northern tribes not found elsewhere in the Chronicler's history. Here their leaders respond appropriately to God's word. This unusual scene challenged the Chronicler's post-exilic readers to reassess their outlooks on the northern tribes (see *Introduction: 2) Northern Israel*).

Victorious Israel Returns Plunder and Prisoners (28:14-15)

The closing step of this narrative contrasts sharply with the beginning of this story. Instead of taking plunder and captives from Judah (see 28:6-8), the northern Israelites sent their Judahite captives home with the plunder.

The soldiers of Israel's army responded positively without a moment's hesitation. Apparently, all the men recognized that the prophetic word was true. More than this, the Chronicler focused on a number of details to make it evident that the army did not merely comply with what had been ordered. They went to great lengths to show contrition and humility. They **clothed all who were naked ... provided them with clothes and sandals, food and drink and healing balm** (28:15). They also put **those who were weak on donkeys** (28:15; see 28:11). With familial language the Chronicler added that the Israelites **took their fellow countrymen** ('brothers' [NAS]) **to Jericho** (28:15; see 28:11). These acts of Israel's army exemplified extraordinary generosity and kindness. In fact, this portion of the story may have been in the background of Jesus' parable of the Good Samaritan (see Luke 10:30-37).

It should be noted that these extraordinary events took place in what the Chronicler called **all the assembly** (28:14). Once again, the Chronicler highlighted the importance of religious assemblies. The splendid display of humility and kindness occurred during an assembly. The importance of gathering for religious assemblies during the post-exilic period becomes evident by this extraordinary blessing (see *Introduction: 5) Religious Assemblies*).

If ever the Chronicler shocked his readers, it must have been here. In this portion of his history the Chronicler had compared the negative behavior of Judah's king with the evil kings of northern Israel (see 28:2). He also depicted the ruthless attack of Israel against Judah (see 28:5-8). But suddenly the portrait of these Israelites changed dramatically, once they heard the word of a prophet, they turned in radical repentance. This story would have given pause to any post-exilic Judahite who had excluded the possibility of repentance among the northern tribes. The Northerners were fully capable of responding to the call of the prophetic word.

Ahaz's Infidelity to God (28:16-25)

After his surprising story about the repentance and faithfulness of northern Israelites, the Chronicler pointed to an ironic contrast in the behavior of Ahaz. At a time when Israelites were obedient to God, Judah's king turned away from God. As we have seen above, much of the basic information contained in this material appears in 2 Kgs. 16:6-18. The Chronicler, however, replaced 2 Kgs. 16:7b-8 with 28:17-20 to explain why Ahaz's kingdom declined. He also summarized 2 Kgs. 16:14-18 in 28:23. Finally, 28:24-25 were added to depict the nadir of Ahaz's apostasy as the cause of severe divine judgment against Judah (see figure 50).

Structure of 28:16-25

The account of Ahaz's infidelity divides into two main sections (see figure 50). These passages record events which display an increasing apostasy in Ahaz's life. He first turned to the king of Assyria for help (28:16-21); second, he turned to the gods of Syria (28:22-25). In the end, he found himself the recipient of severe divine anger.

Ahaz Fails to Receive Help from Assyria (28:16-21)

The Chronicler related Ahaz's appeal to the king of Assyria in two episodes (28:16-20 and 28:21; see figure 50).

Ahaz's Initial Appeal to Assyria (28:16-19)
The skeleton of the first episode consists of two steps: 28:16 and 20. 28:17-19 comprises a parenthetical explanation.

Ahaz Seeks Assyrian Help (28:16)
This two step story begins with Ahaz appealing to **the king of Assyria for help** (28:16). The term **help** is repeated no less than three times in this section (see 28:16,20,21, [see also 28:23 (twice)]). This terminology appears a number of times in Chronicles to describe extraordinary assistance from God for his servants (see *Introduction: 10) Divine Activity*). To find help from anyone but God was to rebel against God. In this regard, the Chronicler's perspective was very similar to that of Isaiah (see Isa. 30:1-5; 31:1-3). Only God was to be the source of help for the people of God, but Ahaz turned to Tiglath-Pileser III of Assyria for assistance instead.

Ahaz's Actions Explained (28:17-18)
Why did Ahaz need help? The Chronicler inserted a parenthetical explanation of the king's desire (28:17-18). The book of Kings focuses on the attacks of Israel and Syria against Ahaz as the basis of Ahaz's need for Assyrian assistance (see 2 Kgs. 16:7). The Chronicler, however, reported Ahaz's troubles in the south and west. The **Edomites** and **Philistines** attacked Judah and took many prisoners (28:17-18). These armies took advantage of Judah's preoccupation with her northern enemies (Syria and Israel) and reasserted their own claims against Judah's southern and western borders.

The Chronicler, however, was not satisfied to leave the matter in purely human terms. He explained that these attacks were successful because **the LORD had humbled Judah** (28:19). Divine purposes were behind these events (see *Introduction: 10) Divine Activity*). Self-imposed humility was a positive quality for the people of God to exhibit (see *Introduction: 18) Humility*). Ahaz's humiliation, however, was imposed on him by God; for this reason the terminology does not bear the positive connotations as it does in other passages.

Beyond this, the Chronicler made it clear why God humiliated Ahaz through these defeats. It was because **he had promoted wickedness** and **had been most unfaithful to the LORD**. The Chronicler had already catalogued Ahaz's wicked deeds (see 28:1-4); here he added that the king was **unfaithful**, a term which he frequently used to indicate flagrant violation of Israel's covenant with God (see *Introduction: 21) Unfaithfulness*). In this parenthetical aside, the Chronicler made it clear that Ahaz found himself in need of help because his sins had turned God against him.

Ahaz Receives Negative Response (28:20)
28:20 picks up the narrative sequence from 28:16 by describing the response of Assyria's king. In 734 BC Tiglath-Pileser III subjugated Israel and came as far south

as the regions of Judah. His presence was a mixed experience for Ahaz. It relieved him of trouble from the North, but it also placed Ahaz in a position of dependence on Assyria (see 2 Kgs. 16:10,17-18). In this sense, the Assyrian king **gave him trouble, instead of help** (28:20). Although Ahaz had sought help from Assyria, he received none because genuine help comes only from God (see *Introduction: 10) Divine Activity*).

In this short episode, the Chronicler demonstrated the futility of Ahaz's efforts. His attempt to acquire help from someone other than the Lord failed miserably. In fact, he brought himself into more trouble.

Ahaz's Further Appeal to Assyria (28:21)

The second episode in this section (28:21) intensifies the outcome of the first. It too divides into a two step presentation (see figure 50).

Ahaz Intensely Seeks Assyrian Help (28:21a)

In an effort to gain the approval of Tiglath-Pileser III, Ahaz gave the Assyrians some of the treasures **from the temple ... the royal palace ... and from the princes** (28:21a). Giving enormous tributes to Suzerains was required for the protection the Suzerains provided their vassals. To pay a tribute of this sort was an acknowledgment of vassalage, a curse on Judah (see *Introduction: 26) Prosperity and Poverty*).

Ahaz Receives Further Negative Response (28:21b)

Despite Ahaz's efforts, the king of Assyria still **did not help him**. In fact, Ahaz had to rob the temple (see also 28:24), as well as others, to pay for his dependence on Assyria (see *Introduction: 9) Temple Contributions*). The cost of Ahaz's infidelity was great. By this example, the Chronicler noted the failure that was sure to follow if his post-exilic readers sought alliances with foreign powers instead of relying on God (see *Introduction: 3) International Relations*).

Ahaz Fails to Receive Help from Syrian Gods (28:22-25)

In this section the Chronicler gave an account of another way in which Ahaz sought help from someone other than his God. This time he turned to the gods of Syria.

Structure of 28:22-25

This account divides into five symmetrical steps (see figure 50). Ahaz increases his rebellion (28:22) and receives God's judgment in the end (28:25b). His worship of the Syrian gods (28:23a) is balanced by further syncretism (28:24-25a). The middle portion of the episode explains that his worship of other gods caused Judah's downfall (28:23b).

Ahaz's Increasing Infidelity (28:22)

In the first step, the Chronicler began with the notice that this time Ahaz was **unfaithful to the Lord** (28:22). The theme of infidelity has already been introduced in the preceding episodes (28:19). The purpose of this story was to show that he had become **even more unfaithful** than before (28:22; see *Introduction: 21) Unfaithfulness*).

Ahaz's Worship of Syrian Gods (28:23)

The second step (28:23a) focuses on Ahaz's **sacrifices to the gods of Damascus,** the capital of Syria. Instead of seeking help from a human king, Ahaz reasoned that the gods of Syria **helped** the Syrians. Therefore, sacrifices will move them to **help** him as well. The pursuit of **help** is central in this episode as it was in the preceding section (see 28:16-21). Ahaz turned away from the Lord as his source of help once again (see *Introduction: 10) Divine Activity*).

Ahaz's Downfall Explained (28:23b)

The third step (28:23b) forms a turning point in the episode. Although Ahaz sought help from the Syrian gods, they **were his downfall and the downfall of all Israel** (28:23b). The desire to gain assistance from foreign gods brought about a terrible turn of events for Ahaz and the nation.

Ahaz's Further Worship of Other Gods (28:24-25a)

The fourth step balances with the second portion of this episode in that it returns to the theme of sacrifice and worship. To demonstrate the depth of Ahaz's apostasy the Chronicler noted that the king stopped all worship of the Lord. He went so far as to remove **the furnishings from the temple** for use in pagan worship and **shut the doors of the LORD's temple** (28:24; see 28:21). Beyond this, his devotion to other gods was so thorough that the king **set up altars at every street corner in Jerusalem** (28:24) and **in every town in Judah he built high places and sacrificed** (28:25a; see 21:11; 33:3). The Chronicler's outlook is evident, Ahaz had sunk so far into infidelity that he no longer even made pretense of serving the God of his fathers. He had completely turned **to other gods** (28:25a).

Ahaz's Judgment (28:25b)

The final step balances with the opening of the story in that it returns to the matter of Ahaz and the God of Israel. Because he had been **even more unfaithful** (28:22), he **provoked the LORD ... to anger** (28:25b). The king's flagrant rebellion against God had made him the object of God's judgment.

Contrary to his usual practice, the Chronicler did not spell out how the great anger of God showed itself in Ahaz's reign. His goal was reached merely by establishing that Ahaz had become an apostate and incurred divine wrath.

The record of Ahaz is shaped to make it clear that Judah's condition had worsened to the point that the southern kingdom was no more faithful than northern Israel. Earlier in the history, King Abijah accused the Northerners of apostasy and rebellion against the God of their fathers (see 13:4-12). At this time, Ahaz had taken Judah into the very same kinds of rebellion. In fact, northern Israelites had shown themselves to be humble before the Lord at a time when apostasy was widespread in the South (see 28:5-15). Judah's special status had diminished to the point that something new was on the horizon for the people of God. That new order would come in the reign of Hezekiah (see 29:1-32:33). In his kingdom, the faithful of the North and the South joined together symbolically to form a reunited kingdom.

The Chronicler's outlook on Ahaz's reign spoke to several dimensions of the post-exilic situation. First, the restored community consisted of members of the northern tribes as well as Judahites (see 1 Chr. 9:3). By noting the contrast between Ahaz's rank apostasy and northern Israel's fidelity, the legitimacy of all members of the post-exilic community was established. Moreover, the returnees should learn from this contrast that the restored community still faced the dangers of infidelity like Ahaz and those tribes outside the restored community may still find the favor of God through repentance.

Closure of Ahaz's Reign (28:26-27)

The Chronicler returned to the record of 2 Kgs. 16:19-20 to close out the reign of Ahaz. He followed Kings closely for the most part, noting sources, the king's death, and his successor (28:26-27). At one point, however, the Chronicler made his outlook on Ahaz evident once again. 2 Kgs. 16:20 notes that Ahaz 'rested with his fathers and was buried with them in the city of David'. The Chronicler wanted his readers to understand that in Ahaz's case this notice did not mean he was buried in the royal tombs. For this reason, he added that **he was not placed in the tombs of the kings of Israel** (28:27). As in several other reigns (see 21:20; 24:25; 26:23; 33:20), the Chronicler noted the dishonor of Ahaz's final resting place (see *Introduction: 28) Healing and Long Life/Sickness and Death*).

Part Four

The Reunited Kingdom
(2 Chr. 29:1–36:23)

With the reign of Hezekiah the Chronicler reached the beginning of the last major division of his history. We have designated this period 'The Reunited Kingdom' because the Chronicler emphasized the symbolic rejoining of the faithful northern Israelites with Judah during this period. The northern kingdom had so violated her covenant responsibilities that it fell to the Assyrians (see 2 Kgs. 17:1-23). At the same time, Judah had become as corrupt as northern Israel during the reign of Ahaz (see 2 Chr. 28:1-4, 22-25). On the heels of this leveling of North and South, Hezekiah reinstituted a national Passover celebration which reunited the faithful in the North and South around the temple and the Davidic king (see 30:1-31:1).

From this point forward, the Chronicler's perspective was that events taking place in Judah involved the faithful from the North and South. Together they experienced times of revival and blessing as well as hardship and trouble. During this time, a series of minor exiles took place, but always with a positive end of returning to the land. Repeated apostasy, however, eventually led to the fall of Jerusalem, and **the remnant** was exiled to Babylon (36:20). Nevertheless, even this great exile was followed by the release of the remnant and the commission to rebuild the kingdom of Israel (see 36:23).

The Reunited Kingdom divides into five parts (see figure 51).

Hezekiah (29:1-32:33)
Manasseh (33:1-20)
Amon (33:21-25)
Josiah (34:1-35:27)
Final Events (36:2-23)

Outline of 29:1-36:23 (figure 51)

The Reign of Hezekiah (29:1-32:33)

The reign of Hezekiah (716/15–687/86 BC) marked an important turning point in the Chronicler's history. Following the demise of the North and the corruption of the South, Hezekiah brought the fires of revival to the tribes of Israel. A new phase of history began as Hezekiah re-established the temple and king at the center of a reunited nation. Hezekiah was not without serious shortcomings, but the Chronicler presented him as an embodiment of many ideals which he held before his post-exilic readers.

Comparison of 29:1-32:33 with 2 Kgs. 17:1-20:21

The Chronicler's perspective on Hezekiah's reign becomes clear when his presentation is compared with the corresponding portions of Kings. The following large scale comparison provides a helpful orientation. More detailed analyses appear in smaller sections which follow (see figure 52).

2 Chr.		2 Kgs.
———	Fall of Israel I (omitted)	17:1-41
29:1-2	Hezekiah's Reign Begins (loosely parallel)	18:1-3
29:3-31:21	Hezekiah's Worship Reforms (expanded)	18:4-8
———	Fall of Israel II (omitted)	18:9-12
32:1-23	Sennacherib Invasion (abbreviated)	18:13-19:37
32:24-26	Hezekiah's Illness (abbreviated)	20:1-11
32:27-30	Hezekiah's Wealth (added)	———
32:31	Emissaries from Babylon (abbreviated)	20:12-19
32:32-33	Hezekiah's Reign Ends (loosely parallel)	20:20-21

Comparison of 2 Chr. 29:1-32:33 and 2 Kgs. 17:1-20:21 (figure 52)

This overarching comparison of the reign of Hezekiah in Chronicles and Kings reveals the major contours of the Chronicler's distinctive presentation. He depended heavily on Kings only at the beginning and end of his record (compare 29:1-2 // 2 Kgs. 18:1-3 and 32:32-33 // 2 Kgs. 20:20-21). Elsewhere he either omitted, added, greatly expanded or abbreviated the record before him.

First, in his usual style the Chronicler omitted material dealing with the fall of the northern kingdom (2 Kgs. 17:1-41). He also omitted the second account of northern Israel's defeat (2 Kgs. 18:9-12). As in the rest of his history, the Chronicler was concerned with events in the North only as they touched on the southern kingdom (see *Introduction: 2) Northern Israel*).

Second, the Chronicler added 32:27-30. This section summarizes blessings of wealth which Hezekiah received from God because of his repentance (32:24-26). As such, it fit well with the Chronicler's theology of divine judgment and blessing.

Third, three sections represent significant abbreviations of the records in Kings.

1) The Sennacherib invasion is shortened (32:1-23 // 2 Kgs. 18:13-19:37). As argued below, the Chronicler's version simplifies the event to illustrate divine judgment and blessing in Hezekiah's life.

2) The story of Hezekiah's illness is also much shorter (32:24-26 // 2 Kgs. 20:1-11). The Chronicler barely reported the king's prayer and used it to show Hezekiah's reward for repenting of pride.

3) The story of Babylonian emissaries and strong condemnation from Isaiah the prophet (2 Kgs. 20:12-19) is reduced to a mere notice (32:31). The Chronicler did not want this terrible event to mar his portrait of Hezekiah.

Fourth, the most impressive aspect of the Chronicler's presentation is his enormous expansion of Hezekiah's reforms. Kings merely reports Hezekiah's destruction of idolatry in a brief notice (2 Kgs. 18:4) and his success due to compliance with the Law of Moses (2 Kgs. 18:5-7). The Chronicler loosely adapted this material to his own purposes (31:1 // 2 Kgs. 18:4 and 31:20-21 // 2 Kgs. 18:5-8). Yet, he greatly expanded the theme of Hezekiah's worship reforms throughout all Judah and Israel (29:1-31:2). For the Chronicler, Hezekiah's re-establishment of the temple and its services was the most important aspect of the king's reign.

Structure of 29:1-32:33

Hezekiah's reign divides into four main sections (see figure 53). A typical opening and a closure appear (29:1-2; 32:32-33). The middle portion separates into times of exemplary fidelity and times of inconsistency (29:3-31:21; 32:1-31).

Opening of Hezekiah's Reign (29:1-2)

The Chronicler began his record of Hezekiah's reign with a very positive orientation. On the whole, Hezekiah was a remarkably righteous king.

As noted above, the Chronicler omitted the lengthy material in Kings that describes and explains the fall of Samaria (2 Kgs. 17:1-41). In addition, he also omitted the synchronization of Hezekiah's reign with the northern kingdom (18:1). This was always his practice with one exception (see 13:1). From the Chronicler's perspective, the history of Judah was more important for his post-exilic readers (see also *Introduction: 2) Northern Israel*).

As with many reigns, the Chronicler began by depending on Kings for his basic information. Here he drew from 2 Kgs. 18:2 and reported the name of the king's mother and provided a chronological framework. (For the Chronicler's treatment of royal mothers, see 2 Chr. 13:2.)

This passage reports that he became king at **twenty-five** and that he reigned **twenty-nine years** (29:1). As noted earlier (see 28:1), if we take the information at face value, it would appear that Ahaz was extremely young when he fathered Hezekiah. The possibility of one or more textual corruptions during transmission cannot be ruled out (see *Introduction: Translation and Transmission*).

Like a number of other kings, Hezekiah **did what was right ... just as his father David** (29:2; see 17:3; 29:2; 34:2). This positive evaluation of Hezekiah's reign derives entirely from 2 Kgs. 18:3. This statement was a generalization evaluating the king's reign as a whole; both Kings and Chronicles record some of Hezekiah's failures (see 32:25-26,31 // 2 Kgs. 20:12-19). For the Chronicler's use of this evaluative terminology, see comments on 2 Chr. 24:2.

Hezekiah Re-establishes Temple Worship (29:3-31:21)

The first step in Hezekiah's reign is his most important. Three long chapters (81 verses) describe the first seven months of the king's reign as fully devoted to the restoration of the temple and its services. This material displays the most significant aspect of the Chronicler's presentation of the king's life.

Comparison of 29:3-31:21 with 2 Kgs. 18:4-8

At this point, the records of Chronicles and Kings are very different. The book of Kings devotes only one verse to Hezekiah's worship reforms (2 Kgs. 18:4); it roughly parallels 31:1. Moreover, the notice of Hezekiah's conformity to the Law of Moses (2 Kgs. 18:5-8) roughly parallels 31:20-21. The writer of Kings gave less attention to Hezekiah's temple effort in order to highlight Josiah's restoration a few generations later (see 2 Kgs. 23:1-20 // 2 Chr. 34:4-7, 29-33). The Chronicler, however, was intent on using Hezekiah's efforts as a model for his post-exilic readers. For this reason, he expanded these five verses into three full chapters.

Structure of 29:3-31:21

The Chronicler's record of Hezekiah's re-establishment of temple worship divides into three large sections. The arrangement of these materials follows a thematic as well as a chronological progression (see figure 53). The chronological progression of these three chapters appears explicitly in the text. The temple was cleansed in the first month of the king's reign (29:3); the Passover celebration occurred in the second month (30:13); the provisions for continuing temple service were arranged from the third to the seventh month (31:7). The thematic symmetry is evident as well. Hezekiah prepared the temple and its personnel (29:3-36); this initial reorganization was maintained by the king's other arrangements (31:2-21). The national Passover celebration formed the pivotal event between the initial establishment and permanent arrangements (30:1-31:1).

Hezekiah Initiates Temple Service (29:3-36)

Hezekiah's first step toward restoring the temple and its services was to cleanse the temple from its defilement under Ahaz. The Chronicler's record of this event presented Hezekiah as a paradigm of devotion to God.

Comparison of 29:3-36 with Kings

This material has no parallels in Kings. It represents the Chronicler's emphasis on what Hezekiah did in his first month as king of Judah.

Structure of 29:3-36

The account of Hezekiah's temple cleansing divides into five sections. These portions display symmetrical thematic concerns that focus not only on the cleansing itself, but on the preparations and results of the cleansing (see figure 53). The passage opens with Hezekiah beginning the process of restoring the temple (29:3). This opening balances with the indication that the king had finished the restoration (29:35b-36). In the center of the chapter stands the actual account of the ceremony of sacrifices for the sins of the people of God (29:20-30). On either side of this turning point are the symmetrical accounts of preparations for and results of Hezekiah's temple sacrifices (29:4-11, 31-35a).

■Opening of Hezekiah's Reign (29:1-2)

♦Hezekiah Re-establishes Temple Worship (29:3-31:21)

•Hezekiah Initiates Temple Service (29:3-36)
- Hezekiah Begins Temple Restoration (29:3)
- Hezekiah's Preparations for Temple Service (29:4-19)
*Hezekiah Commissions the Priests and Levites (29:4-11)
Hezekiah's Commission is Performed (29:12-17)
*Hezekiah Receives Report (29:18-19)
- Hezekiah Offers Sacrifices in the Temple (29:20-30)
*Sacrifices Offered (29:20-24)
*Musical Accompaniment (29:25-30)
- Hezekiah's Results from Temple Service (29:31-35a)
*Hezekiah's Invitation (29:31a)
*Assembly's Response (29:31b)
*Quantity of Service (29:32-35a)
- Hezekiah Completes Temple Restoration (29:35b-36)

•Hezekiah Unites Israel in Passover Celebration (30:1-31:1)
- Tribes Invited to Jerusalem (30:1)
[Regression: Attention to Northern Israelites (30:2-12)]
[Hezekiah Plans the Invitation (30:2-5)]
[Hezekiah Sends Invitation (30:6-9)]
[Hezekiah Receives Reactions to Invitation (30:10-12)]
- Gathering and Reforms before Passover (30:13-14)
Passover Observed (30:15a)
[Regression: Attention to Northern Israelites (30:15b-20)]
- Worship and Reforms after Passover (30:21-31:1a)
First Seven Days (30:21-22)
Seven Day Extension (30:23-31:1a)
- Tribes Return Home (31:1b)

•Hezekiah's Enduring Provisions for Temple Service (31:2-21)
- Hezekiah Permanently Establishes Temple Personnel (31:2-8)
Hezekiah Arranges for Priests and Levites (31:2-3)
Hezekiah Orders Contributions (31:4)
Hezekiah's Orders Enthusiastically Obeyed (31:5-7)
Hezekiah Rejoices in Provisions (31:8)
- Hezekiah Establishes Permanent Distribution (31:9-21)
Hezekiah Evaluates Provisions (31:9-10)
Hezekiah Orders Storehouse Preparations (31:11a)
Hezekiah's Orders Enthusiastically Obeyed (31:11b-19)
Hezekiah Blessed for His Provisions (31:20-21)

♦Hezekiah's Inconsistencies During the Assyrian Invasion (32:1-31)

- Hezekiah's Inconsistent Military Strategy (32:1-23)
    - Hezekiah is Threatened by a Foreign Nation (32:1)
        - Hezekiah Depends on Human Strength (32:2-8)
        - Hezekiah Depends on God (32:9-21)
    - Hezekiah is Highly Regarded by Foreign Nations (32:22-23)

- Hezekiah's Inconsistent Pride (32:24-26)
    - *Hezekiah's Blessing (32:24)
        - Hezekiah's Prayer (32:24a)
        - Divine Healing (32:24b)
            - *Hezekiah's Judgment (32:25)
                - Hezekiah's Pride (32:25a)
                - Divine Wrath (32:25b)
    - *Hezekiah's Blessing (32:26)
        - Hezekiah's Repentance (32:26a)
        - Divine Forbearance (32:26b)

- Hezekiah's Inconsistent Alliance (32:27-31)
    - Hezekiah's Successes (32:27-30)
    - Hezekiah's Failure (32:31)

■Closure of Hezekiah's Reign (32:32-33)

Outline of 2 Chr. 29:1-32:33 (figure 53)

Hezekiah Begins Temple Restoration (29:3)
The Chronicler made it clear that this chapter dealt with the very first things Hezekiah did as the king of Judah. Similar reforms of worship in Judah took place at other points in the history (see *Introduction: 6) Royal Observance of Worship*). Hezekiah began to restore the temple **in the first month of the first year** (29:3). By this means, Hezekiah is likened to Solomon whose first major act after receiving wisdom from God was to begin work on the temple (see 2:1).

The king's efforts began with opening **the doors of the temple** (29:3). It is likely that these doors were those separating the Main Hall (i.e. the Holy Place) from the Outer Court (probably the courtyard of the priests; see *Introduction: Appendix B – The Structures, Furnishings and Decorations of Solomon's Temple*). We cannot know the extent of these initial repairs. Some light may be shed by 2 Kgs. 18:16 which indicates that Hezekiah covered the doors of the temple with gold (see 3:7; 4:22). Opening and repairing the doors leading to the Main Hall was essential to the temple renovation. These were the ceremonial doors through which the priests entered as they performed their duties.

Hezekiah's father, Ahaz, had shut the doors of the temple, thereby making it impossible for Judah to carry out the worship of God (see 28:24). As such, the Chronicler made it evident that Hezekiah reversed the apostasy of his father. A new day had dawned for Judah, symbolized in the opening of the temple doors.

Hezekiah's Preparations for Temple Services (29:4-19)
As the Chronicler's account moves toward the full scale renewal of the temple, he reported Hezekiah's preparatory work. His focus in these verses was on the king's establishment of priests and Levites to cleanse the temple of its defilement.

Structure of 29:4-19
This portion of the account divides into three sections (see figure 53). The dramatic flow of this material is apparent. It begins with the king commissioning (29:4-11) and ends with a report from those commissioned indicating that the king's wish had been fulfilled (29:18-19). Between these events, Hezekiah's commission is enacted (29:12-17).

Hezekiah Commissions the Priests and Levites (29:4-11)
The king began his preparations by commissioning **the priests and Levites** to begin the work of cleansing the temple (29:4). This portion of the record consists of a description of the setting (29:4) and the king's speech (29:5-11).

Hezekiah called for an assembly of **the priests and Levites** (29:4). Normally, the Chronicler reserved these terms for Zadokites and non-Zadokites respectively. In Hezekiah's speech, however, he designated both groups under the rubric of **Levites** (29:5).

Hezekiah's speech is one of four speeches in the Chronicler's account of his reign (see 29:31; 30:6-9; 32:7-8). This speech began and ended with the king giving orders (29:5,11) and contained an historical explanation of his orders (29:6-10).

Hezekiah ordered the priests and Levites to **consecrate** themselves and **the temple** (29:5). In reporting these words, the Chronicler not only connected Hezekiah's actions with those of David (see 1 Chr. 15:2), but also showed Hezekiah's intention to conform his efforts to the Law of Moses. The Mosaic Law offered detailed instructions for the consecration of priests and Levites (see Exod. 29:1-35; 30:19-21, 30; 40:31-32; Num. 8:5-14). These rituals of consecration symbolized God's setting apart priests and Levites from ordinary occupations to perform the service of the tabernacle and Temple. To this end, they were ceremonially cleansed, dressed, and restricted from going places that might contaminate them. In fact, the priests were anointed with the same oil as the tabernacle furniture (see Exod. 30:22-30), thereby indicating that they were to share in the holiness of the dwelling place of God. The consecration of the temple itself involved removing **all defilement from the sanctuary** (29:5) by destroying foreign objects and by setting all temple furnishings in proper order (29:15-17). Rituals of consecration appear frequently in Chronicles as examples of proper worship which the post-exilic readers were to imitate in their day (see *Introduction: 6) Royal Observance of Worship*).

The consecration Hezekiah ordered was a large project. For this reason, he offered an explanation to motivate the priests and Levites (29:6-10). He explained that the previous generation was **unfaithful ... and forsook** the Lord (29:6). The terms **unfaithful** and **forsook** were the Chronicler's typical terms for describing flagrant violation of Israel's covenant with the Lord (see *Introduction: 21) Unfaithfulness*; see also *22) Abandoning/Forsaking*). Judah had demonstrated infidelity by neglecting the temple and its holy services (29:6-7).

As a result of this apostasy, Hezekiah argued that **the anger of the LORD has fallen on Judah and Jerusalem** (29:8). This terminology parallels earlier descriptions of northern Israel's terrible conditions (see 28:9,11,13,25). Northern Israel received the wrath of God, but now Hezekiah declared that in Ahaz's day Judah had sunk to the same level as her northern neighbor (see *Introduction: 2) Northern Israel*).

The similarity between Israel and Judah was taken one step further. Judah had become an **object of dread and horror and scorn.** Usually, these terms depict the tragedy of exile (see Deut. 28:25,41; Jer. 15:4; 19:8; 25:9, 18; 34:17; Ezek. 23:46). Hezekiah explained that the judgment of God had caused **'our fathers to die by the sword'** ... and had led **'our sons and daughters and our wives in captivity'** (29:9).

Because Old Testament prophets used these expressions to describe the Babylonian exile, it would appear that the Chronicler intended for his readers to draw a connection between their own post-exilic situation and that of Hezekiah. The Chronicler presented Hezekiah as living in a situation similar to theirs. Many Judahites were taken captive to Damascus during Ahaz's reign (see 28:5). This event adumbrated the larger exile of Judah to Babylon. As a result, Hezekiah's attention to worship came after an exile and provided a model for the post-exilic readers of

Chronicles as they lived after an even greater exile.

The last step in Hezekiah's explanation focuses on his own intention. He planned **to make a covenant with the Lord** (29:10). The language of this verse suggests that Hezekiah did not have in mind a national covenant renewal, but his own devotion to royal obligations. Much like Asa before him (see 15:12), Hezekiah saw that he had to affirm his responsibilities as king. Renewing his covenant with God was the only way Hezekiah could hope that God's **fierce anger will turn away** (29:10). Hezekiah understood that Judah could expect God's blessing only when the Davidic king was fully devoted to leading the nation in righteousness, especially in the area of temple worship. The Chronicler's message was plain. The same benefit would come to the post-exilic community only when they served a new Davidide with the same commitments (see *Introduction: 13) Covenant*).

Hezekiah concluded his speech with a final exhortation to the priests and Levites. He warned them not to be **negligent** (29:11). They too played a vital role in the restoration of the temple because **the Lord has chosen** them to serve in the temple. The roles of priests and Levites are highlighted throughout the Chronicler's history (see *Introduction: 4-9) King and Temple*). This emphasis spoke directly to those who held these offices within post-exilic Judah. Priests and Levites shared responsibility with political families for reinstituting the temple as the place for the worship of God.

Hezekiah's Commission is Performed (29:12-17)

After reporting Hezekiah's exhortation to the priests and Levites, the Chronicler immediately added that the king's order was initiated. The priests and Levites consecrated themselves and then cleansed the temple.

Structure of 29:12-17

The account of Levitical efforts divides into two main parts (see figure 53): lists of Levitical participants (29:12-14), reports of Levitical activities (29:15-17).

Levite Participants (29:12-14)

The Chronicler wasted no time forming a list of the **Levites** who **set to work** (29:12). His list contains fourteen names that represent groups of Levites who served at Hezekiah's command. Two representatives appear from each Levitical family (see 1 Chr. 6:1-80): **Kohathites**, **Merarites**, and **Gershonites** (29:12).

In addition to these names, two men are listed from the important Kohathite clan of **Elizaphan** (29:13a). **Elizaphan** was one of two Levites whom Moses ordered to purify the Tabernacle by carrying out the dead bodies of Nadab and Abihu (see Lev. 10:4-5). David had the descendants of Elizaphan help bring the ark to Jerusalem (see 1 Chr. 15:8,10-11). Now once again, descendants of Elizaphan helped to purify the Temple and restore acceptable worship. Two names also appear from the families of **Asaph** ... **Heman** and **Jeduthun** (29:13b-14), the three clans of Levitical singers (see 1 Chr. 25:1-31).

This list of Levites participating in Hezekiah's restoration is only representative; **their brothers** joined them in the work as well (29:15). Yet, the breadth of this list points out that all the families of Levi participated. In this manner, the Chronicler drew another connection between Hezekiah and the ideal reigns of David and Solomon. All three kings set all the Levitical families in order (see 1 Chr. 15:4-24; 23:1-32; 24:20-26:32; 2 Chr. 5:4-5,12-14; see also *Introduction: 4-9) King and Temple*).

Levite Activities (29:15-17)

After his representative list of participants, the Chronicler shifted attention to the actual activities which cleansed the temple (29:15-19). The Chronicler's report focuses on three matters: initiation (29:15), process (29:16), and temporal notices (29:17).

The priests and Levites initiated their work by gathering others to their company. Then they **consecrated themselves** (see 29:5) and began to **purify** the temple (29:15). The Chronicler succinctly evaluated their efforts, saying that they did **as the king had ordered** (29:15; see 29:5). Moreover, Hezekiah's orders were according to **the word of the LORD** (29:15). By this means the Chronicler made it clear that everything was done just as it should have been (see *Introduction: 14) Standards*). In sharp contrast with the apostasy of Ahaz his father, Hezekiah and the priests and Levites under his command treated temple worship as a holy duty to be performed according to divine instruction (see Deut. 12:2-4). Once again a strong connection appears between Hezekiah and the idealized reigns of David and Solomon (see 1 Chr. 15:2-15; 16:39-42; 2 Chr. 5:1-7:10; 8:12-13).

The process of purification also took place with the sanctity of the temple in mind (29:16). The Chronicler explained a twofold process. First, **priests went into the sanctuary** (29:16). The term **sanctuary** ('inner part' NAS, NRS) is not altogether specific. It may refer to the Most Holy Place where the Ark of the Covenant was kept (see 3:8-14; 4:22; 5:7; 1 Chr. 28:11; Exod. 26:34). The **priests** alone were allowed into the inner sanctuary of the temple (see 5:4-11). It could also refer, however, to the Main Hall (see *Introduction: Appendix B – The Structures, Furnishings and Decorations of Solomon's Temple*). The **priests** brought **everything unclean** out of the inner portions of the temple **to the courtyard** surrounding the temple proper (29:16).

Second, in the courtyard the **Levites** took charge and carried the unclean items to the **Kidron Valley,** a burial site near Jerusalem that was considered unclean and therefore appropriate for these items (see 15:16; 30:14; 2 Kgs. 23:4,6,12).

The details of the process indicate the Chronicler's desire to show the care with which Hezekiah's temple restoration took place. His efforts illustrated the care with which the post-exilic community must treat the temple and its services.

The Chronicler also added a chronological notice. It took from **the first day of the first month** until **the sixteenth day of the first month** to complete the cleansing of the temple (29:17). At least two purposes lie behind this temporal reference.

On the one hand, it makes evident the extensive nature of the effort. The task was performed carefully and thoroughly. On the other hand, it foreshadows a problem with which Hezekiah must deal in the next chapter. The temple and its services were not ready by the time of Passover on the fourteenth of the first month (see 30:3).

Hezekiah Receives Report from Priests and Levites (29:18-19)
After completing their tasks, the priests and Levites reported to Hezekiah. They announced that they had cleansed **the entire temple of the Lord** (29:18); no defilement remained in the entire temple complex. Moreover, their report focused specifically on the preparation and replacement of various furnishings and **utensils** which **King Ahaz removed** (29:19). The Chronicler repeated his description of Ahaz's life as one of **unfaithfulness** (29:19; see 29:6), a term which he used frequently in his history to describe serious sins (see *Introduction: 21) Unfaithfulness*).

The utensils of worship were a special concern to the early post-exilic community. The utensils of Solomon's temple (see 4:19-22; 1 Chr. 28:14-17) were taken to Babylon and brought back in the early days of restoration (see 36:18; 2 Kgs. 25:14-15; Ezra 1:7-11; Dan. 5:2-3). This particular focus of the Levitical report to Hezekiah spoke clearly to the post-exilic community. Apparently, the Chronicler thought it was important to stress that restoration of the temple included attention to the purification and restoration of the instruments of worship brought back by those returning from Babylon.

Hezekiah Offers Sacrifices in the Temple (29:20-30)
Following the cleansing of the temple by the priests and Levites, the Chronicler recorded the sacrifices which atoned for national apostasy during the years of Ahaz. This material is marked off by the introductory temporal expression **early the next morning** (29:20). It divides into two parts: the sacrifices (29:20-24), and the music (29:25-30). Both of these sections describe the same events from different perspectives. The first part emphasizes the actual slaughtering of the animals; the second part emphasizes the music accompanying the sacrifices.

Sacrifices Offered (29:20-24)
This portion begins with a reference to **King Hezekiah** ... and the **city officials** (29:20). The king and his officials began the ceremonies of sacrifice when they **went up to the temple** (29:20). They brought with them an assortment of animals, seven of each kind for sacrifice (29:21). **Bulls** ... **rams** and **lambs** were brought as **whole burnt offerings;** the **male goats** were brought **as a sin offering** (29:21).

The Chronicler noted that these sin offerings were **for the sanctuary and for Judah** (29:21). The closest parallel to this statement appears in Ezek. 43:18-27 where the prophet predicts that the cleansing of the post-exilic temple will be accomplished by a sin offering. Moreover, Ezekiel insisted that the cleansing of the prince and people for Passover would occur in the same way (see Ezek. 43:21-23). It is likely that both the Chronicler and Ezekiel viewed Hezekiah's sacrifices similarly. Ministering during the exile, Ezekiel employed Hezekiah's action as a model for his predictions of the future renewal of the temple. After the exile, the Chronicler used Hezekiah's actions as a model for the renewal of temple worship in his day.

Hezekiah ordered the **priests** to sacrifice (29:21b). In response, **they** (i.e. the priests) killed the animals for the burnt offering and **sprinkled the blood on the altar** (29:22). In addition, they **laid their hands** on the goats in symbolic transference of their sin to the animal. This ritual alludes to the similar practice outlined for the day of Atonement (see Lev. 16:21).

Throughout the reign of Hezekiah, the Chronicler designated the king's gatherings around the temple as an **assembly** (29:23, 28, 31-32; 30:2, 4, 13, 23-25; 31:18). This terminology connected this event with many other assemblies in the Chronicler's history. The language of **assembly** raised Hezekiah's actions to the level of these numerous exemplary events (see *Introduction: 5) Religious Assemblies*).

As mentioned before, the purpose of these sacrifices was for the cleansing of the temple and for national atonement. While in 29:21 the focus of sacrifice was **for the sanctuary and for Judah**, the Chronicler's description in 29:24 clarified the extent of the human recipients of the atonement. Twice he noted that the sacrifices were not simply for Judah but for **all Israel** (29:24), his favorite way of describing the entire nation (see: *Introduction: 1) All Israel*). In fact, the word order in the Hebrew of the last clause (**'because the king had ordered ... for all Israel'** [29:24]) stresses that the extent of the atonement was the entire nation. By this means the Chronicler revealed that one of Hezekiah's chief motivations for reestablishing the temple was to atone for all the tribes of Judah and Israel.

As we will see in the next chapter, Hezekiah invited the faithful from Israel and Judah to attend Passover in Jerusalem (see 30:1). Moreover, his temple renewal led to reforms throughout the North and South (see 31:1-3). The cleansing of the temple and the atoning sacrifices of this day were intended for all of these people of God. Once again, the Chronicler drew a connection between Hezekiah, David, and Solomon. The Chronicler emphasized that David and Solomon reigned over all the tribes (see *Introduction: 1) All Israel*). Here he indicated that Hezekiah was intent on unifying the kingdom in his day.

Musical Accompaniment (29:25-30)

Having described the sacrifices in the temple with particular concern for the role of the priests, the Chronicler revisited the event with a focus on its musical dimension (29:25-30). Throughout the reigns of David and Solomon, the Chronicler stressed the importance of music in the worship of the Lord (see 1 Chr. 15-16; 25:1-6; 2 Chr. 7:6; see also *Introduction: 8) Music* and *27) Disappointment and Celebration*). In this scene of temple renewal, his delight in the wonder of music moves to the foreground once again.

The Chronicler made it evident that Hezekiah did these things in the proper way. He arranged the Levites with **cymbals, harps and lyres** (29:25). These arrangements were not made according to Hezekiah's whims, but **in the way prescribed by David and Gad ... and Nathan**. The appeal to Davidic and prophetic arrangements confirmed that Hezekiah did things in the proper manner (see *Introduction: 14) Standards*). This passage is the only place where **Gad** or **Nathan** are given a role in the ordering of music. The purpose for this reference is made clear in the next phrase. These arrangements were ordered by **the LORD through his prophets**. Hezekiah did precisely as he should have. His arrangements were supported by David, his prophets, and the Lord himself. As a result, the Levites were ready **with David's instruments** (see 29:27 and 1 Chr. 15:16; 23:5) and the **priests** were ready **with trumpets** (see 1 Chr. 15:24). The Chronicler presented these arrangements as models for his post-exilic readers. Their temple worship must be according to the same standards.

The performance of music on this day appears in two phases. First, the Chronicler noted that the music **began** as the **offering began** (29:27). The **singing ... accompanied by trumpets and the instruments of David ... continued until the sacrifice ... was completed** (29:28). In this ideal worship, music played all during the time of sacrifice. Second, after **the offerings were finished** (29:29), **Hezekiah and his officials ordered the Levites** to continue to play and sing (29:30). As a result, **they sang praises with gladness and bowed their heads and worshipped**.

One of the reasons for the Chronicler's interest in worship music comes to the foreground again. The music of worship brought **gladness** to the hearts of the worshipers (29:30). This snippet of insight into the emotional quality of the event served as a positive incentive for the Chronicler's post-exilic readers. The way to celebrative gladness in their day was through the proper arrangement of temple worship (see *Introduction: 8) Music*; see also *27) Disappointment and Celebration*). Once again, the use of the term **assembly** (29:28, 30, 31) as a designation for this event supported this implication for the Chronicler's readers (see *Introduction: 5) Religious Assemblies*). For the designation of Asaph as a **seer** see *Introduction: 15) Prophets*.

Hezekiah's Results from Temple Service (29:31-35a)

Having described how Hezekiah brought atonement for the temple and all Israel, the Chronicler moved to the immediate results. The people responded overwhelmingly to the king's invitation to sacrifice at the temple.

Structure of 29:31-35a

This portion of the narrative divides into three sections (see figure 53): the king's invitation (29:31a), the assembly's response (29:31b), and a report of quantities (29:32-35a).

Hezekiah's Invitation (29:31a)

At this point in the narrative, the Chronicler moved beyond the activities of the king, his officials, and the priests and Levites (see 29:4-30) to the whole assembly gathered at the temple. The king turned to the crowd and noted, **'you have now dedicated yourselves to the LORD'** (29:31a). The terminology of 'dedication' or 'consecration' as it is translated elsewhere, alluded to the earlier words of Hezekiah (see 29:15). Rituals of consecration appear frequently in Chronicles as examples of proper worship which the post-exilic readers were to imitate in their day (see *Introduction: 6) Royal Observance of Worship*). Hezekiah announced that the crowd was consecrated by the atoning sacrifices. On the basis of their devotion to the temple, the king invited the assembly to **bring sacrifices and thank offerings to the temple** (29:31a). It is likely that the **sacrifices** here are to be identified with **the fellowship offerings** ('peace offerings' NAS, NKJ; 'offerings of well being' NRS) of which **thank offerings** were a type (see Lev. 7:11-15). If this understanding is correct, all of these sacrifices were voluntary, given out of gratitude for the forgiveness bestowed by God through the atoning sacrifices (see 29:22-24). Put simply, Hezekiah invited the assembly to show its gratitude for the blessing of forgiveness and renewal.

Assembly's Response (29:31b)

The assembly responded to Hezekiah's invitation with enthusiasm. In addition to **sacrifices and thank offerings**, those **whose hearts were willing** brought **burnt offerings**. The focus on the willingness of the people brings this passage once again into contact with David. In his final assembly the 'willingness' of the people appears a number of times (see 1 Chr. 29:5, 6, 9, 14, 17). The enthusiasm of Hezekiah's assembly reflected the kind of enthusiasm the Chronicler hoped his own audience would have for the temple in their day. As they remembered that the temple held the possibility of atonement for their sins, they too would delight in its services with voluntary offerings (see *Introduction: 16) Motivations*).

Quantity of Service (29:32-35a)

To highlight the splendor of this event, the Chronicler summarized the numbers of sacrifices and offerings (29:32-35). He focused on large numbers of sacrifices in a number of passages (see 1:6; 5:6; 7:4-5; 24:14; 29:32-35; 35:8-9). In each case, his intention was to convey the enthusiasm for the temple and its services (see *Introduction: 6) Royal Observance of Worship*). He mentioned that the people offered **seventy bulls, a hundred rams, and two hundred male lambs** as **burnt offerings** (29:32). Hundreds more animals were **consecrated as sacrifices** (29:33). This terminology probably refers to animals that were not completely burned on the altar but partially given to the priests as food. The priests were given a portion of all three types of fellowship offerings (thanksgiving, votive, free will; see Lev. 7:11-36), as well as portions of some but not all sin offerings (see Lev. 6:24-30) and guilt offerings (see Lev. 7:1-6).

In the middle of his report on the numbers of sacrifices, the Chronicler paused to mention extraordinary measures that had to be taken at this time (29:34). Lev. 1:5-6 indicates that worshipers were suppose to skin their own sacrifices. For some unknown reason, however, on this occasion the **priests** skinned the burnt offerings. Perhaps the widespread apostasy of the generation before Hezekiah made it necessary to take extra precautions against syncretism among the laity. In all events, the priests **were too few** to handle all of the work. So, **the Levites helped them**. Interestingly enough, the Chronicler added an explanation that cast a favorable light on the Levites. **The Levites had been more conscientious in consecrating themselves than the priests had been**. It is likely that this comment addressed some controversy among the priests and Levites in the Chronicler's day. In a time when Zadokite priests reasserted their leadership over the Levites, such controversies were unavoidable. Rituals of consecration appear frequently in Chronicles as examples of proper worship which the post-exilic readers were to imitate in their day (see *Introduction: 6) Royal Observance of Worship*).

The Chronicler closed his portrait of this glorious event with a catalog of the offerings that took place **in abundance** (29:35). Along with the **burnt offerings** were **fellowship ... and drink offerings** (29:35).

Hezekiah Completes Temple Restoration (29:35b-36)

The Chronicler completed his record of Hezekiah's first act as king with a brief notice. He first stated that the atoning sacrifices and voluntary offerings had reestablished **the service of the temple of the LORD** (29:35b). Hezekiah had accomplished what the Chronicler hoped his own readers would do.

The result of Hezekiah's accomplishment was also important for the Chronicler's purposes. **Hezekiah and all the people rejoiced** (29:36). In this and many other passages, the Chronicler connected joy for Israel with the proper functioning of the king and the temple (see *Introduction: 27) Disappointment and Celebration*). His repeated focus on this connection spoke directly to the needs of his readers. They too desired the happiness and rejoicing. In Hezekiah's day they rejoiced **at what God had brought about**. They were sure it was an act of God **because it was done so quickly**. Enthusiastic devotion to the Davidic family and the re-establishment of temple services brought a swift response of blessing from God. The Chronicler's advice was plain enough. The post-exilic readers could enjoy the same blessing if they devoted themselves fully to the king and temple in their day.

Hezekiah Reunites the Kingdom through Temple Worship (30:1-31:1)

In the preceding portion of Hezekiah's reign, the Chronicler noted that Hezekiah's actions provided atonement for northern Israel and southern Judah (see 29:24). At this point, the Chronicler developed this theme by reporting how Hezekiah celebrated the Passover with representatives of the entire nation. Through this Passover, the faithful of the southern and northern kingdoms were reunified around the temple and under the leadership of David's son.

Comparison of 30:1-31:1 with Kings

This portion of the Chronicler's record is an enormous expansion of one verse in Kings; 31:1 borrows information from 2 Kgs. 18:4. Apart from this connection, however, the account of Hezekiah's Passover is from the Chronicler's hand. The writer of Kings chose to emphasize Josiah's Passover celebration (see 2 Kgs. 23:21-23). The Chronicler, however, had much more interest in Hezekiah's Passover. The distinctive quality of Hezekiah's celebration was that it involved the migration of Northerners after the fall of Samaria (722 BC). The reunification of all Israel was so important to the Chronicler that he could not neglect the opportunity to bring this aspect of Hezekiah's reign to the foreground.

Structure of 30:1-31:1

The structure of this chapter is complex and deserves a few words of explanation. As the outline above suggests, this material consists of one narrative which contains two lengthy temporal regressions (see figure 53). The skeleton of Hezekiah's Passover celebration follows a straightforward five step symmetrical pattern. The passage begins with the tribes invited to Jerusalem (30:1); it ends as they return to their homes (31:1b). The turning point of the story is the observance of Passover at the beginning of the feast of Unleavened Bread (30:15a). Prior to the day of Passover the people gathered in Jerusalem and removed foreign worship from the city (30:13-14); after the day of Passover the people extended the celebration of Unleavened Bread and removed foreign worship even outside Jerusalem (30:21-31:1a).

This main story line is interrupted twice by temporal regressions. Unfortunately, most English translations do not make these temporal shifts clear. First, the Chronicler added an explanation of why and how Hezekiah extended invitations to the tribes, especially the northern tribes (30:2-12). Second, he paused to explain why and how the king was able to celebrate Passover with the northern tribes (30:15b-20). In both of these regressions the simple past tense of most English translations should be replaced by the past perfect. See the comments in each section below.

Recognizing when the Chronicler diverged from his central plot illumines some of his chief concerns in this chapter. Both temporal regressions (30:2-12, 15b-20) focus on Hezekiah's special attention to the northern Israelites. Winning the attendance of Northerners presented special challenges to the king (30:2-12). Once the Northerners arrived and participated, even more problems arose (30:15b-20). The Chronicler's interest in this chapter is not simply to record the bare essentials of Hezekiah's celebration. His two regressions demonstrate that he was particularly concerned with the efforts Hezekiah put forth to include the faithful from the northern tribes (see *Introduction: 2) Northern Israel*).

Tribes Invited to Jerusalem (30:1)

The Chronicler portrayed Hezekiah taking his temple restoration to a higher level by re-introducing **the Passover to the LORD**. The roots of Passover extend from Israel's exodus from Egypt (see Exod. 12:1-28). It was a major religious event in the first month of Israel's calendar commemorating the nation's deliverance from slavery. It was only appropriate that Hezekiah should desire to have Passover celebrated in his newly restored temple.

The Chronicler began his record of this Passover with the notice that Hezekiah was not satisfied simply to celebrate with his fellow Judahites. He invited **all Israel and Judah and ... Ephraim and Manasseh** (30:1). The piling up of terms here expresses the Chronicler's conviction that Hezekiah invited everyone without exception. Later he mentioned that invitations went out **from Beersheba to Dan** (30:1; see comments on 1 Chr. 21:2). In a word, the entire nation was invited. Northern Israel had fallen to Assyrian domination at this time and the capital of Samaria had been destroyed. Hezekiah extended himself to those left behind in the lands of the northern tribes by inviting them to Jerusalem for Passover.

As suggested above, 30:1 summarizes events which are explained more fully in 30:2-5. In many ways, this chronologically displaced verse draws attention to the central concern of this entire chapter. The Chronicler wanted his readers to know from the outset that Hezekiah's Passover celebration was devoted to the reunification of the nation. The motif of national reunification appears several times in this chapter (see 30:5-6,10-12). Moreover, this theme links this chapter with the preceding narrative. In 29:24 the Chronicler twice pointed out that Hezekiah's preparation of the temple included sacrifices for the sins of all the tribes. In 30:1 Hezekiah put the temple to use in the Passover and he invited the whole nation to attend.

This connection was critical to the efforts of the original post-exilic readers. Reestablishing temple service was to be joined with a desire for national reunification in their day as well.

Attention to Northern Israelites (30:2-12)

As mentioned above, in 30:2-12 the Chronicler regressed temporally to provide a lengthy explanation of how Hezekiah invited the entire nation for Passover celebration. For this reason, all of the main verbs in this section should be translated in the past perfect (...*had* **decided** ... **had not been able** ... **had not consecrated** ... **had not assembled** ... *had* **seemed right** ... *had* **decided** ... etc. [30:2-12]).

Structure of 30:2-12

This passage divides into three steps (see figure 53). It begins with the king's plan to invite Northerners (30:2-5). It ends with mixed reactions to the invitation (30:10-12). The turning point of this material is Hezekiah's distribution of the invitation (30:6-9).

Hezekiah Plans the Invitation (30:2-5)

The Chronicler explained that instead of holding the Passover at its prescribed time in the first month (see Lev. 23:5), Hezekiah held the celebration **in the second month** (30:2). Hezekiah's decision to postpone for a month was not entirely without precedent. Num. 9:10-11 made an exception for individuals who were far away or were unclean because they had touched a corpse. These people could celebrate in the second month. Hezekiah's situation was not exactly that envisioned in Num. 9, but apparently he thought it was close enough to warrant postponement of the entire event.

The Chronicler mentioned three factors that legitimized Hezekiah's decision.

1) The decision was made by **the king and his officials and the whole assembly** (30:2). The same explanation is repeated in 30:4. The Chronicler emphasized that the postponement was not simply the king's choice; the entire community supported the move. (For a summary of the Chronicler's outlook on popular consent, see comments on 1 Chr. 13:1-4.)

2) The reason for postponement was that **not enough priests had consecrated themselves and the people had not assembled in Jerusalem** (30:3). Proper consecration was so important that the king postponed the Passover. Rituals of consecration appear frequently in Chronicles as examples of proper worship which the post-exilic readers were to imitate in their day (see *Introduction: 6) Royal Observance of Worship*).

The Chronicler's implicit approval of Hezekiah's reasoning reveals much about the manner in which he understood the application of the Law of Moses. He was no pedantic legalist, insisting on precise and wooden applications of the Law. Hezekiah's situation was unusual and this extraordinary situation required the application of precedents in Mosaic Law in creative ways. The fact that Hezekiah postponed only one month demonstrates the king's desire to adhere to Mosaic standards, but his unique situation required ingenious application.

3) Hezekiah's motivation for this entire event is spelled out plainly. He did not seek the reunification of the people primarily for economic or political reasons. He invited all the tribes because Passover **had not been celebrated in large numbers according to what was written** in the Law of Moses (30:5 see also 30:12). Throughout this chapter Hezekiah is hailed as a king determined to enforce the observance of the Law in his day. As such he was a model king for the post-exilic readers of this book (see *Introduction: 14) Standards*).

The king's desire to see **large numbers** (30:5) join the celebration, led him to send invitations **throughout Israel, from Beersheba to Dan** (30:5). Once again, the Chronicler reversed the traditional 'Dan to Beersheba' as he referred to all the tribes of Israel (see comments on 1 Chr. 21:2). His southern orientation stemmed from his focus on Judah and Jerusalem as the center of hope for all of the tribes. It should also be noted that all of the tribes are now simply called **Israel** (30:5). From the Chronicler's point of view, Israel and Judah were joined again in this great event because Hezekiah was determined to make it possible to have the entire nation at his Passover.

Once again, the Chronicler designed this event as an **assembly** (see 30:2, 4, 13, 23-25). Time and again, he pointed to religious assemblies as examples of ways in which the post-exilic community was to observe the worship of God. This assembly in Hezekiah's day was no exception to this focus (see *Introduction: 5) Religious Assemblies*).

Hezekiah Sends Invitations (30:6-9)

This step continues the elaboration in Hezekiah's invitation. It consists of a summary of the letters he sent to the tribes. This material divides into a brief introduction (30:6a) and the text of the letters (30:6b-9).

In continuity with motifs which have appeared in this and the previous chapters, the Chronicler introduced Hezekiah's letter with the notice that **the king and ... his officials** (2 Chr. 30:2,6) sent letters **throughout Israel and Judah** (30:6a). The unity among the leaders and the participation of the whole nation are in view once again.

The letter which follows was addressed to northern Israelites only (see 30:6b). It is likely that other letters went out to Judahites. At this point, however, the Chronicler emphasized that all the tribes received letters from Hezekiah and the officials of Judah. Hezekiah's letter consists of exhortations to the northern tribes.

Hezekiah's letter contains eight exhortations. These exhortations may be divided in the following manner (see figure 54):

return (30:6b)	Guiding Principle
do not be like your fathers (30:7a) **do not be stiff-necked** (30:8a)	Negative Requirement
submit (30:8b) **come** (30:8c) **serve** (30:8d)	Positive Requirement
if you return (30:9a) **if you return** (30:9b)	Guiding Principle

Outline of 2 Chr. 30:6b-9 (figure 54)

Hezekiah's speech focused on a basic principle which he elaborated at the beginning and end of his letter (30:6b, 9). The repetition of **return** forms an inclusion for the entire correspondence. The inner portion of the invitation explains the two dimensions of what it meant to 'return' (i.e. repent) to the Lord. On the negative side (30:7-8a), the Northerners must reject the practices of their forebears. On the positive side (30:8b-c), they must worship at the temple in Jerusalem.

The irenic quality of Hezekiah's opening words should be noted. He addressed the northern tribes as the **people of Israel** and affirmed their common ancestry with Judah in **Abraham, Isaac and Israel** (30:6b). Hezekiah's tone is open and inviting. As a political entity, northern Israel had turned away from God's temple and king in Jerusalem (see 13:4-9). Even so, the faithful within those tribes were to be given opportunity to join with Judah (see *Introduction: 2) Northern Israel*).

Hezekiah described his addressees as **you who are left, who have escaped**

(30:6b). The Northerners who had been spared from death and deportation by the **hand of the kings of the Assyrians** were invited to repent and join with Judah at the temple (30:6b). These descriptions of the North are very close to the manner in which the Chronicler described those who were eventually carried into exile in Babylon. They were **the remnant, who escaped from the sword** (36:20). This common terminology suggests that the Chronicler identified those who joined Hezekiah's Passover and those who went to exile in Babylon. Both groups were the remnant who could receive a brighter future by returning to the Lord and to Jerusalem.

Hezekiah established the basic principle of his letter at its beginning and reiterated it at the end. The Northerners must **return to the LORD** (30:6b, 9a,c). To return to God (or 'to repent' as it may be translated) was to acknowledge failure and to reaffirm submission to the standards of his covenant with Israel (see *Introduction: 22) Repentance*).

The central portions of the letter explained that returning to the Lord had negative and positive dimensions. Negatively, it meant that the Israelites must reject the apostasies of the past (30:7-8a). The North had been **unfaithful** (30:7; see *Introduction: 21) Unfaithfulness*) and **stiff-necked** (30:8a; see 36:13). These flagrant violations of the covenant were to be rejected by those returning to the Lord. Positively, to return to the Lord meant that they were to **submit to the LORD** (30:8b), i.e. obey his commands, **come to the sanctuary** (30:8c), and **serve** (or 'worship') **the LORD** (30:8d). In short, repentance required rejecting the old ways and endorsing Hezekiah's invitation to worship in Jerusalem. The book of Kings makes it clear that Jeroboam's great sin was the establishment of worship at Dan and Bethel (see 1 Kgs. 12:29). Hezekiah called on the faithful of northern Israel to reaffirm Jerusalem as their only place of worship.

The opening and closing portions of this letter also specify the results of returning to covenant fidelity. If the northern Israelites will return, then the Lord will **return to** [them] (30:6a). Moreover, those taken away **will be shown compassion by their captors and will come back** (30:9a). Beyond this, Hezekiah even promised that their **brothers and ... children** taken away would return to the land of promise (30:9a).

The words of Hezekiah certainly spoke clearly to the Chronicler's post-exilic readers. In many respects, they stood in very similar circumstances. They had suffered at the hands of foreign powers; many of their relatives remained outside the land; they had the opportunity to give temple worship its rightful place again. If they would only return to the Lord in their day, then the promises of divine blessing, including the ingathering of those remaining outside the land, would be theirs.

Hezekiah Receives Reactions to Invitation (30:10-12)

Having explained why and what Hezekiah wrote to the tribes of Israel, the Chronicler reported the results of his invitation. He mentioned that Hezekiah's **couriers** traveled throughout **Ephraim and Manasseh, as far as Zebulun** (30:10). Their mission was to reach the distant tribes as well as those nearby. The Transjordanian tribes may not be listed here because they were probably under stricter Assyrian control. In all events, the reaction to Hezekiah's invitation was mixed. Many of **the people scorned and ridiculed** the couriers (30:10), but **some men** from several northern tribes **humbled themselves and went to Jerusalem** (30:11). The theme of humility appears a number of times in Chronicles as recognition of guilt and surrender to God's requirements (see *Introduction: 18) Humility*). These Northerners took Hezekiah's message to heart and returned to their God (see 30:6-9). In addition to a number of faithful northern Israelites, Hezekiah also received positive responses from many Judahites. As a result of **the hand of God**, the Judahites **had unity of mind** about Hezekiah's Passover (30:12). Once again, the Chronicler pointed to God's purposes behind human events (see *Introduction: 10) Divine Activity*). Moreover, God brought about a remarkable unity among Judahites. This notice of popular unity fit well with the Chronicler's emphasis on the need for cooperation between Israel's people and her leaders. (For a summary of the Chronicler's outlook on popular consent see comments on 1 Chr. 13:1-4.) The reunification of the nation in Hezekiah's day did not just involve the repentance of northern Israelites. It also resulted from the overwhelming popular support of Judahites. They were eager to follow **the word of the LORD** (30:12; see *Introduction: 14) Standards*).

The Chronicler painted an ideal portrait for his readers in these words. At the command of David's son, repentant Israelites came to Jerusalem and met alongside Judahites fully supportive of temple worship. Nothing less was required of the post-exilic community (see *Introduction: 2) Northern Israel*).

Gathering and Reforms before Passover (30:13-14)

At this point, the Chronicler returned to his main narrative begun in 30:1. In these verses, the crowd gathered and began the celebrations.

The group in Jerusalem was **a very large crowd of people** (30:13). Hezekiah's Passover was no minor event. As decided by **the king and his officials and the whole assembly**, the celebration took place **in the second month** (30:13; see 30:2). **The Feast of Unleavened Bread** was largely a continuation of the Passover marked by celebration, corporate worship, and the instruction of children (see Exod. 12:14-20; Lev. 23:4-8; Num. 28:16-25; Deut. 16:1-8).

As the reunified people of God joined together for worship, they purged the city of evil. They **removed the altars in Jerusalem and cleared away the incense altars** to other gods (30:14). In the previous chapter, the priests and Levites had purified the temple of the objects of foreign religions (see 29:15-17). Now the people purify the entire city in much the same way. They too threw the detestable objects **into the Kidron Valley** (30:14, see 29:16). While the worship reforms here extended beyond that which Hezekiah had accomplished earlier (from the temple to the entire city), these actions merely adumbrate a much greater cleansing to take place later in this chapter (from the city to the entire nation [see 31:1]). This enthusiasm for purity in Jerusalem was exemplary for the Chronicler's readers. Receiving the blessings of God in their day required the destruction of all false worship (see 2 Chr. 15:8; see also *Introduction: 6) Royal Observance of Worship*).

Passover Observed (30:15a)

This passage forms the turning point of the main narrative of this chapter. The Passover lamb was slaughtered **on the fourteenth day**. The killing of the lamb began the celebration of the Feast of Unleavened Bread. This verse is purposefully ambiguous when it reads **they slaughtered**. In the normal scenario, the laity slaughtered their own lambs. But these were these extraordinary times. As we will see, special measures had to be taken.

More Attention to Northern Israel (30:15b-20)

At this point, the Chronicler turned again from his main narrative to a temporal regression (see figure 53). He explained how the Passover slaughter had taken place (30:15b-19). The verbs in these verses should be translated in the past perfect (*had been* **ashamed and** *had* **consecrated themselves and** *had* **brought burnt offerings ...**). They describe three things that took place on the **fourteenth day** (30:15a).

First, the **priests and the Levites** had to deal with their own spiritual condition (30:15b-16). The priests and Levites who had helped Hezekiah in the re-establishment of the temple had already consecrated themselves (see 29:4, 15, 34). In all likelihood these worship leaders came from outside Jerusalem in response to Hezekiah's invitation. The condition of priests outside Jerusalem had already been noted in 30:3 as one of the reasons for postponing the Passover. Once these priests and Levites were ceremonially prepared, they performed their duties **as prescribed in the Law of Moses** (30:16). Once again, the Chronicler highlighted Hezekiah's concern for observing Passover in the proper manner (see *Introduction: 14) Standards*).

Second, many of the laity who came from outside Jerusalem **had not consecrated themselves** either (30:17). For this reason, extraordinary measures were taken. **Levites had to kill the Passover lambs**. Normally, the laity were to slaughter their own Passover lambs on the evening of Passover (see Deut. 16:5-6; Exod. 12:3-6, 21). The Levites, however, protected the sanctity of the feast by slaughtering the lambs for them.

Third, **most of the many people who came** from the northern regions had not been purified, but **they ate ... contrary to what was written** (30:18). 30:20 explains that these people had become sick (compare 1 Cor. 11:27-30). In response to this crisis, **Hezekiah prayed for them** (30:18). Instead of condemning or excluding the northern Israelites for their violation, Hezekiah interceded on their behalf. The king's prayer constitutes one of many examples in Chronicles of Solomon's dedicatory prayer in action (see 6:29-31; see *Introduction: 17) Prayer*). In times of sickness, Israel was to offer prayers in and toward the temple (see 6:29). Hezekiah appealed to the mercy of God and asked that he forgive the violation of each one **who sets his heart on seeking God ... even if he is not clean according to the rules of the sanctuary** (30:19). Here the Chronicler touched on the important theme of 'seeking' God. Sincere repentance and devotion are implied by the term (see *Introduction: 19) Seeking*). Although Hezekiah was concerned with the details of worship regulations (see 30:5, 18; 31:3), it is apparent that the king recognized that the heart of the worshippers from the North was more important than mere external conformity to **the rules of the sanctuary** (30:19; see Lev. 15:31). This focus on the heart fit well with the Chronicler's concern elsewhere with motivations and desires (see *Introduction: 16) Motivations*). It also fit well with the concern of God; **the LORD heard Hezekiah and healed the people** (30:20).

The purpose of this lengthy aside (30:15b-20) is evident. The participation of northern Israelites in Hezekiah's day called for a number of extraordinary measures. Patience and flexibility were required. The Chronicler drew attention to these aspects of Hezekiah's celebration to instruct his post-exilic readers. Uniting the people of God from distant places would require extraordinary measures in their day as well. Fear of corruption from unschooled or unprepared Israelites should not forestall the higher goal of gathering all the tribes to the son of David and the worship of God in Jerusalem (*Introduction: 2) Northern Israel*).

Worship and Reforms after Passover (30:21-31:1a)

In balance with the report of gathering and worship reforms in Jerusalem before the Passover (30:13-14; see figure 53), the Chronicler turned to the worship and reforms that followed the Passover (30:21-31:1a).

Structure 30:21-31:1a

This material consists of two sections (see figure 53): the first seven days (30:21-22) and the seven day extension (30:23-31:1a).

First Seven Days (30:21-22)

Once again, the Chronicler's designation of this event as a religious **assembly** indicated his keen interest in this gathering (see 30:23-25). Time and again, he pointed to religious assemblies as examples of ways in which the post-exilic community was to observe the worship of God at the temple (see *Introduction: 5) Religious Assemblies*). This assembly in Hezekiah's day was no exception to this focus.

The Chronicler first reported that the **Feast of Unleavened Bread** was celebrated **for seven days** (30:21). This length of time was true to the instructions of Mosaic Law (see Exod. 12:15). The striking feature of this festival was that it took place **with great rejoicing** (30:21). In fact, **all who had assembled ... including aliens ... rejoiced** (30:25). The Chronicler often highlighted events in his history by pointing to their celebrative quality (see *Introduction: 27) Disappointment and Celebration*).

This **rejoicing** was connected with the **Levites and priests** performing their musical duties (30:21). The text even notes that Hezekiah encouraged the Levites for their faithful service in the celebration (30:22). As in other portions of his history, the Chronicler emphasized the joy of worship as it was expressed in music (see *Introduction: 8) Music*). This picture of celebration was designed to encourage his readers by demonstrating the positive effects of Hezekiah's efforts. If they wanted to rise to these heights of joy, they must devote themselves to the reunification of Israel at the temple much like Hezekiah did in his day.

Seven Day Extension (30:23-31:1a)

The wonder of Hezekiah's Passover was so great that a decision was made to extend the feast for **seven more days** (30:23). This choice was not imposed by the king; the decision was made when **the whole assembly… agreed**. The Chronicler touched on the cooperation between Judahite kings and their citizens on a number of occasions. Several honorable kings developed consensus among their people before implementing policies (see 30:2). (For a summary of the Chronicler's view on popular consent, see comments on 1 Chr. 13:1-4.)

In an effort to highlight the wonder of Hezekiah's celebration, the Chronicler drew close parallels between Hezekiah and Solomon in several ways.

1) He noted that the celebration in Jerusalem was extended **seven more days** (30:23). The same length of extension occurred in the temple assembly in Solomon's reign (see 7:8-10).

2) The Chronicler made one explicit comparison with Solomon. Hezekiah's Passover was greater than all celebrations in Jerusalem **since the days of Solomon** (30:26).

3) Also like Solomon, Hezekiah provided large numbers of sacrifices (30:24, see 2 Chr. 7:5). The numbers here are less than in Solomon's day, but they are still remarkably high.

4) It was also a time when **the priests and Levites stood to bless the people** (30:27). These were not empty pronouncements, but efficacious prayers. **God heard them** from **his holy dwelling place**. The allusion here to Solomon's prayer (6:21, 33, 39) indicates that Hezekiah had at last brought the temple back in line with the Solomonic ideal as the place of effectual prayers.

After describing the actual celebrations, the Chronicler moved to the religious fervor that resulted. When the people first gathered in Jerusalem for the festival, they removed foreign worship altars from the city (see 30:14). In balance with this report, the Chronicler turned to the reforms that took place after the festival (31:1a). At this point, however, the destruction of foreign objects of worship went far beyond the city of Jerusalem. The Chronicler paraphrased the content of 2 Kgs. 18:4 at this point. The people who had worshipped with Hezekiah went throughout **the towns of Judah**, destroying the altars and sacred objects of other religions (31:1a).

To support the central theme of reunification, the Chronicler also mentioned that these reforms took place **throughout Judah and Benjamin and in Ephraim**

and Manasseh (31:1a). Hezekiah's Passover celebration brought recommitment to the worship of the Lord in all of these families.

These same tribes were represented among the first returnees to the land (see 1 Chr. 9:3). In the Chronicler's day the remnants of these tribes had the opportunity to experience these blessings again.

Tribes Return Home (31:1b)

The story of Hezekiah's Passover reunification closes with a simple note that **the Israelites returned to their own towns and to their property** (31:1b). With this brief ending, the Chronicler rounded off his focus on the participation of northern Israelites. The Northerners returned home with their faith renewed. This final scene was fitting for the portrait of the future the Chronicler offered his post-exilic readers. Through reunification around Judah's king and temple, all the tribes would revive their faith in the Lord and return to their tribal lands. (For the Chronicler's geographical hopes, see comments on 1 Chr. 2:42-55.) This portion of Hezekiah's reign provided a compelling motivation for the post-exilic readers to renew their own commitments to David's line, the temple, and the unity of the people of God.

Hezekiah's Enduring Provisions for Temple Services (31:2-21)

Having described how Hezekiah re-established the temple for all Israel (29:1-36) and then reunified the nation in Passover celebration at the temple (30:1-31:1), the Chronicler turned next to Hezekiah's enduring provisions for the temple (31:2-21). In this passage he completed his portrait of Hezekiah as the son of David who brought the people of God together around the temple in Jerusalem.

Comparison of 31:2-21 with Kings

With the exception of the possibility that 31:20-21 paraphrases 2 Kgs. 18:5-7, nothing of this portion of Hezekiah's reign appears in Kings. The account appears only in Chronicles and emphasizes the importance of temple service and personnel.

Structure of 31:2-21

This portion of the Chronicler's record divides into two parallel episodes. Each episode falls into the pattern of four symmetrical steps (see figure 53). As the outline indicates, this material has two main concerns. First, Hezekiah established the priests and Levites in their proper roles and provided for their needs (31:2-8). Second, the king established a distribution system of provisions made for the priests and Levites (31:9-21). These episodes parallel each other in several ways. Hezekiah initiated each action (31:2-3,9-10) and he ordered others to work toward the goal (31:4, 11a). Hezekiah's commands were thoroughly obeyed (31:5-7, 11b-19) and the king was blessed by God (31:8,20-21).

Hezekiah Permanently Establishes Temple Personnel (31:2-8)

The first episode of this material focuses on the king's efforts to establish the **priests and Levites** in a permanent fashion (31:2). The Chronicler had already noted that

Hezekiah's temple restoration involved both priests and Levites (see 29:4, 12-17, 21-24, 25-26, 30, 34; 30:3, 15-17, 21-22, 23-25, 27), but these previous efforts were only temporary arrangements. Here the Chronicler showed how Hezekiah set the temple personnel in their proper order for the ongoing work of the temple.

Structure of 31:2-8

The record of these events presents a four step symmetry (see figure 53). The king makes preliminary arrangements for the priest and Levites (31:2-3). In the end, he rejoices that provisions have been made so well (31:8). The middle of this episode divides into the king's order for contributions (31:4) and the fulfillment of that order (31:5-7).

Hezekiah Arranges for Priests and Levites (31:2-3)

The first step in this episode gives notice that the king **assigned the priests and Levites to divisions** (31:2). The duties of various divisions of temple personnel were diverse. In this passage, the Chronicler focused on how Hezekiah established these divisions so that **burnt offerings** and **fellowship offerings** could be offered (31:2).

Moreover, the Levites were to **minister** to or 'serve' the Lord (see 1 Chr. 15:2). The term **minister** applied to the many tasks performed in and around the temple because they were performed for the pleasure and honor of God. Yet, the Chronicler quickly specified that much of this ministering to God also involved the music of worship (31:2). Hezekiah insisted that these temple personnel were to **give thanks** and **sing praises** just as David had in his day (see 1 Chr. 16:9, 23, 33). Various positions are noted for singers throughout the book of Chronicles (see 1 Chr. 15:16,27; 2 Chr. 5:13; 23:13; 29:28; 35:25). Regular daily singing was performed **at the gates**.

Beyond this, Hezekiah gave **from his own possessions** for the sacrifices of the temple (31:3). A number of passages suggest that it was considered the king's responsibility to provide for these regularly occurring offerings. The examples of David and Solomon established this precedent (see 1 Chr. 16:37-40; 29:1-5; 2 Chr. 2:4; 8:12-13; 9:10-11). Moreover, Ezekiel the prophet gave such instructions for the post-exilic temple (see Ezek. 45:17,22; 46:2). These royal provisions made it possible for the priests and Levites to fulfill their responsibilities every **morning and evening** (see Num. 28:1-8), every **Sabbath** (see Num. 28:9-10), at monthly **New Moons** (see Num. 28:11-15), as well as during the annual feasts (see Num. 28:26-31).

Chronicles ties Hezekiah to David and Solomon once again to establish that Hezekiah's efforts were in the spirit of these great kings of Israel. After the tragic fall of the northern kingdom and the apostasy of the South (see 28:5-9, 22-25), Hezekiah brought the temple back toward its ideal order.

Up to this point, Hezekiah had merely reopened the temple (see 29:3) and held the Passover (see 30:1-31:1). At this point, the king also demonstrated a commitment to the permanent arrangement of temple services. This focus spoke directly to the needs of the post-exilic readers. Their concern with the temple was not to be temporary; they also had to be committed to the permanent functioning of the temple.

Hezekiah Orders Contributions (31:4)

Having arranged and provided for the temple services to be performed by priests and Levites, Hezekiah sought popular support for the temple personnel. **He ordered** the citizens of Jerusalem **to give the portion due**. The Chronicler frequently touched on the importance of temple contributions (see *Introduction: 9) Temple Contributions*). He focused on a particular reason for these gifts. The priests and Levites received their livelihood from contributions made through tithes, first fruits, and by sharing in some sacrifices (see Lev. 6:14-7:36; Num. 18:8-32; Deut. 14:27-29; 18:1-8; 26:1-15). In all likelihood, these offerings were neglected during Ahaz's apostasy (see 28:24-25).

In much the same way, support for the temple had suffered during the exile. Moreover, even the post-exilic community neglected these offerings (see Neh. 13:10-13; Mal. 3:8-12). Through Hezekiah's example, the Chronicler insisted that the system of support for priests and Levites be maintained in his day.

The text gives special attention to the purpose of these offerings. They were necessary so that temple personnel **could devote themselves to the Law of the LORD**. Hezekiah was deeply concerned that after the apostasy of Ahaz's reign the temple personnel should learn the ways of the Law once again. The priests and Levites could support themselves by working the lands devoted to them among the tribes. (For the Chronicler's concern with Levitical lands, see comments on 1 Chr. 6:64.) Yet, to do so would distract them from the more important task of studying and applying the Law. For this reason, Hezekiah hoped that the people of Jerusalem would relieve the temple personnel from all responsibilities except temple service and the Law.

Hezekiah's command to the citizens of Jerusalem touched on a subject that would certainly have been problematic for the post-exilic community. They lived after a period in which the temple personnel needed to learn the Law of Moses once again (see Ezra 7:6). Hezekiah's actions addressed these concerns. Although supporting the temple personnel was a heavy responsibility, it was necessary so that they could learn the ways of the Law (see *Introduction: 14) Standards*).

Hezekiah's Orders Enthusiastically Obeyed (31:5-7)

The Chronicler followed Hezekiah's orders with an extraordinary account of the response of the people. He described the event as a sudden dramatic response: **as soon as the order went out** (31:5). The term **went out** is usually translated 'broke out', or 'broke through'. The Chronicler chose this unusual way of depicting the event to indicate how these events were unexpected. Hezekiah had only ordered **the people living in Jerusalem** (31:4). Now, however, **Israelites** representing the entire nation responded (31:5). Moreover, their response was immediate and they gave **generously** (31:5).

To further heighten the drama of the event, the Chronicler listed the offerings brought to the temple. Those who lived in the outlying agricultural regions brought **the firstfruits** of different items (31:5). These offerings were an acknowledgment that the land and all it produced were expressions of God's love and provision. The firstfruits of **grain, new wine,** and **oil** were given to the priests (31:5; see Num. 18:12-13). The tithe was normally given to the Levites (see Num. 18:21). Here, however, the Chronicler noted that their contributions amounted to **a tithe of everything** (31:5). In other words, much more than was required of the Law was given to the temple. Those people of **Israel and Judah who lived in the towns of Judah** contributed **a tithe** of their livestock (31:6) as well as **a tithe of the holy things to be dedicated** (see Lev. 27:1-34). Once again, the Chronicler focused on the extraordinary amount given. In fact, the people of Israel were so enthusiastic that they had to put their offerings **in heaps** (31:6) as the process continued for five months (31:7).

The Chronicler emphasized the tremendous enthusiasm of the people for at least three reasons. First, he drew another connection between Hezekiah and David. The people contributed generously in David's day as well (see 1 Chr. 29:6-9). Second, he encouraged all of the population of post-exilic Israel to give generously to the temple. Just as all the people contributed in Hezekiah's reign, they should do so again after the exile. Third, the Chronicler's portrait encouraged his Jerusalem readers. In Hezekiah's day, the example of the citizens of Jerusalem encouraged others to give. The response of post-exilic Jerusalem could serve as encouragement to the entire nation once again (see *Introduction: 9) Temple Contributions*).

Hezekiah Rejoices in Provisions (31:8)

Hezekiah's establishment of the priests and Levites closes with a brief scene of the king **and his officials** (see 2 Chr. 29:20,30; 30:2,12) noticing **the heaps** of contributions (31:8). As a result, Hezekiah and his officials were filled with joy. They **praised the LORD** and **blessed his people Israel**. This scene parallels the prosperity coming to Hezekiah at the end of this chapter (see 31:20-21; see figure 53). The nation's devotion to the temple brought delight to the king. In this manner, the Chronicler alluded again to David and Solomon's similar situations (see 1 Chr. 16:2; 2 Chr. 6:3). They too praised God and blessed the people in response to temple activities. The post-exilic readers of Chronicles could hope for the same joy and celebration only as they imitated Hezekiah's actions (see *Introduction: 27) Disappointment and Celebration*).

Hezekiah Establishes Permanent Distribution (31:9-21)

With widespread enthusiastic support for the temple personnel, Hezekiah turned to establishing a stable system of distribution for the priests and Levites. The continuation of the temple as the center of his Reunited Kingdom depended on his ability to provide ongoing support.

Structure of 31:9-21

The Chronicler reported this event in four major steps which reflect the pattern of the preceding episode (see figure 53). The king notes the need for storehouses (31:9-10) and is blessed for his efforts in the end (31:20-21). In the middle portion of the episode, he orders that storehouses be prepared (31:11a) and his orders are obeyed (31:11b-19).

Hezekiah Evaluates Provisions (31:9-10)

This episode begins where the previous section ended. Hezekiah noticed the heaps of offerings brought to the temple, and inquired **about the heaps** (31:9). The focus of his inquiry becomes clear from the answer he received. Apparently, the king asked if the heaps of contributions were adequate. **Azariah the chief priest**, who had responsibility for all the priests and Levites, told the king that the contributions of the people provided them **enough to eat and plenty to spare** (31:10). In fact, **a great amount** was **left over**.

The surplus of contributions brought by the people of Israel was certainly exemplary for the Chronicler's readers. They were not to be satisfied with merely meeting the minimal needs of the temple personnel. In imitation of Hezekiah's day, they too were expected to supply the temple in abundance.

Hezekiah Orders Storehouse Preparation (31:11a)

The surplus of offerings created a need which Hezekiah immediately met. As he had previously ordered the collection of offerings (see 31:4), he now ordered the priests and Levites **to prepare storerooms in the temple**. The expression **'to prepare'** does not specify whether new buildings were erected or existing structures were simply renovated. In all events, these storerooms were part of the outer structure of the temple and were used to store foods, equipment and weapons, and to house temple personnel (see 2 Kgs. 20:13; 1 Chr. 9:26; 23:28; 26:22; 28:12; 2 Chr. 31:11,14).

Hezekiah's Orders Enthusiastically Obeyed (31:11b-19)

The text first simply notes that Hezekiah's order was obeyed (31:11b). The scene is one of unhindered, speedy accomplishment. No one raised objections or made the project difficult. No doubt the Chronicler presented these actions to guide his readers.

Next, he described how the storerooms of the temple were used. The record focuses first on collection of goods (31:12-13), and then on their distribution (31:14-19).

Offerings were brought to Hezekiah's storerooms (31:12-13). The Chronicler described the collection of **contributions, tithes and dedicated gifts** (31:12). These categories of offerings have appeared earlier in this chapter (see 31:5,6).

Special notice is given to **Conaniah and his brother Shemei** who were in charge of the collections (31:12b-13). **Hezekiah and Azariah**, the high priest (see 31:10), placed this responsibility in their hands and ten men were under their command. The Chronicler mentioned these names to instruct the post-exilic readers that Levites, especially Conaniah's descendants, were to be responsible for these kinds of duties in the post-exilic temple.

With offerings filling the temple storerooms, attention turned to the distribution of the goods (31:14-19). **Kore ... the Levite** was in control of **distributing** the goods as was necessary (31:14). Once again, the Chronicler pointed out that Levites instead of priests had this responsibility. Many of the goods which Kore distributed were from **freewill offerings** which the people gave above the required tithe (see Exod. 35:29; 36:3; Lev. 7:16; Num. 29:39; Ezra 1:4,6; Ps. 54:6). They also came from **contributions made to the Lord** as well as **the consecrated gifts** (31:12, 14). Although the focus of this passage is on distributions to the priests, Kore was also in charge of goods for the Levites (see 31:17).

Six men assisted Kore in the distribution effort (31:15). They took care of the needs of those who lived **in the towns of the priests**, cities outside Jerusalem allotted to the priesthood (see Josh. 21:9-19). Chronicles makes reference to the geographical holdings of the priests and Levites on several occasions (see *Introduction*: *1) All Israel*). The Chronicler was concerned that these cities return to their rightful owners in the post-exilic period. Hezekiah's example also made it clear that the post-exilic temple was to supply the inhabitants of these cities.

Kore was also responsible for distributing to those **who would enter the temple ... to perform the daily duties** (31:16). In other words, those priests and Levites living in Jerusalem and serving directly in the temple were not ignored. These distributions included **the males three years old or more**. The families of priests and Levites **twenty years old or more** also received distributions (31:17). Moreover, the **little ones, ... wives, ... sons and daughters of the whole community** were all counted (31:18).

The distribution of goods to those who **lived on the farm lands around their towns or in any of their towns** (31:19) was slightly different. Other **men were designated** to deal with these matters. The standard for those outside Jerusalem was different because they could provide more of their own sustenance than the priests and Levites in Jerusalem. Outside of Jerusalem, provision was made for **every male ... recorded in the genealogies**.

Four times in these passages, the Chronicler mentioned that **genealogical records** were instrumental in guiding these distributions (31:16-19). There can be little doubt that the Chronicler gave this detail to provide practical guidance for his own day. This aspect of his record also explains some of his motivation for concentrating on priestly and Levitical genealogies in the opening chapters of his work (1 Chr. 6:1-30).

Hezekiah Blessed for His Provisions (31:20-21)

The account of Hezekiah's enduring provisions closes with a very positive assessment of his efforts. In some respects, these verses may be seen as a paraphrase of 2 Kgs. 18:5-7, but the resemblance is not extensive. The Chronicler believed that

Hezekiah had done **what was good and right and faithful** (31:20). Hezekiah's fidelity was perhaps the most important feature of the Chronicler's initial assessment. The theme of fidelity appears again in 32:1. To be **faithful** was to be one who did not forsake or prove disloyal to God or his Law (see *Introduction: 21) Unfaithfulness*). As the Chronicler noted, Hezekiah had re-established the temple and its services **in obedience to the law and the commands** (31:21). As on several other occasions, the Chronicler pointed out that Hezekiah was careful to do things in accordance with the Law (see 30:16; 31:3; see also *Introduction: 14) Standards*).

Beyond this, the Chronicler employed two more of his favorite expressions to describe the king in 31:21. He **sought** the Lord (see *Introduction: 19) Seeking*) and worked **wholeheartedly** (see *Introduction: 16) Motivations*). This piling up of positive descriptions indicated the Chronicler's enthusiasm for Hezekiah. He added these chapters on Hezekiah's re-establishment of the temple because they exemplified the kind of obedience he highly admired.

In line with his outlook on divine judgment and blessing, the Chronicler closed this material with the notice that Hezekiah **prospered** because of his wholehearted obedience (31:21). Prosperity often appears in Chronicles as a demonstration of divine blessing (see *Introduction: 26) Prosperity and Poverty*). Hezekiah's devotion to the temple and its personnel brought divine favor to his kingdom. The postexilic readers longed for prosperity in their day. Hezekiah's example demonstrated the only way to see this longing fulfilled.

Hezekiah's Inconsistencies During the Assyrian Invasion (32:1-31)

The Chronicler began this section of Hezekiah's reign with the introductory phrase **after all that Hezekiah had so faithfully done** ... (32:1). As we will see, this clause separates Hezekiah's devotion to the re-establishment of the temple (29:1-31:21) from his response to the Sennacherib invasion (32:1-31). It divides Hezekiah's reign into the early period of faith (29:3-31:21) and a latter period in which he falters (32:1-31). In the divided kingdom, the Chronicler frequently arranged the reigns of kings into period of varying moral and religious quality (see *Introduction: 10-27) Divine Blessing and Judgment*). His account of Hezekiah follows this pattern as well.

Comparison of 32:1-31 with 2 Kgs. 18:13-20:19 (and Isa. 36:1-39:8)

Although we will not compare the Chronicler's text with Isa. 36:1-39:8, it should be noted that much of this material is parallel to this portion of Isaiah. The parallels between Chronicles and 2 Kgs. 18:13-20:19 are more important because the Chronicler depended directly on Kings for much of his material. At this point, we will note several general comparisons between Chronicles and Kings; more detailed discussions of specific portions appear below.

First, throughout this chapter the Chronicler abbreviated larger sections of Kings.

1) The story of Hezekiah's reaction to the Sennacherib invasion is reduced from 62 verses (2 Kgs. 18:13-19:37) to 23 verses (32:1-23).

2) The healing of Hezekiah receives only three verses (32:24-26) by comparison with eleven in Kings (2 Kgs. 20:1-11).

3) Hezekiah's reception of Babylonian emissaries (2 Kgs. 20:12-19) amounts to only one verse in Chronicles (32:31).

The Chronicler's abbreviated style in these three passages may be due in part to his intention to simplify matters in Kings in order to draw attention to his own concerns. Nevertheless, as the comments below will illustrate, the Chronicler expected his readers to know the information in Kings.

Second, the Chronicler added a notice of blessings Hezekiah received from God (30:27-30). These verses provide a counterpoint to a final hint of inconsistency in Hezekiah's actions during the Assyrian crisis (30:31).

Structure of 32:1-31

This portion of the Chronicler's record of Hezekiah divides into three main parts (see figure 53). Hezekiah is inconsistent in the manner in which he responded to Sennacherib's invasion (32:1-23). He falls into pride (32:24-26) and he forms an illegitimate alliance with Babylon (32:27-31). No obvious structural symmetry appears in this section beyond the fact that the first and last sections (32:1-23, 27-31) deal with Hezekiah in relation to foreign powers. The three episodes cluster around the theme that Hezekiah failed to be consistently faithful during the Sennacherib invasion.

Hezekiah's Inconsistencies in Military Strategy (32:1-23)

The first episode in this cluster reveals a side of Hezekiah not provided in the preceding chapters. When threatened by the Assyrian invader, Hezekiah first turned to human strength. Only after this serious failure did Hezekiah turn to God for help. Although this episode does not state why Hezekiah shifted from human to divine strength, we will see that this change is explained in the following episode.

Comparison of 32:1-23 with 2 Kgs. 18:13-19:37 (Isa. 36:2-38)

As noted above, the account of Chronicles is much shorter than Kings, but connections between the texts are apparent. The variations between these accounts fall into several categories (see figure 55).

The variations between Kings and Chronicles are of three types. First, three sections may be described as loosely parallel.

1) The opening verse (32:1 // 2 Kgs. 18:13) omits the synchronization with the northern kingdom as in many other portions of Chronicles (see *Introduction: 2) Northern Israel*). Instead, the Chronicler began this verse with the temporal and thematic notice: **after all that Hezekiah had so faithfully done** (32:1). As we will see below, these introductory words indicate that the Chronicler is shifting away from the king's great accomplishments (29:1-31:21) to a period of inconsistency and failure.

Another shift occurs in the description of Sennacherib's invasion of Judah (32:1).

2 Chr.		2 Kgs.
32:1	Sennacherib Invades (loosely parallel)	18:13
32:2-8	Hezekiah's Preparations (added)	———
———	Hezekiah's Submission (omitted)	18:14-16
32:9-19	Sennacherib's Propaganda (loosely parallel)	18:17-35
32:20	Reactions to Threats (severely abbreviated)	18:36-19:34
32:21	Divine Intervention (loosely parallel)	19:35-37
32:22-23	Hezekiah's Exaltation (added)	———

Comparison of 2 Chr. 32:1-23 and 2 Kgs. 18:13-19:37 (figure 55)

Kings reads that Sennacherib 'took them [the cities of Judah]' (NIV, 2 Kgs. 18:13), but Chronicles reads that the king was simply **thinking to conquer them** (32:1). This variation may have resulted from the Chronicler's desire to downplay the effectiveness of Sennacherib's invasion (note also the omission of 2 Kgs. 18:14-16).

2) Sennacherib's public threats against Jerusalem are only loosely parallel (32:9-19 // 2 Kgs. 18:17-35), but the Chronicler's paraphrase of Kings offers no substantial difference in perspective.

3) The account of God's intervention against Sennacherib is also paraphrased with little difference (32:21 // 2 Kgs. 19:35-37).

Second, the Chronicler completely omitted 2 Kgs. 18:14-16. This portion of Kings describes Hezekiah's attempt to appease Sennacherib by paying him tribute from the royal treasuries and the temple. The Chronicler's desire to present Hezekiah as exemplary in matters related to the temple led him to omit this serious failure.

Third, Hezekiah's reaction to Sennacherib's threat (2 Kgs. 18:36-19:34) is reduced to just one verse (32:20). Chronicles omits the interactions between Hezekiah and Isaiah that led to prayers offered on behalf of the city. The reason for this abbreviation is unclear.

Fourth, two portions of this episode constitute full additions. 1) In 32:2-8 the Chronicler added a list of actions Hezekiah took in preparation for Sennacherib's invasion. As we will suggest, the Chronicler added this material to point to Hezekiah's wavering faith during the invasion. 2) The Chronicler also added 32:21-22 to demonstrate the blessings Hezekiah received once he turned to God for help against his enemy.

Structure of 32:1-23

The Chronicler's variations from the record of Kings shape this material into four symmetrical steps (see figure 53). This episode begins with Hezekiah severely threatened by the approach of a foreign power (32:1). By the end of the passage, however, Hezekiah is not only delivered from this threat, but highly esteemed by foreign powers on every side (32:22-23). Hezekiah's initial reaction to the approaching Assyrian army was to prepare weapons and fortifications and to deliver a speech to his people (32:2-8). This portion balances with the third part of the story where the Assyrian's threatening speech is followed by Hezekiah's appeal to God for help (32:9-21). These two inner segments of the story illustrate the inconsistency of Hezekiah's actions at this time. At first, he relied on human strength, but eventually he turned to God for help.

Hezekiah Threatened by a Foreign Nation (32:1)

The Chronicler began this portion of Hezekiah's reign by adding an important chronological notice to the record of 2 Kgs. 18:13. He commented that these events took place **after all that Hezekiah had so faithfully done**. These introductory words allude to the assessment of the king's previous actions in 31:20. The first part of Hezekiah's reign was one of extraordinary fidelity.

These words also raise a very important interpretative problem. Many interpreters take this comment as an indication that the following account continues the theme of Hezekiah's fidelity. As we will suggest below, however, it is more likely that the Chronicler used this terminology to draw a contrast between what had gone on before and what was about to happen. It was his frequent practice to divide a king's reign into years of fidelity and infidelity, blessing and judgment. This introductory clause appears to fall in line with this practice.

The initiating event of this passage is the Assyrian invasion of Judah. From the time Ahaz sought help from Assyria against the Syrians and Israelite coalition (see 28:16-21), Judah had served as one of Assyria's vassal nations. Hezekiah, however, sought independence and Sennacherib invaded the land to bring Judah back into submission (see 2 Kgs. 18:13,21). The Sennacherib invasion itself has been the subject of much controversy among biblical historians. Some historians believe that the book of Kings presents two invasions of Judah, the first ending in Hezekiah paying tribute (see 2 Kgs. 18:14-16) and the second ending in a plague on the Assyrian army (see 2 Kgs. 19:35-38). Contrary to this interpretation of Kings, the Chronicler understood that only one invasion took place. He omitted the record of Hezekiah's tribute (2 Kgs..18:14-16) and combined elements of the so-called first invasion (32:1-20) with elements of the so-called second invasion (32:20-23).

Hezekiah Depends on Human Strength (32:2-8)

The story of Sennacherib's invasion continues with Hezekiah's preparations for battle. Hezekiah first prepared for battle by relying on his own ingenuity.

Structure of 32:2-8

This material divides into two parts: Hezekiah's defensive action (32:2-5), and Hezekiah's encouragement to Jerusalem (32:6-8). These two sections balance with the two parts of the next section: Assyrian threats against Jerusalem (32:9-19) and Hezekiah's prayer (32:20-21; see figure 53).

Hezekiah's Defensive Preparations (32:2-5)

In 32:2-5 Hezekiah took steps to prepare for the Assyrian army. Before looking into specific aspects of his preparations, it is necessary to comment on the Chronicler's general outlook on the events of these verses. Nowhere does the Chronicler explicitly approve or disapprove of what Hezekiah did. This absence of comment has left the matter somewhat ambiguous. Did Hezekiah do the right thing in response to the Assyrian threat? To begin with, we should note that building armies and defenses is not categorically condemned in Chronicles. In fact, building projects and large armies are usually viewed as blessings from God (see *Introduction: 24) Building and Destruction*; see also *23) Victory and Defeat*). Nevertheless, a number of factors mitigate against applying a positive outlook to Hezekiah's actions.

1) As noted above, all three episodes in this portion of Hezekiah's reign (32:1-31) take place during the Assyrian invasion of Judah. The second (32:24-30) and third (32:31) episodes clearly point to Hezekiah's failures during the crisis. It would appear that the Chronicler had little interest in idealizing Hezekiah in this context.

2) It is apparent, however, that the Chronicler softened Hezekiah's infidelity in the second and third episodes. He mentioned Hezekiah's pride after healing, but quickly resolved the matter with the king's repentance (32:26). Similarly, he abbreviated Hezekiah's attempt to gain the favor of the Babylonians (2 Kgs. 20:16-18). The Chronicler merely mentioned that **God left him to test him** (32:31). In this light, it is not entirely unexpected that the Chronicler would merely insinuate Hezekiah's failure in the first episode of this section as well.

3) Unlike other examples of building and enlarging armies, Hezekiah's actions were in direct response to the Assyrian threat. Asa, for instance, built up defenses and the numbers of his soldiers (14:7-8), but the Chronicler commented that this action was *because* he and Judah had previously **sought the Lord** (14:4). In other words, Asa's military build up was a demonstration of blessing from God for past dependence on him, not a way to handle an impending threat. The same assessment applies to other examples of building projects and military strength (see *Introduction: 24) Building and Destruction*). The Chronicler made it clear, however, that Hezekiah's military preparations resulted precisely because he **saw that Sennacherib had come ... to make war on Jerusalem** (32:2). The implication of dependence on human strength, rather than divine strength seems evident (see *Introduction: 23) Victory and Defeat*).

4) The prophecies of Isaiah directly condemned Hezekiah's actions. The book of Isaiah notes that Hezekiah 'saw that the City of David had many breaches ... stored up water in the Lower Pool ... and tore down houses to strengthen the wall ...

but ... did not look to the One who made it, or have regard for the One who planned it long ago' (Isa. 22:9-11). The prophet viewed Hezekiah's military preparations as a rejection of dependence on God. The evidence weighs heavily in favor of understanding Hezekiah's actions in this section as an example of wavering faith.

Once Hezekiah became convinced that Sennacherib **intended to make war on Jerusalem** (32:2), he began to prepare for conflict. His preparations included military and defensive build up (32:2-5) and a public speech to raise popular confidence (32:6-8).

Hezekiah took several steps to prepare himself militarily. First, he **blocked all the springs that flowed through the land** (32:4). This strategy was designed to slow the advance of Sennacherib's army, if not to stop its move toward Jerusalem. As the text demonstrates, however, the plan did not work (see 32:9).

Beyond this, Hezekiah also looked to the defenses of Jerusalem. He repaired **the wall** and erected **towers on it**. He also built **another wall** (32:5) and he **made a large number of weapons and shields** (32:5). These preparations were also designed to protect against Sennacherib's attack should he reach the city. As we have noted, Isaiah condemned these efforts (see Isa. 39:5-7; 2 Kgs. 20:16-18).

Hezekiah's Hypocritical Speech (32:6-8)

With physical defenses strong, Hezekiah determined to encourage the people with a public speech (32:6-8). The Chronicler's record of this event divides into three parts: the setting (32:6), the speech itself (32:7-8a), and the results (32:8b).

Hezekiah placed **military officers over the people** and **assembled them** (32:6). The king's desperation is evident in that he militarized the entire citizenry of Jerusalem.

Then Hezekiah spoke (32:7-8a). His speech appears on the surface to proclaim reliance on God for victory (see *Introduction: 23) Victory and Defeat*). Hezekiah undoubtedly said the appropriate things, as any wise king would in these circumstances. Yet, it is difficult to avoid the suspicion that the Chronicler assumed his readers knew Hezekiah's inward motivations from the prophecies of Isaiah. Isaiah offered insight into Hezekiah's deeper motivations when he rebuked the king saying, 'The Lord ... called you on that day to weep and wail ... but see, there is joy and revelry ...' (Isa. 22:12-14). From this evidence we must conclude that the religious dimensions of Hezekiah's speech were mere outward conformity to the royal rites of Holy War (see 13:4-12; 20:15-17).

Hezekiah played his political role well. He alluded to God's word to Joshua at the beginning of Israel's conquest: **Be strong and courageous** (32:7 see Josh. 1:6,9; see also 15:7; 1 Chr. 19:13; 22:13; 28:10,20). Several times, he affirmed the Holy War ideal that God would be 'with' his people and 'help' them (32:7b-8; see 13:12; see also *Introduction: 10) Divine Activity*). All the while, however, Isaiah's prophecies revealed that Hezekiah's confidence was actually in the help he hoped to gain from his own military might and alliances with other nations (see 32:31; Isa. 31:1-9), a strategy which the Chronicler repeatedly denounced (see 2 Kgs.

18:20-25; see also *Introduction: 3) International Relations*).

The Chronicler closed this section by noting that Hezekiah's speech worked wonderfully. The people **gained confidence** (32:8b). Yet, once again the Chronicler hinted at the true nature of the event. The confidence of Judah was **in what Hezekiah king of Judah said**, not in the Lord (32:8b). There was much 'eating of meat and drinking of wine' (Isa. 22:13), at a time when the people should have 'put on sackcloth' (Isa. 22:12).

Hezekiah Depends on God (32:9-21)

The mood of the story shifts as Sennacherib boldly moved toward Jerusalem and directly threatened its inhabitants. In the end, the threats of Assyria brought Hezekiah to the point that he turned to God for help.

Structure of 32:9-21

This portion of the narrative divides into two parts (see figure 53). First Sennacherib threatened Hezekiah (32:9-19). Then Hezekiah responded appropriately (32:20-21).

Hezekiah Threatened (32:9-19)

In balance with Hezekiah's speech (32:6-9), the Chronicler reported Sennacherib's threats against Jerusalem in the form of a public message. His record of these threats consists of a setting (32:9), Sennacherib's message (32:10-15), and summaries of other threats (32:16-19).

The setting of Sennacherib's threats provides some important information (32:9). These words came to Jerusalem **when Sennacherib** was **laying siege to Lachish**. From the time of Rehoboam, Lachish had been an important military installation in Judah midway between Jerusalem and Gaza (see 2 Chr. 11:9). The fact that Sennacherib had come as far as Lachish was a terrible defeat to Hezekiah. From the prophecy of Micah 1:13, it would appear that much false confidence had been placed in the military strength represented by Lachish. Sennacherib's success there troubled Hezekiah despite his earlier confidence (see *Introduction: 23) Victory and Defeat*).

While in Lachish Sennacherib sent a **message** by his officers to Hezekiah (32:9b). The Chronicler summarized this message (32:10-15) and noted a number of other threats the Assyrian king made (32:16-18). The Chronicler's version of Sennacherib's letter is much shorter than its counterpart in Kings (see 2 Kgs. 18:19-37). It divides into three main parts: an introductory question and response (32:10, 11), supporting evidence (32:12-14), and a concluding exhortation (32:15).

The heart of Sennacherib's communication appears in the opening question and response (32:10, 11). Where were the people of Jerusalem putting their **confidence** so that they do not flee from Sennacherib (32:10)? The Assyrian king recognized the degree of confidence it took for the people to resist him. He was not, however, actually asking for information. Instead, he asked the question simply to counter their confidence. Naturally, the Assyrian assumed that the people of the city had put their confidence in the words of Hezekiah. So he referred to Hezekiah's assurance that **'our God will save us'** and insisted that the king was **misleading** the people, and would abandon them to **hunger and thirst**.

The middle portion of Sennacherib's message amounted to a series of rhetorical questions (32:12-14). These questions and their assumed answers supported the opening assertion that Hezekiah and his God could not be trusted to deliver Jerusalem.

First, the Assyrian king indicated that the people's confidence was misplaced because Hezekiah had insisted that they **worship before one altar** in Jerusalem (32:12 // 2 Kgs. 18:22). While in the Chronicler's view Hezekiah's re-establishment of the temple was positive (see 29:3-36), the difficulties of travel, ritual cleansing, etc. imposed on the general population was enough to make many of them wonder if Hezekiah could be trusted. Moreover, in the ancient Near East the common assumption was that gods were pleased to have many altars. Sennacherib based his criticism of Hezekiah on the assumption that Israel's God could not be pleased with having only one altar.

Second, Sennacherib appealed to Assyrian military successes (32:13-14 // 2 Kgs. 18:33-35). Sennacherib reminded the inhabitants of Jerusalem of what he and his fathers had done **to all the peoples of the other lands** (32:13). Assyria was well-known for its military conquests. Moreover, in the ancient Near East military conflicts were not viewed as mere human affairs. Gods lost and won as their human armies lost and won. On the basis of this common belief, Sennacherib insisted that **the gods of** [other] **nations** were unable **to deliver their land from** [his] **hand** (32:13). In fact, **all the gods** of the lands were unable to withstand the Assyrians (32:14a). It was only reasonable to wonder how Israel could expect her God to **deliver** (32:14b).

Third, the Assyrian king concluded his message with a series of directives (32:15 // 2 Kgs. 18:29). The people of Jerusalem were not to **let Hezekiah deceive** them. They were not to **believe him** because **no god of any nation or kingdom has been able to deliver** (32:15). If this was true for the gods of nations greater than Judah, **how much less** was it possible for Israel's God to save Jerusalem.

The Chronicler paraphrased the account of 2 Kgs. 19:14 by noting that Sennacherib's men **spoke further** (32:16). Sennacherib also **wrote letters insulting the Lord** (32:17). Moreover, the Assyrian officers **called out in Hebrew** to the inhabitants of Jerusalem (32:18-19 // 2 Kgs. 18:28). The diplomatic language of the day was Aramaic, but the messengers of Sennacherib wanted the people of the city to understand in order **to terrify them and to make them afraid** (32:18). These public speeches also placed the **God of Jerusalem** on par with the gods of other nations which the Chronicler and his readers knew to be **the work of men's hands** (32:19).

This description of Assyrian activities reveals the emotional quality of this material for the Chronicler and his post-exilic readers. Time and again the Chronicler pointed out that the Assyrians treated the God of Israel as if he were nothing more than another god. This rhetoric was not only **insulting** to the Lord (32:17), but it also insulted the Chronicler and his readers. As men and women who lived long after the destruction of the Assyrian kingdom, the post-exilic community knew how ridiculous Sennacherib's claims were. While the people of Hezekiah's day were frightened by these words, the readers of this narrative mocked the Assyrian hubris.

In striking contrast to his earlier preparations for battle (see 32:2-6), Hezekiah reacted to Sennacherib's success and confidence by turning to God in prayer (32:20-21). As noted above, this material is severely abbreviated from 2 Kgs. 18:36-19:38. In Kings, Hezekiah succumbed to fears and finally donned sackcloth under the direction of Isaiah (see 2 Kgs. 19:1; see also Isa. 22:12). The Chronicler's account, however, simply states that **Hezekiah and the prophet Isaiah ... cried out in prayer to heaven** (32:20). The Chronicler did not explain why Hezekiah changed his strategy from self-reliance to dependence on God. He waited until the next episode to reflect on some of the things that influenced the king in this direction (see 32:24-26). Nevertheless, the allusion to Solomon's temple dedicatory prayer is evident (6:12-42). This event is yet another example of Solomon's specific hopes for the temple being realized in accordance with the purpose of the temple (see *Introduction: 17) Prayer*). The king and prophet turned directly to God for help in their threatening circumstance and the enemy was driven away (see *Introduction: 23) Victory and Defeat*).

God responded immediately to Hezekiah's prayer. He **sent an angel** against the Assyrian army (32:21). The sending of an angel to execute divine deliverance and victory was a central motif in the exodus of Israel from Egypt (see Exod. 33:2; Num. 20:16). As an angel was God's instrument in the greatest event in Israel's history, so an angel would be employed to rescue them in dramatic fashion against Sennacherib. As post-exilic Israel contemplated the nation's future in the light of their exodus from Babylon, the Chronicler reminded them of the superlative ways in which God brought salvation in Hezekiah's day. An interesting contrast appears between this passage and 1 Chr. 21:12-30. This is the only other reference to an angel in Chronicles. God sent his angel to destroy Jerusalem because of David's self-reliance. In Hezekiah's situation, however, the angel of the Lord moved against the Assyrians on Israel's behalf.

The Chronicler shortened the account of Kings (// 2 Kgs. 19:35-37) in a number of ways, but two changes should be specially noted. Kings mentions that 'a hundred and eighty-five thousand' Assyrians died (2 Kgs. 19:35). The Chronicler heightened the force of God's intervention by saying that the angel **annihilated all the fighting men and the leaders and officers** (32:21). Also, Kings merely says that Sennacherib 'went home' (2 Kgs. 19:36). The Chronicler added that he returned to his land **in disgrace** (32:21). Beyond this, Kings quickly points away from Sennacherib's death to speak of Esharhaddon (see 2 Kgs. 19:37). The Chronicler ended his account with a report of patricide committed by Sennacherib's sons (32:21).

This notice drew attention to the king's dishonorable demise. These variations continue the Chronicler's mockery of the Assyrian king who had so vigorously threatened Jerusalem and her God.

Hezekiah is Highly Regarded by Foreign Nations (32:22-23)

The Chronicler added a new ending to the account of Hezekiah's encounter with Sennacherib (32:22-23). These final notices balance with the opening of this section (32:1; see figure 53). At this point Hezekiah was safe from foreign powers and actually received honor from them.

The Chronicler's description of Hezekiah's blessing unfolds in a crescendo. First, he reported that Hezekiah and Jerusalem were **saved from the ... king of Assyria** (32:22). In effect this statement summarized the preceding account. The Sennacherib threat had disappeared.

Second, God's deliverance included safety from **all others ... on every side** (32:22). No other enemies troubled Hezekiah on any front. It should be noted that the Greek version of Chronicles reads 'he gave them rest on every side' (NRS and NIV marginal note). If this reading is correct, then the Chronicler heightened Hezekiah's blessing by connecting his reign with the theme of 'rest' in David and Solomon's reigns (see *Introduction: 23) Victory and Defeat*).

Third, **many** (the nearest antecedent of which is **all others** [32:22]) brought **offerings** for the temple and **valuable gifts** to Hezekiah (32:23). Jerusalem's economy prospered as a result of God's blessing on the king.

Fourth, **from then on** Hezekiah **was highly regarded by all the nations** (32:23). Much like David (1 Chr. 14:17), Solomon (9:1-12), Jehoshaphat (17:10; 20:29) and Uzziah (26:8), Hezekiah gained the honor and respect of the surrounding nations (see *Introduction: 3) International Relations*).

This grand reversal of Hezekiah's condition fit well with a perspective the Chronicler offered on several occasions. When the kings of Judah repent of infidelity, they receive the blessing of God. The next episode of Hezekiah's reign follows this pattern (32:24-26). Here Hezekiah had wavered in his dependence on God (32:25). In the end, however, he relied not on human strength, but called on God through prayer (32:26a). This shift prompted immediate blessings from God.

The Chronicler reported this example of Hezekiah's inconsistent faith and prayer to speak to the needs of his post-exilic readers. As those who had returned from exile struggled with the harsh realities of reuniting and rebuilding the kingdom, they certainly failed to live up to the ideals of perfect fidelity. What hope was there for those who had wavered? The example of Hezekiah illustrated that even those who failed could find mercy as they called upon God for help. Blessings were not reserved for those who reached perfect obedience, but for those who in the end came to repentance.

Hezekiah's Inconsistent Pride (32:24-26)
The Chronicler's second look at the Sennacherib invasion involves another example of inconsistency in Hezekiah's faith. Sometime during the troubles with Assyria, Hezekiah became ill and received a miraculous healing. Instead of humbling himself in gratitude, however, Hezekiah became proud and incurred divine anger. Nevertheless, Hezekiah repented of this pride and finally received God's blessing.

Comparison of 32:24-36 with 2 Kgs. 20:1-11 (Isa. 38:1-22)
The Chronicler's version of Hezekiah's sickness and healing both simplifies and complicates the account of Kings. The following figure displays the relation between the records (see figure 56).

2 Chr.		2 Kgs.
32:24a	Hezekiah Becomes Sick (abbreviated)	20:1
32:24b	Hezekiah Prays (severely abbreviated)	20:2-8
32:24c	God Answers Hezekiah (abbreviated)	20:9-11
32:25-26	Hezekiah's Pride, Repentance and Blessing (added)	———

Comparison of 2 Chr. 32:24-30 and 2 Kgs. 20:1-11 (figure 56)

A cursory comparison of these two accounts reveals two kinds of variations between Chronicles and Kings. In the first portion of his record (32:24) the Chronicler abbreviated Kings by omitting Isaiah's oracle of judgment against the king (2 Kgs. 20:1b). He also severely abbreviated Hezekiah's prayer and Isaiah's response (2 Kgs. 20:2-8). Moreover, he shortened the discussion between Isaiah and the king concerning God's sign (2 Kgs. 20:9-11). This abbreviated style accords with the other episodes within this half of Hezekiah's reign (32:1-3). By comparison with Kings, the Chronicler softened Hezekiah's inconsistencies in each of the episodes to avoid a strongly negative appraisal. The Chronicler's chief interest in this material appears in his addition to Kings (32:25-26b). Hezekiah became full of pride after his healing, but his repentance led again to blessings from God.

Structure of 32:24-26
This episode consists of three brief scenarios. Each scenario is initiated by Hezekiah's action and closes with an act of God (see figure 53). Hezekiah began with a dramatic experience of God's mercy (32:24). He incurred the wrath of the Lord (32:25), but finally received the mercy of God again (32:26).

Hezekiah's Blessing (32:24)
The Chronicler followed 2 Kgs. 20:1 and introduced this episode of Hezekiah's sickness with the phrase **in those days** (32:24). This temporal reference indicates that Hezekiah's sickness occurred during the Sennacherib invasion reported in the previous chapter. The fuller account of Kings makes this chronological orientation plain. Isaiah responded to Hezekiah's prayer saying, '[God] will add fifteen years to your life... and ... will deliver you and this city from the hand of the king of Assyria' (2 Kgs. 20:5-6). The healing of the king took place while Hezekiah was under the Assyrian threat before the deliverance of city. For this reason, it would be appropriate to translate the verbs of this section of Chronicles in the past perfect ('In those days Hezekiah *had* become ill ... *had* come to the point of death ... *had* prayed ... etc.').

Hezekiah had become sick **to the point of death** (32:24). The reason for this sickness is not altogether clear, but 2 Kgs. 20:1-11 indicates that it was the judgment of God against Hezekiah. Such a perspective on illness accords with the Chronicler's theology as well (see *Introduction: 28) Healing and Long Life/Sickness and Death*). Perhaps, Hezekiah's illness resulted from his infidelity in preparation for war (see 32:1-31). If so, his sickness probably contributed to his change of heart. Whatever the case, Hezekiah had **prayed to the LORD** and God had provided **a miraculous sign** indicating that his healing and the deliverance of the city would occur (32:24 see 2 Kgs. 20:8-11). As such, Hezekiah's healing demonstrated that Solomon's hopes for the temple as a place of prayer were realized in Hezekiah's life for a second time (see 6:28-31; 32:20-21; see also *Introduction: 17) Prayer*).

Hezekiah's Judgment (32:25)
Having abbreviated the record of Kings in 32:24, the Chronicler now added information not found in Kings. Once Hezekiah had been healed he **did not respond to the kindness shown him** with humility and gratitude (32:25). Instead, his **heart was proud** (32:25). Ingratitude entered Hezekiah's heart following a time of blessing. (For the Chronicler's warning against permitting blessings to lead to infidelity, see comments on 1 Chr. 5:24.) The Chronicler focused on the heart of the king as he did in many passages (see *Introduction: 16) Motivations*). In this case, however, the king's heart was full of pride. As a result of Hezekiah's arrogance, **the LORD's wrath** came on the king and **Judah and Jerusalem**. The Chronicler's notice that divine wrath was against **Judah and Jerusalem** may be an oblique reference to Sennacherib's turn toward Jerusalem (see 32:9). If so, Sennacherib's success at Lachish may have occurred in part because of Hezekiah's ingratitude for his healing. Such a view supports the earlier suggestion that Hezekiah's speech was not sincere (see 32:2-8). At any rate, Hezekiah was full of pride as he reflected on his healing and this ingratitude brought the city under the judgment of God. For other examples of pride as the cause of sin see 25:18; 26:16; 32:26.

Hezekiah's Blessing (32:26)

As the wrath of God became evident, Hezekiah came to his senses and **repented of the pride of his heart** (32:26; see 32:25). Moreover, the Chronicler noted that similar repentance took place among **the people of Jerusalem** as well. Apparently, Hezekiah's healing had engendered pride in both the king and the people. Once again, the Chronicler's concern with the devotion of the inner person is evident (see *Introduction: 16) Motivations*).

The Hebrew word translated **repented** in the NIV may be translated 'humbled himself' (NRS, NKJ). It is the same term translated 'humble' in many places in Chronicles (e.g. 2 Chr. 7:14; 12:6,7). Humility was one way in which the Chronicler taught that God's people could avoid judgment and receive God's blessing (see *Introduction:18) Humility*).

As expected in Chronicles, when the king and people humbled themselves before God, **the LORD's wrath did not come upon them**. The city of Jerusalem was delivered from Sennacherib. Yet, the Chronicler quickly noted that Jerusalem's deliverance from wrath was not permanent. It did not **come upon them during the days of Hezekiah**. The account of Kings explains this matter more fully (2 Kgs. 20:12-19; see also 2 Chr. 32:31). Sometime after his healing, Hezekiah sought to make an alliance with Babylon against Assyria. Isaiah responded to this infidelity by saying that a future generation would see the treasures of Jerusalem carried to Babylon. Despite this undercurrent of future doom, Hezekiah and Jerusalem were delivered from the judgment of God in the Sennacherib invasion.

Once again, the Chronicler offered hope to his post-exilic readers. In many respects, the post-exilic community faced a situation very similar to Hezekiah's circumstance. God had displayed miraculous power in response to their prayers for deliverance from exile, but they had taken this grace as an opportunity for ingratitude by refusing to follow the ways of God. This episode of Hezekiah's life offered them the hope that judgment did not necessarily follow such failure. Even the proud of the post-exilic community could avoid the wrath of God, if they would humble themselves as Hezekiah and the people of Jerusalem had in the past.

Hezekiah's Inconsistent Alliance (32:27-31)

The third episode of Hezekiah's inconsistency during the Assyrian crisis follows a similar pattern to its predecessor. The Chronicler offered an elaborate description of Hezekiah's blessings and success only to follow it with a brief reminder of the king's failure.

Comparison of 32:27-31 with 2 Kgs. 20:12-19

This portion of Chronicles compares to Kings in two ways. First, the Chronicler added 32:27-30. These verses consist of a list of successes Hezekiah experienced which are not mentioned in Kings. Second, in 32:31 the Chronicler briefly alluded to the visit of emissaries from Babylon recorded in 2 Kgs. 20:12-19. Apparently, the Chronicler assumed his post-exilic readers knew this story and his allusion would suffice to make his point.

The chronological framework of this passage is ambiguous as it stands in Chronicles. At first glance, it would appear that the Chronicler spoke of a time after the Sennacherib invasion. It is more likely, however, that the Chronicler assumed that his readers knew the chronology from the book of Kings.

Several factors place these events during the Sennacherib invasion.

1) 2 Kgs. 20:12 introduces the visit of Babylonian emissaries with the notice that it occurred 'at that time...' This temporal reference corresponds to **in those days** in 32:24 (// 2 Kgs. 20:1) and places this event squarely in the days of the Sennacherib invasion.

2) Moreover, both Kings and Chronicles indicate that the Babylonians came to inquire about Hezekiah's healing (32:31; 2 Kgs. 20:12). His healing also occurred during the Sennacherib campaign.

3) The Chronicler already associated Isaiah's threat of Babylonian captivity with these events (2 Kgs. 20:16-19) and with Hezekiah's humility after his pride (32:26).

As a result, it is best to understand this material as a temporal regression offering yet another description of events that took place during the Assyrian crisis. For this reason, it is appropriate once again to translate the verbs in this section as past perfects ('**Hezekiah** *had* acquired **very great riches** ... **he** *had* **made** ... **he** *had* **also made** ... etc.').

Structure of 32:27-31

This section consists of two main parts (see figure 53). The first portion of this material consists of a series of three reports and a summary (32:27-30). The final verse stands in contrast, reminding the readers of another of the king's failures during the Sennacherib invasion (32:31).

Hezekiah's Successes (32:27-30)

As noted above, the Chronicler regressed temporarily to set the stage for another example of Hezekiah's inconsistency during the Sennacherib invasion. After reestablishing the temple (see 29:3-31:21), God blessed Hezekiah in many ways. Hezekiah had acquired **very great riches and honor** (32:27a). He had also engaged in an assortment of building projects to contain his wealth: **treasuries** (32:27), **storehouses** for agricultural surpluses, **stalls** for livestock (32:28) as well as **villages** (32:29). To form an inclusio around these accomplishments, the Chronicler explained that **God had given him very great riches** (32:29b see 32:27). After his work with the temple, Hezekiah reached heights of prosperity. These reports of Hezekiah's riches aligned him once again with the ideal reigns of David and Solomon (see *Introduction: 26) Prosperity and Poverty*).

The Chronicler also noted Hezekiah's well-known water system (32:30). He had **blocked ... the spring and channeled the water** across the city. This water channel, known to archaeologists as the Siloam Tunnel, was a monumental achievement.

The Chronicler summed up Hezekiah's condition just prior to the Sennacherib invasion in a characteristic manner. **He succeeded in everything he undertook** (32:30). The theme of 'success' or 'prospering' occurs a number of times in Chronicles to indicate divine approval of a king (see *Introduction: 26) Prosperity and Poverty*).

Hezekiah's Failure (32:31)

To bring this episode into conformity with his other accounts of Hezekiah's behavior during the Assyrian crisis, the Chronicler followed notices of Hezekiah's successes with a brief allusion to the visit of Babylonian emissaries. According to 2 Kgs. 20:12-19, Hezekiah showed his riches to the Babylonians. This move was an attempt to establish an alliance with Assyria's eastern enemy at the time of Sennacherib's preoccupation with matters in the west. Isaiah rebuked Hezekiah for this attempt (see 2 Kgs. 20:14-19), much as he had earlier warned Ahaz against an alliance with Assyria (see Isa. 7). In fact, the prophet told Hezekiah that any attempt to join with Babylon would eventually lead to the removal of the royal treasures to Babylon.

The Chronicler's version of this event is different from Kings in at least two ways. First, Kings reports that the envoys came to Jerusalem because they had heard that Hezekiah **had been sick** (2 Kgs. 20:12). The Chronicler emphasized instead that the Babylonians had noticed **the miraculous sign**, probably a reference to the reversal of the sun that accompanied the king's healing (see 2 Kgs. 20:10-11).

Second, instead of describing the details of events that occurred during the visit, the Chronicler offered a theological summary of the whole matter. He noted that **God left him to test him and to know everything that was in his heart** (32:31). As he did elsewhere in his history, the Chronicler went behind the scene to explain the divine purposes in events that took place (see *Introduction: 10) Divine Activity*). God brought the Babylonians to Hezekiah to **test** not just the actions of Hezekiah, but **his heart**. David had warned Solomon that God searches the inward motivations (see 1 Chr. 29:9). Here God tested the heart of Hezekiah. As the record of Kings demonstrates, he failed the test. Once again, the Chronicler revealed his interest in the inner motivations of his characters. Fidelity grew out of a wholehearted commitment to God (see *Introduction: 16) Motivations*).

In his profoundly subtle closure to this portion of Hezekiah's reign, the Chronicler challenged his post-exilic readers to compare themselves carefully with Hezekiah. Although Hezekiah was a great king and accomplished much, God was not satisfied with mere external obedience. He desired the wholehearted devotion of his people.

Closure of Hezekiah's Reign (32:32-33)

The end of Hezekiah's reign in Chronicles closely parallels 2 Kgs. 20:20-21. Nevertheless, several changes should be noted. First, Kings draws attention to records of 'all his achievements ... the pool and the tunnel ...' (2 Kgs. 20:20). Chronicles has already mentioned these facts and substitutes **his acts of devotion** (32:32).

Second, the Chronicler recommended a prophetic source, **the vision of the prophet Isaiah son of Amoz** (32:32), much as he did elsewhere (see 1 Chr. 29:29; 2 Chr. 9:29; 12:15; 13:22; 20:34; 26:22; see also *Introduction: 15) Prophets*). This record is not to be confused with the biblical book of Isaiah for it is further identified as being contained **in the book of the kings of Judah and Israel** (32:32; see *Introduction: Historical and Theological Purposes*).

Third, the Chronicler expanded 2 Kgs. 20:21 in two ways to give honor to the king. 1) He added that the king **was buried on the hill where the tombs of David's descendants are** (32:33a). 2) The Chronicler also added that **all Judah and the people of Jerusalem honored him when he died** (32:32).

This final portion of Hezekiah's reign amounts to a series of reports focusing on the king's records (32:32), demise, burial, and successor (32:33). The Chronicler's emphases appear in those portions which he added.

As noted above, the Chronicler drew attention to other records of Hezekiah's **acts of devotion** (32:32). Instead of merely mentioning that Hezekiah had achieved much (2 Kgs. 20:20), the Chronicler gave a moral evaluation. In general, Hezekiah's reign was one of devotion to God. The account of Hezekiah closes with a positive evaluation of the king just as it began (see 29:2).

Moreover, the Chronicler also added that Hezekiah received an honorable burial. He was placed **on the hill where the tombs of David's descendants are** (32:33a). The expression translated **on the hill** is not altogether clear. It may refer instead to an 'upper chamber' [NKJ, NAS] within the tombs themselves. If so, it denotes the prestige afforded Hezekiah at his burial. Here the Chronicler again honored Hezekiah as one of the great kings of Judah (see *Introduction: 28) Healing and Long Life/Sickness and Death*).

In much the same way, the Chronicler mentioned that **all Judah and the people of Jerusalem honored him when he died** (32:32b). In all likelihood, the Chronicler had in mind the ritual burial fire which accompanied the deaths of Judah's honorable kings (see 16:14), but was withheld from dishonorable kings (see 21:19).

This closing to Hezekiah's reign brought the Chronicler's evaluation of the king to the foreground. Despite Hezekiah's inconsistencies during the Sennacherib invasion, on the whole the Chronicler was very positive. Hezekiah was one of the greatest kings of Judah.

The Reign of Manasseh (33:1-20)

Having reflected on Hezekiah's great accomplishment in the reunification of the nation around the temple, the Chronicler turned next to Manasseh's reign (697/96–643/42 BC). His record of Manasseh pointed to the wonder of God's mercy and the responsibility of post-exilic Israel to respond properly to that mercy.

Comparison of 33:1-20 with 2 Kgs. 21:1-18

The Chronicler's account of Manasseh's reign depends to varying degrees on 2 Kgs. 21:1-18. On a large scale the accounts of Chronicles and Kings may be compared as follows (see figure 57).

2 Chr.		2 Kgs.
33:1-10	Manasseh's Early Sins (closely parallel)	21:1-10
———	Manasseh's Condemnation (omitted)	21:11-16
33:11-17	Manasseh's Exile and Restoration (added)	———
33:18-20	Closure of Reign (loosely parallel)	21:17-18

Comparison of 2 Chr. 33:1-20 and 2 Kgs. 21:1-18 (figure 57)

This comparison reveals that Chronicles follows Kings closely at the beginning (33:1-10 // 2 Kgs. 21:1-10) and rather closely at the end (33:18-20 // 2 Kgs. 21:17-18). The middle portions, however, are very different. The Chronicler omitted the lengthy prophetic condemnation of Manasseh (2 Kgs. 21:11-16) and replaced it with his own account of Manasseh's personal exile, repentance, and restoration (33:11-17). This variation reflects a significant difference of perspective. 2 Kgs. 21:11-16 focuses on Manasseh's sins as the final cause for the destruction of Jerusalem. The Chronicler's text treats Manasseh as a model of one who was exiled, repented of sin, returned to the land of promise, and restored the nation to God.

A number of smaller differences appear in the first and last portions of Manasseh's reign. Some of these variations are corruptions introduced through textual transmission (see *Introduction: Translation and Transmission*). Several items, however, deserve comment.

In the opening section (33:1-10) several significant variations appear. First, in 33:1 (// 2 Kgs. 21:1) the Chronicler omitted the reference to Manasseh's queen mother. The reason for this omission is not clear, but this was his practice from here until the end of the book (33:21 // 2 Kgs. 21:19; 34:1 // 2 Kgs. 22:1; 36:2 // 2 Kgs. 23:31; 36:5 // 2 Kgs. 23:36; 36:9 // 2 Kgs. 24:8; 36:11 // 2 Kgs. 24:18.

Second, the Chronicler probably intended to emphasize Manasseh's apostasy by shifting from singular 'Baal' and 'Asherah' (2 Kgs. 21:3) to **Baals** and **Asherahs** (33:3). The plural of **sons** (33:6) as opposed to 'son' (2 Kgs. 21:6) may not have been a shift introduced by the Chronicler. The difference in Hebrew amounts to only one internal letter which could easily have confused copyists (see *Introduction: Translation and Transmission*). Moreover, the Septuagint (Greek version) of 2 Kgs. 21:6 also reads 'sons'.

Third, the omission of the comparison between Ahab and Manasseh (33:3 // 2 Kgs. 21:3) probably resulted from the Chronicler's view that Ahaz – and not

Manasseh – was the worst king of Judah. Elsewhere, Ahaz was compared to the northern king (see 28:2-4).

Fourth, **in the Valley of Ben Hinnon** is added in 33:6 (// 2 Kgs. 21:6) to specify the place of human sacrifice. Perhaps the reference was important for some unknown reason to the post-exilic readers of Chronicles.

Fifth, 33:7-10 paraphrases portions of 2 Kgs. 21:7-10 for no apparent reason.

Sixth, at one point, the Chronicler specified that Manasseh seduced **Judah and the people of Jerusalem** (33:9 // 2 Kgs. 21:9). Perhaps his purpose here was to help his post-exilic Jerusalemite readers more easily identify with the characters of the story.

The closing section (33:18-20) also contains several variations. First, Chronicles substitutes a reference to Manasseh's prayer in the place of his sins (33:18 // 2 Kgs. 21:17). This shift demonstrates that the Chronicler's chief interest in the reign of Manasseh was his prayer of repentance. Second, the Chronicler also added the literary source from which he derived his account of Manasseh's prayer (33:19). Once again, his chief concern is evident. Third, the reasons for the variations in the burial notice are uncertain (33:20 // 2 Kgs. 21:18).

Structure of 33:1-20

The Chronicler's variations from Kings gave a distinctive shape to his account. His record of Manasseh's reign divides into a five step symmetrical pattern (see figure 58).

■Opening of Manasseh's Reign (33:1)

■Manasseh's Heinous Sins (33:2-9)

■Manasseh's Exile and Restoration (33:10-13)
Manasseh Ignores God (33:10)
Manasseh Taken Captive from Jerusalem (33:11)
Manasseh Prays for Deliverance (33:12)
Manasseh Brought Back to Jerusalem (33:13a)
Manasseh Acknowledges God (33:13b)

■Manasseh's Extensive Restorations (33:14-17)

■Closure of Manasseh's Reign (33:18-20)

Outline of 2 Chr. 33:1-20 (figure 58)

Manasseh's reign begins and ends in the usual fashion (33:1,18-20). The middle portion of the account reports Manasseh's change of heart while in exile (33:10-13). On both sides of this central material are two series of reports. Lengthy notices of the various sins he and Judah committed appear first (33:2-9). This catalog of sins is balanced by reports of the king's reforms after he returned from exile (33:14-17).

Opening of Manasseh's Reign (33:1)

The Chronicler began by closely following the account of 2 Kgs. 21:1 with the exception of omitting Manasseh's mother. Manasseh was **twelve years old** when his reign began and remained king for **fifty-five years**. Many historians have argued that Manasseh was co-regent with Hezekiah for about ten years. This suggestion seems likely and brings the king's reign within the limits established by some archaeological findings. Whatever the case, Manasseh reigned longer than any other Judean king.

Given the entirely negative portrait of 2 Kgs. 21:1-18, the length of Manasseh's reign may have prompted the Chronicler to search for another perspective on the king. He considered long life a blessing from God, and the record of Kings gave no reason to expect such a blessing for Manasseh. (For a summary of the Chronicler's outlook on the blessing of long life, see comments on 1 Chr. 29:28.) The explanation of Manasseh's longevity becomes clear in the Chronicler's presentation of the king's repentance and reforms (33:10-17).

Manasseh's Heinous Sins (33:2-9)

Chronicles continues to follow closely the record of 2 Kgs. 21:2-9. This material is separated from the surrounding context by repetitions in 33:2a and 33:9b. Both verses note that Manasseh **did evil** like **the nations the LORD had driven out before the Israelites**. A similar connection exists between **evil in the eyes of the LORD** in 33:2a and 33:6b. As a result, this series of reports on Manasseh's violations of God's Law falls into two sections: Manasseh's various sins (33:2-6) and Manasseh's image in the temple (33:7-9).

33:2-9 depends heavily on the language of Deut. 18:9-13 (see also 28:2-4). There Moses warned Israel not to 'imitate the detestable ways of the nations' (Deut. 18:9). Moses even listed several specific sins mentioned by the Chronicler in 33:2-9. The first report of Manasseh's various sins (33:2-5) follows the lead of Deut. 18:9-13. It begins with the note that the king **did evil** in God's sight by **following the detestable practices of the nations** driven from the land (33:2 see also 33:9b). In a word, Manasseh had violated the warning of Deut. 18.

A number of passages indicate that the Canaanites were particularly wicked people deserving the judgment of Israel's conquest (see Gen. 15:16; Deut. 18:9-12; Lev. 18:28; 20:23). This accusation against Manasseh highlights the severity of his apostasy. Like Ahaz before him (see 28:2-4) and the leaders of Judah in Zedekiah's day (see 36:14), Manasseh had reached such depths of sin that he deserved the judgment laid against the Canaanites.

The text follows this opening accusation against Manasseh with a catalog of different sins: **high places, Baals and Asherahs, starry hosts** (33:3; see 21:11; 28:25), **foreign altars** in the temple (33:4-5), child sacrifice, **sorcery**, **divination, witchcraft, mediums**, and **spiritists** (33:6).

One aspect of this passage is repeated in the report that follows. Both 33:4-5 and 33:7-9 focus on the violation of the temple where the **Name** of God dwelled (see

Introduction: 11) Name of God). Here the text focuses on **altars to all the starry hosts in both courts of the temple** (33:5). Later, a more serious violation occurs in the temple (33:7-9). The repetition of these themes strongly suggests that the Chronicler considered the violation of the temple Manasseh's worst sin. He defiled the place of God's holy presence and thereby incurred the wrath of God (see comments on 33:7-9).

The list of Manasseh's various sins concludes with the comment that they were **provoking** [the Lord] **to anger** (33:6b). The king of Judah stirred the wrath of God against himself and eventually suffered personal exile to Babylon (see 33:11).

The second report focuses on one of Manasseh's particular sins (33:7-9). The king **took the carved image** ('carved Asherah pole' [2 Kgs. 21:7]) and **put it in God's temple** (33:7). As in the similar scene in the previous report (33:4-5), the severity of this violation is highlighted by the mention that the temple was the place where God promised to put his **Name forever**. As Solomon's dedicatory prayer explained (see 6:14-42), the temple was the place of God's Name so that prayers could be heard and the people could be blessed in all kinds of circumstances (see *Introduction: 11) Name of God*).

To demonstrate the severity of Manasseh's sins, the text elaborates on the promise of the permanent presence of the Name. God's presence in the temple was the assurance that the **Israelites** would not have to **leave the land** again ... **if they will be careful to do everything** [God] **commanded them** (33:8). The Chronicler added the explanation that these commandments included **all the laws, decrees and ordinances given through Moses**. The standard of the Mosaic Law was the standard for divine judgment and blessing (see *Introduction: 14) Standards*). If Israel kept the Law then access to the Name would be available. Serious violations of the Law, however, would lead to judgment (see *Introduction: 10-27) Divine Blessing and Judgment*).

Manasseh hardly met the conditions for the preservation of the nation. As the Chronicler made clear, he **led Judah and the people of Jerusalem astray** (33:9). Neither Manasseh nor the people observed the conditions of fidelity required for continuance in the land. Instead, the text returns to the opening of this section and explains that he **did more evil than the nations the LORD had destroyed before the Israelites** (33:9; see 33:2). With these words, the Chronicler closed on an extremely somber note. Manasseh was condemned to the judgment of God.

Manasseh's Exile and Restoration (33:10-13)

The middle portion of Manasseh's reign (33:10-13) forms a turning point between the king's sins (33:2-9) and his reforms (33:14-17).

Structure of 33:10-13

This central portion of Manasseh's reign consists of five balanced steps (see figure 58). This episode begins with Manasseh ignoring God's warnings (33:10), but ends with him acknowledging God (33:13b). In the center of the story is the king's cry to

God for help (33:12). Leading to Manasseh's cry is his exile to Babylon (33:11); following the prayer is Manasseh's return to Jerusalem (33:13a).

Manasseh Ignores God (33:10)

The Chronicler began this segment of Manasseh's reign by indicating the rebellious attitude of the king and nation. This material abbreviates the record of 2 Kgs. 21:10-16 where the prophetic word came against the king to no avail. **The LORD spoke** through his prophets against the sins of **Manasseh and his people**. As in 33:9, the Chronicler made it clear that Manasseh was not alone in his guilt. He led the nation astray so that all the people of Judah shared in his violations of God's Law. The prophetic word against Manasseh and the nation was intended to illicit a response of repentance and humility (see 12:5). Yet, despite these warnings **they paid no attention** (33:10).

Once again, the importance of prophets in the Chronicler's history is evident (see *Introduction: 15) Prophets*). To heed the prophets brought divine blessing; to ignore them was to insure judgment. The repetition of this motif throughout Chronicles suggests that the Chronicler was deeply concerned that his own post-exilic readers were in danger of ignoring the prophets of their day. Among these prophets was the Chronicler himself whose message needed to be heard.

Manasseh Taken Captive from Jerusalem (33:11)

At this point the Chronicler entirely turned away from the record of Kings to focus on a different dimension to the reign of Manasseh. God responded to Judah's rejection of the prophets by sending **against them the army ... of the king of Assyria**. During the reign of Manasseh, several widespread rebellions took place among Assyria's vassal nations. It is likely that Manasseh was somehow involved in one of these rebellions. Whatever the case, the king of Assyria came against Manasseh to punish him for his disloyalty.

As the instrument of divine judgment, the king of Assyria made Manasseh his **prisoner**. The Chronicler's description highlighted the dishonor of this imprisonment. Judah's king was led away with **a hook in his nose** and in **bronze shackles**. Archaeological discoveries verify that the Assyrians actually inserted hooks through the noses of captives and attached them to chains (see also 2 Kgs. 19:28; Ezek. 19:4). Manasseh's **bronze shackles** allude to the captivity and exile of Jehoiachin, the last king of Judah (see 36:6). These descriptive details drew attention to the dishonor which Manasseh suffered. The Assyrians publicly humiliated him for his rebellion (33:10).

Interestingly enough, the Chronicler reported that the Assyrians took Manasseh **to Babylon**. At first glance, this destination is unexpected because the capital city of Assyria was Nineveh. Nevertheless, the Assyrians controlled Babylon at this time and may have dishonored Manasseh even further by taking him to the capital of another defeated people. The Chronicler's purpose for including this information is apparent. He mentioned Babylon to draw a connection between his post-exilic readers and Manasseh. They had gone into exile to Babylon just as Manasseh. This parallel opened the way for the Chronicler's readers to relate Manasseh's experience to their own experience.

Manasseh Prays for Deliverance (33:12)

Manasseh's captivity was one of **distress**, but he prayed for deliverance. The Chronicler used two characteristic phrases to describe the king's prayer. First, Manasseh **sought the favor of the LORD**. This expression may be translated more literally, 'he entreated the face of God'. To entreat the face of God was to seek his benevolent countenance, his favor (see Num. 6:24). This phraseology alludes to God's promise after Solomon's dedicatory prayer. There God commanded the people to **seek my face** to find deliverance from trouble (7:14; see *Introduction: 19) Seeking*). Manasseh prayed toward the temple as the people were to do when outside the land (see 6:34; Dan. 6:10). His model prayer was designed to inspire the Chronicler's readers to see the importance of prayer in their day (see *Introduction: 17) Prayer*).

Second, the Chronicler noted that Manasseh **humbled himself greatly**. Once again, the allusion to 7:14 is evident. Manasseh recognized his disloyalty to God and appealed humbly to be restored through divine mercy (see *Introduction: 18) Humility*).

By noting this remarkable turn of events the Chronicler drew another strong connection between his readers and Manasseh. Solomon's temple not only served as the locus of prayer in Manasseh's day, but in the days of their own exile as well. Humble petitioning in and toward the temple of Jerusalem was their only hope for future blessing from God.

Manasseh Brought Back to Jerusalem (33:13a)

The Chronicler wasted no time describing the results of Manasseh's humble prayers. Just as Solomon had hoped in his dedicatory prayer (see 6:36-39), the Lord heard Manasseh's prayer and **brought him back to Jerusalem**. Even the severe punishment of exile from the land was reversed by prayers offered toward the temple. Moreover, God also brought Manasseh back **to his kingdom**. A throne and crown replaced the humiliation of hook and shackles. God's forgiveness led to a complete reversal of Manasseh's misfortune.

It is apparent that the Chronicler intentionally drew attention to yet another parallel between the experience of Manasseh and his post-exilic readers. Just as the king was brought back to Jerusalem and his kingdom, they too had returned to Jerusalem.

Manasseh Acknowledges God (33:13b)

Upon his arrival in Jerusalem, Manasseh's attitude toward God was radically changed. He **knew that the LORD is God**. Similar expressions occur frequently in Ezekiel's prophecies as descriptions of experiencing the power of God (e.g. Ezek. 6:10, 13). In these and many other cases, to **know** is more than to have factual awareness. It is to be so fully persuaded that Israel's God is supreme that proper responses follow. Earlier Manasseh had worshipped a number of gods (see 33:3). His experience of deliverance from exile convinced him that true divinity rested in the God of Israel alone. By implication, Manasseh would no longer ignore divine instruction; a new life would follow his new conviction.

At this point the Chronicler drew another parallel between Manasseh and post-exilic Judah. Many of those who returned from exile had also come to see the importance of loyalty to the Lord alone. Their experiences had caused them to renew their commitments to Israel's God. Nevertheless, as time went by, these convictions grew stale. Manasseh's example, however, reminded them of the condition of the restored community when it first returned from Babylon. It was a time of strong devotion to the Lord. As we will see, this initial commitment now needed to grow into a fuller commitment of action.

Manasseh's Extensive Restorations (33:14-17)

In juxtaposition to the sins that led to Manasseh's exile (33:2-10), the Chronicler added further material to the account in Kings. He noted the changes which Manasseh brought to the land following his return. His account divides into two parts: military (33:14) and religious reforms (33:15-17).

Two military projects were high on Manasseh's list of restorations (compare 27:3-4). First, he **rebuilt the outer wall** of Jerusalem (33:14a). It is likely that the Assyrians breached this wall when they came to take Manasseh away to Babylon. In all events, to make the wall **much higher** was one of the demonstrations of God's blessings to Manasseh (see *Introduction: 24) Building and Destruction*).

Second, Manasseh placed troops **in all the fortified cities of Judah** (33:14b). Military outposts were important to the defensive strategy of Judah's kings. They were especially designed to control the routes likely to be used by an enemy. Restoring the military strength of Judah required the re-establishment of these posts.

Beyond this, Manasseh turned to re-establishing proper worship in Judah (33:15-17). These actions were twofold as well. First, he **got rid of the foreign gods ... the image ... the altars** ... and **threw them out of the city** (33:15). These actions were direct reversals of the catalogs of sins earlier in this chapter (33:2-6). Manasseh removed the foreign defilements of worship because he had come to recognize the Lord as God (see 33:13b). That conviction led him to destroy the ways of syncretism he had introduced after the reign of Hezekiah.

Second, Manasseh re-established proper worship in a positive manner. He **restored the altar** in the temple (33:16). The reference here is to the bronze altar established by Solomon (see *Introduction: Appendix B – The Structures, Furnishings and Decorations of Solomon's Temple).*

Moreover, he **sacrificed fellowship offerings** and **thank offerings** on the altar (33:16). Much like other faithful kings, Manasseh not only purified the temple of foreign corruptions, but also re-established the active worship of God in the temple (see *Introduction: 6) Royal Observance of Worship*).

The Chronicler closed this material with an aside in 33:17. Although Manasseh himself had been faithful in his attempts to restore worship, **the people** were not able to free themselves completely from the ways of the past. They only worshipped **the LORD their God**, but they did so **at the high places**. This verse anticipates problems that will arise later in the Chronicler's history. Corruption in Judah was not entirely eliminated.

The significance of Manasseh's restoration efforts for the Chronicler's post-exilic audience is evident. Manasseh had focused on military and religious reform. The post-exilic community must do the same (see Neh. 2:17; 13:1-22). The book of Kings presents Manasseh as the worst miscreant of Judah's history (see 2 Kgs. 21:1-18). This feature of Kings made the Chronicler's point even more dramatic. If the great villain of Judah did these things after returning from exile, surely the post-exilic community should not stop short of working for the full restoration of Israel's military strength and the purity of her worship.

Closure of Manasseh's Reign (33:18-20)

In balance with the opening of Manasseh's reign (33:1), the Chronicler returned to the record of 2 Kgs. 21:17-18. He paid Manasseh honor by noting that he was buried **with his fathers and in his palace** (i.e. in the palace area, see 2 Kgs. 21:18 // 33:20). Manasseh's repentance and restoration efforts gained him this honored status in the Chronicler's eyes (see *Introduction: 28) Healing and Long Life/Sickness and Death*).

The most important aspect of this closing, however, appears in the Chronicler's additions to the record of Kings. Twice he varied from 2 Kgs. 21:17-18 to note the sources of Manasseh's prayer as well as the prophetic word against him (33:18). The Apocryphal 'Prayer of Manasseh' is of a much later origin and not in view here. Even so, it is evident that Manasseh's prayer was a central feature in Manasseh's reign (see *Introduction: 17) Prayer*). The Chronicler also used his characteristic word, **unfaithfulness** as a way of indicating the severity of the king's violations (33:19; see *Introduction: 21) Unfaithfulness*). These additions make it evident that Manasseh's sins and his prayer formed the heart of the Chronicler's concern with the king. He left his readers to contemplate further the relevance of these events for their situation.

The Reign of Amon (33:21-25)

Amon reigned in Jerusalem for only a short while (643/42–641/40 BC). Little is known about his brief time on the throne except that he was relentless in his wickedness. Amon's reign comes on the heels of Manasseh's experience of restoration and blessing (see 33:14-17). As such, it posed a dreadful possibility to the post-exilic readers. Even after a gracious restoration after exile, infidelity will lead to further judgment.

Comparison of 33:21-25 with 2 Kgs. 21:19-24
The Chronicler depended heavily on Kings for his information about Amon. Nevertheless, several variations from Kings occur in his account.

First, the Chronicler omitted the reference to Amon's royal mother (33:21 // 2 Kgs. 21:19). This was his practice from Manasseh to the end of his history (see comments on 2 Chr. 33:1).

Second, while 2 Kgs. 21:21 says that Amon "walked in all the ways of his father," the Chronicler omitted this description and only specified that Amon **worshipped and offered sacrifices to all the idols Manasseh had made** (33:22). As noted in 33:2, 9, the Chronicler considered Manasseh's idolatry his worst sin. Amon followed his father's example in the worst way possible.

Third, the most important difference between Kings and Chronicles is the addition of 33:23. There the Chronicler reported one way in which Amon was not like his father. Instead of humbling himself, Amon simply **increased his guilt** (33:23).

Fourth, Chronicles does not mention other sources, the king's burial, or the formal succession of Josiah as found in 2 Kgs. 21:25-26. This variation is difficult to understand. The absence of the material may have resulted from the Chronicler's intention to dishonor Amon (compare Athaliah's death 23:15). Yet, these verses may also have been lost through textual transmission (see *Introduction: Translation and Transmission*). The Hebrew translated '... Josiah his son in his place' (2 Kgs. 21:24 // 2 Chr. 33:25) and 'Josiah his son succeeded him ...' (2 Kgs. 21:26) is precisely the same in both verses. It is possible that a copyist skipped the content of 2 Kgs. 21:25-26 accidentally.

Structure of 33:21-25
The short account of Amon's reign divides into three parts (see figure 59).

Opening of Amon's Reign (33:21)
    Amon's Relentless Sins (33:22-23)
Closure of Amon's Reign (33:24-25)

Outline of 2 Chr. 33:21-25 (figure 59)

As the record now stands in Chronicles (without the formal ending of 2 Kgs. 21:25-26), Amon's story begins with his rise (33:21) and his balanced by his dishonorable death (33:24-25). The middle portion of the account (33:22-23) explains why Amon's kingdom ended so abruptly.

Opening of Amon's Reign (33:21)
The Chronicler repeated the opening verse of 2 Kgs. 21:19 which indicates that Amon reigned only **two years** (33:21). The brevity of Amon's time on the throne fit well with the Chronicler's outlook on divine blessing and judgment (see *Introduction: 28) Healing and Long Life/Sickness and Death*). The obvious contrast with Manasseh's lengthy reign of fifty-five years suited the Chronicler's purpose

in portraying Amon as a king whose unceasing rebellion against God brought his kingdom to a swift end.

Amon's Relentless Sins (33:22-23)

The middle portion of Amon's reign focuses exclusively on his sins. The Chronicler began with the language of 2 Kgs. 21:20, indicating that he **did evil in the eyes of the LORD, as his father Manasseh** (33:22a; for the Chronicler's use of this evaluative terminology see comments on 2 Chr. 24:2). The name Manasseh is repeated three times in these verses because Manasseh's reign served as the interpretative framework for the reign of Amon. This correlation is easily understood in the record of Kings; both Manasseh and Amon are presented in an entirely negative light. As we have seen, however, the Chronicler offered a more balanced assessment of Manasseh. For this reason, the comparison between Manasseh and Amon involved both similarity and dissimilarity.

The first comparison summarizes the content of 2 Kgs. 21:21 which reported that Amon **worshipped ... all the idols Manasseh had made** (33:22b). The Chronicler's keen interest in the worship of Israel makes it only fitting that this sin was the Chronicler's central concern (see *Introduction: 4-9) King and Temple*).

The second comparison is one of dissimilarity (33:23). The Chronicler added this element to the account of Kings (compare 2 Kgs. 21:21). From the Chronicler's perspective, the key difference between the kings is that **unlike his father Manasseh,** Amon **did not humble himself before the LORD** (33:23; see *Introduction: 18) Humility*). Chronicles emphasizes how Manasseh humbled himself and prayed while in exile (see 33:12). The king's humility led to significant reforms in the later years of his reign (see 33:15-16) and explained how he could have enjoyed such a long reign. Amon, however, never repented of his sins. As a result, he **increased his guilt** and his reign endured only **two years** (33:21).

Closure of Amon's Reign (33:24-25)

The Chronicler derived the last portion of his account from 2 Kgs. 21:24. It tells a two step story of conspiracy and counter-conspiracy.

In the first step, Amon's **servants ... killed him in his house** (33:24). This description of Amon's death alludes to the similar circumstances surrounding the demise of Joash (see 24:25). Amon's death in his own home reflected his political impotence and thereby dishonored him.

In the second step, Amon's death left the nation of Judah in political disarray. Those who assassinated Amon became the objects of a counter-conspiracy. The Chronicler mentioned **the people of the land** elsewhere (32:25; for the Chronicler's use of this terminology see 1 Chr. 5:25; 2 Chr. 23:13, 20-21; 26:21; 36:1). It would appear that the Chronicler had in mind common people. Whatever the case, the divine judgment against Amon left Judah without an orderly transfer of power (see 21:1; 23:20-21; 26:1; 36:1). Josiah came to power by means of this counter-conspiracy.

As noted above, it is possible that the Chronicler's original text included at least portions of 2 Kgs. 24:25-26. Whatever the case, the negative ending of Amon's life left no room for mistaking the Chronicler's perspective. He impressed upon his readers the dire consequences of remaining in rebellion against the Law of God, especially as it pertains to worship. Infidelity itself was not the serious problem facing the post-exilic community. Repentance and humility could remedy that. Continued infidelity, however, was sure to bring swift judgment in their day as it did in Amon's time.

The Reign of Josiah (34:1-35:27)

The largely positive reign of Josiah (641-609 BC) follows the terrible downfall in Amon's day. As such, Josiah served as another model of fidelity. Nevertheless, later in his life Josiah failed to be faithful to God's command and suffered the judgment of defeat and death. As a result, Josiah's reign also warned the Chronicler's post-exilic readers to continue in faithful service to God.

Comparison of 34:1-35:27 with 2 Kgs. 22:1-23:30

At this point we will compare the record of Kings and Chronicles on a large scale. More detailed comparisons will appear in the comments on each section. The Chronicler's account of Josiah's reign follows Kings closely for the most part. Yet, his version includes several expansions, abbreviations, and rearrangements of the material in Kings (see figure 60).

As this figure demonstrates, each major portion of Kings is reflected in the Chronicler's account. At this point, however, it is important to note that two sections have been rearranged.

2 Chr.		2 Kgs.
34:1-3a	Josiah's Rise (slightly expanded)	22:1-2
34:3b-7	Widespread Worship Reforms (loosely parallel)	23:6-20
34:8-28	Discovery of the Book (slightly expanded)	22:3-20
34:29-33	Covenant Renewal (slightly expanded)	23:1-5
35:1-19	Passover (greatly expanded)	23:21-27
35:20-25	Death in Battle (expanded)	23:29-30a
35:26-27	Death, Burial, and Successor (slightly expanded)	23:28

Comparison of 2 Chr. 34:1-35:27 and 2 Kgs. 22:1-23:30a (figure 60)

First, the Chronicler moved the description of Josiah's general worship reforms (34:3b-7 // 2 Kgs. 23:6-20) from after Josiah's discovery of the Book and subsequent covenant renewal (2 Kgs. 22:3-23:5 // 2 Chr. 34:8-33) to a position prior to the discovery and renewal. This rearrangement does not reflect an historical disagreement with Kings. The writer of Kings must have known that some worship reforms took place prior to the temple reparations that led to the discovery. Instead, Kings is arranged more topically. By contrast, Chronicles is arranged more chronologically. It first notes the worship reforms that **began** in Josiah's **twelfth year** (34:3b) and continued with specific aspects of those reforms. Chronicles focuses on the events of discovery, renewal and Passover that took place in Josiah's **eighteenth year** (34:8; 35:19). Consequently, the Chronicler's rearrangement provided a general context of worship reforms in which the momentous eighteenth year occurred.

Second, the book of Kings places Josiah's battle with Neco (2 Kgs. 23:29-30) after the reference to other sources (2 Kgs. 23:28). This unusual arrangement led the Chronicler to reverse the order by listing the battle first (35:20-25) and then other sources (35:26-27).

Apart from these rearrangements, the Chronicler's text follows the basic patterns of the record of Kings. A number of smaller variations occur (mostly expansions) which we will describe below.

Structure of 34:1-35:27

The record of Josiah's reign divides into four main parts (see figure 61 below).

In his typical fashion the Chronicler began with the rise of the king to power (34:1-3a) and closed with a balancing closure of his reign (35:26-27). The middle portion of Josiah's reign divides into two parts. The first of these parts focuses on Josiah's years of faithful service to God, especially his worship reforms (34:3b-35:19). The second part of the main body consists of a brief account of his failure to remain loyal to the Lord in battle with Neco of Egypt (35:20-25). This division between times of fidelity and infidelity is typical of the Chronicler's approach to the kings of Judah (see *Introduction: 10-27) Divine Blessing and Judgment*).

Opening of Josiah's Reign (34:1-3a)

The reign of Josiah begins with material derived from 2 Kgs. 22:1-2. With the exception of the omission of Josiah's royal mother (2 Kgs. 22:1b; see comments on 2 Chr. 33:1), the Chronicler closely followed Kings for the first two verses. Josiah became king at the young age of **eight years old** (34:1); only Joash began at a younger age (see 24:1). Like Joash, Josiah probably was under adult tutelage in his early years.

The Chronicler conveyed a very positive evaluation of Josiah. First, he followed the judgment of Kings (34:2 // 2 Kgs. 22:2). Many kings are said to have done **right in the eyes of the LORD.** (For the Chronicler's use of this evaluative terminology, see comments on 2 Chr. 24:2.) A number of kings are also compared with **David** (see 2 Chr. 17:3; 28:1; 34:2; see also *Introduction: 14) Standards*).

■Opening of Josiah's Reign (34:1-3a)

♦Josiah's Fidelity in Worship Reforms (34:3b-35:19)

•Josiah's Earlier Reforms (34:3b-7)
Reforms in the South (34:3b-5)
Reforms in the North (34:6-7)
•Josiah's Later Reforms (34:8-35:19)
-Josiah Repairs the Temple (34:8-13)
Initiation of Temple Repairs (34:8)
Money Designated for Temple Repairs (34:9)
Money Given to Supervisors (34:10a)
Money Paid for Temple Repairs (34:10b-11)
Completion of Temple Repairs (34:12a)
[Afterword Concerning Levitical Supervisors (34:12b-13)]
-Josiah Renews Covenant (34:14-33)
*Josiah Recognizes Sin through the Book (34:14-21)
Josiah's Leaders Discover the Book (34:14-15)
Josiah Hears the Book (34:16-18)
Josiah Reacts to the Book (34:19-21)

*Josiah Receives Prophecy about the Book (34:22-28)
Josiah's Leaders Approach Huldah (34:22)
Huldah Speaks to Leaders (34:23-28a)
Josiah's Leaders Return from Huldah (34:28b)
*Josiah Renews Covenant According to the Book (34:29-33)
Josiah Gathers Judah for Covenant Renewal (34:29-30a)
Josiah Reads the Book (34:30b)
Josiah and Judah Renew Covenant (34:31-33)
-Josiah Observes Passover (35:1-19)
Josiah's Passover Introduced (35:1)
Josiah's Preparations for Celebration (35:2-9)
Josiah Readies Priests and Levites (35:2-6)
Josiah Readies Sacrifices (35:7-9)
Josiah's Performance of Celebration (35:10-15)
Josiah's Passover Summarized (35:16-19)

♦Josiah's Infidelity in Deadly Battle (35:20-25)
Josiah Goes Out for Battle Against Neco (35:20)
Josiah Hears Warning from Neco (35:21)
Josiah Defiantly Enters Battle (35:22)
Josiah is Seriously Wounded (35:23)
Josiah Returns and Dies (35:24a)
[Afterword Concerning Mourning (35:24b-25)]

■Closure of Josiah's Reign (35:26-27)

Outline of 2 Chr. 34:1-35:27 (figure 61)

Nevertheless, Josiah is the only king about whom the Chronicler added that he did not turn **to the right or to the left** (34:1). This description is a traditional way of describing fidelity to the Law of God (see Deut. 17:20; 28:14; Josh. 1:7; 1 Sam. 6:12). This general outlook, however, must be balanced by Josiah's failure in battle (35:20-24 // 2 Kgs. 23:29-30).

To heighten the importance of Josiah, the Chronicler added to the record of Kings that Josiah's loyalty to God began at a very early age. Here we find the first of several chronological references in Josiah's reign. **In the eighth year** Josiah was already taking positive steps toward reform; **he began to seek the God of his father David** (34:3a). 'Seeking' the Lord is one of the Chronicler's regular ways of describing an attitude of humility and devotion to God (see *Introduction: 19) Seeking*).

The Chronicler drew attention to the remarkable character of Josiah by noting that he put his faith into action **while he was still young** (34:3a). In this manner, the opening verses of this material raise high expectations from the Chronicler's readers. If Josiah was loyal to God from such a young age, what great things did he accomplish as an adult? The Chronicler's account turns directly to these great accomplishments.

Josiah's Fidelity in Worship Reforms (34:3b-35:19)
The Chronicler first reported the positive reforms that took place under Josiah's direction. Similar reforms took place at other points in Judah's history (see *Introduction: 6) Royal Observance of Worship*). Here the text highlights the extensive and enduring quality of these changes.

Comparison of 34:3b-35:19 with 2 Kgs. 22:3-20; 23:1-27
As noted above, the greatest difference between this portion of Chronicles and Kings is that the Chronicler rearranged the order of the presentation. Kings reports the events in this order: discovery of Book (2 Kgs. 22:3-20), covenant renewal (2 Kgs. 23:1-5), reforms (2 Kgs. 23:6-20) and Passover (2 Kgs. 23:21-27). Chronicles, however, presents these events in this manner: reforms (34:4-7), discovery of Book (34:8-28), covenant renewal (34:29-33), Passover (35:1-19). No historical conflict exists between these accounts. The writer of Kings merely moved his account of the discovery of the Book forward to highlight it (perhaps the book of Deuteronomy) as the main event of Josiah's reforms.

To understand the Chronicler's outlook, we should also note at this point that his account is governed by a definite chronological framework. To begin with, the Chronicler added a notice in 34:3b that Josiah's reforms began **in his twelfth year**. This point in time is to be distinguished from the temporal note of 34:8 (// 2 Kgs. 22:3) that the cleansing of the temple began **in the eighteenth year** which forms an inclusio with the remark that the Passover also occurred **in the eighteenth year** (35:19 // 2 Kgs. 23:23).

These chronological notes combine with the Chronicler's rearrangement of material to shape Josiah's reforms into two stages: those changes that took place in year twelve and those that took place in year eighteen.

Structure 34:3b-35:19

The Chronicler's variations from Kings result in the following outline (see figure 61). Josiah's reform efforts divide into his earlier (34:3b-7) and later (34:8-35:19) efforts. As we will see below, the king's early reforms cover his work in the South (34:3b-5) and the North (34:6-7). The king's later reforms are more complex. They divide into a large dramatic structure involving the repair of the temple (34:8-13), covenant renewal (34:14-33), and the celebration of Passover (35:1-19).

Josiah's Earlier Reforms (34:3b-7)

The Chronicler first reported the reforms Josiah began to perform **in his twelfth year** (34:3b). This chronological notice separates this material from events in **his eighth year** (34:3a) and in **the eighteenth year** (34:8).

Comparison of 34:3b-7 with 2 Kgs. 23:6-20

A number of significant differences appear between Kings and Chronicles at this point. First, we have already noted that the Chronicler moved this material from after the discovery of the book and covenant renewal (2 Kgs. 22:3-23:5) to a position before these events. He also added the notice that these events took place **in his twelfth year** (34:3b) to make his chronological framework clear.

Second, a number of smaller additions occur.

1) The Chronicler noted the destruction of **altars of the Baals** and their **incense altars** (34:4).

2) He clarified that the expression 'graves of the common people' (2 Kgs. 23:6) meant **the graves of those who had sacrificed to** [idols] (34:4).

3) To divide his record into events in the South and then in the North, the Chronicler added a description of events in the North (34:6-7).

Third, some details of Josiah's reforms (2 Kgs. 23:7-16a, 17-18) are omitted.

1) In usual fashion, references to cult prostitutes operating in the temple do not appear (2 Kgs. 23:7 see 1 Kgs. 14:24; 15:12; 22:46).

2) The list of specific foreign gods which Josiah destroyed is absent (2 Kgs. 23:8-14). The reason for this omission is not evident.

3) In order to divide the record between events in the North and South, the Chronicler also omitted Josiah's destruction of the altar at Bethel (2 Kgs. 23:15-16a, 17-18) and changed the focus of burning priests' bones in Bethel to his similar actions in Judah (34:5 // 2 Kgs. 23:16b).

Structure 34:3b-7

The result of these variations from Kings is that Chronicles presents a much simpler record (see figure 61). Josiah's reforms are described in reports concerning changes in the South (34:3b-5) and in the North (34:6-7).

Reforms in the South (34:3b-5)

The focus of the first set of reports (34:3b-5) appears explicitly in the repetition of phrases in 34:3b and 5. In both verses the Chronicler mentioned that Josiah began to **purge Judah and Jerusalem**. Two vignettes describe the king's actions in the southern kingdom. These scenes overlap to some extent, but they have distinctive features.

First, Josiah got rid of **high places** in Judah with their various **Asherah poles** ... **idols** ... **images** ... **altars of the Baals** ... and **incense altars** (34:3b-4). Like several kings before him (see 11:15; 21:11; 28:4), Josiah destroyed the syncretistic worship sites in Judah (see *Introduction: 6) Royal Observance of Worship*).

Second, the king **burned the bones of the priests on their altars** (34:5). In this verse, the Chronicler paraphrased the notice of similar actions in the North (see 2 Kgs. 23:15-18). The Chronicler, however, applied them to Josiah's actions in Judah. Josiah executed the false priests following the examples of Jehu (2 Kgs. 10:11) and Jehoiada (23:17 // 2 Kgs. 11:18). The apostate priests of Josiah's day were subject to severe punishment for leading the people of Judah astray (Deut. 13:1-5).

Reforms in the North (34:6-7)

The Chronicler turned briefly to Josiah's reforms in the northern kingdom. Like Jehoshaphat and Hezekiah (2 Chr. 19:4; 31:1), Josiah sought to reform worship in the North as well as in the South (see *Introduction: 6) Royal Observance of Worship*). The Assyrian empire was weak during this time of Josiah's reign. As a result, Josiah had the freedom to extend his religious reforms into the North.

The record of Kings is expanded to identify specific tribes touched by Josiah's efforts (34:6-7). In language that alludes to Hezekiah sending couriers throughout the North (see 30:10), Josiah's reforms reached **towns of Manasseh, Ephraim and Simeon, as far as Naphtali** (34:6). His efforts were felt **throughout Israel** (34:7) to the point that contributions from all of these tribes were brought to the temple (34:9).

The Chronicler's distinct emphasis on the extent of Josiah's reforms drew a firm connection between Josiah and Hezekiah. After the fall of the Northern kingdom to Assyria (722 BC), these two kings saw their religious responsibilities extending beyond the borders of Judah. From the Chronicler's point of view, the Passover celebration under Hezekiah had brought a symbolic unity to the nation. He had this unity in view as he reported Josiah's early reforms in the North.

Josiah's actions challenged the Chronicler's post-exilic readers in at least two ways. They should see their need to reform the religious practices of Jerusalem. Whatever syncretistic practices had crept into their community must be eradicated (see Ezra 9:1-15; Neh. 13:23-30). Even so, Josiah's example showed that religious reform was not to be limited to the southern region alone. They must look northward in their day even as Josiah did in his reign.

Josiah's Later Reforms (34:8-35:19)

The Chronicler continued his focus on Josiah's reforms by moving to his renewal of the temple services. During the reign of Amon, Manasseh's reforms were reversed and the temple was filled with foreign gods once again (see 33:22). Josiah brought the temple back to his proper order and celebrated a national Passover much like that of Hezekiah (see 30:1-31:1). The Chronicler separated this material from its surrounding context by several chronological notes. He began by stating that these events took place **in the eighteenth year** (34:8) and closed with the reminder that Josiah's celebration was **in the eighteenth year** (35:19).

Comparison of 34:8-35:19 with 2 Kgs. 22:3-20; 23:1-5; 23:21-27

As we noted above (see figure 60), the Chronicler has shifted the order of the record of Kings to arrange events along a chronological framework. For the most part, the Chronicler's record of these events follows the parallels in Kings. As we will see, however, at a number of points significant variations occur in each section.

Structure of 34:8-35:19

This material divides into three symmetrical sections (see figure 61). Josiah began repairing the temple only to encounter the threat of curses in the book discovered in the temple (34:8-13). This difficulty was corrected by Josiah's covenant renewal in which he reaffirmed his determination to obey the Law of God (34:14-33). As a result of this recommitment, Josiah was able to complete the renewal of the temple and to lead the nation in a grand celebration of Passover (35:1-19).

Josiah Repairs the Temple (34:8-13)

Having established general reforms throughout the land from his twelfth year, Josiah began major repairs on the temple. This effort took the king's reforms to new heights.

Comparison of 34:8-13 with 2 Kgs. 22:3-7

A cursory comparison of Chronicles and Kings indicates that the Chronicler depended heavily on 2 Kgs. 22:3-7. A number of small variations, however, bring the Chronicler's distinctive emphases into view.

First, the Chronicler added some details to provide more information than Kings. 1) In 34:8a (// 2 Kgs. 22:3) he added that the temple renovations took place **to purify the land and the temple**. The Chronicler had already given account of these reforms (34:3b-7). 2) In 34:8b (// 2 Kgs. 22:3) he mentioned the names of more people leading temple renovations.

Second, the Chronicler omitted the comment that no auditing was required of those in charge of purchases (2 Kgs. 22:7). This omission may have been motivated by contemporary concerns about the need for auditing those in charge of such matters in the post-exilic community.

Third, in four places the Chronicler varied from Kings in order to stress his characteristic concerns.

1) He gave the Levites a more important role in these events. For instance, he stated explicitly that those who collected funds for the temple were **Levites** (34:9 // 2 Kgs. 22:4). Moreover, he added the names of Levites who worked in the renovation effort (34:12-13).

2) The Chronicler emphasized the breadth of support for Josiah's efforts by shifting from 'the people' (2 Kgs. 22:4) to an enumeration of various tribes, including northern Israelites who were involved (34:9b).

3) In 34:11b the Chronicler demonstrated his interest in the broader temple complex by reporting that funds were not simply used 'to repair the temple' (2 Kgs. 22:5). They also paid for materials used **for the buildings that the kings of Judah had allowed to fall into ruin** (34:11b).

4) Josiah's role in temple renovations is emphasized. In 2 Kgs. 22:4, Josiah's men were to have Hilkiah 'get ready the money that has been brought into the temple'. The Chronicler, however, made it clear that these representatives of the throne virtually **gave him the money that had been brought into the temple** (34:9). In this way the text highlights royal support for the temple.

Structure of 34:8-13

The Chronicler's record of these events divides into five symmetrical steps followed by an afterword (see figure 61). This episode begins with Josiah sending men to supervise the repair of the temple (34:8) and ends with the repairs being completed (34:12a). The middle portions of the story focus on the money used in the effort. The supervisors designate money for repairs (34:9). This money is spent for materials and laborers (34:10b-11). The turning point of the episode consists of the money being given to the supervisors of the work (34:10a). The final scene (34:12a) is expanded by an afterword concerning the names of Levites who supervised the laborers (34:12b-13).

Initiation of Temple Repairs (34:8)

Josiah commissioned supervisors for repair work on the temple (34:8). The Chronicler had a slightly different list of these men than Kings (// 2 Kgs. 22:3), but both texts make it plain that these men were civilian leaders. Both **the ruler of the city** of Jerusalem and **the recorder** (or financial accountant) were among those who represented the king's interests (34:8). In Judah and other ancient Near Eastern cultures, it was usual for monarchs to be involved in temple building and renovation (see 1 Chr. 28:1-29:9; 2 Chr. 2:1-5:1; see also *Introduction: 24) Building and Destruction*). From the Chronicler's perspective every ideal king had the temple as a high priority of his reign. For this reason, he noted that Josiah specifically commissioned his representatives **to repair the temple**.

Money Designated for Temple Repairs (34:9)

The first task of Josiah's representatives was to authorize **Hilkiah the high priest** to use funds for temple renovation. Hilkiah appears in the Chronicler's genealogies (see 1 Chr. 6:13). He played a major role in the events that follow this episode (see

34:14-28). As high priest, he had charge of the renovations of the temple.

The record of 2 Kgs. 24:4 makes it clear that Josiah's representatives did not actually give money to Hilkiah from the royal treasuries. They gave him permission 'to get ready the money' that had already been brought to the temple. As noted above, the Chronicler wrote that these men **gave him money**, but his words must be understood in the sense of approving or designating the collection. The money in view was not a gift from Josiah; it **had been brought into the temple of God**.

The Chronicler highlighted the role of Levites in these affairs. He added to 2 Kgs. 22:4 that these monies had been collected by **the Levites**. He described these same Levites as **doorkeepers**. Thus the text focuses on funds collected at the temple gates (see 2 Kgs. 22:4), but other revenue may have been gathered by Levites who traveled outside Jerusalem. Both methods were used to gather funds in Joash's time (see 24:5-6,8-9).

The Chronicler also emphasized the broad base of support for Josiah's efforts. 2 Kgs. 22:4 simply reports that the money came 'from the people'. The Chronicler expanded this statement to include **all the people from Manasseh, Ephraim and the entire remnant of Israel and from all the people of Judah and Benjamin and the inhabitants of Jerusalem**. Earlier he had noted that Josiah's reforms extended far beyond the boundaries of Jerusalem (34:6-7); now the financial support for temple renovations came from all of these tribes.

By expanding his record in this manner the Chronicler highlighted the ideal nature of Josiah's temple renovation. The entire nation supported the effort just as all the tribes should support the post-exilic re-establishment of the temple and its services (see *Introduction: 1) All Israel*; see also *9) Temple Contributions*).

Money Given to Supervisors (34:10a)

Once Hilkiah had designated money for the work, he distributed it to **the men appointed to supervise the work**. We learn later that these men were Levites (see 34:12b-13). They served under the direction of Hilkiah and dealt with the practical matters related to temple renovation.

This detail which the Chronicler derived from 2 Kgs. 22:5 fit well with his interest in the diversity of duties among priests and Levites. As in many passages, he made it clear that the Levites were to serve under the direction of the Zadokite priesthood (see *Introduction: Appendix A: The Families of Levi*).

Money Paid for Temple Repairs (34:10b-11)

The supervisors of the laborers **paid the workers** (34:10b). The monies were used precisely as Josiah had ordered. The Chronicler omitted 2 Kgs. 22:7 which indicates that no auditing was necessary because of the honesty of these supervisors. While accounting may not have been necessary at that time, the Chronicler apparently did not want to suggest that this practice be imitated in his day.

In 34:11 the Chronicler varied from 2 Kgs. 22:6 by focusing on the repairs of **the building that the kings of Judah had allowed to fall into ruin**. Here he probably had in mind the storehouses and treasuries in the temple complex (see 1 Chr. 26:20; 2 Chr. 5:1; 16:2). Just as he highlighted Hezekiah's focus on these structures (see 31:11-12), this broader concern reveals the Chronicler's encouragement to his post-exilic readers that they should devote themselves to restoring all the buildings and services of the temple.

Completion of Temple Repairs (34:12a)

The Chronicler added a new ending to this episode. He simply stated that **the men did the work faithfully** (34:12a). No disputes interrupted the work. Josiah's desire to see the temple repaired was accomplished by the full cooperation of priests, Levites, and workers. This simple statement raised yet another element in the Chronicler's desire for his readers. They must be eager to cooperate in completing their temple efforts as well.

Afterword Concerning Levitical Supervisors (34:12b-13)

The Chronicler added an afterword to this episode. In this material he named a number of Levites who supervised the renovations of the temple. Interestingly enough, he noted that the Levites in charge were **all who were skilled in playing musical instruments** (34:12b see 1 Chr. 15:22; 25:7; see also *Introduction: 8) Music*) and others were **secretaries, scribes and doorkeepers** (34:13). Levites supervised renovation projects in other settings as well (see 1 Chr. 26:20; 2 Chr. 24:5; 29:4-5). In the ancient Near East musicians often played for construction workers, but here they have more of a supervisory role. It is likely that these details addressed particular questions rising from controversies among the Levites in the post-exilic community. By appealing to this example, the Chronicler insisted that certain divisions of Levites were to have supervisory roles in temple service in his own day.

Josiah Renews Covenant (34:14-33)

Having described how Josiah repaired the temple, the Chronicler narrowed his focus to a major event that took place during the renovations. He reported the discovery of the **Book of the Law of the LORD** (34:14) and the covenant renewal that took place in response to the Book.

Comparison of 34:14-33 with 2 Kgs. 22:8-23:3

On several occasions Chronicles paraphrases Kings, but for no obvious reason. A number of other differences are best accounted for as problems in textual transmission. Nevertheless, some variations deserve special attention.

First, the opening verse (34:14) is added to the account of Kings. It provides a temporal orientation to the events that follow by setting them within Josiah's temple renovations.

Second, Shaphan's report to Josiah is expanded in Chronicles to read **'Your officials are doing everything that has been committed to them'** (34:16). This variation highlights the exemplary character of Josiah's restoration of the temple.

Third, in 2 Kgs. 22:13 Josiah ordered inquiry 'for me and for the people and for all Judah'. The Chronicler, however, shifted this language to **for me and for the remnant in Israel and Judah** (Hebrew = 'and in Judah' [NRS, NKJ]). Here the Chronicler's perspective on the 'remnant' moves to the foreground.

Fourth, the Chronicler clarified the focus of Huldah's prophecy. In Kings she said, 'everything written in the Book' (2 Kgs. 22:16). Chronicles reads **all the curses written in the book** (34:24).

Fifth, the Chronicler expanded the prophetic response to Josiah's repentance by repeating his 'humbling' motif twice in the same verse. He added, **and you humbled yourself before God** (Hebrew = 'before me', 34:27). The Chronicler frequently used the terminology of 'humbling' to describe the act of genuine repentance (see *Introduction: 18) Humility*).

Structure 34:14-33

The Chronicler's text is so similar to Kings that the structure of this passage is not greatly influenced by his variations. This material divides into a symmetrical three step pattern (see figure 61). The symmetry of this episode is evident. It begins with Josiah realizing Judah's sins through the reading of the Book (34:14-21). It ends with Josiah and the nation renewing commitment to righteousness according to the Book (34:29-33). The turning point of the story concerns the prophecy which Huldah gave to the King (34:22-28).

Josiah Recognizes Sin through the Book (34:14-21)

The Chronicler begins this portion of his record with Josiah facing the severity of sin in Judah. As he discovered, the sins of the nation were great.

Structure 34:14-21

As noted in figure 61 above, the opening of this material divides into three steps. This story develops from the discovery of the Book (34:14-15) to Josiah's humble reaction (34:19-21). Between these events lies the scene in which Josiah heard the Book (34:16-18).

Josiah's Leaders Discover the Book (34:14-15)

The Chronicler expanded the beginning of this section to provide a setting for this narrative. He noted that these events took place **while they were bringing out the money that had been taken into the temple of the LORD** (34:14). The nearest antecedent of **they** is the Levitical supervisors mentioned in 34:12-13. We can be sure that money was brought out many times during temple renovations. Yet, at some point these Levites carried out their supervisory tasks and a major event took place.

Hilkiah the priest, who was in charge of all the temple renovations (see 34:9), **found the Book of the Law of the LORD that had been given through Moses** (34:14). It is not possible to determine the identity of this book with complete certainty. Two proposals are common.

First, some interpreters have argued that the Book was the entire Pentateuch. The Pentateuch is called the 'Torah' or 'Law of Moses' in the biblical tradition (see Dan. 9:13; Mal. 4:4; Luke 2:22; 24:44; John 1:45; Matt. 7:12; 11:13; 22:40). It seems unlikely that the entire Pentateuch would have been referred to as a single Book at this time, but this possibility cannot be ruled out.

Second, it is more common to identify this book as Deuteronomy. A number of evidences point in this direction.

1) This story comes from the book of Kings which depends heavily on Deuteronomy as its standard for evaluating the kings of Israel and Judah.

2) This book is called **the Book of the Covenant** (34:30), a designation that may have reflected the concentration of covenantal motifs in Deuteronomy (but note also Exod. 24:7).

3) Deuteronomy has lists of curses (see Deut. 27:9-26; 28:15-68) which may explain the Chronicler's focus on **the curses written in the book** (34:24).

4) The centralization of worship and the exclusion of high places are important themes in Deuteronomy (see Deut. 12:2-5). These motifs guided Josiah's reforms (34:33).

5) The Passover is emphasized in Deut. 16:1-8 as it was in Josiah's reforms (35:1-19).

In the final analysis, it seems likely that Hilkiah discovered the Book of Deuteronomy.

This reference is one of the few clues as to how sacred texts in ancient Israel were kept safe. Apparently, the **Book of the Law** had been stored within the temple and was forgotten during the days of Amon (see 33:21-24), and perhaps even during the reign of Manasseh (see 33:1-20). While other books may have also been kept in royal archives, apparently this **Book of the Law** had not been in Josiah's possession. As a result, when temple service was neglected the result was that the Scriptures of Israel were also neglected.

Upon discovering this book, Hilkiah reported to his superior, **Shaphan the secretary** (34:15a). Josiah had sent Shaphan to give royal supervision to the collection and distribution of funds (34:8). He reported directly to the king. Hilkiah realized that the Book had important implications for Josiah's kingdom. For this reason, he **gave it to Shaphan.**

Josiah Hears the Book (34:16-18)

Shaphan brought an official report to Josiah, but he may not have realized the significance of Hilkiah's discovery. He did not mention the Book until after a general description of the work's progress. Moreover, when he introduced the subject of the Book, he did not use Hilkiah's words, **the Book of the Law** (34:15). Instead, it simply referred to it as **a book**, or 'some book' as it might be translated (34:16). Despite Shaphan's indifference, Josiah realized that the Book had an important message for his kingdom.

Shaphan began with an account of the work in general. The Chronicler's version of Shaphan's report is very similar to 2 Kgs. 22:9-11. One notable exception is the additional information that [the] **officials are doing everything that has been committed to them** (34:16a). The Chronicler added these words to present the reform effort as a model for his post-exilic readers. The priests and Levites were fully cooperative with the royal program of reform, even as they should be in the Chronicler's day. In addition to this general report on the progress of work, Shaphan informed the king of Hilkiah's discovery. He said that Hilkiah had given him **a book** and he **read from it in the presence of the king** (34:18).

Josiah Reacts to the Book (34:19-21)

After hearing Shaphan read, Josiah reacts (34:19-21). In a context where reform is going well, the text surprisingly reports that Josiah heard **the words of the Law** and **tore his robes** (34:19). Huldah later referred to this act as an aspect of Josiah's sincere contrition (see 34:27). Throughout Scriptures heart-felt repentance expressed itself by the tearing of clothing (see 1 Kgs. 21:27; Isa. 36:22; 37:1) and other similar physical actions (see Ezra 9:3; Job 1:20; Jon. 3:6). Josiah's reaction demonstrated the depth of his commitment to the Law of God, a motif that appears frequently in Chronicles (see *Introduction: 14) Standards*).

Josiah also ordered the leaders of his reforms to **go and inquire of the LORD** (34:21). Although this phrase derives from 2 Kgs. 22:13, it fits well with the Chronicler's theological use of this terminology. 'Seeking' or 'inquiring' of God alludes to the promise of God given to Solomon in 7:14. It is frequently one of the chief characteristics of those who find the blessing of God (see *Introduction: 19) Seeking*). In this case, to **inquire of the LORD** meant specifically to ask for prophetic insight into the situation (34:22).

The Chronicler changed the wording of Josiah's order in 2 Kgs. 22:13 to express his view of the condition of Judah and Israel at this time. Josiah ordered an inquiry **for** [himself] **and for the remnant in Israel and** [in] **Judah** (34:21). In this context, the term **remnant** had both negative and positive connotations. On one side, Josiah referred to those remaining in Israel and Judah as a remnant because warfare in Israel and Judah in previous years had so decimated the population (see 2 Kgs. 17:3-5; 2 Chr. 28:5b-8; 32:1; 33:11,24-25). On the other side, the term **remnant** had the positive connotation of future potential. From the time of Hezekiah the remnant of North and South had been reunited under the leadership of David's sons. Those who remained were the root of Israel's future glory. Josiah appears to have focused largely on the negative sense of this terminology (34:21b), but his reform efforts demonstrate that the positive dimension was not far from his thoughts.

The implications of this change for the Chronicler's readers is evident. They too were the remnant of Israel and Judah. Similar negative and positive connotations applied to them as they contemplated their own condition.

Josiah emphasized the importance of this inquiry by acknowledging that **the LORD's anger ... is poured out on us** (34:21). Israel and Judah had experienced divine judgment time and again. The reason for this divine anger was that their **fathers have not kept the word of the LORD ... that is written in this book**. As Shaphan read the warnings of Deuteronomy to Josiah, the king realized that both the North and South were suffering the results of serious infidelity. This realization caused Josiah to wonder what would now happen to him and his kingdom. For this reason, he sent his men to seek prophetic instruction.

Josiah's decision to consult a prophet points to one of the primary functions of prophets in Israel. The king already knew from the reading of the Book that he and the nation were deserving of divine curses. Yet, this general knowledge did not help him understand how these curses were going to be applied to his specific situation. To have this kind of understanding, he needed a prophetic oracle. In this light, we see one of the central functions of prophets. They mediated between the general principles of the Scriptural blessings and curses and the specific historical situations, explaining how God would enforce his covenant sanctions (see *Introduction: 15) Prophets*).

Josiah Receives Prophecy about the Book (34:22-28)

The narrative continues with an episode describing the prophecy of Huldah in response to Josiah's inquiry.

Structure of 34:22-28

This material divides into three balanced sections (see figure 61). The leaders first approach Huldah (34:22). She speaks to them (34:23-28a) and they leave the prophetess (34:28b).

Josiah's Leaders Approach Huldah (34:22)

Josiah's commission was that his men **speak to the prophetess Huldah** (34:22). Huldah is identified several ways here.

1) She is called a **prophetess**, one of four female prophets in the Old Testament (see Exod. 15:20; Judg. 4:4; Neh. 6:14). It is interesting to note that although a number of well-known prophets were ministering at this time, Josiah's men went to the prophetess instead.

2) Huldah is further specified as **the wife of Shallum**, descendant of **the keeper of the wardrobe** (34:22). This is the only place in the Hebrew Bible where this precise occupational terminology appears. It may refer to the service of maintaining priestly and Levitical garments or it may refer to him simply as a tailor.

3) Huldah is said to have lived **in the Second District** (34:22). The identity of this area is uncertain. It is possible that it refers to the 'second quarter' of the city (see Zeph. 1:10; Neh. 11:9).

Josiah's Men Receive Prophecy (34:23-28a)

Huldah responded to Josiah's representatives with two oracles in 34:23-25 and 34:26-28. The first follows the form of an oracle of judgment (34:23-25); the second amounts to an oracle of deliverance or salvation (34:26-28). In a word, Huldah confirmed that the judgments of the Book would come to Judah, but she also assured Josiah that they would not come upon the nation during his lifetime.

Huldah's oracle of judgment (34:23-25) divides into a preliminary instruction (34:23), followed by a messenger formula (34:24a), sentencing (34:24b), accusation (34:25a) and a second sentencing (34:25b).

The prophetess first instructed Josiah's representatives that they are to **tell the man who sent** them her words of judgment (34:23). She then announced that her message was **from the LORD** (34:24a).

The first sentencing (34:24b) consisted of assurances that God was **going to bring disaster on this place**. This disaster is explained in an addition from the Chronicler's hand as **all the curses written in the book**. Huldah made it plain from the outset that the nation had been sentenced to the curses of the covenant, the greatest of which was exile (see Deut. 4:27-28; 27:1-29:25-28).

Huldah moved to the reasons for this sentence in the form of accusation (34:25a). Although this accusation appeared from 2 Kgs. 22:17, it fit well with the Chronicler's own theological vocabulary. The prophetess said, **'they have forsaken [God]'** (34:25a). To 'forsake' is to become disloyal to the Lord and to seek help either in human strength or other gods (see *Introduction: 22) Abandoning/Forsaking*). Here the prophetess specified that the nation had **burned incense to other gods**.

The prophetess then moved to a second sentencing. Because of the nation's idolatry God's **anger will be poured out on this place and will not be quenched** (34:25b). In other words, Jerusalem will be utterly destroyed. The record of Kings already brought this matter to the foreground in the reigns of Hezekiah (see 2 Kgs. 20:16-18) and Manasseh (see 2 Kgs. 21:12-15), but the Chronicler omitted these passages. Perhaps he waited until this time when his record focused on Josiah's concern for the **remnant in Israel and** (in) **Judah** (34:9) to make it clear that the destruction of Jerusalem and the exile were experienced by the entire remnant to which his readers traced their heritage.

Despite the terrible prediction of eventual judgment against Jerusalem, Huldah offered some relief to Josiah in her second oracle (34:26-28). This message followed the pattern of an oracle of salvation or deliverance (34:26-28a). It began with an introductory instruction (34:26a), and a messenger formula (34:26b) which were followed by a justification and statement of hope (34:27), as well as an elaboration (34:28).

The instruction and messenger formula are very similar to the first oracle (34:26; see 34:23-24a). Huldah said that Josiah's representatives were to **tell the king of Judah, who sent** [them] **to inquire of the LORD**. The mention of 'inquiring' or 'seeking' implied from the outset an approval of Josiah's actions (see *Introduction: 19) Seeking*). Huldah also made it plain that her second oracle was also from God. She claimed only to say **what the LORD says concerning the words you have heard**, i.e. the words of the Book (34:23-25). Thus, Huldah had more to say about the application of the covenant curses to Josiah.

Huldah's second message to Josiah was much more positive than the first. The reason for this shift is stated forcefully. Huldah acknowledged on God's behalf, **'Your heart was responsive and you humbled yourself ... you humbled yourself ... and tore your robes and wept in my presence'** (34:27). The prophetess began with the king's heart, an issue that was very important for the Chronicler (see *Introduction: 16) Motivations*). Josiah's deep conviction led to humility, a motif the Chronicler's addition causes to be repeated twice here (see *Introduction: 18) Humility*). As an earlier scene reported, Josiah ripped his clothes in mourning and he wept before God (34:19, 27). These actions demonstrated the sincerity of Josiah's repentance and regret for the sins of the nation. Because of this sincerity, God declared, **'I have heard you'** (34:27). In other words, God announced his intention to respond favorably to Josiah's contrition.

The initial declaration of divine benevolence toward Josiah was followed by an elaboration of the blessing Josiah would receive (34:28a). First, God said the king **will be buried in peace** (34:28a). This promise is somewhat problematic because Josiah actually died in battle (see 35:20-24). For this reason, the second element of blessing should be taken as an explanation of the meaning of the first. Josiah will die **in peace** in the sense that he **will not see all the disaster ... on this place and on those who live there** (34:28a). In other words, Josiah will not experience the downfall of Jerusalem. Although the judgment against Jerusalem was not reversed, King Josiah's repentance postponed the destruction of the city to a future generation and permitted him to experience the blessing of peace (see *Introduction: 23) Victory and Defeat*). Similar mercy was shown to Hezekiah in his day (see 32:26).

Josiah's Leaders Return from Huldah (34:28b)

To close off this section, the text reports that Josiah's representatives brought Huldah's words **back to the king**. This final scene balances with the opening of this episode (34:22). Josiah's men fulfilled their task.

Josiah Renews Covenant According to the Book (34:29-33)

Once Josiah's men brought Huldah's words back to him, the king determined to renew covenant with the Lord.

Structure of 34:29-33

The Chronicler's record of this event divides into three scenes (see figure 61). The first scene depicts Josiah gathering the nation for covenant renewal (34:29-30a). This scene is balanced by the completion of covenant renewal (34:31-33). The turning point of this episode is Josiah's reading from the Book (34:30b).

Josiah's covenant renewal followed the pattern established in Exod. 24:3-7. There the people gathered (verses 3-7), the Book of the Covenant was read (verse 7) and the people unanimously committed themselves to obedience to the Law of God (verse 7b).

Josiah Gathers Nation for Covenant Renewal (34:29-30a)
The first step in Josiah's renewal of the covenant was to gather **all the elders of Judah and Jerusalem** (34:29) and to go **up to the temple** (34:30). The text emphasizes that this was no small band of followers. Along with the elders were **the men of Judah, the people of Jerusalem, the priests and the Levites** (compare 'the prophets' [2 Kgs. 23:2]). The Chronicler frequently associated Levites with prophetic functions in the worship of Israel. (For the Chronicler's view of Levites as prophets, see comments on 1 Chr. 25:1.) Put simply, **all the people** assembled, **from the least to the greatest** (34:30). Josiah's humble response to the Book motivated large crowds of people to join him at **the temple of the LORD** (34:30).

Although this material stems from 2 Kgs. 23:1-2, it suited well the Chronicler's frequent emphasis on widespread national support for the actions of righteous kings (see *Introduction: 1) All Israel*). In this way, he used Josiah's covenant renewal as another model for his post-exilic readers. They too were in need of national covenant renewal.

Josiah Reads the Book (34:30b)
The actual ceremony of covenant renewal first required the reading of the Law. Josiah **read in their hearing all the words of the Book of the Covenant**. The text makes it clear that this terminology refers to the Book **which had been found in the temple**. Although this is the only time when the Book receives this name, the covenantal character of Deuteronomy certainly warrants this designation. Perhaps this title was intended to draw attention to the similarities between this event and the pattern of Exodus 24 where the 'Book of the Covenant' played such an important role (see Exod. 24:7). The Chronicler's interest in covenant renewal in the post-exilic community may have caused him to maintain this designation from Kings (see *Introduction: 13) Covenant*).

Josiah and the Nation Renew Covenant (34:31-33)
Following the reading of the Book, Josiah **renewed the covenant** (34:31). The text describes the nature of this covenant renewal in some detail. First, it speaks of Josiah's commitment **to follow the LORD and keep his commands**. The king recommitted himself to obedience to the full range of the Mosaic Law. Second, Josiah made this commitment **with all his heart and all his soul**. Here the text points to Josiah's sincerity and deep devotion to the Law in ways which the Chronicler emphasized throughout his history (see *Introduction: 16) Motivations*). Third, the focus narrows to the specific Book that sparked this revival. Josiah devoted himself to the goal of obeying **the words of the covenant written in this book** (34:31).

Beyond Josiah's personal commitment, 2 Kgs. 23:3b reads, 'Then all the people pledged themselves to the covenant.' The Chronicler omitted these words and added a more descriptive elaboration on the same theme in 34:32-33. In order to demonstrate that the entire nation joined Josiah, he added that Josiah brought about renewed commitments from **everyone in Jerusalem and Benjamin** (34:32) as well as **all who were present in Israel** (34:33). In agreement with the covenant, the king **removed all the detestable idols** that were found in **all the territory belonging to the Israelites**. Both in the South and North, Josiah enforced the covenant among the people of God.

The closing words of the Chronicler's addition displays his estimation of Josiah's efforts. Judah and Israel remained faithful to the covenant **as long as he lived** (34:33). Josiah's reforms lasted his entire life.

The Chronicler's version of Josiah's covenant renewal spoke directly to the needs of his post-exilic readers. They too were in need of reviewing the Law of God and renewing their loyalties to the covenant. Such renewal, however, must include the leadership, the inhabitants of Jerusalem, Judahites and all other Israelites (see *Introduction: 13) Covenant*).

Josiah Observes Passover (35:1-19)

The final event of Josiah's eighteenth year was his observance of Passover. This event represents the height of Josiah's efforts to re-establish proper worship in Jerusalem. Having recounted how the king readied the temple (34:8-13) and renewed the covenant (34:29-32), the Chronicler turned to the Passover of Josiah's reign.

Comparison of 35:1-19 with 2 Kgs. 23:21-27

In this passage, the Chronicler greatly expanded the record of 2 Kgs. 23:21-27. The relative sizes of the accounts indicates the importance which the Chronicler placed on Josiah's Passover. The Chronicler's distinctive concerns appear by comparing the two accounts (see figure 62).

2 Chr.		2 Kgs.
35:1a	Introduction to Passover (loosely parallel)	23:21
35:1b-17	Preparations and Ceremonies (added)	———
35:18-19	Summary of Passover (slightly expanded)	23:22-23
———	Josiah's Further Reforms	23:24-27

Comparison of 2 Chr. 35:1-19 and 2 Kgs. 23:21-27 (figure 62)

A number of significant points of comparison should be noted. First, the Chronicler began this material by paraphrasing the opening of 2 Kgs. 23:21 (// 35:1a) so that Josiah's Passover is idealized. Second, the greatest difference between the two accounts is the Chronicler's additional details on how Josiah celebrated the event

(35:1b-17). Third, he also expanded the summary of the event (35:18-19 // 2 Kgs. 23:22-23), noting that Josiah's Passover was greater than all others because it was kept by so many of the people. Fourth, the Chronicler omitted Josiah's further reforms after Passover (2 Kgs. 23:24-27) in order to keep the celebration itself as the climax of the king's efforts.

Structure of 35:1-19

The Chronicler's expansion of the record of Kings formed his account into four symmetrical parts (see figure 61). The opening (35:1) and closing (35:16-19) of this passage form general statements that describe the Passover in its entirety and frame the middle portion. As a result, the middle portion regresses chronologically and explains some of the details of the preparations (35:2-9) and performance (35:10-15).

Josiah's Passover Introduced (35:1)

The Chronicler paraphrased 2 Kgs. 23:21 as he opened his account of Josiah's Passover. His record specified a number of details not appearing in Kings that raise the celebration to the level of a model for his readers (see *Introduction: 27) Disappointment and Celebration*).

First, he noted that the Passover was observed **in Jerusalem**, the city which formed the center of religious life in the post-exilic period. In Hezekiah's previous celebration of Passover, the Chronicler gave much attention to the fact that the king sent couriers with invitations to encourage all the tribes to come to Jerusalem (see 30:5-6). In Josiah's case, no record of such an invitation appears, but it is evident that the Chronicler was concerned that his readers remember that Jerusalem was the only place Passover was to be observed.

Second, the Chronicler added that the slaughtering of the Passover lamb took place **on the fourteenth day of the first month.** The most likely reason for this notice is the contrast it presents with Hezekiah's celebration. Hezekiah observed Passover during the second month because preparations could not be made soon enough (see 30:2-3). Josiah, however, was able to commemorate the event as decreed in the Mosaic Law (Exod. 12:18; Lev. 23:5; Num. 28:16). By this means, the Chronicler not only made it clear that Hezekiah's practice was unusual; he also exalted Josiah's celebration as a model for his post-exilic readers.

Josiah's Preparations for Celebration (35:2-9)

These verses present a chronological regression. As we have seen, the opening verse of this material (35:1) focuses on the day of the Passover slaughter. Now we come to events that preceded the fourteenth day. As a result, it would be appropriate to translate the verbs in this section as past perfects ('**he** had **appointed** ... **and** had **encouraged** ... **He** had **said** ...' etc.).

Structure of 35:2-9

This material divides into two reports of Josiah's preparations for the actual slaughtering of the Passover lambs (see figure 61). He first prepared the priests and Levites (35:2-6) and then the sacrifices (35:7-9).

Josiah Readies Priests and Levites (35:2-6)

The Chronicler focused first on Josiah's appointment of priests and Levites to perform Passover duties. This material presents two concerns: the appointment of priests (35:2), and the exhortation to the Levites (35:3-6).

Josiah **appointed the priests to their duties** (35:2). The king had already interacted intensely with the priesthood during the renovations of the temple (see 34:9,14). It is unlikely that his widespread reforms took place without their help. Here the Chronicler had in view the appointment of priests to specific duties related to the Passover. Josiah **encouraged them in the services of the LORD's temple** (35:2). That is, he instructed them to perform their duties in relation to the Levite divisions he ordered for the celebration (see 35:10).

Along with the priests, Josiah also exhorted the Levites (35:3-6). The Chronicler's record of Josiah's exhortation divides into an introduction (35:3a) and the exhortation itself (35:3b-6).

The introduction of Josiah's exhortation describes these Levites in two ways that indicate the Chronicler's concerns (35:3a). First, they were those **who instructed all Israel**. The Levites were teachers of the Law (see 17:7-9; Neh. 8:7-9). The reference here to **all Israel** may indicate that Josiah brought together Levites who lived outside Jerusalem. If so, this description highlights the fact that Levites from all the tribes (in preparation for people from all the tribes) were present at Josiah's Passover (see *Introduction: 1) All Israel*). The allusion to Hezekiah's Passover is evident (see 30:1-12); Josiah also brought the nation together at this time.

Second, the Levites are described as those **who had been consecrated to the LORD**. This notice demonstrates the Chronicler's concern with presenting this event as a model for his readers. Rituals of consecration appear frequently in Chronicles as examples of proper worship which the post-exilic readers were to imitate in their day (see *Introduction: 6) Royal Observance of Worship*). Only those who had cleansed and committed themselves to the Lord were permitted to participate in the Passover. This qualification was especially important because these Levites probably included many who were dispersed throughout the North and South.

Josiah then gave instructions to the Levites (35:3b-4). The Chronicler's record of these instructions amounts to seven imperatives. These commands touch on different aspects of the Levitical functions and portray Josiah as devoted to proper worship at the temple.

First, the Levites were to **put the sacred ark in the temple** (35:3b). This command is difficult to understand for there is no evidence that the ark had been removed. Yet, we must assume that for some reason, either Manasseh or Amon had removed the ark from the temple. Perhaps they had begun a practice of carrying it through the city for Josiah said it was **not to be carried** any more.

Second, the Levites were to **serve** both **the LORD** and **his people**. As mediators between God and the people of Israel, the Levites performed duties whose object was service to God and to the worshippers.

Third, they were to **prepare** themselves **by families** and **divisions, according to the directions written by David ... and by his son Solomon** (35:4). David's arrangements of the Levites appear in 1 Chr. 24:4, 19-20, 30-31; 28:19-21. Solomon's directions may be found in 2 Chr. 8:14. Apparently, these Levitical arrangements appeared in some written form which is no longer extant. The Chronicler considered the orders of David and Solomon as normative for Israel (see *Introduction: 14) Standards*).

Fourth, the Levites were to **stand in the holy place with a group of Levites** (35:5). The initial organization was to take place within the temple, but later various Levites would move in and out of the temple as they served **each subdivision of the families of ... the lay people**. By this organization, Josiah insured that no family group within Israel would be overlooked at the Passover.

The fifth, sixth, and seventh imperatives appear in rapid succession and should be taken together. As in Hezekiah's day, the Levites were to **consecrate** themselves (see 35:3). Special consecration was required before sacred duties and included washings, the shaving of their bodies, various offerings, and the presenting of the Levites before the Lord (see *Introduction: 6) Royal Observance of Worship*).

The Levites were also to **slaughter the Passover lambs** (35:6), probably for themselves (see 35:8-9). They were then to **prepare the lambs for** (their) **fellow countrymen**.

The importance of these instructions finds expression in Josiah's closing words. Not only did Josiah make certain that things were done **according to the directions written by David ... and Solomon** (35:4). He also insisted that all things were to be done according to **what the LORD commanded through Moses** (35:6). Josiah was intent upon observing the Passover as God had ordered through these men.

One difficulty rises at this point. According to Exod. 12:3 each family was to sacrifice its own lamb. Here the Levites are involved in the Passover sacrifices. This apparent conflict may be resolved by distinguishing between the actual **slaughter of the Passover lambs** and the preparation of lambs (i.e. gathering, inspecting, etc.) for their **fellow countrymen** (35:6). The Levites actually sacrificed all Passover lambs in Hezekiah's day (see 30:17) to protect the sanctity of the rite following a period of apostasy. In all events, the Chronicler made it plain that Josiah's preparations for the Passover were exemplary for his post-exilic readers. They must also arrange for the performance of temple rites in accordance with the standard of Moses' Law (see *Introduction: 14) Standards*).

Josiah Readies Sacrifices (35:7-9)

Not only did Josiah prepare the priests and Levites; he also provided sacrifices. The Chronicler's report of this effort divides into two parts: provisions from Josiah

(35:7), and provisions from Josiah's officials (35:8-9).

Josiah gave **sheep and goats** for sacrifices from **the king's own possessions** (35:7). Hezekiah had done the same in his day (30:24). These contributions were designated **for all the lay people**.

His officials gave numerous sacrifices as well, but their contributions were **to the people and the priests and Levites** (35:8). Both Josiah and his officials gave more than lambs for Passover. They also contributed **goats** (35:7) and **cattle** (35:7-9) for other sacrifices as well (see 35:12).

The Chronicler noted that these gifts were **contributed voluntarily** (35:8). He emphasized the voluntary nature of contributions to the temple services on several occasions (1 Chr. 29:6-9,17; 2 Chr. 17:16; 31:14; see *Introduction: 9) Temple Contributions*). The Chronicler's hope was that the post-exilic community would not support such services under constraint but voluntarily and enthusiastically. Moreover, the number of animals provided for offerings is very large, 8400 in all (35:8-9). Chronicles often points to large numbers of sacrifices to inspire the post-exilic community to enthusiastic observance of worship in their day (see 1:6; 5:6; 7:4-5; 24:14; 29:32-35; 35:8-9; see also *Introduction: 6) Royal Observance of Worship*).

Josiah's Performance of Celebration (35:10-15)

The Chronicler described several aspects of the actual celebration of Passover. He focused on different aspects of the activities of the **priests** and **Levites** (35:10). The Chronicler's record divides between the activities directed toward the lay people (35:10-13), and those directed toward the priests and Levites (35:14-15).

The priests and Levites performed a number of tasks related to **all the people** (35:14). They arranged themselves **as the king had ordered** (35:10 see 35:4). The **lambs were slaughtered** (35:11) probably by the lay people (see 35:6; see also Lev. 3:2,8,12-13). The priests **sprinkled blood handed to them** (35:11 see 29:22; 30:16). This priestly rite corresponded to the original familial practice of sprinkling the doorposts (see Exod. 12:7).

The Levites then **skinned the animals** (35:11; see 29:34) and **set aside the burnt offerings** (35:12). This statement probably does not refer to separate burnt offerings, but to those portions of the Passover lamb that were burned on the altar. This ritual was also done **as is written in the Book of Moses** (35:12). In all likelihood the Chronicler had in mind the regulations concerning peace or fellowship offerings, of which Passover was a type. The same was also done **with the cattle** (35:12), the other sacrifices that were made (see 35:7-9).

Beyond this, the Levites **roasted the Passover animals** (35:13). This act was also done **as prescribed** by Moses (see Exod. 12:2-11). Finally, after cleansing the instruments, the Levites **served them quickly to all the people**. The speed with which the ceremony was carried out also stemmed from Mosaic instruction (see Exod. 12:11). Once again, the Chronicler was careful to point out that this event was true to the regulations of Moses (see *Introduction: 14) Standards*).

The Chronicler not only depicted how the Levites served **all the people** (35:13); he turned next to their services to other priests and Levites (35:14-15). First, the Levites made **preparations for themselves and for the priests** (35:14). The **descendants of Aaron** were too busy to sacrifice the Passover lamb for themselves. So the Levites provided for them. Second, the Levites also provided for the **descendants of Asaph** (35:15), the musical Levites. The Chronicler noted that these men **were in the places prescribed by David** to exalt them as models (compare 35:4; see also *Introduction: 14) Standards*). Here Jeduthun is called **a seer**, identifying the Levitical musicians as prophets once again. (For the Chronicler's outlook on Levitical prophets see comments on 1 Chr. 25:1; see also *Introduction: 15) Prophets*.) They, as well as the **gatekeepers**, were able to remain in their positions **because their fellow Levites made the preparations for them**.

All of these details of Levitical activity probably interested the Chronicler because of questions raised in his day. As the temple service of the post-exilic period was restored to full operation, many practical questions must have risen. Who was to perform certain rituals? When? How? For this reason, the Chronicler exalted the Levites as fully devoted to the task at hand and careful to follow the instructions of Moses, David, and Solomon.

Josiah's Passover Summarized (35:16-19)

The Chronicler closed his account of Josiah's Passover by returning to a general description of the event which balances with his introductory summary in 35:1. Having regressed chronologically in 35:2-15, the Chronicler returned to the **fourteenth day** (35:1) by beginning this section with the expression **at that time** (Hebrew = 'on that day' [NAS] 35:16). Most of this material is part of the Chronicler's addition to the book of Kings and therefore reflects his unique perspectives.

The Chronicler first noted that **the entire service of the LORD was carried out** (35:16). Nothing was omitted, including **Passover** and **burnt offerings**. Everything took place just **as King Josiah had ordered**. The Chronicler's desire to idealize this event is evident. He saw it as a model of proper observance.

To add to this positive portrait, the Chronicler also reported that **the Israelites who were present** joined in the celebration of **Passover** and **Unleavened Bread** (35:17). As in the days of Hezekiah, northern Israelites joined in the celebration (30:11, 18, 21). Thus Josiah's Passover solidified the reunion of North and South around the Davidic monarch and the temple.

In 35:18 the Chronicler returned to the record of Kings (// 2 Kgs. 23:22), but expanded Kings in several significant ways. For instance, he wrote that Josiah's Passover was greater than any Passover celebration **since the days of the prophet Samuel**. Perhaps because of the unusual actions taken in Hezekiah's celebration (see 30:2-3,17-20), the Chronicler exalted Josiah's Passover over Hezekiah's. Moreover, he reported that this supreme Passover included **priests, the Levites and all Judah and Israel who were there with the people of Jerusalem**. As we have seen, the Chronicler's account of Josiah's Passover emphasized that all the temple personnel were in proper order (see 35:5-6,10). Moreover, the presence of both northern Israelites and Judahites also contributed to the wonder of the event (see *Introduction: 1) All Israel*). The temple worship of that time was not limited to a small number in Jerusalem; it involved the entire nation. Josiah's Passover served as a perfect model for the Chronicler's post-exilic readers.

To close off this portion of his record of Josiah's reign, the Chronicler drew upon 2 Kgs. 23:23 to note once again that all these things took place **in the eighteenth year of Josiah's reign** (35:19). This verse forms an inclusio around the events described in 34:8–35:18 and opened the way for the Chronicler to move to a later time in Josiah's reign.

Josiah's Infidelity in Deadly Battle (35:20-25)

Having described Josiah's ideal worship reforms, the Chronicler turned to an event which revealed a failure. As in the record of Hezekiah, the positive features of Josiah's life far outweighed his failures. Nevertheless, the Chronicler decided that one of Josiah's shortcomings provided an important lesson for his post-exilic readers.

Comparison of 35:20-25 with 2 Kgs. 23:29-30

The Chronicler expanded the record of Kings from two to six verses. Several of these differences are noteworthy.

First, the Chronicler introduced the story with his own words, **after all this, when Josiah had set the temple in order** ... (35:20a). This introduction revealed the Chronicler's tendency to divide kings' reigns into periods of fidelity and infidelity (see *Introduction: 10-27) Divine Blessing and Judgment*).

Second, the Chronicler added the words of Neco which Josiah rejected along with his own interpretation of these words (35:21-22).

Third, the Chronicler expanded 2 Kgs. 23:29b-30 (// 35:23-24a) to explain some of the circumstances surrounding Josiah's death.

Fourth, the Chronicler added a report of widespread mourning for Josiah, including the lament of Jeremiah (35:24b-25). This addition honored Josiah as one of Judah's great kings.

Structure 35:20-25

The Chronicler's version of battle between Josiah and Neco takes the form of five symmetrical steps and an afterword (see figure 61). This episode begins with Josiah going out to meet Neco for battle (35:20). This beginning balances with Josiah returning to Jerusalem and dying (35:24a). The turning point consists of Josiah ignoring the warning of Neco and entering battle (35:22). Prior to this turning point, Neco warns Josiah that harm will come to him if he fights (35:21). After the turning point, Josiah is fatally wounded in battle (35:23). The story itself is followed by an afterword which explains some details about the mourning over Josiah (35:24b-25).

Josiah Goes Out for Battle against Neco (35:20)

As noted above the Chronicler added a transitional introduction to this story. Josiah went up against Neco **after all this, when Josiah had set the temple in order**. The years of Josiah's exemplary fidelity had come to an end (see 34:1-35:19). Like many kings before him, Josiah's time of blessing led to infidelity. (For the Chronicler's warning against permitting blessings to lead to infidelity, see comments on 1 Chr. 5:24.)

The initiation of the action of this episode consists of **Neco king of Egypt** going **to fight at Carchemish on the Euphrates**. This event took place in 609 BC some thirteen years after the Passover in Josiah's eighteenth year (622 BC). Neco was on his way to fight with Assyria against the Babylonians (see 2 Kgs. 23:29).

Josiah did not favor Neco's intentions and **marched out to meet him in battle** (35:20). Josiah's motivations are not altogether clear. It is likely, however, that from the time of Hezekiah (see 32:31 // 2 Kgs. 20:12-15), Judah looked to Babylon as a potential source of help against Assyria. To keep the Egyptians from helping Assyria would have been in Josiah's own self-interest.

In a subtle manner, the Chronicler raised the issue of foreign alliances once again. Throughout his history he condemned the times when Judah joined with other nations in military alliances (see *Introduction: 3) International Relations*). Here Josiah fights against Egypt but in alliance with Babylon. This involvement with Babylon will prove to be devastating.

Josiah Hears Warning from Neco (35:21)

Neco learned of Josiah's approach and sent word to the king of Judah. It was common for kings to send messages to their opponents before battle (see 1 Chr. 11:4-5; 2 Chr. 13:4-12; 25:17-19; 32:10-19). Neco sent word to Josiah to dissuade him from attacking. He protested that there was no quarrel between Judah and Egypt; he merely wanted safe passage. In fact, Neco supported his request with a theological assertion. He claimed, **'God has told me to hurry; so stop opposing God who is with me, or he will destroy you.'** The Chronicler cast the Egyptian's message in terms that appear elsewhere in his history. Neco claimed that God was **with** him, indicating that God would fight for him (see 13:12; see also *Introduction: 10) Divine Activity*). To resist the Egyptian army was to resist God himself and to incur destruction at God's hand.

Josiah Defiantly Enters Battle (35:22)

Although the Egyptian king had warned him, Josiah **disguised himself to engage him in battle**. Josiah's actions are reminiscent of the time when Ahab disguised himself in battle against Syria (see 18:29). The reason for Josiah's behavior is not altogether clear. Either he hoped to hide his identity from Neco, God, or both. Whatever the case, his actions proved futile. Although he hid, an archer's arrow still found its way to Josiah (see 35:23).

The Chronicler explained that Josiah's pursuit of battle was not rightly motivated. Josiah refused to pay attention to Neco, even though he had spoken **at God's command**. Neco claimed to be speaking for God (35:21), but nothing prior to this verse indicates that his claim was true. Apparently, the Chronicler assumed his audience knew other information that authenticated the divine origin of Neco's message. Interestingly enough, an apocryphal explanation appears in 1 Esdras 1:26 where Jeremiah is said to have confirmed that Neco's words were from God. This scenario is feasible. Josiah certainly had prophets about him, perhaps even Jeremiah. A message from an approaching enemy would have motivated Josiah to seek confirmation from his prophets (see 18:3-4,6). If this series of events lies behind the Chronicler's words, we have another example of the importance he placed on obedience to the prophets (see *Introduction: 15) Prophets*). In all events, the Chronicler made it clear that Josiah not only rejected Neco's warning, but also defied the word of God given through the king.

Josiah is Seriously Wounded (35:23)

The Chronicler paraphrased 2 Kgs. 23:29 to describe how Josiah was killed. He had already alluded to Ahab's battle against Syria (see 18:28–19:3) by noting that Josiah had disguised himself (see 35:22). Here the Chronicler noted that **archers shot King Josiah** and the king demanded, **'Take me away; I am badly wounded.'** The connection between this passage and Ahab's fatal wounding is apparent. In Ahab's case, **someone drew his bow at random and hit the king**. Then the king ordered, **'Wheel around and get me out of the fighting. I've been wounded'** (18:33). The similarities make it likely that the Chronicler expected his readers to treat 35:23 as an elliptical description of a similar scenario. Just as God's judgment against Ahab came through the arrow shot **at random**, so Josiah came under divine displeasure through the arrow of an enemy's bow (see *Introduction: 10) Divine Activity*).

Josiah Returns and Dies (35:24a)

The Chronicler expanded the account of 2 Kgs. 23:30a to explain that Josiah returned from battle and died in Jerusalem. This scene closes the episode in balance with the opening scene where Josiah left Jerusalem for war (35:20). The king's disregard for the word of God led to a tragic end. The Chronicler's message to his readers is evident. As he had illustrated many times, when the kings of Judah proved unfaithful, tragedy often followed (see *Introduction: 10-27) Divine Blessing and Judgment*).

Nevertheless, Josiah is honored. The Chronicler noted that he was not simply 'buried' (2 Kgs. 23:30a). He was **buried in the tombs of his fathers** (35:24). Attitude of high regard is often indicated for a king by mentioning his burial in the royal tombs (see *Introduction: 28) Healing and Long Life/Sickness and Death*).

Afterword Concerning Mourning (35:24b-25)

The Chronicler emphasized Josiah's honor even further by adding an afterword to this episode. In this brief report, he noted that **all Judah and Jerusalem mourned** the death of Josiah (35:24b). Jer. 22:10, 15-16 confirm that Jeremiah was moved to laments when Josiah died. Jeremiah's laments were sung **to this day** (35:25). In fact, they had become a **tradition** (35:25). Apparently, the Chronicler appealed here to customs which his readers knew. (For the Chronicler's use of the terminology 'to this day', see comments on 1 Chr. 4:41.) He conveyed the sad circumstance of Josiah's death by these recognizable allusions. By these means the Chronicler made it clear that Josiah was greatly honored despite his failure.

Closure of Josiah's Reign (35:26-36:1)

In balance with the opening of Josiah's reign (see figure 61), the Chronicler brought his record to a close in his typical manner. Depending on 2 Kgs. 23:28, the Chronicler noted where more information on Josiah could be found (35:26-27; see *Introduction: Historical and Theological Purposes*). Moreover, he complimented Josiah with the observation that he lived according to the **Law of the Lord** (35:27). The standard of Mosaic Law is evident again (see *Introduction: 14) Standards*). The Chronicler then added that **the people of the land** (i.e. commoners; see 1 Chr. 5:25; 2 Chr. 23:13, 20,21; 26:21; 33:25) made Jehoahaz **king in Jerusalem** (36:1). The Chronicler noted that the transfer of power was left up to the people because of Josiah's untimely death.

The Final Events (36:2-23)

As the Chronicler neared the exile of Judah to Babylon, he reported on the final kings of Judah in rapid succession. This material has a number of motifs that occur on several occasions and reveal his outlook on these events.

Comparison of 36:2-23 with 2 Kgs. 23:30b-25:30 and Ezra 1:1-3

The Chronicler relied on Kings for most of his closing chapter. The final portion (36:22-23) parallels Ezra 1:1-3. Despite these similarities, a number of significant variations occur which reveal the Chronicler's unique perspectives (see figure 63).

Several types of variations occur. First, the Chronicler omitted all maternal notices for these kings (2 Kgs. 23:31b, 36b; 24:8b, 18b). The reason for these omissions is not clear. He kept and omitted such notices in earlier portions of his history for no apparent reason, but dropped all such notices after Hezekiah (see comments on 2 Chr. 13:1-2a). Here he may have dropped these notes to avoid distracting his readers' attention from more important matters in these passages.

Second, the Chronicler repeated all evaluations of these kings (36:5b // 2 Kgs. 23:37; 36:9b // 2 Kgs. 24:9; 36:12a // 2 Kgs. 24:19) with the exception of Jehoahaz (36:2-3 // 2 Kgs. 23:31-33). In this case the deposing and taxation of Judah's king served as sufficient evidence that the Chronicler evaluated his reign negatively.

Third, the Chronicler either loosely followed the descriptions of trouble and exile experienced by each king or severely abbreviated them (36:6-7 // 2 Kgs. 24:1-4; 36:10a-b // 2 Kgs. 24:10-16; 36:15-21 // 2 Kgs. 25:1-30). As we will see below, the Chronicler shaped his record of these events to emphasize his own theological perspectives on this period in Israel's history.

2 Chr.		2 Kgs.
	Jehoahaz	
36:2	Summary of Reign	23:30b-31a
———	Maternal Notice	23:31b
———	Evaluation	23:32
36:3-4	Trouble and Exile	23:33-34
	Jehoiakim	
———	Tribute to Egypt	23:35
36:5a	Summary of Reign	23:36a
———	Maternal Notice	23:36b
36:5b	Evaluation	23:37
36:6-7	Trouble and Exile (loosely parallel)	24:1-4
36:8a-c	Other sources	24:5
———	Death	24:6a
36:8d	Successor	24:6b
———	Babylonian Dominance	24:7
	Jehoiachin	
36:9a	Summary of Reign	24:8a
———	Maternal Notice	24:8b
36:9b	Evaluation	24:9
36:10a-b	Trouble and Exile (severely abbreviated)	24:10-16
36:10c	Successor	24:17
	Zedekiah	
36:11	Summary of Reign	24:18a
———	Maternal Notice	24:18b
36:12-14	Evaluation (expanded)	24:19-20
36:15-21	Trouble and Exile (severely abbreviated)	25:1-26
———	Jehoiachin Released	25:27-30
36:22-23	Return from Exile	Ezra 1:2-3

Comparison of 2 Chr. 36:1-23 with 2 Kgs. 23:30b-25:30 and Ezra 1:2-3 (figure 63)

Fourth, beyond these regular variations, the Chronicler significantly shortened his account of two reigns.

1) Jehoiakim's reign omits his tribute to Egypt (2 Kgs. 23:35), his death (2 Kgs. 24:6a) as well as a note explaining Babylonian dominance in the period (2 Kgs. 24:7). These omissions had the effect of simplifying Jehoiakim's reign and conforming it to the literary pattern established in the records of the other kings of this chapter (see figure 64 below).

2) The Chronicler omitted the closing episode of 2 Kings 25:27-30 which

describes Jehoiachin's release from prison. This event had given hope to the readers of Kings that release from exile may have been imminent. By the time of the Chronicler's writing Jehoiachin's release had proven to be insignificant. For this reason, the Chronicler replaced it with a record of the return from Babylon under the Cyrus edict (36:22-23).

Fifth, the Cyrus edict of 36:22-23 does not appear in the book of Kings, but it parallels Ezra 1:1-3. The Chronicler's version of the edict is only half as long as Ezra 1:2-4. 36:23 closely parallels Ezra 1:2-3a, but it has no correspondent for Ezra 1:3b-4. Explanations of these differences have taken at least four main directions.

1) Some interpreters see the passages as separate accounts based on a common source.

2) Some argue that the material was duplicated because the books of Chronicles and Ezra were originally one and later divided.

3) Still others have urged that Chronicles copied from the book of Ezra.

4) Finally, other interpreters have suggested that the book of Ezra copied from Chronicles.

As these positions illustrate, one's outlook on the relationship between these two texts depends on much more basic issues of authorship and date (see *Introduction: Authorship and Date*). Although the first option seems most likely, it is impossible to prove beyond doubt.

Structure of 36:2-23

This last section of Chronicles consists of a series of four fairly uniform accounts, the last of which extends beyond the others to include the release of Israel's remnant from Exile (see figure 64).

As this outline indicates, each section of this material presents the pattern of summary and evaluation followed by trouble leading to exile. The only break from this pattern occurs in the reign of Zedekiah which adds Israel's release from Babylon (36:22-23).

Jehoahaz (36:1-4)

The death of Josiah (35:20-25) in 609 BC brought such political turmoil to Judah that two other kings reigned before the year came to an end (see 21:1; 23:20-21; 26:1; 33:25; 36:1). Jehoahaz (also named Shallum [1 Chr. 3:15]) was the second of the three kings who reigned in 609. Although the Chronicler followed the record of Kings more closely here than in the other parts of this final series, his thematic concerns are evident.

Summary of Jehoahaz's Reign (36:1-2)

The Chronicler summarized Jehoahaz's reign with a report consisting of two brief notices. Following 2 Kgs. 23:31, he noted that Jehoahaz was **twenty-three years old** and only reigned **three months** (36:2). The brevity of Jehoahaz's reign immediately indicated that conditions were not good for the Judahite king. He reigned

Jehoahaz (36:2-4)
   Summary of Jehoahaz's Reign (36:2)
   Exile, Tribute, and Successor (36:3-4)

Jehoiakim (36:5-8)
   Summary of Jehoiakim's Reign (36:5)
   Exile, Tribute, and Successor (36:6-8)

Jehoiachin (36:9-10)
   Summary of Jehoiachin's Reign (36:9)
   Exile, Tribute, and Successor (36:10)

Zedekiah (36:11-21)
   Summary of Zedekiah's Reign (36:11-14)
   Exile, Tribute, and Restoration (36:15-23)
      God Has Pity on Israel (36:15)
         God's Anger Stirred against Israel (36:16)
         God Sends Punishment against Israel (36:17-20)
      God Has Pity on Israel (36:21-23)

Outline of 2 Chr. 36:1-23 (figure 64)

under the judgment of God (see *Introduction: 10-27) Divine Blessing and Judgment*). As we suggested above, the omission of Jehoahaz's evaluation (2 Kgs. 23:2) is unusual for this chapter, but the Chronicler probably felt Jehoahaz's terrible experience sufficiently exposed the nature of his kingdom.

Tribute, Exile, and Successor (36:3-4)

In a fashion that will appear throughout this chapter, the Chronicler included three elements in his description of Jehoahaz's trouble and exile. First, he noted that a fine was imposed on Judah by a foreign power (36:3). The other examples of such impositions in this chapter involved the removal of temple treasures (see 36:7,10,18). This connection emphasized that the sins of Judah's kings brought harm to the temple itself. Here, however, the temple is not explicitly noted.

Second, the Chronicler mentioned in each case that the king of Judah was exiled to a foreign land. In this example, **Neco ... carried him off to Egypt** (36:4). In the other cases, King Nebuchadnezzar took Judah's kings to Babylon (see 36:6,10,20).

Third, the Chronicler mentioned the successor to the king who had been exiled. Neco put Eliakim in the place of Jehoahaz (36:4). Notices of succession appear for all the kings in this final chapter except Zedekiah, the last king of Judah (see 36:8,10). Following 2 Kgs. 23:34, the Chronicler noted that Neco changed Eliakim's name to **Jehoiakim** (36:4). Neco's ability to set up Judah's king and to change his name indicated his dominance over Judah. The king of Judah was little more than a puppet of Egypt. A similar circumstance occurs in 36:10 when Nebuchadnezzar made Zedekiah king.

Put simply, the Chronicler quickly covered the reign of Jehoahaz as entirely negative, and left Judah under foreign control. As far as the Chronicler was concerned, Jehoahaz had no redeeming qualities worth mentioning.

Jehoiakim (36:5-8)

Continuing his rapid coverage of the last kings of Judah, the Chronicler turned to the third king who reigned in 609 BC. Jehoiakim ruled Judah 609-598/7 BC.

Summary of Jehoiakim's Reign (36:5)

As expected in this chapter, the Chronicler began his record of Jehoiakim by noting that he began to reign when he was **twenty-five years old**; his reign lasted **eleven years**. Despite the length of his reign, the Chronicler characterized Jehoiakim's reign as entirely negative. He did **evil in the eyes of the Lord his God** (see 36:9, 12; for the Chronicler's use of this evaluative terminology, see comments on 2 Chr. 24:2).

Tribute, Exile and Successor (36:6-8)

The Chronicler omitted Jehoiakim's interaction with Neco (see 2 Kgs. 23:35) in order to concentrate on trouble caused by Nebuchadnezzar. The three main themes of this chapter appear in this material. First, the theme of exile appears. As the Chronicler put it, **Nebuchadnezzar ... attacked him and bound him with bronze shackles to take him to Babylon** (36:6). It is unclear whether or not Jehoiakim was actually taken to Babylon. The Chronicler merely noted that he had been bound in order to be taken. Perhaps the threat of exile sufficed to subdue Jehoiakim. If the king was actually taken away, he left in 605 BC when Daniel and his companions were exiled (36:7; see Dan. 1:1-3; Jer. 46:2).

Second, the motif of tribute occurs again in this passage (see 36:10,14,18-19). **Nebuchadnezzar ... took to Babylon articles from the temple ... and put them in his temple there** (36:7). By mentioning that these treasures came from the temple, the Chronicler joined together the fate of Jerusalem's king and temple. Just as his history set forth these two institutions as indispensable for the blessings of God (see *Introduction: 4-9) King and Temple*), here he connected the fall of one with the other (see 36:10,14,18-19).

Third, after mentioning other records of **the detestable things** Jehoiakim did as well as **all that was found against him** (36:8), the Chronicler noted that Jehoiachin succeeded Jehoiakim. As the account of Kings reports, Jehoiakim was submissive to Nebuchadnezzar for three years and then rebelled (see 2 Kgs. 24:1). It is not clear how Jehoiakim died, but Jer. 22:18-19 suggests that he did not die by natural causes. In all events, it is clear that the Chronicler had nothing positive to say about this king of Judah.

Jehoiachin (36:9-10)

The next king of Judah was Jehoiachin. He reigned in the year 598/97 BC, but was taken to exile in that same year.

Summary of Jehoiachin's Reign (36:9)
The Chronicler abbreviated his record of Jehoiachin's reign so that it would match the pattern of presentation throughout this chapter (36:9-10 // 2 Kgs. 24:8-17). It should also be noted that the Chronicler omitted Jehoiachin's release from prison in Babylon (2 Kgs. 25:27-29). This scene is the last segment of the book of Kings and was probably intended to inspire hope in the readers of that book for release from exile through the Davidic line. The Chronicler, however, shifted attention away from Jehoiachin's release because he wrote after this event had been eclipsed by the Cyrus edict (see 36:22-23).

Consequently, the Chronicler merely summarized Jehoiachin's reign. He became king at **eighteen years** of age and reigned **in Jerusalem** only **three months and ten days**. Jehoiachin also received a thoroughly negative evaluation from the Chronicler's hand. **He did evil in the eyes of the LORD** (36:9b; see 36:5,12; for the Chronicler's use of this evaluative terminology, see comments on 2 Chr. 24:2).

Tribute, Exile and Successor (36:10)
Once again the Chronicler noted three things that occurred in this king's reign. First, **Nebuchadnezzar ... brought him to Babylon**. Second, **articles of value from the temple** were also brought to Babylon. The vital connection between monarch and temple continues in this passage (see 36:7,14,18-19). Third, the nation of Judah was at such a low state that Nebuchadnezzar **made Jehoiachin's uncle, Zedekiah, king over Judah** (36:10). As Neco had imposed Eliakim on Judah (36:4), so Nebuchadnezzar put the man of his choice over the people of God. By any measure, the kingdom of Judah was barely surviving at this point in its history.

Zedekiah (36:11-21)
At last the Chronicler reached the final king of Judah, Zedekiah (597-586 BC). This account follows patterns similar to those of other kings in this chapter, but the record of Zedekiah is unique in several important ways.

Summary of Zedekiah's Reign (36:11-14)
The Chronicler began with very basic information about the king. Zedekiah rose to power when he was **twenty-one years old** and his rule lasted for **eleven years** (36:11). As the other kings in this final series, Zedekiah **did evil in the eyes of the LORD** (36:12a; see 36:5,9; for the Chronicler's use of this evaluative terminology, see comments on 2 Chr. 24:2).

Up to this point, Zedekiah's record is very similar to 2 Kgs. 24:18-19 as well as the overarching patterns of this chapter. As noted above, however, the Chronicler expanded the summary of Zedekiah's reign beyond the account of 2 Kgs. 24:19-20. Perhaps he derived this information from the record of Zedekiah's life in Jeremiah (see Jer. 27:1-28:17; 34:1-22; 37:1-38:28). Zedekiah was the king whose sins sealed the final destruction of Jerusalem. For this reason, the Chronicler gave special attention to the evil he did.

The Chronicler added that Zedekiah not only **did evil**, but also **did not humble**

himself (36:12b). The Chronicler focused on humility on a number of occasions in his history (see *Introduction: 18) Humility*). Humility averted disaster (see 7:14; 12:7, 12; 33:12-13; 32:26) and pride brought tragedy (see 25:19; 26:16; 32:25,26). In addition, the Chronicler added that Zedekiah did not yield himself **before Jeremiah the prophet** (36:12). Throughout the Chronicler's history blessings came to those who responded properly to prophets; disaster came to those who did not submit themselves to the prophetic word (see *Introduction: 15) Prophets*). To stress the severity of the king's sin, the Chronicler also noted that Jeremiah **spoke the word of the LORD** (36:12). To refuse humility before the prophet was to resist God himself.

Zedekiah's failure to give proper regard to the prophet warranted his punishment, but the Chronicler went further into the king's sin. Zedekiah **also rebelled against King Nebuchadnezzar** (36:13). Jeremiah had urged Zedekiah to submit to the Babylonian emperor (see Jer. 27:1-28:17; 37:1-38:28), but the king of Judah refused. To explain why this act ranked among Zedekiah's great sins, the Chronicler noted that Nebuchadnezzar **had made him take an oath in God's name** (36:12). This oath is not mentioned in Kings or Jeremiah, but Ezekiel noted it (see Ezek. 17:12-17). By rebelling against the Babylonian king, Zedekiah not only rejected the prophet, but also broke his sacred vow in the Name of God (see *Introduction: 11) Name of God*). As a result, Zedekiah became **stiff-necked** (see 30:8); he **hardened his heart** against God rather than serving him wholeheartedly (see *Introduction: 16) Motivations*); he also refused to **turn to the LORD** in repentance (see *Introduction: 22) Repentance*). By describing the king in this manner, the Chronicler specified the severity of the monarchy's failures.

In addition to describing the corruption of the king, the Chronicler also noted the failure of temple worship. He pointed out that **all the leaders of the priests and the people became more and more unfaithful** (36:14). The Chronicler used the term 'unfaithful' on a number of occasions to describe disloyalty to the Law of God (see *Introduction: 21) Unfaithfulness*). Here the focus is on worship. Not only did the Chronicler specify that the priesthood had failed to be faithful, he also noted that their infidelity reached the point that they imitated the **detestable practices of the nations** (36:14; for the Chronicler's use of this comparison, see comments on 2 Chr. 33:2-9). These practices probably included idols in the temple as well as pagan ceremonies. By describing Judah's sins in this manner, the Chronicler made it plain that the distinctive holiness of Judah had vanished. The priests had gone so far astray that they were **defiling the temple which** [God] **had consecrated** (36:14).

By adding these priestly sins to those of Zedekiah, the Chronicler repeated a theme that occurs throughout this chapter. The throne and temple in Jerusalem shared the same fate. As kings were exiled, the temple treasuries were depleted (see 36:7,10,18; see also *Introduction: 4-9) King and Temple*). Now the Chronicler made it clear that the corruption of the monarch was paralleled by the corruption of temple worship. The two central institutions of Israel had fallen into utter ruin during the reign of Zedekiah.

Trouble, Exile and Restoration (36:15-23)
Having established that the monarchy and the temple were severely corrupted, the Chronicler moved toward God's reaction. This portion of the account abbreviates 2 Kgs. 25:1-30. It amounts to the Chronicler's own summary of events leading to the fall of Jerusalem, the Babylonian exile, and the Cyrus Edict.

Structure of 36:15-23
This material divides into a four step narrative (see figure 64). Throughout this material the Chronicler made God the principle character. The story begins with God sending prophets because he had pity on his people and the temple (36:15). It ends with God showing mercy to Israel once again (36:21-23). The rising action involves the people stirring God's anger by rejecting his prophets (36:16). God responded to this rejection in the falling action by sending Nebuchadnezzar to destroy them (36:17-20).

God Has Pity toward Israel (36:15)
The preceding passage established that Zedekiah and the priests were in serious violation of the Law of God. Nevertheless, contrary to his normal way of describing God's acts as immediate retribution (see *Introduction: 10-27) Divine Blessing and Judgment*), the Chronicler pointed out that God displayed great patience. God first sent **word to them through his messengers**. Instead of immediately destroying Israel, God sent his prophets to instruct and warn the nation. In fact, he sent them **again and again**. The book of Kings does not note these events, but this scenario looks much like the course of events in Kings' account of Manasseh. Manasseh sealed the fate of Judah because he refused to listen to the many prophets God sent to him (see 2 Kgs. 21:11-15; 23:26-27; 24:3). A similar series of events took place in Zedekiah's reign. This material illustrates the Chronicler's repeated emphasis on the role prophets played in Israel's blessing and judgment (see *Introduction: 15) Prophets*).

The book of Jeremiah records many of the prophecies given by Jeremiah during the reign of Zedekiah. In fact, the language of this passage echoes Jer. 26:5; 29:19. The Chronicler mentioned Jeremiah in this passage three times (36:12, 21, 22) and certainly had him in mind as he spoke of these **messengers**. It is not clear, however, what other prophets he may have counted along with Jeremiah.

The Chronicler also noted the reason why God sent prophets to Zedekiah. It was **because he had pity on his people and on his dwelling place**. The purpose of these prophetic warnings was to stir repentance so that the people and the temple could be spared from divine wrath. This mercy balances with the final portion of this narrative where mercy is shown once again to **his people** and the **temple** (36:22-23).

God's Anger Stirred against Israel (36:16)
Unfortunately, Judah did not respond properly to the prophets whom God had sent. Instead they **mocked** ... **despised** ... and **scoffed**. As a result, the **pity** of God (36:15)

turned to **wrath**. Throughout his history, the Chronicler pointed to the dire consequences of rejecting the prophetic word (see *Introduction: 15) Prophets*). Here God's anger was so **aroused** that **there was no remedy** (see Prov. 29:1; Jer. 7:26; 20:8; 25:4; 30:12). Although the prophets spoke to bring repentance, the repeated rejection of prophetic warnings eventually led to a course of events that could not be averted. God became so angry that no annulments, mollifications, or postponements were possible. The judgment of God was coming against his people.

God Sends Punishment against Israel (36:17-20)

The Chronicler turned next to spell out the manner in which God's wrath came against Israel. God **brought up against them the king of the Babylonians** (36:17a). The Chronicler's readers knew the disaster that Nebuchadnezzar brought to Judah. They lived in its aftermath. But the Chronicler emphasized that it had not been a mere human affair. God himself moved the king of Babylon to attack (36:17a). God's active involvement in these events is stressed here as well as in two other places in this material (36:17c, 21-22).

The Chronicler spelled out four specific ways in which God punished Israel through Nebuchadnezzar. First, he engaged in much killing. Nebuchadnezzar **killed young men in the sanctuary** (36:17b). Presumably, these young men were Levitical soldiers who sought to protect the temple. On a number of occasions the Old Testament describes a military function for some Levites (see 1 Chr. 23:7). The fact that these killings took place **in the sanctuary** (i.e. the main hall; see *Introduction: Appendix B – The Structures, Furnishings and Decorations of Solomon's Temple)* of the temple indicates that God had already begun to desert the temple.

Moreover, the Chronicler pointed to the severity of Nebuchadnezzar's killings by noting that he **spared neither young man nor young woman, old man or aged** (36:17). Whereas the Chronicler considered increases of the population of Judah a divine blessing, the judgment of God meant the death of many. To draw attention to the fact that this event resulted from divine wrath, the Chronicler noted that **God handed all of them over** (see *Introduction: 10) Divine Activity*).

Second, Nebuchadnezzar depleted Jerusalem of her riches **from the treasuries of the LORD's temple and the treasures of the king and his officials** (36:18). Once again, the Chronicler tied the fate of the temple and king together (see 36:7, 10,14,19). To depict the extent of this plundering, the Chronicler noted that the Babylonian king took **all the articles from the temple ... large and small**. Just as Nebuchadnezzar showed no restraint in his killings, he robbed the temple of all it had. The accumulation of riches and wealth was the blessing of God, but the judgment of God reversed this blessing.

Third, the Chronicler reported that the Babylonians also destroyed the buildings and fortifications of Jerusalem (36:19). Elsewhere in Chronicles success in building and fortification was a sign of God's favor (see *Introduction: 24) Building and Destruction*). Here the destruction of buildings indicates his curse. The Babylonians **set fire to God's temple and broke down the wall of Jerusalem**. They also set fire to **all the palaces**. To emphasize once again the extent of the damage, the Chronicler noted that the Babylonians actually **destroyed everything of value there** (36:18; see 36:7,10,17).

Fourth, the Chronicler reported that **the remnant** was **carried into exile to Babylon** (36:20). The term **remnant** has both negative and positive connotations in this passage. On the one hand, it indicates that which is left over after severe destruction. These are the people of Israel who barely survived (see Isa. 10:22; Jer. 8:3). On the other hand, the remnant of Israel is positive because it is that source out of which renewal may come (see Isa. 11:16; 37:31-32; Ezek. 6:8; Mic. 2:12). Both connotations apply in this context. These people are **those who escaped from the sword**, a relatively small group of survivors. Yet, the Chronicler will point out in the next section that these same people are the beginning of a great restoration as well. In fact, the Chronicler had already pointed in this direction in his list of those who had returned from exile (see 1 Chr. 9:2-21). They were descendants of those who had been spared and represented all Israel (see *Introduction: 1) All Israel*). The Chronicler closed this section with the note that the **remnant** remained **servants** (i.e. subjects) of Nebuchadnezzar **until the kingdom of Persia came to power**. The exile to Babylon continued as long as the kingdom of Babylon endured.

God Has Pity toward Israel (36:21-23)

At this point, the Chronicler closed his entire history with a record of God's mercy toward Israel. He noted the benefit of the exile for the land (36:21) and the commission of Cyrus that Israel should rebuild the temple (36:22-23). This positive material balances with the opening scene of God's pity toward the people and temple (36:15).

The NIV obscures the paragraph break between 36:20 and 36:21. The thematic shift is evident; the Chronicler moved from divine curse to blessing. This break is supported by the grammar of the Hebrew text. Literally, the Hebrew of 36:21 begins, 'to fulfill the word of the Lord ...' This clause may refer to what has gone before (i.e. the exile in Babylon [see NAS]), or it may refer to the sentences that follow (i.e. the land's Sabbath rest [see NIV]). If we read this clause as connected to the following sentences (as NIV), the text states that **the land enjoyed its Sabbath rests** to fulfill the word of the Lord ... This understanding is preferred.

In all events, the Chronicler's main idea is plain enough. The exile had a positive benefit: **the land enjoyed its Sabbath rests; all the time of its desolation it rested** (36:21). This understanding of the purpose of the exile stems from Lev. 26:34-35 which states that 'the land will enjoy its Sabbath years all the time that it lies desolate ... the land will have the rest it did not have during the Sabbaths you lived in it.' Mosaic Law required that the land not be worked for crops every seventh year (see Lev. 25:1-7). These years were to give the land rest and to demonstrate Israel's reliance on God. The Chronicler interpreted the exile as a time for the land to enjoy the years of rest it had not received in the past. By means of the exile, the land was refreshed and prepared for new occupants, those who returned from Babylon.

The Chronicler mentioned that these years of rest for the land were in fulfillment of Jeremiah's prediction (see Jer. 25:11; 29:10) that the exile would last **until seventy years** (36:21). The Chronicler associated the end of Jeremiah's seventy years with the Cyrus edict of 539/8 BC (36:22). This association has led to several attempts to calculate when the Chronicler believed the seventy year period began. At least three lines of interpretation deserve consideration.

1) Some interpreters calculate the seventy years from the Babylonian victory at Carchemish (605 BC, see Jer. 46:2ff.) to the Cyrus Edict (539 BC), a period of approximately 67 years.

2) Other interpreters note that Zechariah still looked for the fulfillment of the seventy years after the Cyrus Edict (see Zech. 1:12). Apparently, he connected the prophecy more directly with the building of the temple. The period from the destruction of the temple (586 BC) to the completion of the temple (516/5) is precisely seventy years. It is possible that the Chronicler had this chronology in mind as well, and simply treated the Cyrus edict and temple reconstruction as one complex event.

3) Some extra-biblical ancient Near Eastern texts suggest that the number 'seventy' was a symbolic designation of a time when kingdoms would suffer under the wrath of their gods. This period of time could be shortened or lengthened depending on the actions of the king and nation. This symbolic understanding would explain how the Chronicler could connect the seventy years to Cyrus and Zechariah to the completion of the temple. It would also explain how Daniel's prophecy could extend Jeremiah's seventy years to 490 years (see Dan. 9:1-27).

In all events, the Chronicler turned his post-exilic readers' attention to the positive benefits of the exile. From his perspective, the time of desolation for the land was a time of rest and preparation for a new day. That new day began with the return of his readers, the remnant, to the land of Judah in 538 BC.

The final scene of the Chronicler's history reminded the post-exilic community of its origins and goal (36:22-23). First, the edict originated with **Cyrus king of Persia** who made **a proclamation throughout his realm** (36:22). The Chronicler explained the importance of this edict by emphasizing God's role in the matter. In three ways, he stressed that God was actually behind the Cyrus edict (see *Introduction: 10) Divine Activity*).

1) It occurred **in order to fulfill the word of the LORD spoken by Jeremiah** (36:22).

2) **The LORD moved the heart of Cyrus** to give his edict; it was not the king's initiative (36:22).

3) Cyrus himself acknowledged **the LORD, the God of heaven** as the source of his authority (36:23). The divine authorization of the Cyrus edict showed the proclamation to be more than a mere human event. God himself gave the decree binding authority.

Second, the importance of this divine authorization becomes clear when we note the goal of the Cyrus edict.

1) The Persian king announced that God had ordained him **to build a temple**

for him at Jerusalem in Judah (36:23). Throughout his history the Chronicler had made it clear that the post-exilic community was to reinstitute proper worship in the Jerusalem temple (see *Introduction: 4-9) King and Temple*). Without the completion of this project the Chronicler's readers could have no hope for divine blessings. To resist or neglect this effort was to insure divine judgment because God had decreed it through Cyrus.

2) The emperor invited **anyone of** [God's] **people** to go to Jerusalem to build (36:22). The invitation was open to all Israelites throughout **all the kingdoms of the earth** (36:22). In every portion of his history, the Chronicler emphasized the need for all Israelites to be involved in the restoration program. Here the emperor's words reinforced the Chronicler's call that those outside the land should return and join those who had already returned (see *Introduction: 1) All Israel*).

3) Cyrus also blessed those who returned saying, **may the LORD his God be with him** (36:23). These words reminded the Chronicler's readers of a theme that appeared time and again in his history. Success in the post-exilic temple project could come only with the help of God. God must be 'with' the post-exilic community, protecting them from enemies and giving them success in all their efforts (see 2 Chr. 13:12; see also *Introduction: 10) Divine Activity*).

The Chronicler closed his history on this positive note to leave his readers with a clear understanding of their privileges and responsibilities. They had received tremendous grace from God through the Cyrus edict. Yet, this same edict required all Israel to join in the restoration of the temple to its proper place in order to bring the abundant blessings of God to the people of God.

Index